# Principles of Services Marketing

Seventh Edition

D0248714

# Principles of Services Marketing

## Seventh Edition

Adrian Palmer

BATH SPA UNIVERSITY
NEWTON PARK LIBRARY
Class No.
658·8 PAL
DISCARD
2/12/2015

Principles of Services Marketing, Seventh Edition
Adrian Palmer
ISBN-13 9780077152345
ISBN-10 0077152344

Published by McGraw-Hill Education
Shoppenhangers road
Maidenhead
Berkshire
SL6 2QL
Telephone: 44 (0) 1628 502 500
Fax: 44(0) 1628 770 224
Website: www.mcgraw-hill.co.uk

**British Library Cataloguing in Publication Data**
A catalogue record for this book is available from the British Library

**Library of Congress Cataloging in Publication Data**
The Library of Congress data for this book has been applied for from the Library of Congress

Acquisitions Editor: Peter Hooper
Marketing Manager: Geeta Kumar
Production Editor: Alison Davis

Text design by Hardlines
Cover design by Adam Renvoize

Published by McGraw-Hill Education (UK) Limited an imprint of The McGraw-Hill Companies, Inc., 1221 Avenue of the Americas, New York, NY 10020. Copyright © 2010 by McGraw-Hill Education (UK) Limited. All rights reserved. No part of this publication may be reproduced or distributed in any form or by any means, or stored in a database or retrieval system, without the prior written consent of The McGraw-Hill Companies, Inc., including, but not limited to, in any network or other electronic storage or transmission, or broadcast for distance learning.

Fictitious names of companies, products, people, characters and/or data that may be used herein (in case studies or in examples) are not intended to represent any real individual, company, product or event.

ISBN-13 9780077152345
ISBN-10 0077152344

© Adrian Palmer 2014. Exclusive rights by The McGraw-Hill Companies, Inc. for manufacture and export. This book cannot be re-exported from the country to which it is sold by McGraw-Hill.

# Brief table of contents

# Detailed table of contents

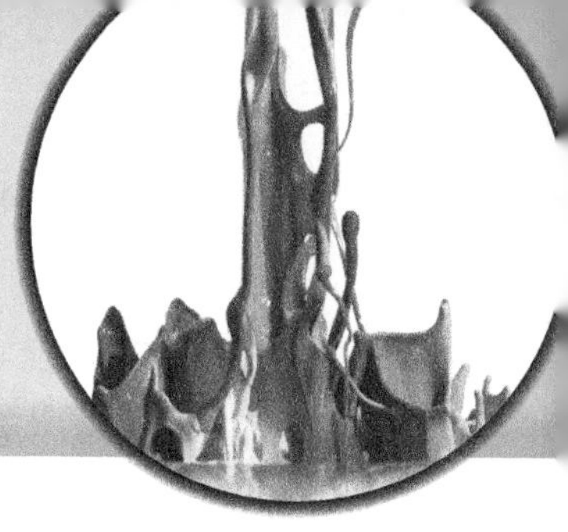

# About the author

Adrian Palmer is Professor of Marketing at ESC Rennes, France, a *Grand Ecole* which has been listed in the Financial Times rankings of the World's Top 50 schools for Masters in Management programmes. The School has an active group of researchers in the field of Services Marketing and Customer Experience Management. He was previously Professor of Marketing at Swansea University, UK and before entering academia held marketing positions in the transport and travel sectors. The author is Associate Editor of the Journal of Marketing Management and has published articles in many leading journals, including Journal of Services Marketing, European Journal of Marketing, Journal of Marketing Management and Tourism Management. Consultancy projects, previous work in the services sector and courses delivered throughout the world have informed the cases and examples used in this new edition.

# Preface

Today, more people in the Western world earn a living from producing services than from making manufactured goods. For consumers, increasing wealth has resulted in opportunities to buy services which were previously unattainable. For businesses, services are not a luxury, but have become essential inputs as firms concentrate on their core business activities and buy in specialist services from outside. Services have become a component of almost all products that we buy, and in this sense, all businesses are services businesses. The book explores the concept of 'service dominant logic' which puts services at the centre of all value creation

The growth of the services sector has presented many apparent paradoxes. Despite the efforts of services organizations to improve their quality standards, dissatisfaction has been seen to grow in many sectors, simply because firms have not kept up with consumers' rising expectations. There is the paradox of many services companies developing relationship marketing programmes with their customers, but which result in poor perceptions by customers of their relationships, as firms 'industrialize' their service processes. One explanation of such apparent paradoxes is that service benefits can only be defined in consumers' minds. With few tangible cues to go on, the same service can be perceived quite differently by two different consumers.

This book develops frameworks for understanding services and the effective marketing of them. Central to this are the characteristics of intangibility, inseparability, perishability and variability, which have profound implications for the way that marketing managers in the services sector develop their service offer, promote it and then deliver it. Traditional marketing-mix frameworks that apply to manufactured goods do not always work well for services. Services are about processes as much as outcomes and these processes often involve considerable interaction between customers and operations people. It follows therefore that marketing cannot be seen as an isolated function within an organization. Successful services companies make sure that their front-line staff can competently deliver the promises which marketing people make to customers. Services marketing cannot be separated from services management.

The book begins by trying to define services and assessing the impacts of core service characteristics on marketing activities. In some aspects of marketing, for example pricing and promotion, there may be relatively few differences between goods and services in the application of the general principles of marketing. In other aspects, new principles are called for. For this reason, a chapter is given to studying service systems in which the customer becomes a co-producer of a service, something which doesn't generally occur for goods where production and consumption are separated. Another chapter is devoted to studying the interface between human resource management and marketing, something that is vital for the success of people-based services. Other themes that are emphasized in this book are the importance of information technology as a tool for producing, distributing and promoting services, and the increasingly important role of buyer–seller relationships as a service benefit in its own right. The final chapter considers the problems and opportunities open to firms expanding overseas in increasingly competitive global markets for services.

To illustrate the general principles of services marketing, each chapter contains contemporary In Practice vignettes of good practice drawn from successful services organizations around the world, while Thinking Around the Subject boxes illustrate some of the operational challenges of putting theory into practice. The division of the material in this book into 14 chapters is to some extent arbitrary, and successful marketing must recognize the interrelatedness of all of the subjects covered. For this reason, each chapter concludes with a summary of key linkages to other chapters. Suggestions are made for further reading.

This new edition has been revised to take account of the most recent developments in services marketing. There is extensive coverage of Internet-based service delivery, noting the evolution of Web 2.0 to incorporate greater peer-to-peer interaction. The concept of 'customer experience' has aroused recent interest, and a new chapter is given to exploring experiential aspects of service consumption.

Adrian Palmer
mail@apalmer.com

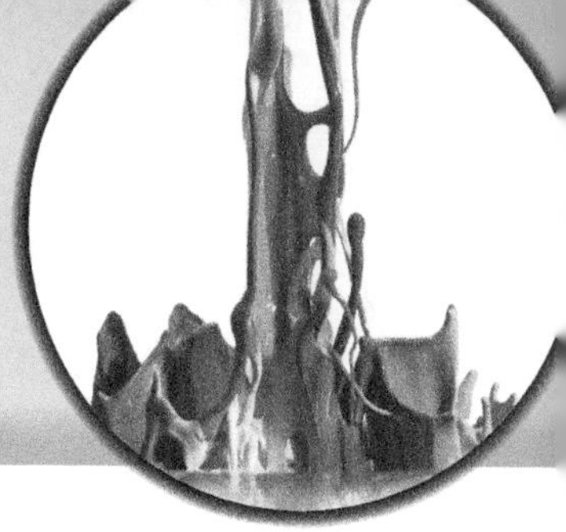

# Acknowledgements

The author and publishers would like to thank the following reviewers for their comments at various stages in the text's development:

Annie Chen, University of Westminster
Jill Brown, University of Portsmouth
Sangwon Park, University of Surrey
Andrea Beetles, University of Cardiff
Danilo Brozovic, Stockholm University
Saima Bantvawala, VU University Amsterdam
Solomon Russom Habtay, Witwatersrand

For the provision of case studies for the new edition we would also like to thank:

Paul Custance, Harper Adams University College, Shropshire, UK
Irena Descubes, ESC Rennes of School Business, France
Michael Etgar, College of Management, Tel-Aviv, Israel
Nicole Koenig-Lewis, Swansea University, UK
Rod McColl, ESC Rennes of School Business, France
Alexander Moll, Virtual Identity AG, Germany
Una McMahon-Beattie, University of Ulster, UK
Steve Worthington, Monash University, Melbourne, Australia

We would also like to thank the following organizations for allowing us permission to republish material:

Air Berlin
Amazon.co.uk
Birmingham International Airport
British Airways
British Telecom
Cheltenham Tourism
Childbase Nursery
Confused.com
Corbis Images
Crocus.co.uk
Domino's Pizza
easyJet
Expedia.co.uk
Experian
Fitness First
Gloucestershire County Cricket Club
Google
i-Stock
Jet2.com
Kallkwik
Lastminute.com
Lifestyle Marketing (Mother & Baby) Ltd
McDonald's Corporation
Orange
Sainsbury's
Timpson
TripAdvisor
Virgin Galactica
Virgin Media
Whitbread PLC (Premier Inn)

Every effort has been made to trace and acknowledge ownership of copyright and to clear permission for material reproduced in this book. The publishers will be pleased to make suitable arrangements to clear permission with any copyright holders whom it has not been possible to contact.

# Guided tour

Chapter 1

What is services marketing?

## Opening vignette

Each chapter opens with a short reflective example which illustrates the chapter's key themes in practice, setting the scene for the issues that will be addressed in the chapter.

*Joey was visiting the capital of an Asian country where he had read in his guidebook about a ne which incorporated an imitation volcano. Every hour, spectacular lighting effects, rumbling sc movement in the tables and chairs simulated the eruption of a volcano, which were a great tou region. For Joey, this was a 'must see' to be experienced, but his friend entered the restaura He just wanted to eat and he got no enjoyment from sitting through the light and sound disp American visitors from California were traumatized by the experience, bringing back memorie were living in an active earthquake zone. Joey might have enjoyed the experience of the volcan even he had to admit that after the third or fourth time, it became repetitive and boring – now the restaurant for eating. When services companies move from providing purely utilitarian ben istic benefits, the nature of the value that they deliver to customers becomes much more comp the case of a restaurant with an imitation volcano, the 'experience' might have been exciting to so and bad for yet others. Even those who found the experience good one day might find that anoth different and that what once generated positive emotions is now dominated by negative fee we will explore some of the complexities of designing services which provide a high level of ' beginning with the conceptual issues about defining the term, and working through to practica*

### Learning objectives

After reading this chapter, you should understand:

- Theoretical underpinnings of the concept of 'customer experience'
- Frameworks for understanding and managing customer experience
- The effects of other customers on individuals' experience of a service
- Issues and problems for the services marketer that arise from having to produce a se of customers in a safe and secure environment

## Learning objectives

Learning objectives clearly summarize what knowledge, skills and understanding readers should acquire from each chapter.

### In practice: A smarter way to communicate

Matching the target market with media audiences is key to successful communication. A message sent to the wrong audience is a message wasted. For this purpose, target markets have traditionally been defined in terms of economic, social and demographic factors, and the stage that a consumer has reached in the buying process. Timing has always been crucial, and a message that is too late or too early for the target audience may be wasted. Increasingly, the place that a message is received is becoming a basis for defining a target audience. Newspapers, television and radio stations have for a long time segmented their audience by time and place (e.g. leisure attractions advertising in the local press just before the weekend). With the advent of smartphones, the ability to target messages to geographically very specific audiences is greatly increased. This is particularly important for inseparable and perishable services, so for example a restaurant with spare capacity can send special offer messages to people on its database who are in the area at the time. Smartphones also offer the chance of two-way feedback communication; for example, the recipient of a message smartphone to book a table at the restaurant immediately. There is some evidence t received at exactly the right location may increase a consumer's expenditure (Hui et al., 2

## In practice examples

Each chapter includes numerous boxed examples of concepts and ideas, illustrating how services are delivered and experienced by customers in practice.

## Figures and Tables

Each chapter contains photos, models and tables with descriptive captions clearly making links to chapter content.

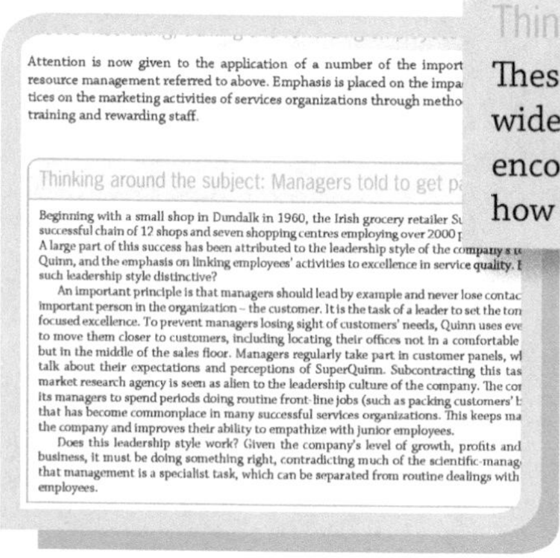

## Thinking around the subject

These boxes help you to see the real-life application and wider implications of services marketing decisions. They encourage you to explore 'the bigger picture' and question how the issues work in practice.

## Case studies

Each chapter ends with a longer case study designed to test how you can apply the main concepts you have learned. All the case studies are based on real-life examples taken from a variety of service contexts, and contain questions to test your understanding.

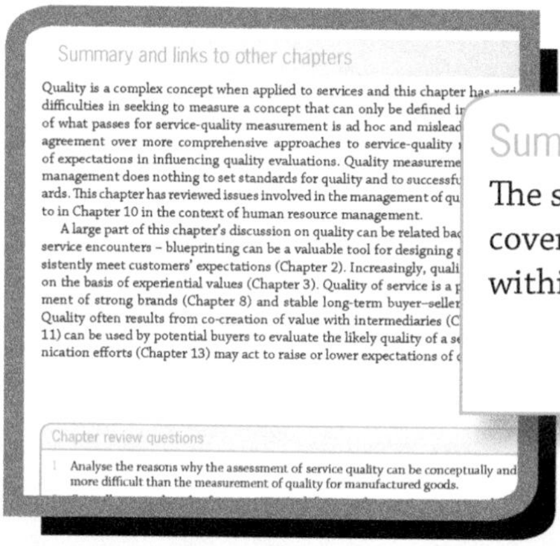

## Summary and links to other chapters

The summary briefly reviews and reinforces the main topics covered, and clearly shows how they link to other chapters within the book.

## End of chapter activities

Chapter review questions help you review your learning, while Activities give you the opportunity to apply what you've learned in practice.

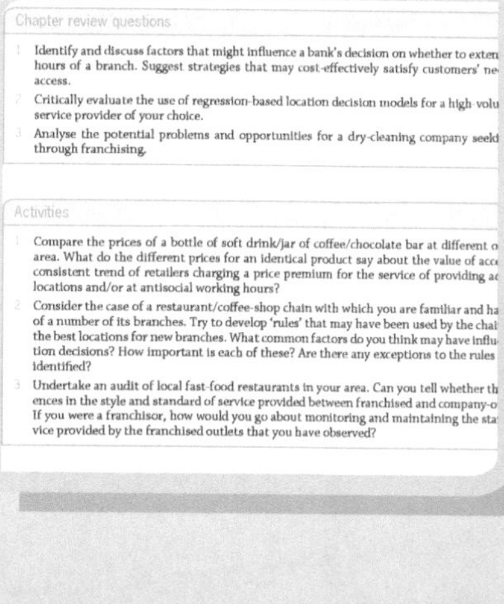

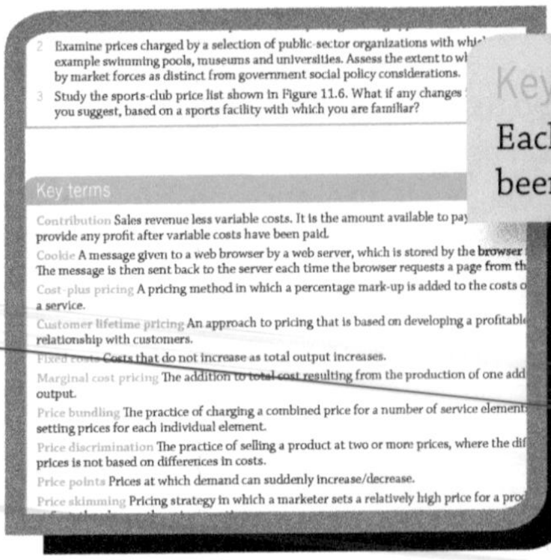
2 Examine prices charged by a selection of public-sector organizations with whi... example swimming pools, museums and universities. Assess the extent to wh... by market forces as distinct from government social policy considerations.
3 Study the sports-club price list shown in Figure 11.6. What if any changes ... you suggest, based on a sports facility with which you are familiar?

Key terms

Contribution Sales revenue less variable costs. It is the amount available to pay ... provide any profit after variable costs have been paid.
Cookie A message given to a web browser by a web server, which is stored by the browser ... The message is then sent back to the server each time the browser requests a page from th...
Cost-plus pricing A pricing method in which a percentage mark-up is added to the costs o... a service.
Customer lifetime pricing An approach to pricing that is based on developing a profitabl... relationship with customers.
Fixed costs Costs that do not increase as total output increases.
Marginal cost pricing The addition to total cost resulting from the production of one add... output.
Price bundling The practice of charging a combined price for a number of service element... setting prices for each individual element.
Price discrimination The practice of selling a product at two or more prices, where the dif... prices is not based on differences in costs.
Price points Prices at which demand can suddenly increase/decrease.
Price skimming Pricing strategy in which a marketer sets a relatively high price for a pro...

## Key terms

Each chapter has a short glossary of key terms which have been introduced in the chapter.

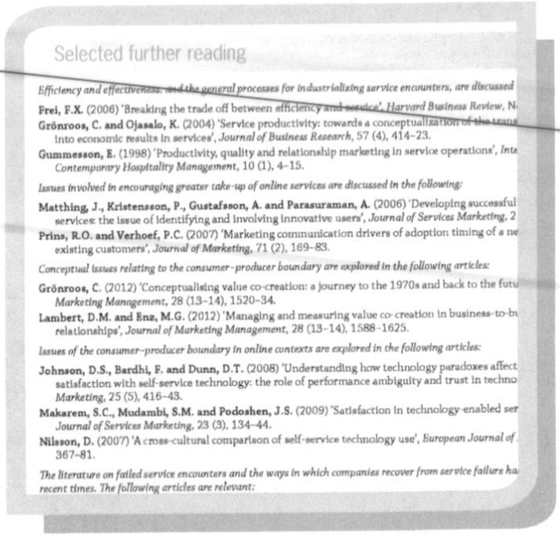
Selected further reading

*Efficiency and effectiveness, and the general processes for industrialising service encounters, are discussed ...*

**Frei, F.X.** (2006) 'Breaking the trade off between efficiency and service', *Harvard Business Review*, N...
**Grönroos, C. and Ojasalo, K.** (2004) 'Service productivity: towards a conceptualization of the trans... into economic results in services', *Journal of Business Research*, 57 (4), 414–23.
**Gummesson, E.** (1998) 'Productivity, quality and relationship marketing in service operations', *Int... Contemporary Hospitality Management*, 10 (1), 4–15.

*Issues involved in encouraging greater take-up of online services are discussed in the following:*

**Matthing, J., Kristensson, P., Gustafsson, A. and Parasuraman, A.** (2006) 'Developing successful ... services: the issue of identifying and involving innovative users', *Journal of Services Marketing*, 2...
**Prins, R.O. and Verhoef, P.C.** (2007) 'Marketing communication drivers of adoption timing of a ne... existing customers', *Journal of Marketing*, 71 (2), 169–83.

*Conceptual issues relating to the consumer–producer boundary are explored in the following articles:*

**Grönroos, C.** (2012) 'Conceptualising value co-creation: a journey to the 1970s and back to the futu... *Marketing Management*, 28 (13–14), 1520–34.
**Lambert, D.M. and Enz, M.G.** (2012) 'Managing and measuring value co-creation in business-to-bu... relationships', *Journal of Marketing Management*, 28 (13–14), 1588–1625.

*Issues of the consumer–producer boundary in online contexts are explored in the following articles:*

**Johnson, D.S., Bardhi, F. and Dunn, D.T.** (2008) 'Understanding how technology paradoxes affect ... satisfaction with self-service technology: the role of performance ambiguity and trust in techno... *Marketing*, 25 (5), 416–43.
**Makarem, S.C., Mudambi, S.M. and Podoshen, J.S.** (2009) 'Satisfaction in technology-enabled ser... *Journal of Services Marketing*, 23 (3), 134–44.
**Nilsson, D.** (2007) 'A cross-cultural comparison of self-service technology use', *European Journal of ...* 367–81.

*The literature on failed service encounters and the ways in which companies recover from service failure ha... recent times. The following articles are relevant:*

## Selected further reading and references

In addition to a comprehensive list of references, each chapter contains a list of annotated further reading. These suggestions have been chosen as the ideal starting point for any additional reading or further research on the chapter's themes.

# Technology to enhance teaching and learning

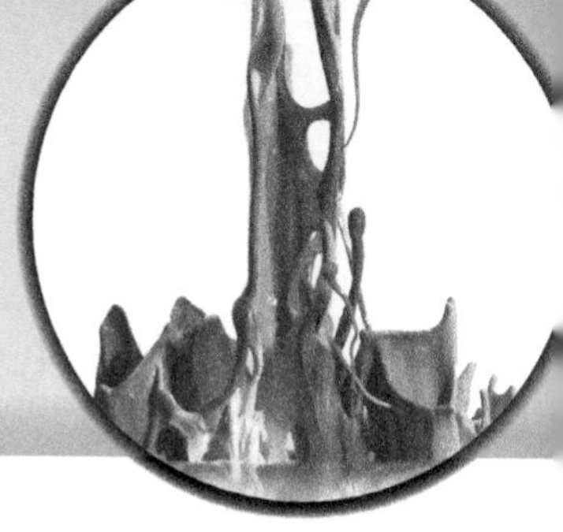

*Visit www.mheducation.co.uk/textbooks/palmerservices7 today*

## Online Learning Centre (OLC)

The new seventh edition website provides lecturers with additional time-saving tools to help them to prepare their module materials. Students will also find the website provides a number of useful supporting resources for revision and self-test.

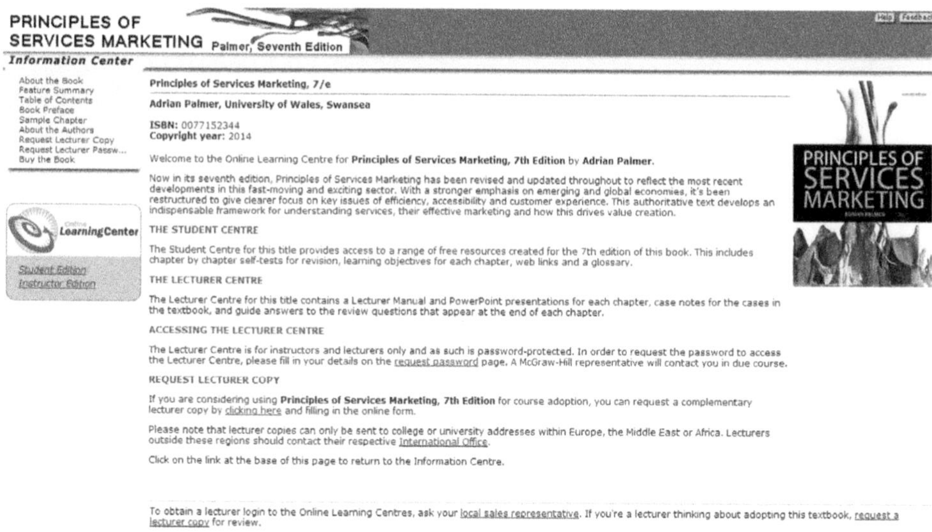


## For lecturers

The site provides a number of key teaching resources to help you to prepare your seminars and lectures using this textbook.

**PowerPoint Presentations** – chapter by chapter PowerPoint presentations have been prepared by the author. These can be used in lectures or seminars and can be edited to suit your module.

**Lecturer Manual** – A fully revised and updated manual of teaching tips and suggestions has also be provided for the new edition

**Case Study Solutions** – A set of suggested answers have been written to help lecturers to prepare for to deliver a case from the book in class or as a student assignment

**Answers to Chapter Review Questions** – The author has also provided some guide answers to the questions that appear at the end of the chapters in the book.

To request the password for the resources, either visit the site **www.mheducation.co.uk/textbooks/palmerservices7** and fill out on the online form or ask your McGraw-Hill Education representative to help you.

## For students

**Multiple Choice Self-Test Questions** – the new edition provides students with a set of multiple choice questions for each chapter in the book. Students can take the quiz and get instant results to see how well they have understood the topics in the chapter.

**Glossary** – a glossary containing all the key terms and their definitions from the textbook will also be available free online.

Visit the site to find all of these free resources and more . . .

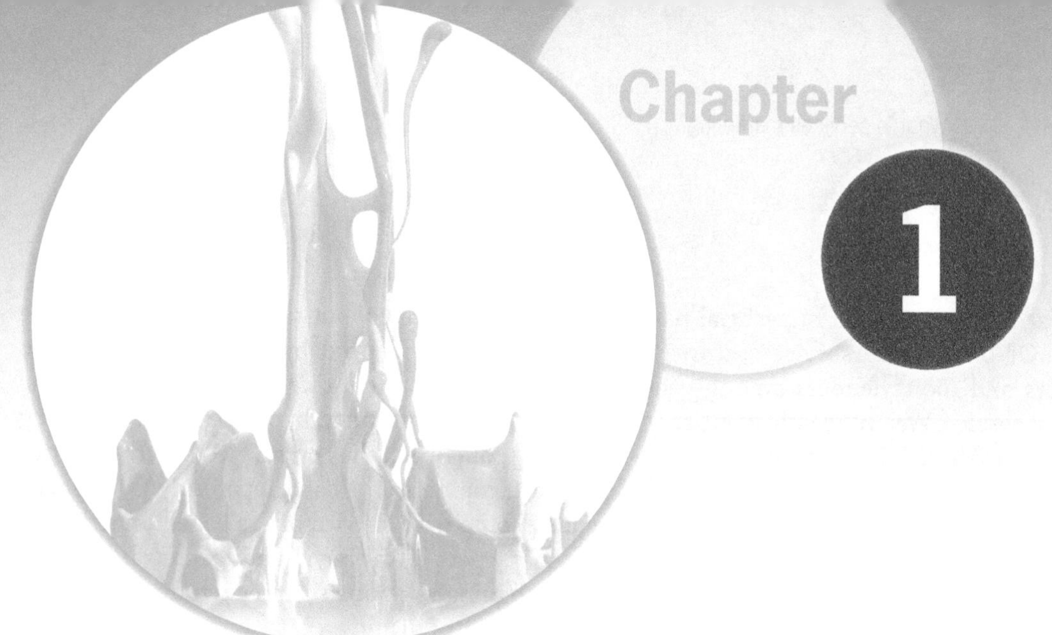

Chapter 1

# What is services marketing?

*Consider two major items that a private household is likely to buy – the annual holiday and a new large-screen television. Which would you rather have marketing responsibility for? They probably cost about the same, but think about all the ways in which trying to sell the holiday may be much more difficult than the television. Buyers will not be able to examine the holiday until they are committed to it, unlike the television which can be seen and examined before purchase. You would have to overcome holiday buyers' perception of risk, especially given widespread reports of 'nightmare' holidays. On the other hand, how often do televisions go wrong? And if they do, a buyer probably got a guarantee so would just take it back and get a new one. These are the kinds of issues we will be exploring in this first chapter. Do services really differ from goods? Indeed, are the two quite distinct categories? If you were selling the television, you would probably be very keen to sell additional services such as finance, installation, a warranty and maybe even subscription television services.*

## Learning objectives

After reading this chapter, you should understand:

- What is meant by the term services
- How national economies have become dominated by services
- The theoretical underpinnings of 'service dominant logic'
- The distinguishing characteristics of intangibility, perishability, inseparability and variability
- Differences between the marketing of goods and services
- The extended marketing mix for services
- The role of marketing in a service-based economy

## 1.1 Introduction

Services are not a minor or superficial part of Western economies, but go to the heart of value creation. Of course, the service sector is nothing new, as evidenced by biblical references to innkeepers and moneylenders among others. Today most products that we buy include some element of service. We can readily identify activities such as accountancy, banking and hairdressing as being service based. In addition to these, a wide range of goods relies on service-based activities to give them value in use, and a marketing advantage over competitors. Many apparently 'pure' goods such as television sets and washing machines usually come with service offers based on delivery, financing, insurance and maintenance benefits. For many people, car buying has been transformed from an infrequent but major capital purchase to an ongoing relationship in which finance, insurance and maintenance services help to provide a key benefit of owning a car – movement.

Although there has been a big growth in interest in the services sector in recent years, the academic literature has not always recognized its value. Some early economists paid little attention to services, considering them to be unproductive, adding nothing of value to an economy. Adam Smith, writing in the mid-eighteenth century, included intermediaries, doctors, lawyers and the armed forces as groups whom he described as 'unproductive of any value' (Smith, 1977, p. 430). Attitudes towards services began to change from the latter part of the nineteenth century, when Alfred Marshall argued that a person providing a service was just as capable of giving utility to the recipient as a person producing a tangible product. Indeed, Marshall recognized that tangible products may not exist at all without the services performed in order to produce them and to make them available to consumers. To Marshall, an agent distributing agricultural produce performed as valuable a task as the farmer himself. Without the provision of transport and intermediary services, agricultural products produced in areas of surplus would be of no value (Reisman, 2012).

Today, despite some lingering beliefs that the services sector is in some way an 'inferior' sector of the economy, considerable attention is paid to its direct and indirect economic consequences. Indeed, in an important article which talked about the 'service-centric' organization, services were seen as the driving force behind all value creation in the economy (Vargo and Lusch, 2004). Services, in effect, are vital for creating 'value in use' for goods, and goods effectively become a subsidiary part of a service offer. We will return to this point later.

There are many definitions of what constitutes a service. Modern definitions of services focus on the fact that a service in itself produces no tangible output, although it may facilitate the production of tangible goods. Perhaps one of the simplest definitions of a service was given by *The Economist*, which described services as:

> anything that cannot be dropped on your foot.

The definition of services that will be used to define the scope of this book is:

> The production of an essentially intangible benefit, either in its own right or as a significant element of a tangible product, which, through some form of exchange, satisfies an identified need.

This definition recognizes that most products are in fact a combination of goods elements and services elements. In some cases, the service element will be the focal element of the service (e.g. hairdressing and management consultancy), while in other cases the service will simply support the provision of a tangible good (e.g. a loan facility provided to support the sale of a new car).

We should also mention here how service (singular) has been distinguished from services (plural). In everyday usage, the two terms are often used interchangeably. However, some, for example Vargo and Lusch, see an important distinction. In the context of their service dominant logic framework, service indicates a *process* of using resources for the benefit of serving a consumer. These resources could be provided by both the service provider and the consumer, who co-operate through a process of co-creation. *Services*, on the other hand, refer to intangible units of *output* – a ride on a bus, an SMS message or a haircut, for example. Expressed another way, service can be thought of as a verb and services as a noun (Vargo and Lusch, 2008).

In the evolution of the services marketing literature, there has been argument about the extent to which services should be considered a distinctive area of study in marketing. On the one hand, some have argued that a service contains many important elements common to goods, which makes services marketing obsolete as a separate discipline. Thus, Levitt (1972) observed:

> . . . there is no such thing as service industries. There are only industries where service components are greater or less than those of other industries.

On the other hand, many have pointed to the limitations of traditional marketing principles when applied to the marketing of services. Grönroos (1978), Lovelock (1981), Shostack (1977), Berry (1980) and Rathmell (1974) were among early critics who argued that there were such big differences between goods and services that the marketing tools used for goods marketing cannot easily be translated to services marketing. In reality, many of the principles of goods marketing – such as the importance of understanding customers' needs – can be applied to services with relatively little refinement. But in some cases – such as the analysis of service encounters – a new area of marketing thought needs to be opened up.

In addition to the grey area between a pure good and a pure service, some marketing activities do not easily fit on this scale at all. The first of these is the marketing of ideas, whether these be the ideas of a political party, a religious sect or an idea on a specific subject, such as road safety. The second – and related – area is the marketing of a cause, such as famine relief in Africa or a campaign to prevent the construction of a new road. Both of these types of activity are distinguished from normal goods and services marketing as there is no exchange of value between the producer and the individuals or organizations at whom the marketing effort is aimed. To take an example, the consumer of transport services enters into an exchange and pays for services received, either directly and willingly (as in the case of a train fare), or indirectly (and possibly unwillingly) through general taxation, as is the case for the use of roads. By contrast, when a pressure group mounts a campaign to stop the building of a new road, the concept of exchange of value becomes extremely tenuous.

Generally, the concept of services does not offer an appropriate framework for analysing the marketing of ideas and causes where these do not form part of an exchange-based service process. Of course, in many cases, consumers of a service are buying into an idea promoted by the service provider, or may identify with a cause that the provider promotes. Many customers of coffee shops using Fairtrade coffee, for example, choose their coffee shop because of its identification with the cause of developing-world producers. In this case, there is a market-based transaction (the purchase) to support the idea. At other times, a service exchange may be based almost entirely on an idea. Copywriters and consultants may be selling little more than an idea, but again there is an exchange between the parties (a payment in return for a creative idea). We return to the subject of ideas, or knowledge-based services, later in this chapter.

### 1.1.1 The growth of service-based economies

There is little doubt that the services sector has become a dominant force in national economies. Within the European Union (EU)-27 countries, *services* (including public administration) accounted for 74.1 per cent of total gross value added in the EU economy *in 2009* (Eurostat, 2011). Business activities and financial services accounted for 29.2 per cent of the EU-27's gross value added, followed by other services (largely made up of public administration and education and health services, as well as other community, social and personal service activities (24.0 per cent)) and trade, transport and communication services (20.9 per cent) (Eurostat, 2011). Manufacturing in the EU is playing a steadily diminishing role in both employment and output. In contrast, the services sector accounted for around three-quarters of all growth in employment and GDP since 2000 (European Investment Bank, 2010).

There appears to be a close correlation between the level of economic development in an economy (as expressed by its gross domestic product – GDP – per capita) and the strength of its services sector. The more highly developed economies are associated with a high proportion of employees in the services sector. Within the EU-27 there is variation in the share of value-added derived from services, with more developed member states having higher proportions (e.g. UK 76 per cent, France 78 per cent) and less developed member states lower (e.g. Bulgaria 64 per cent, Slovakia 63 per cent) (World Bank, 2011).

According to the International Labour Organization, 72.8 per cent of all workers from developed economies were employed in the services sector in 2009 (e.g. USA 79.4 per cent, UK 77.6 per cent, France 73.9 per cent, Japan 67.8 per cent, Hong Kong 86.7 per cent). Lower figures are found in many of the emerging economies, for example Mexico 60.9 per cent, Malaysia 57.9 per cent, the Philippines 50.3 per cent and Turkey 45.8 per cent. The lowest levels of service employment are found in the less developed countries, for example Indonesia 41.0 per cent and Thailand 38.1 per cent (ILO, 2011). Within the 27 EU countries, 69.8 per cent of all employment was within the services sector in 2011, having risen from 62 per cent in 2000 (Eurostat, 2012).

Figure 1.1 indicates the close correlation between GDP per head and services sector employment.

While there is undoubtedly a close correlation between the level of a country's economic development and the level of services activity within its economy, which is the cause and which is the effect? Does the existence of a services sector result in growth, or are services an outcome of that growth? To answer this question, we need to distinguish between business-to-business services and consumer services. Business-to-business services provide inputs to other companies' production processes. They have often had a major impact on national economies and many service industries have allowed improved productivity elsewhere in the manufacturing and agricultural sectors. As an example, transport and distribution services have often had the effect of stimulating economic development at local and national levels (e.g. following the improvement of rail or road services). One reason for agriculture not having been fully exploited in some developing countries has been the ineffective service-based distribution systems available to food producers. *Consumer services*, on the other hand, consume wealth rather than create it. As national economies become more prosperous, we have a tendency to increase our consumption of a wide range of consumer services, such as holidays, entertainment and eating out.

Although it is conventional wisdom that the services sector has grown strongly in recent years, we need to qualify this with the following observations:

- A common practice in recent decades has been for manufacturing companies to 'outsource' many of their support activities, such as accounting, distribution, cleaning and catering. Often, staff who were previously employed by the manufacturer have transferred to the new outsourced service supplier. National statistics record this as a reduction in manufacturing sector employment and an increase in services sector employment, even though the employees involved are doing exactly the same work as before and there has been no net increase in service

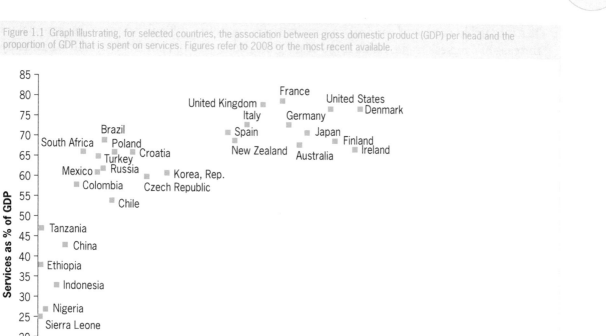

Figure 1.1 Graph illustrating, for selected countries, the association between gross domestic product (GDP) per head and the proportion of GDP that is spent on services. Figures refer to 2008 or the most recent available.

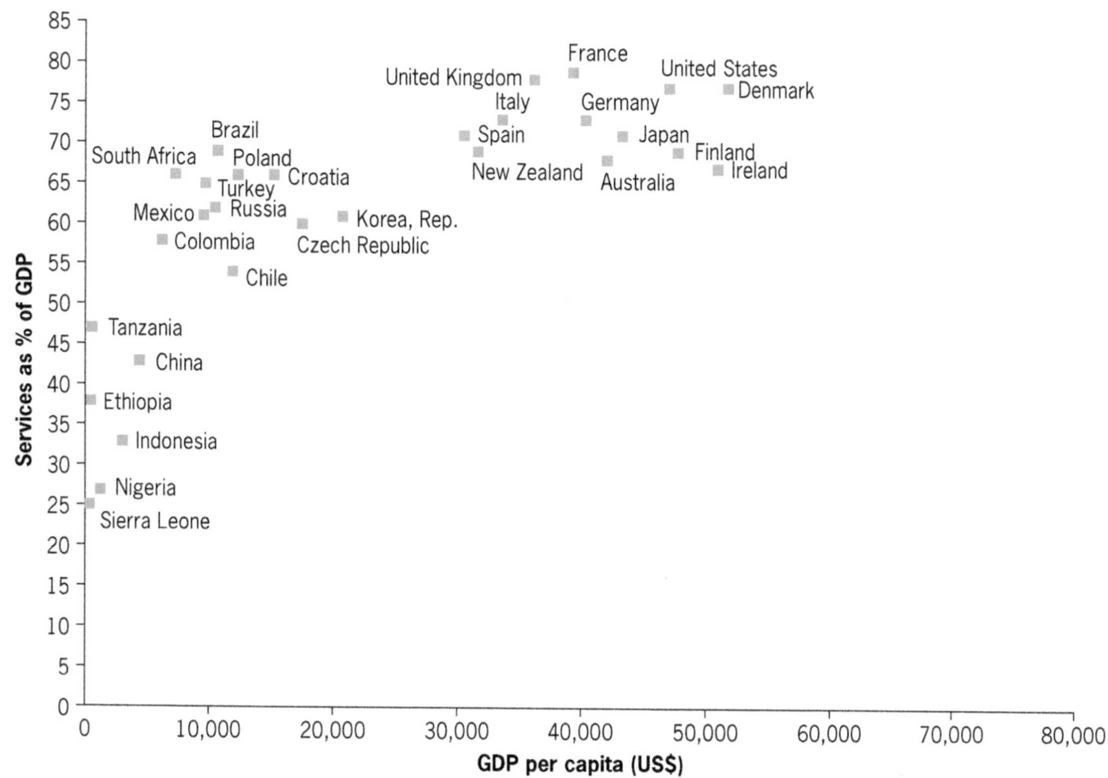


*Source*: based on World Bank, 2012

production. The key difference is that the services are now market mediated rather than internally produced.

- The system of Standard Industrial Classifications (SICs) for a long while did not disaggregate the services sector in the same level of detail as manufacture or agriculture. Many products are classified as manufactured goods, when in fact they are sold with a substantial service component. Further refinement of SICs has led to some new counting of services as separate activities which might previously have been included in manufacturing output.
- Methods used to measure services differ between countries, and this may explain some of the observed variation in the size of countries' services sectors. In 2006, the Chinese government revised its estimates of the country's GDP figure for 2004. It suddenly 'found' $40 billion worth of services that had previously not been recorded using the country's material product system, developed in the 1980s under the centrally planned economic system. As a result of this change, the proportion of the country's GDP accounted for by services rose overnight from 31.9 to 40.7 per cent.
- Many services are produced within household units and not counted in statistics of national output. Families who look after young children or elderly relatives are producing service-type benefits comparable to those of a kindergarten or care home, but the latter would be included in statistics of national economic output, while the former would not.

- The intangible nature of services can make them relatively difficult to measure, especially in the case of overseas trade. While flows of tangible goods through ports can usually be measured relatively easily, trade flows associated with services are much more difficult to identify and measure. Furthermore, cutbacks in government statistical collection have sometimes reduced the accuracy of many series. As an example, the UK trade figures relating to tourism and financial services frequently have to be revised after initial publication.

Services can have a **multiplier effect** on local and national economies, where initial spending with a service producer triggers further expenditure. The services multiplier works like this. The first producer spends money buying in supplies from other suppliers (including labour) and these suppliers in turn purchase more inputs. The multiplier effect of this initial expenditure can result in the total increase in household incomes being much greater than the original expenditure. The local multiplier effects of additional service activity will depend on the proportion of the subsequent spending that is kept within the local area. A good example of the multiplier effect was used to argue the case for London's successful bid to host the 2012 Olympic Games. Among many multiplier effects, expenditure on new transport and accommodation facilities brought long-term employment benefits to relatively deprived parts of East London.

One approach to understanding the contribution of services to other areas of economic activity is input–output analysis, a methodology attributed to the economist Wassily Leontief. This uses matrices to show data on production, labour and capital inputs by sector and/or region. Wood (1987) used this approach to estimate the effects of productivity improvements in the services sector on productivity levels in all other sectors. Some apparently high-productivity sectors were shown to be held back by the low productivity of some of their inputs, including service inputs. On the other hand, efficiency improvements in some services such as transport and distribution were shown to have had widespread beneficial effects on the productivity of other sectors.

Should Western developed economies focus on becoming service-based economies, even at the expense of the manufacturing sector? This may sound appealing, but the logic of this argument can be pushed too far. In particular:

1. A large part of the growth in the service sector has reflected the prosperity of the manufacturing sector. As manufacturing industry increases its level of activity, the demand for business-to-business services such as accountancy, legal services and business travel increases. However, during a period of decline in manufacturing, demand for associated services will decline. As an example, the level of house-building in the UK fell sharply following the 'financial crisis' of 2008, resulting in reduced demand for architecture, estate agency and financial services.
2. For Western developed economies, it may be naïve to assume that they can depend on services while other emerging economies focus on low-cost manufacturing. Many Western countries, including the UK, lost their competitive advantage in many manufacturing sectors to emerging economies from the 1960s and 1970s. Could the same pattern be repeated for services? Software support services, which have been a major export of the UK, are increasingly challenged by competitors in India. Improved telecommunications have offered an opportunity for Indian-based call-centre providers to challenge British-based call centres. High levels of training in competing nations have allowed those countries first to develop their own indigenous services and then to develop them for export. Banking services which were once a net import of Japan are now exported by the Japanese throughout the world.
3. Over-reliance on the services sector could pose strategic problems for a country. A diverse economic base allows a national economy to be more resilient to changes in world trading conditions.

Figure 1.2 Plant growing has traditionally been associated primarily with the agricultural sector. However, crocus. co.uk has shown how even such a basic agricultural activity can be transformed into a service. The company does not just grow and sell plants, but can offer a complete service to the buyer which includes delivering and planting, as well as continuing to give advice about caring for the plant. The company realizes that the benefits of owning a plant may last long after the purchase of the plant, so these service-type activities create 'value in use' during the lifetime of the plant. Instead of selling a simple plant as a commodity product, it now offers a service in which the plant is just one component of the product offer. (Reproduced courtesy of crocus.co.uk)

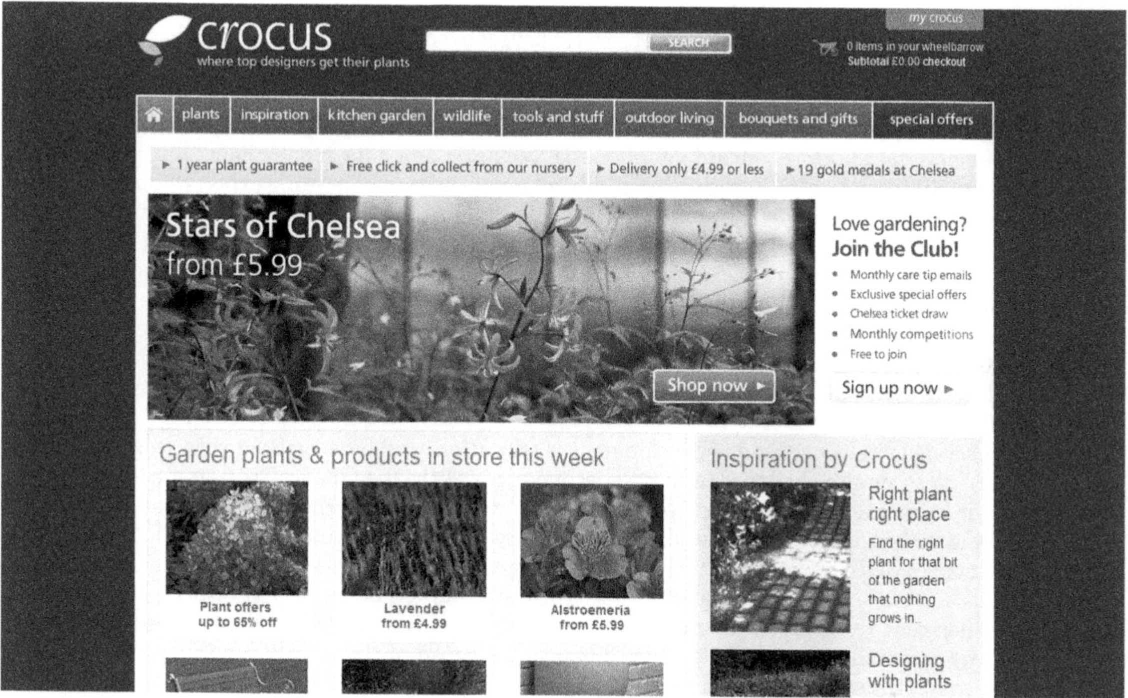


4 Some have suggested that many newer service industries such as call centres may destabilize local economies because they can be set up and closed down easily, unlike manufacturing industry which must invest in fixed and immovable capacity. This is particularly true where service production can be separated from service consumption. But, against this argument, we will see later in this chapter that the inseparability of services generally reduces their locational flexibility.

## 1.2 Distinguishing features of services

Services have a number of distinctive characteristics that differentiate them from goods and have implications for the manner in which they are marketed. These characteristics are often described as **intangibility**, **inseparability**, **variability**, **perishability** and the inability to own a service. These characteristics will be a recurrent theme throughout this book, and their nature is briefly introduced below.

### 1.2.1 Intangibility

A pure service cannot be assessed using any of the physical senses – it is an abstraction that cannot be directly examined before it is purchased. A prospective purchaser of most goods is able to examine goods for physical integrity, aesthetic appearance, taste, smell etc.

## Thinking around the subject: BRICS need their services too

'Brics' countries (Brazil, Russia, India and China) have seen spectacular growth in GDP in recent years, but could services bottlenecks eventually slow their growth? Just as Britain needed vital business-to-business services to fuel its growth during the nineteenth-century industrial revolution, the Brics countries need them today. However, some observers have looked to Brazil to illustrate what can happen when poorly developed services impede growth.

The World Economic Forum's 2013 Global Competitiveness Report assessed the quality of countries' infrastructure and ranked Brazil 107th of 144 countries, putting it below the other Brics countries and many other emerging countries, including Indonesia, Mexico, Cambodia and Thailand. Brazil's airports and ports – crucial to sustaining its agricultural, raw material and manufacturing exports – ranked Brazil among the 10 worst countries in the world. The poor quality of the country's ports and roads was highlighted in a report by management consultancy McKinsey (2013) which estimated that about 12 per cent of all grain produced in Brazil was wasted, not because of a lack of buyers, but because of shortcomings of the country's transport and storage infrastructure. McKinsey also noted that on an average day, severe congestion at the port of Paranaguá resulted in 89 ships waiting to dock, costing money in terms of lost utilization of the ships and crew, and also resulting in unreliable supply chains. Even getting to the ports was difficult, with only an estimated 5 per cent of roads in Brazil being paved, much less than in China (50 per cent) or Russia (80 per cent).

Another service vital to economic development is education, and here again Brazil's services sector has been seen by some as a challenge for further economic growth. The OECD's Programme for International Student Assessment (2012) noted that Brazil was some way behind other countries that it surveyed in 2012 (it was ranked 53 out of 65), resulting in some key sectors struggling to find qualified staff.

In 2012, Brazil's GDP grew by an estimated 1.3 per cent, down from 7.5 per cent in 2010, and seemingly dwarfed by the growth rates of China and India which had slowed down to still respectable levels of 7.8 and 5.4 per cent respectively. Some commentators blamed Brazil's falling growth rate on falling demand for its commodities, especially from China; appreciation of the Brazilian currency, making its exports less competitive; and controls on capital movements introduced by the Brazilian government. Were these just passing concerns? Or was the country having to face up to a more important reality that the availability of high-quality, key services are vital for continuing industrial growth?

Many advertising claims relating to these tangible properties can be verified by inspection prior to purchase. On the other hand, pure services have no tangible properties that can be used by consumers to verify advertising claims before the purchase is made. The intangible process characteristics that define services, such as reliability, personal care, attentiveness of staff, their friendliness etc., can only be verified once a service has been purchased and consumed.

The level of tangibility present in the service offer derives from three principal sources:

- tangible goods, which are included in the service offer and consumed by the user (e.g. the food in a restaurant);
- the physical environment in which the service production/consumption process takes place (the restaurant building);
- tangible evidence of service performance (seeing the cooks at work in the kitchen).

Where goods form an important component of a service offer, many of the practices associated with conventional goods marketing can be applied to this part of the service offer. Restaurants provide a mix of tangibles and intangibles and, in respect of the food element, few of the particular characteristics of services marketing are encountered. Therefore, production of the food can be separated from its consumption and there may be opportunities for potential customers to sample food beforehand, or to see a representation of it. The presence of a tangible component gives customers

Figure 1.3 Some implications of service intangibility

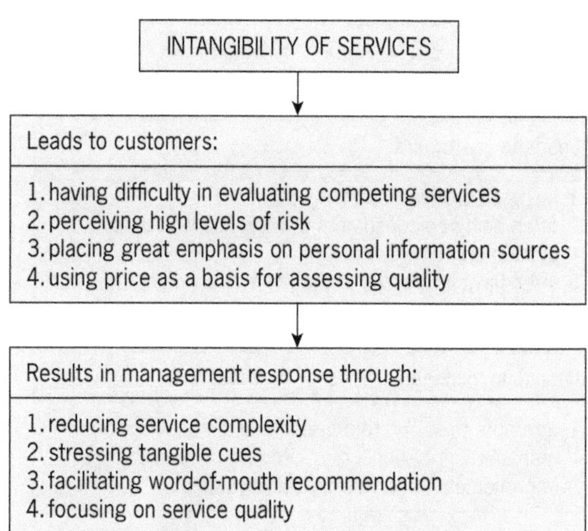


a visible basis on which to judge quality. While some services are rich in such tangible cues (e.g. restaurants, shops), other services provide relatively little tangible evidence (e.g. life insurance).

INTANGIBILITY OF SERVICES
Leads to customers:
1. having difficulty in evaluating competing services
2. perceiving high levels of risk
3. placing great emphasis on personal information sources
4. using price as a basis for assessing quality
Results in management response through:
1. reducing service complexity
2. stressing tangible cues
3. facilitating word-of-mouth recommendation
4. focusing on service quality

Intangibility has a number of important marketing implications (Figure 1.3), which will be examined in more detail in later chapters. The lack of physical evidence that intangibility implies increases the level of uncertainty a consumer faces when choosing between competing services. An important part of a services marketing programme will therefore involve reducing consumers' perceived risk by such means as adding physical evidence and the development of strong brands. It is interesting to note that pure goods and pure services tend to move in opposite directions in terms of their general approach to the issue of tangibility. While services marketers often seek to add tangible evidence to their product, pure goods marketers often augment their products by adding intangible elements such as loan finance and after-sales service.

### 1.2.2 Inseparability

The production and consumption of a tangible good are two separate activities. Companies usually produce goods in one central location and then transport them to the place where customers most want to buy them. In this way, manufacturing companies can achieve economies of scale through centralized production and have centralized quality-control checks. The manufacturer is also able to make goods at a time that is convenient to itself, then make them available to customers at times that are convenient to customers. Production and consumption are said to be separable. To see this effect, just look at the label of a typical shirt – it may be made in low-cost Vietnam, but sold in London's relatively wealthy Oxford Street. On the other hand, the consumption of a service is said to be inseparable from its means of production. Producer and consumer must interact in order for the benefits of the service to be realized – both must normally meet at a time and a place that is mutually convenient in order that the producer can directly pass on service benefits. In the extreme case of personal care services, the customer must be present during the entire production process – a surgeon cannot sensibly undertake an operation on a patient without the involvement of the patient. For services, marketing becomes a means of facilitating complex producer–consumer interaction, rather than being merely an exchange medium.

Figure 1.4 Some implications of service inseparability

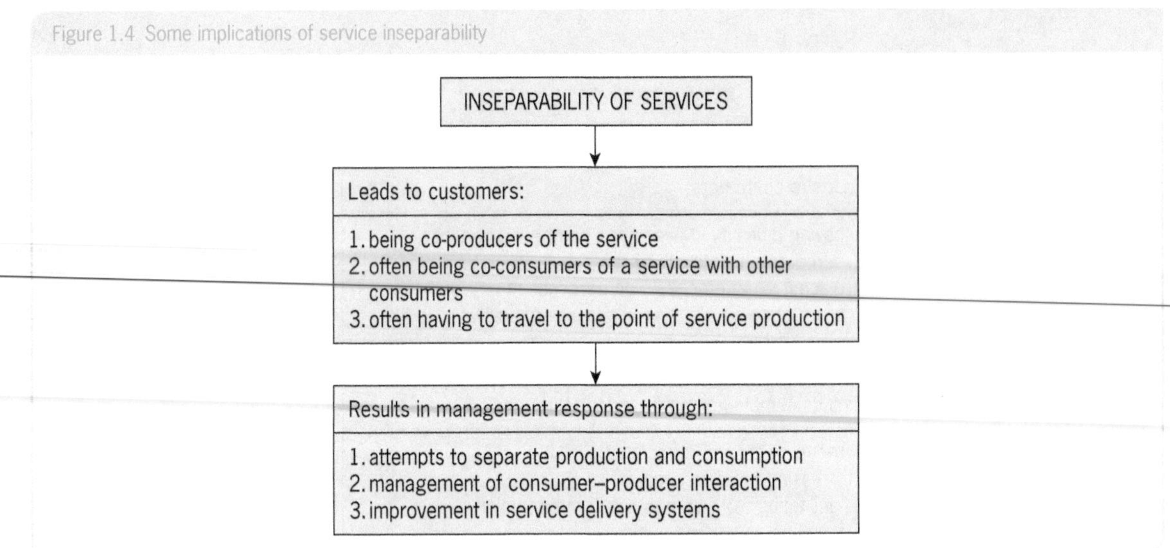


Inseparability occurs whether the producer is human – typical of healthcare services – or a machine (e.g. a bank automated teller machine – ATM). The service of the ATM can only be realized if the producer and consumer interact. In some cases, it has been possible to reduce the effects of inseparability, especially where the need for personal contact is low and the intangible information content is high. Customers of a bank no longer need to go into a branch and interact with bank employees in order to obtain information about their account. Nowadays, this can often be done just as easily using the Internet or a call centre, possibly located thousands of miles away. Inseparability still requires producer and consumer to interact, but technology has facilitated a more flexible and impersonal basis for interaction.

Inseparability has a number of important marketing implications for services (Figure 1.4). First, whereas goods are generally first produced, then offered for sale and finally sold and consumed, inseparability causes this process to be modified for services. They are generally sold first, then produced and consumed simultaneously. Second, while the method of goods production is to a large extent (though not always) of little importance to the consumer, production processes are usually critical to the enjoyment of services.

For goods, the consumer is not usually a part of the process of production and, in general, so long as the product that they take delivery of meets their expectations, they are satisfied (although there are exceptions, for example where the ethics of production methods cause concern, or where quality can only be assessed with a knowledge of production stages that are hidden from the consumer's view). With services, the active participation of the consumer in the production process often makes this process as important as defining the outcome of the service process. In some cases, an apparently slight change in service production methods may totally destroy the value of the service being provided. A person buying a ticket for a concert by Cliff Richard may derive no benefit at all from the concert if it is subsequently given by Lady Gaga instead.

### 1.2.3 Variability

There are two aspects of variability that affect services:

- the extent to which production performance varies unintentionally from a norm, in terms both of outcomes and of production processes;
- the extent to which a service can be deliberately varied to meet the specific needs of individual customers.

For services, variability impacts upon customers not just in terms of outcomes but also in terms of processes of production. It is the latter point that causes variability to pose a much greater problem for services, compared with goods. Because the customer is usually involved in the production process for a service at the same time as they consume it, it can be difficult to carry out monitoring and control to ensure consistent standards. The opportunity for pre-delivery inspection and rejection that is open to the goods manufacturer is not normally possible with services (Figure 1.5). The service must normally be produced in the presence of the customer without the possibility of intervening quality control.

Figure 1.5 We are all familiar with buying clothing and shoes made in countries such as China and Bangladesh where production costs are low. The production of goods in a low-cost country can be separated from their consumption in a high-income country. This opportunity for separation has not generally been possible for services, as the consumer and producer normally need to interact with each other. The development of telecommunications is allowing new opportunities to lessen the effects of service inseparability. Many service companies have located call centres in low-cost countries such as India, and customers may be quite unaware that their call is being answered several thousand miles away. (Reproduced with permission of Iserve Systems Ltd)

Variability in production standards is of greatest concern to services organizations where customers are highly involved in the production process, especially where production methods make it impractical to monitor service production (Figure 1.6). This is true of many labour-intensive personal services provided in a one-to-one situation, such as healthcare. Some services allow greater scope for quality-control checks to be undertaken during the production process, allowing an organization to provide a consistently high level of service. This is especially true of machine-based services; for example, telecommunication services can typically operate with very low failure rates (British Telecom claims that in over 99 per cent of all attempts to obtain service, customers are able to make a connection to their dialled number at the first attempt).

The tendency today is for equipment-based services to be regarded as less variable than those that involve a high degree of employee intervention in the production process. Many services organizations have sought to reduce variability – and hence to build strong brands – by adopting equipment-based production methods. Replacing human telephone operators with computerized voice systems and the automation of many banking services are typical of this trend. Sometimes

Figure 1.6 Causes and consequences of service variability

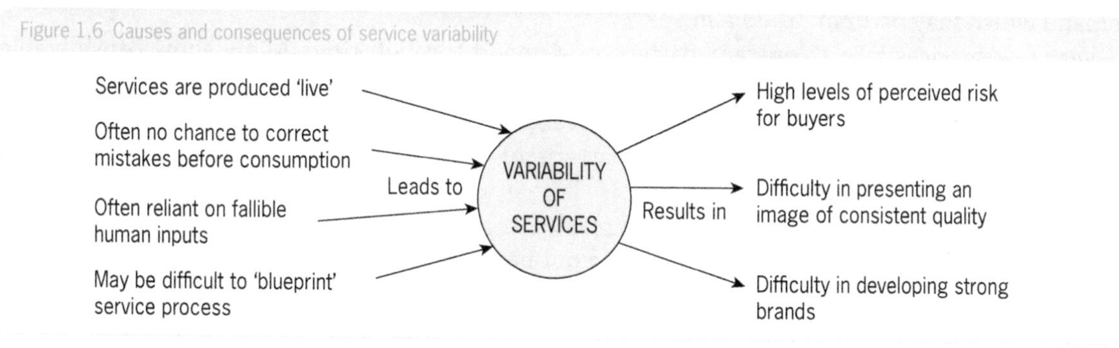
Services are produced 'live'
Often no chance to correct mistakes before consumption
Often reliant on fallible human inputs
May be difficult to 'blueprint' service process
Leads to
VARIABILITY OF SERVICES
Results in
High levels of perceived risk for buyers
Difficulty in presenting an image of consistent quality
Difficulty in developing strong brands

reduced personnel variability has been achieved by passing on part of the production process to consumers, in the way that self-service petrol filling stations are no longer dependent on the variability of forecourt serving staff.

The second dimension of variability is the extent to which a service can be deliberately customized to meet the specific needs of individual customers. Because services are created as they are consumed, and because consumers are often a part of the production process, the potential for customization of services is generally greater than for manufactured goods. The extent to which a service can be customized is dependent upon the production methods employed. Services that are produced for large numbers of customers simultaneously may offer little scope for individual customization. The production methods of a railway do not allow individual customers' needs to be met in the way that the simpler production methods of a taxi operator may be able to (e.g. the taxi can leave ten minutes later than planned at the request of the customer, but the train operator is unlikely to be willing or able to delay departure following a request from one individual passenger).

The extent to which services can be customized is partly a function of management decisions on the level of authority to be delegated to front-line service personnel. While some service operations give discretion to front-line staff, the tendency is for service firms to 'industrialize' their encounters with customers. Industrialization implies following clearly specified standardized procedures in each encounter. While industrialization often reduces the flexibility of producers to meet customers' needs, it also has the effect of reducing variability of processes and outcomes. We will return to the subject of industrialization in Chapter 2.

The variability of service output can make the development of strong brands more difficult for services than for goods. For the latter it is usually relatively easy to incorporate monitoring and quality-control procedures into production processes in order to ensure that a brand stands for a consistency of output. The services sector's attempts to reduce variability concentrate on methods used to select, train, motivate and control personnel, issues which are examined in Chapter 10. In some cases, service offers have been simplified, jobs have been 'deskilled' and personnel replaced with machines in order to reduce human variability.

### 1.2.4 Perishability

Services differ from goods in that they cannot be stored. A producer of cars that is unable to sell all of its output in the current period can carry forward stocks to sell in a subsequent period. The only significant costs are storage costs, financing costs and the possibility of loss through obsolescence. By contrast, the producer of a service that cannot sell all of its output produced in the current period gets no chance to carry it forward for sale in a subsequent period. An airline which offers seats on a 9.00 a.m. flight from Warsaw to Paris cannot sell any empty seats once the aircraft has left at 9.00 a.m. The service offer disappears and spare seats cannot be stored to meet a surge in demand which may occur at 10.00 a.m.

Very few services face a constant pattern of demand through time. Many show considerable variation, which could be a daily variation (city-centre sandwich bars at lunchtime), weekly (the Friday-evening peak in demand for railway travel), seasonal (hotels, stores at Christmas time), cyclical (mortgages) or an unpredictable pattern of demand (e.g. emergency building-repair services following heavy storms).

The perishability of services (Figure 1.7) results in greater attention having to be paid to the management of supply and demand by evening out peaks and troughs in demand, and in scheduling service production to follow this pattern as far as possible. Pricing and promotion are two of the tools commonly adopted to tackle this problem and these are discussed in Chapter 11.

Figure 1.7 Causes and consequences of service perishability

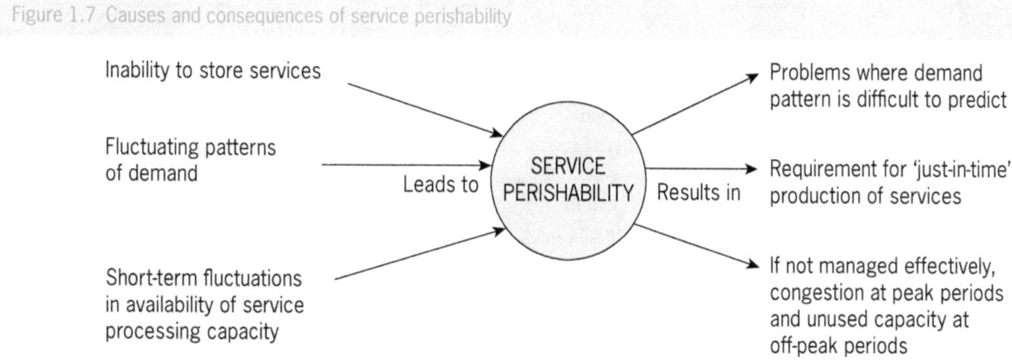


### 1.2.5 Ownership

The inability to own a service is related to the characteristics of intangibility and perishability. In purchasing goods, buyers generally acquire title to the goods in question and can subsequently do as they wish with them, including selling them on to somebody else. On the other hand, when a service is performed, no ownership is transferred from the seller to the buyer. The buyer is merely buying the right to a service process such as the use of a car park or a solicitor's time. A distinction should be drawn between the inability to own the service act and the rights that a buyer may acquire to have a service carried out at some time in the future (a theatre ticket, for example). To some (e.g. Lovelock and Gummesson, 2004), the concept of rental/rights to access defines a service where it is otherwise impossible to transfer ownership of a product through an exchange transaction.

The inability to own a service has implications for the design of distribution channels, so a wholesaler or retailer cannot take title, as is the case with goods. Instead, direct distribution methods are more common and, where intermediaries are used, they generally act as a co-producer with the service provider.

## 1.3 The service offer

A further approach to defining a service begins by asking what it is that a consumer is buying, and distinguishing between two levels of service purchase:

- the core service;
- the secondary service.

The core service is best understood in terms of the essential benefit that a service provides. Grönroos (1984) used the term *service concept* to denote the core of a service offering. Grönroos stated that it could either be general, such as offering a solution to transport problems, e.g. car hire, or it could be more specific, such as offering Chinese cuisine in a restaurant.

There seems to be little difference between services and tangible goods when considering this fundamental level of a firm's offer. All customers' needs and wants are intangible – they cannot be seen or touched. The offer should be developed, produced and managed with consumers' benefit in mind in such a way that they perceive it as being successful in satisfying their needs and wants. The offer can be a tangible good, a service or a combination of both. It follows that an understanding of customers' needs and wants is vital.

## In practice: Fitness First?

Gyms and fitness centres have boomed in recent years, as increasing numbers of people recognize the importance of health and fitness. In many areas, potential members of a gym have a wide choice open to them, but how do they arrive at a decision on which gym to join? The service on offer at a gym is essentially intangible and, in many cases, the outcome of attending a gym – a fitter, leaner body – can be just as important as enjoyment of the service process itself. In this advert (Figure 1.8), Fitness First is stressing a desirable outcome of attending its service process. The challenge for a gym is then to get potential members through its door so that they can see and experience the quality of the intangible service process on offer. Many gyms recognize buyers' limited ability to evaluate fully an intangible service, and so provide trial membership periods. Consumer co-production is an essential part of the service provided by a fitness centre, and consumers will only achieve the desired results of the service process by continued personal commitment. Fitness centres enrol large numbers of new members after Christmas, but typically half of the new members who take out an annual subscription have stopped attending regularly after six months. The inseparability of services requires consumers to take responsibility for service production, as well as consumption.

Figure 1.8 A Fitness First trial offer. (Reproduced with permission of Fitness First)

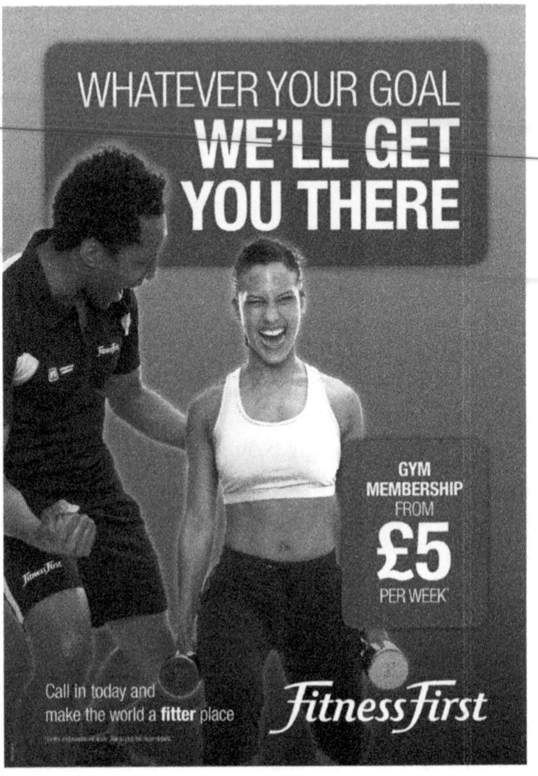


The secondary service offer refers to the manner in which the core service offer is actually delivered, covering issues such as installation, delivery, credit availability and after-sales service. There are, however, a number of specific difficulties involved in determining the particular combination of tangibles and intangibles that are used in this process. One major difficulty is the actual articulation of the elements – it is generally much easier to articulate the tangible aspects than it is to produce and display the intangibles. In addition, the intangible elements are relatively difficult to control and therefore there is a tendency for service managers to emphasize the controllable, i.e. tangible, elements rather than the more difficult intangibles. Shostack (1977) believed that the more intangible the service, the greater the need for tangible evidence and the importance of managing tangible evidence.

Another major conceptual problem in defining the service offer is that because of the inseparability of production and consumption, some elements of the secondary service level are not actually provided by the service provider but by customers themselves, for example the student who 'reads around' a subject before attending a seminar.

A further problem arises from intangibility giving a potential buyer very little opportunity to assess the manner in which a service will be delivered until the service has actually been consumed. Many of the differentiating features of goods can be examined and evaluated before purchase, but

Figure 1.9 The core and secondary service elements of an insurance product

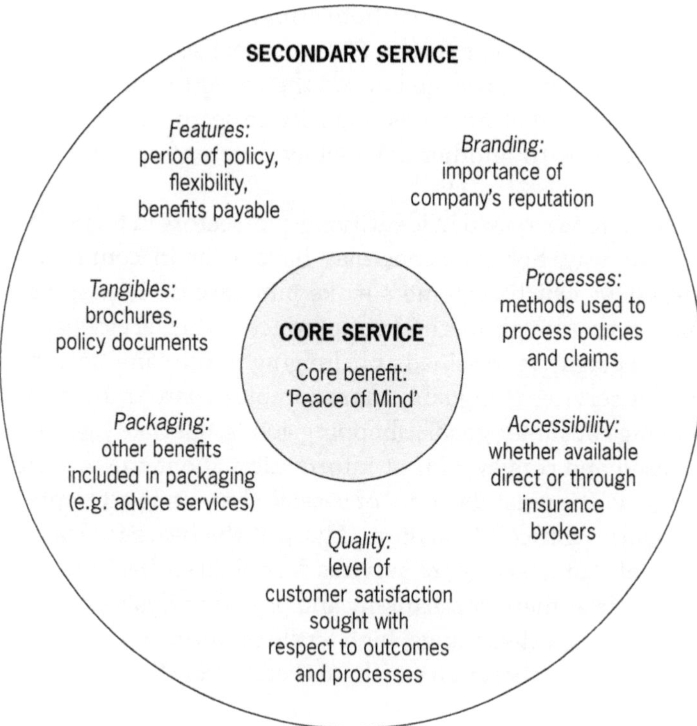


for services these generally only become apparent after consumption. Rushton and Carson (1985) also noted that in many cases, services could also be mentally intangible in that they are concepts that are difficult to grasp.

An example of the core and secondary elements of a service, applied in the context of an insurance product, is illustrated in Figure 1.9.

## 1.4 Classification of services

Earlier in this chapter, it was noted that services typically account for around three-quarters of the size of developed economies. The very size of the services sector implies great diversity in the nature of services activities that make up the major part of modern economies. The contrast between a simple local window-cleaning service and a complex international banking corporation illustrates this diversity. Because of this diversity, any general analysis of the services sector will be very weak unless smaller categories of services can be identified and subjected to an analytical framework that is particularly appropriate to that category of service.

The most common basis for classifying services has been the type of activity that is performed. Statistics record services activities under headings such as banking, shipping and hotels, based largely on similarity of production methods. In this way, shipping is defined in terms of organizations that are largely engaged in movement by sea, even though freight movement between the USA and China is quite different from the operation of a car ferry between Britain and France.

Such simple classification systems are not particularly helpful to marketers. In the first place, a single production sector can cover a very diverse range of activities with quite different marketing needs. Small guest-houses and international hotels may fall within the same sector, but their marketing needs are likely to be quite different. Second, most services are in fact a combination of services. Retail stores, for example, often go beyond their traditional retail boundaries by offering banking facilities. Third, the marketing needs of a service sector defined by production methods may share more in common with another completely different sector than with other services within the same sector.

Marketers should be more interested in identifying sub-sectors in terms of similarity of marketing requirements. In this way, hotel services may have a lot in common with airline services in terms of the processes by which customers make purchase decisions, methods of pricing and promotional strategies, even though methods of producing the services are completely different and they would not at first sight be classified as belonging to the same sector.

Defining categories of services is arguably more complex than for manufactured goods, where terms such as fast-moving consumer goods, shopping goods, speciality goods, white goods, brown goods etc. are widely used and convey a lot of information about the marketing requirements of products within a category. The great diversity of services has made attempts to reduce services to a small number of categories difficult to achieve. Many of the bases for classifying services derive from the five fundamental characteristics of services described earlier in this chapter. For example, groups of services as diverse as merchant banking and psychoanalysis show similar levels of intangibility, which result in, among other things, high levels of uncertainty in the buying process. The following sections discuss further bases on which marketers can classify groups of services in order to identify common marketing needs.

### 1.4.1 Marketable vs unmarketable services

This first classification distinguishes between those services that are considered marketable and those where the social and economic environment of the time considers it desirable that benefits should be distributed by non-market-based mechanisms. Among the latter group, many government services are provided for the public benefit but no attempt is made to charge users of the service. For example, it is not possible in practice for a local authority to charge individuals for the use of local footpaths. The benefits are essentially external in that it is not possible to restrict the distribution of the benefit to those who have entered into some form of exchange relationship.

A second major group of services that many cultures do not consider to be marketable are those commonly provided within household units, such as the bringing up of children, cooking and cleaning. While many of these services are now commonly marketed within Western societies (e.g. childcare services; Figure 1.10), many societies – and segments within societies – would regard the internal provision of such services as central to the functioning of family units. Attempts by Western companies to launch family-based services in cultures with strong family traditions may result in failure because no market exists.

### 1.4.2 Business-to-business vs consumer services

Consumer services are provided for individuals, who use the service for their own enjoyment or benefit. No further economic benefit results from the consumption of the service. In this way, the services of a hairdresser can be defined as a consumer service. On the other hand, business-to-business services are those that are bought by a business in order that it can produce something

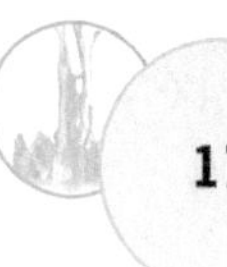

Figure 1.10 Childcare services have emerged as an important new service sector in many Western countries. Changing family structures and growing career orientation among women have led many people to seek outside childcare services, rather than caring for children entirely within the family unit. Some cultures may regard childcare as central to family life, and so the abhorrence of the idea of putting children out for care would render commercial childcare services essentially unmarketable. Attitudes in Western countries have changed, and a growing proportion of people would regard it as quite normal to buy in professional help to look after their children. Many service providers, such as this one, have emerged to satisfy this new market. (Reproduced courtesy of Child Base Nurseries)

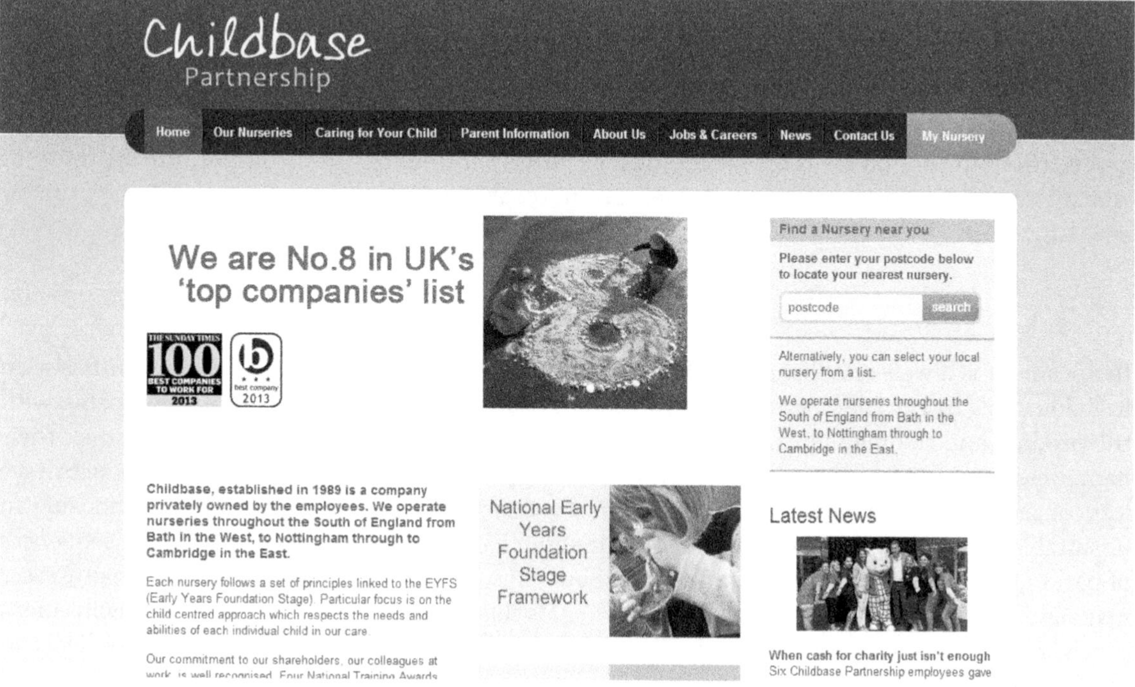


else of economic benefit. A road haulage company sells services to its industrial customers in order that they can add value to the goods that they produce, by allowing their goods to be made available where customers want them.

Many services are provided simultaneously to both consumer and business markets. Here, the challenge is to adapt the marketing programme to meet the differing needs of each group of users. In this way, airlines provide a basically similar service to both consumer and business markets, but the marketing programme may emphasize low price for the former and quality and greater short-notice availability for the latter.

The distinction between the two classifications can sometimes appear blurred. It has, for example, been suggested that business buyers of services do not simply judge a service on its ability to profitably add value to their own production process, but the personal, non-organizational goals of individuals within an organization may cause some decisions to be based on personal consumption criteria. A mobile Internet service may be judged for its personal status value as well as its productive value.

### 1.4.3 The significance of the service to the buyer

The marketing of a service will be affected by its significance to the buyer. Some services are purchased frequently, are of low value, are consumed very rapidly and are likely to be purchased on impulse with very little pre-purchase activity. Such services may represent a very small proportion of the purchaser's total expenditure and correspond to the goods marketer's definition of fast-moving consumer goods ('fmcgs'). A casual purchase of a lottery ticket would fit into this category. At the other end of the scale, long-lasting services may be purchased infrequently and, when they are, the decision-making process takes longer and involves more people. Pension policies and package holidays fit into this category.

We can also distinguish between services which are merely ancillary to another product, and services which are fundamental to the product offer. Research may be needed to identify which parts of the total product offer are of most significance to the buyer. For example, a satellite navigation device may be offered with the benefit of a service-based package to update maps and to provide live traffic information. Is the service package merely incidental, or an important attribute to which buyers pay a lot of attention in their pre-purchase searching, and may even be the primary evaluation factor?

### 1.4.4 Extent of customer involvement

Involvement is a well-established marketing concept, referring to the level of attachment that an individual has to a product. For high-involvement products, buyers have a close relationship with the product and the manner in which the product is used has the capacity to deeply affect their happiness. Many personal medical services fall into this category. Low-involvement products have less consequence for an individual's psychological well-being. If a mistake were made in choosing an unsuitable product, we would not worry about it unduly. We can normally live with the consequences of parking our car in an inconvenient car park, but choosing the wrong hairstyle at the hairdresser may significantly affect our self-image. Involvement is closely associated with risk. High-involvement purchase decisions are seen as being more risky in terms of their outcomes, so we are likely to spend more time and effort in trying to avoid a bad purchase for such services.

In the services sector, involvement also refers to the extent to which a customer personally interacts with the service production process. Some services can only be provided with the complete involvement of customers, whereas others require them to do little more than initiate the service process. In the first category, personal care services almost by definition require the complete involvement of customers during the service production and delivery process. This can be interactive, as where clients of a hairdresser answer a continuous series of questions about the emerging length and style of their hair. For such a customer, the quality of both the service production process and the outcome is important. For other services, it is not necessary for the customer to be so fully involved in the production process. Customer involvement is generally lower where the service is carried out not on the mind or body directly, but on customers' possessions. The transport of goods, the cleaning of a car or the operation of a bank account does not involve a service being carried out directly on the customer, whose main task is to initiate the service and to monitor performance of it.

### 1.4.5 The pattern of service delivery

The marketing of a service is likely to be affected by the manner in which it is typically delivered:

- Some services are supplied on a continuous basis (e.g. the provision of a fixed phone line to a home), whereas other services are only supplied when needed (e.g. repair of a faulty phone).
- Some services are provided on the basis of an ongoing relationship with the service provider (e.g. a season ticket to attend football matches), while other services are typically provided casually (buying a ticket at the gate).

Figure 1.11 The nature of the relationship between producer and consumer

| Relationship of customers to service provider | Discrete transaction | Continuous service delivery |
|---|---|---|
| Ongoing relationships | Telephone calls from home<br>Rail tickets purchased with railcard | Insurance<br>Subscription TV service |
| Casual transactions | Taxi service<br>Fast-food restaurant<br>Public telephone kiosk | Radio station<br>Public services (e.g. roads, parks) |

Nature of service delivery

Service marketers generally try to move customers into the category where service is provided continuously rather than through separate, discrete transactions, and by an ongoing relationship rather than casually. The former can be achieved by offering incentives for the purchase of a continuous stream of service benefit (e.g. offering attractively priced annual travel insurance policies rather than selling individual short-term policies as and when required). The latter can be achieved by a number of strategies, which are discussed further in Chapter 5. At its simplest, relationships could be developed through a communication programme to inform existing customers regularly of new service developments. It could develop into methods to tie customers to a single service provider by offering a long-term supply contract. In this way a bus company may seek regular custom from individuals by offering season tickets that restrict the consumer's choice to one particular service provider.

Services are classified according to the nature of their supply in Figure 1.11.

### 1.4.6 People-based vs equipment-based services

Some services involve very labour-intensive production methods. A fortune-teller employs a production method that is almost wholly based on human actions. At the other extreme, many services can be delivered with very little human involvement – a pay-and-display car park involves minimal human input in the form of checking tickets and keeping the car park clean.

The management of people-based services can be very different from that of those based on equipment. While equipment can generally be programmed to perform consistently, personnel need to be carefully recruited, trained and monitored. People-based services can usually allow greater customization of services to meet individual customers' needs. These issues are considered further in Chapter 10.

### 1.4.7 Process vs outcome-based services

It has already been noted that services are essentially about processes. However, in some cases, the outcome of the process is more important than the process itself. This applies particularly to services that maintain an individual's tangible or intangible assets. For a car-repair garage, many invisible processes may be involved in repairing a customer's car. However, other than the brief encounter that occurs at the time of delivering the car and picking it up, the customer gets to see very little of the service process. They are more likely to be concerned with whether the car that they collect performs to their satisfaction. Similarly, with the maintenance of an intangible financial portfolio, the customer is more likely to be concerned with the performance of their portfolio, rather than the many investment management processes that the service provider may have undertaken invisibly on the customer's behalf.

Contrast a service that is highly outcome-orientated with one that is high in process considerations. A visit to a cinema has no clear outcome (except possibly memories). It follows that the evaluation criteria for the cinema will be quite different compared with that for the financial portfolio management service, where outcomes dominate evaluation.

### 1.4.8 High-knowledge vs low-knowledge services

Sometimes, a service provider has to take very few actions, other than providing knowledge to the buyer. Where a particular type of knowledge is in scarce supply, the credibility of that knowledge may overshadow all of the service activities that surround it, for example the way in which the knowledge is delivered and after-sales enquiries.

Examples of services that are highly knowledge based include top barristers, who give their knowledge on a narrow specialist area of the law, and medical consultants, who have specialized in a narrow field of medicine and give a diagnosis based on symptoms presented. If there are only a handful of consultants specializing in rare forms of tropical diseases, their knowledge of the condition is likely to comprise the most important element of the service offer. Evaluation of the claimed knowledge of the specialist may be the primary basis for evaluating the service offer. Relatively little by way of traditional services activities, such as methods of service delivery, may be important in consumers' evaluation. In the case of many medical services, there may be an information asymmetry that can put considerable power in the hands of a doctor (Hogg et al., 2003). As Neuberger (2000, p. 7) noted, the traditional relationship between doctor and patient is one of 'deference, obedience and instruction'.

Of course, all services comprise a knowledge element to some extent. A restaurant offers the knowledge of its chefs and waiting staff, which is applied to make a good meal served in the appropriate environment. An accountant carrying out a client's routine financial audit brings their knowledge of tax law to the service process, which may include extensive analysis of the client's books and producing a report at the end of the process. In both of these cases, knowledge is an implicit element of the service offer, which is used to evaluate competing services, along with their outcomes and processes. In extreme knowledge-based services, many of the frameworks developed in this book will have relatively little meaning. The concept of a **service encounter** (Chapter 2) is reduced in significance where the only encounter is an exchange of expert opinion.

## 1.5 Defining marketing in a services context

This book is concerned with services marketing, but we need to pause to reflect on just what is meant by the term 'marketing'. Indeed, is marketing relevant to all types of services? There has been a lot of debate about just what is meant by marketing, and a useful starting point are two definitions of marketing:

> *"Marketing is the activity, set of institutions, and processes for creating, communicating, delivering, and exchanging offerings that have value for customers, clients, partners, and society at large."*
>
> (American Marketing Association)

> *"The management process which identifies, anticipates and supplies customer requirements efficiently and profitably."*
>
> (Chartered Institute of Marketing)

There are many variations on these definitions, but the essential elements of marketing focus on a company meeting its own objectives by meeting the needs of its customers. Firms who adopt marketing are said to be marketing orientated and there has been a lot of debate about what is meant by market orientation Two frequently cited conceptualizations of market orientation are provided by Kohli and Jaworski (1990) and Narver and Slater (1990).

Kohli and Jaworski (1990) defined market orientation as the organization-wide generation of market intelligence, dissemination of the intelligence across departments and organization-wide responsiveness to it. According to Kohli and Jaworski, the marketing concept is a fundamental business philosophy, whereas the term market orientation refers to the actual implementation of the marketing concept, providing a unifying focus for the efforts of individuals within the organization.

Narver and Slater (1990) consider market orientation as an organizational culture consisting of three behavioural components:

- Customer orientation, meaning that an organization has a sufficient understanding of its target buyers that allows it to create superior value for them. This comes about through increasing the benefits to the buyer in relation to the buyer's costs or by decreasing the buyer's costs in relation to the buyer's benefits. A customer orientation requires that the organization understands value to the customer not only as it is today, but also as it will evolve over time.
- Competitor orientation, defined as an organization's understanding of the short-term strengths and weaknesses and long-term capabilities and strategies of current and potential competitors.
- Interfunctional co-ordination, referring to the manner in which an organization uses its resources in creating superior value for target customers. Many individuals within an organization have responsibility for creating value, not just marketing staff, and a marketing orientation requires that the organization draws upon and integrates its human and physical resources effectively and adapts them to meet customers' needs. This aspect of marketing is crucial to the services sector where production and consumption are inseparable. Later chapters will emphasize the importance to a company of satisfying customer needs through the integration of marketing, human resource management and operations management.

Market orientation first emerged in the relatively affluent countries for goods where competition between suppliers had become fierce. Adoption of marketing by the services sector generally came later, largely due to the effects of significant public-sector monopolies and the existence of professional codes of practice, which until recently have restrained many services organizations' marketing activities.

Of course, there are still many services organizations that operate in an environment with very little competitive pressure, so they can afford to pursue a production orientation rather than a market orientation. Sometimes, local or temporary shortages of service providers may bring this about. During the boom in property prices that occurred in the UK during the early 2000s, plumbers and craftsmen were in short supply relative to customers' demand, especially in prosperous parts of the country. Stories abounded of builders 'selecting' customers and delaying the completion of jobs because they knew that customers had very little choice.

The debate about the nature of marketing has often been linked to debate about the role of the marketing department within organizations (CIM, 2009). It is too simplistic to say that the presence of a marketing department is a sign of marketing orientation, and many have argued that a separate marketing department may actually be a barrier to all individuals within the organization thinking with a marketing perspective. If marketing is a philosophy, it should be inherent in all employees' thoughts and actions. However, some would argue that this is not realistic, and some semblance of a marketing department is always going to be necessary to plan and execute specific marketing tasks such as advertising and market research.

### 1.5.1 Is marketing appropriate for all services?

Marketing has come under increasing critical scrutiny in recent years, and it must not be assumed that a market-based approach is necessarily the best approach to making all types of services available. Markets are motivated by the self-interest of individuals and companies. Without this self-interest, there will be little motivation for firms to provide better services, workers to work harder and consumers to aspire to a higher level of consumption. But some moral philosophers have drawn a fine line between self-interest which helps markets work more effectively for the benefit of all, and a self-interest that becomes greed and a divisive force which undermines communities and is eventually self-destructive. Furthermore, there are many services that money used in market-based transactions cannot – or should not be able to – buy.

#### Thinking around the subject: Can you spot the marketing-orientated company?

It is easy for a service organization to say that it is marketing orientated and puts customers first. But, all too often, it is very easy to spot telltale signs that marketing is only skin deep. Consider some of the following giveaway signs:

- opening hours that are designed to suit the interests of staff rather than customers (very common among many public-sector services);
- administrative procedures that make life easier for the company rather than its customers (e.g. expecting customers to contact several sections of the organization, rather than offering a 'one-stop' facility);
- reserving prime car-parking spaces for staff rather than customers;
- advertising that is aimed at the egos of company managers rather than the needs and aspirations of potential buyers.

Can you think of any further giveaways?

The moral philosopher Michael Sandel has described a process by which markets triumphed during the three decades from the 1980s, but in doing so, undermined many vital public interests such as civic security, national defence, health and welfare, which increasingly became outsourced, delivered or created through market-based mechanisms. Markets may lead individuals to commodify public services and undermine a sense of shared pride and moral righteousness in services provided for the community (Sandel, 2009).

In this section, we consider a number of areas of service provision where the debate about the role of marketing is greatest: 'essential' public services; the provision of services by not-for-profit organizations; and the debate about the environmental impacts of market-based competition.

### 1.5.2 Essential public services

For some essential public services, it may be extremely difficult to introduce a marketing discipline. The core of the work carried out by the police, fire brigades and the armed services cannot be easily subjected to the test of market forces. It is difficult for the consumer to exercise any choice over who polices their town and equally difficult in practice for local authorities to subcontract provision via a competitive tender. In such cases, marketing may be confined to peripheral activities of the provider (for example, UK police forces compete with each other and with private security companies for the provision of crowd-control services at football matches). Alternatively, marketing activities may be confined to periodic negotiations for outsourced contracts to provide vital inputs to service processes, some of which may interface directly with users. As an example, the provision of transport services to move prisoners between prisons and police stations is outsourced in the UK through a competitive market-based bidding process.

What is considered an essential responsibility of government has changed over time and differs between countries. A service such as public transport might be seen in one country as an essential part of the urban infrastructure for which government must take responsibility, while in other countries public transport might be regarded as just another service which can be provided through market forces.

In the UK, some services which were previously considered suited only to distribution through centrally planned methods are now routinely distributed using market-based mechanisms. Electricity supply, for example, was for a long time centrally planned with no semblance of a market. Today, several electricity-generating companies, specialist energy retailers and even supermarkets vie with each other to sell gas and electricity to consumers. Some countries would consider this approach to be wasteful or harmful to planning for long-term energy needs, and have retained more of a planned rather than a market-based approach to electricity and gas distribution. Some have argued that energy companies' preoccupation with short-term profits may lead them to defer investment in new capacity, with the prospect of a long-term energy shortage which will have harmful effects on the national economy.

In theory, markets should punish companies that do not serve the public interest, because they will lose customers and eventually go out of business. Unfortunately, the reality is that markets may not be efficient, or sufficiently rapid, in punishing companies that do not satisfy the wider public good. Consider the following cases that have been cited as evidence of failure of market-based distribution of services:

- The financial services sectors of many Western countries were deregulated from the 1980s, with lending and investment decisions made by banks increasingly free of regulation by government regarding the volume and type of transactions that they should undertake. One consequence was a goal-driven culture which saw a lot of high-risk investments made by and between banks, and which began to unwind during the 'credit crunch' of 2008. Some would argue that as a result of short-term goal orientation by market-orientated banks, the banking system as a whole came close to collapse, with financial institutions drastically reducing the amount of credit made available for investment by companies.
- Consider the case of a privatized, profit-driven railway service. During a period of heavy snowfall, the train operator may make a profit-orientated judgement and choose to cancel all trains, thus avoiding the high costs of maintaining a service during the bad weather. But this may cost businesses and consumers much more when shops, offices and factories have to close because workers cannot get to work because the trains are not running.

Following the banking crisis of 2008, many commentators argued that some public services were simply too important to the rest of the economy to be left to market forces. Advocates of a centrally planned approach to the provision of essential public services pointed to countries such as France and Germany which had retained a much higher level of central control of essential public services, and their economies appeared to be less badly affected by the disruptive effects that occurred when bad, market-based decisions taken earlier by private-sector companies harmed the rest of the economy. In particular, some argued that banking was an essential public service and that the relatively unregulated actions of banks in the UK and USA had precipitated the credit crunch. More regulated financial services sectors in other countries did not suffer such a fallout. The importance of the financial services sector to the rest of the economy was reflected in the decisions by many governments to nationalize failing banks or to provide substantial support for them. In the UK, the government effectively nationalized Lloyds TSB and Royal Bank of Scotland, realizing that if these banks were to become bankrupt, there would be very serious implications for investment and financial transactions in all sectors of the economy.

In practice, service sectors cannot be described simply as being either market based or centrally planned. In between these extremes, a variety of operating environments exist. Many apparently private-sector, market-based service providers, such as telephone, electricity and railway providers, nevertheless are subject to extensive government regulation which may determine, among other things, the markets they serve, the services they offer, the prices that they can charge and the investment that they must make. Some cynics have argued that railway managers in the UK actually had more freedom to serve their customers under state ownership than under their current private, but heavily regulated, ownership.

### 1.5.3 Voluntary and not-for-profit sector marketing

The principles of marketing have increasingly been applied to services provided by voluntary or not-for-profit organizations. Some people remain dubious about their use of marketing – why should you need marketing to promote a school which should be judged by the quality of its teaching, or to encourage donations to a charity whose cause people should recognize as a socially useful one in its own right?

A feature of many services activities in recent years has been for commercial organizations to become involved where previously provision was determined by community interests and involvement. Instead of a church-based group providing child-minding facilities according to local need and the church's mission, parents have increasingly looked to the services of market-based kindergartens. Instead of extended families and community groups looking after elderly or disabled people, a market in retirement homes and disabled living support has emerged. Services which were once undertaken informally between friends and family or within a community have been increasingly 'marketized'. This implies putting a price on everything that goes into a transaction, which is more likely to be formal rather than informal. Competition from commercially provided services has often led to heightened expectations by consumers, and many voluntary and not-for-profit organizations have tried to counter this by adopting many of the principles of marketing themselves. Schools, for example, increasingly use the services of advertising and public relations agencies to attract students.

This creeping **marketization** of traditional community-based services has attracted strong criticism from those who see market forces 'crowding out' the efforts of the voluntary sector. One well-documented example of this is the case of blood donation services, which in many countries are operated as community-based voluntary activities, whereas in others blood donation is based

on the market principles of paying money to individual donors in return for a valuable product. Richard Titmus showed how monetary compensation for donating blood could crowd out the supply of blood donors. Blood had been reduced to a commodity to be bought and sold, and this market-based calculation had crowded out individuals' evaluation based on moral rightness and benefit to the community (Titmus, 1970). In short, there seemed to be evidence that introducing the principles of marketing might actually impede service provision.

Where not-for-profit organizations take on board the principles of marketing, the objectives of activities associated with marketing need to be clearly understood. Very often, these objectives may not be about maximizing sales or profits, but may be based on achieving benefits to the community, for example increasing the number of people completing an educational programme or raising awareness of a region among potential tourists.

There have been many attempts to operationalize marketing concepts to not-for-profit organizations (e.g. Sargeant et al., 2002). Typically, marketing managers' financial objectives and the requirement to meet customers' needs must be further constrained by wider social objectives. In this way, a public library may be set an objective of providing the public with a range of materials that help to develop the knowledge and skills of the population it serves. Therefore, the 'quality press' may be the only newspapers purchased, although customer preferences may call for the purchase of popular tabloids. This apparently centrally planned approach is not incompatible with a marketing philosophy – the library may work within its objectives of developing knowledge and skills by seeking to maximize the number of people reading its quality newspapers. Marketing strategies that might be employed to achieve this could include a promotional campaign, the development of a friendly, welcoming attitude and accessible opening hours. As the example of the library illustrates, not only is it often difficult to specify marketing objectives clearly, it can also often be difficult to monitor performance. Where benefits accrue to the community in general, this can be much more difficult to measure than a marketing manager's traditional metrics of sales and profits. Furthermore, many of the tools of the commercially based marketer, such as pricing, may not be available to marketers within the not-for-profit sectors where services are provided without charge. The strategies and practices of marketing within the sector are likely to attract even more critical awareness than those of the commercial sector marketer, because members of the public may consider that they have a democratic right to influence the decisions of public or quasi-public bodies. As a result, marketers in the sector may feel much more constrained in their decision making.

Many not-for-profit sector services such as museums and leisure services are increasingly being given clearly defined business objectives, which make it much more difficult for managers to continue doing what their professional judgement guides them to do, rather than what the public they serve wants. Marketing orientation has been most rapidly adopted by those public-sector services that provide marketable goods and services, such as swimming pools and local bus services. It is much more difficult to adopt marketing orientation where the public sector is a monopoly provider of a statutory service.

In the provision of school places, the UK government has moved away from the traditional basis of centralized resource allocation to a quasi-market-based system where funding – in principle – follows parents' choices. Those schools that are popular with parents and provide their service at a competitive cost to local and central government funding providers will grow, while those that do not will gradually lose resources. While developing a marketing framework for public services may sound fine in principle, new problems may be created. If consumers of services express their preferences for a provider, there is no guarantee that additional government funding will be provided to make available the additional capacity that consumers have demanded. And how able are government funding agencies to take a view of long-term capital commitments based on possibly short-term changes in consumer preferences? The application of marketing principles to public services such as schools and hospitals has been motivated by the desire to give consumers choice. However, consumers have often shown overwhelming preference for 'good' schools or hospitals, and one consequence of the introduction of market mechanisms has been that the school or hospital ends up choosing whom to accept, rather than the user choosing their service provider. In the short term, at least, the idea of consumer choice can be illusory.

### In practice: Marketing without markets?

Can you have marketing in a situation where there is no market? The link between marketing and markets has been extensively discussed, with some confusion about the role of marketing. Many public-sector services have employed people with titles such as 'marketing officer', often with responsibilities which include services for which consumers may have little or no choice. Even many police forces have appointed marketing officers. Although there may be some instances where such a person would genuinely need to apply the principles of marketing (for example, where police forces compete against each other to provide cover at regional football matches), most of their work is likely to be involved with promotion and possibly learning more about public opinion. For most services provided by police forces, there is no market, and indeed soliciting payment from some groups may sound like corruption. When one police force accepted sponsorship of its cars from the security company Chubb, it was widely accused of leaving itself open to accusations of favouritism if the sponsor was ever considered to be involved in an offence. Many of the tools of marketing such as pricing and market segmentation are clearly not available to the police service. It can also be difficult to identify who the customer is – it may be members of society more generally, who benefit from a safer community, but with whom there is no exchange relationship.

So can we have marketing without markets? Karl Marx once questioned whether you could have capitalism without capital. Perhaps marketing without a market is a similar oxymoron?

## 1.5.4 Marketing and ecological responsibility

Another area of concern about the role of marketing is its effects on the ecological environment. Critics have argued that marketing only takes account of direct resource implications between the parties concerned – normally the buyer and seller. Marketing does not factor in effects that a transaction may have on other people, or on future generations. With climate change being high on the agenda of governments and the public generally, many have blamed marketing for being irresponsible in its pursuit of private benefit at the expense of collective ecological loss. A tsunami in Asia may seem quite far removed from a British family flying away on a package holiday to Spain, but scientists are increasingly making such links and accusing market-based systems of exacerbating ecological problems.

For some time, services were assumed to be a relatively 'clean' form of economic activity. Compared with coal-mining or manufacturing, the kinds of services employment that have often replaced these traditional sources of employment have been seen as an improvement to the natural environment. However, more recently, concerns have grown that some service sectors may pose significant threats. The harm caused by services may not always be as immediately apparent as the visible pollution emitted by a factory, but the long-term consequences may be just as serious. Consider the following cases:

- Consumers have benefited enormously from low-cost air travel as a result of deregulation and improved efficiency by aircraft and airline operators. However, a report by Oxford University's Environmental Change Institute (2006) predicted that by 2050 aviation will be contributing up to two-thirds of the government's total carbon dioxide emission target if uncontrolled demand continues to grow, even if technological and air traffic management improvements are taken into account. This has potentially serious implications for climate change.

- The retail sector has shown remarkable improvement in efficiency by providing an ever wider range of goods at falling real prices. However, one consequence has been a sharp increase in 'food miles' as goods are transported between distant producers, large centralized processing factories, warehouses and, finally, supermarkets. The UK Department for the Environment, Food and Rural Affairs (Defra) has estimated the environmental, social and economic costs of food transport to be £9 billion per year, of which £5 billion is due to road congestion, £2 billion to road accidents, £1 billion to pollution and £1 billion to other factors. The miles that food travelled by trucks increased by 30 per cent between 1997 and 2010 and the miles flown by air by 10 per cent. 'Food miles' accounted for about 2 per cent of UK $CO_2$ emissions (Defra, 2012). Even vegetables sold in hypermarkets as 'locally produced' may have travelled hundreds of miles between farm, processing/packing facility, warehouse and hypermarket. Furthermore, the efficiency of large hypermarkets has to be offset against the increased travelling that it is necessary for shoppers to undertake to go shopping – Defra estimated that the average UK adult travels about 135 miles by car per year to shop for food.
- Tourism development in many countries has led to a shortage of water for local inhabitants. The marketing of a hotel may be improved by offering guests freshly laundered towels each day and large swimming pools, but the tourism sector as a whole can find itself accused of misusing a valuable natural resource.

More profoundly, is commercial organizations' pursuit of more consumption fundamentally opposed to ecological interests? Taken to its logical extreme, consumption of the vast majority of goods and services can result in some form of ecological harm. For example, the most ecologically friendly means of transport is to avoid the need for transport in the first place. The most ecologically friendly holiday is for an individual to stay at home.

Very few services businesses can claim not to be affected by ecological change, especially climate change. As an example, bad weather, such as hurricanes, floods and gale-force winds, which have been attributed to climate change, affects companies when they come to renew their insurance policies. Damage caused to property by storms can close down a company's facilities and affect the reliability of its service offer. Because of their inability to store products, services companies are particularly vulnerable to adverse weather, as witnessed by the major disruption that affects train and airline operators when abnormal weather occurs.

The ecological environment can present opportunities as well as challenges for services businesses. Proactive companies have capitalized on ecological issues by reducing their costs and/or improving their organizational image:

- Many markets are characterized by segments that are prepared to pay a premium price for a product that has been produced in an ecologically sound manner. Some retailers, such as The Body Shop, have developed valuable niches on this basis. What starts off as a 'deep green' niche soon expands into a larger 'pale green' segment of customers who prefer ecologically sound products, but are unwilling to pay such a high price premium.
- Being 'green' may actually save a company money. Often, changing existing environmentally harmful practices primarily involves overcoming traditional mindsets about how things should be done (e.g. fast-food chains using recycled packaging materials and overcoming a one-way logistics mindset by returning their waste materials for recycling).

- In Western developed economies, legislation to enforce environmentally sensitive methods of production is increasing. A company that adopts environmentally sensitive service processes ahead of compulsion can gain a competitive advantage.

We will return to the issue of consumers' evaluation of services organizations' 'green' credentials and the importance of being perceived as a 'good citizen' in Chapter 13.

## 1.6 So, is goods marketing different from services marketing?

In practice, it can be very difficult to distinguish services from goods, for when a good is purchased, there is nearly always an element of service included. Similarly, a service is frequently augmented by a tangible product attached to the service. In this way, a car may be considered to be a good rather than a service, yet cars are usually sold with the benefit of intangible service elements, such as a warranty or a financing facility. On the other hand, a seemingly intangible service such as a package holiday includes tangible elements in the purchase – use of an aeroplane, the hotel room and transfer coach, for example. In between is a wide range of products that are a combination of tangible good and intangible service. A meal in a restaurant is a combination of tangible goods (the food and physical surroundings) and intangible service (the preparation and delivery of the food, reservation service etc.).

Lovelock and Gummesson (2004) are among many who have pointed out that, in fact, many services are tangible rather than intangible, separable rather than inseparable, homogeneous rather than variable, and durable rather than perishable. For example, on the subject of variability, there are some non-services industries – such as tropical fruits – that have difficulty in achieving high levels of consistent output, whereas some services industries such as car parks can achieve a consistent standard of service in terms of availability, cleanliness etc. Similarly, many tangible goods share the problem of intangible services in being incapable of full examination before consumption. It is not normally possible, for instance, to judge the taste of a bottle of wine in a supermarket before it has been purchased and (at least partially) consumed. Services marketers have learnt a lot from the marketing activities in the goods sectors and vice versa.

Lovelock and Gummesson (2004) have also suggested that marketing exchanges that do not result in a transfer of ownership from seller to buyer are fundamentally different from those that do. They argue that services offer benefits through access or temporary possession, instead of ownership, with payments taking the form of rentals or access fees. This rental/access perspective offers a different perspective through which to view services. One implication is the opportunity to market goods in a service format. Some of the points of convergence are illustrated in Figure 1.12.

Figure 1.13 shows schematically that considerable diversity exists within the services sector. In fact, rather than talking about the services sector as a homogeneous group of activities, it would be more appropriate to talk about degrees of service orientation. All productive activities can be placed on a scale somewhere between being a pure service (no tangible output) and a pure good (no intangible service added to the tangible good). In practice, most products fall between the two extremes by being a combination of goods and services.

A distinction can be drawn between a service that is delivered directly by an organization to consumers and services that are delivered by means of the goods that the consumers have purchased. Conceptually, many goods purchases result in a consumer buying a stream of internally produced services. Consider the following examples of goods and the service-type benefits that they produce:

Figure 1.12 The marketing of goods and services has tended to converge in terms of the strategies and tactics employed. This diagram illustrates some of the points of convergence.

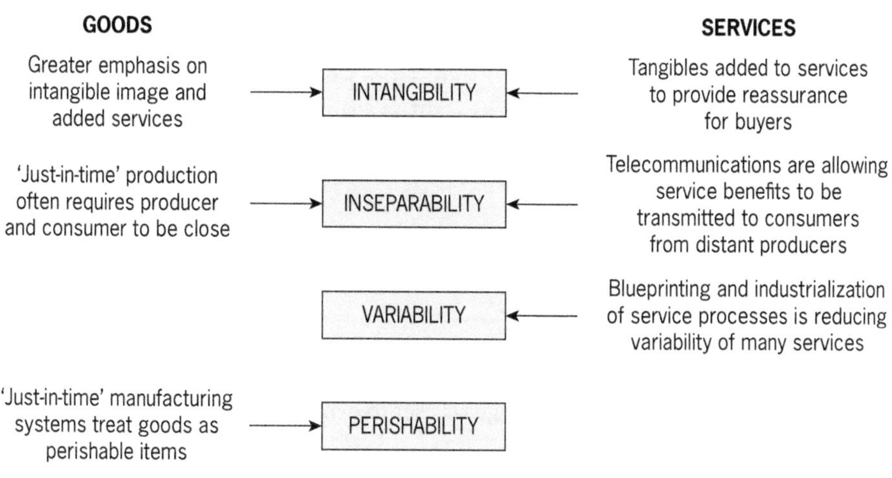
GOODS
SERVICES
Greater emphasis on intangible image and added services
INTANGIBILITY
Tangibles added to services to provide reassurance for buyers
'Just-in-time' production often requires producer and consumer to be close
INSEPARABILITY
Telecommunications are allowing service benefits to be transmitted to consumers from distant producers
VARIABILITY
Blueprinting and industrialization of service processes is reducing variability of many services
'Just-in-time' manufacturing systems treat goods as perishable items
PERISHABILITY

Figure 1.13 The goods and services continuum. All products that we buy are essentially a combination of goods and services components and, rather than talking about goods and services as two separate categories of product, it is more realistic to talk about degrees of 'service orientation', depending on the importance of the service component within the total product offer.

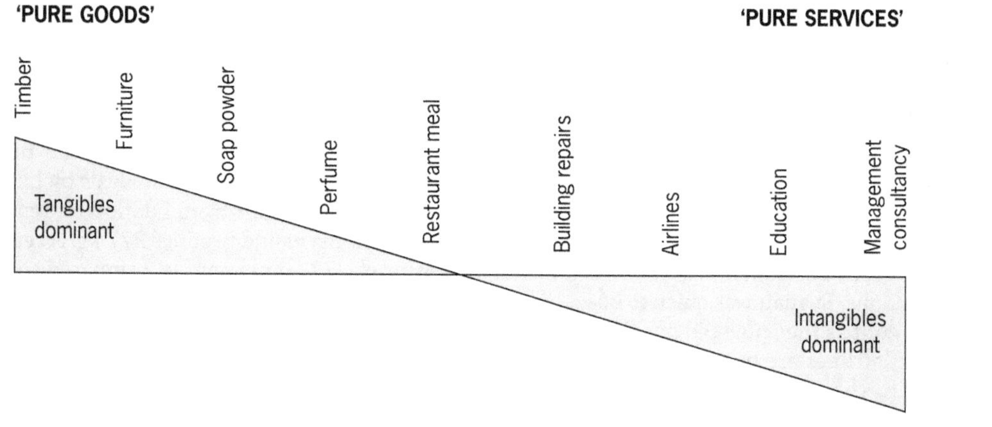
'PURE GOODS'
'PURE SERVICES'
Timber
Furniture
Soap powder
Perfume
Restaurant meal
Building repairs
Airlines
Education
Management consultancy
Tangibles dominant
Intangibles dominant

- A washing machine provides indirect service benefits that may otherwise have been provided directly by a launderette.
- A car provides benefits otherwise provided by taxis and public transport.
- An espresso coffee-maker provides cups of coffee that might otherwise have been provided by a takeaway coffee shop.

Substitutions have been made in economies as the relative costs of goods and services have changed. In general, the real cost of goods has tended to fall, as production and distribution efficiencies have increased. The ability of goods manufacturers to transfer production to low-cost production countries has hastened this trend. On the other hand, the cost of services has tended to rise in real terms, especially for labour-intensive services, which have faced the need to pay rising levels of wages and to comply with growing levels of employment legislation (although some newly deregulated and equipment-intensive service sectors such as telecommunications have experienced rapidly falling costs).

While the rising real costs of some types of services may have led to substitution with goods producing service benefits, this has been offset by rising real incomes. Greater wealth has resulted in the consumption of most services increasing. Where this increased demand is channelled into labour-intensive services industries (e.g. restaurants, personal healthcare), one result is often an acute labour shortage in these sectors.

## In practice: Cheap flights, but high costs to the planet?

Airlines have had cause to feel uncomfortable as concerns mount about the causes and consequences of climate change. Having struggled with the aftermath of the terrorist attacks of 9/11, and a worldwide recession which set in from 2008, climate change was set to become yet another challenge for the airline industry. Could marketing come to the rescue?

The popular press had vilified airlines for their harmful effects on the ecological environment, especially in situations where high-profile schemes, such as a new airport or runway extension, captured the public imagination and threatened large interest groups. But the reality was that most people still liked to travel abroad, escaping to a warmer climate, visiting friends and family or simply exploring somewhere new. Surveys had suggested that there can be a big difference between what people said and what they did – they may have agreed that flying was bad for the environment, but could not resist the £29.99 flight to Spain. Furthermore, it seemed that many people were tiring of claims about climate change and saw this as an excuse for government to raise taxes. A YouGov tracking survey showed that the percentage of people in the UK who thought that human activity was making the world warmer fell between 2008 and 2010, and the proportion who thought the world was *not* getting warmer increased sharply, from 7 per cent in 2008 to 28 per cent in 2013.

Actually assessing the ecological impacts of flying is more problematic than at first sight. The low-cost airlines spotted an opportunity to present themselves as ecologically more friendly than the 'full service' airlines from whom they had been gradually taking away business. According to analysis by Liligo.co.uk, a flight-comparison website, a couple making a return flight with Ryanair from London to Venice have a carbon footprint of 410 kg, while the equivalent journey on Alitalia would produce 977 kg. A return flight from London to Zurich with easyJet has a carbon footprint of 277 kg per couple, compared with 688 kg with Aer Lingus. Ryanair was quick to boast of its 'green' credentials, just in case potential flyers were feeling a sense of guilt as they hovered over the 'buy' button for one of its bargain tickets. The ecological benefits of low-cost airlines are based on a number of factors. First, they tend to fly with more seats occupied – according to the CAPA Centre for Aviation, Europe's two largest budget airlines, easyJet and Ryanair, topped the 'load factor' tables, with 90 and 85 per cent respectively of all seats occupied, compared with 80 per cent for Air France/KLM and 75 per cent for Lufthansa (CAPA, 2011). Second, low-cost airlines squeeze more seats into an aircraft than their full-service rivals. For example, easyJet ('squeezyJet' to some of its passengers) fits 156 seats into an Airbus A319, whereas the average full-service airline has just 124 seats. The carbon footprint per passenger is correspondingly lower. Finally, low-cost airlines promoted the fact that they tended to fly direct between a wide range of dispersed airports, without the need to change planes at a central 'hub' airport, again reducing carbon emissions during take-off and landing.

Are airlines being irresponsible in promoting more flying? Is it realistic for them to encourage alternatives to flying? What else could they do to reconcile the short-term interests of their passengers, the business needs of their shareholders and the long-term needs of the planet?

### 1.6.1 Service dominant logic

The debate about the factors that distinguish or unite goods and services was crystallized in an article by Vargo and Lusch (2004), which talked about a new 'service dominant logic' of marketing.

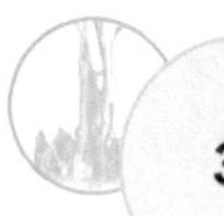



They argued that marketing was originally built on a goods-centred, manufacturing-based model of economic exchange developed during the industrial revolution but, with the aim of broadening its scope to include services, it has been constrained by the language and models of manufactured goods. Factory metaphors have frequently been applied to services, using such terms as inputs, processing, outputs and productivity (Goodwin, 1996). The early phases of service research deliberately drew parallels between production of a tangible good and delivery of an intangible service. Early articles placed consumers in the factory, as contributors to production processes (Lovelock and Young, 1979) or as potential bottlenecks to be processed as quickly as possible (Chase, 1978). However, factory metaphors fail when marketers are forced to recognize the unique aspects of human consumers as inputs to a service production process, as compared to inanimate inputs. The latter can be inventoried in a warehouse for months at a time, whereas customers can become dissatisfied after waiting for just a few minutes in a queue. Vargo and Lusch argue that the characteristics that have been identified as distinguishing services from goods – intangibility, inseparability, heterogeneity and perishability – only have meaning from a manufacturing perspective and do not in themselves distinguish services from goods.

Models of exchange used in marketing have derived from an economic model, in which the exchange was driven by goods, and the focus was the transaction between buyer and seller, in which goods which had an embedded value were exchanged. Over time, newer perspectives have emerged that focus on intangible resources, the co-creation of value, and relationships between buyer and seller. Service dominant logic encapsulates these trends and is driven by a logic in which service provision rather than goods is fundamental to economic exchange.

A fundamental part of service dominant logic is that the customer is always a co-creator of value, rather than merely the target of selling and the passive recipient of a firm's efforts. This idea of co-creation is crucial to understanding the manner in which both good and service exchanges take place. As an example, even the most basic agricultural products must be made accessible to the consumer by means of service-type activities, and decisions must be made about how, when and where the product will be exchanged, and the role in this exchange to be played by producer and consumer. Vargo and Lusch argue, in effect, that the focus of marketing (the dominant logic) has moved from the product (goods and/or services) to what the product does for the consumer, from the consumer's point of view (Vargo and Lusch, 2004).

Service dominant logic is built on ten foundational principles (FPs), some of which overlap:

FP1* **Service is the fundamental basis of exchange.** The application of operant resources (knowledge and skills), as defined in service dominant logic, is the basis for all exchange. Service is exchanged for service.

FP2 **Indirect exchange masks the fundamental basis of exchange.** The service basis for exchange is not always apparent, because service is provided through complex combinations of goods, money, and institutions.

FP3 **Goods are a distribution mechanism for service provision.** Goods (durable and non-durable) provide service-type benefits and derive their value through use.

FP4 **Operant resources are the fundamental source of competitive advantage.** Competition is essentially driven by differential advantages in a company's use of knowledge and skills.

FP5 **All economies are service economies.** Service drives the logic of exchange, therefore all economies could be said to be service based.

FP6* **The customer is always a co-creator of value.** Interaction by the consumer with the product must take place if the value of the product is to be realized by the consumer.

**FP7** **The enterprise cannot deliver value, but only offer value propositions.** Organizations can offer their resources to customers but cannot create value independently of the buyer who must collaborate in a process of value creation.

**FP8** **A service-centred view is inherently customer orientated and relational.** Service can only be defined in terms of customer-determined benefit and is co-created with the customer.

**FP9*** **All social and economic actors are resource integrators.** Production of value cannot be confined to just one party (e.g. the manufacturer), but all individuals and organizations in a network integrate resources.

**FP10*** **Value is always uniquely and phenomenologically determined by the beneficiary.** There is no objective definition of value – it can only be defined idiosyncratically by individuals and even the same individual might attribute different values to the same product in different contexts.

Vargo and Lusch have noted that some of their original foundational principles could be derived from others and subsequently four of them, indicated here by * (FP1, FP6, FP9 and FP10), are particularly important and form the essential basis of service dominant logic.

There has been considerable debate about the validity of the theory underpinning service dominant logic (see suggested further reading at the end of this chapter). Some have argued that it is unrealistic to regard services as being a driving force in the marketing of a tangible product if the tangible product is poorly designed. To give an example of a car, service dominant logic can explain how 'value in use' is generated through the use of intermediaries and the availability of loan finance etc. But if the car is perceived as unreliable and uninspiring, would any amount of service be able to sell it?

## In practice: Servicing your car

Figure 1.14 A service-based approach to car sales

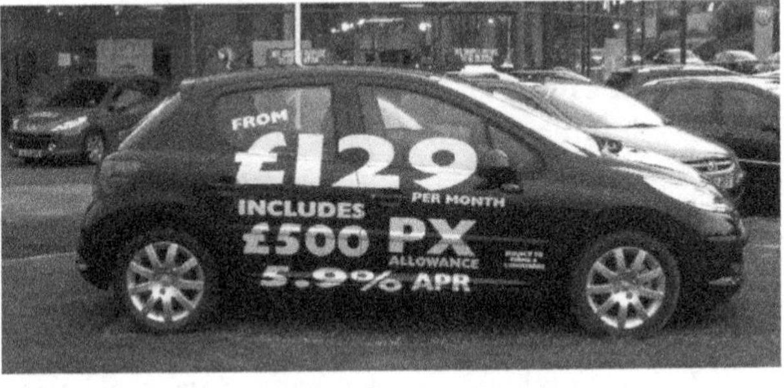


One of the great marketing successes of the car industry in recent years has been to transform the sale of a car into what is effectively an ongoing supply of services. For many private buyers, the traditional way of buying a car has been to pay a sum of money for the car (either as cash or through a loan), keep the car for probably three or four years, then trade it in for a new one and make a fresh payment for the new car. The car – a tangible product – was the focus of the transaction and pre-purchase evaluation was typically dominated by the tangible characteristics of the car. Today, in line with service dominant logic, the emphasis is on services and relationships. A wide variety of service-type benefits are promoted, which aim to create maximum value in use for the car owner. These typically include: a loan, which is repaid over two or three years; an extended warranty; and a breakdown support service. Some of the breakdown services have become increasingly sophisticated in the benefits they offer car buyers to keep them mobile (for example, many support packages include the provision of a temporary replacement car and overnight accommodation if necessary). Many agreements give the car buyer the option of returning their car at the end of a specified period and exchanging it for a newer model. Instead of spending £15,000 every three years for a tangible object, the car buyer now typically pays £200 or £300 a month for a service-based relationship with a car company and its dealers.

## 1.7 An extended marketing mix for services

So far in this introductory chapter we have explored the differences between goods and services, and critically defined the role of marketing for different types of services. It should be apparent that there are many ways in which the marketing of a 'pure' good is likely to differ from the marketing of a 'pure' service. These differences will become more apparent as we work through the subsequent chapters and explore. For now, we will end this chapter by introducing the idea of an **extended marketing mix** for services, which forms a basis for many of the subsequent chapters.

The **marketing mix** is a set of tools available to an organization to shape the nature of its offer to customers. It is not a theoretical framework, but just a list of headings for strategic decisions and tactical actions to be taken by managers. Goods marketers are familiar with the 4Ps of product, price, promotion and place. Early analysis by Borden (1965) of marketing-mix elements was based on a study of manufacturing industry at a time when the importance of services to the economy was considered to be relatively unimportant. More recently, the 4Ps of the marketing mix have been found to be too limited in their application to services. Particular problems which limit their usefulness to services are these:

- The intangible nature of services is overlooked in most analyses of the mix – for example, the product mix is frequently analysed in terms of tangible design properties, which may not be relevant to a service. Likewise, physical distribution management may not be an important element of place-mix decisions.
- The price element overlooks the fact that many services are produced by the public sector without a price being charged to the final consumer.
- The promotion mix of the traditional 4Ps fails to recognize the promotion of services that takes place at the point of consumption by the production personnel, unlike the situation with most fast-moving consumer goods, which are normally produced away from the consumer and therefore the producer has no direct involvement in promoting the good to the final consumer. For a bank clerk, hairdresser or singer, the manner in which the service is produced is an important element of the total promotion of the service.

As well as throwing up ambiguities about the meaning of some of the four elements of the marketing mix, this simple list also fails to recognize a number of key factors that marketing managers in the service sector use to design their service output. Particular problems focus on:

- defining the concept of quality for intangible services, and identifying and measuring the mix elements that can be managed in order to create a quality service;
- the importance of people as an element within the service product, both as producers and as co-consumers;
- the oversimplification of the elements of distribution which are relevant to intangible services.

These weaknesses have resulted in a number of attempts to redefine the marketing mix to make it more applicable to the services sector. While many have sought to refine the marketing mix for general application, the expansion by Booms and Bitner (1981) provided a useful framework for analysing services, although, again, this is not based on an empirically proven theory. In addition to the four traditional elements of the marketing mix, Booms and Bitner add the additional elements of people, process and physical.

The principle of the extended marketing mix (as indeed with the traditional marketing mix) is to break a service offering down into a number of component parts and to arrange them into manageable subject areas for making strategic and tactical decisions. Decisions on one element of the mix can only be made by reference to other elements of the mix in order to give a sustainable product positioning. The importance attached to each element of the extended marketing mix will vary between services. In a highly automated service such as vending machine dispensing, the people element will be a less important element of the mix than in a people-intensive business such as a restaurant.

A brief overview of these marketing mix ingredients is given below, with fuller discussion following in the subsequent chapters.

### 1.7.1 Products

Products are the means by which organizations seek to satisfy consumers' needs. As we saw earlier in this chapter, product in this sense is anything that the organization offers to potential customers, whether it be tangible or intangible. After initial hesitation, most marketing managers are now happy to talk about an intangible service as a product. Thus bank accounts, insurance policies and holidays are frequently referred to as products, sometimes to the amusement of non-marketers, as when pop stars or even politicians are referred to as a product to be marketed.

Product-mix decisions facing a services marketer can be very different from those dealing with goods. Most fundamentally, pure services are best defined using process descriptions rather than tangible descriptions of outcomes. Elements of the product mix such as design, reliability, brand image and product range may sound familiar to a goods marketer, but can assume different roles. There is also a difference from goods in that new service developments cannot be protected by patent.

### 1.7.2 Pricing

Price-mix decisions include strategic and tactical decisions about the average level of prices to be charged, discount structures, terms of payment and the extent to which price discrimination between different groups of customers is to take place. These are very similar to the issues facing a goods marketer. However, the intangible nature of a service can mean that price in itself can be an important indicator of quality. The personal and non-transferrable nature of many services presents additional opportunities for price discrimination within service markets, while the fact that many services are marketed by the public sector at a subsidized, or no, price can complicate price setting.

### 1.7.3 Promotion

The traditional promotion mix includes various methods of using messages to communicate the benefits of a product to potential consumers. In addition, the promotion of services often needs to place particular emphasis on increasing the apparent tangibility of a service. The promotion mix for services is wider than that for goods because services production personnel can themselves become an important element of the promotion mix.

### 1.7.4 Place

Place decisions refer to the ease of access that potential customers have to a service. Place decisions can therefore involve physical location decisions (e.g. where to locate a hotel), decisions about which intermediaries to use in making a service accessible to a consumer (e.g. should a tour operator uses travel agents or sells its holidays direct to customers?) and non-locational decisions that are used to make services available (e.g. the use of Internet-based delivery systems). For pure services, decisions about how to physically move a good are of little strategic relevance. However, most services involve movement of goods of some form. These can either be materials necessary to produce a service (such as fast-food packaging material) or the service can have as its whole purpose the movement of goods (e.g. road haulage, plant hire). For services, the concept of accessibility is more important than the traditionally defined place. Access issues include not only the location of service outlets but, more importantly, how the consumer is to be designed into the service production–consumption process, and who is to be involved in that process. We will return to the issue of accessibility in Chapter 4.

### 1.7.5 People

For most services, people are a vital element of the marketing mix. Where production can be separated from consumption – as is the case with most manufactured goods – management can usually take measures to reduce the direct effect of people on the final output received by customers. Therefore, the buyer of a car is not concerned whether a production worker dresses untidily, uses bad language at work or turns up for work late, so long as there are quality control measures that reject the results of lax behaviour before they reach the customer. In service industries, everybody is what Gummeson (2001) calls a 'part-time marketer' in that their actions have a much more direct effect on the output received by customers.

While the importance attached to people management in improving quality within manufacturing companies is increasing – for example, through the development of quality circles – people planning can be much more important for services, especially where staff have a high level of contact with customers. For this reason, it is essential that services organizations clearly specify what is expected from personnel in their interaction with customers. To achieve the specified standard, methods of recruiting, training, motivating and rewarding staff cannot be regarded as purely personnel decisions – they are important marketing-mix decisions.

People planning within the marketing mix also involves developing a pattern of interaction between customers themselves, which can be very important where service consumption takes place in public, as we will see in Chapter 3.

### 1.7.6 Physical evidence

The intangible nature of a service means that potential customers are unable to judge a service before it is consumed, thereby increasing the perceived riskiness of a purchase decision. An important element of marketing planning is therefore to reduce this level of perceived risk by offering tangible evidence of the nature of the service. This evidence can take a number of forms. At its simplest, a brochure can describe and give pictures of important elements of the service product – a holiday brochure gives pictorial evidence of hotels and resorts for this purpose. The appearance of staff can give evidence about the nature of a service – a tidily dressed ticket clerk for an airline gives some evidence that the airline operation as a whole is likely to be run with care and attention. Buildings are frequently used to give evidence of service nature. Towards the end of the nineteenth century, railway companies outbid each other to produce the most elaborate station buildings. For people wishing to travel from London to Scotland, a comparison of the grandeur of the three terminals in London's Euston Road could give some clue about the ability of the railway to provide a substantial service. Today, a clean, bright environment used in a service outlet can help reassure potential customers at the point where they make a service purchase decision. For this reason, fast-food and photo-processing outlets often use red and yellow colour schemes to convey an image of speedy service.

### 1.7.7 Processes

Grönroos (2001) noted that 'a service firm has no products, only *interactive* processes'. Production processes are usually of little concern to consumers of manufactured goods, but can be critical to consumers of 'high contact' services where consumers are co-producers of the service. A visitor to a restaurant may be deeply affected by the manner in which staff serve them and the amount of delay that is involved during the production process. Issues arise about the boundary between the producer and consumer in terms of the allocation of production functions – for example, a restaurant might require a customer to collect their meal from a counter, or expect them to deposit their own rubbish. With services, a clear distinction cannot be made between marketing and operations management. Service design should therefore pay attention to processes and the manner in which service personnel interact with customers during this process. Service dominant logic recognizes that consumers are co-creators of a service within the production process.

So far, we have considered seven elements of an extended marketing mix, which conveniently all begin with the letter P. Unfortunately, simplicity of presentation may be at the expense of practical relevance to particular service industries. Just as the '4Ps' marketing-mix model may be inappropriate for services as a whole, it can be argued that the '7Ps' marketing-mix model cannot hope to be appropriate for the great diversity of services that was described earlier. What really matters for any service organization is to have a list of headings for strategic and tactical decisions that are of relevance in its particular marketing environment. For some public-sector services, the P for price may be largely irrelevant as a heading for marketing decisions if they do not directly charge their users. On the other hand, there may be additional issues that are not adequately covered by the 7Ps headings. These include:

- *Research and development.* For many services companies involving new technologies, decisions about which new technology to invest in may be crucial to providing competitive advantage through improved benefits to customers, and/or lower costs. Many Internet-based service providers have placed innovation in new technologies high on their marketing agenda.
- *Merchandising.* For retailers, competitive advantage may be based on an ability to source goods as cheaply as possible and to move them through a supply chain quickly, flexibly and reliably. Skills of merchandising at the point of sale may be important in their own right rather than being subsumed as an element of the 'promotion' mix element.
- *Quality/customer satisfaction.* This is such an important topic that it could warrant its own heading as a marketing-mix element. A sound understanding of how consumers evaluate quality can allow services companies to be clearer in the specification of quality levels that they incorporate in their offering, as well as allowing a clearer communication to potential customers of the service level on offer. Because of the importance of quality in the total service offer, the subject of defining, measuring, planning, implementing and monitoring quality standards is considered in more detail in Chapter 9.

Finally, the development of close *relationships* with customers has risen high on the agenda of many companies, who see relationships rather than one-off transactions as a source of competitive advantage. We will return to this subject in Chapter 5.

## Case study

### Old MacDonald had a farm – and a service business too?

By Paul Custance, Harper Adams University College

The children's nursery rhyme about Old MacDonald's farm tells about the cow, the pig, the horse and the sheep that the farmer kept, but says nothing about farm services. Farming in Western countries has shifted from an overwhelming emphasis on growing food to the management of an increasing array of services.

Being a farmer in Britain was not generally a happy experience during the last years of the twentieth century, with numerous food scares such as 'mad cow' disease, and increasing pressure on margins from supermarkets who bought their produce. It seemed that customers were not prepared to pay high enough prices to make it attractive for farmers to grow crops, raise animals and produce milk and eggs. Admittedly, there had been some bright spots in the quest to improve profit margins, with farming becoming ever more intensive from the 1960s onwards, with larger farms using land, machinery and chemicals intensively. But even organic farming – seen as a hope of the 1990s – lost some of its glamour as competition forced down farmers' margins. It hardly seemed surprising, therefore, that farmers should seek to diversify into services. According to the 2009/10 Farm Business Survey produced by Defra, 50 per cent of farms had some form of diversified activity. While much of this related to renting out farm buildings, 27 per cent was not related to buildings and was largely service based (Defra, 2011).

The idea of adding value was nothing new to farmers; after all, many had undertaken some processing of the food that they had produced, such as turning milk into cheese. Many more had ventured into services by selling the produce that they had grown through their own farm shops. These had developed from simple roadside stalls that operated only at harvest time, to become fully fledged services activities in their own right. It was no longer good enough simply to have the right fruit and vegetables, but also opening hours, car parking and customer facilities that met buyers' rising expectations. Some farm shops have even developed into mini out-of-town visitor destinations, which families visit in order to eat, go shopping and provide entertainment for children. In an attempt to get a higher price for their produce, some farmers have developed innovative service-based methods of delivery. Vegetable box schemes have become very popular with some segments of food buyers, who prefer to pay a premium price for freshly delivered local produce. Barcombe Organic Nurseries, in Lewes, Sussex, is typical of many farms that have developed a vegetable box scheme by offering buyers Internet-based ordering, home delivery and food preparation advice. Getting closer to customers is also achieved by selling produce from the farm at the farmers' markets that have sprung up in many towns and cities since the late 1990s.

Increasingly, farmers have diversified into even more wide-ranging service sectors, reflecting the nature of consumer demand. Many farms have diversified into various aspects of tourism, ranging from caravan parks, paintball competitions and bed and breakfast accommodation, to 4 × 4 driving courses and pop concert venues. Some have opened their doors as visitor centres, giving urban visitors an insight into life on a farm. Most farm attractions offer a standard range of 'unthemed' activities such as animals, countryside access, museum/exhibition events, arts and crafts, children's entertainment and retail and catering. Some are thematically linked to the activity on the farm, such as cider farms and vineyards. Nearly one-quarter of diversified farms provide accommodation and catering services to the general public. These days, Old MacDonald's spouse might well be running these services businesses and be a member of Women in Rural Enterprise (WiRE).

Moving the emphasis from growing crops to selling services can demand big changes in the way farmers run their business. No longer is the emphasis on a tangible product that can be quality controlled through increasingly sophisticated growing methods. No longer do farmers simply sell their produce to a merchant, giving them no direct contact with the consumers who eat their food. No longer can they schedule their work around their own convenience and the needs of the crop. Moving into services activities means that farmers must take into account the implications of intangibility, inseparability, variability and profitability. Having customers coming on to their farm poses new challenges, and farmers must now 'design in' customers to their production processes. If customers want to come on

Sundays or in school holidays, farmers will have to change their working patterns to suit the needs of customers. Understanding what makes customers satisfied with a service can be much more complex than assessing the quality of crops against easily defined benchmarks. Farmers must now get inside the mind of customers to try to understand the often complex needs that they seek to satisfy through service-based activities. Understanding why and how a customer decides to take part in a paintball competition can be much more difficult than understanding how they buy an apple, and calls for a more thorough understanding of needs, expectations and the process of evaluating and selecting a service.

It is not only consumers who have seen the results of farmers' diversification into services. Behind the scenes, a wide range of new business-to-business services has developed. The days when farmers would retain staff and equipment to undertake all farming tasks themselves are disappearing, as specialist service suppliers are brought in. True, farmers have always relied on bought-in administrative services, such as those provided by accountants and solicitors. Today, even basic agricultural operations such as crop spraying and harvesting are likely to be bought in from a specialist service supplier. Many farmers have come to realize that it is more cost-effective to get a contractor to harvest their wheat and barley, rather than keep a combine harvester for their own use. Farm labour has been increasingly casualized as many farmers rely on the services of employment agencies to source gangs of workers to cope with the harvesting of fruit and vegetables.

Even the business of applying fertilizer and pesticides has been turned into a service activity. Some pesticide manufacturers, for example, offer farmers an 'integrated pest management' service. They claim to save up to 50 per cent of pesticide costs and at the same time increase yields by the timely application of pesticides. In a more developed version the pesticide provider could even offer a crop insurance service, guaranteeing the farmer that certain pests and diseases will not affect yield. The whole pesticide application would be carried out by the service provider. For some farmers, all of their farm operations are now undertaken by contract services providers. Farmers are not just buyers of business-to-business services such as crop spraying. Many have spotted the opportunities of doing other farmers' work for them, and given their own farming up to become farm services suppliers. Old MacDonald might not recognize today's farm, but services suppliers have certainly spotted the opportunities.

### Case study review questions

1. To what extent is the presence of a well-developed agricultural services sector a prerequisite for an efficient and profitable agricultural sector? Or is the development of the agricultural services sector a consequence of advanced farming methods?
2. From a marketing perspective, discuss the main differences between a crop of potatoes and a camping site.
3. What are the principal challenges that farmers are likely to face as they develop new consumer services to supplement their basic agricultural output?

## Summary and links to other chapters

Services are becoming an increasingly important element of developed economies, and this chapter has traced their development and the thinking that has been associated with their marketing. An important message of this chapter is that services are not a homogeneous group of activities, but rather there is a continuum of products from pure goods to pure services. Intangibility, inseparability, perishability and variability have been introduced as key defining characteristics of a service. The effects on marketing activities of these characteristics have been noted. While the general principles of marketing may apply to all products, an extended marketing mix for services has been suggested that takes account of the staff interaction and intangible process characteristics of services. In the case of services in the not-for-profit sector, further constraints on marketing management have been noted.

This chapter has set the scene for subsequent chapters. Definitions of services introduced here will be elaborated later. Chapter 2 analyses services in terms of systems approaches to production. In Chapter 3 we explore 'softer' experiential bases for defining services. In Chapter 4 we return to the issue of 'place' by considering ways in which access to a service becomes an essential design feature. Buyer behaviour, relationship development and the need to develop new services are considered further in Chapters 5, 6 and 7. The concept of service quality in Chapter 9 brings together various elements of marketing activity and emphasizes the greater difficulty in managing quality of services compared with goods. The extended marketing-mix element of people management is considered Chapter 10. Chapter 11 explores implications of intangibility and inseparability for the pricing of services. Chapter 12 returns to the topic of perishability by examining the management of service capacity. Chapter 13 explores how promotional efforts often try to overcome the greater perceived risk associated with service buying. The final chapter offers an integrated perspective on how service firms might replicate their success in overseas markets.

## Chapter review questions

1. Discuss the relationship between GDP and the size of a nation's services sector. Identify key cause-and-effect relationships.
2. Critically assess the concept of the marketing mix. To what extent is an extended marketing mix of seven Ps suitable for services, or is the extended mix itself too general, given the diversity of services?
3. Critically assess the extent to which the marketing of goods is different from the marketing of services. What does service dominant logic contribute to this debate?

## Activities

1. Develop a checklist of points that you consider to be important indicators of whether a service organization is marketing orientated. Why did you choose these indicators? Now select two or three services organizations from the following: a fast-food retailer; a bank; a college or university; a hotel. Use your checklist to evaluate whether your chosen organizations are truly marketing orientated. If they are not, analyse the reasons why this might be. What, if anything, could or should the organization do to become more marketing orientated?
2. Go through a business directory such as *Yellow Pages* and randomly select 20 business classification headings from the services sector. Critically analyse the nature of the service offer provided by organizations in each of these sectors. Then try grouping your selected service sectors according to the similarity in their marketing needs. On what basis did you arrive at similarity? What lessons can be learnt by sectors that may appear outwardly quite different, but share many underlying similarities?
3. Examine promotional material for the following manufactured products: cars, digital cameras and office equipment. Critically explore the argument of Vargo and Lusch for a 'service dominant logic' by examining the extent to which services create 'value in use' for these goods.

## Key terms

**Business-to-business services** Services that are bought by business organizations for incorporation into their production processes.

**Cause-related marketing** Promoting the interest of a particular cause (e.g. a social issue) without a specific aim of exchange of value.

**Ethics** A set of principles based on moral judgement.

**Extended marketing mix** An extension of the 4Ps marketing-mix framework to make it relevant to services. Usually includes people, processes and physical evidence.

**Inseparability** The production of most services cannot be spatially or temporally separated from their consumption.

**Intangibility** Pure services present no tangible cues that allow them to be assessed by the senses of sight, smell, sound, taste or touch.

**Market** A group of potential customers with similar needs who are willing to exchange something of value with sellers offering products that satisfy their needs.

**Marketing** The management process that identifies, anticipates and supplies customer requirements efficiently and profitably.

**Marketing mix** The aspects of marketing strategy and tactics that marketing management uses to gain a competitive advantage over its competitors. A conceptual framework that for services usually includes elements labelled 'product offer', 'price', 'promotion', 'accessibility', 'people', 'physical evidence' and 'processes'.

**Marketization** Using market mechanisms to distribute services that were previously distributed through non-market mechanisms.

**Multiplier effect** The addition to total income and expenditure within an area resulting from an initial injection of expenditure.

**Perishability** Describes the way in which service capacity cannot be stored for sale in a future period. If capacity is not sold when it is produced, the chance to sell it is lost for ever.

**Productivity** The efficiency with which inputs are turned into outputs. Difficult to measure for services as inseparability means that changes in production inputs often affect consumers' perceptions of the value of service outcomes.

**Pure service** Service that has none of the characteristics associated with goods, i.e. is intangible, inseparable, instantly perishable and incapable of ownership.

**Service encounter** The period during which an organization's human and physical resources interact with a customer in order to create service benefits.

**Variability** The extent to which service processes or outcomes vary from a norm.

## Selected further reading

*The following references are classic articles from the early debate about whether services marketing should be considered to be a separate subject in its own right. They are still useful for identifying the key characteristics of services:*

**Bateson, J.** (1977) 'Do we need service marketing?', in *Marketing Consumer Services: New Insights*, Report 77–115, Marketing Science Institute, Boston.

**Berry, L.L.** (1980) 'Services marketing is different', *Business*, 30 (3), 24–9.

**Levitt, T.** (1981) 'Marketing intangible products and product tangibles', *Harvard Business Review*, 59 (3), 95–102.

**Lovelock, C. and Gummesson, E.** (2004) 'Whither services marketing? In search of a new paradigm and fresh perspectives', *Journal of Service Research*, 7 (1), 20–41.

**Shostack, G.L.** (1977) 'Breaking free from product marketing', *Journal of Marketing*, 41 (2), 73–80.

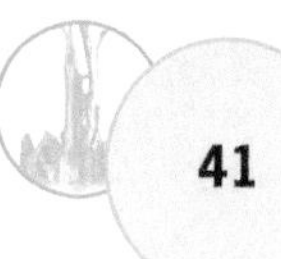

*The debate about whether services should be the focal point for all marketing is explored in the following articles discussing 'service dominant logic':*

**Ballantyne, D. and Varey, R.** (2008) 'The service-dominant logic and the future of marketing', *Journal of the Academy of Marketing Science*, 36, 11–18.

**Grönroos, C.** (2008) 'Service logic revisited: who creates value? And who co-creates?', *European Business Review*, 20 (4), 298–314.

**Vargo, S.L. and Lusch, R.F.** (2004) 'Evolving to a new dominant logic for marketing', *Journal of Marketing*, 68 (1), 1–17.

**Vargo, S.L. and Lusch, R.F.** (2008) 'Service-dominant logic: continuing the evolution', *Journal of the Academy of Marketing Science*, 36, 1–10.

*For a review of the distinctive aspects of the public and not-for-profit sectors and how they impact on marketing, the following is useful:*

**Sargeant, A.** (2009) *Marketing Management for Not-for-Profit Organisations*, 3rd edn, Oxford University Press, Oxford.

*For a general introduction to the principles of marketing, numerous texts are available, including the following:*

**Kotler, P., Armstrong, G., Harris, L.C. and Piercy, N.** (2013) *Principles of Marketing: 6th European edition*, Pearson, London.

**Jobber, D. and Ellis-Chadwick** (2012) *Principles and Practice of Marketing*, 7th edn, McGraw-Hill, Maidenhead.

## References

**Berry, L.L.** (1980) 'Services marketing is different', *Business*, 30 (3), 24–9.

**Booms, B.H. and Bitner, M.J.** (1981) 'Marketing strategies and organization structures for service firms', in J.H. Donnelly and W.R. George (eds), *Marketing of Services*, American Marketing Association, Chicago, IL, 51–67.

**Borden, N.H.** (1965) 'The concept of the marketing mix', in G. Schwartz (ed.), *Science in Marketing*, John Wiley and Sons, New York.

**CAPA** (2011), CAPA – Centre for Aviation, 'European airline traffic and load factors up in Sep-2011, but outlook mixed for major carriers', available at http://centreforaviation.com/analysis/european-airline-traffic-and-load-factors-up-in-sep-2011-but-outlook-mixed-for-major-carriers-60656 (accessed 8 July 2013).

**Chartered Institute of Marketing (CIM)** (2009) *The Future of Marketing*, Chartered Institute of Marketing, Cookham.

**Chase, R.B.** (1978) 'Where does the customer fit in a service operation?', *Harvard Business Review*, 56 (6), 137–42.

**Defra** (2011) *Farm Diversification in England: Results from the Farm Business Survey, 2009/10*, available at http://www.defra.gov.uk/statistics/files/defra-stats-fbs-diversification-2011.pdf

**Defra** (2012) *Food Statistics Pocketbook 2012*, Department for Environment, Food and Rural Affairs, National Statistics, available at http://www.defra.gov.uk/statistics/files/defra-stats-foodfarm-food-pocketbook-2012-121005.pdf

**European Investment Bank** (2010) *Innovation and Productivity Growth in the EU Services Sector*, Luxembourg, by Kristian Uppenberg and Hubert Strauss, available at http://www.eib.org/attachments/efs/efs_innovation_and_productivity_en.pdf (accessed 8 July 2013).

**Eurostat** (2011) *Europe in Figures: Eurostat Yearbook 2011*, Office for Official Publications of the European Communities, Luxembourg.

**Eurostat** (2012) *Eurostat Newsrelease*, based on the 2011 results of the European Labour Force Survey, available at europa.eu/rapid/press-release_STAT-12-142_en.pdf (accessed 8 July 2013).

**Goodwin, C.** (1996) 'Moving the drama into the factory: the contribution of metaphors to services research', *European Journal of Marketing*, 30 (9), 13–36.

**Grönroos, C.** (1978) 'A service oriented approach to marketing of services', *European Journal of Marketing*, 12 (8), 588–601.

**Grönroos, C.** (1984) 'A service quality model and its marketing implications', *European Journal of Marketing*, 18 (4), 36–44.

**Grönroos, C.** (2001) 'Guru's view: the perceived service quality concept – a mistake?', *Managing Service Quality*, 11 (3), 150–2.

**Gummeson, E.** (2001) *Total Relationship Marketing*, Butterworth-Heinemann, Oxford.

**Hogg, G., Laing, A. and Winkelman, D.** (2003) 'The professional service encounter in the age of the Internet: an exploratory study', *Journal of Services Marketing*, 17 (5), 476–94.

**ILO** (2011) *Global Employment Trends 2011: 'The challenge of a jobs recovery'*, Geneva, available at http://www.ilo.org/wcmsp5/groups/public/@dgreports/@dcomm/@publ/documents/publication/wcms_150440.pdf (accessed 8 July 2013).

**Kohli, A.K. and Jaworski, B.J.** (1990) 'Market orientation: the construct, research propositions, and managerial implications', *Journal of Marketing*, 54, 1–18.

**Levitt, T.** (1972) 'Production line approach to service', *Harvard Business Review*, 50 (5), 41–52.

**Lovelock, C.** (1981) 'Why marketing needs to be different for services', in J.H. Donnelly and W.R. George (eds), *Marketing of Services*, American Marketing Association, Chicago, IL.

**Lovelock, C. and Gummesson, E.** (2004) 'Whither services marketing? In search of a new paradigm and fresh perspectives', *Journal of Service Research*, 7 (1), 20–41.

**Lovelock, C.H. and Young, R.F.** (1979) 'Look to consumers to increase productivity', *Harvard Business Review*, 57 (3), 168–78.

**McKinsey** (2013) 'Infrastructure productivity: how to save $1 trillion a year', San Francisco, McKinsey Global Institute.

**Narver, J.C. and Slater, S.F.** (1990) 'The effect of a market orientation on business profitability', *Journal of Marketing*, 54 (4), 20–35.

**Neuberger, J.** (2000) 'The educated patient: new challenges for the medical profession', *Journal of Internal Medicine*, (247), 6–10.

**OECD** (2012) Programme for International Student Assessment, Organisation for Economic Co-operation and Development, Paris, available at http://www.oecd.org/pisa/ (accessed 17 July 2013).

**Oxford University's Environmental Change Institute** (2006) *Predict and Decide: Aviation, Climate Change and UK Policy*, Oxford University Centre for the Environment, Oxford.

**Rathmell, J.M.** (1974) *Marketing in the Service Sector*, Winthrop, Cambridge, MA.

**Reisman, D.** (2012) *The Economics of Alfred Marshall*, London, Routledge.

**Rushton, A.M. and Carson, D.J.** (1985) 'The marketing of services: managing the intangibles', *European Journal of Marketing*, 19 (3), 19–39.

**Sandel, M.J.** (2009) *Justice: What's the Right Thing to Do?* Allen Lane, New York.

**Sargeant, A., Foreman, S. and Liao, M.-N.** (2002) 'Operationalizing the marketing concept in the nonprofit sector', *Journal of Nonprofit & Public Sector Marketing*, 10 (2), 41–64.

**Shostack, G.L.** (1977) 'Breaking free from product marketing', *Journal of Marketing*, 41 (2), 73–80.

**Smith, A.** (1977) *The Wealth of Nations*, Penguin, Middlesex (first published 1776).

**Titmus, R.** (1970) *The Gift Relationship: From Human Blood to Social Policy*, Allen and Unwin, London.

**Vargo, S.L. and Lusch, R.F.** (2004) 'Evolving to a new dominant logic for marketing', *Journal of Marketing*, 68 (1), 1–17.

**Vargo, S.L. and Lusch, R.F.** (2008) 'Service dominant logic: containing the evolution', *Journal of the Academy of Marketing Science*, 36, 1–10.

**Wood, P.A.** (1987) 'Producer services and economic change, some Canadian evidence', in K. Chapman and G. Humphreys (eds), *Technological Change and Economic Policy*, Blackwell, London.

**World Bank** (2011) *World Development Report 2011: 'Conflict, Security and Development'*, Washington, DC, available at http://siteresources.worldbank.org/INTWDRS/Resources/WDR2011_Full_Text.pdf (accessed 8 July 2013).

**World Bank** (2012) *World Development Indicators database*, World Bank, Washington, DC, available at http://data.worldbank.org/indicator/NY.GNP.PCAP.CD (accessed 17 July 2013).

**World Economic Forum** (2013) *The Global Competitiveness Report 2012–2013*, World Economic Forum, Davos, Switzerland.

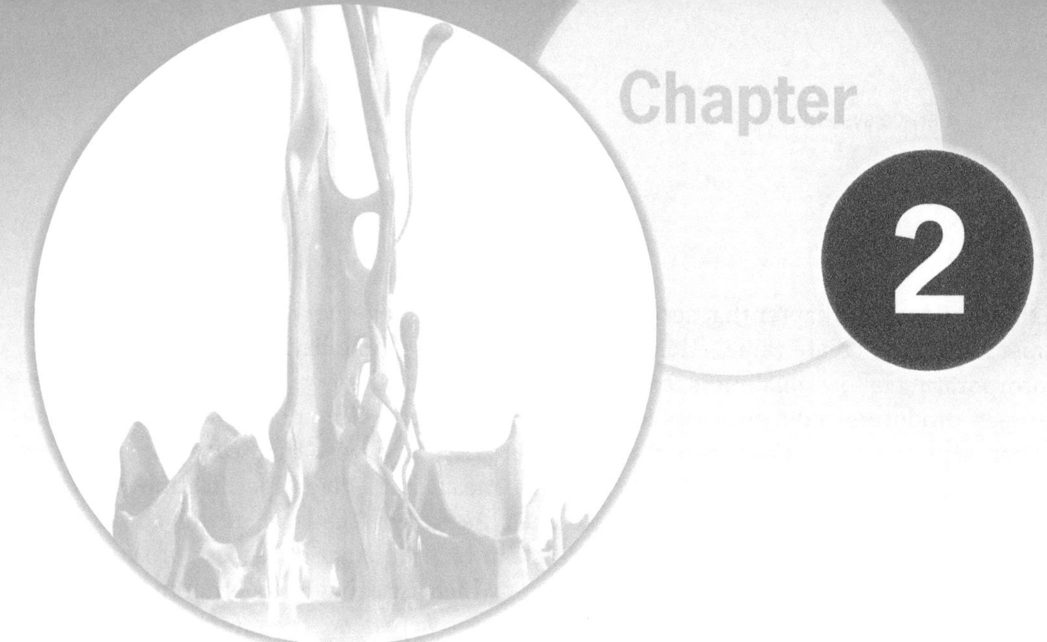

Chapter 2

# Service systems

*A family-run pub/restaurant, 'The King's Arms,' in a northern England town was recently taken over by a national restaurant chain which specializes in affordable family-orientated dining. Out went the former pub owners, George and Freda, who ran their business in a fairly informal way. Menus were flexible and if the customer wanted anything a bit different, one of the waiters would just have a word with the chef. Some days, service was faster than others, and the food itself seemed to have good days and bad days. All of this seemed to change when the national restaurant chain took over. The menu was simplified and based on extensive consumer research and development work carried out at the company's central food technology laboratories. Out went Freda's notepad to take orders, and in came a computerized system for ordering strictly predetermined types of food. Tight specification of the food and of portion size meant that there was now little variation from one day to the next. Instead of Freda's instinctive judgement about how long it should take to serve the food, now there were targets for delivery time and staff bonuses based on the extent to which targets were met. The incoming restaurant chain had well-developed systems, allowing it to achieve significant operating economies which it passed on as lower prices. The consistency of the service offer also helped to build its brand reputation for consistency. Many services companies have gone down the route of defining service processes in systems terms and ruthlessly 'industrializing' their service processes. In this chapter we will explore systems approaches to services marketing management. To some, systems-based services can be quite soulless, and in the next chapter we will look at 'softer' experiential aspects of service consumption.*

## Learning objectives

After reading this chapter, you should understand:

- The concept of a service environment, service system and sub-systems
- Methods of defining services from a systems perspective
- The concept of service productivity and conceptual difficulties raised in measuring productivity for inseparable services
- Methods used to industrialize service processes
- The role of the Internet in improving the efficiency and effectiveness of service processes

## 2.1 Introduction

We saw in the introductory chapter that services involve bringing together the service provider and the consumer in order to create value – this is the essence of inseparability. The process also often involves incorporating fellow consumers to create value. In this chapter we will examine the interactions between producers and consumers in a structured manner. Who does what, when, where and how? Service providers seek to design the encounters they have with their customers in order to improve efficiency and effectiveness. By efficiency, we mean that a given specification of service can be produced with the minimum possible resources. As we will see later in this chapter, the whole concept of efficiency in the context of services can be problematic, because of the diverse nature of consumer-based and producer-based resources which are brought together in the service production/consumption process. When we talk about effectiveness, we are referring to a service which creates the right type of value for the consumer. A service may be very efficient in terms of transforming resource inputs into consumable services, but it may be ineffective if consumers do not place a high value on the actual service which has been produced.

This chapter will concentrate more on the efficiency aspects of service production/consumption by taking a 'hard' systems approach to defining and managing service encounters. We are probably all familiar with systems which might seem tightly scripted and prescribed, but leave us frustrated because the resulting service may seem inflexible or unfriendly. Services can also create value through their 'softer' aspects of design. Rather than asking the question 'who does what, when where and how?', the softer side of service design involves asking 'how does the service make you feel?' We discuss this softer aspect of service design in the following chapter.

An important aspect of service design focuses on how to bring consumer and producer together. In this chapter we will introduce some exploratory concepts of service system design, and in Chapter 4 we will look more specifically at how services are made accessible to consumers – should the consumer come to the producer, or should the producer go to the consumer, for example?

Service design also raises questions about whether the service provider should itself deal with its customers, or would it be better to outsource part of its service process? By taking a systems approach to defining and managing the service, many service providers have identified component parts of their processes which can be performed by a separate outsourced or subcontracted service provider. We will return to these issues in Chapter 5.

## 2.2 Systems approaches to analysing services

What do we mean by systems approaches to services? In its broadest sense, systems theory was proposed in the 1940s by the biologist Ludwig von Bertalanffy as an interdisciplinary study of the abstract organization of phenomena. It investigates the principles common to all complex entities and the models which can be used to describe them. Its early applications focused on systems within mathematics, computing and ecology. More recently, systems theories have been used to understand the complexity of the business environment in which organizations operate. International trade, banking and competition are among many phenomena which have been modelled using systems approaches. Increasingly, services are being seen as systems which operate in a broader system composed of the wider business, economic, social and ecological environment.

A service system has been defined by Spohrer et al. (2007, p. 2), as a

> "value-coproduction configuration of people, technology, other internal and external service systems, and shared information (such as language, processes, metrics, prices, policies, and laws)."

A further definition is provided by Tronvoll et al. (2011), who define a service system as

> "a re-creation of structures with its resources and intended interactions to enhance a value **co-creation** process involving one or a constellation of actors within a given social context."

It is possible to identify service systems at a range of scales, from small-scale systems associated with a small window-cleaning business, through to call centres, hotels and complex hospitals as systems. Service systems can become extremely complex where they incorporate many sub-systems, in the way that an airport incorporates a diverse range of systems to process passengers, their baggage and aircraft, among others. Even cities can be regarded as complex service systems, incorporating separate sub-systems to provide transport, water supply and education services, to name but a few.

Any individual service system exists within a broader environment (sometimes also called an 'ecosystem'). Some parts of this system environment will comprise other service systems which may be complementary or competitive. Other aspects of the service environment, such as the political system of a country, may not be a service system as such, but can have major impacts on individual service systems.

Systems survive, adapt and evolve through interaction with other systems in their environment. For any one service system, interaction with another system may represent an opportunity to grow and to prosper. Interaction with other systems may pose a threat and, in the absence of sufficient adaptability, may even result in the elimination of the system. Vargo et al. (2008, p. 146) noted that 'service systems engage in exchange with other service systems to enhance adaptability and survivability, thus co-creating value – for themselves and others', and noted that like social systems, service systems adapt and survive through interaction and the integration of resources that are mutually beneficial.

Although a number of attempts have been made to apply the principles of systems theory to business organizations, there are major differences between systems based in the natural sciences and service systems. Very often, the natural sciences deal with closed systems in which all the parameters are known, and each can be monitored and controlled (admittedly, this is not always true; for example, in some ecological studies it may not be possible to identify all life forms which might possibly migrate into a system). By contrast, business environments generally comprise an open system in which it is very difficult to place a boundary round the system and to identify the complete set of components within the system. Elements may come into or go from the system and a researcher generally has no control over these elements in the way that a laboratory-based scientist could carry out controlled experiments.

The principal elements of a service system and its environment are shown in Figure 2.1.

### 2.2.1 The service environment (or 'ecosystem')

Before we begin to look in detail at how services systems operate, we need to place these systems in the context of the broader environment in which they operate (or 'ecosystem' to use a term defined by Vargo and Lusch (2008), and which is used interchangeably here). The types of services that are available today are a response to the opportunities and challenges present in this broader

Figure 2.1 Service systems, sub-systems and the service environment. This figure illustrates the basic principles of a service system, and the difficulties in trying to define its boundaries. At the centre of this system is a restaurant, which exists to turn human, physical and financial resources into a service that customers value by exchanging money for service. Without this exchange, the restaurant as a system would probably soon cease to function. The restaurant is also dependent on other systems for its continued existence, for example suppliers for food and equipment, and a labour market system to provide adequate trained employees. The restaurant can be seen as both a system and as a series of sub-systems, which might typically include an operations system, a marketing system and a finance system. Even these sub-systems are likely to have their own sub-systems, so for example the marketing sub-system may have further sub-systems comprising advertising, marketing research and sales systems. These systems and sub-systems are closely connected and this figure simplifies matters by showing only a few of the complex links which connect elements of the system. There is further simplification by showing sharp boundaries between systems, whereas in reality the systems may be very closely interconnected, so for example a supplier of cleaning systems may effectively function as part of the restaurant's operations system. A sharp demarcation of responsibilities between internal systems may have harmful consequences of encouraging a 'silo' mentality in which an organization is perceived as being disconnected and inconsistent in addressing customers' needs. Beyond this constellation of service systems and sub-systems is the service environment, which comprises phenomena which can affect the stability of the system. In its broadest sense, the environment of this service 'ecosystem' comprises a range of economic, technological and ecological forces, identified around the edge of this system. But for any one system within it, other systems can represent that system's environment, so for the restaurant, government regulatory agencies, competitors and suppliers become part of its environment, in that they are external to the restaurant's own system.

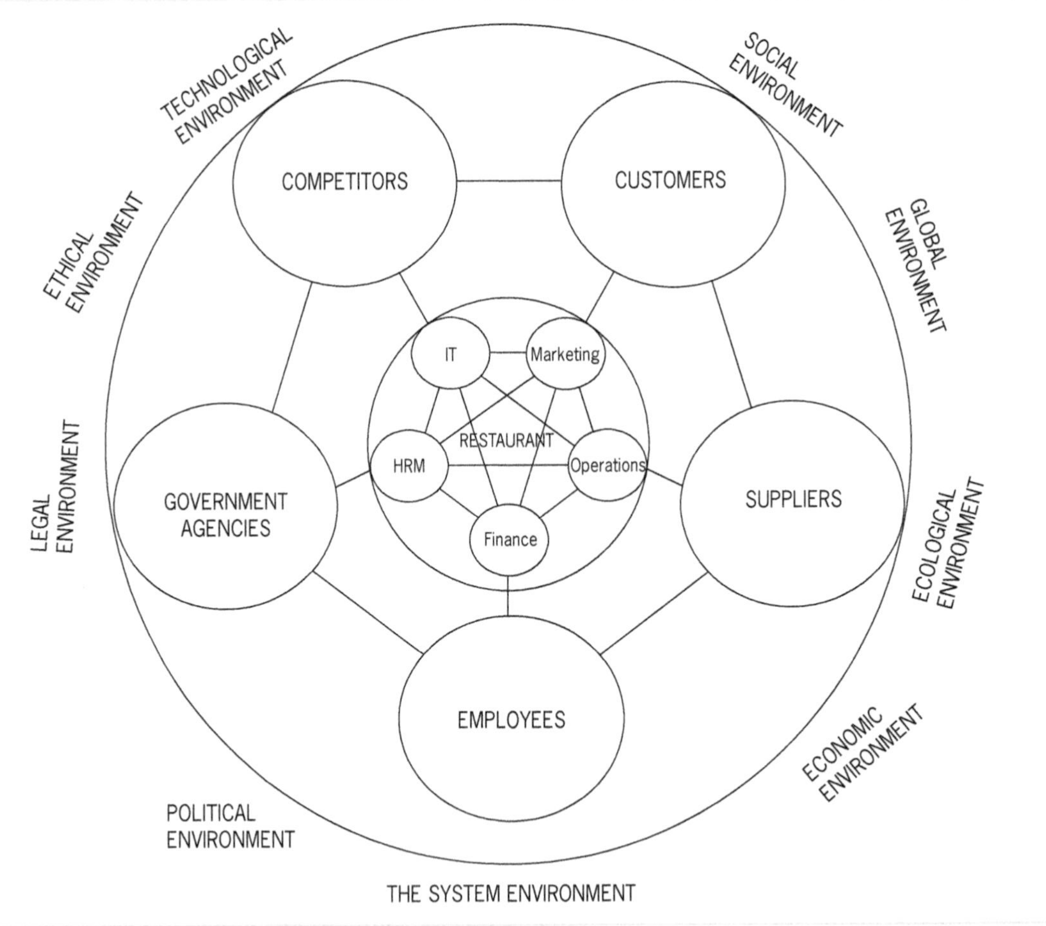


service ecosystem. It is the diversity and nature of the ecosystem which explains why services provided today are different from those which were available to consumers 50 or 100 years ago, and why the services available today in Western Europe are different from those currently available in Saudi Arabia or Bangladesh. The types of service available are a response to changes in the broader service environment. But it also has to be recognized that the service environment itself changes in response to the availability of services.

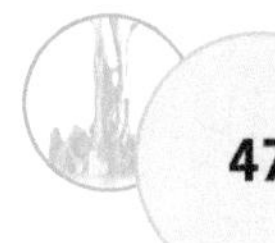



We can begin to analyse the effects of the service environment by identifying different components of the environment and their effects on service provision. The environment facing most service providers is complex and interrelated, so any attempt to define distinct elements of this environment can be quite arbitrary. But in the sections below we explore some of the principal headings for analysing the pressures in the environment which affect service systems.

### Economic

We saw in Chapter 1 that as economies prosper, services tend to account for a growing proportion of GDP. Most services are what economists often define as 'superior' products, meaning that as individuals' incomes rise, they buy more of these types of product. Overseas holidays, eating out more often and elective medical treatments are typical of these superior products. Some goods and services show the opposite pattern and tend to decline as individuals' incomes increase (e.g. local bus services).

Rising incomes of consumers generally reflect a rise in wage levels. While rising wage levels present an opportunity to services companies by allowing wage-earning consumers to spend more on services, they can also pose a major challenge to labour-intensive service providers. We will see later in this chapter how the design of service systems has to balance increasingly wealthy consumers' desire to consume more services with the employers' need to cut the cost of increasingly expensive labour.

### Social

This is a very broad heading for a range of phenomena which influence consumers' and employees' attitudes towards service production and consumption. The size of different social classes has changed over time, and in some cultures fixed cast-systems have given way to a class system in which membership of a group can be achieved other than by accident of birth. Membership of different social classes can be associated with quite distinct patterns of consumption; for example, in many Western societies, consumption of 'bingo' halls and many other lottery-type services has been associated with consumers of lower social status, while stockbroking services have been more typically associated with groups of higher social status. The existence of social classification can have quite subtle implications for services systems, and it is often important to understand the aspirational identity of individuals in order to have a better understanding of the types of services they will seek to consume. As an example, many fast-food chains have positioned themselves in emerging economies by appealing to some individuals' need to identify with a group of upwardly mobile consumers, and which can be manifested through consumption of Western-style services. In Western countries themselves, those same fast-food chains might appeal to groups seeking more utilitarian benefits.

Sociologists have distinguished between values, attitudes and lifestyles. Values tend to be quite enduring and passed down from generation to generation; for example, the family may be at the centre of most societies' value systems. Attitudes may change over time; for example, although there may be continuing belief in the family, attitudes about what is an acceptable form of family have changed over time. Eventually, changing attitudes are reflected in the lifestyles people lead. Service systems must adapt to accommodate changing attitudes and lifestyles; for example, many services have emerged to satisfy the needs of busy professionals who prefer to allocate less of their time to household jobs.

Changing social attitudes also affect the production capabilities of a service system. Employees bring to work attitudes and values which might be alien to the needs of the service system; for example, a social system which places priority on the family above all else may find conflict with a service system which demands flexibility by employees. A society characterized by a slow pace of life may present challenges for a service provider seeking to offer a high-speed service.

Cultures may see some service jobs as glamorous and thereby facilitating recruitment, but at other times a service may be associated with servitude and not compatible with a person's aspirational social standing. Many societies have therefore sought to recruit foreign employees who may have less social stigma (and often a greater economic need) to do the kinds of jobs which the native population would not do.

## Ecological

It is sometimes thought that because of their inherent intangibility, ecological issues are of less concern for services than for manufacturing industries with their visible use of scarce resources and emissions of pollutants to the atmosphere. However, it must be recognized that most services involve some tangible components, for example the food in a restaurant and the aircraft used as part of a holiday package.

The nature of service systems needs to adapt to the issues raised by consumers' preferences and the increasing constraints on production possibilities. Some commentators have suggested that a growing segment of consumers seeks to manifest their positive ecological credentials by purposefully consuming goods and services which are less harmful to the ecological environment. It may currently be only a small segment of consumers who are opposed in principle to the idea of flying to their holiday destination, because of the $CO_2$ emissions which their flight will cause. But if such attitudes became mainstream, service systems of airlines and holiday companies would have to adapt in scale and scope. The ecological challenges facing the production possibilities of service systems are becoming increasingly apparent, typified by debates about the development of tourism resorts in areas of low rainfall, putting pressure on local water supply, and the continuing debate about aircraft emissions and the consequences for airlines of taxation on emissions. In Chapter 7 we will examine the case of 'space tourism', which can be seen either as a great opportunity, targeting a rich and adventurous segment, or ecological irresponsibility which will eventually attract regulatory control.

## Technological

Many service systems have been dramatically transformed by technological innovation. The impacts of technology are most apparent to consumers in the case of completely new services, such as online gambling and home shopping services. But we must not forget technological innovation, which has improved the efficiency of unseen aspects of service processes, for example GPS-based vehicle scheduling and routing systems which have improved the efficiency and effectiveness of distribution systems. We will consider the impacts of technological developments on service systems later in this chapter.

## Ethical

Ethics is about what is considered right and what is considered wrong. Ethical values change over time, with consumers in developed societies generally leading the way in defining expectations about how companies should treat their customers (and indeed how customers should treat companies and their fellow customers). Ethical considerations are particularly important for service-based companies because of the high levels of trust that are typically placed in service providers. Although there have been many cases of manufacturing companies acting unethically in how they manage their production processes, ethics is particularly important in the services sector because intangibility means that services cannot generally be inspected before consumption and the buyer needs to trust a service provider to deliver what it has promised.

## Political

The political environment comprises the processes by which decisions are made about the allocation of resources, rights and responsibilities within a society. As such, it comprises not just formal political processes, such as government agencies, but also the pressure groups who seek to change government policy. Radical political change is rare in Western developed countries, but service systems nevertheless have had to adapt to changes in the political environment. Following the collapse of communism in the 1990s, entrepreneurs in Eastern Europe found themselves creating service systems to fill the gap left by the demise of government-controlled systems. In many Western European countries, the tendency towards further privatization has resulted in the fragmentation of service systems to embrace multiple subcontractors, outsourcing and franchising. Where the political system has placed more emphasis on a market-based economy rather than a centrally planned economy, service system design has had to respond even more vigorously by putting the customer at the centre of the system. The convenience of operating staff and management might have driven service systems in economies which emphasize centralized planning and allocation of resources, but such systems have to change radically to embrace transition to market-based environments.

#### Legal

The legal environment is essentially the embodiment of political statements of rights and responsibilities within a society. As societies develop, there is a tendency for dealings between buyers and sellers increasingly to be governed by legally binding contractual relationships, rather than by moral governance (see Gundlach and Murphy, 1993). A systems approach to designing services tends to be associated with pluralism in relationships between buyers and sellers and greater anonymity. In the absence of networks of trusted service suppliers (and also of trusted customers), legal processes and frameworks take on the role of regulating relationships between different participants in a service system.

#### Global business environment

The economies of countries of the world have become increasingly interlinked, helped by falling real costs of transport and communication and an apparent 'homogenization' of market segments around the world. Service systems have responded to globalization, with many of our well-known hotels, restaurants and retailers, to name but a few, now seeing their systems operating at a global rather than just a local level. From a production perspective, many service providers who are able to overcome problems of inseparability by the use of improving telecommunications have seized opportunities to move part of their production processes to lower-cost overseas bases.

Service organizations need to be constantly alert to changes in the globalized business environment. Is increasing globalization only a one-way process? Is it possible that rising energy prices will actually encourage more local, rather than global, consumption and production? Will the seemingly inexorable trend towards homogenization of markets be replaced by increasing concerns by individuals to assert their distinctive cultural identity through the purchases that they make?

### 2.2.2 Effects of service systems on the wider business environment

Service systems have to continually adapt to change in their business environment if they are to survive. But we can often also observe an opposite effect where the business environment has adapted to change in service systems.

We saw in Chapter 1 that the link between services growth and national economic growth is a two-way process. New services have emerged in response to increasing levels of national income. But the whole national economic environment has been shaped by developments in key service sectors. Banking, transport, education and communication services, to name just a few, continue to be critical to the development of local, regional and national economies. A high-speed rail link to a previously underdeveloped region will most likely stimulate further economic growth in the region. National economies such as Singapore and Ireland have attributed periods of rapid economic growth to the availability of high-quality education services.

We have seen that where service systems fail, there can be profound effects on the broader business environment. Banking is a sometimes forgotten and hidden service which allows other production sectors to function effectively, so the problems which followed the banking crisis of 2008 had effects far beyond the sector. These included firms who were no longer able to borrow money to fund expansion, consumers who were no longer able to borrow money to buy houses and governments who were forced to rescue failing banks with emergency loans which added to government debt and created new political tensions.

### 2.2.3 The service production/consumption system and service dominant logic

You will recall from Chapter 1 that inseparability is one of the defining characteristics of services. Consumers and producers must meet within the service system for the service to be simultaneously produced and consumed. This is in contrast to a manufacturing system in which the production system can generally be clearly separated from the consumption system. In a manufacturing system, value is created exclusively by producers and consumed exclusively by consumers.

Service dominant logic – introduced in Chapter 1 – has contended that analysis of value creation in terms of a service system blurs the distinction between the roles of producers and consumers. Their roles become less distinct and value is co-created during interactions between service providers and consumers.

Service dominant logic has sought to explain why some service systems succeed while others fail, and in pursuit of this has distinguished between operand and operant resources. *Operand* resources comprise 'hard' resources, typically physical items, such as raw materials and computer hardware. *Operant* resources may be regarded as 'softer' resources, typically based on human skills and knowledge; organizational routines, cultures and competencies; information about markets, competitors and technology; and relationships with competitors, suppliers and customers (Hunt and Derozier, 2004). Operand resources tend to be static in nature, while operant resources are dynamic and can be rejuvenated and replenished.

Vargo and Lusch argue that competitive advantage is primarily derived from operant resources, rather than operand resources, because knowledge and skills operate on resources to solve problems, fulfil needs and produce a favorable customer experience (Vargo and Lusch, 2004). Operand resources may be easy to copy, for example an airline may buy the same aircraft as its competitors and its meals and booking systems can be easily replicated. But knowledge of customers' preferences, trust through channels of distribution and loyalty from employees are much harder to copy and are typically a key source of competitive advantage.

A service system integrates operand and operant resources. The system which is best able to integrate these resources will gain a competitive advantage. Service dominant logic argues that both service providers and consumers are involved in resource integration (Lusch and Vargo, 2006; Vargo, 2008); however, it has been pointed out that the nature of this resource integration between suppliers and customers is shaped by the social and political context of co-creation (Edvardsson et al., 2011).

### 2.2.4 Service systems and sub-systems

We are now going to move our focus away from the 'big picture' of the service environment and explore more specifically the service production/consumption system that customers experience. This service system involves a service provider and consumer in a process of co-creating value. But it can be too simplistic to talk just about a service system, because anything except the most basic service will involve multiple sub-systems. In a restaurant, for example a number of sub-systems can be typically identified: a food preparation system; an order taking/delivery system; an accounting system; an inventory/procurement system; a building maintenance system etc. The bigger and more complex the restaurant, especially if it is operating at multiple sites, the more complex its sub-systems are likely to be.

The sub-systems need to be synchronized with each other. The procurement system of a restaurant must ensure that the needs of the food preparation system can be met. The food preparation system must have a capacity which is consistent with the requirements placed on it by the order taking/delivery system. Too many orders relative to food preparation capacity can quickly result in dissatisfied customers. Too much capacity relative to orders may result in unnecessary costs, putting the restaurant at a competitive disadvantage. Even a restaurant may be regarded as a relatively simple service system. Service systems can become much more complex where multiple activities need to be integrated, which can be the case for airlines, hospitals, and even cities if they are regarded as a complex service system.

Service design involves determining who should be involved in each sub-system. The consumer is clearly an important component of the service production/consumption system and we will return later to the issue of how consumers are designed into a service system.

Many service providers decide that it would be more efficient and effective if a third-party service provider took responsibility for a sub-system. In complex systems such as airlines, an outsourced service provider may take complete responsibility for a major sub-system such as baggage handling or aircraft maintenance. These outsourced service providers may in turn outsource part of their work, so the baggage handling company may outsource the maintenance of its vehicles. In Chapter 5 we will look in more detail at networks and relationships in the context of making service systems more efficient and effective.

### 2.2.5 A typology of service systems

Service systems exist to produce quite different types of benefit. Some systems will require the complete involvement of the consumer, by their presence in the service process and often through their emotional engagement. At other times, the consumer will not need to be present for much of the service production process, therefore opportunities for co-creation of value may be fewer.

Service encounters occur where a consumer and producer meet in order for the former to receive the benefits that the latter has the resources to provide. The concept of a service encounter has been defined broadly by Shostack (1985) as 'a period of time during which a consumer directly interacts with a service'. This definition includes all aspects of the service provider with which a consumer may interact, including its personnel and physical assets. In some cases, the entire service is produced and consumed during the course of this encounter. Such services can be described as 'high-contact' services and the encounter becomes the dominant means by which consumers assess their satisfaction with the service. At other times, the encounter is just one element of the total production and consumption process. For such 'low-contact' services, a part of the production process can be performed without the direct involvement of the consumer.

We can define the type of service encounter – and hence the parameters for service system design – by reference to two principal factors:

- first, whether it is the customer him or herself who is the recipient of the service, or whether it is their possessions;
- second, the extent to which tangible elements are present within the service offer.

These two dimensions of the service encounter are shown diagrammatically in matrix form in Figure 2.2 and some of the implications flowing from this for categorizing service systems are discussed below:

Figure 2.2 A classification of service encounter types

| How tangible is the service? | The consumer | Their possessions |
|---|---|---|
| Tangible | 1. HIGH-INVOLVEMENT PERSONAL SERVICES<br>e.g. Healthcare services<br>Hairdressing<br>Public transport | 2. GOODS MAINTENANCE SERVICES<br>e.g. Car servicing<br>Building renovation<br>Road haulage |
| Intangible | 3. SERVICES FOR THE MIND<br>e.g. Education<br>Television programme<br>Radio programme | 4. INTANGIBLE ASSET MAINTENANCE SERVICES<br>e.g. Litigation<br>Accountancy<br>Fund management |

**What is the service performed on?**

1 *High-involvement personal services*. The most significant types of service encounters occur in the upper left quadrant of Figure 2.2, where the consumer is the direct recipient of a service and the service offer provides a high level of tangibility. These can be described as high-contact encounters. Examples are provided by most types of healthcare, where the physical presence of a customer's body is a prerequisite for a series of quite tangible surgical operations being carried out. Public transport offers further examples within this category. The benefits of a bus service are fundamentally to move customers, and without their presence the benefit cannot be received. Services in this quadrant represent the most intense type of service encounter. Customer and producer must physically meet in order for the service to be performed and this has a number of implications for the service system design – most importantly, the customer must be designed into the system from the outset. The customer cannot be external to the system, but the system should focus on them as a key element:

- Quality control becomes a major issue, because the consumer is often concerned with the processes of service production as much as with the end result (not only 'will the surgery make me better?', but also 'will I feel comfortable during the surgery?'). Furthermore, because many services in this category are produced in a one-on-one situation where judgement by the service provider is called for, it can be difficult to implement quality-control checks within the system design before the service is consumed.
- Because the consumer must attend during the production process, the customer's ease of access to the service can be crucial. A service system that is inconveniently located, or has restricted opening hours, may effectively make the system inaccessible to potential users.
- The problem of managing the pattern of demand is most critical with this type of service, as delays in service production can have an adverse consequence not only for the service outcome, but also for consumers' satisfaction with the service process.

2 *Goods maintenance services*. Here, services are performed on a customer's objects rather than on their person, an example being the repair of electrical appliances or the transport of goods. A large part of the service production process can go unseen without any involvement of the customer, who merely initiates the service process (e.g. delivering a car to a repair garage) and collects the results (picking up the car once a repair has been completed). The process by which a car is repaired – the substantive service – may be of little concern to the customer, as long as the outcome – a car that works – is satisfactory. However, the processes by which customers

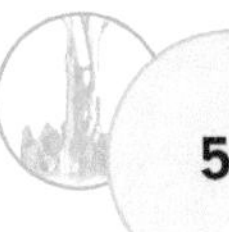


are handled during the pre-service and after-service stages form part of the service encounter. It follows that, while technical skills may be essential for staff engaged in the substantive service production process, skills in dealing with customers are important for those involved in customer encounters. Because the consumer is not physically present during the substantive service production process, the timing and location of this part of the service system allows the service provider much greater flexibility. In this way, the car repairer can collect a car at a customer's home (which is most convenient to the customer) and process it at its central workshops (which is most convenient to the service producer). As long as a job is completed on time, delays during the substantive production process are of less importance to the consumer than would be the case if the customer was personally delayed during the production of the service.

3. *Services for the mind*. Here, the consumer is the direct recipient of a service, but does not need to be physically present in order to receive an essentially intangible benefit. The intangibility of the benefit means that the service production process can often be separated spatially from the consumption of the service. In this way, viewers of an intangible television channel do not need to interact with staff from the television company in order to receive the benefits. Similarly, recipients of 'distant learning' educational services often do not need to be physically present during an encounter with the education provider (although some interaction by phone, mail or email is likely to occur).
4. *Intangible asset maintenance services*. The final category of service encounter comprises intangible services performed on a customer's intangible assets (for example, a financial adviser managing a portfolio of shares, or a solicitor providing legal representation). For these services, there is little tangible evidence in the production process and the customer does not normally need to be physically present during the production process. Here, a large part of the substantive service production process (such as the preparation of sale transaction documents) can be undertaken with very little direct contact between customer and service provider. The service encounter becomes less critical to the customer and can take place at a distance without any need to physically meet. Customers judge transactions not just on the quality of their encounter, but also to a much greater extent on outcomes (e.g. the performance of a financial portfolio).

## 2.3 Designing the customer into the service system

Customers are not passive consumers of a service (as they may be in the case of goods), but are instead active co-creators of the service. The service system has to treat the consumer as part of a production process, rather than merely an outcome, especially in the case of 'high-contact' service encounters. The consumer goes into the producer's 'factory' and the resulting design of the service system involves trade-offs between the level of service desired by the consumer, the price they are prepared to pay for the service and the operational efficiency of the producer, which in turn will affect the price charged to the consumer and the level of personal service offered. Should the service provider position itself as a premium service in which it takes a lot of co-creation responsibility away from the consumer (as in the case of home delivery of groceries), or should it offer a more basic service in which consumers are expected to put in more of their own effort, usually in return for a lower price?

A number of commentators have used the term 'service convenience' to describe the extent to which service systems adapt to consumers' needs, by relieving consumers of the need to perform part of the service production process themselves. Berry et al. (2002) identified five types of service convenience:

- *Decision convenience* refers to consumers' perception of the time and effort needed to choose a service. (Has the service provider guided me through the options that are best for me?)
- *Access convenience* refers to perceptions of the time and effort needed to gain access to a service. (How far is the nearest branch of a bank?)
- *Transaction convenience* is consumers' time and effort needed to complete a transaction. (Do I have to go to a bank branch to open an account?)
- *Benefit convenience* is consumers' time and effort expenditure to experience a service's core benefits. (Does the train go directly to my destination or do I have to wait for a connecting train?)
- *Post-benefit convenience* is consumers' time and effort expenditure following consumption (e.g. in respect of service failures).

We will return to issues of designing the consumer into service systems in future chapters. In this chapter, we explore conceptual frameworks for including the consumer in service processes. Organizations often seek to push the boundary towards the consumer, implying that the consumer undertakes a larger part of the production/consumption process themselves (for example, a restaurant can improve the efficiency of its staff by requiring customers to collect their own food, rather than serving it to their tables). At other times, customers are prepared to pay for additional convenience and the production/consumption boundary moves towards the producer, implying that the consumer is relieved of parts of their role in the production process (for example, a fast-food restaurant may offer a home delivery service, thereby removing the consumer's role of collecting the food from the restaurant). There is evidence that co-creation involving the consumer can actually increase their evaluation of a service rather than reduce it (Troye and Supphellen, 2012).

## In practice: Fast food to your door

As consumers' incomes rise, they are likely to purchase more 'luxury' services. This often means that consumers perform less of the production process themselves, and the service provider does more. This effect can be clearly seen in the market for convenience food. The UK in recent years has seen a growth in the number of convenience food outlets, which have capitalized on consumers' desire to buy ready-cooked food. With increasing wealth, consumers have been able to purchase convenience food routinely, and not just for special occasions. With further increases in wealth, many consumers have decided that they would rather not have to go to collect their food, but would rather have the service provider bring it to them. The delivery of convenience food, such as the service provided by this pizza company, has become a growth area and it effectively represents a shift in the consumer–producer boundary that reduces the input from the consumer. However, one challenge for companies such as Domino's in extending their service system to reach the customer's home is the increasing cost of labour. Rising wages may mean more money in the pockets of consumers to buy more services, but it also implies – all other things being equal – higher real costs of providing labour-intensive services such as home pizza delivery.

Figure 2.3 Pizza delivered to your home. (Reproduced courtesy of Domino's Pizza)

## 2.3.1 Designing other customers into the service system

So far, service design has been described as essentially a process by which a service provider does something to a consumer, who work together to co-create value. This may be a simplification, and there is growing interest in the role of consumers who jointly produce a service between themselves, without recourse to the formally designated 'service provider'. Groups of friends have traditionally done favours for each other by co-producing services which would otherwise have been counted as part of the output of the formal economy, but are nevertheless produced informally. A group of friends taking it in turns to drive their respective children to school reduces the need for a taxi and bus services provided through a formal service provider. Today, with the development of social network media, there has been a lot of interest in consumer–consumer co-production (see vignette 'Diners in the kitchen').

Many companies have used online forums to facilitate co-creation among their customers. Many software companies, for example, have developed online self-help communities where one customer can ask a question and receive comments from other customers. Eager contributors to the forum can save a service provider the cost of employing its own staff and may provide customers with a better experience.

We will explore further the experiential aspects of incorporating fellow customers into service design in the next chapter.

### Thinking around the subject: Co-creation through social media – diners in the kitchen

When does a customer become a producer? The inseparability of services means that customers generally become co-creators of the services that they consume and their role in this co-creation can range from a very minor role to one where they take a dominant role in creating the service. But what about situations where a consumer becomes a seller of services to other consumers?

Individuals have always traded services with friends and relatives, often in a simple bilateral way, or sometimes using more complex multilateral arrangements. So two sets of parents could take it in turn to take their children to school, each effectively co-producing transport services for the other. Or A might take B's children to school, then B does the weekly shopping for C, then C does childminding for A. It's how communities and families have always worked, and without the need for formal marketization of supply.

Recently, there has been renewed interest in the use of social network media to extend this network of sharers, for example through car sharing schemes, music sharing and dining groups. Cooking for others shows how consumers can easily become producers.

There is nothing new in households preparing food for small groups of people on a semi-commercial basis. The tiffin boxes prepared by households in India and distributed to workers have often operated on a small scale. Today, many Western countries have seen the emergence of 'dining clubs' where individuals take it in turns to cook in their own homes for others. Sometimes known as 'dinner co-ops', one person might cook for five people on one night, then be fed by other members of the co-op on other nights with a variety of food which each individual member alone could not prepare. It can be a great idea for people who don't want to cook every night and who enjoy the challenges and opportunities of entertaining. The Internet has made it much easier for dining co-ops to be formed, with many neighbourhood schemes in bigger towns such as New York and Washington. Home cooks can be rated, so a diner who is not so keen on taking a risk with their choice of host can check out their reviews online first.

Some home cooks who have received good reviews have thought about going on to become a 'real' restaurateur, and here again social media have helped. Some have opened 'pop-up' restaurants – temporary restaurants often in unusual venues such as disused offices or shops. They can open easily and close just as easily, and social media can be used to rapidly spread news of the location, helped where the 'pop-up chef' has a loyal following through social media. And just in case they fancy setting up something a bit more permanent, social media can help again with 'crowdsourcing' of funds to set up the restaurant – quicker, easier and some would argue just as secure for all concerned as a loan from a traditional bank.

Like many new technologies, social media can have applications way beyond what people had originally envisaged. Could social media really change our eating habits by allowing customers to take on a role as restaurateur for a day?

## 2.4 Specifying the design of a service system

Services are essentially about processes and cannot be as easily reduced to objective descriptions as in the case of most tangible goods. A fairly precise description of a confectionery bar is usually possible, so that it allows a buyer to judge it and a manufacturer to replicate it. Such a description is much more difficult in the case of a service such as a visit to a restaurant, where a large part of the outcome can only be subjectively judged by the consumer and it is difficult to define all aspects of the service process in such a way that it can be easily replicated. This problem in defining the service encounter has given rise to a number of methodologies, which essentially 'map out' the service process. In this section we begin with the basic process of 'blueprinting' a service.

### 2.4.1 The service 'blueprint'

Where service production processes are complex, it is important for an organization to gain a holistic view of how the elements of the service relate to each other. 'Blueprinting' is a graphical approach proposed by Kingman-Brundage (1989) to overcome problems that occur where a new service is launched without adequate identification of the necessary support functions. The approach essentially attempts to draw a map of the service process.

A customer blueprint has three main elements:

- All of the principal functions required to make and distribute a service are identified, along with identification of the responsible personnel.
- Timing and sequencing relationships among the functions are depicted graphically.
- For each function, acceptable tolerances are identified in terms of the variation from standard that can be tolerated without adversely affecting customers' perception of quality.

The essence of a blueprint is to show how customers, assets and information are processed. The principles of a service blueprint are illustrated in Figure 2.4 with a very simple application of the framework to the purchase of a cup of tea in a café.

A customer blueprint must clearly identify all steps in a service process, that is, all contacts or interactions with customers. These are shown in time sequential order from left to right. The blueprint is further divided into two 'zones': a zone of visibility (processes that are visible to the customer and in which the customer is likely to participate) and a zone of invisibility (processes and interactions that, although necessary to the proper servicing of a customer, may be hidden from their view).

The blueprint also identifies levels of tolerance (for example, the acceptable amount of time that it should take to perform each stage of the service process), and points where consumers may

Figure 2.4 Customer service blueprint – a simplified application to the purchase of a cup of tea in a café

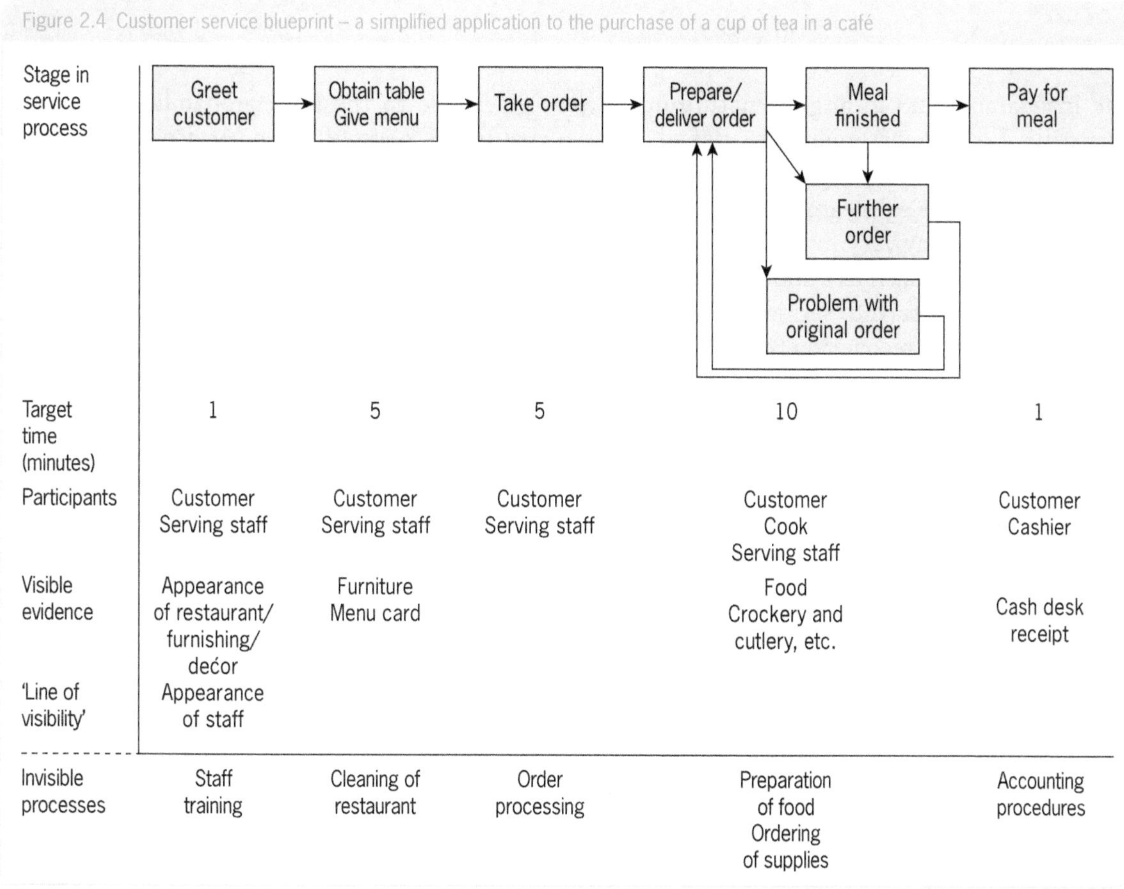


potentially encounter failures in the service production process. Where failure occurs, a feedback loop is shown through which a problem can be rectified (for example, if the wrong meal is delivered in a restaurant, a feedback loop can indicate how this will be rectified and who is responsible for doing so).

Blueprinting is not a new idea, with many precedents in methods of critical path analysis. What is important here is that marketing, operations management and human resource management focus on processes that deliver benefits which are valued by customers and efficient for the company.

The example of a blueprint shown in Figure 2.4 is of course very simplistic. In practice, firms with complex service processes produce lengthy manuals describing procedures for the different components of their service systems.

It does not matter how a blueprint is expressed, whether it is in the form of a diagrammatic portrayal of processes or simply in words. The important point is that it should form a shared and agreed basis for action, which is focused on meeting customers' needs effectively and efficiently. Of course, a blueprint cannot anticipate all contingencies for which a response will be required, for example a bomb explosion in a restaurant or the kidnapping of a bank clerk. Risk management techniques are sometimes used to estimate the likelihood of certain types of events occurring. Nevertheless, if the general nature of a process problem is identified, the outline of possible next steps can be developed.

## 2.5 Service failure and recovery

The inseparable and intangible nature of services gives rise to the high probability of failures occurring, leaving customers dissatisfied. From a customer's perspective, a service failure is any situation where something has gone wrong, irrespective of responsibility. The inseparability of high-contact services means that service failure usually cannot be disguised from the customer. Service failures may vary in gravity from being very serious, such as a food-poisoning incident, to something trivial, such as a short delay.

A systems approach to services marketing management can facilitate the process of identifying service failure and recovering from it. Using a process map such as the blueprint shown in Figure 2.4 can allow a service provider to identify points in a system where failure frequently occurs. A systems approach can allow diagnoses of specific causes of failure; for example, are there particular types of meal orders or times of the day in a restaurant when failure is more likely to occur?

By way of example, a blueprint can be used to identify what employees should do in any of the following circumstances:

- When a dentist has to cancel appointments due to illness, who should inform his patients? When and by whom should alternative arrangements be made? Should some patients be regarded as higher priority than others for rescheduling of appointments?
- A restaurant customer complains of a badly cooked meal. Who should have the authority to decide whether any recompense should be given to the complainant? On what basis should compensation be assessed?
- A hotel overbooks its accommodation. Which alternative hotels should the duty manager approach first to try to obtain alternative accommodation for its guests? Should it actively try to pacify intending guests with free vouchers for use on future occasions? If so, who will authorize them and how will their value be determined?

### 2.5.1 Defining service failure

The service failure literature has produced many typologies characterizing the general nature of service failures (e.g. Bitner et al., 1990; Kelley and Davis, 1994). It has been suggested by Halstead et al. (1993) that a single service failure may have two effects. First, a 'halo' effect may negatively colour a customer's perceptions (for example, if an airline loses a passenger's baggage, the passenger may subsequently associate any communication from the airline with failure). Second, a 'domino' effect may engender service failures in other attributes or areas of a service process. This can occur where a failure in an early stage of a service process puts a customer in a bad mood so that they become more critical of minor failures in subsequent stages. A diner who has been unreasonably delayed in obtaining their pre-booked table may be more ready to complain about minor problems with the subsequent delivery of their food.

During a service process such as that shown in Figure 2.4, there will be many opportunities for service failure to occur (and indeed opportunities for excellent service delivery which is beyond customers' expectations). Each part of the service process where customers interact with the service provider presents an opportunity for failure, and while processes may be quite trivial, others may be critical to customers' enjoyment of the service. At each 'critical incident', customers have an opportunity to evaluate the service provider and form an opinion of service quality.

But what constitutes a 'critical incident'? Service processes can be quite complex, resulting in a large number of potentially critical incidents, many of which involve non-front-line staff. Consider the following list of potential critical incidents which may occur during the course of a flight with an airline:

| | |
|---|---|
| Pre-sales | Clarity of information on airline website |
| | Making reservation online |
| | Receipt of e-ticket |
| Post-sales, pre-consumption | Check-in of baggage |
| | Issue of boarding pass |
| | Advice of departure gate |
| | Quality of airport announcements |
| | Quality of waiting conditions |
| Consumption | Welcome on boarding aircraft |
| | Assistance in finding seat |
| | Assistance in stowing baggage |
| | Reliability of departure time |
| | Attentiveness of in-flight service |
| | Quality of food service |
| | Quality of in-flight entertainment |
| | Quality of announcements |
| | Safe/comfortable operation of aircraft |
| | Fast transfer from aircraft to terminal |
| Post-consumption | Baggage reclaim |
| | Information available at arrival airport |
| | Queries regarding lost baggage etc. |

This list of critical stages in a service system is by no means exhaustive. Indeed, the extent to which any point is critical should be determined by customers' own judgements, rather than relying on a technical definition by the service provider. Where there is a high level of involvement on the part of the consumer, an incident may be considered to be particularly critical.

Successful accomplishment of many of the critical incidents identified above can be dependent upon satisfactory performance by support staff who do not directly interact with customers – for example the actions of unseen baggage handlers can be critical in ensuring that baggage is reclaimed in the right place, at the right time and intact. This emphasizes the need to treat everybody within a service organization as a 'part-time marketer' (Gummesson, 2008).

A series of apparently unrelated service failures may lead to a crisis (Elliott et al., 2005). A major disaster, such as the sinking of the cruise ship *Costa Concordia* off the Italian coast in 2012 with the loss of 32 lives, may be the result of apparently minor failures, including inattentive staff and failure to follow procedures, which when combined result in a major crisis. We will return to the subject of crisis management in the context of service organizations' communications in Chapter 13.

### 2.5.2 Identifying points of service failure

It can be quite easy to say that companies should pay attention to critical points in their service system, but much more difficult to determine when a company has failed in a critical incident. In the academic literature, critical incidents have most often been based on analyses of customers' spontaneous statements following a short interview (Edvardsson and Strandvik, 2000). Such an approach represents top-of-the-mind memories of service interactions that are socially acceptable to report to an unknown interviewer. Often, no probing has been done and respondents have not been asked to elaborate about how negative or positive such an incident has been. More importantly, it can be unrealistic to look at critical incidents in isolation from previous incidents and the whole context of the relationship. To overcome the problem of just looking at a disconnected series of critical incidents, Stauss and Weinlich (1995) have suggested the sequential incident technique (SIT). This technique considers the whole history of a relationship and the incidents that have occurred within it. There is some evidence that the length of a customer relationship may moderate the effects of failure of a critical incident (Palmer et al., 2000).

Having systems for identifying, tracking and analysing service failures allows management to identify common failure situations (Hoffman et al., 1995). More importantly, it allows management to develop strategies for preventing failures occurring in the first place, and for designing appropriate recovery strategies where failure is unavoidable. Firms with formal service recovery programmes supplement the bundle of benefits provided by the core product offer and enhance the service component of the firm's value chain (Hoffman and Kelley, 2000).

Many services companies have tried to facilitate complaints from customers in order that they can more precisely identify points of failure. The use of freefone helplines, customer comment cards and online surveys is evidence of this. There is a suggestion that complaining may in itself lead to a feeling of satisfaction, simply because the complainant has managed to get the feeling 'off their chest'. In one study of members of a fitness centre in the USA, it was found that the greater increase in satisfaction from customers who had been asked for their views came from the most dissatisfied customers (Nyer, 2000). Providing the opportunity to express feelings about a service can prove beneficial to satisfaction levels but must be seen in the context of the business's willingness to correct errors or failures. Against this, it must also be noted that companies may experience an increase in 'bogus complaints'. With such encouragement to complain, some customers may be tempted to push their luck in the hope of getting some form of compensation for quite spurious complaints.

There appears to be variation in different types of consumers' propensity to complain. Heung and Lam (2003) found that female, young and well-educated customers tend to complain more, and confirmed earlier findings that an individual's level of educational achievement is a good predictor of their propensity to complain.

The study of service failure and recovery has built on a number of theoretical frameworks. These include: attribution theory (Heider, 1958; Maxham and Netemeyer, 2002), justice theory (Adams, 1965; Tax et al., 1998), disconfirmation theory (Churchill and Surprenant, 1982; Oliver, 1980; Parasuraman et al., 1985), social exchange theory (Homans, 1961; Kelley and Thibaut, 1978) and fairness theory (Folger and Cropanzano, 1998; McColl-Kennedy and Sparks, 2003; Spreng et al., 1995).

Justice theory probably offers the most comprehensive framework for understanding the complaint resolution process from initial service failure to final resolution. Justice theory has evolved to incorporate three dimensions:

- distributive justice (the fairness of the outcome of the complaint resolution process);
- procedural justice (whether the procedures for resolving the failure were considered to be fair);
- interactional justice (which concerns interpersonal behaviour employed in the complaint resolution procedures and delivery of outcomes).

### 2.5.3 Developing recovery strategies

It is often suggested that a happy customer will go away and tell two or three people about their good service, but a dissatisfied customer will tell probably a dozen about a failure. Businesses commonly lose 15–20 per cent of their customer base each year (Reichheld and Sasser, 1990). Although customers may defect to the competition for a number of reasons (e.g. better prices, better products, change of location etc.), minimizing the number of customers who defect due to poor customer service is largely controllable. However, there is plenty of evidence that firms do not take complaining customers seriously and that unresolved complaints actually strengthen the customer's negative feelings towards the company and its representatives (Hart et al., 1990). Organizations need to have in place a strategy by which they can seek to recover from failure.

Complaint handling can be viewed as a sequence of events, beginning with communicating a complaint about the service failure, that generates a process of interaction leading to a decision and an outcome. Justice literature suggests that each part of the sequence is subject to an assessment of fairness in resolving a problem (Bies, 1987; Tax et al., 1998).

A successful recovery is accomplished when the aggrieved consumer is provided with an appropriate blend of the three justice dimensions noted above (Maxham and Netemeyer, 2002). The importance of the three dimensions depends on several factors, including: the type and magnitude of the service failure (McColl-Kennedy and Sparks, 2003), the service context (Mattila, 2001), the extent of any prior relationship (Hoffman and Kelley, 2000), customer psychographics (McCole and Herwadkar, 2003) and emotional state (Schoefer and Ennew, 2005).

There is a growing body of literature on the methods used by services organizations to recover from an adverse critical incident and to build up a strong relationship once again. Service recovery processes are those activities in which a company engages to address a customer complaint regarding a service failure. There is evidence that a good recovery can turn angry, frustrated customers into loyal ones and may create more goodwill than if things had gone smoothly in the first place (Kau and Loh, 2006; Noone, 2012).

The most important step in service recovery is to find out as soon as possible when a service has failed to meet customers' expectations. Customers who are dissatisfied and do not report this dissatisfaction to the service provider may never come back and, worse still, may tell friends about their bad experience. Services companies are therefore going to increasing lengths to facilitate feedback of customers' comments in the hope that they are given an opportunity to make amends. Service recovery after the event might include financial compensation that is considered by the recipient to be fair, or the offer of additional services without charge, giving the company the opportunity to show itself in a better light. If service recovery is to be achieved after the event, it is important that appropriate offers of compensation are made speedily and fairly. If a long dispute follows, aggrieved customers could increasingly rationalize reasons for never using that service organization again and tell others not only of their bad service encounter, but also of the bad post-service behaviour encountered.

Rather than wait until long after a critical incident has failed, services companies should think more about service recovery during the service delivery process. It can be possible for services organizations to turn a failed critical incident into a positive advantage with their customers. In the face of adverse circumstances, a service organization's ability to empathize with its customers can create stronger bonds than if no service failure had occurred. As an example, a coach tour operator could arrive at a hotel with a party of customers only to find that the hotel has overbooked, potentially resulting in great inconvenience to its customers. The failure to swiftly check its guests into their designated hotel could represent failure of a critical incident, which results in long-term harm for the relationship between the coach tour operator and its customers. However, the situation may be recovered by a tour leader who shows determination to sort things out to their best advantage. This could involve the tour leader demonstrating to his or her customers that they are determined to get their way with the hotel manager and to get their room allocation restored. They could also negotiate with the hotel management to secure alternative hotel accommodation of a higher standard at no additional charge, which customers would appreciate. If the process of rearranging accommodation looked like taking time, the tour leader could avoid the need for customers to be kept waiting in a coach by arranging an alternative enjoyable activity in the interim, such as a visit to a local tourist attraction.

The extent to which service recovery is possible depends upon two principal factors. First, front-line service personnel must have the ability to empathize with customers. Empathy can be demonstrated initially in the ability to spot service failure as it is perceived by customers, rather than some technical, production-orientated definition of failure. Empathy can also be shown in the manner of front-line staff's ability to take action that best meets the needs of customers. Second, services organizations should empower front-line staff to take remedial action at the time and place that is most critical. This may entail authorizing – and expecting – staff to deviate from the scheduled service process and, where necessary, empower staff to use resources at their discretion in order to achieve service recovery. In the case of the tour leader facing an overbooked hotel, taking customers away for a complimentary drink may make the difference between service failure and service recovery. If the tour leader is not authorized to spend money in this way, or approval is so difficult that it comes too late to be useful, the chance of service recovery may be lost for ever.

The role of blueprinting service processes can be emphasized again here. While it may not be possible to anticipate the precise nature of every service failure, a blueprint can indicate what to do in the event of certain general types of failure occurring.

Consider the case of the cancellation of an airline flight, which causes great inconvenience to passengers. A blueprint should be able to immediately show:

- who is responsible for informing intending passengers of the cancellation;
- which passengers will have priority in being rescheduled to alternative services;
- what compensation choices will be offered to passengers;
- who will handle unresolved claims for compensation.

In too many organizations, poor blueprinting of recovery processes merely compounds the problem of the original service failure, as customers gain further evidence that the company is not organized effectively and does not have their best interests at heart. However, although blueprinting may provide a basis for service recovery, it may not be sufficient to turn failed customers into advocates. Understanding the emotional state of the customer can be critical, requiring the service provider's response to be carefully tailored to individual customers' emotional states (see Smith and Bolton, 2002). In one study, it was noted that the warmth shown by employees, and their ability to deal with customers' emotions and to demonstrate empathic behaviours, had a significant effect on customer loyalty following a service failure (Lemmink and Mattsson, 2002). We will return to the experiential aspects of service recovery in the following chapter.

## In practice: Complaints welcome!

It has become conventional wisdom that firms should make it easy for customers to complain, on the basis that unresolved complaints may lead to significant negative word-of-mouth comments being made by aggrieved customers to their friends and colleagues. Also, if the organization does not actually receive a complaint, it may be unaware of the underlying cause of the problem, and therefore it can be difficult to avoid the problem occurring again in future. But can companies go too far in encouraging customers to complain? Does ready availability of channels for complaint result in some customers actually looking for reasons to complain? Does it even raise the idea among customers that service failure is routine, as evidenced by the readily available channels for complaints? In reality, customers are often just as likely to be delighted by exceptionally good service as they are to be disappointed by very bad service. Should a service operation not make similar efforts to understand what makes customers particularly happy? One company that takes a balanced approach is Timpsons, which operates a chain of shoe-repair and key-cutting outlets. The company goes one stage further than most companies, by inviting customers to send their comments not only when their expectations have not been met, but also when they have been exceeded. The inclusion of a positive feedback form (Figure 2.5) helps to create a more balanced set of expectations for customers, and can be valuable for motivating staff whose exceptional efforts are recognized.

Figure 2.5 Customer feedback forms. (Reproduced courtesy of Timpsons)

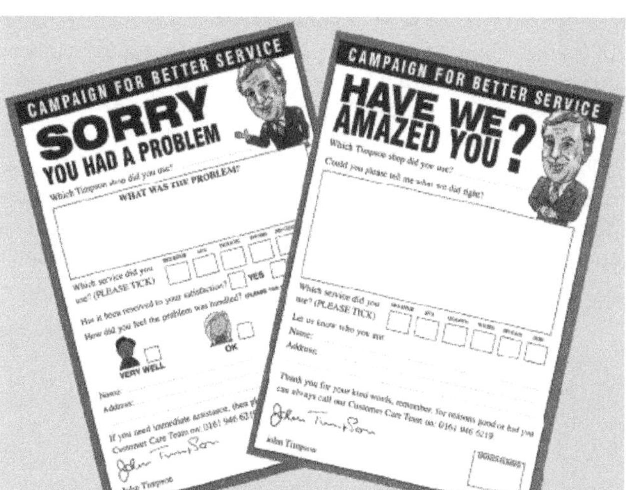


## In practice: Wrong kind of excuses?

Train operators in the UK have a long tradition of giving excuses for service failures that have become stock-in-trade for stand-up comedians. 'Leaves on the line' is a problem that perplexes commuters each autumn, amazed that a few small leaves can halt a 100-tonne train. The greatest ridicule was given to British Rail when 'the wrong kind of snow' grounded the latest Sprinter trains, which had supposedly been tested in the Arctic.

There are signs that the privatized train operating companies have improved their standards of communication with passengers. Many companies have instructed their train crews that blaming delays on 'operating problems' or 'technical difficulties' is just not good enough for intelligent customers who, with a bit of careful thought, could be brought to empathize with the train company and its problems. Crews have also made greater efforts to keep passengers updated on progress towards resolving a problem, helped by improved two-way communication between trains and central control rooms.

At first sight, the strategy might appear to be paying off, with passenger numbers rising sharply despite many rail operators achieving no significant improvement in reliability (although, of course, other factors, such as road traffic congestion, could have explained the increase in passenger numbers). However, the media still enjoys running horror stories about train delays, and went into overdrive in January 2009 when a Christmas and New Year shut-down of the West Coast Main Line at Rugby overran and caused chaos for commuters as they returned to work after the holiday break. Earlier, there had been great scepticism when one commuter train operator seemed to go back to insulting the intelligence of its customers with gobbledegook excuses when it blamed delays on 'atmospheric conditions affecting adhesion of rolling stock', and another where a train conductor apologized for overcrowding on a train, saying this was due to a 'lack of seats'.

Even the 'wrong kind of snow' excuse came back to haunt one rail operator – Eurostar – in December 2009 when thousands of passengers in France and Britain were left scrambling to get home in time for Christmas after six trains became stuck in the Channel Tunnel. Eurostar blamed the closure of their train service on the wrong type of snow, leading to melted snow shorting vital electrical circuits inside the 186 mph trains. The news media were full of scenes of abandoned passengers camping out at London's St Pancras and Paris's Gare du Nord stations, while Eurostar management appeared to give less than convincing reasons for the failure, and even less reassurance about when passengers would finally reach their destination. A leader in the *Independent* newspaper came back with a sharp retort – was this not so much a case of the 'wrong kind of snow' as the 'wrong kind of management'?

## 2.6 Industrializing the service encounter

**Industrialization** is at the heart of many service organizations' efforts to improve the consistency of their services while reducing their cost. A systems-based approach underlies much of what has been described as industrialization within the services sector. Ritzer (1996) used the term 'Macdonaldization' to extrapolate from the practices used by the restaurant chain of that name to services and society more generally.

Services organizations face a dilemma, for, while most seek to maximize the choice and flexibility of services available to customers, they also need to pursue methods for increasing productivity, and in particular for reducing the amount and cost of skilled labour involved in production processes. In addition, they need to reduce the variability of service outcomes in order that consistent brand values can be established.

Complex and diverse service systems can result in personnel being required to use their judgement and to be knowledgeable about a wide range of services. In many service sectors, giving too much judgement to staff results in a level of variability that is incompatible with consistent brand development. The existence of multiple choices in the service offer can make training staff to become familiar with all of the options very expensive, often matched by a minimal level of income that some services generate. For these reasons, services organizations often seek to simplify their service offerings and to 'deskill' many of the tasks performed by front-line service staff. By offering a limited range of services at a high standard of consistency, the process follows the pattern of the early development of factory production of goods.

The industrialization of service processes involves taking a systems approach to each part of a service process, and can manifest itself in a number of ways:

- *Simplifying the range of services available.* Organizations may find themselves offering services that are purchased by relatively few customers. The effort put into providing these services may not be justified by the financial return. Worse still, the lack of familiarity of many staff with little-used services could make them less than proficient at handling service requests, resulting in a poor service encounter, which reflects badly on the organization as a whole. Where peripheral services do not produce significant net revenue, but offer a lot of scope for the organization to make mistakes, a case can often be made for dropping them. As an example, some retailers have sometimes offered a delivery service at an additional charge, only to experience minimal demand from a small segment of customers. Moreover, the lack of training often given to sales staff (e.g. on details of delivery areas etc.) and the general complexity of delivery operations (such as ensuring that there is somebody at home to receive the goods) could justify a company in dropping the service. Simplification of the service range to offering only basic retail services allows a wide range of negative service encounters to be avoided, while possibly driving relatively few customers to competitors. It also allows service personnel to concentrate their activities on doing what they are best at – in this case, shop-floor encounters.

- *Providing 'scripts' for role performance.* It is noted in Chapter 3 that service personnel act out their role expectations in an informally scripted manner. More formal scripting allows service staff to follow the expectations of their role more precisely. Formal scripting can include a precise specification of the actions to be taken by service staff in particular situations, often with the help of machine-based systems. In this way, a telephone sales person can be prompted what to say next by messages on a computer screen. Insurance companies have long experience of simplifying the task of telephone sales personnel so that calculations of premiums are based entirely on data provided by customers, and the sales assistant does not need to use their own judgement. Scripting specifies welcoming and closing messages.
- *Tightly specifying operating procedures.* In some instances, it may be difficult to set out operating procedures that specify in detail how service personnel should handle each encounter. Personal services such as hairdressing rely heavily on the creativity of individual staff, and operating procedures can go no further than describing general conduct. However, many service operations can be specified with much greater detail. At a managerial level, many jobs have been deskilled by instituting formalized procedures, which replace much of the judgement previously made by managers. In this way, bank employees use much less judgement in deciding whether to advance credit to a client – the task is decided by a computer-based credit scoring system. Similarly, local managers in sectors such as retailing and hotels are often given little discretion over such matters as the appearance of their outlets and the type of facilities provided – these are specified in detail from head office and the branch manager is expected to follow closely. In this way, organizations can ensure that many aspects of the service encounter will be identical, regardless of the time or place.
- *Replacing human inputs with machine-based inputs.* Machines are generally more predictable in delivering services than humans. They also increasingly offer cost savings, which may give a company a competitive price advantage. Although machines may break down, when they are functioning they tend to be much less variable than humans, who may suffer from tiredness, momentary inattentiveness or periodic boredom. In addition to reducing the variability of service outcomes, machine-based encounters can offer a number of other advantages over human-based encounters. We turn to these later in this chapter.

## Thinking around the subject: Mayo may not be served this way

A student visited her local branch of McDonald's in Northern Ireland. After she had received her burger and fries she asked the serving assistant for some mayonnaise to accompany her food. No sachets of mayonnaise were available, so the assistant obliged, with typical Irish hospitality, by taking some mayonnaise from a bulk container and putting it on a coffee cup lid for the student. This seemed a pragmatic solution, which the customer was more than happy with. But for the serving assistant, it brought a sharp reprimand from her supervisor. This was evidently not allowed by the service blueprint. Perhaps handing over mayonnaise on a cup lid did not present an image of consistently high professional standards. There may even have been food safety issues involved. But on this occasion at least the customer had been pleased that the server had thought for herself and resolved the problem. How does a company such as McDonald's strike a balance between rigid industrialized procedures and the need for flexibility to meet individual customers' requirements?

## 2.7 Defining and measuring productivity of a service system

An important part of industrialization is the improvement of productivity, and many services organizations have regarded improvement of productivity as an operational priority. **Productivity** can be defined as the efficiency with which an organization's inputs are turned into outputs:

$$\text{Productivity} = \frac{\text{Outputs}}{\text{Inputs}}$$

The industrial revolution in England in the eighteenth century was characterized by dramatic improvements in the productivity of human, equipment and financial resources. Many have pointed to a 'service revolution' during the past couple of decades when productivity in many service sectors has shown a significant improvement. Processes of service industrialization have contributed to this improvement in productivity. However, services are still a relatively low-productivity sector of the economy. Using a measure of 'gross value added' (GVA), the UK Office for National Statistics has calculated that although the services sector provides around three times as many jobs as all other sectors combined, it manages to deliver less than twice as much approximate GVA. Consequently, service-sector labour productivity is about two-thirds that of the production sector. During the two decades 1981–2000, real productivity growth in services was lower than in the manufacturing sector, except for a brief period in 1995–98 (Lau, 2002). Across the EU, it is reported that labour productivity per employee, calculated as value added per person employed, was highest in the mining, quarrying, gas, electricity and water supply sectors, but was lowest in the distributive trades, hotels and restaurant sectors (Eurostat, 2012).

The whole concept of productivity is much more complex for services than for goods. For goods, production can generally be separated from consumption, and consumers are not usually affected by the way in which the item has been manufactured. Provided it performs to standard, a car buyer is not too concerned whether the car has been produced with automated or manual methods of production (although buyers may have concerns about the ethics of production, or may wish to know about the quality of production processes that cannot be immediately verified by inspecting the finished product). However, for the service consumer the nature of production methods can be crucial, because the inseparability of production and consumption means that the whole nature and benefit of the service can change when production methods change. A bank replacing its counter staff with ATMs and telephone banking may appear to have improved its productivity when assessed by such measures as customer transactions per employee or cost per transaction. However, the automated service may be perceived as something quite different from that which went before it. Because of the problem of inseparability, it can be difficult to gain a clear picture of what is happening to the true productivity of the services sector. More efficient does not necessarily mean more effective in meeting consumers' needs.

## In practice: Flying the no-frills skies

Figure 2.6 No-frills flying

No-frills airlines typically claim much higher levels of productivity than their full-service rivals, when measured using a variety of indicators, such as passengers carried per employee or utilization of aircraft. However, straightforward productivity comparisons between the two airline sectors can be misleading, because the service provided, and the value delivered to customers, can be quite different between the two sectors. The no-frills airlines may achieve much higher levels of aircraft utilization, for example by typically operating five return flights a day on short-haul European trips, compared with the four return flights which are more typical of full-service airlines. However, tight scheduling can have an effect on reliability, with fewer opportunities available to the no-frills airline to recover from bad weather or technical problems, resulting in delays or cancelled flights. Also, many would argue that the experience of using a full-service airline is quite different from that of a no-frills airline, evidenced by better in-flight services. Increased productivity by the no-frills airlines invariably results in the production of quite a different service, which many consumers would value less highly than the service provided by full-service airlines. But the no-frills sector has shown remarkable growth in recent years, indicating that large numbers of airline travellers are prepared to sacrifice some service benefits in return for the lower prices that are made possible by the ruthless pursuit of productivity improvements by no-frills airlines.

## 2.8 Managing the consumer–producer boundary

A common method used by services organizations to improve their productivity is to involve the consumer more fully in the production process through a process of co-creation. As real labour costs have increased and service markets become more competitive, many services organizations have sought to pass on a greater part of the production process to their customers in order to try to retain price competitiveness. At first, customers' expectations may hinder this process, but productivity savings often result from one segment taking on additional responsibilities in return for lower prices. This then becomes the norm for other follower segments. Examples where the boundary has been redefined to include greater production by the customer include:

- petrol stations that have replaced attendant service with self-service;
- mail delivery companies that give discounts to bulk mail users who do some pre-sorting of mail themselves;
- banks that encourage customers to enter personal data through a website, rather than being entered by the bank's employees in a branch or a call centre;
- television repair companies that require equipment for repair to be taken to them, rather than collecting it themselves;
- restaurants which replace waiter service with a self-service buffet.

While service production boundaries have generally been pushed out to involve consumers more fully in the production process, some services organizations have identified segments in which customers are prepared to pay higher prices in order to relieve themselves of parts of their co-production responsibilities. Examples include:

- car repairers who collect and deliver cars to the owner's home;
- fast-food firms that avoid the need for customers to come to their outlet by offering a delivery service;
- tour operators who arrange a taxi service from the customer's home, avoiding the need for customers to get themselves to the airport.

Is the service provider more productive as a result of passing on part of the service production process to customers, and less productive if its staff provide additional services? Is a self-service restaurant more productive than a full-service restaurant, or one offering home delivery? Based on productivity indicators of meals served per employee, the self-service restaurant would almost certainly be more productive. But the nature of the meals delivered may be substantially different, and what really matters is consumers' evaluation of the service that is delivered. The restaurant may be more efficient, but it may be less effective in meeting customers' needs. If consumers are prepared to pay the same price for a meal delivered to the table as for one that they have to collect from a serving counter, then there could be a case for stating that the restaurant's labour productivity has genuinely improved. But it is quite likely that customers may perceive a self-service restaurant as inferior, and only be prepared to pay, say, 30 per cent less than the price of a similar meal at a restaurant that offers table service. Their perceived value added is lower. For the restaurant operator, the key issue is whether their cost of production falls by more than consumers' valuation of the service. If consumers are only prepared to pay 30 per cent less than in a 'full-service' restaurant, yet operating costs have gone down by only 20 per cent, the restaurant has effectively destroyed value. However, if it managed to reduce its costs by 40 per cent, greater than consumers' fall in valuation of the service, then value in a wider economic sense has been created. Managing this balance between what consumers value and the costs to the supplier is a difficult aspect of services marketing management and may involve experimentation through trial and error. Successful companies have managed to lower their costs through greater productivity, while at the same time improving consumers' perception of value. An example is Internet banking, which many consumers find much more convenient than branch-based banking transactions, yet is also much more efficient for a bank to provide, compared with the cost of undertaking transactions in a bank branch.

## 2.9 Computer-mediated service systems

There is nothing new in the use of technology to intervene in a producer–consumer encounter. Banks, for example, have for some time reduced the amount of contact that their staff have with customers through the use of ATMs, so Internet banking could be seen as an extension of this technological development. The extent to which service companies are able to use the Internet to intervene in service encounters is influenced by the type of service in question (refer back to section 2.2). For high-contact services where the service process requires direct contact with the customer's body (as in the case of many medical services), the possibilities for computer-based intervention are likely to be small (although 'tele-medicine' may nevertheless be used to provide support services such as booking facilities for a doctor or a remote diagnostic facility). Where services involve processes being carried out on the customer's physical assets (e.g. car repairs), there is still a need for a point of contact where the assets are collected/delivered, although reservation and accounting facilities may be undertaken without direct human encounters. It is in the area of pure services with few tangible components that the development of the Internet has had greatest impact. Many 'pure' information services, such as gambling services and the provision of bank savings accounts and share price information, can be done with very little, if any, physical encounter between a customer and a company's employees.

Computer-mediated encounters can impact on traditional face-to-face encounters in a number of ways:

- Computer mediation can completely replace the need for a face-to-face encounter; for example, airlines use the Internet to reduce face-to-face contact at the point of purchase, and online check-in further reduces the need for face-to-face contact at the airport.
- Computer mediation may facilitate face-to-face encounters; for example, train companies sell tickets through their website for collection at a customer's local station, reducing pressure on the station ticket office.
- Sometimes, a website can be used to 'educate' a customer prior to a face-to-face encounter. For example, one study of medical practitioners showed how patients who engaged in virtual, parallel service encounters through the Internet changed the nature of their primary encounter with the doctor and presented challenges and opportunities to medical professionals both in terms of doctor–patient relationships and their professional judgement (Hogg et al., 2003).
- The service provider may be able to offer a much wider range of encounter possibilities. For example, Internet banking and ATMs allow many bank transactions to be undertaken at a time that is convenient to the customer, and at a place that is convenient.
- It is often possible to program machinery to provide a range of services reliably in a manner that would not have been possible if the encounter was based on a human service producer. Telephone companies now offer a wide range of automated telephone services (e.g. call interception services), which can be delivered at lower cost and with higher levels of reliability than if human operators had to be used.
- Automated encounters can give some customers a feeling of greater control over an encounter. Bank customers phoning their local branch to ask for the balance of their account may feel that they are having to work hard to get the information out of a bank employee and may feel intimidated by asking additional questions. By calling an automated banking information system or using an Internet banking service, some customers may feel they have greater 'locus of control' over their dealings with the bank (although, against this, many service users may feel uncomfortable with computer-mediated services and would feel much happier with face-to-face encounters).
- In some cases, the Internet has allowed completely new services to be developed. Downloadable music services, for example, had no direct service-based predecessor.
- The Internet has been used to gain access to customers who would previously have been considered inaccessible. Small independent hotels can now get much easier access to overseas customers, and universities can create awareness of their specific courses to clearly targeted overseas students.
- The information-gathering and analysis power of the Internet has allowed companies to build a much clearer picture of their markets in general, and individual customers in particular. This has resulted in improvements in efficiency (for example, fewer wasted mailshots that are sent to uninterested target buyers), as well as improvements in effectiveness (improving the content of the mailshot so that it addresses target buyers' principal concerns). More importantly, it has been suggested that measurability, which is an inherent aspect of the Internet, has led to a change in organizational culture, from one based on a lot of intuition and judgement to one where measurement of targets, processes and outcomes is key.

Computer-mediated service systems need to take account of all the stages involved in a service process. Building on the discussion of systems-based approaches earlier in this chapter, a number of stages in a typical online service process can be identified:

- *Access phase*. This may involve customers gaining access to an Internet-connected computer.
- *Check-in phase*. In this phase, consumers identify themselves to the service organization, for example by supplying a user name and PIN. How does a service provider balance the sometimes-conflicting requirements for ease of checking in with the need for security and privacy?
- *Diagnosis stage*. The consumer presents himself or herself and the system must identify his or her needs as quickly as possible. For example, a bank's website should quickly be able to establish whether a visitor to the site wants to make a transfer, view his or her account details or request information about other services.
- *Delivery stage*. The customer's needs are fulfilled (e.g. the statement of recent account transactions is printed).
- *Check-out stage*. During this stage, the consumer is securely disengaged from the service delivery system, for example by logging off the website.

Of course, service encounters which are computer mediated need to be designed with the same care and attention to detail as those that involve human encounters. It is not uncommon to find websites that are slow and confusing in their layout and operation or that fail to bring about the desired service. Just as in the failure of a human-based critical incident, failure during a web-based encounter may result in defection of the customer to a competitor. The study of human–computer interaction (HCI) has become an important area of study in its own right (see below).

Some segments of consumers may be slow to embrace computer-mediated exchanges, as we shall see below. However, it is not only service users who may be slow to adapt to new self-service technologies. Research has found that designing, updating and maintaining websites proves particularly difficult for small firms (Blackburn and Athayde, 2000).

The Internet is now so firmly embedded in most services organizations' marketing activities that it is referred to in most chapters of this book. Companies' strategies for making their services accessible to customers in a wider range of locations, and for extended time periods, have often focused on the Internet as a means of achieving better accessibility. We will return to this in Chapter 4. The Internet has had a profound effect on buyer behaviour, with potential buyers typically searching numerous companies' websites and referring to customer review sites. We will return to this topic in Chapter 5. Companies increasingly deal not with very broad segments of customers, but with specifically targeted individuals whose information can be retained and used to develop an ongoing relationship. We will see in Chapter 6 how the Internet has facilitated this. Such individualization is reflected in organizations' increasing use of the Internet not only as a distribution mechanism, but as a central part of their promotional strategy, and we will return to this in Chapter 13.

## Thinking around the subject: The Internet and the law of unintended consequences

'The world will never be the same again.' This was the bold message being proclaimed by many advocates at the dawn of the Internet age. In one sense, these people were quite right, because the Internet has had significant effects on how individuals have gone about their lives. Business processes have been transformed, often resulting in great cost savings and improvements in service to customers. But, in many respects, the nature of the change that has resulted from the development of the Internet has not quite been what was expected. The complex interaction between the technological, social and economic environments has produced some unexpected consequences of technological development.

Consider the following predictions, which were made in 2000 when 'dot.com' mania was at its height:

- Predictions were made that there would be less commuting as people work from home using the Internet to communicate with their work colleagues. Traffic congestion would reduce and commuter rail services would lose customers. In fact, technology has allowed many people to choose a pleasant residential environment and to live much further away from their work, because they now only have to travel to the office on a couple of days each week rather than every day. Overall, the travelling distances of many people in this situation have actually increased, resulting in more rather than less total commuting.
- Conferences were predicted to disappear in favour of video conferencing. Why bother travelling to a meeting or conference when you could meet 'virtually' from the comfort of your own desk or armchair, and at lower cost? However, face-to-face conferences have continued to prosper. The technology that causes many people to work in isolation may have indirectly contributed to a desire to counter this with more face-to-face meetings with a greater social content.
- 'High street' shops were being written off in 2000, when quite extraordinarily, the pure Internet company Lastminute.com had a market capitalization value far in excess of the Debenhams store chain with 110 outlets. The convenience and social benefits of shopping in the high street or at out-of-town shopping centres and the problems of arranging home delivery of Internet suppliers were underestimated by advocates of Internet-based shopping.
- Predating all of these predictions was the expectation that we would need to work fewer hours, as we live in a world of leisure where machines do the work, leaving consumers with more leisure time. In reality, average working hours have tended to increase, not fall.

We seem to have an inherent tendency to overstate the short-term effects of technological change, but to understate the long-term effects on our behaviour. With the development of new technologies enabling high-speed mobile Internet services, further predictions have been made. Will large numbers of people really want to download full-length feature films to watch on smartphones or tablets? Would there be unforeseen 'killer applications' such as SMS text messaging, which was almost left out of the specification of first-generation mobile phones, because no useful role for it was foreseen? Perhaps the long-term effects of the Internet may be more subtle by contributing to individuals' sense of connectedness with narrowly selected commercial and social groups, no matter where they may be located, while the sense of community with diverse groups of people forced to live together in close proximity may be reduced.

The unforeseen consequences of the Internet emphasize how difficult it can be for organizations to understand the consequences of new technologies. Understanding social attitudes has become a key to predicting the success of new technologies, and led in 2006 to one leading service provider, Yahoo!, appointing an anthropologist to give it a better understanding of how users interacted with its website.

### 2.9.1 Encouraging take-up of Internet-based services

Services companies' industrialization strategies often focus on methods to migrate their customers from face-to-face encounters to computer-mediated encounters. Financial incentives and additional benefits online have been used by banks, among others, to get more of their transactions undertaken online. However, while service providers may try to move customers to the new self-service technology, they often face resistance from some segments of consumers. Why do buyers of services differ in their readiness to use computer-mediated methods?

Several models of technology acceptance have emerged which seek to explain the processes by which consumers come to accept self-service technologies (e.g. Curran et al., 2003; Dabholkar and Bagozzi, 2002). Parasuraman (2000) developed a 'Technology Readiness Index' designed to assess consumers' likelihood of adopting new technologies on the basis of four dimensions (their optimism, innovativeness, discomfort and insecurity). It has been noted that consumers' adoption of self-service technologies is likely to be facilitated where the technology fits in with their existing lifestyle and they have a low perception of risk (Bobbitt and Dabholkar, 2001).

Models of technology adoption have their origins in the disciplines of psychology, information systems and sociology (Venkatesh et al., 2003). The Technology Acceptance Model (TAM) (Davis et al., 1989), based on the Theory of Reasoned Action (Ajzen and Fishbein, 1980; Fishbein and Ajzen, 1975) has become well established as a model for predicting acceptance of new information technology (IT)-based services (Venkatesh and Davis, 2000). The model shown in Figure 2.7 introduces two specific beliefs that are relevant for technology usage, namely perceived usefulness (U) and perceived ease of use (E). Actual behaviour is determined by behaviour intention (BI); however, behavioural intention is jointly determined by the individual's attitude towards a technology (A) and perceived usefulness (U). Finally, perceived ease of use (E) is a direct determinant of attitude (A) and perceived usefulness (U). In the case of older bank customers, where there are often no perceived benefits to be gained by switching to computer-mediated banking because other banking methods are available, it is likely that perceived ease of use would have a stronger influence on behavioural intentions than would perceived usefulness. However, in a business banking context, perceived usefulness is likely to be a stronger predictor of behavioural intention than attitude. Although the TAM model has been widely used, more recent advances have integrated performance expectancy, effort expectancy, social influence and facilitating conditions in a unified theory of acceptance and use of technology (UTAUT) (Venkatesh et al., 2003).

Services companies often promote the fact that service users can obtain additional benefits by using an automated form of service delivery. However, many service users may remain deeply sceptical, failing to see the benefits to themselves, and influenced by horror stories in the media of how

Figure 2.7 The influences of perceived usefulness and attitude on consumers' intention to use and actual use of new technology. (Based on Davis et al., 1989, p. 985)

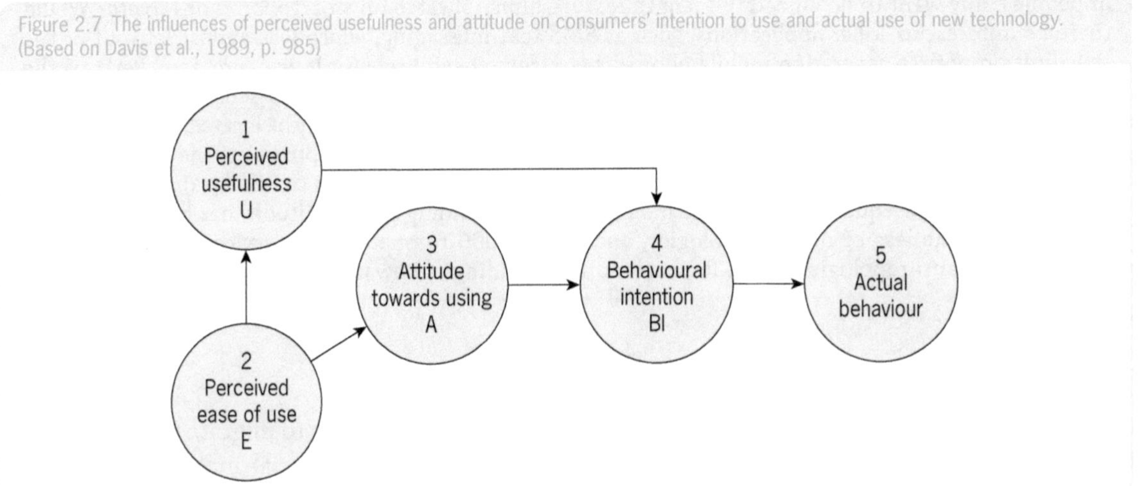

the new technology has previously let customers down (for example, many people remain cautious about giving their credit card details over the Internet, although, rationally, this is safer than giving details over the telephone). There is a danger that customers may perceive a loss of value when they are required to jointly co-create the service, effectively becoming partial unpaid employees (Hilton et al., 2013).

When planning the expansion of self-service facilities, companies need to be able to estimate the take-up rate, so that queues do not form or capacity remain unused. The model in Figure 2.7 has been developed to explain the influences of perceived usefulness and attitude on consumers' intention to use and actual use of new technology.

In one study of the use of the Internet and telephone for financial services, it was found that individuals' willingness to adopt was influenced by their sense of personal capacity or capability to engage with these service systems, the perceived risks and relative advantages associated with their use, and the extent to which contact with service personnel is preferred or deemed necessary (Walker and Johnson, 2006).

It has been noted that consumers who use computer-mediated service delivery may experience a number of post-purchase paradoxes, which a service provider should seek to address (Mick and Fournier, 1998):

- *Freedom/enslavement.* Consumers are likely to experience feelings of freedom when their use of new technology gives them new levels of independence, but on the other hand are likely to experience enslavement when they become dependent on the technology.
- *Control/chaos.* A feeling of control arises when consumers can use new technology and use it to direct their activities, but chaos results when the technology inhibits their activities and causes turmoil.
- *Engaging/disengaging.* Technology can be engaging when customers enjoy the facilities and activities it brings. But disengagement can occur where it results in distraction and it inhibits activities.
- *Fulfils/creates needs.* While technology may fulfil one set of needs, it may merely serve to emphasize other needs that are not fulfilled.
- *Competence/incompetence.* A feeling of competence may arise out of the successful use of new technology, but incompetence when the technology either fails or is not fully understood.

### 2.9.2 From e-services to m-services

Many organizations industrialized their service processes by moving face-to-face encounters to the Internet. There were big savings to the service provider and often benefits to customers too. But what about more recent developments of the mobile Internet? M-services, or 'location-based services', have the potential to improve efficiency and to make service delivery more effective by allowing customers to access a service wherever they are located. Banking was at the forefront of the service sectors that sought to migrate customers from face-to-face transactions to computer-mediated transactions. With the development of m-commerce, similar expectations have been held out that much banking activity that is currently carried out online through fixed-line Internet terminals will migrate to mobile devices. M-banking enables customers to access their bank accounts through mobile devices to check their balance or to conduct financial transactions. The range of services that can be undertaken while mobile has increased with the development of 'apps', and mobile phones are likely to evolve as ubiquitous payment devices (Wilcox, 2009). However, it has been claimed that m-banking does not provide significant cost-saving benefits for banks in comparison to those that can be achieved by migrating customers to online banking (Laukkanen et al., 2007). Therefore the development of m-banking is more likely to proceed only if customers see significant benefits in a bank which offers it, compared to those which do not (Mallat et al., 2004). If consumers do not see advantages in m-banking, it is unlikely that banks will significantly increase resources used to support it. We will return to the subject of m-services in Chapter 7.

## Case study

### Should MOOCs spook universities' traditional service delivery systems?

Universities have engaged in 'distance learning' for many years, but from around 2010 a potentially game-changing development appeared in universities' business environment – 'MOOCs', or 'Massive Open Online Courses'. Were they just another technological fad that appeared every now and again before disappearing, or could they be a disruptive technology that would change the face of universities and the way they deliver education for ever? For universities, should they join the 'MOOC' movement, or stand aside in the hope that the world would always prefer their more traditional approach to education?

In 2013, a report published by the Institute for Public Policy Research argued that the forces of technology and globalization that had transformed service delivery systems in the banking and finance sectors were now ready to challenge higher education (IPPR, 2013). The case was made that information-based services could easily dispense with the need for premises from which the service was provided, with plenty of evidence of information-based services which had rapidly gone online, often making technological innovators the market leaders in their sector. Travel-related services typically don't need any physical presence, which allowed new technology-based entrants such as Expedia and Travelocity to steal a march on their traditional shop-based rivals, many of whom went out of business or drastically scaled back their physical branches. Financial services, book retailing and gambling had all experienced a similar phenomenon – new technology brought low costs and high convenience to a mass market, leading physical outlets to reduce in number and to cater for smaller niches. One observer noted, 'recent history shows us that the internet is a great destroyer of any traditional business that relies on the sale of information' (Harden, 2013).

Would universities go the way of the book shop and travel agent? Pedagogically, numerous studies had suggested that classroom-based learning is not particularly effective for imparting knowledge and skills. Sitting in a class, taking notes in a room full of maybe over 100 other people, with little opportunity for interaction may not correspond to many people's idea of effective 'student-centred learning'. Having to be at a class at a specified time each week may not meet the busy lifestyles of students who juggle part-time jobs or family responsibilities between classes.

MOOCs would appear to offer many advantages to educational service providers and students alike, and follow a fairly familiar pattern of service industrialization. Typically, students enrolled in a MOOC watch video lectures, often streamed in digestible segments of 10 or 15 minutes. Instead of listening to a well-qualified lecturer live in their classroom, they can tune into a 'celebrity' lecturer beamed in from the other side of the world. Some academics have become celebrity big hits with MOOCs, including the historian Simon Scharma and Harvard's Michael Sandel who has been described as the 'rock star' of moral philosophy. Now their audiences are not limited to a few hundred who can get into their lecture theatre at a given time and place, but typically tens of thousands who can watch by video at any time and in any place. A key claimed advantage of MOOCs over traditional classroom-based classes is their convenience. They allow students to learn at a pace which they can determine themselves. MOOCs give students the opportunity to watch again parts of a lecture that they did not understand first time round. Some MOOCs invite, or require, students to take online tests or quizzes with multiple choice answers that can be graded automatically. Many MOOCs incorporate some form of peer-to-peer learning and review of assessments.

So far, MOOCS would seem to meet the criteria which define the service industrialization process: they have transformed learning from a small-scale classroom-based craft activity to one which is produced centrally and distributed widely; in doing so, costs per student have been drastically cut; variability of output has been reduced due to the possibility of editing videos before they are put online; as a consequence, some would argue that adaptability to individual students' needs has been reduced (e.g. interaction by the student with the lecturer is generally not possible in an online class seen by many thousands of students, but probably would be face-to-face in class); finally, MOOCs industrialize by passing much more of the co-creation of value to students themselves (e.g. peer review of students' assignments).

Given this apparently overwhelming logic, should we expect the traditional university to disappear soon? Perhaps not. In service sectors where industrialization has played a big role, small-scale providers often coexist alongside their larger industrialized competitors. Many small restaurants and cafés continue to prosper without using the industrialized processes of McDonald's, and small niche retailers coexist with larger industrialized chains.

Many critics of MOOCs have been quick to come to the defence of the traditional university. Attendance at class can have a distinctive atmosphere, as students laugh together and share surprises together – can this atmosphere be re-created when students are studying by themselves online? It has also been argued that it is not just the nature of the knowledge that students learn that is important, but *how* they learn it. Learning in a university environment with fellow students, and learning the value of co-operation, can help develop problem-solving abilities in a way that is not possible online. Simply attending a university with a known set of values and ethos makes a statement about a student which cannot easily be provided by enrolment in a MOOC. Some universities provide students with employability skills, for example through internship programmes and real-life company case-study presentations. How could this be industrialized online?

Efficiency of MOOCs may be one thing, but their effectiveness can be another. Some educationalists have argued that MOOCs would create a generation of celebrity lecturers who were judged like 'X-Factor' contestants not so much for their knowledge but for their screen appeal. And how would you keep the attention of young online students, accustomed to switching between applications every few minutes?

When industrialized services go online, security issues are likely to be not far away, and this can be true of MOOCs. If students are to be assessed as a basis for an award, how confident can we be that the work submitted reflects the students' own efforts? How can we be sure that a multiple choice test being taken by a student is not actually being done by a hired expert several hundred miles away? Furthermore, can industrialized online testing ever match the abilities of traditional coursework for developing students' analytic and reasoning abilities?

There is an apparent paradox that while people are undoubtedly doing more things online, this has often been balanced by an increase in shared activities offline. Although the business of selling (and reading) books is now done increasingly online, attendance in person at book festivals such as the Hay Festival has increased, with the latter achieving over a quarter of a million ticket sales in 2012, and it has spawned sister festivals around the world, for example in Mexico and Bangladesh. Similarly, the rise in online music consumption has been matched by a rise in attendance at live music festivals. Maybe there is an experiential benefit of 'being there' with your friends – is education any different? Commentators even noted the ultimate paradox in March 2013 when many leaders from universities and private educational providers met in person in Boston to attend a conference hosted by MIT and Harvard University to debate the future of MOOCs. If they had to travel from around the world to attend this 'class', should we consider the traditional student class to be safe?

Another issue facing MOOCs is the development of a sustainable business model. Many online social media, such as Facebook and Twitter, have found popularity with users, but difficulty in making profit for their owners. Among MOOCs, some have been created as not-for-profit ventures, but many profit-seeking companies entered the market. How could they make money from MOOCs?

Among the for-profit operators, Coursera had signed up 62 universities by March 2013 and based its business model on earning fees as an employment agency. The argument was proposed that a MOOC should give it a good overview of students' interaction and performance, from which it can earn fees by brokering people looking for work and employers with positions to fill. Other business models are based on providing individual charged-for one-to-one tuition, and awarding qualifications. Some online organizations associated with MOOCs, such as DeVry University in Illinois, have the power to award degrees. However, going down this route raises issues about quality control.

MOOCs could be the next big idea which industrializes a huge sector of the service economy. Or, like many big new ideas on the Internet, the hype could be ahead of the substance. In practice, the reality will probably be somewhere between these two extremes. Should universities be worried? Should they sit back on the assumption that the experiential bases of going to university will never be replaced by MOOCs? Or should they start following those universities who have begun engaging with MOOCs to try to find a way that they can coexist in the emerging ecosystem of higher education delivery?

### Questions

1 Discuss the concepts of efficiency and effectiveness in the context of MOOCs.

2 Identify ways in which the principles of industrialization can be applied to higher education and summarize the strengths and weaknesses of this approach to higher education delivery.

3 Discuss the role and limitations of 'co-creation of value' in a MOOC.

## Summary and links to other chapters

This chapter has introduced the principles of service systems, and later chapters will build on these principles. The next chapter will be something of an antidote to the 'hard' systems described in this chapter, by exploring 'softer' experiential aspects of services. Providing high levels of accessibility to the service system will be the focus of Chapter 4. The concept of the service ecosystem will be returned to in Chapter 5 with a closer look at relationships between service suppliers and their network of suppliers. Systems are continually developing and innovation in system design will be explored in Chapter 7. We will return to issues of productivity measurement in Chapter 10 when we look at the marketing impacts of service-sector employees.

### Chapter review questions

1 In the context of industrialization, critically discuss the concept of service productivity and methods used to measure it.

2 To what extent do you think that models of the service encounter developed for face-to-face encounters, e.g. blueprinting, are applicable in an online service context? Illustrate your answer with examples of points of similarity and difference.

3 What is meant by service failure? Critically evaluate strategies that a fast-food restaurant can employ to recover from service failure.

## Activities

1 Reflect on medium/large-size mid-market restaurants that you may have visited recently. What evidence of industrialization of service processes was apparent? Critically assess the advantages and disadvantages for consumers and the service provider of the industrialization processes that you noted. What do you understand by the concept of 'productivity' in the context of the restaurant? Would you consider the restaurant to be highly productive? Why? Could it be improved further?

2 Choose one of the following service processes: taking a car into a garage to have an exhaust system renewed; minor building repairs to a house; hair styling and colouring. Draw a service blueprint that describes the service processes involved. Your blueprint should identify the different stages involved in the service production process, target times for each stage to be undertaken, the participants involved in each stage, visible evidence of the service process and the invisible processes involved.

3 Consider a visit to a dentist or a doctor's surgery. Identify possible critical incidents during the service process. Suggest how the service provider could identify critical incidents and diagnose whether it has failed or succeeded in respect of these. Use frameworks such as blueprinting to suggest methods by which recovery from service failure could be facilitated. What do you think is the effect on the service failure/recovery process of the professional status of the doctor/dentist?

## Key terms

**Apps** Programs that run on a mobile phone or tablet computer.

**Co-creation** The consumer is a contributor to the service production process.

**Ecosystem** The broader environment in which a service system operates.

**Hard system** Elements of a system which can be easily defined and measured.

**Human–computer interaction** The study of how humans interact with computers, physically, psychologically and socially.

**Industrialization of services** The process of deskilling and simplifying service production processes with the aim of improving efficiency and reducing variability in outcomes and processes.

**Open system** A system with no clearly defined boundaries.

**Peer-to-peer sites** Websites on which content is ostensibly defined by users, rather than being centrally determined by a commercial sponsor.

**Productivity** The ratio of inputs to outputs in a production process.

**Service system** A set of connected processes, actors and phenomena forming a complex whole, and existing within a shared environment.

**Soft system** Elements of a system which are difficult to define and measure.

**Technology Acceptance Model (TAM)** A theory that models how users come to accept and use new technology. The model suggests that acceptance is influenced by perceived usefulness and perceived ease of use.

**Theory of Reasoned Action** A theory that suggests that a person's behavioural intention is dependent on their attitude to behaviour and to subjective norms.

## Selected further reading

*Efficiency and effectiveness, and the general processes for industrializing service encounters, are discussed in the following:*

**Frei, F.X.** (2006) 'Breaking the trade off between efficiency and service', *Harvard Business Review*, November, 1–10.

**Grönroos, C. and Ojasalo, K.** (2004) 'Service productivity: towards a conceptualization of the transformation of inputs into economic results in services', *Journal of Business Research*, 57 (4), 414–23.

**Gummesson, E.** (1998) 'Productivity, quality and relationship marketing in service operations', *International Journal of Contemporary Hospitality Management*, 10 (1), 4–15.

*Issues involved in encouraging greater take-up of online services are discussed in the following:*

**Matthing, J., Kristensson, P., Gustafsson, A. and Parasuraman, A.** (2006) 'Developing successful technology-based services: the issue of identifying and involving innovative users', *Journal of Services Marketing*, 20 (5), 288–97.

**Prins, R.O. and Verhoef, P.C.** (2007) 'Marketing communication drivers of adoption timing of a new e-service among existing customers', *Journal of Marketing*, 71 (2), 169–83.

*Conceptual issues relating to the consumer–producer boundary are explored in the following articles:*

**Grönroos, C.** (2012) 'Conceptualising value co-creation: a journey to the 1970s and back to the future', *Journal of Marketing Management*, 28 (13–14), 1520–34.

**Lambert, D.M. and Enz, M.G.** (2012) 'Managing and measuring value co-creation in business-to-business relationships', *Journal of Marketing Management*, 28 (13–14), 1588–1625.

*Issues of the consumer–producer boundary in online contexts are explored in the following articles:*

**Johnson, D.S., Bardhi, F. and Dunn, D.T.** (2008) 'Understanding how technology paradoxes affect customer satisfaction with self-service technology: the role of performance ambiguity and trust in technology', *Psychology & Marketing*, 25 (5), 416–43.

**Makarem, S.C., Mudambi, S.M. and Podoshen, J.S.** (2009) 'Satisfaction in technology-enabled service encounters', *Journal of Services Marketing*, 23 (3), 134–44.

**Nilsson, D.** (2007) 'A cross-cultural comparison of self-service technology use', *European Journal of Marketing*, 41 (3/4), 367–81.

*The literature on failed service encounters and the ways in which companies recover from service failure has been growing in recent times. The following articles are relevant:*

**Hocutt, M.A., Bowers, M.R. and Donavan, D.T.** (2006) 'The art of service recovery: fact or fiction?', *Journal of Services Marketing*, 20 (3), 199–207.

**Michel, S., Bowen, D. and Johnston, R.** (2009) 'Why service recovery fails: tensions among customer, employee, and process perspectives', *Journal of Service Management*, 20 (3), 253–73.

**Noone, B.M.** (2012) 'Overcompensating for severe service failure: perceived fairness and effect on negative word-of-mouth intent', *Journal of Services Marketing*, 26 (5), 342–51.

## References

**Adams, J.S.** (1965) 'Inequality in social exchange', in L. Berkowitz (ed.), *Advances in Experimental Social Psychology*, vol. 2, Academic Press, New York.

**Ajzen, I. and Fishbein, M.** (1980) *Understanding Attitudes and Predicting Social Behavior*, Prentice Hall, Englewood Cliffs, NJ.

**Berry, L.L., Seiders, K. and Grewal, D.** (2002) 'Understanding service convenience', *Journal of Marketing*, 66 (3), 1–17.

**Bies, R.** (1987) 'The predicament of injustice: the management of moral outrage', *Research in Organizational Behavior*, 9, 289–319.

**Bitner, M.J., Booms, B.H. and Tetreault, M.S.** (1990) 'The service encounter: diagnosing favourable and unfavourable incidents', *Journal of Marketing*, 54 (1), 71–84.

**Blackburn, R. and Athayde, R.** (2000) 'Making the connection: the effectiveness of Internet training in small businesses', *Education + Training*, 42 (4/5), 289–99.

**Bobbitt, L.M. and Dabholkar, P.A.** (2001) 'Integrating attitudinal theories to understand and predict use of technology-based self-service: the internet as an illustration', *International Journal of Service Industry Management*, 12 (5), 423–50.

**Churchill, G.A. and Surprenant, C.** (1982) 'An investigation into the determinants of customer satisfaction', *Journal of Marketing Research*, 19 (4), 491–504.

**Curran, J.M., Meuter, M.L. and Surprenant, C.F.** (2003) 'Intentions to use self-service technologies: a confluence of multiple attitudes', *Journal of Service Research*, 5 (3), 209–24.

**Dabholkar, P.A. and Bagozzi, R.P.** (2002) 'An attitudinal model of technology-based self-service: moderating effects of consumer traits and situational factors', *Journal of the Academy of Marketing Science*, 30 (3), 184–201.

**Davis, F.D., Bagozzi, R.P. and Warshaw, P.R.** (1989) 'User acceptance of computer technology: a comparison of two theoretical models', *Management Science*, 35 (8), 982–1003.

**Edvardsson, B. and Strandvik, T.** (2000) 'Is a critical incident critical for a customer relationship?', *Managing Service Quality*, 10 (2), 82–91.

**Edvardsson, B., Tronvoll, B. and Gruber, T.** (2011) 'Expanding understanding of service exchange and value co creation', *Journal of the Academy of Marketing Science*, 39 (2), 327–39.

**Elliott, D., Harris, K. and Baron, S.** (2005) 'Crisis management and services marketing', *Journal of Services Marketing*, 19 (5), 336–45.

**Eurostat** (2012) *Key Figures on Europe – Statistical Pocketbook 2012*, Eurostat, Luxembourg.

**Fishbein, M. and Ajzen, I.** (1975) *Belief, Attitude, Intention, and Behavior: An Introduction to Theory and Research*, Addison-Wesley, Reading, MA.

**Folger, R. and Cropanzano, R.** (1998) *Organizational Justice and Human Resource Management*, Sage, Thousand Oaks, CA.

**Gummesson, E.** (2008) *Total Relationship Marketing*, 3rd edn, Oxford, Butterworth-Heinneman.

**Gundlach, G.T. and Murphy, P.E.** (1993) 'Ethical and legal foundations of relational marketing exchanges', *Journal of Marketing*, 57, 35–46.

**Halstead, D., Drogue, C. and Cooper, M.B.** (1993) 'Product warranties and post purchase service: a model of consumer satisfaction without complaint resolution', *Journal of Services Marketing*, 7 (1), 33–40.

**Harden, N.** (2013) 'The end of the university as we know it', *The American Interest*, January/February.

**Hart, C.W.L., Sasser, W.E. Jr and Heskett, J.L.** (1990) 'The profitable art of service recovery', *Harvard Business Review*, 68 (4),148–56.

**Heider, F.** (1958) *The Psychology of Interpersonal Relations*, John Wiley and Sons, New York.

**Heung, V.C. and Lam, T.** (2003) 'Customer complaint behaviour towards hotel restaurant services', *International Journal of Contemporary Hospitality Management*, 15 (5), 283–9.

**Hilton, T., Hughes, T., Little, E. and Marandi, E.** (2013) 'Adopting self-service technology to do more with less', *Journal of Services Marketing*, 27 (1), 3–12.

**Hoffman, K.D. and Kelley, S.W.** (2000) 'Perceived justice needs and recovery evaluation: a contingency approach', *European Journal of Marketing*, 34 (3/4), 418–33.

**Hoffman, K.D., Kelley, S.W. and Rotalsky, H.M.** (1995) 'Tracking service failures and employee recovery efforts', *Journal of Services Marketing*, 9 (2), 49–61.

**Hogg, G., Laing, A. and Winkelman, D.** (2003) 'The professional service encounter in the age of the Internet: an exploratory study', *Journal of Services Marketing*, 17 (5), 476–94.

**Homans, G.C.** (1961) *Social Behavior*, Harcourt Brace and World, New York.

**IPPR** (2013) *An Avalanche is Coming*, Institute for Public Policy Research London.

**Kau, A.K. and Loh, E.W.Y.** (2006) 'The effects of service recovery on consumer satisfaction: a comparison between complainants and non-complainants', *Journal of Services Marketing*, 20 (2), 101–11.

**Kelley, H.H. and Thibaut, J.** (1978) *Interpersonal Relations: A Theory of Interdependence*, John Wiley and Sons, New York.

**Kelley, S.W. and Davis, M.A.** (1994) 'Antecedents to customer expectations for service recovery', *Journal of the Academy of Marketing Science*, 22 (1), 52–61.

**Kingman-Brundage, J.** (1989) 'The ABCs of service system blueprinting', in M.J. Bitner and L.A. Crosby (eds), *Designing a Winning Service Strategy*, American Marketing Association, Chicago, IL.

**Lau, E.** (2002) 'Productivity measures – ONS strategy', *Economic Trends*, (581), 1–20.

**Laukkanen, P., Sinkkonen, S., Kivijarvi, M. and Laukkanen, P.** (2007) 'Segmenting bank customers by resistance to mobile banking', *Proceedings of the 6th International Conference on the Management of Mobile Business (ICMB 2007)*, IEEE.

**Lemmink, J. and Mattsson, J.** (2002) 'Employee behavior, feelings of warmth and customer perception in service encounters', *International Journal of Retail & Distribution Management*, 30 (1), 18–33.

**Lusch, R.F. and Vargo, S.L.** (2006) 'Service-dominant logic: reactions, reflections and refinements', *Marketing Theory*, 6 (3), 281–88.

**Mallat, N., Rossi, M. and Tuunainen, V.K.** (2004) 'Mobile banking services', *Communications of the ACM*, 47 (5), 42–6.

**Mattila, A.S.** (2001) 'The effectiveness of service recovery in a multi-industry setting', *Journal of Services Marketing*, 15 (7), 583–96.

**Maxham, J.G. and Netemeyer, R.G.** (2002) 'A longitudinal study of complaining customers' evaluations of multiple service failures and recovery efforts', *Journal of Marketing*, 66 (4), 57–71.

**Mccole, P. and Herwadkar, A.** (2003) 'Towards a more inclusive model for understanding service failure and service recovery', in *ANZMAC Annual Proceedings 2003*, University of Adelaide.

**McColl-Kennedy, J.R. and Sparks, B.** (2003) 'Application of fairness theory to service failures and service recovery', *Journal of Service Research*, 5 (3), 251–66.

**Mick, D.G. and Fournier, S.** (1998) 'Paradoxes of technology: consumer cognizance, emotions, and coping strategies', *Journal of Consumer Research*, 25 (2), 123–43.

**Noone, B.M.** (2012) 'Overcompensating for severe service failure: perceived fairness and effect on negative word-of-mouth intent', *Journal of Services Marketing*, 26 (5), 342–51.

**Nyer, P.U.** (2000) 'An investigation into whether complaining can cause increased consumer satisfaction', *Journal of Consumer Marketing*, 17 (1), 9–19.

**Oliver, R.** (1980) 'A cognitive model of the antecedents and consequences of satisfaction decisions', *Journal of Market Research*, 17 (4), 460–9.

**Palmer, A., Beggs, R. and Keown-Mcmullan, C.** (2000) 'Equity and repurchase intention following service failure', *Journal of Services Marketing*, 14 (6), 513–28.

**Parasuraman, A.** (2000) 'Technology Readiness Index (TRI): a multiple-item scale to measure readiness to embrace new technologies', *Journal of Service Research*, 2 (4), 307–20.

**Parasuraman, A., Zeithaml, V. and Berry, L.L.** (1985) 'A conceptual model of service quality and its implications for future research', *Journal of Marketing*, 49 (4), 41–50.

**Reichheld, F.E. and Sasser, W.** (1990) 'Zero defections: quality comes to services', *Harvard Business Review*, 68 (5), 105–11.

**Ritzer, G.** (1996) *The McDonaldization of Society*, Sage, Thousand Oaks, CA.

**Schoefer, K. and Ennew, C.** (2005) 'The impact of perceived justice on consumers' emotional responses to service complaint experiences', *Journal of Services Marketing*, 19 (5), 261–70.

**Shostack, G.L.** (1985) 'Planning the service encounter', in J.A. Czepiel, M.R. Solomon and C.F. Suprenant (eds), *The Service Encounter*, Lexington Books, Lexington, MA.

**Smith, A. and Bolton, R.** (2002) 'The effect of customers' emotional response to service failures on their recovery effort valuations and satisfaction judgements', *Journal of the Academy of Marketing Science*, 30 (1), 5–23.

**Spohrer, J., Maglio, J. and Gruhl, D.** (2007) 'Steps toward a science of service systems', *Computer*, 40 (1), 71–7.

**Spreng, R.A., Harrell, G.D. and Mackoy, R.D.** (1995) 'Service recovery: impact on satisfaction and intentions', *Journal of Services Marketing*, 9 (1), 15–23.

**Stauss, B. and Weinlich, B.** (1995) 'Process oriented measurement of service quality by applying the Sequential Incident Method', in *Workshop on Quality Management Proceedings*, University of Tilburg.

**Tax, S.S., Brown, S. and Chandrashekaran, M.** (1998) 'Customer evaluation of service complaint experiences: implication for relationship marketing', *Journal of Marketing*, 62 (2), 60–76.

**Tronvoll, B., Edvardsson, B. and Vargo, S.L.** (2011) 'What we see depends on how we look at it; using an ontological framework to describe service systems', Forum on Service, Capri, June.

**Troye, S.V. and Supphellen, M.** (2012) 'Consumer participation in coproduction: "I made it myself" effects on consumers' sensory perceptions and evaluations of outcome and input product', *Journal of Marketing*, 76 (2), 33–46.

**Vargo, S.L.** (2008) 'Customer integration and value creation: paradigmatic traps and perspectives', *Journal of Service Research*, 11 (2), 211–15.

**Vargo, S.L. and Lusch, R.F.** (2004) 'Evolving to a new dominant logic for marketing', *Journal of Marketing*, 68 (1), 1–17.

**Vargo, S.L. and Lusch, R.F.** (2008) 'Why "service"?', *Journal of the Academy of Marketing Science*, 36 (1), 25–38.

**Vargo, S.L., Maglio, P.P. and Akaka, M.A.** (2008) 'On value and value co-creation: a service systems and service logic perspective', *European Management Journal*, 26 (3), 145–52.

**Venkatesh, V. and Davis, F.D.** (2000) 'A theoretical extension of the technology acceptance model: four longitudinal field studies', *Management Science*, 46 (2), 186–204.

**Venkatesh, V., Morris, M.G., Davis, G.B. and Davis, F.D.** (2003) 'User acceptance of information technology: toward a unified view', *MIS Quarterly*, 27 (3), 425–78.

**Walker, R.H. and Johnson, L.** (2006) 'Why consumers use and do not use technology-enabled services', *Journal of Services Marketing*, 20 (2), 125–35.

**Wilcox, H.** (2009) Press release: 'Mobile banking users to exceed 150m globally by 2011 according to Juniper Research', Juniper Research, available at http://juniperresearch.com/shop/viewpressrelease.php?pr=120 (accessed 8 July 2013).

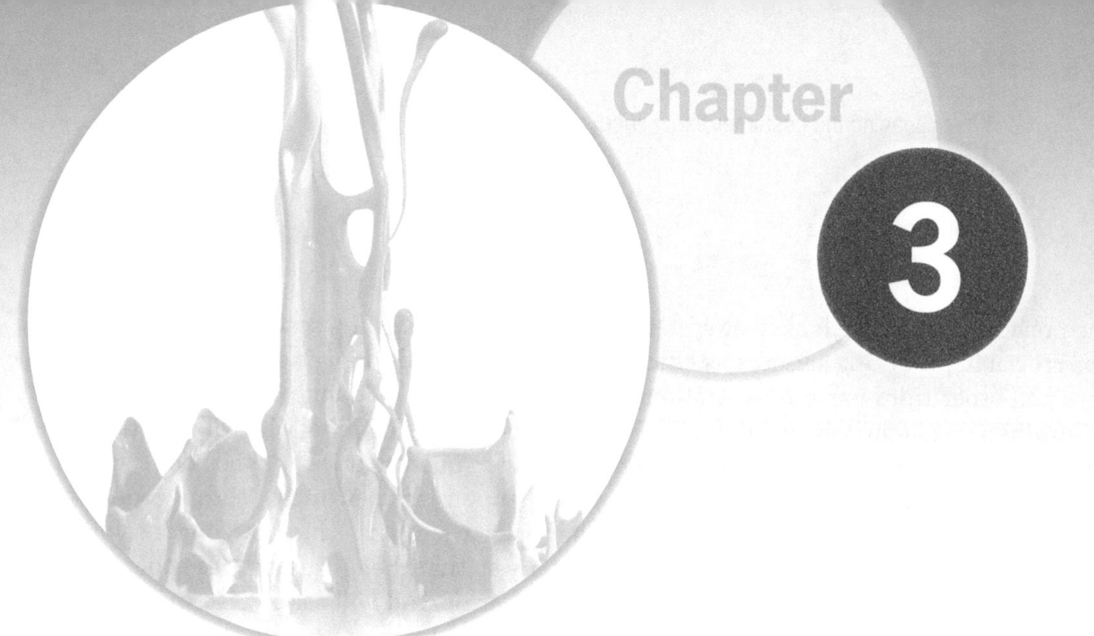

Chapter 3

# Managing the customer experience

*Joey was visiting the capital of an Asian country where he had read in his guidebook about a new themed restaurant which incorporated an imitation volcano. Every hour, spectacular lighting effects, rumbling sounds and a feeling of movement in the tables and chairs simulated the eruption of a volcano, which were a great tourist attraction in the region. For Joey, this was a 'must see' to be experienced, but his friend entered the restaurant tired and hungry. He just wanted to eat and he got no enjoyment from sitting through the light and sound display. Worse still, some American visitors from California were traumatized by the experience, bringing back memories of the fact that they were living in an active earthquake zone. Joey might have enjoyed the experience of the volcano first time round, but even he had to admit that after the third or fourth time, it became repetitive and boring – now he just wanted to use the restaurant for eating. When services companies move from providing purely utilitarian benefits to more* **hedonistic benefits**, *the nature of the value that they deliver to customers becomes much more complex to understand. In the case of a restaurant with an imitation volcano, the 'experience' might have been exciting to some, neutral to others, and bad for yet others. Even those who found the experience good one day might find that another day their needs are different and that what once generated positive emotions is now dominated by negative feelings. In this chapter, we will explore some of the complexities of designing services which provide a high level of 'customer experience', beginning with the conceptual issues about defining the term, and working through to practical issues of delivery.*

## Learning objectives

After reading this chapter, you should understand:

- Theoretical underpinnings of the concept of 'customer experience'
- Frameworks for understanding and managing customer experience
- The effects of other customers on individuals' experience of a service
- Issues and problems for the services marketer that arise from having to produce a service 'live' in front of customers in a safe and secure environment

## 3.1 Introduction

In the previous chapter we looked at systems approaches to designing services. Systems thinking can be crucial in producing services as efficiently as possible and for giving guidance to staff, customers and other third-party organizations about who should be doing what, where and when. Just imagine a restaurant which did not have systems in place for defining who will take customers' orders, who will order supplies for the kitchen, and how frequently this should be done; what processes will be used for checking that customers are happy with their meal. With a good system, waiting staff will clearly know which customers they will have to serve and how long it should take them to be served; supplies of food will arrive regularly so that the restaurant has enough food to satisfy all customers' requests; and a designated member of staff will ask if customers are happy with their meal at a predetermined time and will have a blueprint for action to take if the customers are not satisfied.

But having good systems is a necessary, but not a sufficient basis for customer satisfaction. The actual length of waiting time in a restaurant may not be as important as how the waiting is subjectively perceived; waiters in the restaurant may follow their service blueprint and ask customers if they are satisfied, but the way in which they ask can be just as important as the timing of their intervention. Systems approaches may maximize efficiency, but often it is customers' subjective experiences of service effectiveness which may create value in their eyes.

The systems approaches described in Chapter 2 may be described as 'hard' approaches to designing services, where service design can be reduced to phenomena which can be relatively easily measured and managed. In this chapter, we will turn to relatively 'soft' approaches to designing the service by focusing on more qualitative and subjective aspects of service design. So instead of focusing on the utilitarian benefits that consumers receive from a service, we will instead focus more on hedonic benefits and customers' subjective experience of the service.

## 3.2 Customer experience

Companies are increasingly using the framework of 'customer experience' to define what they offer to their customers. Although the term has become widely used, there are many definitions of just what constitutes customer experience. An all-embracing definition is provided by Gupta and Vajic (2000), who stated that an experience occurs when a customer 'has any sensation or knowledge acquisition resulting from some level of interaction with different elements of a context created by the service provider'. Some authors have broadened the concept of customer experience, with sometimes seemingly circular definitions, for example 'total customer experience emphasizes the importance of all contacts that a consumer has with an organization and the consumer's holistic experience' (Harris et al., 2003). Such broad definitions take us back to an early definition of Abbott who noted that:

> *"What people really desire are not products, but satisfying experiences. Experiences are attained through activities. In order that activities may be carried out, physical objects for the services of human beings are usually needed . . . People want products because they want the experience which they hope the products will render."*
>
> (Abbott, 1955, cited in Holbrook, 2006, p. 717)

Unfortunately, use of the term 'experience' has been confused by its frequent association with the hedonistic values of a product rather than the more basic utilitarian value defined by Abbott. As a result of such confusion, its use runs counter to a lot of consumer behaviour literature, which emphasizes how consumers' repeated experience of a phenomenon leads to a learned response. While repeated exposure may lead to a learned response, hedonistic definitions of customer experience imply that the value of an experience may lie in the lack of a learned response. The true benefit may lie in attitudinal outcomes of 'surprise', 'delight' and 'excitement'. The first encounter with a stimulus may be highly valued because of its novelty, but the stimulus is less likely to be subsequently sought because of its lack of novelty value.

If 'customer experience' is regarded as comprising essentially non-utilitarian benefits that a consumer seeks from a purchase, it could be expected that interest in customer experience advances during periods of prolonged economic prosperity. In the field of leisure and tourism, it has been suggested that the most rapid developments analogous to 'customer experience' occurred in the UK during periods of prosperity, notably the 1890s, 1930s, 1950s and, more recently, the late 1990s (Urry, 2002). As well as growth in overall GDP per head, these periods have also been associated with increasing disparity in income distribution, with an affluent group able to afford high-experience services, while poorer groups can afford only basic utilitarian services. More recently, there has been evidence of growing inequalities within some societies, and in January 2010, the National Equality Panel reported that the gap between the richest and poorest segments in the UK had widened. This widening disparity may explain the apparent anomaly of simultaneous rapid growth in 'low-cost, low-frills' (and therefore by implication 'low-experience') sectors within the airline, retail and hotel markets. To detractors of the 'experience economy' the growth of 'no-frills' sectors is evidence of consultants' hype and the limited applicability of the customer experience model. They also point to falling demand for many high-experience services following the 'credit crunch' and recession of 2008, pointing to Starbucks' decision to close over 900 of its coffee shops worldwide. It seemed that interest in customer experience could decline in the post-2008 years of austerity just as quickly as it rose in the preceding boom years. However, given a growing disparity in income, price-driven and experience-driven business models can coexist. Moreover, with continuing rising expectations, it could be expected that non-utilitarian dimensions of experience will continue to become a more important component of the total service offer.

Creating a customer experience is about more than the sum of its individual components, which may typically comprise:

- the physical setting (Grove et al., 1992; Gupta and Vajic, 2000);
- customer-focused product design with expected levels of quality (Price et al., 1995);
- the service delivery processes (Harris et al., 2001);
- aspirational or utilitarian brands (de Chernatony and McDonald, 2003);
- supporting relationships (Gummesson, 1997).

A number of authors have recognized the importance of sequencing to the development of a memorable customer experience (e.g. Chase and Dasu, 2001; Pine and Gilmore, 1998, 1999). According to Chatman (1978), experiences should have a sequence structure with a story structured in a manner similar to musical pieces. Creating a story-like time pattern in experience design can provide sequences of emotions similar to those provided by episodes in human life (Deighton, 1992). Pine and Gilmore (1999) noted that experience of an emergent phenomenon should be designed for enhancement over time. The sequence of events in an experience design should improve over time and end on a positive note because an unpleasant ending dominates the memory of the entire experience. Returning to the drama analogy, this is similar to musicals invariably ending on a high note.

Sequencing issues have been addressed in discussion of '**flow**', described as an experiential state 'so desirable that one wishes to replicate it as often as possible' (Csikszentmihalyi, 1988). To remain in flow, an individual must be presented with progressively more challenging scenarios in order to ensure that the level of complexity is consistent with their motivation and skills. Flow has been examined in relation to a number of leisure services, including gambling, adventure parks and computer-mediated environments that involve individuals becoming completely engrossed (Hoffman and Novak, 1996; Csikszentmihalyi, 1990; Trevino and Webster, 1992). It has been suggested that the experience of flow may be particularly high where an individual is uncertain about the outcome (Arnould and Price, 1993). Operators of online gambling services have recognized the importance of understanding flow, as we will see in the next chapter.

When does a customer experience begin and end? It may be too simplistic to believe that it begins when the consumer initiates a service process and ends on completion of the agreed service. Prior to the service process beginning, individuals may gain experiential benefits through anticipation. For example, many people enjoy the experience of looking through holiday brochures before they choose a holiday, and long before they begin their holiday. There is increasing evidence that anticipation of an event may be recognized as an important experiential benefit, evidenced by the way that some organizations use queues and waiting time to generate emotions of excitement and anticipation for the main event (Cowley et al., 2005). After the event, an experience may be extended through the purchase of memorabilia. Memorabilia contribute to an experience in two important ways. First, they are a visible reminder of the experience, extending the memory of it after the actual encounter; second, memorabilia can facilitate peer discussion of the experience (Goulding, 1999).

What are the boundaries of a customer experience? Service providers may be interested in perceptions of that part of a service encounter that they control, but consumers' perception of their 'total experience' may embrace other non-controllable components. As an example, a dominant element of the experience of dining at a restaurant may be the lack of available public parking spaces or perceived levels of street crime in the vicinity of the restaurant.

### 3.2.1 Understanding customers' emotions

A crucial aspect of defining a successful customer experience lies in understanding individuals' emotional states, before, during and after the service encounter. When involvement with an item or service is high, consumers can experience strong emotional reactions to a stimulus. Emotions act as a source of information, which is used to evaluate the stimulus and lead to the formation of an attitude. Emotions are more likely to play an important role in attitude formation and change when they are relevant to the product or service being consumed (Koenig-Lewis and Palmer, 2008; Price et al., 1995). For example, an individual who is tired and hungry may see a restaurant primarily as a source of food, and efforts by restaurant management to provide an experiential environment may fail to appeal to that individual's emotional state. It should follow that the consumer's selective perception is directed towards the food rather than the environment, and therefore the experience retained in memory will focus on the food component. For an individual on vacation and visiting the restaurant for a leisurely social meal, selective perception is more likely to be directed towards environmental cues, which will be retained in memory. Emotional involvement is not an attribute of a product or service; rather it is the importance of it to the consumer. The same product or service can be low-involving for some and high-involving for others. Emotions can transform an event into an experience.

Emotions have been difficult to define, and it was noted by Fehr and Russell that 'everyone knows what an emotion is, until asked to give a definition' (1984, p. 464). Furthermore, emotions should be differentiated from the related affective term 'mood'. According to Westbrook and Oliver (1991, p. 85), emotions have a 'relatively greater psychological urgency, motivational potency, and situational specificity'. Bagozzi et al. (1999) additionally noted that mood is perceived as longer lasting and lower in intensity than emotion, and defined emotions as a mental state of readiness that occurs from cognitive evaluations of events or thoughts and may result in specific actions. A further distinction between moods and emotions was made by Frijda (1993), who noted that emotions are intentional and associated with a specific stimulus while moods are more diffuse and generally unintentional. Therefore, emotions are relatively easier to identify and to measure and of more interest to consumer researchers (White and Scandale, 2005).

From the debate about the nature of emotions, two dominant bases for their conceptualization and measurement have emerged. The 'dimensional approach' conceptualizes all emotions as belonging to three independent bipolar constructs of pleasure, arousal and dominance (Mehrabian and Russell, 1974). The 'basic emotion approach' does not attempt to aggregate emotions in this way, but seeks to measure individual emotions that are relevant to a context. The interrelationship between individual emotions was developed by Russell (1980) who used a spatial model to organize these emotions into bipolar pairs of opposites, for example pleasure–displeasure and excitement–depression. This approach has been widely used and found to be appropriate to a variety of contexts (Liljander and Bergenwall, 2002; Liljander and Strandvik, 1997; Mano and Oliver, 1993; Oliver, 1997; Russell, 1980). A number of authors have sought to classify emotions into negative and positive emotions, with some evidence that they are separate constructs and not polar extremes of a single construct with structurally different impacts on future buying behaviour (Smith and Bolton, 2002; Varela-Neira et al., 2008), and on response to advertising messages (Homer, 2006).

Actually measuring emotions in a service context can be very difficult. Previous studies of emotions have frequently involved retrospective recall, which may be subject to reporting error as intervening experience may moderate the reporting of experienced emotions. The nature of affective expectations may be more complex than cognitive expectations and it has been suggested that high-involvement services are able to elicit emotional responses before the service consumption starts (see Bagozzi and Pieters, 1998; Perugini and Bagozzi, 2001; Perugini and Conner, 2000). Bagozzi and Pieters (1998) state that the emotional experiences anticipated for a future service will influence goal-directed behaviour. There is evidence in the literature that consumers' forecasts about how much they will enjoy a service encounter will have an effect on how much they actually enjoy the service (see the Affective Expectations Model by Wilson and Klaaren, 1992). Baumgartner et al. (2008, p. 695) propose that '. . . such mental simulations about future states may lead to actually experiencing the future emotion at present, when the affective forecast leads to the feelings, thoughts, motivational goals, and action tendencies that accompany actual emotions'. Such anticipation of emotions may be manifested in the way that an individual becomes excited about a forthcoming vacation, or fearful about future surgery. An implication of this is that a positive pre-consumption affect is likely to lead to positive post-experience satisfaction levels and repurchase intention (Mattila and Wirtz, 2000). However, in an educational context, Athiyaman (1997) found that pre-enrolment attitude had little or no effect on post-enrolment attitude.

Given the complexity of emotions, it is probably not surprising that on a day-to-day basis, most service providers settle for the quite simple measures, rather than the complex multiple-item measures described above. One approach to understanding the holistic nature of a customer

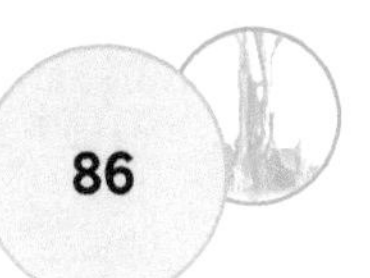



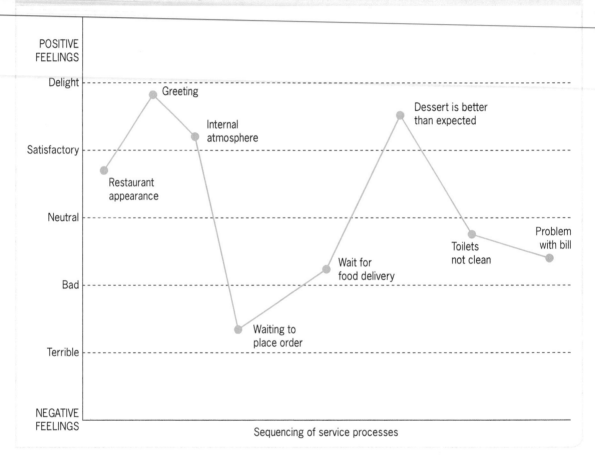

Figure 3.1 Complex service processes typically have high points and low points in terms of the feelings and emotions evoked in customers as they pass through the process. Based on survey research, an experience map can seek to identify where these points occur, in order that management can improve on the low points and review the sequence of experience states, and so ensure that customers leave the service process with positive feelings. For example, if payment is a major source of frustration, could this process be moved from the end to the beginning of the service process, so that customers are more likely to leave the restaurant with positive feelings? Of course, an event that generates positive feelings for one customer may generate negative feelings for another, and even the same customer may experience different feelings from one day to the next, reflecting variability in the service process and variability in customers' prior emotional states. With these caveats, this simplified diagram shows how a customer's overall emotional state may fluctuate during a visit to the restaurant.



experience is to draw an experience map showing the general level of positive/negative emotions evoked as an individual makes their journey through a service process. There may at first sight appear to be similarities between this approach and blueprinting, which was discussed in the previous chapter. The difference, however, is that, while a blueprint is driven by operational systems and sub-systems, the customer experience map focuses on customers' feelings and emotions at different points in what should be a seamless service process. An example of a customer experience map applied to a full-service restaurant is shown in Figure 3.1.

Can a customer experience be defined in the objective and operational manner that is possible for the more sub-systems-based approaches such as blueprinting? Probably the greatest problem in developing a simple and operationally acceptable framework for customer experience is the complexity of context-specific variables. The discussion above indicated that experience is conditioned by differences between individuals, differences over time in an individual's emotional state and a variety of situation-specific factors. To be of managerial usefulness in planning and control, a measure of experience must take account of these moderating influences. A further conceptual problem in measuring and managing experience is the identification of an optimal level of experience. For parallel and contributory constructs such as quality and satisfaction, there is an implicit assumption that consumers will prefer outcomes with higher scores on these scales. However, experience is more complex, and non-linearity may imply lower cut-off points at which an experience is not recognized, and a higher point beyond which 'more' experience may be associated with negative benefits (imagine a restaurant with excessive sounds and video screens). An alternative, qualitative approach adopted by Holbrook focuses on the 'three Fs' of fantasies (dreams, imagination or unconscious desires), feelings (emotions such as love, hate, anger, fear, joy and sorrow) and fun (hedonic pleasure derived from playful activities or aesthetic enjoyment) as key aspects of the consumption experience (Hirschman and Holbrook, 1982; Holbrook and Hirschman, 1982). However, far from being a new approach to studying consumer behaviour, the authors accepted that this experiential approach had a long lineage, dating back to Alfred Marshall in the nineteenth century and Adam Smith in the eighteenth century (Reisman, 2012).

Figure 3.2 Many consumers regard a service outlet not so much as a functional place where a service can be delivered efficiently, but rather an experience to be enjoyed in its own right. Hard Rock Cafés provide food and drink, but this is only a small part of the total service offer. At Hard Rock Cafés throughout the world, consumers are not just buying a cup of coffee, but are buying an experience in an imaginatively themed bar.

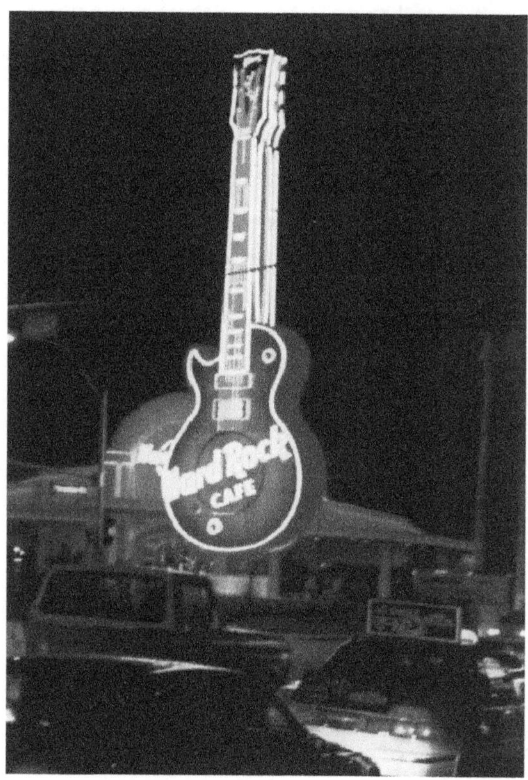


## 3.3 Frameworks for managing the customer experience

So far, customer experience has been presented as a series of ideas for defining what a service feels like to consumers. But how can such abstract ideas be transformed into strategies and tactics for managers to implement? One school of thought holds that if a concept cannot be measured, then it cannot be managed. But another view might hold that some of the most successful services businesses have been developed on the basis of entrepreneurs having an eye for detail and understanding the subjective bases for value in the eyes of consumers.

The ideas underlying customer experience are not new, and historically many successful entrepreneurs have used essentially qualitative research techniques to develop distinctive customer experiences. The development of Joe Lyons coffee shops and Butlins holiday camps in the early twentieth century were based on a process of inspired listening combined with a trial and error approach to new service development. Developing a new customer experience involves risk, and research techniques – especially quantitative techniques – may be incapable of eliciting a response from potential customers where the proposed experience is hypothetical, and devoid of the emotional and situational context in which it will be encountered.

Services marketing management benefits from a number of proposed frameworks for understanding how the subjective experience of a service is perceived by consumers. We will begin by looking at the concept of a servicescape, which incorporates some elements of a systems approach, followed by an approach referred to as servuction, which emphasizes the consumer's role in subjectively constructing the service concept in their mind. Dramaturgy models have been proposed and draw heavily on analogy with theatre. Finally, we will look at models of 'flow', which emphasize consumers' engagement in an interactive process.

## 3.3.1 The 'servicescape'

The concept of a '**servicescape**' was developed by Booms and Bitner to describe the environment in which a service process takes place (Figure 3.3). If you were to try to describe the differences a customer encountered when entering a branch of McDonald's, compared with a small family-owned restaurant, the concept of servicescapes may be useful. Booms and Bitner defined a servicescape as 'the environment in which the service is assembled and in which seller and customer interact, combined with tangible commodities that facilitate performance or communication of the service' (Booms and Bitner, 1981, p. 36). There is evidence of the effect of servicescape on consumers' intention to use a service (e.g. Hooper et al., 2013).

The design of a suitable service environment should explicitly consider the likely emotional states and expectations of target customers. Booms and Bitner distinguished between 'high-load' and 'low-load' environments, both of which can be used to suit particular emotional states and customer types. They noted that:

Figure 3.3 Servicescape – a conceptual framework

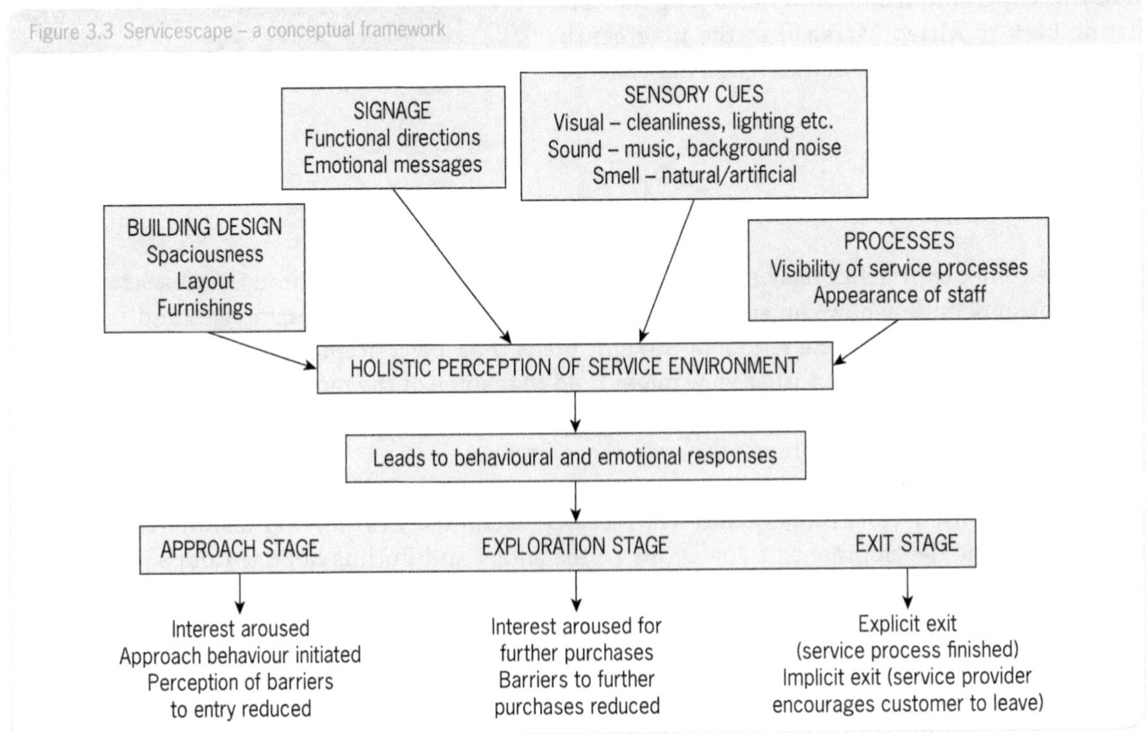

> *"A high-load signifies a high information rate; a low-load represents a low information rate. Uncertainty, novelty, and complexity are associated with high-load environments; conversely a low-load environment communicates assurance, homogeneity, and simplicity. Bright colours, bright lights, loud noises, crowds, and movement are typical elements of a high-load environment, while their opposites are characteristic of a low-load environment. People's emotional needs and reactions at a given time determine whether they will be attracted to a high- or a low-load environment."*
>
> (Booms and Bitner, 1981, p. 39)

The servicescape must encourage target customers to enter the service environment in the first place. Booms and Bitner discuss 'approach behaviour' in terms of physically moving customers towards exploring an unfamiliar environment, affiliating with others in the environment through eye contact and performing a large number of tasks within the environment. Avoidance behaviour includes an opposite set of responses. The likelihood of approach behaviour is directly linked to the two dimensions of pleasure and arousal, with a stimulating and pleasing environment being most likely to attract custom. Brightly lit window displays, a prominent and open front door, and front-of-house greeting staff are typical actions designed to induce approach. A door that is hard to find or difficult to open is more likely to achieve the opposite effect. Having induced an approach, the servicescape should encourage further exploration (for example, a bank branch may try to promote related financial services to customers with attractively designed information posters and video screens). Finally, the servicescape may need to encourage customers to leave (restaurants and coffee shops that rely on fast turnaround of customers may design seats that become uncomfortable after a time, thereby discouraging customers from staying too long and denying their table to the next paying customer).

After entry to the service production system, the servicescape must be efficient and effective for the service provider in securing customers' co-operation in the production system. Clearly explained roles for the customer, expressed in a friendly way, will facilitate this process of compliance. The physical aspects of the environment are brought to life by the actions of employees; for example, staff could be on hand to help customers who find themselves lost in the service process. Ultimately, the servicescape should encourage customers to repeat their visit.

## In practice: Welcome to the servicescape

Service consumption usually takes place in a building provided by the service provider (although, of course, many services take place in the consumer's own home). 'Servicescape' is a term used to describe the environment in which a service is delivered and, to be successful, the servicescape has to do a number of things. First, it has to attract customers. Eye-catching displays such as those found in this coffee shop (Figure 3.4) must grab attention from potential customers who are passing by. Prospective customers should be encouraged to explore further and so restaurants place their menus in the window and try to give customers a good view of the inside of the restaurant, either through clear windows or by using pictures showing tables that may be upstairs or

Figure 3.4 Designing an inviting servicescape

otherwise not visible. Barriers to further exploration must be reduced and, for this reason, many service establishments deliberately leave their front door open – even the effort of pushing the door may act as a barrier and deter some people. Inside, many restaurants employ 'greeters', who seek to rapidly commit the prospective customer to the restaurant and initiate the service process. Inside the restaurant, the servicescape must be functional for the employees, as well as creating the right ambience for the target customers. Sometimes, the servicescape can be subtly changed to meet different needs; for example, soft lighting may be used in the evening to create a leisurely atmosphere, while bright lighting is used for more hurried lunchtime diners. For special occasions, completely new servicescapes can be created; for example, restaurants often create a festive environment in the run-up to Christmas. It is not just the visual aspects of the servicescape that can be managed – restaurants also pay close attention to ambient music, which is typically faster at lunchtime and slower in the evening. Restaurants also use smells such as fresh baking or coffee to tempt prospective customers in. Although a lot of effort is spent on encouraging entry and exploration, the servicescape may also need to discourage customers from staying too long. At closing time, for example, staff typically want to clean up and go home as soon as possible, and a variety of subtle and not-so-subtle hints are used in an attempt to speed the customer's departure, such as seating which may provide welcome relief at first, but begins to feel uncomfortable after half an hour or so.

## 3.3.2 Service ambience

Ambience is an important aspect of the servicescape and can be very difficult to define (see Rollo et al., 2009). A pleasant ambient environment may be taken for granted and ambient factors are often only noticed by customers when they are particularly bad. In a typical service, ambience can be attributed with a number of dimensions: lighting, colours, sounds, smell, temperature and the availability of signage to guide customers through the service system. These individual elements must work together to encourage initial approach to the service system, further exploration and finally exit from the service process. The elements of service ambience can work subconsciously to create a favaourable emotional response and this has led some commentators to ask whether it is ethical to manipulate customers' response through ambient cues. When used together, ambient cues can create a unique signature identity for a service business to distinguish it from its near competitors. Chains of coffee shops may offer a fairly generic type of service, but in terms of ambient values, many people might consider a branch of Starbucks to be quite different from branches of Café Nero or Costa Coffee, for example.

The ambience of a service environment becomes particularly important for consumer evaluations where the purpose of service consumption satisfies hedonistic rather than utilitarian needs. Wakefield and Blodgett (1994) suggested that in situations of hedonic consumption, ambience had the capacity to increase approach and exploration behaviour, and resulted in longer duration of a visit to a service outlet. Ambience has less effect where the purpose of the visit to a service outlet is utilitarian. Atmospherics may be effective for a restaurant in obtaining a favourable response from diners dining out in the evening, but would be less effective for customers at lunchtime who seek the utilitarian benefits of eating quickly and cheaply, rather than the hedonic and social benefits of a leisurely meal.

Researchers have identified three patterns of responses to ambient cues – cognitive, affective and behavioural:

- Cognitive responses include the development of attitudes towards the service environment and service provider (e.g. Kang and Hillery, 1998), and evaluations of the credibility of the service provider (e.g. Sharma and Stafford, 2000).
- Affective responses include pleasure and arousal (Donavan and Rossiter's, 1982) and a range of individual context-specific positive and negative emotions such as excitement, boredom and anger (Izard, 1977).

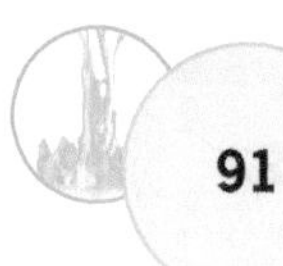

- Behavioural responses include approach-avoidance behaviour (e.g. Kim and Runyan, 2011); time spent in the service environment (e.g. Harrell et al., 1980); level of consumption/purchase (Mattila and Wirtz, 2008).

Service providers frequently undertake experiments to test the consequences of different types of service ambience. These can range from a very small scale of variation in one aspect of ambience, for example new signage in the entrance area, through to a complete redesign of the whole outlet. A large chain would compare performance of the changed, experimental outlets with performance of a control group of service outlets which are similar in terms of size, location, local competitive pressure etc., the only difference being that their design is not changed. In a well-designed experiment, any change in performance in the experimental group could therefore be attributed to the new design treatment, and if change in performance is positive and cost-effective, this treatment will in due course be rolled out to the whole network of service outlets. As with any experimental marketing, there is a danger that not only will the company conducting the experiment by closely looking at the results, its competitors may be observing as well. If they notice that patronage appears to be greater in the experimental stores, they may use the knowledge gained from the experiment to redesign their own outlets.

Although ambience may be a matter of subjective judgement, service providers seek to specify the elements of ambience quite precisely in order to reproduce a similar customer experience from one service outlet to another and consistently over time. To some, such consistency is the basis of powerful brand building. To others, such consistency may become synonymous with boring uniformity and undermine the excitement of new discovery which many would define as an essential element of customer experience.

### Lighting

The intensity, location and hue of lighting can transform a space by picking out positive features of a service environment and allowing other less pleasant aspects to disappear into the background. Many service outlets seek to exclude natural light with the aim of controlling the environment and reducing the temptation for customers' eyes to wander outside. Retailers, for example, typically want customers to focus their attention on the stock in the store, and the sight of external cues is a distraction from this. Lighting also has a safety function by ensuring that hazards are adequately lit at all times.

As well as having a practical function in inducing a cognitive response, lighting can also seek to induce an affective response. Soft lighting can create a warm inviting ambience which can encourage approach behaviour and further exploration within the service outlet. The effects of lighting can be very subtle, and many retailers have realized that soft hues can flatter the appearance of individuals while harsher lighting has the opposite effect. Lighting can be adjusted during the day or week to suit different types of service encounters; for example, a large open space within a hotel which is brightly lit during the working day as a conference centre can be transformed by lighting to make a dance floor for a wedding reception at the weekend.

### Colours

Colour can have a role in attracting customers to a service outlet and encouraging exploration. Colour has now been extensively studied in a range of marketing and service-based contexts (e.g. Grimes and Doole, 1998; Gorn et al., 1997), and while it is difficult to define universal rules of colour, a number of findings can inform the design of the service environment.

Bright colours such as yellows and reds have come to be associated with speed, which might explain their use in many chains of fast-food outlets. Subdued pastel shades are associated with a calming influence and can be effective in service environments where customers face potentially high levels of stress, for example airport terminals and dentists' waiting rooms.

Although researchers have sought universal rules governing response to colour, there appear to be significant distortions based on race, gender, age and personality. It has been noted that colours associated with pleasure and fear are culturally determined and differences have been noted in responses to colour dependent upon age and gender (Silver and Ferrante, 1995).

### Smells

Distinctive smells can encourage approach behaviour and further exploration by customers once within the service environment. Smells have a powerful ability to evoke memories and companies go to great lengths to understand which smells attract and which repel. Smell is often used in conjunction with other atmospheric cues to create an ambience of authenticity, for example the Eastern authenticity of a Chinese restaurant where smell combined with colour and décor can create the illusion of being in the Far East rather than Western Europe. The use of smells raises practical as well as ethical issues, and some of these are raised in the vignette 'Smells sell?'.

#### In practice: Smells sell?

Smell has been used for a long time by organizations to create a pleasant service environment. Coffee shops have often circulated the smell of freshly roasted beans by the entrance door in the hope that such smells would be an irresistible invitation to passers-by to enter. Supermarkets have managed smells carefully, for example by extracting unpleasant smells of fish and detergents, and instead circulating fresh bread smells. The effect of smell on consumers' evaluation of a service experience, and their subsequent purchase/repurchase/recommendation, has been well researched (see, for example, Bosmans, 2006). Among a number of reported findings, the smell of mulled wine has been seen to increase sales of Christmas food, and the smell of toast has been associated with sales of electric toasters. Improvements in technology no longer constrain a service provider to those smells that are an inherent part of their production processes – such as bread smells for a bakery and coffee smells for a coffee shop. Manufactured smells that are completely unrelated to production processes can be imported. The electrical shop selling toasters, for example, would almost certainly have to import an artificial smell, rather than producing it naturally by toasting bread.

Why are companies so keen to spend money creating artificial smells? Most simply, if a smell is seen to work, its use will be further developed. A large multi-outlet chain can experiment with smells by measuring the effects of specific smells on sales in experimental outlets, compared with sales in matched control outlets. More fundamentally, smell can act as part of a service organization's distinctive identity, in much the same way as its distinctive visual identity. Even with a blindfold, many book-buyers may be able to recognize the distinctive smell of a Waterstone's bookshop, or of a Starbucks coffee shop. Why do smells have such effects on buyers? Stimulus–response models can provide some explanation. Some responses may be part of our basic psychological make-up; for example, the smell of fresh food to a hungry person is likely to create a desire for food. However, other stimuli may have a more indirect effect through association with evoked memories. There is no physiological reason why the smell of popcorn should help a video rental business to hire out more videos, but an effect arises from association of popcorn with previous visits to the cinema, maybe associated with happy childhood memories. Of course, a smell that evokes such a response in one person may have no effect in another, and services organizations expanding overseas need to understand cultural definitions of smell, as well as basic physiological responses.

Is the use of smells in the service environment ethical? Can the use of artificial smells be justified where there is no link to actual production methods, and some would argue the company is cynically exploiting consumers' subconscious memories? Are some groups of customers particularly vulnerable to such an approach, for example children, who may be attracted to a store by the smell of confectionery? Or is the use of smell evidence of services organizations' strong customer focus and their determination to create a pleasant experience, whose success can be measured by customers returning and recommending the business to others?

### Sounds

Similar to smells, the sound present in the service environment may be very subtle and its effects only noticed by customers when it becomes intrusive. One extreme form of sound environment is complete silence, which may be reminiscent of the study area in a traditional library. Many customers may find silence intimidating because of the presumed social-norm pressure to maintain silence. Dialogue between customers and the service personnel may be perceived as being more difficult where the customer's requests may be the focus of unwanted attention from others in the environment, rather than having their dialogue lost in the anonymity of background noise.

Sound can have utilitarian and hedonic functions. The pace of music can quicken bodily processes; for example, fast music may be associated with more rapid movement around the store, whereas slow music will slow the pace of customers' movement. Sounds can also create a distinct identity for a service outlet; for example, Italian music may reinforce the Italian-style décor to suspend diners' belief that they are not in the centre of Manchester, but eating in a little piece of Italy.

Service providers carefully choose their music to match their target audiences. A service business targeting customers in their fifties may identify with 1960s music played in the service setting and this may cause a behavioural response of prolonging the time spent there. The same audience of fifty-year-olds may be alienated by the sound of a modern boy band and this may reinforce avoidance behaviour and a feeling of not being able to identify with the service provider.

### Temperature

Many physiological studies have demonstrated the effects of temperature and humidity on human performance (e.g. Van De Vliert and Van Yperen, 1996). Particularly high levels of temperature and humidity may induce a lethargic response which is often contrary to service providers' desire to encourage exploration and activity within the service environment. For this reason, many retailers install air conditioning in their outlets to encourage greater exploration behaviour.

In cases where a compliant response is sought, temperatures may be raised. During the middle section of a long-haul flight, airlines typically raise the temperature to induce sleep by passengers, thereby allowing the perception of the length of the flight to be shortened.

### Signage

Signage has a practical function of guiding customers around the service environment, but signs can vary in their degree of perceived friendliness and formality. Signs in uniform colours such as black on white or yellow, using a standard font such as Arial, may be very functional in a hospital or railway station, but convey little feeling. Friendly fonts, varied colours and imaginative forms of guidance (for example footprints painted on the floor and 'racetracks' cut into carpeted areas to guide people through the store) can help to induce affective as well as cognitive responses.

### Décor

The décor of a service outlet comprises the furniture and general style of decoration applied. Most service environments have to balance practicality against aesthetic appeal. Tables and chairs which look smart and trendy may be much more difficult to clean and maintain than their practical and plain alternatives.

Décor can be used with colour, sound and smell to make a distinctive identity for a chain of service outlets; for example, the style of tables, chairs, floors and the wall covering may differ from one chain of coffee shops to another, creating a distinctive identity for each.

### Appearance of employees

We will look at the role of employees in making successful service encounters in Chapter 10. For now, we can note that the appearance of employees may be considered to be part of the ambience of the service environment. Physical attributes of front-line employees include their demographics (e.g. age, sex and ethnicity), physical attractiveness and non-verbal cues (e.g. posture, facial expression, smile). The dress of employees contributes to the ambience of the service environment. Some have taken dress to include not just the clothes that people wear, but also body modifications, such as hairstyle, nails, jewellery and tattoos (Eicher and Roach-Higgins, 1993).

Customers should be able to identify with the physical characteristics of front-line employees. The physical characteristics should also be in accordance with their expectations. For a wine bar targeting young professional people, the ambience is likely to be much improved if front-line staff are young, fit and glamorous rather than elderly, overweight and with tattoos (Söderlund and Julander, 2009).

It has been found that front-line employees' dress can influence customers' initial response towards the service provider. One study found that where front-line staff wore a professional uniform, customers rated the service quality of the outlet more highly compared to a situation where they wore casual personal clothes (Shao et al., 2006). The appropriateness of front-line employees' dress has been shown to influence customers, expectation of service quality and their subsequent purchasing (Kim and Ok, 2010).

Sometimes the ethnicity of front-line serving staff can add to the ambience and authenticity of the service experience. A Chinese restaurant employing non-Chinese front-line staff will probably lack the authenticity of a restaurant in which Chinese personnel are visible.

## 3.3.3 Dramaturgical approaches

Service encounters can be conceptualized as a drama, similar to a theatrical production. At first sight there would appear to be many similarities between service encounters and theatrical drama:

the stage – where the service encounter takes place;
roles –the purpose of service employees (and customers);
scripts – specified procedures for providing service;
costumes – uniforms worn by employees.

The stage is the location where the encounter takes place and can itself affect the role behaviour of both buyer and seller. A scruffy service outlet may result in lowered expectations by the customer and in turn a lower level of service delivery by service personnel (see Bitner, 1990). Both parties work to a **script** that is determined by their respective role expectations. An air stewardess is acting out a script in the manner in which she performs her safety and customer service duties. The script might include precise details about what actions should be performed, when and by whom, including the words to be used in verbal communication. In reality, there may be occasions when the stewardess would like to do anything but wish an awkward customer a nice day.

The theatrical analogy extends to the costumes that service personnel wear. When a doctor wears a white coat or a bank manager a suit, they are emphasizing to customers the role they are playing. Like the actor who uses costumes to convince his audience that he is in fact Henry VIII, the bank manager uses the suit to convince customers that he is capable of taking the types of decision which a competent bank manager takes.

The concept of **role playing** has been used to apply the principles of social psychology to explain the interaction between service producer and service consumer (e.g. Solomon et al., 1985). It sees people as actors who act out roles that can be distinguished from their own personality. In the sociological literature, roles are assumed as a result of conditioning by the society and culture of which a person is a member. Individuals typically play multiple roles in life, as family members, workers, members of football teams etc., each of which comes with a set of socially conditioned role expectations. A person playing the role of worker is typically conditioned to act with reliability, loyalty and trustworthiness. An analysis of the expectations associated with each role becomes a central part of role analysis. The many roles that an individual plays may result in conflicting role expectations, as where the family role of a father leads to a series of role expectations that are incompatible with his role expectations as a business manager. Each role may be associated with competing expectations about the allocation of leisure time.

In a service encounter, both customers and service personnel are playing roles that can be separated from their underlying personality. Organizations normally employ staff not to act in accordance with this personality, but to act out a specified role (although, of course, personality characteristics can contribute to effective role performance). It follows that employees of banks are socialized to play the role of cautious and prudent adviser and to represent the values of the bank in their dealings with customers. Similarly, customers play roles when dealing with service providers. A customer of a bank may try to act the role of prudent borrower when approaching a bank manager for a small business loan, even though this might be in contrast to his fun-loving role as a family member.

Both buyers and sellers bring role expectations into their interaction. From an individual customer's point of view, there may be clear expectations of the role that a service provider should play. Most people would expect a bank manager to be dressed appropriately to play his or her role effectively, or a store assistant to be courteous and attentive. Of interest to marketers are the specific role expectations held by particular segments within society. As an example, a significant segment of young people might be happy to be given a train timetable by an enquiry office assistant and expected to read it themselves. On the other hand, the role expectations of many older people might be that the assistant should go through the timetable and read it out for them. Similarly, differences in role expectations can be identified between different countries. While customers of supermarkets in the USA often expect the checkout operator to pack their bags for them, this is not normally part of the role expectation held by UK shoppers.

It is not just customers who bring role expectations to the interaction process. Service producers also have their idea of the role that their customers should perform within the co-creation process. In the case of hairdressers, there may be an expectation that customers should give clear instructions at the outset, arrive for the appointment on time and (in some countries) give an adequate tip. Failure of customers to perform their role expectations can have a demotivating effect on front-line personnel. Retail sales staff who have been trained to act in their role may be able to withstand abusive customers who are acting out of role – others may resort to shouting back at their customers.

The service encounter can be seen as a process of simultaneous role playing in which a dynamic relationship is developed. In this process, both parties can adapt to the role expectations held by the other party. The quality of the service encounter is a reflection of the extent to which each party's role expectations are met. An airline that casts its cabin crews as the most caring crews in the business may raise customers' expectations of their role in a manner that the crews cannot deliver. The result would be that customers perceive a poor-quality service. By contrast, the same standard of service may be perceived as high quality by a customer travelling on another airline, which had made no attempt to try to project such a caring role on their crews. The quality of the service encounter can be seen as the difference between service expectations and perceived delivery. Where the service delivery surpasses these expectations, a high quality of service is perceived (although sometimes, exceeding role expectations can be perceived poorly, as where a waiter in a restaurant offers incessant gratuitous advice to clients who simply want to be left alone).

Over time, role expectations change on the part of both service staff and their customers. In some cases, customer expectations of service staff have been raised, as in the case of standards expected from many public services. In other instances, expectations have been progressively lowered, as where customers of petrol stations no longer expect staff to attend to their car, but are prepared to fill their tank and to clean their windscreen themselves. Change in customers' expectations usually begins with an innovative early adopter group and subsequently trickles through to other groups. It was mainly young people who were prepared to accept the simple, inflexible and impersonal role played by staff of fast-food restaurants, which many older segments have subsequently accepted as a role model for restaurant staff.

Goodwin (1996) has described how a role-playing drama can involve game-based strategies to outwit an opponent. Service providers sometimes manipulate customers' perceptions of reality, for example by concealing queues to make them appear shorter than they actually are. Some customers also play games, by trying to obtain a higher level of service than the one to which they are entitled (e.g. airline customers seeking an upgrade). Customers may seek reward by abusing guarantees and complaint-handling policies, complaining about non-existent problems and demanding refunds.

## In practice: All the world's a stage

An analogy is often drawn between front-line service workers and actors in a theatre. Typically, both may seek to create an illusion in the eyes of their audiences. The actor playing Romeo in Shakespeare's *Romeo and Juliet* can use costumes and a stage set to take his audience back to Italy in the Middle Ages. The members of the audience suspend belief in the reality around them until they leave the theatre and sixteenth-century Italy suddenly becomes twenty-first-century Manchester again. Many service providers similarly aim to suspend belief through the use of costumes and 'stage' props. Many people go to a coffee shop to escape from the rush of everyday life, and some UK chains have tried to create the illusion of escape to a typical Viennese or Parisian coffee house, for example. But is the analogy between theatre actors and front-line service personnel a valid one? The front-line coffee-shop worker arguably has a much harder task than the stage actor. Unlike the actor, he has to interact with his 'audience', treating each customer as an individual and entering into a dialogue, in contrast to the typical stage actor, who, with a few exceptions, does not directly interact with the audience. Nevertheless, many services organizations base their recruitment on 'audition'-type practices, in which the ability to 'perform' can be just as important a selection criterion as formal qualifications.

Figure 3.5 Acting a part?

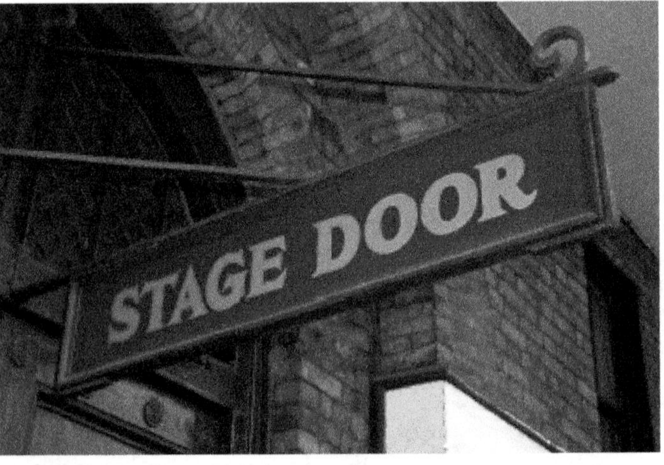

### 3.3.4 Flow

The concept of flow has featured frequently in studies of users' interaction with service processes. The concept of flow has been defined by Csikszentmihalyi as a:

> "*. . . mode of experience when an individual becomes absorbed in their activity. This mode is characterised by a narrowing of the focus of awareness, so that irrelevant perceptions and thought are filtered out; by loss of self-conscious, by a responsiveness to clear goals and unambiguous feedback; and by a sense of control over the environment . . .*"
>
> (Csikszentmihalyi, 1975, p. 36)

In a state of flow, use of a service should be autotelic, that is, intrinsically motivated by a task which is worth doing for its own sake. From being simply a context for undertaking a simple transaction, an individual in a state of flow may enjoy the experience of finding out about related services, or other product/price offers that better meets their needs.

In one study, the antecedents of flow were described as the perception of clear goals, an immediate feedback and challenges that are matched with skills. Indicators of flow and its intensity have included scores that measure:

- the balance between an individual's skills and the challenges they face;
- their focus of attention;
- loss of self-consciousness;
- feelings of control;
- momentary loss of anxiety and constraint;
- significant feelings of pleasure.

However, researchers have noted context-specific effects on flow, with a suggestion that some personal characteristics may enable individuals to engage in flow experiences more frequently, more intensely and for longer periods than others (Csikszentmihalyi and Csikszentmihalyi, 1988).

The study of flow originated in challenging sports contexts, for example white water rafting, but has since been applied to many other leisure-based service contexts. More recently, the concept of flow has been extensively applied to web-based situations. Web-based service providers consider the achievement of a state of flow in their customers to be desirable for a number of reasons. Individuals are presumed to lose self-consciousness and distort the passage of time. Lengthy periods of time may pass by, but the site user may only be conscious of having been at the site for a few minutes. A positive flow discourages a desire to leave and in many online service encounters the longer an individual is at a site, the more profitable they are, whether they are spending money directly or simply clicking through on advertisers' links.

Interactivity is a key to the achievement of a state of flow, and rapid feedback facilitates flow. To remain in flow, users need to be presented with challenges that they perceive as achievable and that are subsequently and rapidly reinforced through feedback. This may be something simple, such as planning a train journey and getting the best possible time and fare information through a process of exploration and comparison. Many online service providers have developed the concept of flow to a much greater extent, especially where a website is a destination for service fulfilment in itself (such as a music download site or chat room), rather than the means of obtaining information about a service that will substantially be provided elsewhere (for example, an airline ticket booking site). The concept of flow is well illustrated in the numerous online gambling operations that have developed (see Thinking around the subject, below). A root cause of online gambling's success is its ability to capture flow through users' desire to take risks and to attain rapid feedback.

## Thinking around the subject: Taking a punt online

The gambling industry in Britain is substantial, with a turnover of over £84 billion in 2006/07 (Gambling Commission, 2009). The most popular gambling activities in 2007 were the National Lottery Draw (57 per cent of the UK population had participated in the past year), scratchcards (20 per cent), betting on horse races (17 per cent) and playing slot machines (14 per cent).

Gambling in Britain has been in long-term decline. Statistics provided for the Gambling Bill in 2005 showed that the number of people participating in gambling activities had declined from 37.5 million in 1966 to 28 million in 2004. However, online gambling has been increasing rapidly and a Keynote report published in 2011 showed that expenditure online had reached £11.9 billion (Keynote, 2011). The Gambling Commission had estimated that 6 per cent of the population had used an Internet site for gambling. The National Lottery was the most popular gambling site for punters, making it one of the 40 most-visited sites in the UK. William Hill came in second, followed by Partypoker.com.

The appeal of online service to gambling companies is overwhelming. Growth in the UK has been driven by a range of gambling, betting and online casino sites, and not just by the National Lottery. Gamblers have been attracted by the speed and convenience of betting online, facilitated by greater availability of broadband Internet access.

Many of the traditional high-street betting shops have developed a web presence, where they have much lower transaction costs compared to their town-centre and racecourse shops, for which they have to pay high overheads. By moving their customers online, the overhead costs of running a branch network can be greatly reduced. Companies can also use the Internet to overcome problems of inseparability by locating their operations in obscure offshore countries where taxation is lower. By going online, betting companies can get access to customers who might not traditionally have considered visiting a betting shop. The Internet also allows access to groups of people who may otherwise be prevented by law from being served. The Internet recognizes no international boundaries, and it has proved difficult to prevent citizens of a country where gambling is illegal from using a gambling website based in another country. It can also in practice be much more difficult to prevent access to under-age players, whose identity cannot be as readily established online as face to face.

Above all else, gambling companies like to go online because of the addictive nature of the Internet. Once an individual achieves a state of 'flow', they have a tendency to distort time and lose self-consciousness. Gambling meets many of the criteria for establishing flow, especially the interactivity of challenges and the rapid feedback.

Of course, online gambling has raised many ethical and legal issues. Many countries restrict access to gambling services, in the belief that they may be associated with a range of social disorders. However, the nature of the Internet makes the medium both particularly attractive to gambling operators and, at the same time, particularly difficult to control. The US government, frustrated by the inability of its anti-gambling laws to control offshore online operations, has resorted to a number of more indirect approaches to control these companies, including making it illegal for American banks to carry out transactions with such companies, and effectively preventing executives of the gambling companies from visiting the USA for fear of being arrested.

Is online gambling the perfect business model for online service delivery? Is the market so attractive that competition between companies would inevitably intensify, forcing down profitability? Or would intense competition result in even more devious practices being used to make customers addicted to gambling online? Given the international environment in which online companies cross national borders, how could governments hope to regulate this sector? Indeed, should it be regulated?

### 3.3.5 Servuction

The frameworks that we have looked at so far take fairly company-focused definitions of the service environment. **Servuction** takes a slightly different perspective by concentrating on *consumers'* perceptions of a service environment, and effectively, they define the service concept, rather than the service provider. The framework, developed by Eiglier and Langeard (1987), emphasizes

Figure 3.6 Servuction – a conceptual framework

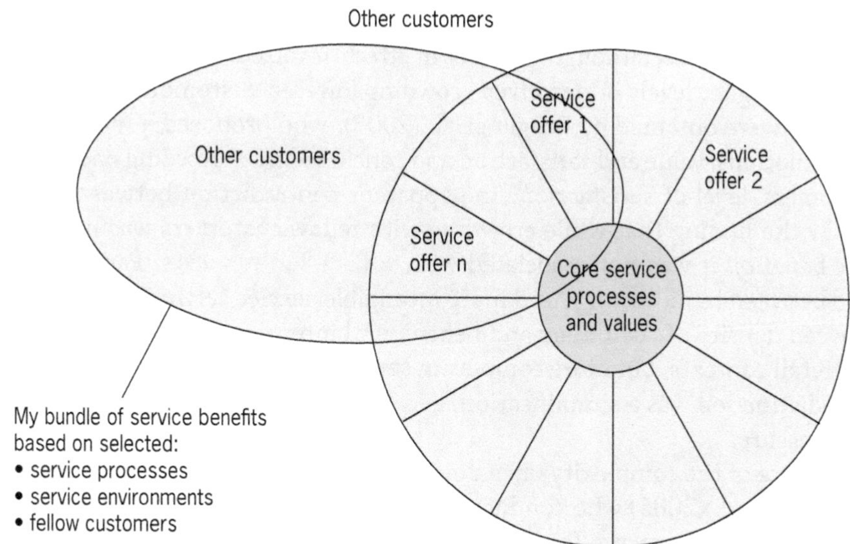


experiential aspects of service consumption and is based on the idea of organizations providing consumers with complex bundles of benefits (Figure 3.6).

Components of the servuction model combine to create the experience for the consumer. These other components comprise the physical environment, contact personnel of the service provider and customers. In addition, the servuction system comprises unseen processes of the service provider. Everyone and everything that comes into contact with the consumer is effectively delivering the service. Bateson (1989) has noted that identifying the servuction system can be difficult because of the often large number of contacts between the service provider and the customers. The servuction approach is particularly relevant to services that involve high levels of input from fellow consumers or third-party producers. Consumers essentially create their own bundle of benefits from the contributory elements of the service offer. The servuction model has been applied to the marketing of towns as tourism and shopping destinations (Warnaby and Davies, 1997) in which consumers must essentially define their own bundle of benefits from the complexity of facilities provided by multiple organizations within the town. One person's definition of the benefits of a leisure visit to Paris may be quite different from another person's – only consumers can define the service offer that matters to them.

## 3.4 The effects on customer experience of other customers

Many services can only sensibly be produced in large batches, while the consumers who use the service buy only individual units of the service. It follows therefore that services such as train journeys, meals in a restaurant and visits to the theatre are consumed in the presence of other customers. Here, there is said to be an element of joint consumption of service benefits. A play cannot be produced just for one patron and a train cannot run for just one passenger – a number of customers jointly consume one unit of service output. An environment is created in which the behaviour pattern of any one customer during the service process can directly affect the experiential values of the service for all consumers. In the theatre, the visitor who talks during the performance spoils the enjoyment of the performance for others.

Researchers have observed an effect on consumers' satisfaction of the density of other customers present in the service process, although evidence of effects is mixed. In a retail context, Machleit et al. (2000) found that higher levels of perceived crowding lowered customers' satisfaction. Somewhat different findings were obtained by Eroglu et al. (2005), who proposed a model linking perceived crowding with emotions, value and satisfaction and concluded that crowding had a positive influence on retail customers' level of satisfaction. The apparent contradiction between these studies may be explained by the finding that while crowding with fellow customers was negatively associated with hedonic benefits, it was not associated with utilitarian benefits. Pan and Siemens (2011) distinguished between retail settings and more intangible service settings and found that the relationship between density of customers and behavioural intention was relatively simple and linear in the case of retail contexts, but more complex in service settings such as hairdressers. They noted that even this distinction was a simplification, because the results changed where customers were under a time pressure.

Further evidence of the complexity of customer satisfaction across a range of levels of crowding was found by Argo et al. (2005) who conducted field experiments in a retail context by manipulating the number of fellow shoppers. They found a non-linear V-shape function, indicating that when the number of shoppers increases from zero to one person, negative emotions decrease. But they found that when the number increased from one person to three, negative emotions increased.

It is not just the absolute number of other customers in the service environment that may affect any individual's satisfaction, but also the nature of those other customers and what they are doing. A study by Söderlund (2011) found that visible consumption and purchasing activities by other customers had an effect on an individual's attitude towards a retailer and their overall evaluation of it – if lots of people were busy eating, drinking, or buying and generally looking happy, this would result in the customer having a more favourable evaluation of the service provider and being more likely to purchase. It has also been suggested that satisfaction with the service environment will be greater where there is perceived similarity of social standing between an individual and their fellow consumers. In a study of retailers, Dickson found that individuals tended to avoid stores that were used by people perceived as being different from their own perceived social status. Many bar owners realize that an important factor influencing consumers' decision about whether to enter and stay at the bar is based on whether the people in the bar are considered to be 'their kind of people'.

The actions of fellow consumers are often therefore an important element of the service experience and service companies seek to manage customer–customer interaction. By various methods, organizations seek to remove adverse elements of these encounters and to strengthen those elements that add to all customers' enjoyment. Some commonly used methods of managing encounters between customers include the following:

- *Selecting customers on the basis of their ability to interact positively with other customers*. Where the enjoyment of a service is significantly influenced by the presence of other customers, formal or informal selection criteria can be used to try to ensure that only those customers who are likely to contribute positively to service encounters are accepted. Examples of formal selection criteria include tour companies who set age limits for certain holidays – people booking an 18–30 holiday can be assured that they will not be holidaying with children or elderly people whose attitudes towards loud music might prevent enjoyment of their own lifestyle. Formal selection criteria can include inspecting the physical appearance of potential customers – many nightclubs and restaurants set dress standards in order to preserve a high-quality environment in which service encounters take place. Informal selection criteria are aimed at encouraging some groups who add to customers' satisfaction with the service environment, while discouraging those who detract from it. Colour schemes, service ranges, advertising and pricing can be used to discourage certain types of customer. Bars that charge high prices for drinks and offer a comfortable environment will be informally excluding the segment of the population whose aim is to get drunk as cheaply as possible.

- *Determining rules of behaviour expected from customers.* The behaviour of one customer can significantly affect other customers' enjoyment of a service. Examples include smoking in a restaurant (which is now against the law in many countries), talking during a cinema show and playing loud music in public transport. The simplest strategy for influencing behaviour is to make known the standards of expected behaviour and to rely on customers' goodwill to act in accordance with these expectations. Where rules are not obeyed, the intervention of service personnel may be called for. Failure to intervene can result in a negative service encounter continuing for the affected party, and the service organization may be perceived as not caring by its failure to enforce rules. Against this, intervention that is too heavy-handed may alienate the offender, especially if the rule is perceived as one that has little popular support. The most positive service encounter results from intervention that is perceived as a gentle reminder by the offender and as valuable corrective action by other customers.
- *Facilitating positive customer–customer interaction.* For many services, an important part of the overall benefit is derived from positive interaction with other customers. Holidaymakers, people attending a conference and students of a college can all derive significant benefit from the interaction with their peer group. A holiday group where nobody talks to each other may restrict the opportunities for shared enjoyment. The service providers can seek to develop bonds between customers by, for example, introducing customers to one another or arranging events where they can meet socially.

## In practice: A day at the races

Services are often produced and consumed in public. Indeed, one of the benefits of a service may be the ambience that is provided by a crowd of fellow customers. One reason for the continuing high attendances at horse-race meetings, in the face of increasing levels of televised racing and online gambling, is the atmosphere that is generated by thousands of fans simultaneously cheering their horse on. But this atmosphere needs to be carefully managed if it is not to detract from the overall service offer. The horse-racing authorities are keen to avoid problems that have been experienced in the past by football clubs. The latter increasingly manage the expected behaviour of supporters, mindful of the fact that live football increasingly targets women and family groups, rather than being the traditional all-male preserve. Football clubs have become more vigilant in curbing antisocial behaviour, such as racially sensitive chanting and the use of flags and banners that obscure fellow fans' view of the game, as well as in controlling drunken and disorderly behaviour.

Figure 3.7 Cheltenham Races. (Copyright Cheltenham Tourism/David Sellman)

### 3.4.1 The Internet service delivery environment

'Servicescape' was discussed earlier in this chapter as a model for understanding service processes and the environment in which consumer–producer interaction takes place. You will recall that the model recognized the importance of environmental cues for encouraging approach behaviour, exploration and, eventually, departure. Can a similar approach be applied to online environments?

A number of studies have sought to extend the principles of Bitner's original servicescape model to online environments. Many such approaches have used Bitner's stimulus–organism–response model, initially developed by Mehrabian and Russell (1974). But what are the electronic equivalents of stimuli such as store atmosphere, layout, smells and the body language used by staff during the service encounter? Web-based stimuli are much narrower in their scope than those typically encountered in a face-to-face encounter. Smell and body language, for example, are just two of the cues that have been difficult or impossible to emulate in an online environment. Many studies have therefore focused on the content and design of a website.

Shih (1998) developed the concepts of 'telepresence' (defined as the extent to which a website visitor feels a real presence of the company behind the website) and information vividness (defined as the way in which the breadth and depth of information are presented and appeal to the senses). To what extent did the website provide all the information that a visitor was looking for, and how vividly did the required information stand out from other information that was of no interest? Did the imagery used create liking for the organization or specific service processes?

The web environment must encourage potential visitors to click through to the site in the first place, so the design of banner ads elsewhere on the Internet becomes an Internet version of a greeter at the door beckoning people to enter. When they have arrived at the site, the design of the site should encourage exploration. Links to other pages must be clearly and logically laid out, and combine both rational and emotional reasons for a visitor to follow through to another page. The information content of the site must appear relevant to a visitor and be of such a high quality that it develops credibility in the source and a desire to click through to additional pages. A number of studies have demonstrated the importance of high-quality information for visitors' evaluations of a website (e.g. Elliott and Speck, 2005; Park and Kim, 2003).

As well as providing credible factual information about the service on offer, a website often needs to develop an emotional appeal. The use of aesthetics and imagery that are appropriate to the target audience can help to differentiate otherwise similar websites. However, a balance must be struck, as in real-life service encounters, between providing information that users really need and the danger that this becomes lost among emotional messages.

Finally, the online environment must be user friendly. Human–computer interaction has emerged as a field of study of the way people use technology, and the study of how visitors use a website has parallels with how visitors interact in a face-to-face encounter. Website usability refers to the ease of navigation around a site, the ease of learning how to use the site and the level and quality of support available. The speed of download, or the time taken to receive a reply to a request, is analogous to the time that a consumer waits for service in a face-to-face encounter. Bachelder (2000) noted that slow download speeds could be just as off-putting as a queue for service. A number of studies have shown that fast download speeds are crucial to achieving a high rate of flow, discussed in Section 3.2 (McMillan and Hwang, 2002; Novak et al., 2000). There is evidence that slow download speed has a negative effect on consumers' emotional responses (Rose and Straub, 2001), leading to early exit from a site. Page and Lepkowska-White (2002) noted a significant correlation between download speeds and the number of pages visited, the time spent at the website and attitudes towards a business.

## 3.5 The effects on customer experience of health, safety and security considerations

Often, the experience that marketers want to offer their customers may not be the same as what operations managers and employees are able or willing to deliver. The desire for a high level of customer experience may sound fine in theory, but be difficult to deliver in practice. A true marketing orientation and focus on customers is increasingly being challenged by the need to ensure that a service is provided safely and securely.

The inseparability of services implies that customers effectively walk into the 'factory' where their service is produced. This analogy is important when it comes to understanding the need to ensure a safe and secure environment in which a service is produced. As we will see in this section, services organizations often face challenges in reconciling the need to maximize customer experience, while at the same time maintaining a safe and secure service process.

A contemporary example of the issues raised concerns smoking in service outlets such as bars and restaurants. For many bars and restaurants, smokers may have been good customers, spending more than average, and likely to defect to an alternative venue if smoking was restricted. Marketers had to make the initial calculation whether the loss of smokers would be offset by attraction of additional customers for whom a smoke-free environment was more attractive. But there was a bigger consideration that goes beyond marketing. Should a company run the risk that its employees may sue it for the harmful effects of passive smoking? Marketers may now be frustrated by legislation to ban smoking in workplace environments, now adopted in many European countries. Given the inseparability of services, a ban on smoking at work to protect employees effectively reduces marketers' discretion, even if market research indicates that a segment of customers would prefer a smoking environment.

At the heart of many decisions about the service encounter is the idea of risk assessment. What is an acceptable risk has changed over time, and varies between countries. Very few services could be considered completely risk-free – even serving a cup of coffee from a coffee takeaway stall runs the risk that the water may be too hot and scald the customer. But the likelihood of this happening, coupled with having reasonable processes in place to make sure this does not happen, means that coffee shops quite happily accept the risk of serving coffee. Sometimes, risk is a central concern of a service encounter, and marketing people generally do not need any reminder of its importance. An outward-bound adventure centre offering courses in abseiling and canoeing, for example, must have robust risk assessment procedures in place, with clearly specified guidelines for managing these risks (for example, allocating a minimum supervisor-to-student ratio and requiring the use of safety equipment and compulsory training for supervisors). At other times, it may be very easy to ignore risk, and companies may fail to undertake a proper risk assessment. What about the risk to the health of staff and customers working in a shop or leisure facility with inadequate ventilation or poor lighting?

There have been a number of cases of reported conflicts between the marketing function of a service business, wanting to improve customer experience at lower cost, and the operating departments, which must ultimately carry responsibility for shortcomings in operating practice. An inquiry into the sinking of the passenger ferry *Herald of Free Enterprise* in 1987 noted the operational pressure to depart on time (and therefore reduce customer complaints about delays), even if this meant the ship leaving with its doors open, a consequence of which was the capsizing of the ship and the loss of 193 lives.

## In practice: Dress to impress

Figure 3.8 A traditional Oktoberfest waitress

Visitors to Bavaria's beer festivals come away with memories of the beer and barmaids. The service encounter is made memorable by the distinctive dress worn by barmaids, which combines tradition with visual appeal (especially to men, who make up a large part of the festivals' market). The barmaids' dress, known as a 'dirndl', comprises a figure-hugging dress and apron with a tight, low-cut top. The sight of a barmaid dressed in a dirndl and carrying several glasses of beer helps to transform a drink into an experience. Customers love the dress, brewers love it and apparently the barmaids do too. But this apparently happy service environment was threatened in 2006 by the EU's Optical Radiation Directive, by which employers of staff who work outdoors, such as those in Bavaria's beer gardens, must ensure that staff are protected against the risk of sunburn. The serious point underlying the EU legislation is that in the UK alone about 70,000 new cases of skin cancer are diagnosed each year. Faced with this directive, how should the provider of an outdoor service encounter react? If they leave scantily dressed employees exposed to the sun, they could face fines, and possible legal action by employees who subsequently develop skin cancer. But, contrary to many newspaper reports, the EU directive does not specifically require Bavarian barmaids (or outdoor workers elsewhere) to cover up their low-cut dresses. Management must undertake a risk assessment and consider what is appropriate to a specific service encounter. Perhaps the unique character of the Munich Oktoberfest could be preserved with the help of sun cream and by reducing each barmaid's hours of exposure to the sun.

Managers must be very careful to specify a service encounter in a manner that rigorously addresses the issue of risk. Too often, when a service encounter results in injury or death, the initial reaction is to blame the low-level operative who made a mistake. However, this mistake has to be seen in the context of pressures from other sources within the service production process. For example, the immediate cause of a train crash might be a driver who wrongly crossed a red signal. Although this driver may take the immediate blame for the crash, further enquiry often reveals a catalogue of service design failures, for example raising questions about the recruitment and training of drivers, failure by management to rectify a problem which had previously been reported to it, and management's commitment to the installation of the latest safety equipment that would have prevented this type of accident. There have been calls for greater use of the charge of corporate manslaughter against managers of companies who design and implement unsafe services, and it has been argued that pursuing a prosecution against an errant junior employee would not serve the public interest as much as a prosecution of the managers who designed poor service processes in the first place.

Service marketers must increasingly be aware of the possibilities for terrorism to disrupt their service encounters. Terrorism can impact on marketing in a number of ways:

- The need to take security measures may make a service process unattractive to some consumers, who no longer use the service. For example, there has been a suggestion that increased delays at airports due to security screening have led some people to believe that the hassle of flying is too great, and so they have chosen other means of transport, or not travelled at all.

- The fear of terrorism itself may deter some people from using a service. For example, few people ventured into the restaurants and bars of central Belfast during the periods of the 'troubles' in Northern Ireland. With the return of peace, restaurants in Belfast's 'Golden Mile' are busy once more.
- By contrast, rigorous security measures may be perceived by many customers as a price worth paying in order to ensure that they can consume the service without fear of interruption. For example, the Israeli airline El Al is acknowledged to have the strictest security of any airline, which has been used by the airline to promote reassurance to consumers.

Although terrorism has become a much more important item on the agenda of many services organizations since the events of 11 September 2001, terrorism is of course not new. Companies operating in Northern Ireland and Israel have long experience of designing the threat of terrorism into their service blueprint.

Terrorist attacks can affect manufacturers as well as service organizations, but their effects on service organizations can be very much greater. Manufacturing companies can take steps to protect the security of their production facility by controlling and confining access to employees only. Cases of deliberate damage to manufactured goods are rare, and manufacturers have taken steps to reduce this risk throughout their distribution channels, for example by introducing tamper-evident packaging. This is in contrast to services organizations, where customers typically enter the production process and cannot be easily screened out in the way that unauthorized entry to a factory can be prevented. Indeed, the whole point of most services is for customers to enter the service 'factory', so, with relatively open access, risks are much greater.

Services organizations have become targets for terrorist groups. Sometimes, the group may be campaigning against a specific company. This has been the case, for example, with the direct action that has been taken against the companies who supplied services to Huntingdon Life Sciences, a company that has undertaken experiments on live animals and which has been targeted by numerous animal rights groups. At other times, a service company may simply represent the values of a group that protestors are opposed to, and an attack is a means of making this point publicly and with maximum impact. When left-wing groups of protestors smashed windows at a branch of Royal Bank of Scotland during the G20 summit of leaders of the richest nations in London in April 2009, they probably did not have any particular grudge against the bank, but the bank symbolized a set of capitalist values and interventions in the world to which the group was opposed. Whatever the reason, services offer relatively easy opportunities for terrorist groups to have great impact through the publicity and disruption that their actions cause. Attacks on underground trains, aircraft and shopping centres can attract considerable publicity for a cause.

What lengths should an organization go to in order to reduce the possibilities of a disruptive attack on its service processes? There are a number of issues here:

- What is the best estimate of the probability of a terrorist attack actually occurring? Many services organizations use risk assessment methodologies, often employing specialist risk assessors.
- What will be the downside cost of an attack actually occurring, in terms of physical damage and damage to an organization's reputation?
- What is the public's perception of the probability of an attack and its likely consequences? Consumers often make apparently irrational choices; for example, over the past couple of decades it has been estimated that the probability of being injured or killed in a terrorist aircraft attack is much less than the probability of being injured or killed in a road traffic accident. Despite this, it is quite common for the fear of flying to be much greater than fear of driving.

- What is the public's perception of measures taken to reduce the threat of terrorism? Are consumers likely to be deterred by extensive security measures, such as body searches and identity checking, or do these provide a source of reassurance?
- What security measures are operationally feasible? Would it, for example, be feasible to search all passengers entering a busy commuter train station during the peak period?

## In practice: A serious threat from a funny comedian?

'Security' has become a blanket reason used by many services companies to explain why they cannot fulfil a customer's request. Of course, there are often good security reasons that explain the response, but there are many instances where apparently silly 'security' responses are made. Consider the case of the veteran comedian Joan Rivers, 76 years old, much loved by the public and hardly likely to cause any danger for an airline. But in January 2010 she was 'bumped' off a Continental Airlines flight from Costa Rica to New York, because of an apparent anomaly in her passport. Like many American celebrities, her passport gave her married name (Joan Rosenberg) as well as the words 'AKA Joan Rivers'. Her ticket was issued in the name by which she was best known. According to Rivers, 'some stupid bitch' at the gate decided that she couldn't understand an 'Also Known As' passport. Rivers was deemed a danger to national security and removed from the New York-bound flight. It seemed that while the gate agent had difficulty working out who she was, there were fans in the departure area asking for autographs and taking pictures.

In many services industries, empowered staff would use their common sense and would weigh up the situation and come to a decision. But the security industry is labour intensive and there can be fierce competition for contracts between security services providers, who operate on low margins. Staff tend to be paid the minimum wage level and opportunities for choosing top-quality staff and training them in judgement skills are limited. So, in order to comply with government requirements, it is easier for companies to rely on strict rules-based blueprint approaches to security checking.

Fans of Joan Rivers who were waiting in New York for her to perform may have been disappointed when she was late. Disappointment may have also been experienced by the thousands of little old ladies who have innocently tried to take nail scissors on board an aircraft, but have had them confiscated because 'those are the rules'. Despite the 'rules', a smart and determined terrorist might have developed a much more ingenious method of smuggling harmful objects on board the aircraft.

Often, the appearance of a strictly enforced security policy may give some reassurance to customers that management is taking measures to avoid a terrorist attack. But sometimes the visible appearance of security may be a front for much deeper flaws. In the case of Joan Rivers, 'security' may have been a catch-all excuse to hide operational problems. It had been reported that her flight to New York was overbooked, so 'security' made a convenient and politically acceptable reason for ejecting passengers, rather than admitting that the airline had overbooked. While there may have been few reported cases of little old ladies using their nail scissors as weapons to overpower cabin crew, it may be easier to imagine a determined terrorist breaking a glass bottle to use as a much more lethal weapon. Little old ladies with nail scissors may be an easy and visible sign that security was being treated seriously by an airline, but would airlines voluntarily enforce a bottle ban, thereby annoying even more passengers, and causing a loss of valuable duty-free sales in airport shops?

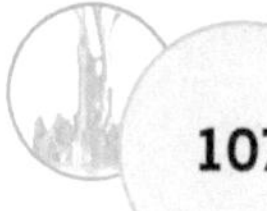



## Case study

### Creating a drama at T.G.I. Friday's

Is it a pub? Is it a restaurant? Or is it theatre? The operators of T.G.I. Friday's would hope that their customers see it as all three. For diners who tire of the scripted industrialized service processes of many fast-food chains, the service encounter at a branch of T.G.I. Friday's may come as welcome relief.

T.G.I. Friday's is a themed American restaurant and bar group in the USA and in 2010 had over 900 restaurants operating in 59 countries. In the UK, the chain operated since 1986 as a franchise through Whitbread plc (in 2007 Whitbread sold the operating rights of its 45 UK restaurants back to a consortium consisting of Carlson Restaurants Worldwide and ABN Amro Capital).

The credo of T.G.I. Friday's, according to Richard Snead, president and chief executive officer (CEO) of Carlson Restaurants Worldwide, parent company of T.G.I. Fridays, is 'to treat every customer as we would an honoured guest in our home, and it is reflected in everything we do'.

There are four crucial components of the company philosophy which contribute to successful service encounters at their restaurants:

- *Employees*. These are seen as the key to service quality. This applies not only to front-line staff who visibly contribute to guests' experience, but also to back-room staff.
- *Product*. A meal is a focal point of a customer's visit and consistency of standards is important.
- *Package*. This comprises the building and furnishings which must be kept well maintained.
- *Ambience*. This is an important part of the meal experience that is difficult to specify, but memorable to customers.

The first T.G.I. Friday's was opened at First Avenue and 63rd Street in New York City in 1965 and featured the now familiar red and white stripes. Inside were wooden floors, Tiffany lamps, bentwood chairs and striped tablecloths. Décor has become a key element in the T.G.I. Friday's experience, transforming an otherwise bland and boring industrial-type building into a theatrical stage. For T.G.I. Friday's interior décor, a full-time antique 'picker' travels extensively to auctions and flea markets. Memorabilia have to be authentic and, if possible, unique to the area where a new restaurant would be located.

T.G.I. Friday's offers 'mass customization' in which the company offers a basically standard service to all customers, but the customer can personalize their meal through an extensive range of menu permutations. The company's approach to managing the service encounter distinguishes between 'hard' and 'soft' elements. Hard elements include core service processes and tangible elements of the product offer, such as car parking facilities, the menu offered and target service times. The fundamental design of T.G.I. restaurants is remarkably similar throughout the world, with a large central bar area with dining facilities surrounding the bar and authentic American decorative memorabilia. Even the location of the toilets is standard, and an American guest visiting the T.G.I. Friday's restaurant in Coventry would immediately know where to look for them. Each restaurant offers a range of approximately 100 American/Mexican food menu items and approximately the same number of cocktails. Service target times form part of the 'hard' element of the service encounter and the company requires that starters should be served within seven minutes of receipt of a customer's order. A computer program helps managers to monitor the achievement of these service times. The hard elements of the service encounter tend to be specified by head office and branch managers are expected to achieve specified standards. Menus and the product range are designed and priced centrally at head office.

However, it is the 'soft' elements of the service encounter that distinguish T.G.I. Friday's from its competitors. Crucial to the distinction is the empowering of employees to take whatever actions they see fit in order to improve customers' experience. Employee performance requires, therefore, more than the traditional acts of greeting, seating and serving customers. Employees have to be able to provide both the behaviours and the emotional displays to match with customers' feelings. Getting serving staff to join in a chorus of 'Happy Birthday' may not be easy to script, but spontaneous singing when a meal is served to a group of diners celebrating a birthday can make all the difference in customers' experience of their meal. Of course, recruitment of the right kind of people becomes crucial and prospective candidates are selected as much for their sense of fun as on the strength of their CV. Initial interviews take the form of 'auditions' in which potential recruits are set individual and group tasks to test their personality type. Opportunities are given for trained staff to express their personality and individuality, for example by wearing outlandish clothes that make a statement about their personality.

T.G.I. Friday's has become a preferred place of employment for restaurant staff, who have enjoyed relatively good working conditions, above-average earnings for the sector – especially when tips are taken into account – and a sense of fun while at work. The chain has won numerous awards as a good employer, and in 2013 was third overall winner in the annual UK 'Sunday Times Best Places to Work' awards. In the voting process, for the awards, 87 per cent of employees said they felt a strong sense of 'family' in their teams, and 84 per cent said that working with their colleagues gave them a real 'buzz'. Staff also said that their managers were 'excellent role models' who gave confidence through their leadership skills and that they felt motivated to give their best every day.

Is the pattern of service encounters developed by T.G.I. Friday's a sustainable business model? Among the portfolio of restaurant formats formerly operated by Whitbread plc, T.G.I. Friday's has been a star performer, in contrast to some of its more traditional formats such as Beefeater, which have become less popular with consumers. A glance at the customer review site www.ciao.co.uk provides an insight into customers' experience of the service encounter. Overall, contributors seem to be happy with the format, although a number of people observed that service standards could decline when a restaurant becomes very busy. It may be fine for serving staff to sing to customers when times are quiet, but how can they do this and still meet their service delivery-time targets when the restaurant is busy? A number of customers also commented on the very high prices charged by T.G.I. Friday's, with more than one person describing them as 'rip-off prices'. But, in order to get the best staff who can create a memorable experience, is it worth paying staff a little more and passing this on to customers as higher prices?

### Case study review questions

1. What are the connections between theatre and T.G.I. Friday's? Is the dramaturgical analogy a good one?
2. Identify the types of benefits that consumers may seek from a visit to T.G.I. Friday's. How would you define the experiential benefits of a visit?
3. Identify and critically evaluate the contributions of 'hard' systems approaches and 'soft' experiential approaches to managing service encounters at T.G.I. Friday's.

## Summary and links to other chapters

This chapter has built on the previous chapter by supplementing a 'hard' systems approach to service design with a 'softer' experiential-based approach. Attempts to measure the quality of a service encounter are considered in more detail in Chapter 9. In labour-intensive services, the quality of the service is influenced by the efforts of employees, and their role is explored in Chapter 10. Delays during a service process can impact directly upon consumers; therefore, service providers aim to avoid bottlenecks by carefully matching their capacity with the level of demand, and these issues are explored in Chapter 12.

## Chapter review questions

1. If you were a customer experience manager for a consumer services company, what issues would likely be on your agenda? What challenges would you need to address in implementing a programme to improve customers' experience of the service?
2. Many analyses of the service encounter have drawn analogies with the theatre. Critically assess the extent to which this analogy is valid.
3. What is the value to services marketers of the concept of 'flow'? Are there any important differences between application of the concept in online and offline environments? What ethical issues are raised by the concept?

## Activities

1. Consider a high-contact service that you have consumed recently, such as a visit to a bar, restaurant, library or dentist. Construct an experience map, using the principles shown in Figure 3.1. Be careful to consider when your experience began and ended, and identify all the sensory cues that you picked up during the service process. What elements of experience stand out in your memory? Why is this? Why is it important for the service provider to understand your long-term memory of the encounter?
2. Visit a website such as YouTube.com or MySpace.com that is a 'destination' website in its own right, rather than merely a means of undertaking a specific transaction. Try to apply the framework of servicescape to the website. In particular, explore the methods used by the website operator to encourage approach behaviour and subsequent exploring of the website. What similarities are there between real-life service environments and virtual service environments? Is the analogy a good one or do we need fundamentally different frameworks for analysing the two?
3. Reflect on the concept of 'flow' in Internet environments. Have you ever noticed that the time spent at a website passed by faster than you thought? Were you encouraged to click through to additional pages on the site? What factors about the design of the website encouraged you to achieve a state of 'flow'?

## Key terms

**Banner ads** Paid for advertising on websites, which typically targets a predetermined profile of visitors to the website.

**Co-creation** A service benefit can be realized only if more than one party contributes to its production, e.g. customer–producer co-creation implies that customers take a role in producing service benefits.

**Flow** A mode of experience when an individual becomes absorbed in their activity and feels a sense of control over the environment.

**Hedonistic benefits** Benefits that are essentially based on pleasure rather than practicality.

**Role playing** Behaviour of an individual that is a result of his or her social conditioning, as distinct from innate predispositions.

**Script** A pattern of behaviour that is tightly specified by another party.

**Servicescape** A description of the environment in which service delivery takes place.

**Servuction** A description of the producer–consumer service production system.

**Utilitarian benefits** Benefits that are essentially based on practical use rather than pleasurable outcomes.

## Selected further reading

*The central role of the encounter between an organization's staff and its customers has led to a considerable literature in defining service encounters and prescribing methods for improving the quality of encounters. The following are important early papers in the development of this stream of literature:*

**Bitner, M.J., Booms, B.H. and Tetreault, M.S.** (1990) 'The service encounter: diagnosing favourable and unfavourable incidents', *Journal of Marketing*, 54 (1), 71–84.

**Shostack, G.L.** (1984) 'Designing services that deliver', *Harvard Business Review*, 62 (1), 133–9.

*Experiential aspects of service environment design are explored in the following:*

**Grayson, R.A.S. and McNeill, L.S.** (2009) 'Using atmospheric elements in service retailing: understanding the bar environment', *Journal of Services Marketing*, 23 (7), 517–27.

**Harris, L.C. and Ezeh, C.** (2008) 'Servicescape and loyalty intentions: an empirical investigation', *European Journal of Marketing*, 42 (3/4), 390–422.

**Rollo, A.S., Grayson, L. and McNeill, S.** (2009) 'Using atmospheric elements in service retailing: understanding the bar environment', *Journal of Services Marketing*, 23 (7), 517–27.

**Slåtten, T., Mehmetoglu, M., Svensson, G. and Sværi, S.** (2009) 'Atmospheric experiences that emotionally touch customers: a case study from a winter park', *Managing Service Quality*, 19 (6), 721–46.

**Kim, N. and Lee, M.** (2012) 'Other customers in a service encounter: examining the effect in a restaurant setting', *Journal of Services Marketing*, 26(1), 27–40.

*The following papers offer further discussion of role playing and scripting, which is an important aspect of service encounters:*

**Goodwin, C.** (1996) 'Moving the drama into the factory: the contribution of metaphors to services research', *European Journal of Marketing*, 30 (9), 13–36.

**Harris, K., Harris, R., Elliott, D. and Baron, S.** (2010) 'A theatrical perspective on service performance evaluation: the customer critic approach', *Journal of Marketing Management*, 27 (5–6), 477–502.

**Parker, C. and Ward, P.** (2000) 'An analysis of role adaptations and scripts during customer-to-customer encounters', *European Journal of Marketing*, 34 (3/4), 341–58.

**Williams, J.A. and Anderson, H.H.** (2005) 'Engaging customers in service creation: a theatre perspective', *Journal of Services Marketing*, 19 (1), 13–23.

*The subject of customer experience management is discussed in the following:*

**Tynan, C. and McKechnie, S.** (2009) 'Experience marketing: a review and reassessment', *Journal of Marketing Management*, 25 (5/6), 501–17.

**Ferguson, R.J., Paulin, M. and Bergeron, J.** (2010) 'Customer sociability and the total service experience: antecedents of positive word-of-mouth intentions', *Journal of Service Management*, 21 (1), 25–44.

**Meyer, C. and Schwager, A.** (2007) 'Understanding customer experience', *Harvard Business Review*, 85 (2), 116–26, 157.

**Palmer, A.** (2010), 'Customer experience management: a critical review of an emerging idea', *Journal of Services Marketing*, 24 (3), 196–208.

**Pine, B.J. and Gilmore, J.H.** (1999) *The Experience Economy: Work is Theatre and Every Business a Stage*, Harvard Business School Press, Boston, MA.

**Price, L., Arnould, E. and Tierney, P.** (1995) 'Going to extremes: managing service experiences and assessing provider performance', *Journal of Marketing*, 59 (2), 83–97.

*A number of articles have sought to develop frameworks for analysing the online service environment, using analogies with the frameworks that were introduced in this chapter:*

**Harris, L.C. and Goode, M.M.H.** (2010) 'Online servicescapes, trust, and purchase intentions', *Journal of Services Marketing*, 24 (3), 230–43.

**Karakas, F.** (2009) 'Welcome to World 2.0: the new digital ecosystem', *Journal of Business Strategy*, 23 (4), 23–30.

**Rosenbaum, M.S.** (2005) 'Meet the cyberscape', *Marketing Intelligence & Planning*, 23 (7), 636–47.

# References

**Abbott, L.** (1955) *Quality and Competition*, Columbia University Press, New York.

**Argo, J.J., Dahl, D.W. and Manchanda, R.V.** (2005) 'The influence of a mere social presence in a retail context', *Journal of Consumer Research*, 32 (2), 207–12.

**Arnould, E. and Price, L.** (1993) 'River magic: extraordinary experience and the extended service encounter', *Journal of Consumer Research*, 20 (1), 24–45.

**Athiyaman, A.** (1997) 'Linking student satisfaction and service quality perceptions: the case of university education', *European Journal of Marketing*, 31 (7), 528–40.

**Bachelder, B.** (2000) 'The art of e-biz – the good and not good enough of web site design', *Information Week*, 14, 42–6.

**Bagozzi, R.P. and Pieters, R.** (1998) 'Goal-directed emotions', *Cognition & Emotion*, 12 (1), 1–26.

**Bagozzi, R.P., Gopinath, M. and Nyer, P.U.** (1999) 'The role of emotions in marketing', *Journal of the Academy of Marketing Science*, 27 (2), 184–206.

**Bateson, J.E.G.** (1989) *Managing Services Marketing – Text and Readings*, 2nd edn, Dryden Press, Forth Worth, TX.

**Baumgartner, H., Pieters, R. and Bagozzi, R.P.** (2008) 'Future-oriented emotions: conceptualization and behavioral effects', *European Journal of Social Psychology*, 38, 685–96.

**Bitner, M.J.** (1990) 'Evaluating service encounters: the effects of physical surroundings and employee responses', *Journal of Marketing*, 54 (2), 69–82.

**Booms, B.H. and Bitner, M.J.** (1981) 'Marketing strategies and organisation structures for service firms', in J. Donnelly and W.R. George (eds), *Marketing of Services*, American Marketing Association, Chicago, IL.

**Bosmans, A.** (2006) 'Scents and sensibility: when do (in)congruent ambient scents influence product evaluations?', *Journal of Marketing*, 70 (3), 32–43.

**Chase, R.B. and Dasu, S.** (2001) 'Want to perfect your company's service? Use behavioral science', *Harvard Business Review*, 79 (6), 78–84.

**Chatman, S.B.** (1978) *Story and Discourse: Narrative Structure in Fiction and Film*, Cornell University Press, Ithaca, NY.

**Cowley, E., Farrell, C. and Edwardson, M.** (2005) 'The role of affective expectations in memory for a service encounter', *Journal of Business Research*, 58 (10), 1419–25.

**Csikszentmihalyi, M.** (1975) *Beyond Boredom and Anxiety: Experiencing Flow in Work and Play*, Jossey-Bass, San Francisco.

**Csikszentmihalyi, M.** (1988) 'The flow experience and its significance for human psychology', in M. Csikszentmihalyi and I.S. Csikszentmihalyi (eds), *Optimal Experience: Psychological Studies of Flow in Consciousness*, Cambridge University Press, Cambridge.

**Csikszentmihalyi, M.** (1990) *Flow: The Psychology of Optimal Experience*, Harper and Row, New York.

**De Chernatony, L. and McDonald, M.** (2003) *Creating Powerful Brands*, Butterworth-Heinemann, Oxford.

**Deighton, J.** (1992) 'The consumption of performance', *Journal of Consumer Research*, 19 (3), 362–72.

**Donovan, R.J. and Rossiter, J.R.** (1982) 'Store atmosphere: an environmental psychology approach', *Journal of Retailing*, 58 (1), 34–57.

**Eicher, J.B. and Roach-Higgins, M.E.** (1993) 'Definition and classification of dress', in R. Barnes and J.B. Eicher (eds), *Dress and Gender: Making and Meaning*, Berg, Oxford, 8–28.

**Eiglier, P. and Langeard, E.** (1987) *Servuction*, McGraw-Hill, New York.

**Elliott, M.T. and Speck, P.S.** (2005) 'Factors that affect attitude toward a retail website', *Journal of Marketing Theory and Practice*, 13 (1), 40–51.

**Eroglu, S.A., Machleit, K. and Barr, T.F.** (2005) 'Perceived retail crowding and shopping satisfaction: the role of shopping values', *Journal of Business Research*, 58 (8), 1146–53.

**Fehr, B. and Russell, J.A.** (1984) 'Concept of emotion viewed from a prototype perspective', *Journal of Experimental Psychology: General*, 113 (3), 464.

**Frijda, N.H.** (1993) 'Moods, emotion episodes, and emotions', in M. Lewis and J.M. Haviland (eds), *Handbook of Emotions*, Guilford Press, New York.

**Gambling Commission** (2009) *Industry Statistics 2008/09*, Gambling Commission, London.

**Goodwin, C.** (1996) 'Moving the drama into the factory: the contribution of metaphors to services research', *European Journal of Marketing*, 30 (9), 13–36.

**Gorn, G.J., Chattopadhyay, A., Yi, T. and Dahl, D.W.** (1997) 'Effects of color as an executional cue in advertising: they're in the shade', *Management Science*, 43 (10), 1387–400.

**Goulding, C.** (1999) 'Heritage, nostalgia, and the "grey" consumer', *The Journal of Marketing Practice: Applied Marketing Science*, 5 (6/7/8), 177–99.

**Grimes, A. and Doole, I.** (1998) 'Exploring the relationships between colour and international branding: a cross cultural comparison of the UK and Taiwan', *Journal of Marketing Management*, 14 (7), 799–817.

**Grove, S.J., Fisk, R.P. and Bitner, M.J.** (1992) 'Dramatizing the service experience: a managerial approach', in T.A. Swartz, D.E. Bowen and S.W. Brown (eds), *Advances in Services Marketing and Management*, vol. 1, JAI Press, Greenwich, CT.

**Gummesson, E.** (1997) 'Relationship marketing as a paradigm shift: some conclusions from the 30R approach', *Management Decision*, 35 (4), 267–72.

**Gupta, S. and Vajic, M.** (2000) 'The contextual and dialectical nature of experiences', in J.A. Fitzsimmons and M.J. Fitzsimmons (eds), *New Service Development; Creating Memorable Experiences*, Sage, Thousand Oaks, CA.

**Harrell, G.D., Hutt, M.D. and Anderson, J.C.** (1980) 'Path analysis of buyer behavior under conditions of crowding', *Journal of Marketing Research*, 17 (2), 45–51.

**Harris, K., Harris, R. and Baron, S.** (2001) 'Customer participation in retail service: lessons from Brecht', *International Journal of Retail and Distribution Management*, 29 (8), 359–69.

**Harris, R., Harris, K. and Baron, S.** (2003) 'Theatrical service experiences: dramatic script development with employees', *International Journal of Service Industry Management*, 14 (2), 184–99.

**Hirschman, E.C. and Holbrook, M.B.** (1982) 'Hedonic consumption: emerging concepts, methods and propositions', *Journal of Marketing*, 46 (3), 92–101.

**Hoffman, D.L. and Novak, T.P.** (1996) 'Marketing in hypermedia computer-mediated environments: conceptual foundations', *Journal of Marketing*, 60 (3), 50–68.

**Holbrook, M.B.** (2006) 'Consumption experience, customer value, and subjective personal introspection: an illustrative photographic essay', *Journal of Business Research*, 59 (6), 714–25.

**Holbrook, M.B. and Hirschman, E.C.** (1982) 'The experiential aspects of consumption: consumer fantasies, feelings and fun', *Journal of Consumer Research*, 9 (2), 132–40.

**Homer, P.M.** (2006) 'Relationships among ad-induced affect, beliefs, and attitudes: another look', *Journal of Advertising*, 35 (1), 35–5.

**Hooper, D., Coughlan, J. and Mullen, M.R.** (2013) 'The servicescape as an antecedent to service quality and behavioral intentions', *Journal of Services Marketing*, 27 (4).

**Izard, C.E.** (1997) 'Emotions and facial expressions: a perspective from differential emotions theory', in J.A. Russell and J.M. Fernandez-Dols (eds), *The Psychology of Facial Expression*, Cambridge University Press, New York.

**Kang, J. and Hillery, J.** (1998) 'Older salespeople's role in retail encounters', *Journal of Personal Selling and Sales Management*, 18 (4), 39–53.

**Keynote** (2011) *Betting & Gaming Market Report 2011*, London, Keynote.

**Kim, J.H. and Runyan, R.** (2011) 'Where did all the benches go? The effects of mall kiosks on perceived retail crowding', *International Journal of Retail & Distribution Management*, 39 (2), 130–143.

**Kim, W. and Ok, C.** (2010) 'Customer orientation of service employees and rapport: influences on service-outcome variables in full-service restaurants', *Journal of Hospitality & Tourism Research*, 34 (1), 34–55.

**Koenig-Lewis, N. and Palmer, A.** (2008) 'Experiential values over time – a comparison of measures of satisfaction and emotion', *Journal of Marketing Management*, 24 (1), 69–85.

**Liljander, V. and Bergenwall, M.** (2002) *Consumption-Based Emotional Responses Related to Satisfaction*, Occasional Paper, Swedish School of Economics and Business Administration, Department of Marketing.

**Liljander, V. and Strandvik, T.** (1997) 'Emotions in service satisfaction', *International Journal of Service Industry Management*, 8 (2), 148–69.

**Machleit, K.A., Eroglu, S.A. and Mantel, S.P.** (2000) 'Perceived retail crowding and shopping satisfaction: what modifies this relationship?', *Journal of Consumer Psychology*, 9 (1), 29–42.

**Mano, H. and Oliver, R.L.** (1993) 'Assessing the dimensionality and structure of the consumption experience: evaluation, feeling, and satisfaction', *Journal of Consumer Research*, 20 (3), 451–66.

**Mattila, A.S. and Wirtz, J.** (2008) 'The role of store environmental stimulation and social factors on impulse purchasing', *Journal of Services Marketing*, 22 (7), 562–67.

**Mattila, A. and Wirtz, J.** (2000) 'The impact of preconsumption affect on service satisfaction', *Psychology & Marketing*, 17 (7), 587–605.

**McMillan, S.J. and Hwang, J.S.** (2002) 'Measures of perceived interactivity: an exploration of the role of direction of communication, user control, and time in shaping perceptions of interactivity', *Journal of Advertising*, 31 (3), 29–42.

**Mehrabian, A. and Russell, J.A.** (1974) 'A verbal measure of information rate for studies in environmental psychology', *Environment and Behavior*, 6, 233–52.

**National Equality Panel** (2010) *An Anatomy of Economic Inequality in the UK*, London, Government Equalities Office.

**Novak, T.P., Hoffman, D.L. and Yung, Y.F.** (2000) 'Measuring the customer experience in online environments: a structural modeling approach', *Marketing Science*, 19 (1), 22–42.

**Oliver, R.L.** (1997) *Satisfaction: A Behavioural Perspective on the Consumer*, McGraw-Hill, London.

**Page, C. and Lepkowska-White, E.** (2002) 'Web equity: a framework for building consumer value in online companies', *Journal of Consumer Marketing*, 19 (3), 231–48.

**Pan, Y. and Siemens, J.C.** (2011) 'The differential effects of retail density: an investigation of goods versus service settings', *Journal of Business Research*, 64 (2), 105–12.

**Park, C.H. and Kim, Y.G.** (2003) 'A framework of dynamic CRM: linking marketing with information strategy', *Business Process Management Journal*, 9 (5), 652–71.

**Perugini, M. and Bagozzi, R.P.** (2001) 'The role of desires and anticipated emotions in goal-directed behaviours: broadening and deepening the theory of planned behaviour', *British Journal of Social Psychology*, 40 (1), 79–98.

**Perugini, M. and Conner, M.** (2000) 'Predicting and understanding behavioral volitions: the interplay between goals and behaviors', *European Journal of Social Psychology*, 30 (5), 705–31.

**Pine, B.J. and Gilmore, J.H.** (1998) 'Welcome to the experience economy', *Harvard Business Review*, 76 (4), 97–105.

**Pine, B.J. and Gilmore, J.H.** (1999) *The Experience Economy*, Harvard Business School Press, Boston, MA.

**Price, L., Arnold, E. and Tierney, P.** (1995) 'Going to extremes: managing service experiences and assessing provider performance', *Journal of Marketing*, 59 (2), 83–97.

**Reisman, D. (2012)** *The Economics of Alfred Marshall, London, Routledge.*

**Rollo, A.S., Grayson, L. and McNeill, S.** (2009) 'Using atmospheric elements in service retailing: understanding the bar environment', *Journal of Service Marketing*, 23 (7), 517–27.

**Rose, G.M. and Straub, D.W.** (2001) 'The effect of download time on consumer attitude toward the e-service retailer', *e-Service Journal*, 1 (1), 55–76.

**Russell, J.A.** (1980) 'A circumplex model of affect', *Journal of Personality and Social Psychology*, 39 (6), 1161–78.

**Shao, C.Y., Baker, J.A. and Wagner, J.** (2004) 'The effects of appropriateness of service contact personnel dress on customer expectations of service quality and purchase intention: the moderating influences of involvement and gender', *Journal of Business Research*, 57 (10), 1164–76.

**Sharma, A. and Stafford, T.F.** (2000) 'The effect of retail atmospherics on customers' perceptions of salespeople and customer persuasion: an empirical investigation', *Journal of Business Research*, 49 (2), 183–91.

**Shih, C.F.E.** (1998) 'Conceptualizing consumer experiences in cyberspace', *European Journal of Marketing*, 32 (7/8), 655–63.

**Silver, N.C. and Ferrante, R.** (1995) 'Sex differences in color preferences among an elderly sample', *Perceptual and Motor Skills*, 80 (3), 920–2.

**Smith, A. and Bolton, R.** (2002) 'The effect of customers' emotional response to service failures on their recovery effort evaluations and satisfaction judgements', *Journal of the Academy of Marketing Science*, 30 (1), 5–23.

**Söderlund, M.** (2011) 'Other customers in the retail environment and their impact on the customer's evaluations of the retailer', *Journal of Retailing and Consumer Services*, 18 (3), 174–82.

**Söderlund, M. and Julander, C.R.** (2009) 'Physical attractiveness of the service worker in the moment of truth and its effects on customer satisfaction', *Journal of Retailing and Consumer Services*, 16 (3), 216–26.

**Solomon, M.R., Surprenant, C., Czepiel, J.A. and Gutman, E.G.** (1985) 'A role theory perspective on dyadic interactions: the service encounter', *Journal of Marketing*, 49 (1), 99–111.

**Trevino, L. and Webster, J.** (1992) 'Flow in computer-mediated communication', *Communication Research*, 19 (5), 539–47.

**Urry, J.** (2002) *The Tourist Gaze*, 2nd edn, Sage, London.

**Van De Vliert, E. and Van Yperen, N.-W.** (1996) 'Why cross-national differences in role overload? Don't overlook ambient temperature', *Academy of Management Journal*, 39 (4), 986–1004.

**Varela-Neira, C., Vázquez-Casielles, R. and Iglesias-Argüelles, V.** (2008) 'The influence of emotions on customer's cognitive evaluations and satisfaction in a service failure and recovery context', *The Service Industries Journal*, 28 (4), 497–512.

**Wakefield, K.L. and Blodgett, J.G.** (1994) 'The importance of servicescapes in leisure service settings', *Journal of Services Marketing*, 8 (3), 66–76.

**Warnaby, G. and Davies, B.J.J.** (1997) 'Cities as service factories? Using the servuction system for marketing cities as shopping destinations', *International Journal of Retail & Distribution Management*, 25 (6–7), 204–10.

**Westbrook, R.A. and Oliver, R.L.** (1991) 'The dimensionality of consumption emotion patterns and consumer satisfaction', *Journal of Consumer Research*, 18 (1), 84–91.

**White, C. and Scandale, S.** (2005) 'The role of emotions in destination visitation intentions: a cross cultural perspective', *Journal of Hospitality and Tourism Management*, 12 (1), 168–78.

**Wilson, T.D. and Klaaren, K.J.** (1992) ' "Expectation whirls me round": the role of affective expectations on affective experiences', in M.S. Clark (ed.), *Review of Personality and Social Psychology: Emotion and Social behavior*, vol. 14, Sage, Newbury Park, CA.

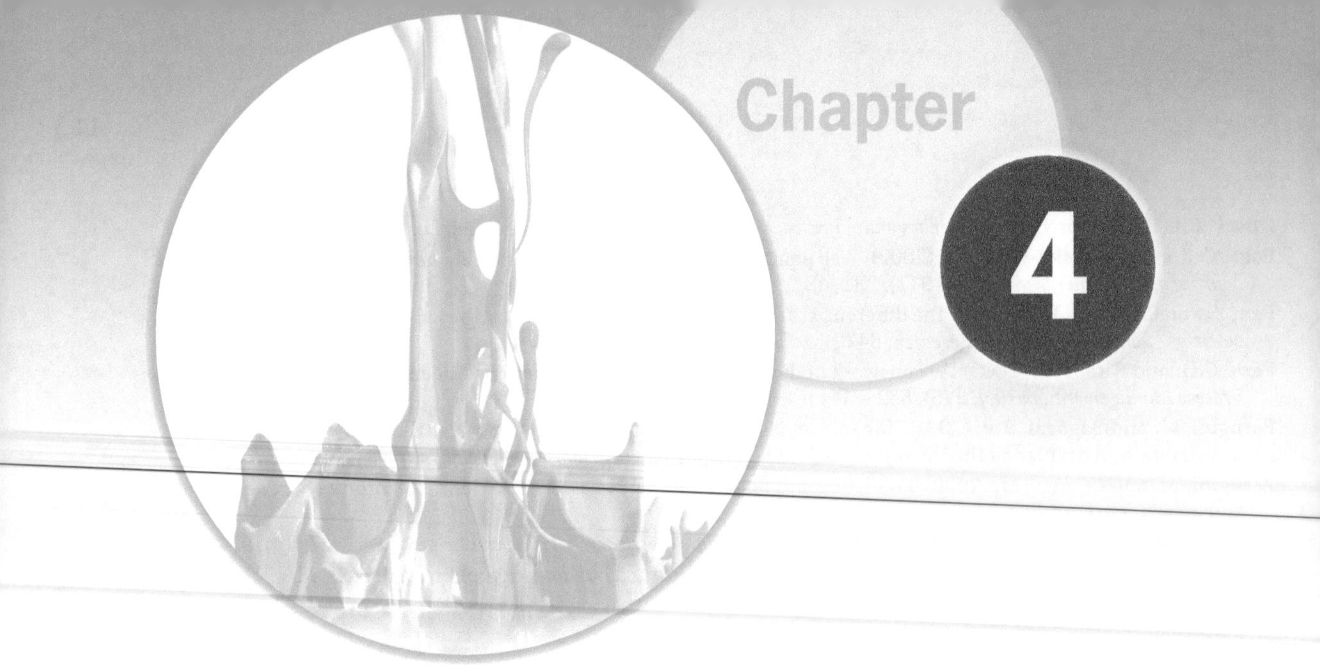


# Making services accessible to consumers

*We take coffee shops for granted, and find them in most towns. But stop and think about all the decisions that had to be made by the owners of a chain of coffee shops to make its service accessible to you, just in the place that you want it, and just at the time that you want a cup of coffee. Where should the coffee shop be located? What hours should they open? Who should be involved in the task of bringing coffee shops to towns throughout the country? This chapter explores further the concept of inseparability by looking at how accessibility to a service becomes a key design feature.*

## Learning objectives

After reading this chapter, you should understand:

- The effects of inseparability on decisions about the time and place of the service production/consumption process
- Accessibility as a key foundation of value for customers
- Methods used to design accessibility into the service offer
- Models to assist service location decisions
- The role of service intermediaries as co-producers of a service
- Types of service intermediary, including agents and franchisees
- Methods used to select, motivate and monitor service intermediaries

## 4.1 Introduction

Consider the following successful service innovations:

- First Direct telephone banking from home;
- McDonald's out-of-town 'drive through' restaurants;
- Domino's Pizzas home delivery service.

In each case, success has been based on making an existing service more readily accessible to customers. So bank customers no longer need to visit their local branch to carry out many types of transactions, and they can do it at any time of day rather than just during bank branch opening hours; somebody looking for a Big Mac need no longer leave their car; and a pizza eater need not even leave home.

Achieving these high levels of accessibility calls for a strategy that is capable of achieving desired levels within a specified time period. For the pizza company to be able to put a pizza in anybody's home requires an effort that is probably not achievable by the company acting alone. It may therefore seek a variety of arrangements, such as franchising, with local companies who are able to provide widespread accessibility faster and more cost-effectively than it could itself.

This chapter can be thought of as dealing with the 'P' for place of the extended marketing mix – the concept of accessibility builds on this. Think back to the discussion in Chapter 1 on 'service dominant logic' and you will recall the argument that services can be crucial for creating 'value in use'. Accessibility is a key aspect of creating value in use. Products in a shop that is inconveniently located for customers, or which has limited opening hours, are of less value than the same products made available just at the time and place that the customer wants them.

The inseparability of services makes the task of passing on service benefits much more complex than is the case with manufactured goods. Inseparability implies that services are consumed at the point of production; in other words, a service cannot be produced by one person in one place and handled by other people to make it available to customers in other places. A service cannot therefore usually be produced where costs are lowest and sold where demand is greatest – customer accessibility must be designed into the service production system.

In this chapter, strategies to make services accessible to customers will be analysed by focusing on four important, but related, issues:

- When and where is the service to be made available to the consumer?
- What is the role of intermediaries in the process of service delivery?
- How are intermediaries selected, motivated and monitored?

There are close links between this chapter and the Chapter 2 covering service systems. Many service providers have found that a very cost-effective way of making services available anywhere and at any time is through the Internet. In the case of many 'pure' services, the Internet has become a very important aspect of accessibility strategy, which is explored further in this chapter.

## 4.2 *When* should the service be made accessible?

We have seen that the inseparability of services generally requires producer and consumer to meet in order that service benefits can be simultaneously produced and consumed. Unfortunately, a problem often occurs when the consumer wants to consume a service at a time when the producer is unable or unwilling to produce it. The perishability of services makes this a particular problem because the service producer does not have the goods manufacturer's ability to make the product at a time of its choice, then make it available when consumers want to buy it. Services must be produced 'live' when the consumer requires them. Time of availability can add value to a service (Dacko, 2012).

What are the factors that inhibit a service provider's ability or willingness to move towards continuous service delivery, in other words, to make services accessible to consumers at all times?

- Demand from consumers for a service may not be uniform throughout the day, week or year and, at quiet times, the limited level of demand may not cover the service provider's cost of providing the service.
- Costs of production may be higher at some times than others; for example, staff may only be induced to work in the evenings or at holiday periods if they are paid at a higher rate.
- In some service processes with high fixed costs, it may not be easy to downsize the level of resources used in response to relatively low levels of demand. As an example, an airport needs a very high minimum level of staff to remain open, including minimum levels of staffing at check-in, security, passport control etc., regardless of the number of passengers handled.
- Government legislation may prevent a service being accessible at a time when consumers prefer, and when producers are able and willing to provide it. Many countries, for example, restrict the ability of retailers and other service businesses to open on Sundays.

Against these inhibitors, there are many reasons why services companies in many sectors have been keen to move towards much greater accessibility by time:

- Consumers' expectations have been rising, and a 'snowball' effect occurs where consumers who experience extended access hours for one category of service come to expect extended hours of access for other services. If my supermarket can stay open late into the evening, why can't my bank? Or my public library service?
- Service companies with high levels of investment in fixed infrastructure (e.g. buildings and equipment) have often been keen to offer extended access in order to spread their fixed costs over a greater volume of customers. A shop that has invested millions of pounds in a new store may be keen to increase the utilization of that store by opening on Sundays and later into the evenings.
- For individual companies, extended access may be a competitive response to actions by competitors. If other shops in an area are opening on Sundays, a shop that remains closed may lose part of its business to competitors.

Accessibility to service can be an important point of differentiation between service providers, and in some circumstances can allow a company to charge a price premium. In retailing, supermarkets with high fixed costs may not be able to justify opening throughout the night, despite the economies of scale present when they are open during the daytime. Their competitive advantage is therefore based on low prices during opening hours that are convenient for the mass market. On the other hand, small convenience retailers have lower fixed costs, but the volume of demand during the night may be sufficient to pay the running costs of the small store, especially if customers are prepared to pay a premium price for the convenience of all-night access.

Services organizations use a number of methods to improve time accessibility:

- Where demand is uneven during the day, week or year, the development of an appropriate cost structure can allow the company to operate profitably during periods of low demand. Sometimes this can involve renegotiating agreements with employees over staffing levels or using technology to change the cost base (see below).
- A limited format of a service process can be offered during quiet periods; for example, a bank may offer a lobby service that customers can use to draw cash, pay in cheques and check balances at any time of day, but restrict a full-service staffed branch to times of day when demand is greatest.
- Technology can be used to lower the cost of providing service during quiet periods. The cost to banks of providing 24-hour Internet access can be not much more than the cost of providing the service only during normal working hours. Some retailers have developed self-service shops in which customers during quiet hours can select the most popular items from a machine located outside the shop.
- It was noted above that greater accessibility can provide an opportunity for service providers to charge a premium price, thereby offsetting higher costs of operation.
- Customers can often be segmented according to their flexibility with respect to the timing of service consumption. Airlines and train operators offer a range of tickets, from low-priced tickets, which are only available in advance and give access to a service only at a specific time, through to full-priced tickets that allow access to service at any time and at short notice.

Extended availability of services raises issues of social concern, and many countries have been debating whether restrictions on trading should be relaxed. Some see an inevitable process of market forces leading to ever-longer availability of services, fuelled by a process of spiralling consumers' expectations. Others have argued that wider time access to services favours wealthy consumers at the expense of an army of low-paid service-sector workers. We will return to the subject of stress among front-line employees required to work unsocial hours in Chapter 10.

## In practice: Open all hours?

Figure 4.1 Extending opening hours at Tesco

For many services providers, a point of competitive differentiation is based on the times that a service is available to customers. When all the shops in town are closed, a shop with extended opening hours, or even round-the-clock opening, will have a competitive advantage. There has been a gradual tendency in most cultures for consumers to expect greater access to services, with even some traditionally conservative professional service providers, such as solicitors and dentists, offering late-night opening. Many professional services providers have even forsaken their traditional weekend closing, providing service at weekends. Legislation that has prevented the provision of services in the evenings or on Sundays remains in place in some European countries, but there has been a general tendency to liberalize restrictions on the hours during which services may be provided. How does a service provider determine whether it is profitable to extend its hours of availability to customers? In the UK, the easing of restrictions on opening hours for shops and pubs has been followed by extension of firms' opening hours, only to be followed by cutbacks by some service providers when the expected numbers of shoppers or drinkers in the middle of the night failed to be sufficient to cover the additional costs of extended opening hours.

## 4.3 *To whom* should the service be made accessible?

In Chapter 6, we will consider the issue of segmentation and the methods that companies use to target individuals, or categories of individuals. The basic principles of segmentation and targeting are similar for goods and services companies. However, services companies face an additional practical problem that they may wish to specifically exclude access for some individuals. The main problem here is that service consumers come into the 'production factory' and service providers often wish to exclude some 'inputs' (consumers) because they will be too costly to process, or may be disruptive to other co-consumers. The goods manufacturer does not generally face this problem. Its customers do not normally go into the factory, and a manufacturer cannot normally prevent the onward sale of goods to 'bad' consumers. In any case, the consequences of a 'bad' consumer are not likely to be great for the manufacturer (there are exceptions; for example, the Burberry brand of clothing is reported to be have been harmed when it was 'adopted' by 'chavs' and other downmarket groups).

There are many examples of types of consumer that services organizations may prefer not to serve, because they are considered likely to be difficult to process:

- Schools and universities have been accused of being reluctant to take academically weak students because of the extra remedial support they may require. Weak students may also disrupt student-to-student interaction in class.
- Banks decline applications from individuals whose characteristics suggest that they may be a bad credit risk, and likely to occupy a disproportionate amount of management time.
- Disabled consumers often cost more to process than able-bodied consumers, because of the requirement to redesign buildings and vehicles etc. The level of additional demand from disabled consumers may not be sufficient to justify investment in suitable facilities.

In each of these cases, services providers must recognize wider social pressures to provide access to groups who may be considered to be socially disdvantaged. What may be seen initially as antisocial behaviour by service providers is likely, sooner or later, to be translated into government legislation requiring service providers to address these wider social concerns. In short, if the market does not provide access to disadvantaged groups, legislation is likely to intervene to provide it. So, throughout the EU, governments have developed policies to ensure that children or students from disadvantaged socio-economic groups are not denied access to schools or universities. Denying a bank account to an individual denies that individual the opportunity of benefiting from online services that are only available to individuals with a bank account. In the UK, the government has put pressure on banks to offer a basic bank account to individuals who would not normally qualify for full banking facilities. In the case of access to disabled groups, the UK Disability Discrimination Act (based on an EU directive) is progressively requiring services companies to make reasonable adaptations to their service processes to accommodate disabled customers. Case law is being developed as to what are reasonable measures that a company should take in order to provide access. As the Act is implemented, specific requirements on services providers are increasing; for example, all new buses must be capable of access by wheelchairs.

Some services providers have taken an early cue from social pressures, and learned how to handle disadvantaged groups ahead of legislation. This experience has sometimes put them at a competitive advantage when the sector as a whole has been required to adopt wider access policies. Those universities that had developed outreach projects to disadvantaged communities found government pressure for wider access relatively easy to manage, compared with those universities that had been set in their traditional ways. However, in markets where cost leadership is crucial to gaining competitive advantage, government pressure, and indeed legislation, may be tested to the limit, and companies may continue to avoid their obligations as far as possible. The airline Ryanair, which has built a successful business model based on ruthlessly controlling costs, has faced a legal challenge in respect of its provision for disabled customers. It has argued that disabled customers should pay for the use of wheelchairs, in much the same way as its able-bodied customers pay for additional services such as baggage and in-flight food. Is the airline's low-cost model and charging for use of wheelchairs compatible with the Disability Discrimination Act?

### Thinking around the subject: Welcome to the bank (if you are rich)

'Sorry, you are too poor to come into this bank branch' was the message many people read into the actions of HSBC when, in April 2007, it converted its branch at Canford Cliffs near Poole, UK into a centre for 'Premier Banking' customers. To qualify, Premier customers were required to have savings of at least £50,000, or a mortgage of £200,000, or a salary of £75,000 a year. Customers who did not meet these criteria had to travel a mile to the nearest HSBC branch where full-service facilities were available to them.

Local community groups expressed dismay at the bank's action, with the local Member of Parliament describing the bank as moving towards social exclusion, rather than financial inclusion, which was high on the government's policy agenda. The local Citizens Advice Bureau described the bank as providing second-class access for people on moderate incomes. The elderly and those on low incomes would be disadvantaged most by the need to travel to a bank. Despite great developments in online access to banking facilities, these groups are the least likely to have Internet access.

Was the bank being socially irresponsible by denying access to the branch to all except the financially well-heeled? Are the bank's actions compatible with its stated agenda for corporate social responsibility? Or is its decision based on sound principles of segmentation and targeting? With Canford Cliffs having among the highest household incomes and property prices in the United Kingdom, is it not just good business sense that the bank provides enhanced facilities for customers of high net worth? Other banks have opened offices specifically for such customers, but did HSBC inflame the social exclusion debate by restricting a branch that was previously accessible to all, rather than building a completely new facility? Instead of complaining about HSBC's actions, shouldn't UK bank customers be celebrating the fact that they have one of the best networks of bank branches in the world, especially compared to many emerging economies, as the absence of bank braches in areas where poor people live can cause much greater social problems?

## 4.4 Where should the service be made accessible?

In this section, choices facing services providers about the place at which a service is to be provided are considered. First, it should be repeated that because consumers of services are usually involved as co-creators of the service, the time and place at which they are expected to take part in this process becomes an important criterion for evaluation. Production location decisions therefore cannot be taken in isolation from an analysis of customers' preferred place of consumption. While services organizations often have a desire to centralize production in order to achieve economies of scale, consumers usually seek local access to services. Service location decisions therefore involve a trade-off between the needs and flexibility of the producer on the one hand and the needs and flexibility of the consumer on the other. This is in contrast to goods manufacturers, who can manufacture goods in one location where production is most economic, then ship the goods to customers where their goods are most valued.

For some services, production is very inflexible with respect to location, resulting in production-led location decisions. In other cases, production techniques may allow much greater flexibility, and location decisions are constrained by the inflexibility of consumers to travel to a service outlet, because of either their physical inability or merely their unwillingness. In the case of some intangible, low-contact services, it is possible to separate production from consumption, using some of the methods described later in this chapter. In such cases, services can be produced in the most economic location and made available wherever customers are located.

### 4.4.1 Flexibility in production

The extreme case of inflexibility in production is provided by services where the whole purpose of the service is to be at one unique location – for example, tourism-related services based on a unique historic site by their very nature cannot be moved. A further group of services are locationally inflexible because they can only sensibly be produced in large-scale centralized production facilities. This can be the case where the necessary supporting equipment is expensive and offers opportunities for significant economies of scale. Where this equipment is also highly immobile, customers must come to a limited number of central service points to receive service. This is true with much of the specialized and expensive equipment needed for complex medical care, such as trauma care, which tends to be provided at a small number of central locations. In cases where the equipment offers less scope for economies of scale and is more easily transported, service production can be distributed more widely. This explains why breast-screening services are frequently taken to users, while users must travel to trauma centres.

Some services organizations operate a '**hub and spoke**' system where the benefits of large-scale, centralized production of specialized services is combined with locally accessible outlets. In the banking sector, specialized business and investment services can often only be competitive if they are produced in units that have a high enough critical mass to support the payment of experts in that field of activity. Banks have accordingly developed specialized business advisory centres located in a few key locations. Their services are subsequently made available through local branches by a combination of telephone, mail, computer link or a personal visit from the centrally based expert. Similarly, much of the processing work involved in producing a service can be transferred to an efficient regional centre, leaving local outlets to act as an interface with customers. In this way, many banks have transferred mortgage processing from local branches, leaving these to act as little more than sales outlets. The principal components of a hub and spoke system are illustrated in Figure 4.2.

As well as internal economies of scale, external economies of scale are sometimes an important influence on a firm's location decisions. The first kind of external economies occur where a location close to other service producers reduces a firm's input costs. For this reason, many diverse financial services companies have congregated in the City of London. A ship-broking agency may find significant benefits from being located within walking distance of Lloyd's insurance market and banks for sources of finance. Similarly, clusters of advertising agencies, graphic designers, typographers and typesetters can be found to maximize benefits from internal trading, to the benefit of suppliers and customers alike. However, the importance of such external economies of scale to location decisions is declining as technological developments allow production to be separated from consumption. In both of the above examples, service benefits can now be delivered electronically, reducing the need for direct interaction, although the importance of social contact between companies remains.

A second source of external economies of scale can result from locating in a recognized local marketplace, as occurs where jewellers or real estate agents locate in one neighbourhood of a town.

Figure 4.2 A hub and spoke system of service production and delivery. Much of the processing of a service can often be undertaken in a central processing facility, and then made available locally to customers through branch networks. For highly intangible services, many customers have opted to deal directly with the central processing centre by telephone, Internet or mail, rather than accessing the service through the branch network.

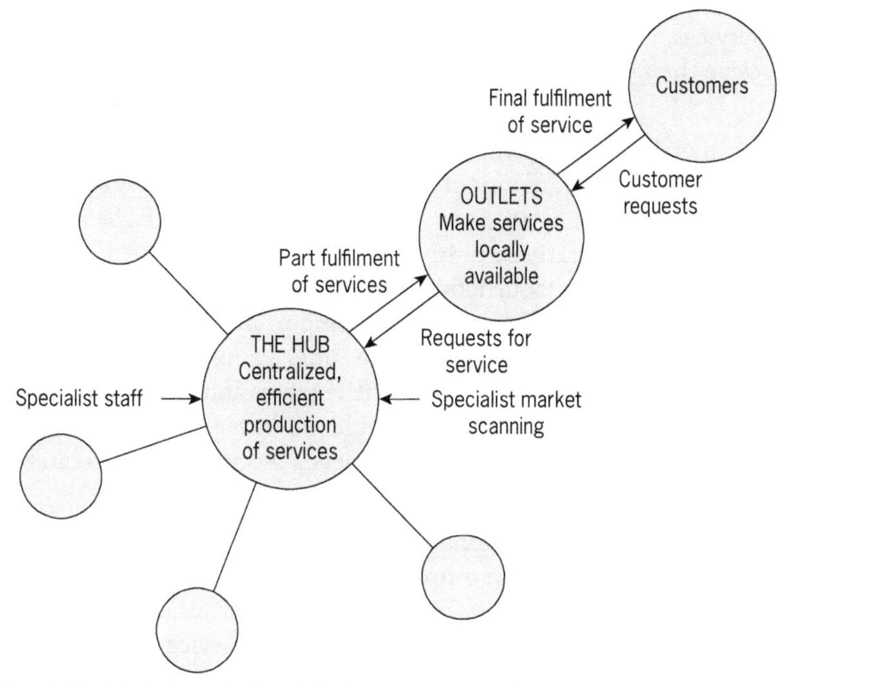


Because the existence of the marketplace is widely recognized, any firm locating within it will need to spend less on promotion to attract potential customers to its location.

Production considerations are likely to be a less important influence on location decisions where economies of scale are not significant. In a market environment, competitive advantage will be gained by maximizing availability through more widespread distribution outlets, rather than any cost saving through centralization. To illustrate this, hairdressing offers fairly limited scope for economies of scale and competitive advantage is gained by providing small outlets that are easily accessible to customers.

Finally, the competitiveness of the market environment can affect the locational flexibility of service producers. A service producer that is able to be flexible in its location decisions may nevertheless be unwilling to be flexible if its customers have little choice of supplier. For this reason, many government-provided services (e.g. tax offices) have often been provided through centralized administrative offices, which may be inconveniently located for most users.

### 4.4.2 Flexibility in consumption

Decisions on service location are also influenced by the extent to which consumers are willing or able to be flexible in where they consume a service. Inflexibility on the part of consumers can arise for a number of reasons:

- Where a service is to be performed on a customer's possessions, those possessions may themselves be immovable, requiring the supplier to come to the customer (e.g. building repairs).

- Sometimes, the customer may also be physically immobile (e.g. physically disabled users of healthcare services).
- For impulse purchases, or services where there are many competitive alternatives, customers are unlikely to be willing to travel far to seek out a service.
- For specialist services, customers may show more willingness to be flexible in where they are prepared to receive the service, compared to routine purchases that they would be unwilling to travel for.

In reality, most consumers' decisions involve a trade-off between the price of a service, the quality of delivery at a particular location, the amount of choice available and the cost to the consumer in terms of time and money involved in gaining access to a service. For the buyer of a few odd items of groceries, price and choice are likely to be relatively unimportant compared to ease of access – hence the continued existence of many small neighbourhood shops. For a consumer seeking to purchase the week's groceries, price and selection may become much more important relative to ease of access. For more specialized services, such as the purchase of expensive audio equipment, consumers may be willing to travel longer distances to a retailer who offers competitive prices and/or a wide selection of equipment.

It follows therefore that access strategies should be based on an identification of market segments made up of users with similar accessibility needs. Access strategies can then be developed that meet the needs of each segment:

- Age frequently defines segments in terms of the level of access sought. For many elderly users of personal care services, there is sometimes an unwillingness or inability to leave the home, making home availability of a service a sought attribute. For other groups, such as older teenagers, the very act of getting away from home to receive a service may be attractive. This could explain continuing interest in going out to see a film at a cinema in the face of the competing alternatives provided by video rental services and satellite television services.
- Segmentation on the basis of an individual's economic status can be seen in the willingness of more affluent segments to pay premium prices in order to consume a service at a point and time that is convenient to themselves rather than the service provider. Evidence of this is provided by home delivery food services which typically target groups with higher disposable incomes.
- Psychographic segmentation can be seen in the way groups of people seek out services that satisfy their lifestyle needs. As an example, some segments of the population are prepared to travel long distances to a restaurant whose design and ambience appeal to them.
- The cultural background of some individuals can predispose them to seek a particular kind of accessibility. This can be seen in the reluctance of some groups to become involved in service delivery methods that remove regular personal contact with the service provider. Insurance companies that collect premiums from the homes of customers may give reassurance to some segments who have been brought up to distrust impersonal organizations, whereas telephone banking or annual payment by post may satisfy the needs of other segments.
- Access strategies can be based on the type of benefit that users seek from a service. As an example, customers are often prepared to travel a considerable distance to a restaurant for a celebration meal, but would expect it to be easily accessible for a lunchtime snack.
- High-frequency users of a service may place a higher premium on easy accessibility than casual users.
- In the case of business-to-business services, the level of access to a service can directly affect the customer's operating costs. A computer repair company that makes its services available at buyers' offices avoids the costs that the latter would incur if it had to perform part of the service – delivery and collection – itself.

For some services, the location of the service delivery point is the most important means of attracting new business. This can be true for low-value services for which consumers show little willingness to pre-plan their purchase or to go out of their way to find. Location is also very important in the case of impulse purchases. Petrol filling stations, tea shops in tourist areas and many tourist attractions are typically chosen as a result of a customer encountering the service outlet with no prior planning. It is unlikely for instance that many motorists would follow media advertisements and seek out a petrol station that is located in a back street – a visible location is a vital factor influencing consumers' choice.

### 4.4.3 A typology of service location influences

An attempt to develop a typology of service location decisions is shown in Figure 4.3, where inseparable services are classified in a matrix according to their degree of flexibility in production and consumption.

Services in the upper left quadrant of Figure 4.3 often have little locational flexibility because they are associated with a unique site, for example outstanding scenery or a historical association. Nevertheless, attempts have sometimes been made to replicate the original site at a point that is closer to consumers; for example, the creation of Disneyworld Paris was an attempt to bring the unique features of the American Disneyland to a European audience.

Services in the bottom right quadrant may have little locational flexibility because consumers are unable to move themselves or their possessions. In the case of some fixed assets such as buildings, this inflexibility may be absolute and the service provider must come to the consumer. However, consumers may merely be unwilling to be flexible or it may be part of their expectations that a service should come to them.

It is in the upper right quadrant where trade-offs between convenience for the consumer and for the producer are greatest. Here, both the producer and consumer are potentially flexible, and markets can often be segmented by accessibility preferences, with producers adapting their production methods to the price/convenience preferences of each segment. The retailing sector shows a wide variation from large hypermarkets, which are efficient for the producer but relatively inaccessible to most consumers, through to corner shops, which are more accessible but less efficient. Many consumers are prepared to pay a premium for ease of access, even to have goods delivered to their door.

Where both producer and consumer are inflexible, it may be difficult for any service to take place at all and, where it does, it may be under distress conditions (e.g. hospital emergency admissions).

Figure 4.3 Locational flexibility in production and consumption of inseparable services

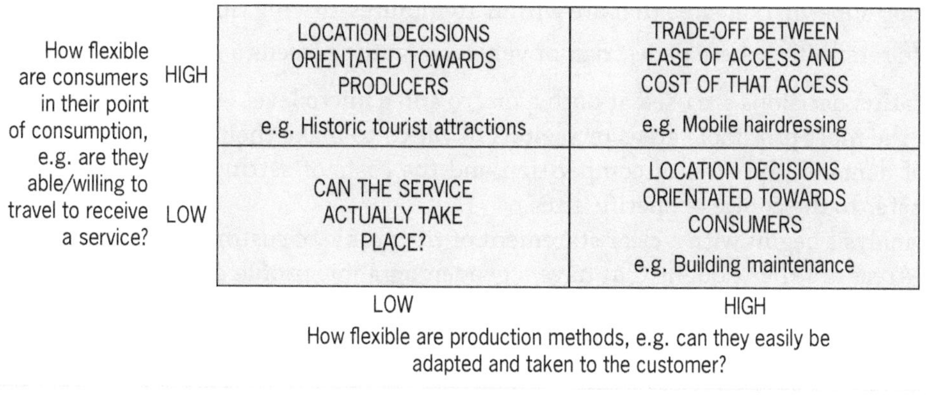

| How flexible are consumers in their point of consumption, e.g. are they able/willing to travel to receive a service? | | | |
|---|---|---|---|
| | HIGH | LOCATION DECISIONS ORIENTATED TOWARDS PRODUCERS<br>e.g. Historic tourist attractions | TRADE-OFF BETWEEN EASE OF ACCESS AND COST OF THAT ACCESS<br>e.g. Mobile hairdressing |
| | LOW | CAN THE SERVICE ACTUALLY TAKE PLACE? | LOCATION DECISIONS ORIENTATED TOWARDS CONSUMERS<br>e.g. Building maintenance |
| | | LOW | HIGH |

How flexible are production methods, e.g. can they easily be adapted and taken to the customer?

With developments in technology, it is sometimes possible to increase the production flexibility (e.g. through mobile operating theatres and tele-medicine).

We will consider later in this chapter the case of services whose production can be separated from their consumption, for example through the use of the Internet.

### 4.4.4 Service location models

Before a network of service outlets can be designed, an organization must clearly define its accessibility objectives. In particular, it must have a clear idea of the volume of business, market share and customer segments that it seeks to attract. Accessibility objectives derive from the positioning strategy for a service, for example a high level of accessibility may only be compatible with business objectives if it is also associated with a premium price position. By contrast, a strategy that involves a low level of accessibility may need to rely heavily on promotion to make potential customers aware of the location of service outlets.

Suppliers of goods and services must consider the location where their products will have greatest value for end-consumers. Many supermarket operators have identified groups of consumers who would prefer to have the services of the shop taken to them, rather than the customer having to go to the shop. The development of the Internet has resulted in home delivery of groceries being a growth area for many supermarket operators, fuelled by rising real household incomes and increasingly busy lifestyles. However, although the cost of using the Internet has fallen, the cost of delivering goods and services to the home has tended to increase, in line with rising wage costs and employment legislation (see Figure 4.4).

Figure 4.4 In affluent countries with relatively low minimum wage rates and flexible labour legislation, home delivery of groceries allows retailers to extend their service offer to customers' front doors. However, patterns of home delivery have varied between countries, for example in France relatively restrictive labour legislation and high employment costs have resulted in fewer grocery delivery vans being seen than in the UK. Instead, 'click and collect' is much more popular, allowing customers to order online and collect their shopping from a 'drive through' counter at the supermarket. (Reproduced with permission of Sainsbury's Supermarkets Ltd)

Examples of accessibility objectives include:

- to provide a hotel location in all towns with a population of 200,000 or more;
- to develop supermarket sites that are within 10 minutes' driving time of at least 50,000 people;
- to locate retail sites where pedestrian or vehicular traffic exceeds a specified threshold.

Service location decisions are used at both a macro and a micro level. At the macro level, organizations seek the most profitable areas or regions in which to make their service available, given the strength of demand, the level of competition and the costs of setting up in an area. Micro-level decisions refer to the choice of specific sites.

Macro analysis begins with a clear statement of the profile of customers that an organization is targeting. Areas are then sought that have a geodemographic profile closely matching that of the target market. At its simplest, indicators can be used to identify potentially attractive locations. A financial services company seeking to set up a national chain of outlets offering home equity loans to elderly people may select the most promising areas on the basis of three pieces of information:

the average value of houses in an area (in the UK, available from the Royal Institution of Chartered Surveyors' regular monitoring report); the percentage of the population who are elderly (available from the national census of population); and the percentage of the population who are owner-occupiers (available from government census or financial regulation data). The attractiveness of a market could be indicated by a weighted index of these factors and subjected to a more detailed analysis of competitor activity in each area. A number of more specialized segmentation methods have been developed that allow organizations to evaluate the profile of an area. An example is Mosaic developed by Experian Ltd, which is based on an analysis of postcodes.

Methods used by an organization to select service outlet locations tend to become more complex as the organization grows. In the early stages of growth, simple rule-of-thumb methods may be acceptable. With further growth, simple indexes and ratios are commonly used. With more service outlets established, an organization can begin to gather sufficient data to analyse the performance of its existing outlets, and from this to develop models that can be used to predict the likely performance of proposed new locations. Regression techniques are used to identify relationships between variables and the level of significance of each variable in explaining the performance of a location. The development of regression models requires considerable initial investment in creating an information base and calibrating the model, but once calibrated they can help to reduce the risk inherent in new service location decisions. It should be noted, however, that models cannot be extrapolated to cover types of decisions that were not envisaged in the model as originally calibrated – for example, a model calibrated for UK site location decisions may be inappropriate for making site location decisions in France.

## Thinking around the subject: Where are the supermarket customers?

The level of risk associated with opening a new supermarket in a fiercely competitive environment can be considerable, yet large retailers claim that they can predict the turnover of a new store opening to within a few percentage points. While a small general retailer may be able to rent shop space on low-risk short-term leases, modern supermarkets require considerable investment in purpose-built facilities that meet customers' ever-increasing needs and expectations. A study by Jones and Mock (1984) of a small American supermarket chain illustrates the value of regression modelling techniques. The supermarket chain being studied had previously relied on rule-of-thumb methods for store location, but, as the size of its new stores increased, so too had the level of risk. As its business grew, it was also able to gather more data to understand the factors that are associated with the success of a particular store.

The regression modelling started by grouping sites according to similarities in their environments. On the basis of socio-economic data, five distinctive environments were identified: city centre, suburbs, old-established shopping streets, the urban fringe and non-metropolitan locations. To find out which of the many variables available were the most relevant for each retailing environment, a series of cross-tabulations between individual key variables was carried out. The relevant variables were then put into a series of stepwise regression models, one for each environment, allowing the identification of the variables that were most effective in explaining sales performance. In the case of suburban stores, variation in store sales was best explained by three measures: the percentage of the neighbourhood that had recently been developed, accessibility of the site by car and the number of competitors located within three blocks. Each increase of 1 per cent in the share of new houses resulted in an additional weekly sales turnover of $120, whereas each nearby competitor reduced sales by $656.

Such models tend to give good results when the business environment is stable. But how useful are they when it is possible for operators to set up rival facilities quickly, changing the assumptions on which the model is based? After all, if one supermarket is running such a model, its competitors are probably doing the same and coming up with similar results. Should they be concentrating on flexibility so that the start-up and close-down costs are reduced?

A number of additional problems in the application of regression modelling techniques can be noted. Because such techniques require large amounts of data for calibration, they are only really suited to high-volume services. It can also be difficult to identify the key variables that cause variation in sales turnover, or to exclude interaction among the variables. Simple linear regression models may not be adequate to explain complex non-linear relationships (for example, one or two nearby competitors for a restaurant may detract from sales at a prospective site; however, a large number of competitors may actually increase sales, if the clustering of restaurants creates a hot spot that attracts diners looking for a choice of restaurants). Finally, regression is essentially an incremental planning technique and is less appropriate for designing networks of service outlets, such as may occur following the merger of two service organizations resulting in a need to rationalize outlets. For the latter, an alternative approach is to use a spatial location-allocation model.

Spatial location-allocation models measure the geographical dispersion of demand and seek to allocate this demand to service outlets on the basis that the probability of a consumer using a particular outlet will be:

- positively related to the attractiveness of that outlet;
- negatively related to its distance from the points where demand is located.

These principles are developed in the following model (Huff, 1966), which has frequently been used as a basis for retail location models, but also has applications in locating leisure facilities, health services, etc.:

$$P_{ij} = \frac{\dfrac{A_j^a}{d_{ij}^b}}{\displaystyle\sum_{n=1}^{i} \frac{A_j^a}{d_{ij}^b}}$$

where $P_{ij}$ = the probability of a trip from origin $i$ to destination $j$
$A_j$ = the attractiveness of destination $j$
$d_{ij}$ = the distance between origin $i$ and destination $j$
$a$ and $b$ = parameters to be empirically determined.

The intuitive appeal and simplicity of such a model can hide a number of conceptual and practical problems in its application and this has triggered considerable research in an attempt to operationalize the basic model. The concept of attractiveness can be difficult to measure. Fishbein (1967) has pointed out that, although an individual may have a belief that a location is attractive, this attractiveness may not be of importance to that particular individual and may consequently not affect their behaviour. Distance itself can be difficult to measure and can be measured objectively (e.g. mileage or average travelling times) or subjectively according to users' perceptions of distance. As an example of research into the distance components of such models, Mayo and Jarvis (1981) showed that subjectively perceived distances increase proportionately less than the objective measured distance.

Spatial location-allocation models are powerful tools that emphasize long-term marketing strategies rather than short-term decisions about opening or closing a specific location. They can be used to evaluate all possible combinations of location possibilities in relation to the geographical pattern of demand. The criteria for selecting the most efficient network of outlets usually involve

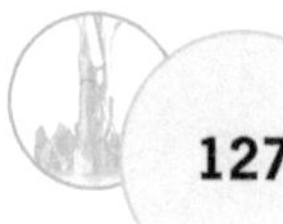


balancing the need to maximize its attractiveness to customers against the service provider's need to minimize the cost of operating the network. Sophisticated computer models allow assumptions about consumer behaviour to be varied – for example, the maximum distance which people are prepared to walk to an outlet. Such models are expensive to develop in view of the data requirements and the need to use specialized staff to develop them. Where the risks associated with a bad location decision are low, it may be more cost-effective to use rule-of-thumb methods than to commission such a model. In the UK, the high cost of acquiring and refurbishing property in the mid-1980s led to spatial location-allocation models becoming very popular as risk reducers. However, the fall in property-related costs – and associated risk levels – that occurred following the recession of 2007 saw some companies reverting to more opportunistic cost-effective rule-of-thumb methods or regression models. In some service sectors, fashionability of formats has sometimes led companies to view a project over a relatively short timescale, facilitated by flexible leases and low start-up/close-down costs. In short, if a new outlet did not work, the close-down costs would not be too prohibitive.

Spatial location-allocation models do, however, continue to be used extensively in both the private and public sectors (e.g. in planning a network of clinics that minimizes patients' travel distances).

## Thinking around the subject: You travel miles to find a restaurant, then half a dozen appear all together

Many towns have local concentrations of services businesses where competitors locate close to each other – café bar districts, and streets lined with restaurants or estate agents are not uncommon. But why should a restaurant apparently choose to expose itself to direct competition from a restaurant next door, rather than locating in a part of town where it could potentially have a unique locational advantage?

In 1929, Harold Hotelling developed a model of spatial competition that helps to explain this phenomenon. He developed his model using a number of assumptions, notably that the product on offer was uniform and customers were evenly dispersed and would buy from the nearest seller. His model assumed a linear dispersion of buyers and sellers – that is, they were all located at some point along a straight line (Hotelling, 1929). Such an assumption may be true of buyers and sellers of ice cream located on a beach (the example that he used), but the principles can apply in more complex spatial environments. Consider first the situation in Figure 4.5(a) where a 1 km length of beach is occupied by two sellers, who are located at the quarter points along the beach. The two sellers would each capture one half of the beach ice-cream market. If buyers were evenly distributed along the beach, then this arrangement would have the advantage of minimizing the amount of walking by buyers.

However, Hotelling demonstrated that this arrangement is not stable. Seller A would have a profit incentive to move towards Seller B, in fact to move almost up to the location of Seller B and thereby capture three-quarters of the ice-cream market (based on the assumption that buyers would walk to their nearest seller). Likewise, Seller B would be tempted to move towards Seller A. They would eventually find that the only sustainable location is the centre of the beach (Figure 4.5b). Each seller still gets one half of the market (the same as in Figure 4.5a), but the average distance buyers have to walk is now double what it was when the sellers were located at the quarter points.

Hotelling noted that, if buyers were not evenly distributed along the beach, the tendency of the ice-cream sellers would be to locate at the median point, where half of the customers are to the west of that point and half are

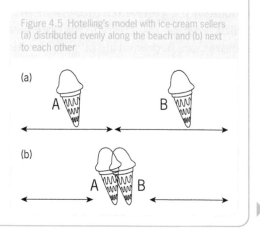

Figure 4.5 Hotelling's model with ice-cream sellers (a) distributed evenly along the beach and (b) next to each other

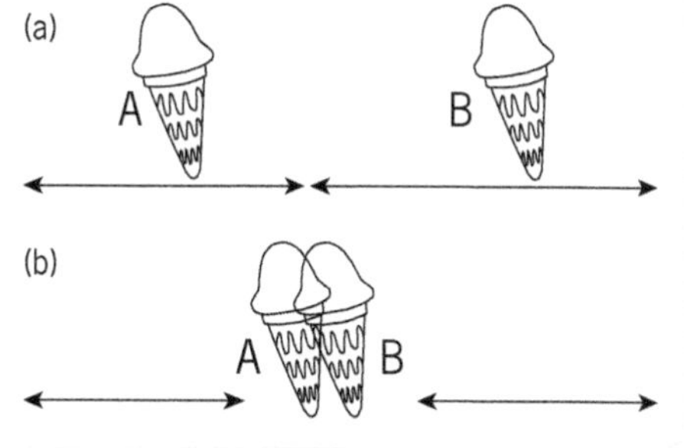

to the east of it. A number of attempts have subsequently been made to relax Hotelling's assumption of linearity, most notably Salop's circle model, which assumes that buyers are dispersed equally around a circle, rather than along a straight line.

According to Hotelling's analysis, competitive markets would appear to be inherently bad for maximizing consumers' access to a service, because market forces had the effect of requiring consumers to walk further to gain access to centrally located outlets. Some might argue that a centrally planned system of service location may prevent this apparently bad outcome arising. There are many examples of government intervention to prevent such outcomes; for example, in the UK, the government issues licences to chemists to dispense National Health Service (NHS) prescriptions partly on the basis of the need to maintain local access to service, rather than requiring users to travel to a central facility.

Was Hotelling too severe in his assumptions about buyers' and sellers' preferences? Do buyers actually prefer to go to a central location where they can find choice? Is the prospect of a choice of restaurants a sufficient temptation to lure diners away from their home neighbourhood to the restaurant district of their town? And for sellers, is the idea of a homogeneous service offer untenable in markets where service providers seek to differentiate their offer so that consumers will seek it out, wherever it is located?

### 4.4.5 Reducing locational dependency by overcoming problems of inseparability

The traditional idea that service production and consumption are inseparable would appear at first sight to pose problems in achieving both maximum productive efficiency and maximum accessibility to a service. One method of resolving this apparent problem is to try to make production and consumption separable – that is, to design a service that can be produced where it is most efficient and consumed where it is most valued.

We saw in Chapter 2 how telecommunications can be used to allow the substantive element of a service to be produced at a central processing unit and made available at any point of consumers' choice. Banks have recognized the distribution implications of improved telephone and Internet technology and most large banks have developed telephone and Internet-based banking services. Increasingly, such services are being made available at almost any point of the customer's choosing through mobile Internet devices. The bank may actually answer the telephone call in a relatively low-cost country, such as India, which is distant from the customer. Telephone and Internet banking have extended the possibilities for spatial separation of customer and provider. The locational implications of such delivery systems are quite significant. Banks have been steadily reducing their costly branch networks and seeking to channel more of their business through electronic media. As well as cutting costs through the use of an efficient centralized administration centre, Internet banking makes the banks' services available to customers at any location and at any time of day. Nevertheless, problems remain with excessive reliance on the Internet, as many services usually involve a tangible benefit, which must be transferred from producer to consumer at some point. Bank customers usually require cash, necessitating physical locations to supplement the Internet-based service delivery.

The issue of location decisions arises in cyberspace, and a number of attempts have been made to use the principles of spatial location models to define access strategies for web-based service providers (e.g. Sen et al., 2006). Just as a service outlet in a busy shopping street may be an attractive option for a business relying on a high level of passing trade, so too the right location on the Internet is essential if the business model is based on capturing passing trade. A link from the main page of Yahoo! or Google can be the equivalent of having a prime shopping location, but, like the prime shopping location, the best sites on the Internet are expensive. If a company locates its services (and links to its services) away from main Internet hit sites, this is equivalent to locating outlets in a quiet street in a quiet part of town. In both cases, a strategy is needed to promote awareness of the location.

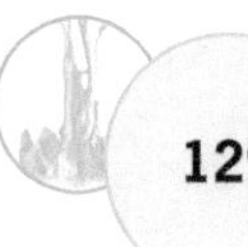



## 4.5 *How* should access be provided? The role of intermediaries

Having now discussed issues of when and where services should be made available to consumers, this chapter now considers *how* they should be made available. More specifically, *who* should be involved in the process of delivering the benefit of a service to consumers? Should a company seek to perform the whole service process itself? If not, whom should it involve, and at what stages of the production process?

In the context of goods marketing, the concept of an intermediary can be understood as being a person or company that handles goods as they pass from the organization that manufactured them to the individual or business that finally consumes them. The intermediary may physically handle the goods, splitting them into progressively smaller volumes as they pass through channels of distribution, or it may simply buy and sell the rights to goods in the role of a commodity dealer.

Any discussion of service intermediaries immediately raises a number of conceptual issues:

- Services cannot be owned; therefore it is difficult to talk about service ownership being transferred through channels of distribution.
- Pure services are intangible and perishable; therefore stocks cannot exist.
- The inseparability of most services should logically require an intermediary to become a co-producer of a service.

A distinction should be made between intermediaries as co-producers and their role as mere sales agents. While the former is an active part of the production process, the latter does not actually deliver a service itself, only the right to a service. As an example, a shop selling postage stamps is not significantly involved as a co-producer of postal services. It can be difficult to distinguish between these two situations – a theatre ticket agency, in addition to merely selling the right to a service, may provide a valuable service for consumers in procuring specific seats.

Service intermediaries perform a number of important functions on behalf of services organizations (the latter are often referred to as 'service principals'). The role expectations of intermediaries vary according to the nature of the service in question and some of the most important are described below:

- As a co-producer of a service, an intermediary assists in making a service available locally to consumers at a place and time that is convenient to consumers. A newsagent's store selling mobile phone payment vouchers is assisting in the process of producing and making mobile phone services available to consumers. In other cases, an intermediary may become the dominant partner involved in co-production. A national key-cutting or shoe-heeling service may leave almost the entire service production process in the hands of intermediaries, leaving the principal to provide administrative and advertising support and to monitor standards.
- Intermediaries usually provide sales support at the point of sale. For some customers of personal services, a two-way personal dialogue with a local intermediary may be more effective in securing a sale than advertising messages derived centrally from a service principal.
- Consumers may prefer to buy services from an intermediary who offers a wide choice, including the services offered by competing service principals. Visiting the website of an airline which only sells tickets for its own flights may seem much less convenient to a buyer than visiting the website of an agent that offers a choice of flights from many airlines.
- Consumers may enjoy trusting relationships with intermediaries and prefer to choose between competing alternatives on the basis of the intermediaries' advice. In the financial services

sector, intermediaries develop trust with their clients in guiding them through often complex choices. To be successful with such segments of buyers, a financial services company must establish its credentials with the intermediary if its products are to enter the final consumer's shortlisted choice set.

- An intermediary as co-producer of a service often shares some of the risk of providing a service. This can occur where a service principal requires intermediaries to contribute some of their own capital to the cost of acquiring equipment and both share any subsequent operating profit or loss.
- The use of independent intermediaries can free up capital which a service principal can reinvest in its core service production facilities. An airline that closes its own ticket shops and directs potential customers to travel agents is able to reinvest the proceeds in updating its aircraft or reservation systems, which may give it greater competitive advantage than having its own ticket outlets.
- Once the initial service is completed, there may be a requirement for 'after-sales' services to be provided. Intermediaries can make this support more accessible to the consumer and assist the service principal as co-producer of the after-sales support. Insurance is a good example where many segments of the insurance-buying public feel happier with easy local access to a local agent, who can give advice about making a claim. The agent in turn simplifies the task of the insurance company by handling much of the paperwork involved in making a claim, thereby reducing the latter's workload.

### 4.5.1 Push and pull relationships with intermediaries

**Push and pull channels** of distribution are familiar concepts in the marketing of goods, but they also have relevance within the services sector. A traditional push channel of distribution involves a service principal aggressively promoting its service to intermediaries by means of personal selling, trade advertising and the use of trade incentives. The intermediary in turn aggressively sells the service to final consumers, often having to strike a balance between maximizing the customer's benefit and maximizing the incentives offered to the intermediary by the service principal. This approach sees the service as essentially a commodity – the consumer starts with no preference of service principal and seeks the best value available from an intermediary. A push channel is typical of the way in which basic motor insurance is made available to customers. For many buyers, insurance is a 'distress' purchase, where the only perceived difference between policies is the price. Many people rely on their intermediary to suggest the lowest-cost insurance available to them. Intermediaries will be most aggressive in the sale of policies that meet buyers' criteria and on which they receive the most attractive commission payments.

For service principals, push strategies can be quite risky, as any product differentiation policy can only be effective if the intermediary communicates the unique benefits effectively to potential customers, rather than relying on price alone as the point of differentiation. To try to reduce this risk, service principals can aim messages directly at consumers, seeking to establish at an early stage in the buying process the values for which their brand stands. Having developed an attitude towards a brand, consumers are more likely to ask specifically for that brand from an intermediary or to express a preference for it when offered a choice by the intermediary. For a pull strategy, the intermediary's role is reduced to one of dispensing pre-sold branded services. The pensions sector in many countries has seen considerable activity by companies seeking to build up favourable images of their organization so that potential customers enter discussions with intermediaries with a favourable predisposition towards their organization. Buyers may know very little about the

Figure 4.6 Push and pull strategies for making services available to consumers

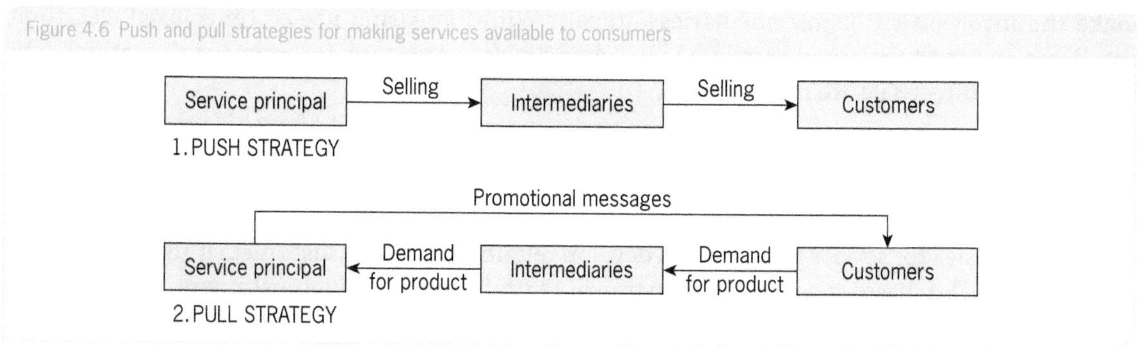


merits of one pension policy over another, but they approach an intermediary with attitudes about their preferred principal. Push and pull strategies are compared in Figure 4.6.

### 4.5.2 Service characteristics as an influence on the role of intermediaries

Services are not homogeneous and this is reflected in the diversity of roles played by intermediaries. While some services can be handled by a large number of intermediaries, others cannot easily be handled by intermediaries at all. The characteristics of services and of customers' expectations need to be considered before a strategy for intermediaries is developed:

- Some services experience highly variable outcomes, making efforts to control quality through intermediaries very difficult to achieve. This is particularly true of personal services, such as hairdressing, which are most commonly provided by small businesses direct to final consumers without the use of intermediaries.
- Some services may be highly specialized and likely to be neglected by intermediaries with inadequate training or knowledge. A service principal may gain no competitive advantage if intermediaries are incapable of giving appropriate sales and co-production support. Where a service is complex, the service principal must pay careful attention to the selection of intermediaries, or alternatively deal directly with consumers. Within the package holiday industry, trekking and activity holidays are quite specialized services, about which most travel agents have inadequate knowledge to handle them effectively. Some operators of these holidays have chosen to operate through specialized intermediaries such as specialist outdoor pursuit agencies, while many more prefer to deal directly with their target markets.
- Margins available on a service may be insufficient to support many intermediaries, if any at all. Domestic and industrial cleaning services often operate on very low margins, resulting in most services being provided direct to consumers.
- Legislation or voluntary codes of conduct may limit the choice of intermediary available to a service principal, or make it impossible to act through them at all. In the UK, the Financial Services Act 1986 is a good example of legislation that directly constrains the distribution opportunities available for certain services. The Act requires that specified financial services may only be handled by authorized intermediaries.

### 4.5.3 Direct sale

Should a service principal involve intermediaries at all? Direct sale is a particularly attractive option for service providers where the service offer is complex and variable and where legal constraints make the involvement of intermediaries difficult. With increasing use of centralized electronic databases and the Internet, direct sale is becoming more important for many organizations. The attractions of direct sale are numerous:

- The service provider is in regular direct contact with consumers of its service, making faster feedback of customer comments a possibility. This can facilitate the process of improving existing services or developing new ones.
- It can be easier for service principals to develop relationships with customers if they are in regular contact. Databases can be built up to provide a profile of individual customers, allowing more effective targeting of new service offers.
- Intermediaries may jealously guard their customers from the service principal, in the fear that any initial contact between the service principal and consumer could result in the role of the intermediary being diminished. Having spent time and effort attracting their customer, they do not wish to see the service principal picking up the long-term benefits of repeat business without the revenue-earning involvement of the intermediary. The service principal therefore loses a lot of valuable feedback. In the travel industry, agents have deliberately not passed on the addresses of customers to the tour operating company with whom they are booked, disclosing only a telephone number for emergency use.
- In the public sector, political considerations or fears over confidentiality may prevent services being provided by private-sector intermediaries. Definitions of what is politically acceptable change over time. In the UK many have considered that school catering and leisure-centre services are vital public services that can only be supplied directly by public-sector bodies. However, it is now widely accepted that these can be provided through service intermediaries of one form or another, although debate continues about whether more contentious services such as prisons and security services should be provided through private-sector intermediaries. From the opposite approach, the use of public-sector organizations as intermediaries has been increasingly accepted. As an example, hospitals are being used to make a range of private-sector health-related services available.
- The service principal can retain for itself the profit margin that would have been paid to an intermediary. This could be beneficial where its own distribution costs are lower than the commission that it would have paid to an intermediary.

Quite often, service principals choose to make their services available both directly and through intermediaries. This can be an attractive option as it allows the principal to target segments that may have very different accessibility preferences. As an example, one segment of the holiday-buying public may seek the reassurance provided by being able to walk into a travel agency and talk to an agent, while another segment may be more confident, price sensitive and short of time, for whom direct booking with a tour operator by telephone or the Internet is attractive. Against the advantages of segmenting the market in this way can come significant problems. Intermediaries can become demotivated if they see a principal for whom they are working as agent selling the same services direct to the public. To make matters worse, direct-sale promotional material often emphasizes the benefits of not using an intermediary, typically lower prices and faster service. One solution is to split an organization into two distinct operating units with their own brand identity, one to operate through intermediaries and the other to sell direct to the final consumer. This was the solution adopted by the Tui Travel group, which in addition to selling holidays through travel agents under the Thomson brand name (among others) also sells basically similar holidays direct to the public under the Portland brand name.

### 4.5.4 Electronic distribution of services

Services were early to adopt the Internet within their distribution strategy. With typically no (or very little) tangible product needing to be delivered to a customer, the Internet has been ideal for making intangible services available to consumers. Change in technology has called for new thinking on distribution, and while many would argue that the basic principles of making services available to consumers has not changed with the advent of the Internet, many practices have certainly changed.

In the early days of the Internet, it was widely predicted that many service principals would be able to dispense with intermediaries and distribute their services directly to each customer. The growth of direct-selling intermediaries such as Direct Line Insurance appeared to confirm the ability to cut out intermediaries, who were often portrayed as parasitic and delaying middlemen. The inelegant term '**disintermediation**' has been used to describe the process of removing intermediaries from a distribution channel and developing direct communications.

There is a lot of evidence that services companies have used the Internet to strategically make their distribution activities more efficient. For example, some retailers have closed a number of branches or reduced their sales force and instead offer customers access to their product range via a website.

The Internet does not change one of the basic roles of intermediaries, which is to simplify buyers' choice processes. When several companies seek to develop direct relationships with their customers, buyers are faced with a confusing array of messages. Faced with dozens of insurance companies seeking to sell insurance directly, consumers are likely to simplify their choice process by using an intermediary who can carry out some of the buyer's search activity on their behalf. The result has therefore been the emergence of a new generation of Internet intermediaries, or 'informediaries'. In the travel sector, numerous informediaries such as Expedia and Travelocity have emerged to simplify consumers' buying process, fulfilling very much the same type of role as the traditional high-street travel agent. Many service principals have realized that gaining the attention of the final consumer is becoming increasingly difficult in a congested cyberspace. 'Electronic shelf-space' may be almost infinite, but service principals need to be sure that target customers will come past their site. So instead of (or as well as) heavily promoting their own site, many companies have resorted to using informediaries. Disintermediation has turned into reintermediation and the basic principles of channel design are little changed.

In the era of Internet-based distribution, a lot of thought has to go into how to get access to potential buyers most cost-effectively. The options for achieving this seem to grow in number each year. Search-based advertising has become a very big part of many services organizations' promotional expenditure and we will return to it again in Chapter 13 as a promotional tool. Increasingly, companies are bidding to search engines such as Google for key search terms to be listed at the top of the visitors' search results, and this often involves apparently devious practices. For example, one company may bid for a search term that is associated with its main competitor, so every time a person searches for the competitor, the company itself will appear at the top of the page of search results.

Many companies have also developed networks of 'affiliates', whereby a site that refers an individual to the company's site through a web page link receives an agreed level of commission. As a further refinement of this model, some websites, such as www.topcashback.com, pass part of this commission back to the end-customer. Another type of affiliate relationship is the use of comparison websites, which allow a visitor to enter their specific service needs and the site then lists alternatives available to them, based on price, rating, or some other criteria. Comparison sites exist for most search-based services provided in a competitive market, for example gas and electricity (www.uSwitch.com); loans and savings accounts (www.moneysupermarket.com) and car insurance (www.confused.com). The price comparison site generally receives a payment for each visitor to its site who clicks through and subsequently makes a purchase. Companies also offer a range of coupons and voucher codes to segment their markets, and again, a number of intermediaries such as myvouchercodes.co.uk and ukdiscountvouchers.co.uk have appeared to facilitate the process of bringing buyer and seller together.

In all of these cases of affiliate-type relationships, companies have to consider the benefits of paying affiliates to introduce customers, against the possible costs of pulling out from such arrangements completely. With increased popularity of price comparison sites, many buyers may limit their choice set to services providers who are listed, and some comparison sites may refuse to list a service provider who does not agree to pay them a fee, thereby denying access by the company to customers who rely solely on a comparison site. Price comparison sites compete among themselves to attract visitors to their site, including television advertising campaigns. The additional overhead cost of supporting these electronic distribution channels has led some companies to cut them out completely and to use their own advertising to inform potential buyers that information about their company's services will not be found on any comparison site, and that the company's best deals can only be found on its own site, which it heavily promotes.

Another important, related consideration in e-distribution design is the role of social network sites to distribute messages, and also to listen to customers' comments. Many buyers may only make a purchase from a company if it has a high approval rating from people using their favourite blog or social network site. Unhappy customers are increasingly willing to use such sites to protest about poor service standards. Companies must increasingly have a strategy for listening and responding to what customers are saying in social network media. We will return to this subject in Chapter 13.

Of course, it is not just in business-to-consumer markets that the Internet is reshaping distribution channels. In business-to-business channels, the Internet (and intranets and extranets) has replaced previous electronic data interchange (EDI) systems for handling transactions between businesses. Government and not-for-profit organizations have also incorporated the Internet into their distribution channels, both for procuring purchases and for making services available to users (for example, hospitals which make appointments systems available online).

Despite the enormous potential of the Internet to simplify communication between a company and its customers, problems remain where tangible goods are involved (see Yrjölä, 2001). The cost of delivering tangible goods has tended to increase in real terms. Many goods can only be evaluated by experiencing them through touch or smell, something that is difficult to achieve online. The failed Internet clothes retailer boo.com found that many people would probably find it much easier and reassuring to try on clothes in a shop than rely on a computer image, thereby ensuring a continuing role for traditional high street retailers.

There have been hopes that three-dimensional virtual reality systems may help to make tangible these services, for example by allowing potential buyers to have a virtual tour of a hotel, or have the semblance of a face-to-face meeting with an employee of a bank. Many companies now use 'virtual assistants' in their websites to put a face to answers provided for the most frequently asked questions or to allow customers some limited experience of a product (e.g. the use of personalized avatars to try on clothes). However, large-scale virtual environments, such as 'Second life' (www.secondlife.com), do not yet appear to have gained the widespread popularity that many had expected.

Many organizations appear to have succeeded by integrating online and offline access to their services. Retailers who have a physical presence in shopping centres can use their stores as

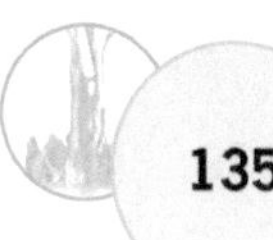

showcases for products that can be ordered online, or as collection points for goods ordered online. They can also facilitate returns of unwanted items, providing reassurance to buyers. In the market for online retail sales, some have suggested that the local stores networks of retailers such as Tesco and Argos could give these companies an important competitive advantage over pure online retailers such as Amazon.

## In practice: easy to book

easyJet was a pioneer in transforming the sale of airline tickets from a face-to-face encounter to one undertaken through the Internet. By 2012, the company claimed that 95 per cent of its customers used the Internet for booking its tickets, saving administrative costs for the airline, which are passed on in lower prices to customers. easyJet was at the forefront of refusing to pay commission to travel agencies and instead sold direct only. Many other airlines have now followed its lead, as buyers' expectations have changed and they learnt that in order to get the best price, they need to book online. However, easyJet realized that it was missing out on potential business passengers who are likely to book all of their travel arrangements through a nominated business travel agency. Some large organizations have formalized procedures which require use of the nominated agency, and many employees needing to make business travel arrangements would find it much easier to go to the travel agency, rather than spending their own time searching for a bargain online and using their own credit card to pay for it. For this reason, easyJet now makes its booking system available to business travel agencies through Global Distribution Systems (GDS). The price charged by travel agencies is usually greater than the same ticket available directly from the easyJet website, and many business buyers may consider this premium to be good value for the easier access to easyJet services that is provided.

Figure 4.7 Online booking promotion from easyJet

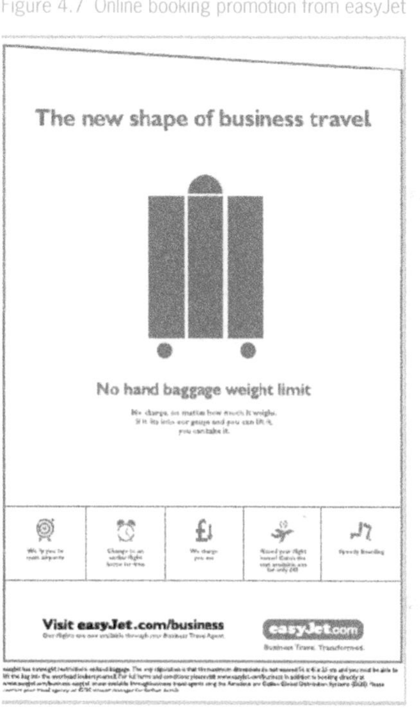


## 4.5.5 Defending the integrity of the Internet environment

Ease of access to online services may be a key point of competitive advantage, but can access be made too easy for 'good' customers as well as criminals? And can customers unwittingly find themselves giving their credit card details to a website which isn't that of the real service provider? Security and privacy have emerged as major concerns in the Internet service delivery environment. When a customer evaluates a real-life service facility, such as a shop or a hospital, they can visit it and observe staff and processes. Admittedly, there can be no guarantee that the process they actually go through will be similar to the observations on which they based their expectations. However, in the case of online evaluation, there may be even fewer cues available to make a judgement about whether a service provider will deliver its service promises, and whether it will respect their privacy. Sadly, there are too many examples of online companies that have simply disappeared after giving promises to customers in return for customers' money. In the run-up to the 2010 World Cup in South Africa, it is reported that many bogus websites appeared, but soon disappeared after taking money for tickets which did not exist (*Daily Mail*, 2010). Some apparently legitimate websites have been set up to obtain customers' personal information, which has then been used fraudulently after the company has disappeared.

There has now been a lot of research investigating the factors that affect consumers' perceptions of the trustworthiness of an online service provider. Gefen et al. (2003) noted that perceived trust in an online service provider derives from two sources: familiarity with the company's offline marketing presence, including its service outlets, employees and advertisements; and familiarity with the company gained through visits to its website.

Where an online service provider has no real-life presence, and has no local facilities that can be checked out, the task of establishing credibility with new customers can be particularly difficult. A high level of advertising, both offline and online, may eventually bring about familiarity in the eyes of potential customers, on the basis that a company with an ability to communicate so widely is likely to be around long enough to deliver their promise.

Approach behaviour for an online service provider may be facilitated by a number of measures. A strong offline presence would reassure many individuals that the company is a real one, and helps to provide reassurance that they can go to speak to somebody in person if necessary. Simply having a local contact address and telephone number may reassure some people. In addition, many companies have adopted industry association standards to certify their security and privacy credentials, such as VeriSign and Thawte. These specify standards for the manner in which the company deals with customers and handles their information. Where such schemes are backed by specific industry sector associations, they may provide some recompense against deviant members. In a study of the banking sector, Yousafzai et al. (2005) found that banks that displayed on their websites a security policy, a privacy policy and a statement of compliance with banking codes were more likely to be trusted than those that did not.

It is not just customers who need be wary of rogue companies; companies also need to be wary of rogue customers. In a real-life service environment, a company can see who is coming into its site and remove potentially disruptive elements, such as people entering a restaurant who are already visibly drunk. In the case of online service processes, it can be much more difficult to judge whether visitors to a company's website are benign, or malicious. Malicious visitors may disrupt a company's service processes by planting viruses, bombing it with mass emails, or disrupting the codes of its operating system. The reasons for this action may be a grudge against the company, or simply the challenge for a computer hacker of beating a system. Where a company is dependent on online transactions for the bulk of its revenue, the effects of such malicious intrusions can be devastating, not only resulting in a short-term loss of revenue, but in long-term harm to its brand reputation where customers' details are obtained or used in an unauthorized way. In designing the online environment, companies must strike a balance between making a site easily accessible to all and difficult for those with malicious intentions.

Online service companies also face the threat from companies offering lookalike service processes, but with fraudulent intentions. A customer visiting a city-centre bank can be fairly certain that the bank is genuine (although there have been reported cases of fraudulent lookalike ATMs capturing innocent visitors' personal details). However, visitors to an online bank may find it difficult to distinguish between the real bank and a lookalike bank. There have been many reported cases of bogus banks luring visitors to their site before 'phishing' for customers' details, and then selling these details on for fraudulent use.

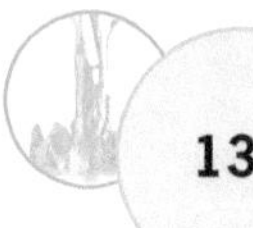



## Thinking around the subject: Providing online service behind the Great Firewall of China

How does a service company get access to potential customers who live the other side of China's great 'firewall'? 'Exporting' services to China should be relatively easy for Western companies, which have an established know-how base and with no physical customs controls to get in the way of trade. But despite the intangibility of services, the firewall has proved difficult to penetrate. Google, the most popular search engine in the Western world, encountered difficulty in China, as Chinese Internet users often regarded the rival search engine Baidu as being more suitable for Chinese culture, for example in the way that finding Chinese music is easier than with Google. Western companies have sometimes misunderstood Chinese attitudes to national pride and collectivism, manifested by the presence of active communities within Baidu. Collectivist Chinese had developed their own online group-buying communities, long before Groupon became popular in the West. Even the mighty Amazon, which has achieved high levels of market penetration in many Western countries, struggled to achieve 2 per cent of the Chinese market for books and music by 2012, as it faced many local competitors.

The online auctioneer and retailer eBay saw the potential of China when it launched there in 2002. However, eBay was soon out maneuvered by a local competitor – Taobao.com, operated by the Alibaba group. Taobao appealed to Chinese national loyalty by using more local cultural context in its website than the very American appeal of eBay. Taobao allowed Chinese eBay customers to list their items for sale free of charge, positioning Taobao as a patriotic and more cost-effective operator than the American eBay. In the following years, Taobao innovated in ways which were more appropriate to the Chinese context, with payment systems which were widely accessible. Taobao offered its own 'Zhifubao' currency which is a kind of online shopping currency playing the role of Chinese money, and linked to users' bank accounts. It innovated with distribution strategies (Blog, Weibo in Chinese), advertising messages and customer services which Chinese people felt they could trust.

eBay recognized that the only way to get access to the huge Chinese market was to work with a local company who had a better understanding of the habits of local consumers. In November 2012 it announced a partnership with xiu.com, which would allow eBay to list its vast inventory of global clearance stock through xiu.com. eBay was no longer a simple auction site, but had developed as a site for selling last seasons' clearance stock from leading brand names such as Calvin Klein and Burberry, which brand-conscious middle-class Chinese consumers were increasingly eager to buy. Xiu.com, which had only been founded in 2008, would translate and list stock offered for sale by eBay and offer it on its site. Xiu would handle all payments, shipping and customer services. It would also handle all regulatory issues, something which many exporters of both goods and services to China have found to be a minefield. Faked goods have been a big concern of Chinese online buyers and eBay had to match the practice of Taobao which provided a guarantee system – buyers pay their money to Taobao and Taobao only pays this money to sellers after the customer is satisfied with receipt of the goods. Sellers will not deliver their goods if Taobao has not given them a payment received notice.

The Chinese services market may be seen by Western companies as a huge market waiting to be exploited. But Western companies should not overlook the differences in buying behaviour and the often intense loyalty of Chinese consumers to their country. They should also not forget that China has an ancient tradition of trading which predates the Internet age by hundreds if not thousands of years. Should the West worry about the prospect of Chinese companies doing with online services what they have already done with cheap manufactured goods, by flooding the West with their services?

A sign of possible things to come occurred in 2012 when 360buy, China's largest online retailer (by volume of transactions), targeted Western consumers with an English-language website initially selling Chinese goods to consumers in Europe and the USA. Would this develop into a general online site selling a much wider range of Chinese and Western goods? Could it be that Chinese service businesses have a better understanding of Western consumers than Western businesses have of the Chinese? And if this happens, what would this say for the assumption that the West should concentrate on services while China concentrates on manufacturing?

## 4.5.6 Future developments in Internet-based distribution strategy

History tells us that a key to success for many services organizations has resulted from being first to offer a new method to make a service available more cheaply and cost-effectively. Start-up businesses such as Lastminute.com have spotted opportunities and gone on to great success. Others have seen their ideas flop. What will be tomorrow's innovative methods of making services available to customers?

The Internet has evolved from its fixed-line constraints and is increasingly mobile. Mobile phone handsets, which were initially used almost exclusively for voice calls, are now often used to transmit data and undertake commercial transactions (often generically referred to as 'm-commerce'). In recent years, mobile phones have become very popular, with a penetration rate in many parts of Europe approaching 100 per cent (Eurostat, 2012), and a growing proportion of these are equipped to handle data, as well as voice calls. The availability of online services no longer needs to be restricted to where a customer is within reach of a fixed-line computer. Mobile Internet services and 'apps' are also increasingly being linked to global positioning systems (GPS) which use satellites to locate the precise position of a customer. This can give users information that is much more relevant to their needs, for example apps can help to find a taxi that is nearby or to show the location of the nearest railway metro station and the time of the next train departing from it. Whole new categories of services using 'apps' have emerged to provide location-specific information; for example, subscription traffic advisory services which give real-time, locationally specific information about traffic congestion. For private consumers, such services can avoid the inconvenience of being stuck in a traffic jam. For businesses employing drivers, such mobile information can allow drivers to be redirected and cost savings to be made. Technology providers and financial institutions believe that m-payment services will reach critical mass in the next few years.

Younger people appear to be more predisposed to adopt m-commerce services than other Internet users because these services are usually low-cost entertainment products (e.g. ringtones, songs) which fit with their lifestyle (Bigne et al., 2005).

### In practice: How much to Timbuctoo?

Figure 4.8 A typical travel booking website. (Reproduced with permission of Expedia.co.uk)

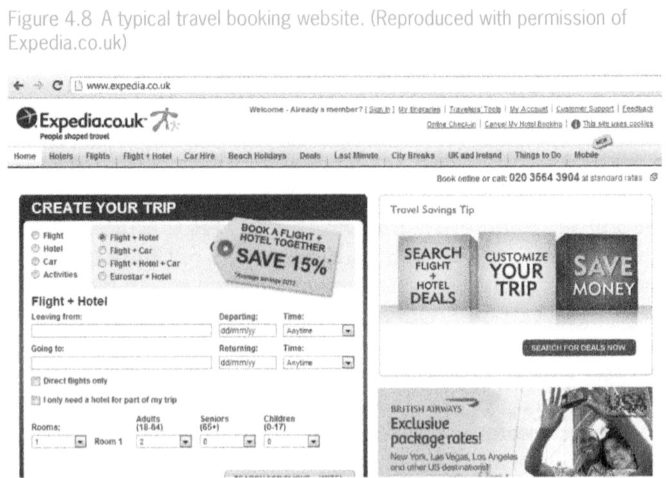


Many people thought that the Internet would fundamentally change the pattern of distribution for services, by allowing service principals to distribute their services efficiently and effectively without the use of intermediaries. In the travel sector, budget airlines have been notable for the way in which they have managed to use their websites to cut out intermediaries and thereby pass on cost savings to customers (easyJet, for example, claims that over 95 per cent of its customers book through its website). However, customers looking for choice may prefer to use the website of one of the many web-based travel intermediaries that have emerged, and whose diversity has continued to grow. Some web-based travel intermediaries such as Skyscanner simply provide a listing of availability on a particular route, but provide no booking facility or customer support.

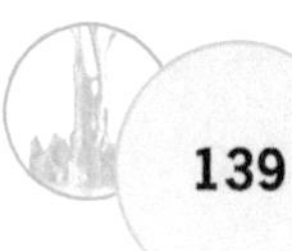



Other intermediaries provide a full service similar to that provided by traditional high-street travel agencies. Expedia.co.uk is a leading online travel agency and is particularly valuable to consumers where guidance is needed on the options available. Airlines and hotels selling online directly to the public generally provide no choice of service providers, therefore the use of an online agency such as Expedia can simplify the search process, especially for more complex long-haul journeys which are not well served by budget airlines' relatively simple websites. Expedia can provide customers with valuable help and reassurance in the booking process, especially where customers are buying multiple services from different service providers (e.g. an airline ticket, hotel and car hire). Where a customer books two or more such elements of a travel booking with a company such as Expedia, European law provides additional protection to buyers and the agency has a greater responsibility to relocate or support the customer if there are any problems with their booking. The use of an online agency such as Expedia can help to overcome the nightmare stories which have been told by travellers who have booked their airline ticket and hotel separately with different providers, then encountered difficulties when one of the bookings changes. For example, an airline might reschedule the flight times of a booking already made, which means that the hotel booking is no longer usable. However, if the hotel was booked separately, the hotel operator may have no obligation to amend or refund the booking.

## 4.6 Selection of intermediaries

Service intermediaries take many forms in terms of their size, structure, legal status and relationship to the service principal. Because of this diversity, attempts at classification can become confused by the level of overlap present. In this section, attention is focused on the characteristics of four non-mutually exclusive types of intermediary – agents, retailers, wholesalers and franchisees.

### 4.6.1 Service agents

A **service agent** is somebody who acts on behalf of a principal and has the authority to create a legal relationship between the customer and service principal as if it were made directly between the two. Agents are usually rewarded for their actions by being able to deduct a commission before payment is passed on to their principal, although in many cases agents may be paid a fixed fee for the work actually done – for example, in preparing a new market prior to the launch of a new service.

For service principals, the use of agents offers many advantages:

- Capital requirements for creating a chain of distribution outlets are minimized.
- Consumers may expect choice at the point of service purchase and it is usually easier for an independent agent to do this rather than for the service principal to set up distribution outlets that sell competing products. (In the case of many financial services, European legislation makes it difficult for service principals to sell both their own products and those of competitors – for example, banks and building societies must choose between becoming a 'tied' agent of one service principal, or offering a genuine choice to customers.)
- Where a service principal is entering a new market, it may lack the knowledge that allows it to understand buyer behaviour and the nature of competition in that market. Some financial institutions with a poor understanding of an overseas mortgage market choose to make mortgage services available by means of independent mortgage brokers.
- In the case of overseas markets, it may be illegal for a service principal to deal directly with the public, a problem that can be remedied by acting through a local licensed agent.

- In some cases, special skills are required by a service principal, which would be very costly to develop in-house. A shipping company may not have the need for a full-time employee to negotiate sale of its capacity in the open charter market, and it may therefore be more sensible to employ an agent to do this on its behalf as and when required, on either a commission or fixed-charge basis.

### 4.6.2 Retail outlets

The notion of a retailer in the services sector poses conceptual problems, for it has already been established that a retailer cannot carry a stock of services, one of the important functions of a retailer of goods. The distinction between a retailer and an agent or franchisee (see below) can be a fine one. In general, a retailer operates in a manner that does not create legal relations between the service principal and the final customer – the customer's relationship is only with the retailer.

Many services that pass through retailers have a significant goods element. As an example, mobile phone retailers are a familiar feature of many shopping centres, but in addition to providing network service contracts on behalf of the network operators, they also provide immediate availability of a choice of handsets. Many retail services which incorporate high levels of tangible goods, such as key cutting and fast-food catering, are often retailed in the form of a franchise agreement, which is discussed below.

Sometimes, service retailers undertake another of the traditional goods retailer's functions in taking risk. A retailer can buy the right to a block of service transactions and if these rights are not sold by the time the service is performed, the value of these rights disappears. This can happen where a ticket agent buys a block of tickets on a no-return basis from an event organizer.

### 4.6.3 Service wholesalers

Similar conceptual problems apply to the role of the wholesaler. For services, the term is most sensibly understood where an intermediary buys the right to a large volume of service transactions and then proceeds to break these down into smaller units of rights to a service for handling by retailers or other intermediaries. Hotel booking agencies that buy large blocks of hotel accommodation earn their margin by buying in volume at low prices and adding a mark-up as a block booking is broken down into smaller units for sale to retailers or agents. As with retailers, it can be difficult to distinguish a wholesaler from an agent. A hotel wholesaler may have some rights to return unsold accommodation to the hotels concerned and may include in their dealings with customers a statement that the transaction is to be governed by conditions specified by the service principal.

## 4.7 Franchised service distribution

The term '**franchising**' refers to a relationship where one party – the franchisor – provides the development work on a service format and monitors standards of delivery, while coming to an arrangement with a second party – the franchisee – who is licensed to deliver the service, taking some share of the financial risk and reward in return. Vertical franchising occurs where a manufacturer allows a franchisee an exclusive right to sell its goods within a specified area. The more recent business-format franchising occurs where an organization allows others to copy the format of its own operations.

The International Franchise Association (2010) has defined a franchise operation as:

> *a contractual relationship between the franchisor and franchisee in which the franchisor offers or is obliged to maintain a continuing interest in the business of the franchisee in such areas as know-how and training; wherein the franchise operates under a common trade name, format or procedure owned by or controlled by the franchisor, and in which the franchisee has made or will make a substantial capital investment in his business from his own resources.*

The services sector has seen considerable recent growth in franchising. According to the annual NatWest/British Franchise Association survey, the total number of franchise systems in the UK in 2011 was 897. These were linked to a total of 36,900 franchisees, with an annual turnover of £12.4 billion and employing an estimated 465,000 people (British Franchise Association, 2012). Franchising offers particular opportunities for service industries that are people intensive, by combining the motivation of self-employed franchisees with the quality control and brand values of the franchisor.

Franchising tends to be a relatively low-risk method of market entry for new businesses, with some evidence to suggest that franchises are less likely to fail than other types of small business organization (Castrogiovanni et al., 1993). In the UK, overall franchisee 'churn' (old franchisees leaving and new ones entering) was 8.8 per cent in 2011, and of those leaving, only 3.1 per cent was attributable to financial failure (British Franchise Association, 2012).

Franchise agreements cover a diverse range of services, from car hire to fast food, kitchen design services, veterinary services and hotels. Of the top 10 UK business franchise operations (in terms of turnover), all are involved in essentially service-based activities. Most franchisees are self-employed individuals or small companies, although they can also be very large organizations. To illustrate this, it is quite common to find corporate franchisees who operate a large number of hotels for a franchisor, making the franchisee a very large organization. Franchising also has applications within the public sector (see Section 4.7.2 below).

Once franchising has taken hold within an organization, it tends to expand rather than contract. If a franchisor has built up a successful brand format, coupled with successful management, it can usually achieve greater returns on its capital by selling the right to use its name rather than operating its own outlets. The sandwich shop chain Subway, for example, has steadily increased the proportion of its restaurants that are franchised from 6 per cent in 1974 to 100 per cent in 2012. Other examples of strongly managed brands that have followed this route include Prontaprint, McDonald's Restaurants and Days Inn hotels.

There is a limit to which operations can be franchised, and many franchisors choose not to franchise their operations entirely. There are two important reasons for this. First, new service development can be easier to carry out in-house rather than at a distance through a franchise. In this way it avoids alienating franchisees should experimental new services fail. Second, some operations may be too specialized to expect a franchisee to have the standard of training to ensure a consistent standard of delivery and the franchisor may choose to retain responsibility for providing these.

Maintaining and motivating franchisees is a constant challenge for franchisors. Franchisees can become only too aware of the payments that the franchisor takes from them on an ongoing basis in return for dubious support. In the USA, some franchisee associations have brought legal actions against their franchisor for granting excessive numbers of franchises, which have adversely affected existing franchisees. In such situations, many franchisees may be tempted not to renew their franchise at the end of their agreement and to either go it alone or sign up with another franchise operation. Where brands are strong, the former route can be very risky – for example, Days Inn hotel franchisees who have used their premises to provide their own competing service format have lost customers when the franchisor creates a new outlet in the locality. Payment of franchise fees represents good value to a franchisee for as long as it receives good back-up from the franchisor and a steady supply of customers who are attracted by the reputation of the franchise brand.

### 4.7.1 The nature of a franchise agreement

A franchise agreement sets out the rights and obligations of the franchisor and franchisee and typically includes the following main clauses:

- The nature of the service that is to be supplied by the franchisee is specified. This can refer to particular categories of service that are to be offered – for example, a car repair franchise would probably indicate which specific service operations (such as brake replacement, engine tuning etc.) are covered by the franchise agreement.
- The territory in which the franchisee is given the right to offer a service is usually specified. The premium that a franchisee is prepared to pay for a franchise usually reflects the exclusivity of its territory.
- The length of a franchise agreement is specified – most franchises run for a period of five to ten years, with options to renew at the end of the period.
- The franchisee usually agrees to buy the franchise for an initial fee and agrees the basis on which future payments are to be made to the franchisor. The level of the initial fee reflects the strength of an established brand – a high initial fee for a strong established brand can be much less risky for a franchisee than a low price for a relatively new franchise. The cost to a business in setting up as a franchise in the first year ranges from £20,000 to £900,000, with the average being £150,000–£170,000 (British Franchise Association, 2012). Franchisees typically pay between 5 and 10 per cent of their sales in recurring fees to their franchisors. Payment of ongoing fees by the franchisee is usually calculated as a percentage of turnover. The agreement also usually requires the franchisee to buy certain supplies from the franchisor.
- The franchisee agrees to follow instructions from the franchisor concerning the manner of service delivery. Franchisees are typically required to charge according to an agreed scale of prices, maintain standards of reliability, availability and performance in the delivery of the service and ensure that any advertising follows the franchisor's guidelines.
- The franchisee usually agrees not to act as an intermediary for any other service principal, insisting that their franchised outlets show the same loyalty to the organization as if they were actually owned by the organization. Thus the operator of a Pizza Express franchise cannot use a franchised outlet to sell the services or goods of a competing organization such as Burger King. Franchising implies a degree of control that the franchisor has over the franchisee, unlike a retail agent, who usually has considerable discretion over the manner in which they conduct their business. For the franchisor, considerable harm could result from its promotion being used to draw potential customers into the franchisee's outlets, only for them to be cross-sold a service over which the franchisor has no control or is not likely to receive any financial benefit. However, in many cases, service franchises are sold on the understanding that they will form just one small part of the franchisee's operations – for example, a franchise to operate a courier service's collection point may be compatible with the business of a petrol filling station or newsagent franchisee.

Figure 4.9 Printing used to demand a high level of craft skills and specialized facilities to accommodate printing presses. However, the development of low-cost offset litho and photocopying machines lowered the entry barriers to printing. At the same time, the structure of business was changing, with companies outsourcing much of their printing and a growing volume of documents that needed to be copied. These conditions led to the rapid development of the fast-printing sector. A number of profitable chains have grown rapidly through franchising. Kallkwik is typical in selling a franchise to people who can demonstrate commitment to high standards and profitable growth. For a small investor looking for a business of their own, a Kallkwik franchise offers the security of a brand name that customers have come to trust. (Reproduced with permission of Kallkwik)

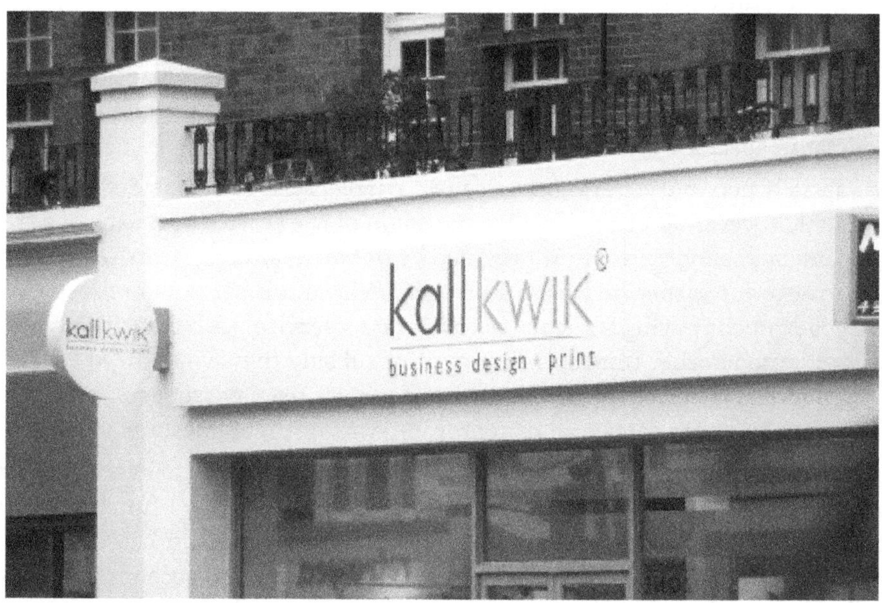


- The franchisor agrees to provide promotional support for the franchisee. The aim of such support is to establish the values of the franchisor's brand in the minds of potential customers, thereby reducing the promotion which the franchisee is required to undertake. The franchise agreement usually requires certain promotional activity of the franchisee to be in accordance with approved guidelines.
- The franchisor usually agrees to provide some level of administrative and technical support for the franchisee. This can include the provision of equipment (e.g. printing machines for a fast print franchise) and administrative support such as accounting.
- Franchise agreements usually give either party the right to terminate the franchise and for the franchisee to sell their franchise. The right to terminate can act as a control mechanism should either party fail to perform in accordance with the conditions of the franchise. A successful franchisee would want a clause in an agreement allowing him or her to sell the goodwill of a franchise that they have developed over time.

### 4.7.2 Public-sector franchising

Public services are increasingly being delivered by franchise agreements in order to capitalize on the motivation of smaller-scale franchisees, which was described above. Franchising can take a number of forms:

- The right to operate a vital public service can be sold to a franchisee, who in turn has the right to charge users of the facility. The franchisee will normally be required to maintain the facility to a required standard and to obtain government approval of prices to be charged. In the UK, the government has offered private organizations franchises to operate vital road links, including the M6 West Midlands Toll Road and the Severn River Crossing, linking England and Wales. In the case of the latter, an Anglo-French consortium acquired the right to collect tolls from users of the bridge and in return paid to develop a second river crossing and agreed to carry out routine maintenance work.

- Government can sell the exclusive right for private organizations to operate a private service that is of public importance. Private-sector radio and television broadcasting is operated on a franchise basis, where the government invites bids from private companies for exclusive rights to broadcast in specified areas and/or at specific times.
- Where a socially necessary, but economically unviable, service is provided in a market-mediated environment, government can subsidize provision of the service by means of a franchise. In the UK, rail passenger services are now provided by private train operators who have a franchise to operate a route for a specified period of time. Where rail services are loss making, this has entailed government paying franchisees to operate a service, with franchisees being selected on the basis of, among other things, the amount of subsidy they would need to operate a service. Successful bidders keep the revenue that they generate from passengers, subject to meeting the minimum requirements of the rail regulator in terms of timetables, reliability, fares etc.
- Even though a public service is not market mediated at the point of delivery, production methods may nevertheless be market mediated and part of the production function provided through a franchise agreement. Such an arrangement can have benefits for customers where the franchisee is rewarded partly on the basis of feedback from users. A recent application of this type of franchise can be found in the field of higher education, where many universities have franchised their courses to local colleges, with one aim being to provide local access to courses.
- In the UK, possibly the longest-established public-sector franchise is seen in the Post Office. In addition to government-owned 'Crown' post offices, 'sub'-post offices have traditionally been operated on a franchise basis in smaller towns. Franchises have been taken up by a variety of small shops and newsagents and generally offer a more limited range of postal services compared to Crown offices.

## In practice: Franchising the railways

Think of making services available through a franchise, and you will most likely first think about fast-food outlets or retailing. In fact, franchising plays a big role in the provision of many public services, where problems of managing the franschisee–franchisor relationship can become even more complex because of the additional need to reconcile the wider public interest.

In the UK, rail services were for a long time provided by a state-run organization, similar to common practice in most European countries. But from the mid-1990s, the UK government embarked on a radical plan to deliver train services through a franchising system, which in principle copied the approach of a fast-food franchise. But implementing a franchising system was much more difficult and threw up many new problems.

The principle of rail franchising is simple. The government defined individual routes or groups of routes and specified a minimum standard of service that it required. It then invited private companies to bid for the right to run the franchise for a specified number of years. For highly profitable routes, the successful bidder would pay the government an annual fee in return for rights to run the service. As with the fast-food franchise, the franchisee could increase its profits by generating more revenue from customers and/or by operating its service more efficiently. In the case of highly profitable routes such as the East Coast Main Line, a bidding war resulted in high payments being made by the franchisee to the government, but in other cases, such as the Valleys Lines of South Wales, it was recognized that these services would never be profitable, and the successful franchisee was the company that could provide the required level of service for the minimum level of government subsidy. In the financial year 2011/2012, the UK government paid £3.9 billion in subsidies to the rail industry.

So far, the similarity with the fast-food franchise may be fairly good, but the implementation then raises some very tricky additional issues. First, railways serve a vital function in life, and many people, such as commuters into central London, are effectively captive, something that cannot really be said of McDonald's restaurants' customers. As a result, franchise agreements include a long list of requirements set by the government to safeguard the interests of passengers and society generally, for example a requirement for inter-availability of tickets on the services of competing rail operators. In recent years, there has been a tendency for the government to 'micromanage' franchisees with ever-increasing detail, leading many to question the purpose of having private-sector entrepreneurs involved when they are so constrained in using their entrepreneurial skills.

A further problem has occurred where franchise rail operators have made inaccurate assumptions about future costs and revenues, and have been forced to renegotiate or hand in their franchise, leaving the government to take over operation. In 2009, the operator of the East Coast Main Line franchise, National Express, found the £1.4 billion franchise fee that it was committed to paying the government over the life of the franchise unsustainable, because it had overbid for the franchise, and assumed an overoptimistic level of passenger growth which was sharply undermined by an economic recession. Many critics of rail franchising have suggested that franchisees would invest very little of their own capital, and take all the benefits when the going was good, but when times got hard, they would simply abandon the franchise by handing it back to the government – was this a fair allocation of risk between the government and franchisee? Even the process of allocating franchises to the winning bidder was described as a shambles following the admission in 2012 that civil servants had incorrectly calculated the value of First Group's 'winning' bid for the West Coast Mainline franchise, and then caused great uncertainty by reopening the bidding process.

There has been debate about the ideal length of a rail franchise – too short, and the franchisee would have little incentive to invest in improvements, knowing that they may lose the franchise in a couple of years to a competitor; too long, and the operator may become too complacent, in which case extensive use of key performance indicators needs to be written into the franchise agreement to allow the government to take action if the terms of a franchise agreement are broken.

A further paradox of the rail franchise system is that it was originally designed to bring private-sector skills to the previous state-run bureaucracy of British Rail, but in practice, Europe's state-owned railways have bought in to British rail operators, either through consortiums, or through outright ownership; for example, Germany's state-owned railway DB operates the Chiltern Railways service between London and Birmingham and owns Arriva Trains. French and Dutch state-owned railways have interests in other franchise operators.

Has franchising been beneficial for the UK rail sector? A report published in October 2008 by the National Audit Office was generally positive, noting that 'rail franchising produces generally well thought through service specifications and generates keen bidding competition. This approach has resulted in better value for money for the taxpayer' (NAO, 2008).

Maybe some of the early problems with rail franchising resulted from policy-makers drawing too much of an analogy with the proverbial fast-food restaurant. As franchising has matured, new models of management have developed, but to critics, if further control is needed by government, why not go the whole way and renationalize the sector and cut out the middleman? The state-owned British Rail had been the subject of many bad jokes when it ran the country's railways, so were sceptics wearing rose-tinted spectacles as they applauded the effective renationalization of the East Coast Main Line in 2009 when the franchise was taken from National Express?

## 4.8 Accessibility through co-production

Some services organizations choose to make their services available to consumers in combination with other goods and services, with the collaboration of another producer. The outputs of the two organizations can be quite diverse – for example, a finance company could offer loan facilities in conjunction with customers buying domestic electrical equipment. Other examples include a combined train fare and museum admission ticket and a combined hotel and travel offer.

On other occasions, a service can be made available in combination with similar services provided by potential competitors. The basis for doing this is that the combined value of the enlarged service offer will generate more business and ultimately be of benefit to all service providers involved. In this way, many regional travel tickets allow passengers to travel on the trains and buses of potentially competing operators, thereby making public transport as a whole a relatively attractive option. Similarly, banks benefit by sharing cash dispenser networks – those sharing gain a competitive advantage over a bank that chooses to go it alone with its own dedicated but smaller network. However, we will see in Chapter 5 that in most Western countries, legislation exists to restrict such collaborative activities where they are deemed to be anti-competitive and therefore against the public interest.

### Case study

#### A bike to rent just whenever and wherever you want it?

Rod McColl and Irena Descubes, ESC Rennes School of Business, France

Cycling has become increasingly popular in recent years, spurred on by many factors, including increasing concern for personal fitness, rising costs of running a car, gridlocked city streets, an increasing number of segregated cycle lanes, and the social acceptability of bike use – once seen as a poor person's means of transport, but now a sign of the fit and ecologically friendly citizen. Like many products, bikes can be bought either as a tangible purchase, or as a service. While bike retailers in Western Europe have been enjoying a boom time, many rental schemes have emerged to loan out bikes as a service. For a long time there have been bike rental companies who rent out bikes to tourists for a day or a week or so. Accessibility to a bike has not generally been a strong point of these operations, as the renter must generally collect the bike from a predetermined place and return it to the same point some time later. More recently, many towns have developed schemes to rent out bikes just at the point where a consumer wants one, and just for the length of time that they need it. The principle is just like hiring a taxi – you pick it up where and when you need it, you leave it at your destination, then repeat the process if you are making a return journey. Making sure that bikes are available just at the time and place that people need them can be very difficult to manage, especially if the bikes are provided as a community service without the full intervention of commercial market principles.

The city of Rennes in Western France has pioneered the development of an urban cycle rental scheme, and learned how to tackle some of the problems of accessibility to the system. The first bike rental scheme was established in Rennes in 1998, and the current scheme, called Vélo STAR, has been operated since 2009 by the leading French transport operator Keolis SA. The contract between Rennes Metropole and Keolis SA has been renewed for the period 2013-2017.

Keolis proposed a maximum distance of 330 metres between each of the 83 city stations (40 of which are within Rennes city centre), using a fleet of 900 bikes (a plan submitted in 2013 to incorporate outlying villages, growing the system to 117 stations and 1285 bikes, was postponed). Bike rental stations vary in size depending on the forecast demand and have 16, 30 or 50 bike parking spaces. Keolis had grand ambitions for making a bike easily accessible to all, with a much higher level of accessibility than had been provided by the previous operator of the cycle scheme – Clear Channel – which provided only 25 stations with 12 cycle stands in each, and limited the number of registered users of the scheme to 5000 at any one time.

The first issue in making bikes accessible was to develop a system for registration and payment by users. One approach could have been to install a coin slot at each bike station by which users paid each time that they wanted to rent a bike. This would have been inconvenient for users and costly for the operator to set up and maintain. The previous system had required individuals to obtain an access card from a central office, which was free but the user had to pay a refundable deposit, and their card was deactivated if they did not use it for three months. The system was not very user-friendly and may have been one factor contributing to the bike scheme 'running out of steam', with just 280 rentals per day citywide in 2008. Keolis made access to a bike easier by allowing renters to use their annual bus/metro pass as a bike access card. Alternatively users could purchase an access card using a credit card at one of the 10 main rental stations at a cost of €1 for 24 hours or €5 for seven-day access.

So far, so good – it was now in principle easier for a user to get access to the bike rental system, but Keolis now had to make sure that bikes were available at the places that users wanted to rent them. It had learned a lot from experience of usage patterns during the previous 10 years. Users tended to be relatively young, with 40 per cent aged under 25 years. Fifty-five per cent of the total system usage was concentrated between seven key city-centre stations. Keolis developed a model to predict patterns of usage, and from its analysis, priority areas for development of new bike rental stations were identified – near to places used by young adults, especially the city's universities. More stations were established at other key points such as bus and train interchanges and suburban employment and shopping centres. The company used a modular system of cycle station, so the capacity of a station could be reduced or enlarged in response to changes in demand, or to correct an error in forecasts of demand.

Having a bike rental station is one thing, but actually having bikes available can be another. In principle, there should be a constant flow of bikes in and out of each station, but unfortunately, stations have a tendency to accumulate bikes or to run out completely. Students travelling to lectures would deplete bikes at the stations near to residential accommodation at the start of the day, and they would pile up at campus stations. Another quirky imbalance that needed to be addressed was the tendency for more bikes to be rented to make short downhill journeys rather than for making the return uphill journey. To resolve the problem of imbalances in flow, the operator uses cycle transporters to move bikes around the system. It has a central control room which collates information about the status of each bike station and can take action in response to this. At first, it was mainly reactive, moving bikes from stations with a surplus to stations with a shortage. With more experience of operation, it has developed a predictive model to better understand when shortages will occur, so that it can move bikes in anticipation. It has found, for example, that Monday and Thursday mornings are particularly busy times for a number of stations used by students.

To avoid the inconvenience of a user trying to rent a bike from an empty bike rack, Keolis has developed a website showing real-time availability of bikes at each rental station (https://www.levelostar.fr/fr/stations/liste-des-stations.html). It has further innovated with a format that is easily available through mobile devices for potential renters who are already on the move, for example a passenger arriving on a train can check before they arrive on the availability of bikes at the station bike rack, and if none is available there, they will be informed about the nearest alternative availability.

Keolis has had to strike a fine balance between making bikes easily accessible to genuine users, and too easily available to thieves. In the past, some towns have operated voluntary bike rental schemes which allow anybody to borrow a bike without prior registration, and they are then trusted to return it. This invariably turned out to be an unsustainable model, as users 'borrowed' bikes without returning them. In Rennes, more than half of the 900 bikes in the system were stolen from the racks between September and November 2009. A defective hook connecting the bike to the console made it relatively easy for bikes to be stolen. Despite the improved design, 220 out of the 900 bikes were stolen between May and September 2012, forcing the temporary closure of eight city-centre stations.

The Rennes bike rental scheme is not intended to be a profit-making venture, and the local municipality subsidizes the scheme for environmental benefits. In fact, only 2 per cent of users use their bike beyond the first 30-minute period which is free of charge to registered users. In commercial markets, money tends to follow individuals' preferences for availability of a service, but in this case, there is only a very weak market signal to guide service access decisions. Instead, accessibility decisions made by Keolis are governed by a variety of key performance indicators (KPIs) specified by the municipality in return for the annual subsidy. This has resulted in some apparently odd behaviour, for example users frequently return their bike to a rack just before the end of the 30-minute free period and then immediately rent the bike again. There is no limit to how often a user can do this. Keolis does not mind, because this action boosts the number of recorded bike rentals – one of its KPIs. The existence of KPIs may have inhibited some possible marketing initiatives; for example, there is a surplus of bikes at the weekend when there could be a great demand for leisure use of bikes for longer periods, but the price mechanism is too inflexible to encourage this, and the company's KPIs wouldn't benefit from such an initiative.

Making a bike more accessible to users has been a key part of the marketing strategy of the Rennes bike rental scheme. It is undoubtedly one factor that has resulted in an increase in usage from just 280 rentals per day in 2008, to almost 3000 in December 2012. What's next? In June 2013 Keolis proposed to offer 220 electric bikes, which may be rented for an annual fee of €150 per year with a 20 per cent discount for existing travel card holders. The introduction of electric bikes sought to broaden the appeal of the bike rental scheme and, according to Rennes Metropole, 'this measure is a kind of a green nudge that will allow users to adopt sustainable modes of transportation during a transitional test period'.

### Case study review questions

1. Evaluate the role of technology in its widest sense in making bikes available to users.
2. In designing their system, what factors should Keolis have considered when estimating the overall number of bikes needed, the location of the rental stations and the number of parking places for each station?
3. How should Keolis balance the need for easy access to bikes by genuine users with the need to prevent theft and abuse?

## Summary and links to other chapters

Making services accessible to consumers involves some different principles compared to goods, largely arising out of the inseparability, intangibility and perishability of services. Because services are produced 'live', accessibility becomes an important design criterion for services, involving issues of time and place convenience. Services vary in the extent to which producers and consumers are able or willing to travel to each other in order for an inseparable service to be performed. Intermediaries become co-producers of a service. Services firms in many sectors have sought to reduce the effects of inseparability through mail, telephone and Internet access systems.

Intermediaries are often the main contact that a customer has with an organization and therefore they can be critical to successful service encounters (Chapter 2) and contribute to the overall quality of a service (Chapter 9). Increasingly, intermediaries are being used to promote service firms' relationship marketing strategies, although problems still remain where intermediaries are suspicious of service principals, who they fear are trying to reduce or eliminate their role (Chapter 5). The level of accessibility to a service is often reflected in the price charged for a service at a particular time and location (Chapter 11). When firms seek to expand overseas, new problems in developing accessibility are raised and these are discussed in Chapter 14.

## Chapter review questions

1 Identify and discuss factors that might influence a bank's decision on whether to extend the opening hours of a branch. Suggest strategies that may cost-effectively satisfy customers' need for greater access.

2 Critically evaluate the use of regression-based location decision models for a high-volume/low-value service provider of your choice.

3 Analyse the potential problems and opportunities for a dry-cleaning company seeking to expand through franchising.

## Activities

1 Compare the prices of a bottle of soft drink/jar of coffee/chocolate bar at different outlets in your area. What do the different prices for an identical product say about the value of access? Is there a consistent trend of retailers charging a price premium for the service of providing access in prime locations and/or at antisocial working hours?

2 Consider the case of a restaurant/coffee-shop chain with which you are familiar and have knowledge of a number of its branches. Try to develop 'rules' that may have been used by the chain for deciding the best locations for new branches. What common factors do you think may have influenced its location decisions? How important is each of these? Are there any exceptions to the rules that you have identified?

3 Undertake an audit of local fast-food restaurants in your area. Can you tell whether there are differences in the style and standard of service provided between franchised and company-owned outlets? If you were a franchisor, how would you go about monitoring and maintaining the standards of service provided by the franchised outlets that you have observed?

## Key terms

**Channels of distribution** A group of individuals and organizations that handles the flow of products from producers to customers.

**Co-producers** Consumers and suppliers that work together to produce the end product or service transaction. Sometimes also referred to as 'co-creation' of value.

**Disintermediation** The removal of intermediaries in a supply chain in order to sell products directly to the end consumer.

**Economies of scale** A productivity improvement occurring when an increase in the scale of the firm causes a decrease in the long-run average cost of each unit of production.

**Franchising** A continuing relationship in which the franchisor provides a licensed privilege to do business, plus assistance in organizing training, merchandising and management in return for a payment from the franchisee.

**Hub and spoke system** A model that uses a centrally located production hub and geographically dispersed outlets linked to the hub.

**Intermediary** A person or business who is acting as a third party that offers mediation services between two trading parties and acts as a conduit for goods or services offered by a supplier to a consumer.

**Push and pull channels** Producers either 'push' goods and services through a distribution channel to the final consumer, or consumers 'pull' them through the channel from the producer through intermediaries.

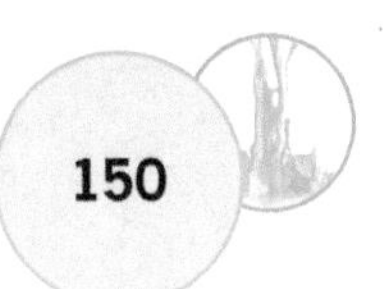

Service agent An intermediary who assists a service principal in making service benefits available to consumers. An agent is usually a co-producer of a service and acts on behalf of the service principal, with whom customers enter into legal relations.

Service principal The primary producer of a service, who may make part of its service available to consumers through intermediaries.

Social network sites Internet sites which facilitate communication between multiple users.

Spatial location-allocation models Models that are developed to locate multiple centres and allocate their demand area simultaneously on a network space of nodes and lines.

## Selected further reading

*For discussion of issues relating to the use of intermediaries by services organizations, the following provide useful insights:*

**Cassab, H. and MacLachlan, D.L.** (2009) 'A consumer-based view of multi-channel service', *Journal of Service Management*, 20 (1), 52–75.

**Doherty, A.M. and Alexander, N.** (2006) 'Power and control in international retail franchising', *European Journal of Marketing*, 40 (11/12), 1292–316.

**Hughes, T.** (2006) 'New channels/old channels: customer management and multichannels', *European Journal of Marketing*, 40 (1/2), 113–29.

**Lambert, D.M. and Enz, M.G.** (2012) 'Managing and measuring value co-creation in business-to-business relationships,' *Journal of Marketing Management*, 28 (13–14), 1588–1625.

*The effects of the Internet on service distribution channels are discussed in the following:*

**Dall'Olmo Riley, F., Scarpi, D. and Manaresi, A.** (2009) 'Purchasing services online: a two-country generalization of possible influences', *Journal of Services Marketing*, 23 (2), 92–102.

**Kim, J.-H., Kim, M. and Kandampully, J.** (2009) 'Buying environment characteristics in the context of e-service', *European Journal of Marketing*, 43 (9/10), 1188–204.

*Franchising of services is discussed in the following:*

**Altinay, L.** (2004) 'Implementing international franchising: the role of intrapreneurship', *International Journal of Service Industry Management*, 15 (5), 426–43.

**British Franchise Association** (2012) *The NatWest/British Franchising Association Annual Survey of Franchising*, British Franchise Association, Henley-on-Thames.

**Combs, J.G., Michael, S.C. and Castrogiovanni, G.J.** (2009) 'Institutional influences on the choice of organizational form: the case of franchising', *Journal of Management*, 35 (5), 1268–90.

*The subject of access to services for socially disadvantaged groups is discussed in the following article:*

**Carbo, S., Gardener, E.P.M. and Molyneux, P.** (2007) 'Financial exclusion in Europe', *Public and Money Management*, 27 (1), 21–7.

*Implications of the 24/7 culture for service firms' accessibility strategy is discussed in the following:*

**Groucutt, J.** (2005) 'Radical strategies may be required in today's 24/7 society', *Handbook of Business Strategy*, 6 (1), 241–5.

## References

**Bigne, E., Ruiz, C. and Sanz, S.** (2005) 'The impact of internet user shopping patterns and demographics on consumer mobile buying behaviour', *Journal of Electronic Commerce Research*, 6 (3), 193–209.

**British Franchise Association** (2012) *The NatWest/British Franchising Association Annual Survey of Franchising*, British Franchise Association, Henley-on-Thames.

**Castrogiovanni, G.J., Julian, S.D. and Justis, R.T.** (1993) 'Franchise failure rates: an assessment of magnitude and influencing factors', *Journal of Small Business Management*, 31 (2), 105–14.

**Dacko, S.G.** (2012) 'Time-of-day services marketing', *Journal of Services Marketing*, 26 (5), 375–88.

**Daily Mail** (2010) 'Hundreds of schoolchildren sold fake World Cup tickets', *Daily Mail*, 19 June, 6.

**Eurostat** (2012) *Eurostat Yearbook*, Statistical Office of the European Communities, Luxembourg.

**Fishbein, M.** (1967) *Readings in Attitude Theory and Measurement*, John Wiley and Sons, New York.

**Gefen, D., Karahanna, E. and Straub, D.W.** (2003) 'Trust and TAM in online shopping: an integrated model', *MIS Quarterly*, 27 (1), 51–90.

**Hotelling, H.** (1929) 'Stability in competition', *The Economic Journal*, 39 (153), 41–57.

**Huff, D.L.** (1966) 'A programmed solution for approximating an optimal retail location', *Land Economics*, 42 (3), 293–303.

**IFA** (2010) *An Introduction to Franchising*, IFA Educational Foundation, Washington, DC.

**Jones, K.G. and Mock, D.R.** (1984) 'Evaluating retail trading performances', in R.L. Davies and D.S. Rogers (eds), *Store Location and Store Assessment Research*, John Wiley, New York.

**Mayo, E.J. and Jarvis, L.P.** (1981) *The Psychology of Leisure Travel*, CBI, Boston, MA.

**National Audit Office (NAO)** (2008) *Major Projects Report 2008*, National Audit Office, London.

**Sen, R., King, R.C. and Shaw, M.J.** (2006) 'Buyers' choice of online search strategy and its managerial implications', *Journal of Management Information Systems*, 23 (1), 211–38.

**Yousafzai, S.Y., Pallister, J.G. and Foxall, G.R.** (2005) 'Strategies for building and communicating trust in electronic banking: a field experiment', *Psychology & Marketing*, 22 (2), 181–201.

**Yrjölä, H.** (2001) 'Physical distribution considerations for electronic home shopping', *International Journal of Physical Distribution & Logistics*, 31 (10), 746–61.

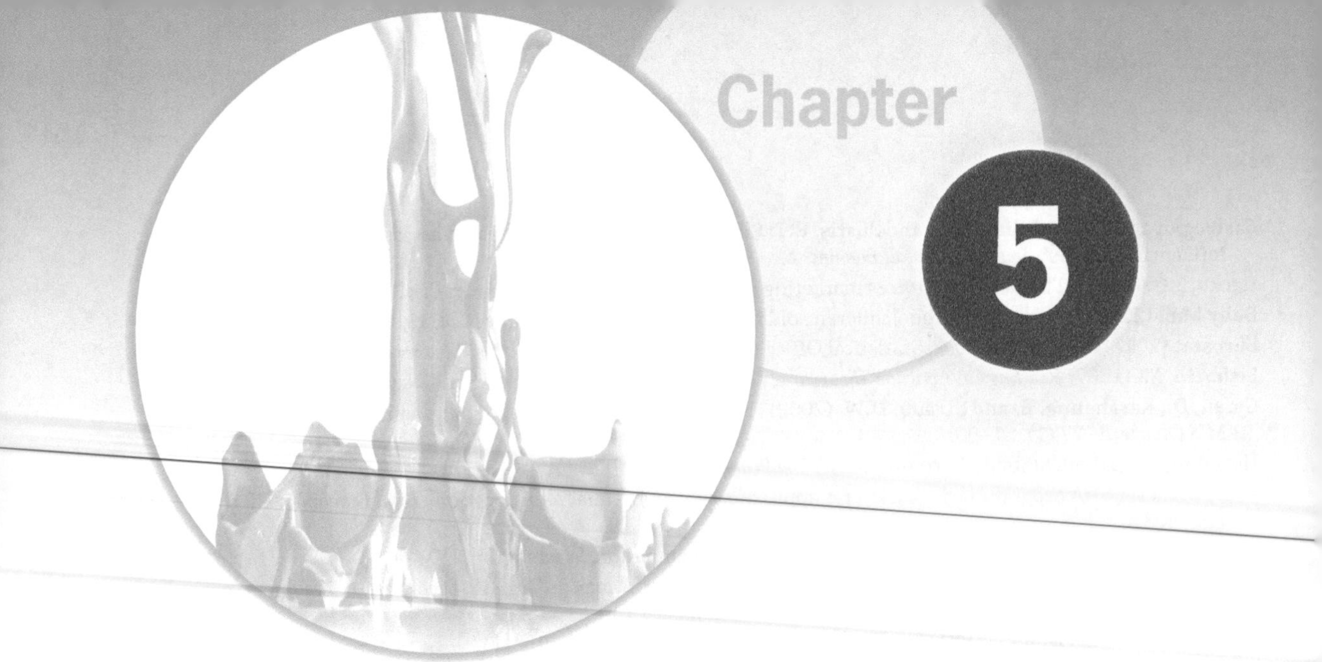


# Relationships, partnerships and networks

*Great, you thought! You had bought an all-inclusive deal to visit a top London show, including the tickets for the show and train travel. Then your excitement was deflated when the eagerly awaited event went wrong. The train was badly delayed, so you missed the show. The travel agent from whom you bought the ticket passed you on to the train operator who blamed the track operator for a problem that was not its fault. The theatre would not give a refund on the unused ticket because it had done nothing wrong and found itself with two empty seats. It might all sound a mess, but reflects the reality of many complex (and not so complex) services that are provided by many co-operating companies. Had the theatre break gone according to plan, we might just have taken for granted the network of companies that made the event a great success for us. In this chapter we explore the nature of networks and relationships that create many of the services that we consume, and what it takes to turn us into loyal customers of a company.*

## Learning objectives

After reading this chapter, you should understand:

- The role of co-production between service providers
- The diversity of networks and relationships that exist between service providers and their customers
- Reasons for the development of buyer–seller relationships
- Theoretical underpinnings of buyer–seller relationship development
- Methods used by companies to turn casual transactions into ongoing loyal relationships

## 5.1 Introduction

The idea of relationships between businesses, and between businesses and their customers, has become central to modern marketing. Indeed, some have talked about 'relationship marketing' representing a 'paradigm shift' (Grönroos, 1994). A relationship implies that a buyer and seller do not simply regard each encounter in isolation, but rather see the relationship in the context of previous transactions, and with an expectation of future transactions. Many manufacturing businesses have transformed their product offer by taking a relational perspective. As we saw in Chapter 1, car manufacturers no longer simply sell a car and then forget about the customer until they come back to replace it in three years' time. They have developed ongoing relationships, which may include warranties, maintenance, finance and insurance to provide support for the customer throughout the lifetime of their vehicle. Many suppliers of generic products, such as building materials, have developed relationships as a source of competitive advantage in the eyes of customers who benefit from easier ordering and delivery tailored to their specific needs. In business-to-consumer markets, service providers now have the ability to know their customers individually, and to tailor the service offer based on an ongoing relationship.

In this chapter, we begin by exploring the complex networks of business-to-business relationships that often underlie the provision of services. We see that parts of the service sector have grown as a result of many manufacturing companies (and indeed other service companies) outsourcing their service provision through networks of relationships with other businesses. We explore the theoretical bases for the growth of relationships and networks. The first part of this chapter will focus on business-to-business relationships and we then move on to consider business-to-consumer relationships. Although the principles are similar, the task of one company managing relationships with thousands, or even millions, of individual customers poses challenges, helped (or in some cases hindered) by developments in technology.

## 5.2 Network perspectives of marketing

All but the very simplest service systems are likely to involve a complex network of relationships between producers, who help to create the service and make it available to consumers. Some links in the network will become particularly important and characterized by long-term co-operative relationships, rather than short-term bargaining over a series of one-off transactions. The idea of networks of producers co-operating to create value is true of both services and manufactured goods sectors. In the manufacturing sector, for example, computer manufacturers have relied on a network of component manufacturers to create value-added products that are worth more than the sum total of the component inputs. They also often rely on independent intermediaries to make their computers available to buyers. As far as consumers are concerned, the network of supplier relationships remains by and large hidden, so that somebody who buys a Dell laptop may not be aware – and may not even care – that the battery has been made by Sony or the disk drive by Seagate. They have no interaction with the component manufacturers, and are generally happy as long as the quality of the complete product meets their expectations.

The big difference with services is that many parts of a service provider's production network impact directly on the consumer. Because of the inseparability of service processes, network providers become embedded in the service offer as a co-producer. This is different from the manufactured components used by a car manufacturer, for which the consumer generally has no interaction with the manufacturer. For services, the performance of network-provided processes can contribute significantly to consumers' evaluation of the total service offer.

An idea of the complexity of networks that may impact on consumers can be provided by the following example of an Air France flight from Birmingham, UK to Paris, France. Consider the following network of partnerships that a customer would have encountered during their journey:

- A customer will probably begin their encounter with one of the many intermediaries (online and offline) with which Air France deals. Travel agents themselves are likely to be linked into one of the major global distribution networks (such as Amadeus).
- Some customers may have bought their ticket with an Air France credit card, which is actually provided by American Express.
- The airport at Birmingham is not owned by Air France, which must rely on service level agreements with the airport operator in order to ensure that facilities available (access facilities, availability of information, general maintenance etc.) are consistent with the total service offer of Air France.
- At Birmingham, check-in and baggage handling for Air France is carried out on its behalf by Servisair. This supplier of ground services operates on behalf of a number of airlines flying into Birmingham and, for many people, is the first face-to-face contact that they have with a representative of Air France.
- Some passengers will be travelling with a ticket issued by another airline. The service from Birmingham to Paris is a 'code share' flight with Alitalia, so Air France must seek to make a seamless journey for Alitalia customers who are travelling to Italian destinations via Paris. Likewise, many Air France customers from Birmingham may be travelling onwards from Paris using an Air France code-share flight that is actually operated by another airline, for example China Eastern.
- Air France is a member of the 'Skyteam' alliance of leading airlines, including Delta, Alitalia, Aero Mexico, Czech Airlines and Korean Air. Passengers on the flight from Birmingham to Paris who are members of the alliance's frequent-flyer programme will earn points that can be redeemed with any of the alliance members.
- After checking in, a customer must pass through immigration and security controls. At many airports, airlines have been frustrated by their relationship with these services, over which they have little control.
- The flight itself is not actually operated by Air France, but is operated on its behalf by the Irish-based airline City Jet. Air France has calculated that it is more cost-effective to subcontract or franchise the operation of its more peripheral routes.
- On arrival in Paris, a new set of network relationships is present, although in this case, because Paris is an important base for Air France, many of the services that are subcontracted in Birmingham (such as check-in) are provided directly by the company itself.

In addition to these visible relationships which a consumer encounters directly, there is a very large network of invisible relationships whose performance is crucial to successful operation of a flight. These include relationships to maintain aircraft, provide technology support for the airlines' self-service check-in facilities, catering supplies etc.

We will use the example of the Air France flight to illustrate some of the principles of networks and relationships as they affect services marketing. Although the following headings do not provide an exhaustive and mutually exclusive analysis, they do provide a useful summary of the literature on distinguishing characteristics of networks and relationships.

### 5.2.1 Horizontal collaborative relationships

There are many situations where two or more service organizations providing an essentially similar service, at the same point in a supply chain, can create greater value for customers by working together. In some cases, these collaborative networks may span an entire industry. There are two principal benefits to such collaboration:

1. Customers may benefit where potentially competing suppliers agree on common technical standards. The growth of the mobile phone sector in Europe has been greatly facilitated by agreement among the main operators on the common global system for mobile communications (GSM) standard. Some have argued that mobile phones developed more slowly in the USA because of a lack of agreement among operators on shared standards. If we consider the Air France case, the airline sector has benefited from many agreements on technical standards brokered through the International Air Transport Association (IATA). Even a simple agreement, such as the common barcodes used to identify bags as they travel through airports throughout the world, has the potential to reduce costs and to improve customer satisfaction by reducing the number of mislaid bags.
2. A second, and sometimes related, form of collaboration occurs where service suppliers recognize that their service offer may be too small to have an impact on customers but, if they collaborate with their competitors, they can offer more choice and achieve a critical mass that has an impact on customer value. Banks in Britain co-operate through the Link network to make their cash machines available to their competitors' customers, and they collaborate at a global level through Maestro to create further benefits to customers, who can use their credit cards at cash machines throughout the world. Bank customers in many countries take the benefits of such collaboration for granted, in contrast to those countries where customers of a bank are only allowed to use the ATMs operated by that bank. Airlines frequently co-operate to provide 'seamless' travel between potentially competing airlines. The code-share flights referred to above allowed Alitalia customers to travel seamlessly on an Air France flight, as if the flight were actually provided by Alitalia. Alitalia was able to reduce the cost of its route network, while offering a more extensive network to its customers than would have been the case had it simply not provided a connection to Birmingham. Global alliances between airlines (for example, SkyTeam and Oneworld) offer further opportunities for customers to seamlessly acquire and use frequent-flyer benefits.

Against these benefits to customers and suppliers resulting from collaboration, competition authorities throughout the world are becoming increasingly concerned about business practices that directly or indirectly have the effect of restricting competition within a market. To refer back to the examples given above, the UK Office of Fair Trading conducted an investigation into an agreement between the main UK banks to charge customers to use ATM cards in machines operated by other members of the Link network. Their report showed that, although banks' sharing of ATMs brought benefits to customers, the banks' collective monopoly supply of ATMs in the UK led to excessive prices charged to customers, and the banks were subsequently ordered to reduce some charges (OFT, 2003). In the case of airlines, the European Commission has taken a growing interest in global alliances and their possible anti-competitive implications. In 2006, it launched an enquiry into alleged price fixing between SkyTeam alliance members (which included Air France, KLM, Delta and Alitalia) for airfreight rates (*Financial Times*, 2006).

Karl Marx observed that capitalists were more concerned with *avoiding* risks rather than *taking* risks. The development of networks of buyer–seller relationships may be seen as a means of reducing entrepreneurs' exposure to risk, thereby reducing some of the presumed benefits of a competitive market environment.

### 5.2.2 Vertical collaborative relationships

Where a service process involves significant tangible content, close vertical collaborative relationships may be crucial for ensuring a timely delivery of these tangible components. Fast-food chains, for example, have developed integrated supply chains reaching back through transport companies, food processors and farms, which have the effect of ensuring that consistent quality products, ethically produced, are available for incorporation into their service processes at exactly the right time and place.

### 5.2.3 Outsourcing

We saw in Chapter 1 that one reason for the apparent growth in the services sector was the trend for businesses to 'outsource' many activities that they previously carried out in-house. Many companies that have traditionally employed their own cleaning, catering and security staff now subcontract or outsource these to specialist suppliers. Sometimes, employees of the organization are transferred to the new supplier and hence become employees of the specialist contractor. This contractor then provides an agreed level of service to the organization for a specified contract period. At the end of this period the organization is able to evaluate competing suppliers before placing the next contract. The specialist supplier assumes profit-and-loss responsibility for the delivery of the service as well as taking on the employment and employment rights of the employees.

Outsourcing has been defined as 'the strategic use of outside resources to perform activities traditionally handled by internal staff and resources' (Cain, 2009). Outsourced contracts range from a small factory replacing kitchen assistants with a contract caterer, to the Greater London Authority's outsourcing of the collection of the London Congestion Charge, to Capita plc.

Outsourcing offers many potential advantages to an organization:

- It builds on the principles of industrialization that were discussed in Chapter 2 by allowing an organization to focus its activities on its core activities.
- Access is given to cutting-edge skills that would be difficult for a company to acquire and learn on its own. The company does not have to worry about continually introducing new technologies.
- The risks of service provision are shared, especially in the case of activities that are new to the company.
- Service quality can be improved where a contract provides rewards for good performance.
- A company's scarce human resources can be freed up and redeployed in activities that add higher value.
- Outsourcing can free up cash flow, allowing it to be reinvested in core business activities (e.g. an airline outsourcing its maintenance operations can use cash that was previously invested in its maintenance facilities to invest in better aircraft).
- It can make the business more flexible to changes in the external environment.

However, outsourcing also has disadvantages:

- Big disruptions can occur if the outsourced service provider ceases to trade (e.g. through bankruptcy).
- Employees may react badly to outsourcing and consequently the quality of their work may suffer.
- Outsourcing may involve redundancy costs and bad feeling among employees who remain.
- There may be a career-progression problem with the loss of talent generated internally.
- Other competing companies may also be using the service provider, resulting in a possible conflict of interest on the part of the outsourced service provider.
- The company may lose direct contact with its customers.

Some have argued that outsourcing undermines a coherent internal focus on meeting customers' needs. An outsourced supplier may be so focused on meeting its narrowly defined performance targets that it overlooks more qualitative aspects of delivering value to customers. The UK's National Health Service has used outsourcing extensively for the cleaning of hospital wards. There may have been significant cost savings from this move, but the cleaners who come in and do their work have been accused of not having the same team spirit as cleaners who are employed by the hospital and directly answerable to the matron. Over time, and through an acculturalization process, a ward-based cleaner may have learnt to be the eyes and ears of nurses, for example, identifying symptoms of medical problems that doctors and nurses may have missed. Now they may just 'tick the box' and do no more than the cleaning specified in their service agreement.

Outsourcing is now being undertaken on a global scale. Although manufacturers have traditionally outsourced the manufacture of component goods to countries with low costs, the inseparability of services has reduced the opportunities for global outsourcing of services. However, improved telecommunications have provided new opportunities, for example call centres and Internet support operations that many Western companies have 'offshored' to relatively low-cost countries such as India. We will return to this subject in Chapter 14.

## Thinking around the subject: Powering up computers through outsourcing

Seeboard, a West-Sussex-based energy company that supplies gas and electricity to approximately 2 million customers in the UK, identified its core competence as being the distribution of energy at lower prices and with higher customer service levels than its competitors. Of course, low prices and top-quality services can easily lead to a loss, so the company has had to keep a very close eye on its costs, as well as ensuring that the best people deliver its services.

Outsourcing has played an important role for the company. Seeboard began its first outsourcing contract with Accenture in 1993, subsequently adding Siemens to its outsourced suppliers. Since 2001, the company has outsourced the management of its desktop computers and network servers to the specialist IT services company Computacenter.

Information technology has become increasingly important to Seeboard. Like many companies, Seeboard is web-enabling more of its business processes, for example an online service for customers to record and submit their own meter readings. The company also realized that expansion of its IT needs would rapidly outgrow the resources of its in-house team.

Computacenter was brought in to manage Seeboard's computers in a contract that covered 3,000 desktops, 400 laptops and 200 servers at various sites across London and the South East. Computacenter was given responsibility for developing standard desktop builds, configuring servers, rolling out new software and hardware, day-to-day support and the disposal of redundant equipment.

One slight complication of the contract was that care had to be taken to avoid a conflict of interest between Seeboard's power supply operations (Seeboard Power Networks) and its distribution business (Seeboard Energy). The deregulation of the industry had meant that energy companies must avoid taking competitive advantage from their ownership of both supply and distribution operations in an area. Separate service provision to Seeboard Power Networks and Seeboard Energy meant separate support contracts and organizations for each business.

By working with Computacenter, Seeboard was able to access a much wider pool of technical knowledge and benefited from Computacenter's experience gained through other IT projects and outsourcing contracts. As a result, Seeboard benefited from worldwide best practice, requiring fewer staff than if it had carried out the work itself in-house, and claimed to have cut its total IT operating costs. Just by implementing a standard desktop configuration, it saw a decrease in support calls and, as a result, in support overheads.

It must not, however, be forgotten that Seeboard's aim was not just to cut costs, but also to improve customer service – a vital source of competitive differentiation. A cheap outsourced operation that left the company's websites down for lengthy periods would not be good for customers and profitability. Seeboard used a balanced scorecard system with internal and external users to assess the service-level standards, responsiveness, customer satisfaction and project performance, and claimed to be happy with the results.

How far can a company such as Seeboard go in its outsourcing? Like many utility services, it saw advantages in supplementing outsourcing with 'offshoring' – moving many of its service processes overseas to lower-cost providers. Some electricity companies have transferred call centres and bill-processing functions to India, where a high-quality workforce can usually undertake the job at lower cost. But, if it went down this route, would it still be able to maintain high levels of customer service? Would customers be as happy speaking to a call-centre worker in Bangalore as a Seeboard worker in Brighton?

## 5.2.4 Public–private partnerships

A significant trend in recent years has been the development of agreements between public- and private-sector organizations to jointly develop and market vital public services. The principal motivation for such agreements is the desire to combine the long-term planning role of the public sector with the resources, energy and entrepreneurship of the private sector. **Public–Private Partnerships (PPP)** is an umbrella name given to a range of initiatives that involve the private sector in the operation of public services. In the UK, the **Private Finance Initiative (PFI)** is the most common initiative, but PPP can also extend to other forms of partnership, for example joint ventures.

Traditionally, governments have procured facilities and services, which the private sector has supplied under contract to the public sector. For example, under a traditional supply relationship, a private-sector contractor would build a new school to the specification of a local education authority, with associated maintenance and services then being provided by a range of private companies and the authority itself.

With a PPP, one contractor provides the school and then operates a range of specific services such as maintenance, heating and school meals on behalf of the education authority through a long-term contract. This new way of working allows the private sector to contribute its expertise to the process, so as to find innovative solutions and secure better value for money. A typical PFI project would be operated by a company set up specially to run the scheme. These companies are usually consortia, which typically include a building firm, a bank and a facilities management company. PFI projects can be structured in various ways, but there are usually four key elements: design, finance, build and operations. In the case of new hospitals funded by PFI schemes, the clinical, medical and nursing services generally continue to be provided by the hospital authority, while the private sector finances the building of the new hospital and runs the non-clinical services in it such as maintenance, cleaning, portering and security.

The transformation from subcontractor to partner in a PPP scheme has a number of implications for marketing. The first major marketing challenge for a private-sector company is to win the selection process for becoming the PPP partner. For major schemes, this process can take several months or years of detailed analysis and assessment of likely costs and revenues, and also of what rival companies may bid. The process may also include lobbying of civil servants and politicians to emphasize the company's credibility as a long-term partner. The company must carefully assess the risks and likely rewards associated with a long-term agreement. The costs of setting up a PPP scheme are reflected in a UK Audit Commission report, which found that the first 15 NHS trust hospital PFIs spent £45 million on advisers, an average of 4 per cent of the capital value. Although one reason for governments pursuing PPPs has been their desire to shift risk to the private sector, this must be acceptable to the private sector. One way of managing the company's exposure to risk is to include a price premium to reflect downside risk. To spread risk, it is common for consortia of firms to submit a joint PPP bid. Where a company takes on a PPP on disadvantageous terms, results can be potentially crippling. This was seen in the case of Metronet, which had been awarded a contract to maintain and upgrade parts of the London underground train network. In 2007, faced with escalating costs and arguments with the public-sector partner – Transport for London – over design standards, the consortium behind Metronet put it into administration, leaving Transport for London to take back operation of the underground lines affected.

Once an agreement is up and running, the opportunities for marketing vary between agreements. In many cases, government sets performance standards, such as the availability of beds in a hospital, or the proportion of time that a telephone system is available, and the private-sector partner earns its profits by careful control of costs and meeting its agreed performance standards. In such cases, the opportunities for revenue development by attracting more customers are absent. In other cases, an agreement will allow for the private-sector partner to generate additional revenue, usually subject to regulatory controls. As an example, the Australian-based Macquarie Bank, which entered an agreement with the UK government to finance and build the M6 toll motorway around Birmingham, is allowed to keep revenues that it charges drivers to use the motorway. As with outsourcing contracts, there is a need for flexibility to be built into the agreement to accommodate environmental and internal changes that can occur over the lifetime of a contract (Ketter, 2008).

## In practice: Working together for 2012

Figure 5.1 The Olympic Games came to London

When London was chosen to host the 2012 Olympic Games (the Games), the initial cheers tended to hide the enormous amount of collaborative work that lay behind London's successful bid, and the even more extensive network of relationships that would be necessary to deliver a successful Olympic Games. Thousands of individual service providers stood to benefit from the Games, ranging from small restaurants catering for construction workers and visitors to the Games through to large infrastructure providers. At the centre of the collaborative relationships that made the Games happen is the Olympic Delivery Authority (ODA). The ODA was given statutory backing through the London Olympic Games and Paralympic Games Act 2006, and has used a combination of power and persuasion to co-ordinate the efforts of multiple service providers, who collectively made up the total Olympic experience for those who visited the Games in person, or who watched on television. The ODA worked closely with key partners such as the London Organizing Committee of the Olympic Games, Transport for London (which was responsible for developing transport infrastructure to serve the Games), the London Development Agency and other regional development agencies such as the London Thames Gateway Development Corporation, in order to ensure not only that the Games were successful, but also that the infrastructure achieves long-term planning goals. The ODA was responsible for making arrangements for building works, which it did through partnerships and subcontractor arrangements. At the same time as managing relationships with numerous suppliers, the ODA had to work closely with the International Olympic Committee to ensure that its standards were met. The ODA had responsibilities for protecting the Olympic logo and rights to use it by sponsors and other commercial users, and this required the ODA to manage a large network of sponsors who contributed to the cost of holding the Games.

From the beginning, many sceptics were convinced that the London Olympics would be an expensive mistake as government spent money that could have been used for other important purposes. But in the summer of 2012 the Olympic Games took place and most people agreed that they were a great success. Without doubt, a large part of this success was due to the complex networks of public- and private-sector organizations who worked hard behind the scenes to deliver the Games.

### 5.2.5 Networks of connected consumers

Finally, we must not overlook the networks that can exist between the customers of a company. The ability of customers to be connected with one another is not new, but today, the development of various Web 2.0 social network technologies has extended the possibilities for such connectedness. A distinguishing feature of social network sites is the apparent willingness and ability of individuals to communicate their thoughts to others, including people whom they do not know. Many strong service brands such as Skype have been built with very little paid-for advertising and instead relied on referral through online communities.

Online communities present a number of opportunities for companies to get close to their markets, including observing and collecting information; hosting or sponsoring communities; providing content to communities (such as music, information or entertainment); and participating as members of online communities (Miller et al., 2009). Companies would generally love their product to be at the heart of a community, and there have been many examples of companies who have developed social network media to put them at the centre of a community. Starbucks, for example, has a Facebook site which claimed to have 34,496,669 'likes' in May 2013; it is present on Twitter; and it has its own YouTube channel and its own online community web pages (MyStarbucksIdeas, Starbucks V2V and StarbucksRed).

A company's involvement in social network sites can result in a wide range of strategic and operational benefits. By inviting feedback, or simply observing conversations, a company can learn about customers' needs and inform its new product development policy. In the language of 'service dominant logic', a company can involve members of the community in the co-creation of value through the generation of ideas (Constantinides and Fountain, 2008).

Online communities can pose a threat as well as an opportunity to companies as they can rapidly spread the views of dissatisfied, angry customers. As an example, the HSBC bank announced in 2007 that it intended to end interest-free overdrafts for students after they had graduated, but was subsequently forced to do a U-turn and restore the facility. Many commentators attributed this change of heart to the strength of feeling expressed through Facebook circles of friends. Another example is provided by two employees from Domino's Pizza in North Carolina who posted a video of disgusting food preparation on YouTube (Vogt, 2009).

## 5.3 Theories underpinning networks and relationships

Several researchers have linked competitive success with a company's ability to develop and manage its array of network relationships. For example, Araujo and Easton (1986) categorize competition on the basis of competitive advantage, conflict, coexistence, co-operation or collusion. They use three theoretical frameworks for their analysis. First there are frameworks based on traditional marketing strategies, second, an interaction approach and, third, a network approach. Before we look at the methods and practices of developing networks and relationships, we will briefly consider some of the underpinning theory that seeks to explain why firms seek relationships through networks of co-producers and customers. A number of overlapping streams of literature are particularly relevant here: contracting theory, transaction cost economic theory and resource dependence theory. In addition, models of consumer choice help to explain why consumers seek relationships with suppliers. This is not an exhaustive list of the theoretical roots of relationship marketing, but the overlapping ideas contained in these theories have made significant contributions to the subject.

*Contract theory*, given prominence by McNeil (1980), discusses the bases of contracts that combine, on the one hand, freedom for both parties to adapt to changing circumstances but, on the other hand, must reduce the temptation for one party to exploit the other. In general, details about the whole range of rights and obligations cannot be defined in advance for complex transactions, and it must be recognized that a formal contract is just a part of the process of governing relations between parties. Overlying this is a shared understanding, which arises when parties develop longer-term relationships with each other rather than making a series of one-off transactions with different parties. Developing on this, Williamson, in his book *Markets and Hierarchies*, addressed the question 'Why do organizations exist?'. He argued that organizations are a means to reduce uncertainty and opportunism in the marketplace (Williamson, 1975). By extension, networks of co-operating organizations reduce the costs and uncertainty associated with acting alone as isolated business units through series of one-off transactions.

*Transaction cost economics*, given prominence by Williamson, is based on the notion that there are costs of doing business that are in addition to readily identifiable resource costs. These costs can include administrative costs and the cost of insuring against contingencies when dealing with unknown customers and suppliers (Williamson, 1985). Williamson noted that the primary objective of economic organizations is to 'economize in both transaction and neo-classical production costs' (Williamson, 1985, p. 28). Transaction costs are affected by information availability and uncertainty. Hybrid forms of organization, such as strategic alliances, networks, equity joint ventures etc., can be attributed to the search for efficiency in transaction costs (Williamson, 1993). In the theoretical model, all transactions lie somewhere on a continuum from being purely market based to being internal to an organization. According to Williamson, firms exist as a means of reducing the risk of dealing with the uncertainties of a market, thereby reducing transaction costs. On the other hand, market forces can stimulate competition, and hence bring down production costs. Firms seek to reduce their total costs and, in reality, 'hybrid' types of organization emerge. Networks of buyer–seller relationships represent a hybrid type of organization, which reduces the uncertainty of pure market-mediated exchanges, while overcoming the inefficiencies of internal (hierarchical) systems of exchange.

Co-operation between firms, which creates value through lowering transaction costs and/or increasing benefits to each party, may result in one or both parties giving preferential treatment to the other. Within a transaction-cost framework, this could come about as a result of growing levels of trust, which reduce the need for contingencies against risk and uncertainty in transactions. It can also arise where scale benefits encourage preference being given to one partner, who is capable of delivering increasing levels of benefits relative to costs.

*Resource dependency theory* approaches commercial relationships by conceptualizing them as a strategic response by firms to conditions of uncertainty (Pfeffer and Salanick, 1978). Firms have been conceptualized as bundles of competencies such as tacit knowledge, skills etc., and this framework has been extended to the study of inter-organizational relationships. Through co-operation, partners can exchange core competencies and thereby avoid the risk of tackling novel products or markets alone. In the discussion on strategic relationships between organizations, the ability of member organizations to exchange their technical and marketing competencies has been noted (Hamel et al., 1989). As an example, many alliances between airlines and hotels are formed where individual companies calculate that there will be benefits in sharing access to each other's customers, who are mutually exclusive in terms of their geographical representation and/or product requirements. The value of networks of relationships has been shown to be particularly valuable where 'strategic holes' exist in the connectivity between members, and the network can create social capital by bringing together disparate individuals and organizations (Baker, 1994; Burt, 1992).

A further school of thought based on models of buyer behaviour sees buyer–seller relationships as being essentially about a process of *choice reduction* (Sheth and Parvatiyar, 2002). From the buyer's perspective, having excessive choice involves spending time and effort evaluating the competing alternatives. Models of buyer behaviour have been developed to show how consumers reduce the total available set of products to a more manageable 'choice set', which typically may involve just five or six products, which are evaluated in greater detail. A relationship is one way of managing this process of choice reduction – in other words, a buyer will initially confine their search to those suppliers with whom they have already established a satisfactory relationship.

*Equity theory* has been used to argue that customers who feel that they are getting a better ratio of benefits to costs than their exchange partner will feel a greater sense of commitment to their exchange partner (Goodwin and Ross, 1992; Kelley and Davis, 1994) and are likely to show greater forbearance in the event of a failure by the supplier. The notion of *reciprocity* has been considered to be a fundamental virtue that builds solidarity and contributes to the creation and maintenance of balance in commercial and social relationships (Bagozzi, 1995; Becker, 1990).

*Anthropological and sociological approaches* have contributed an understanding of individuals' desire to identify with groups and the services that they consume (e.g. Sierra and McQuitty, 2005). Relationships satisfy individuals' affiliation and attachment needs, and there is some evidence that commercial relationships have replaced church, family and work-based relationships as a means of satisfying these needs (Palmer and Gallagher, 2007). The term 'tribal marketing' has been used to explain how marketers can take advantage of individuals' desire to belong to a group (Cova and Cova, 2002).

The concept of identity salience has been used in social psychology to explain why people develop relationships with not-for-profit organizations. Many people have developed a relationship with the Royal Society for the Protection of Birds (RSPB) because they can identify with the society's mission. Many students graduating from a university wish to continue to identify with that university by maintaining a relationship with its alumni association. Identity salience can also apply in the case of profit-orientated service organizations that go out of their way to identify with ethical business practices (Arnett et al., 2003).

Sociologists have also noted the effect of culture on individuals' approaches to business relationships. It has been observed that the pattern of doing business in many countries may be based on a tightly knit network of relationships between buyers, sellers, suppliers and distributors, typified by Japan's manufacturing and distribution *keiretsus* (Cutts, 1992; Ohmae, 1989). In many Asian countries, the idea of a relationship based on tightly specified contracts may be viewed as an insult, and a relationship would only develop over time through mutual trust. An American culture, by contrast, may view a detailed contract as essential for the development of a relationship.

Marketers have developed a number of models and frameworks to try to describe and explain the phenomenon of business relationships, and some of these are summarized here.

A significant contributor to the development of theory and research in this area is the Industrial Marketing and Purchasing (IMP) group. This group of primarily European-based researchers started in the 1970s and has conducted many studies of inter-firm relations, including many in-depth case studies and major empirical surveys of relations and networks in a variety of domestic and international contexts. The focus of IMP researchers has been on the nature and role of interactions, relations and networks in business markets and a central part of their analysis rests on an actors, activities and resources (AAR) model as the fundamental dimensions of relations (see for example Hakansson and Snehota, 1995).

The question has often been raised whether there should be a consistency in an organization's pattern of relationships with the different groups with whom it does business. Can an organization pursue a strategy of relationship marketing with its customers while it pursues one of 'hire and fire' with its employees and suppliers? A useful analytic framework for considering the consistency between an organization's multiple relationships is the 'six markets' model proposed by Christopher et al. (1991) and Payne et al. (2005). The six markets comprise:

- customers;
- suppliers;
- employees;
- other internal departments within the organization;
- referral markets, comprising advocates for the organization (e.g. intermediaries);
- influence markets, comprising bodies such as regulatory agencies that can significantly affect the organization.

Some organizations are notable for the way in which they have managed to create consistency in their dealings with each of their markets. The retailer Marks and Spencer has a long-standing policy of creating long-term relationships with its suppliers and its employment practices have emphasized the development and retention of personnel. In recent years, the company has taken a number of measures to improve the quality of ongoing relationships with its customers. The quality of its goods and customer service has always encouraged buyers to return, and this has been supplemented in recent years by the development of its credit card and related financial services. At the opposite end of the retailing spectrum, some chains of discount shops position themselves as price leaders with little attempt to reward customer loyalty, other than continuing low prices. Negotiations with suppliers are likely to be based on bargaining over individual consignments. Staff may be paid little more than the minimum wage. While consistency between the six markets may seem intuitively attractive, questions are asked where companies try to impose different patterns in each of its markets. In the case of Marks and Spencer, the company has terminated a number of long-standing relationships with suppliers in favour of cheaper sources negotiated elsewhere. Is this consistent with the relational culture within the organization, as manifested by relationships with customers?

The concept of *many-to-many marketing* has been developed by Gummesson in recognition of the limited usefulness of analysing one buyer–seller relationship in isolation from all the other relationships in which each party is involved. Gummesson's framework of a network society reflects the reality that people and organizations live in complex networks. Rather than conceptualizing a single customer meeting a single supplier, his framework comprises a customer network meeting a supplier network. He introduces a network approach to all marketing, be it business-to-business (B2B) or business-to-consumer (B2C), goods or services (Gummesson, 2006).

Finally, researchers in organizational behaviour have noted that an organization's relationships can be very complex, and individuals in one organization may see another organization as a co-operative relational partner in some aspects of business, but competitive in others. Airline sales managers, for example, may compete fiercely with another airline for customers, yet that same company's engineering managers may have co-operative relationships in respect of aircraft maintenance. This has led to exchanges between organizations being seen increasingly as multifaceted, rather than being based on contact solely through their respective buyers and sellers (Figure 5.2).

Figure 5.2 Relational exchange between organizations should occur between all of each organization's main functions. The traditional 'bow-tie' approach, in which communications between firms was focused on firms' buyers and sellers, is increasingly being replaced by the 'diamond' approach in which communication is dispersed through all of their main functions.

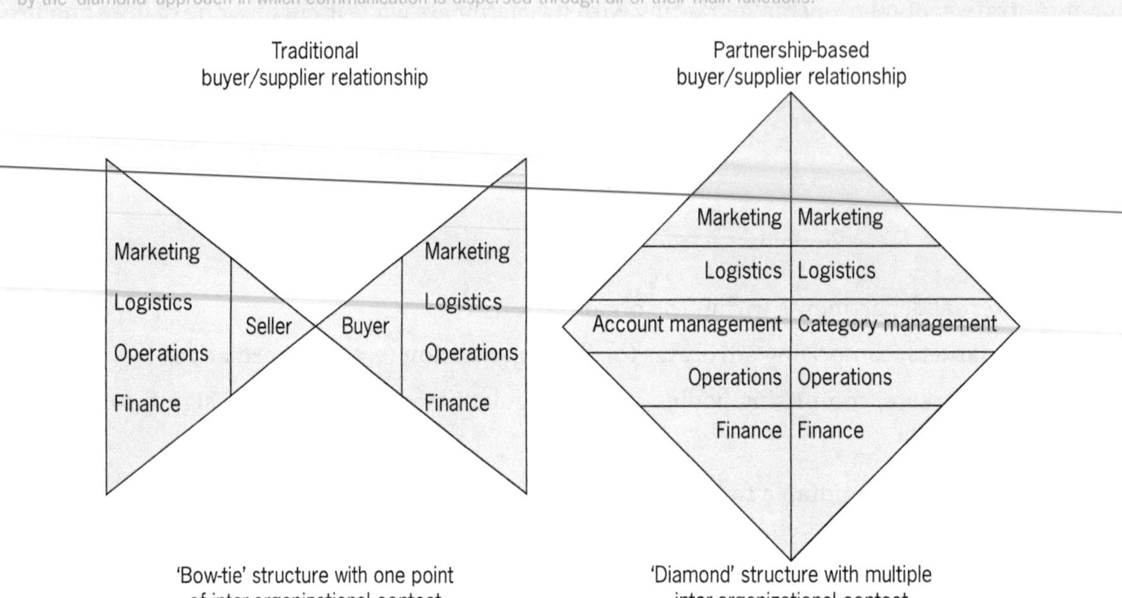


## 5.4 Relationship marketing and consumer services

The term 'relationship marketing' has become very widely used in the field of consumer marketing in recent years. However, as with many ideas in business that come along, confusion has set in as to just what the term means. Some advocates have claimed that relationship marketing represents a paradigm shift in marketing, while some sceptics have argued that it is really all about well-established business practices dressed up as something new. Figure 5.3 illustrates the principal differences between traditional transaction-based marketing and relationship marketing in consumer markets.

Figure 5.3 The components of transactional and relational exchange compared

| Traditional transaction-orientated marketing | Relationship marketing |
|---|---|
| • Focus on a single sale | • Focus on customer retention |
| • Short-term orientation | • Long-term orientation |
| • Sales to anonymous buyers | • Tracking of named buyers |
| • Salesperson is the main interface between buyer and seller | • Multiple levels of relationship between buyer and seller |
| • Limited customer commitment | • High customer commitment |
| • Quality is the responsibility of production department | • Quality is the responsibility of all |

Conceptually, relationship marketing has been positioned variously between being a set of marketing tactics, in which any interaction between buyers and sellers is described as a relationship, and a fundamental marketing philosophy that goes to the core of the marketing concept through its customer lifetime focus. Many have pointed to the central role played by the concepts of commitment, interdependence and trust (e.g. Crosby et al., 1990; Morgan and Hunt, 1994).

Building on Berry's conceptualization of three levels of relationship marketing (Berry, 2002), the published literature on relationship marketing can be classified into three broad approaches:

- At a *tactical* level, relationship marketing is used as a sales promotion tool. Developments in information technology have spawned many short-term loyalty schemes. However, the implementation of such schemes has often been opportunistic, leading to expensive loyalty schemes that create loyalty to the incentive rather than to the supplier (Barnes, 1994).
- At a more *strategic* level, relationship marketing has been seen as a process by which suppliers seek to 'tie in' customers through legal, economic, technological, geographical and time bonds (Perry et al., 2002). Again, it has been pointed out that such bonds may lead to customer *detention* rather than *retention* (Dick and Basu, 1994) and that a company that has not achieved a more deep-seated affective relationship with its customers may be unable to sustain those relationships if the legal or technological environment changes. What often passes as a relationship, therefore, is an asymmetric association based on inequalities of knowledge, power and resources, rather than mutual trust and empathy. Where tying-in is achieved through mutually rewarding co-operation, mutual dependence and shared risk, the relationship is likely to show greater stability and endurance.
- At a more *philosophical* level, relationship marketing goes to the heart of the marketing philosophy. Traditional definitions of marketing focus on the primacy of customer needs, and relationship marketing as a philosophy refocuses marketing strategy away from products and their life cycles towards customer-relationship life cycles. Conceptualizations of marketing as being the integration of a customer orientation, competitor orientation and inter-functional co-ordination (Narver and Slater, 1990) stress the key features of a relationship marketing philosophy, using all employees of an organization to profitably meet the lifetime needs of targeted customers better than competitors.

The language of relationship marketing can be misleading. We saw in Chapter 2 how many services organizations are simplifying and 'industrializing' their processes, usually in an attempt to improve their operational efficiency and consistency of performance. Such companies may talk about relationship development with customers, based on a dialogue that is driven by information technology, but such relationships can be qualitatively quite different from those based on social bonds and trust. While UK banks have become vigorous in their development of customer databases and named personal banking advisers, many customers would feel that the relationship with their bank is qualitatively worse than when a branch manager was able to enter into a more holistic dialogue with customers.

Managers of firms seeking to develop relationships with their customers should avoid the sometimes arrogant belief that customers seek such relationships. Surveys have indicated that many categories of buyers are becoming increasingly confident in venturing outside of a business relationship and reluctant to enter into an ongoing relationship. Relationship marketing strategies may fail where buyers' perception is of reduced choice and less freedom to act opportunistically rather than of added value that can derive from a relationship. Added value must be defined by sellers in terms of buyers' needs, rather than focusing on customers as captives who can be cross-sold other products from a firm's portfolio.

### 5.4.1 Reasons for the development of relationship marketing

There is nothing new in the way that firms have sought to develop ongoing relationships with their customers. In simple economies where production of goods and services took place on a small scale, it was possible for the owners of businesses to know each customer personally and to come to understand their individual characteristics. They could therefore adapt service delivery to the needs of individuals on the basis of knowledge gained during previous transactions, and could suggest appropriate new product offers. They would also be able to form an opinion about customers' creditworthiness. Networks of relationships between buyers and sellers are still the norm in many Far Eastern countries and many Western exporters have found it difficult to break into these long-standing, closed networks.

With the growth in size of Western organizations, the personal contact that an organization can have with its customers has often been reduced. Instead of being able to reassure customers on the basis of close relationships, organizations in many cases have sought to provide this reassurance through the development of strong brands.

Current interest in relationship marketing has occurred for a number of reasons:

- In many markets, relationships have become a new source of differentiation, adding to services as a point of differentiation for many manufactured products. In increasingly competitive markets, good products alone are insufficient to differentiate an organization's products from its competitors. Think back to Chapter 1, where in the context of service dominant logic, the example was given of car manufacturers who traditionally differentiated their cars on the basis of superior design features such as styling, speed and reliability. Once most companies had reached a common standard of design, attention switched to differentiation through superior added service facilities, such as warranties and finance. Once these service standards became the norm for the sector, many car manufacturers sought to differentiate their cars on the basis of superior relationships. So most major car manufacturers now offer customers complete packages that keep a car financed, insured, maintained and renewed after a specified period. Instead of a three-yearly one-off purchase of a new car, many customers enter an ongoing relationship with a car manufacturer and its dealers, which gives the customer the support they need to keep their car on the road and to have it renewed when this falls due (Figure 5.4).

Figure 5.4 The changing focus of marketing from product emphasis to relationship emphasis – an illustration of the car sector

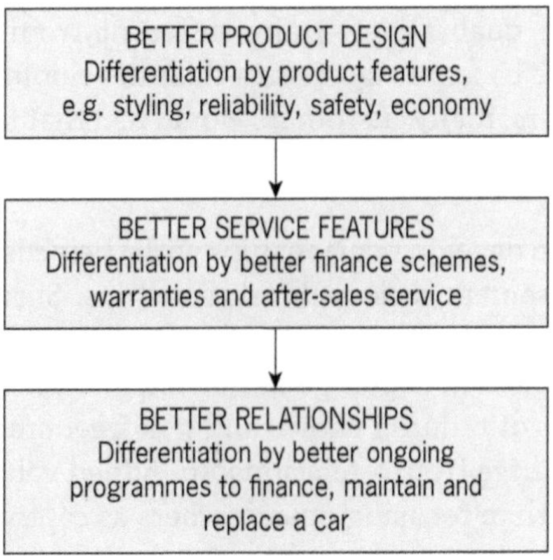

BETTER PRODUCT DESIGN
Differentiation by product features, e.g. styling, reliability, safety, economy

↓

BETTER SERVICE FEATURES
Differentiation by better finance schemes, warranties and after-sales service

↓

BETTER RELATIONSHIPS
Differentiation by better ongoing programmes to finance, maintain and replace a car

Figure 5.5 The 'leaky bucket' model of customer retention and defection. A leaky bucket is costly to maintain because, in order to maintain a constant level of water, new water must be acquired in order to replace the water that has been lost through wastage. Similarly, if a company seeks to maintain a constant number of customers, it is generally easier to avoid wastage of existing customers, so that it does not have to expensively recruit new ones.

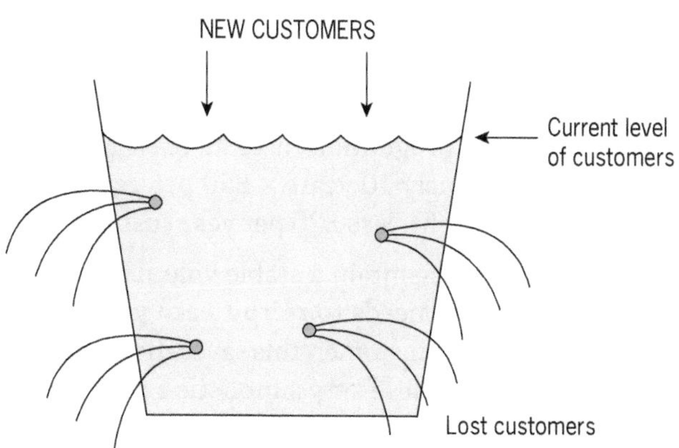


- A second major reason why firms pursue ongoing relationships is because it is generally more profitable to retain existing customers than continually seek to recruit new customers to replace lapsed ones. A 'leaky bucket' has often been used as an analogy to illustrate the effects of high levels of customer 'churn' (Figure 5.5). A bucket that has holes in its sides and bottom will leak water, so if a stable level is required, this can only be achieved by topping up the bucket with fresh water. This may be an expensive process, so it would make more sense to prevent water escaping in the first place, perhaps by investing in a better-quality bucket that does not leak. So too for businesses that 'lose' customers. There have been many exercises to calculate the effects on a company's profits of even a modest improvement in the rate at which customers defect to competitors (e.g. Reichheld, 1993; Reichheld and Sasser, 1990). Fewer defections mean lower expenditure on recruiting new customers to replace lost ones, although some studies have questioned assumptions about the strength of the link between loyalty and profitability (e.g. Helgesen, 2006). The example below illustrates the principles of profitable customer retention.

  Consider this example of the financial effects for a bank of developing customer retention strategies:

  1. Before the development of relationship marketing:
     - Assume that the bank has 500,000 customers and loses 10 per cent of these each year, for one reason or another.
     - This implies that the average length of relationship between the company and its customers is 10 years.
     - It costs £100 to recruit a new customer (in advertising, incentives and processing costs). In order to replace its lapsed customers, it spends £5,000,000 a year (50,000 lapsed customers to replace × £100) on advertising and customer recruitment.
     - The company makes an average profit of £50 per year from each of its customers.
  2. After the introduction of a relationship marketing programme:
     - A customer care programme is introduced which costs £20 per customer (this may include the cost of sending a magazine to all customers, setting up an improved customer service centre or offering rewards for loyalty, etc.).

- The customer defection rate falls from 10 per cent per annum to 5 per cent.
- The average relationship duration is therefore extended from 10 to 20 years.

3 Financial effects on the company:

- Each new customer now represents a profit potential of 20 years × £50 p.a. = £1000, rather than 10 years × £50 = £500, a gain of £500.
- The net effect, after taking into account the additional expenditure of £20 per customer per annum for a customer care programme, is to increase the lifetime profitability of each new customer by £100 (previously 10 years × £50 per year profit = £500 lifetime value; now 20 years × £50 per year profit, less £20 per year customer care programme = £600).
- If the company was content to maintain a stable volume of business, it could cut by half the number of new customers it needs to recruit each year, from 50,000 to 25,000. At a recruitment cost of £100 per new customer, this saves the company £2,500,000 per annum.

  In summary, on the basis of these very simplistic assumptions, revenues (in terms of customer lifetime value) have been increased and costs (recruitment of new customers) have fallen.

  Of course, customers are not all equally profitable, and there may be some categories of customer that a company would rather lose than pursue a relationship with. Being able to identify these segments is therefore also an important part of a relationship marketing strategy. Many companies use past records to develop a profile of the most promising groups to target and do less to encourage those inherently disloyal groups who are likely to leave the company as quickly as they were attracted to it. Sometimes, companies go through their customer list and actively seek to terminate their relationship with groups who are unprofitable. Many UK banks have attracted media criticism when they have closed the accounts of customers who kept only minimal account balances and did not buy any other services offered by the bank. Like many other banks and financial services companies, they had recognized that relationship marketing needs to focus on profitable customers and that an exit strategy may be needed for unprofitable ones. Naturally, one bank's target customers for relationship development may be the same as its competitors' targets, so intense competition can occur for key types of customers. This competition can create a dynamic tension in which customers' loyalty is continually challenged by the efforts of competitors to undermine it.

- Developments in information technology have had dramatic effects on firms' abilities to develop relationships with customers. The development of powerful user-friendly databases has allowed organizations to re-create in a computer what the individual small business owner knew in his or her head. Large businesses are now able to tell very quickly the status of a particular customer, for example their previous ordering pattern, product preferences and profitability. Developments in information technology have also allowed companies to enter individual dialogues with their customers through direct mail and email (although managing databases effectively can present many challenges for services organizations). Increased production flexibility based on improved technology allows many manufacturers and service organizations to design unique products that meet the needs of individual customers, rather than broad segments of customers.
- Just-in-time (JIT) production methods have become very widespread in Western countries, thanks to the lead given by Japanese manufacturing companies. It often makes sense for a manufacturer to keep its holdings of component parts down to an absolute minimum. This way, it ties up less capital, needs less storage space and suffers less risk of stocks becoming obsolete.

So, instead of keeping large stocks of components 'just in case' they are needed, manufacturers arrange for them to be delivered 'just in time' for them to be used in their production process. It is not uncommon to find car manufacturers receiving batches of components that within an hour are incorporated into a car. Just-in-time systems demand a lot of co-operation between supplier and customer, which cannot easily be achieved if each transaction is to be individually bargained. Some form of ongoing relationship between the two is essential. While JIT is essentially a concept of the manufacturing sector, its effects have been to draw the manufacturing and services sectors closer together. Just-in-time implies a system of production in which manufacturing capacity potentially becomes instantly perishable if component parts are not delivered at the right time. Service industries face a very similar problem of perishable output. Just-in-time within the manufacturing sector has given many opportunities to services firms who organize the logistics for just-in-time delivery of materials.

- Finally, it has been commented that an emphasis on one-off transactions in which each transaction is bargained is very much associated with masculine values of conquest and victory. There is an extensive body of literature on differences in personality traits that exist between males and females. One important area of difference is in the way that males and females develop relationships with others, with masculine gender traits being characterized as aggressive and instrumental, while feminine traits are more commonly associated with showing empathy and resolving conflicts through reconciliation (Barry et al., 1957; Meyers-Levy and Sternthal, 1991; Palmer and Bejou, 1995). In one recent study of bank customers, women were found to be significantly more loyal than men (Ndubisi, 2006). Recent moves from warfare approaches to business exchange towards collaborative approaches may appear novel when judged by the stereotypical value systems of males, but may be considered normal by the value system of females. In recent years, females have taken on increasingly important roles in business, both as buyers and sellers of goods and services. Although there is the possibility of role conflict, women as buyers and sellers are likely to bring values to commercial exchanges that are more relational than transactional.

### Thinking around the subject: A lifetime of eating?

What is the lifetime value of a restaurant customer? A first-time customer may be spending only £20 on this occasion, but if they like what they get, how much are they likely to spend in the future? A typical diner eating out just once a month could be worth £1200 in just five years. If they are happy, they are likely to tell their friends. If they are not, they are likely to tell even more of their friends. It follows that customers should be seen as investments, to be carefully nurtured over time. When things go wrong (for example, through overbooking), it would probably be to the restaurant's advantage to spend heavily on putting things right for the customer (e.g. by offering money off a future meal). Judged on the basis of the current transaction, the restaurant may make a loss, but it has protected its investment in a future income stream. Like all investments, some customers are worth more than others. Some attempts have been made to develop predictive models to calculate the likely lifetime value of a customer (e.g. Reinartz and Kumar, 2003), but these have often proved difficult to operationalize. How should a company decide which customers are priority relationships to invest in? And what level of investment can be justified in terms of the expected future profitability from the relationship?

## 5.4.2 Methods of developing buyer–seller relationships

A number of attempts have been made to analyse the development of relationships, often using the principles of life-cycle theories. A theoretical model of relationships proposed by Dwyer et al. (1987) identified five stages of relationship development – awareness, exploration, expansion,

Figure 5.6 Stages in buyer–seller relationship development. (Based on Dwyer et al., 1987)

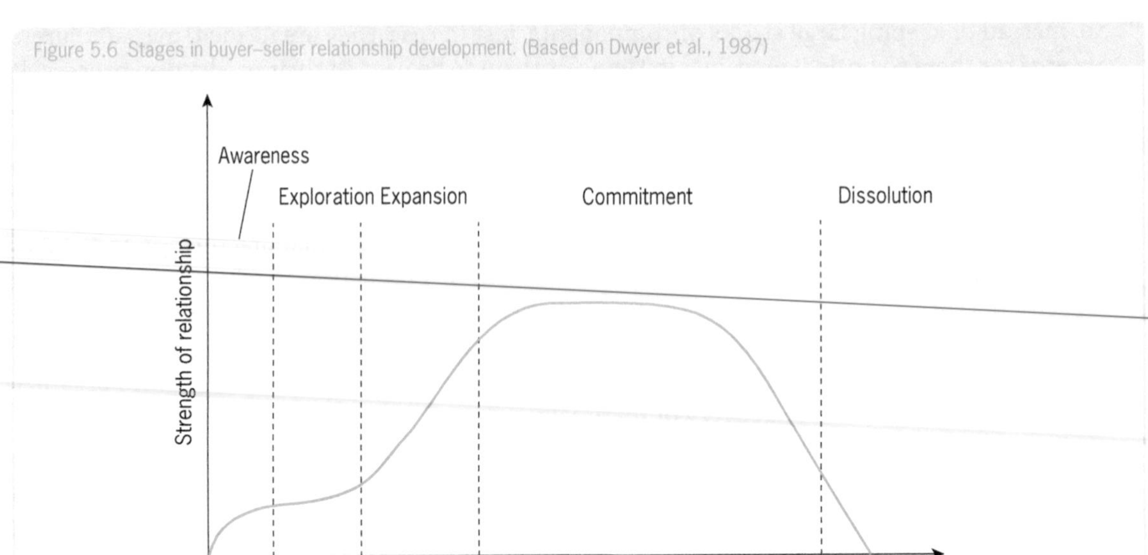


commitment and dissolution (Figure 5.6). Their model proposed that a relationship begins to develop significance in the exploration stage, when it is characterized by attempts of the seller to attract the attention of the other party. The exploration stage includes attempts by each party to bargain and to understand the nature of the power, norms and expectations held by the other. If this stage is satisfactorily concluded, an expansion phase follows. Exchange outcomes in the exploratory stage provide evidence as to the suitability of long-term exchange relationships. The commitment phase of a relationship implies some degree of exclusivity between the parties and results in an information search for alternatives – if it occurs at all – being much reduced. The dissolution stage marks the point where buyer and seller recognize that they would be better able to achieve their respective aims outside the relationship. Subsequent studies have validated the existence of a relationship life cycle (Palmer and Bejou, 1994; Palmatier et al., 2013).

Organizations use a number of strategies to move their customers through the stages of relationship development:

- The possibility of relationships developing can only occur where the parties are aware of each other and of their mutual desire to enter into exchange transactions. At this stage, the parties may have diverging views about the possibility of forming a long-term relationship. The supplier may need to offer potential customers reasons why they should show disloyalty to their existing supplier. In some cases, low introductory prices are offered by organizations that provide a sufficient incentive for disloyal customers of other companies to switch supplier. Non-price-related means of gaining attention include advertising and direct mail aimed at the market segments with whom relationships are sought. Over time, the supplier would seek to build value into the relationship so that customers would have little incentive for seeking lower-price solutions elsewhere. Inevitably, sellers face risks in adopting this strategy. It may be difficult to identify and exclude from a relationship invitation those segments of the population who are likely to show most disloyalty by withdrawing from the relationship at the point when it is just beginning to become profitable to the supplier.
- On entering into a relationship, buyers and sellers make a series of promises to each other (Grönroos, 1989). In the early stages of a relationship, suppliers' promises result in expectations

Figure 5.7 Birmingham International Airport uses the opportunity of an information request to build up a profile of its customers. Like all companies operating in the EU, the airport is required to obtain the consent of respondents before it can use their details for other purposes. Those who consent to receiving further information receive, among other things, a quarterly magazine containing information about new services offered by the airport. The airport has used reader surveys and competitions to further build up a picture of airport users. (Reproduced with permission of Birmingham International Airport Ltd)

**In order to keep our records up to date please fill in all the following details and tick all relevant boxes. (Please use block capitals)**

Are you the travel arranger? Yes ☐ No ☐

Are you the traveller? Yes ☐ No ☐

What is the purpose of your trip? Business ☐ Leisure ☐

PLEASE FILL IN YOUR 3 MOST FREQUENT JOURNEYS AND TICK THE RELEVANT BOXES

| UK DEPARTURE AIRPORT | DESTINATION AIRPORT | FREQUENCY | CLASS |
|---|---|---|---|
| 1. | | ☐ 1–5 times<br>☐ 5–15 times<br>☐ above 15 | ☐ Economy<br>☐ Business<br>☐ First Class |
| 2. | | ☐ 1–5 times<br>☐ 5–15 times<br>☐ above 15 | ☐ Economy<br>☐ Business<br>☐ First Class |
| 3. | | ☐ 1–5 times<br>☐ 5–10 times<br>☐ above 15 | ☐ Economy<br>☐ Business<br>☐ First Class |

NAME: ________

POSITION: ________

COMPANY: ________

ADDRESS: HOME/WORK*________

POSTCODE: ________

COMPANY: ________

*PLEASE DELETE AS APPROPRIATE

OCCASIONALLY WE MAY PASS YOUR DETAILS ON TO OTHER COMPANIES IN THE TRAVEL INDUSTRY. PLEASE TICK THIS BOX IF YOU WISH TO BE INCLUDED IN THESE MAILINGS ☐

Birmingham International Airport

RIA 11.97

being held by buyers as to the standard of service that will actually be delivered. Many studies of service quality have highlighted the way in which the gap between expected performance and actual performance determines customers' perception of quality. Quality in perceived service delivery is a prerequisite for an emotionally committed relationship being developed.

- Many organizations record information about customers that will be useful in customizing service delivery and assessing their future needs (Figure 5.7). This can be used to build up a database from which customers are kept in touch with new product developments of specific interest to them. We will return to customer information management later in this chapter.
- Financial incentives are often given to customers as a reward for maintaining their relationship. These can range from a simple money-off voucher, valid for a reduction in the price of a future purchase, to schemes whereby gifts or cashback incentives are given at the end of a period in proportion to a customer's spending during the period. Incentives that are purely financially based have a problem in that they can defeat the service supplier's central objective of getting greater value out of a relationship. It is often expensive to initiate a relationship and organizations therefore seek to achieve profits at later stages by raising price levels to reflect the value that customers attach to the relationship. There is a danger of buyers becoming loyal to the financial incentive, rather than to the brand that it is designed to promote. Once the financial incentive comes to an end, loyalty may soon disappear.
- Rather than offer price discounts, companies can add to the value of a relationship by offering other non-financial incentives. Value has to be assessed from the perspective of the buyer and can come about in a number of ways, including:
  - *Making re-ordering of services easier*. Information about the preferences of individual customers can be retained in order that future requests for service can be closely tailored to their needs. In this way a travel agent booking accommodation for a corporate client can select hotels on the basis of preferences expressed during previous transactions. By offering

a more personalized service, the travel agent is adding value to the relationship, increasing the transaction costs of transferring to another travel agent. Similarly, many hotels record guests' details and preferences to speed up the checking-in process.

- *Offering privileges to customers who wish to enter into some type of formal relationship*. For example, many retailers hold special preview events for cardholders and send a free copy of the store's magazine.
- *Developing an ability to jointly solve problems*. As an example, a car repair garage may take on board identifying exactly what the problem is that a customer seeks fixing, rather than leaving it to the customer to have to specify the work that they require to be carried out. Such joint problem-solving requires a considerable level of trust to have been developed between the parties.

- A medium-term attempt to create loyalty from customers is sometimes made through the creation of structural bonds whereby buyers are tied to a seller. Structural bonds have been defined by Turnbull and Wilson (1989) in terms of investments that cannot be retrieved when a relationship ends, or when it is difficult to end the relationship because of the complexity and cost of changing relational partners. A structural bond between buyer and seller has the effect of tying one to the other, through the creation of barriers to exit, although such ties may be asymmetric. One way in which buyers can become tied to sellers is by designing services in such a way that transferring to another supplier involves significant switching costs. Within the commercial banking sector, one means by which banks increase their retention rate is to increase switching costs by such means as long-term mortgages with penalties for early closure. Airlines' frequent-flyer programmes have a similar effect in seeking to make the cost of competitor airlines appear more expensive by virtue of the opportunity cost of forgoing loyalty rewards. Where the process of tying-in is achieved through a process of mutually rewarding co-operation, mutual dependence and shared risk, the relationship is likely to show greater stability and endurance (Han et al., 1993).
- A strategy used by some companies is to create relationships by trying to turn one-off service delivery into continuous delivery. In this way, mobile phone service providers often seek to turn casual 'pay-as-you-go' customers into more committed customers with a long-term contract.
- More intensive relationships can develop where customers assign considerable responsibility to another company for identifying their needs. In this way a car supplier may attempt to move away from offering a series of one-off services, initiated by customers, to a situation where it takes total responsibility for maintaining a customer's car, including diagnosing problems and initiating routine service appointments.
- In a competitive marketplace, customer satisfaction is the surest way to ensure that buyers return repeatedly. To achieve high levels of satisfaction requires a customer-focused effort of all functions within an organization. Relationship development cannot be simply left to a relationship manager. There are many notable cases of companies that have not developed any explicit relationship marketing programme, but nevertheless, through providing consistently high levels of service, achieve very high levels of customer advocacy.
- Even companies that have an apparently poor standard of service can achieve high levels of repeat business by charging low prices. Airlines such as easyJet and Ryanair have developed strong loyalty from price-sensitive customers who consider that the total service offer (ease of booking, flight times, range of destinations and reliability etc.) are acceptable in return for the price that they have paid. The danger here is that competitors may enter the market with similarly low prices, but offering higher levels of service. Would customers still remain loyal?

- In some cases, the focus of a relationship is not so much the *customer*, but their *assets*. In the case of high-value, long-life assets, such as industrial machinery and cars, companies may keep a record of all services performed on that asset. The benefit of this approach becomes apparent when an asset changes hands and the new owner can gain access to its complete service history. Value is added in the form of higher resale values that customers achieve.

## 5.5 Customer loyalty

The outcome of the process of relationship development should be a loyal (and profitable) customer. But, as with the concept of relationship marketing itself, there is much debate and confusion about just what is meant by customer loyalty.

The *Oxford English Dictionary* defines loyalty as the state of 'being faithful . . . true to allegiance'. However, too frequently, mere repetitious behaviour by customers has been confused with loyalty as defined above. Repetitious purchasing behaviour may be a result of a market structure in which buyers find themselves with few alternatives, or where available alternatives can only be obtained at a high cost in terms of breaking current ties with a supplier. In many markets, some segments are likely to purchase repetitively out of inertia or lack of awareness of the alternatives available. The loyalty of customers who are influenced by such inertia is likely to be very different from that of a customer who strongly advocates a product and feels emotionally attached to it. Becoming an advocate of a company is the peak of a 'ladder of loyalty' (Figure 5.8).

Dick and Basu (1994) developed the notion of relative attitude as a theoretical grounding to the loyalty construct. Relative attitude refers to 'a favourable attitude that is high compared to potential alternatives' (Dick and Basu, 1994, p. 100). They suggest that loyalty is evidenced both by a more favourable attitude towards a brand (compared with other alternatives) and by repeat buying behaviour. By their analysis, low relative attitude with low repeat purchase indicates an absence of loyalty, while low relative attitude with high repeat purchase indicates 'spurious' loyalty. Satisfaction with a service provider is seen as an antecedent of relative attitude because without satisfaction consumers will not hold a favourable attitude towards the service provider, compared with other alternatives available.

Figure 5.8 The customer loyalty ladder. (Adapted from Christopher et al., 1991)

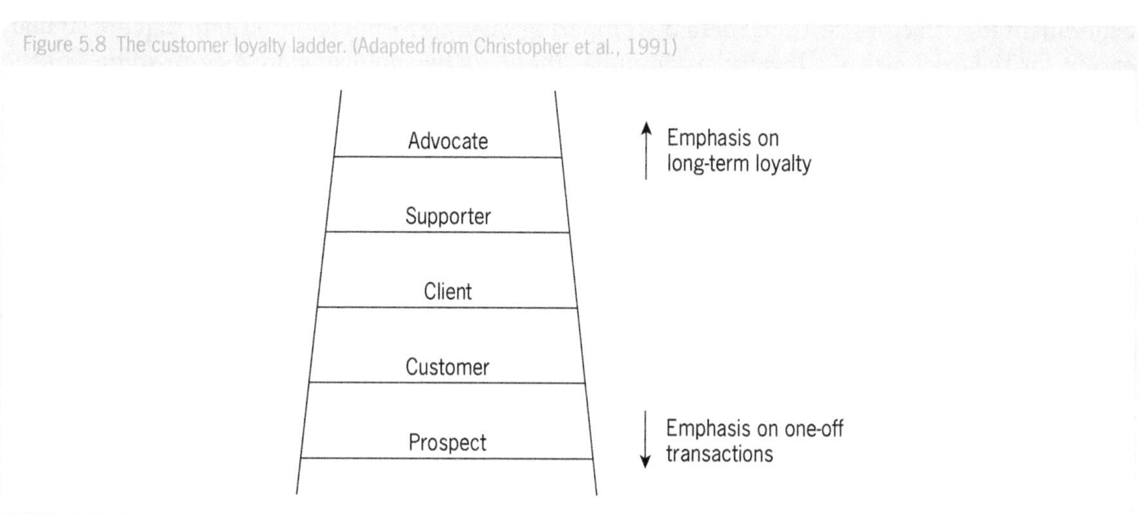

## In practice: Is there loyalty in a traffic jam?

Just because customers repeatedly come back to a company does not necessarily mean that they are loyal to that company. This point was made, tongue-in-cheek, during the continuing war of words between British Airways and Virgin Atlantic Airways. The latter had objected to BA's use of the advertising slogan 'The world's favourite airline'. Statistically, it was true that more passengers travelled internationally with British Airways than with any other airline, but surveys of airline users had consistently put Virgin ahead of BA in terms of perceived quality of service. Virgin's Richard Branson claimed that on BA's logic, the M25, London's notorious orbital motorway, could be described as the world's favourite motorway. Despite coming back to the motorway day after day, few motorists could claim to be loyal to it – they simply have no other choice.

The spat between BA and Virgin serves to underline the point that loyalty is about more than repetitious buying. True loyalty involves customers becoming an enthusiastic advocate of a company.

### 5.5.1 Loyalty programmes and profitability

Customer loyalty is about more than '**loyalty programmes**', which have become popular with companies in many services sectors in recent years (see case study at the end of this chapter). Many loyalty schemes can be seen as classical sales promotion activity in that they offer a short-term incentive to disloyal brand switchers. It has been noted that much sales promotion activity is very short term in effect and can actually undermine the long-term task of developing a strong brand (O'Brien and Jones, 1995). There is evidence to suggest that sales promotion activity, by encouraging brand switching, can bring about a short-term increase in sales for a company. In the case of manufactured-goods companies, this may simply bring forward consumers' purchases, resulting in a subsequent fall as stockpiles are used up. In the case of services, the problem of carrying forward stockpiles does not exist, but disloyal brand switchers who were attracted by one company's offer may be just as easily attracted away by a competitor's incentive.

An important aim of loyalty programmes is to extend a customer's life with a company so that their lifetime profitability is increased. Unfortunately, it can be very difficult to measure the effectiveness of a loyalty programme. The conceptual difficulties in measuring the performance of loyalty programmes stem from the difficulty of comparing the performance of a marketing plan that includes a loyalty programme with a plan that does not include one. Some companies have experimented with cross-sectional data by comparing sales performance at outlets that are similar, except for the existence of a loyalty programme. There are few published long-term studies of the effectiveness of loyalty programmes.

## In practice: Loyalty on the cards?

Boots is one of many retailers offering benefits to customers who sign up for their loyalty programmes. One of the challenges of Boots is to encourage the large number of people who visit its stores each day to spend more during their visit. So, instead of just buying a bottle of shampoo, customers could be tempted to buy a sandwich, camera or a new pair of glasses, rather than going to one of the company's competitors. A loyalty card offers an inducement to customers to place a larger part of their total expenditure with the company, especially where the rewards are seen as significant. However, the biggest benefit of a loyalty programme to a company such as Boots is to get a much deeper insight into the shopping

behaviour of its customers. No longer does it have to base its marketing planning simply on till receipt analysis; it can now understand individuals' patterns of buying over time. It can also link data collected at the point of sale with other demographic data provided by cardholders. Although some retailers have dismissed loyalty programmes as an expensive gimmick that adds to a company's operating costs, many others have taken the view that the additional operating costs involved are a low price to pay for the rich data that is provided.

Figure 5.9 A well-known loyalty card scheme

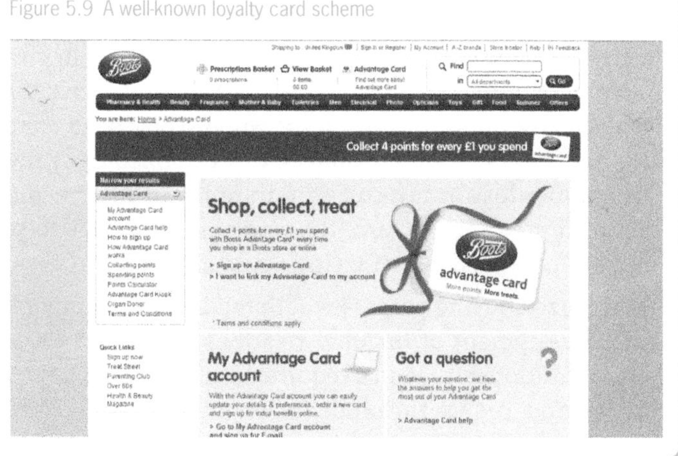


In any given industry sector, there are usually significant benefits in being the first company to offer a loyalty programme. However, while pioneers in a sector may introduce incentive schemes and gain additional profitable business from competitors, incentives can rapidly become a sector norm that buyers expect. Loyalty schemes may fail to give a long-term strategic advantage to a company because they are easy for competitors to copy. There is evidence that once one innovator in a sector introduces a loyalty scheme, competitors soon follow.

A further reason why it is very difficult to evaluate the effectiveness of a loyalty programme is because one of the main benefits to a company is the data that programmes can give them. To many companies, a loyalty programme represents a cost-effective way of gathering longitudinal data about customers' behaviour, particularly as they can also link this to customers' demographic information.

Against these benefits to companies is an increasing realization by some customers of the privacy implications of allowing so much data to be collected about them. While it is probably true that the majority of customers are quite happy to simply collect rewards, unconcerned about the privacy issues, or simply unaware of the amount of data that is collected about them, there are nevertheless many customers who do not use loyalty programmes because of the need to give information about themselves (see case study at the end of this chapter).

## 5.5.2 Challenges to customer loyalty

In developing customer loyalty, service providers face a number of challenges:

- Loyalty may be an unrealistic pursuit where customers have no underlying need to make further purchases of a category of product that a company is able to supply. In the extreme case, a small-scale company may appeal to the curiosity of buyers for whom a second-time purchase will have little of its original value – curiosity. This phenomenon is present in many tourism-related businesses in destinations of symbolic rather than aesthetic quality (for example, many people make a religious pilgrimage once in their lifetime with little incentive to return again). While firms with a diverse product and geographical coverage may be able to build on their initial curiosity contact, opportunities for relationship development by smaller companies in such circumstances are limited.

- In many consumer markets, buyers have become more confident and their need for ongoing trusting relationships has been reduced by legislation, which has had the effect of reducing the risk associated with buying goods and services from previously unknown sources. In the UK, for example, statutory provision for investors' compensation funds has lessened the need for investors to rely on an intermediary whom they have come to trust. Legislation has reduced the chances of a poor relationship being developed and provided means for compensating investors who suffer loss as a result of failure by an intermediary, thereby encouraging greater transactional orientation. Also, the availability of peer-to-peer review websites can help to reduce buyers' perceived fear of trying a new supplier.
- Formalized buying processes adopted by large companies and government bodies may prevent the development of ongoing relationships based on social bonds. Tightly specified supplier–buyer relationships, and a requirement for contracts to be re-submitted for tender after a specified period, reduce the scope for ongoing socially based relationships to be developed within a system of routine competitive tendering. It has been argued that such an approach to obtaining value for money has stressed cost reduction at the expense of more qualitative measures of efficiency and effectiveness.
- Much of the literature on relationship marketing has focused on *suppliers'* needs to develop relationships (e.g. Day and Wensley, 1983; Webster, 1992), overlooking the perspective of *buyers'* needs or lack of need to develop ongoing relationships. Commitment by a customer to one supplier relationship can imply forgoing alternative opportunities when they present themselves. Buyers may deliberately seek to minimize risk of dependency by developing a portfolio of suppliers.
- Recent developments in IT have emphasized the benefits to producers of being able to gain an asymmetrical position of power in private buyer–seller relationships. With further development, IT is strengthening the willingness and ability of private consumers to engage in multiple sourcing of purchases at the expense of ongoing relationships. For example, online price comparison sites such as Go Compare.com are increasingly allowing consumers to search quickly and easily for the best deal when their car insurance comes due for renewal, reducing the chances of renewal through inertia.
- Individuals differ in their level of optimum stimulation level, implying that some individuals have a greater propensity than others to seek out variety or to take risks, compared with those who seek out the security and predictability of an ongoing relationship. There is evidence of a demographic effect on loyalty. In one study of customers of dentists, hairdressers and travel agents, it was found that older age groups displayed significantly more loyal behaviour than their younger counterparts. Additionally, it was found that older clients had different motives (social benefits, special treatment and confidence) for staying loyal compared to the younger clients (Patterson, 2007).
- The excessive use of financial incentives to create loyalty may put a firm at a cost disadvantage in a market where cost leadership is important, while securing little underlying loyalty. While pioneers in a sector may introduce incentive schemes and gain additional profitable business from competitors, incentives for loyalty can rapidly become a sector norm that customers expect. In the case of airlines' frequent-flyer programmes, a cycle of development has been described that began in the 1980s, when the first companies to launch achieved revenue benefits. By the end of the 1980s, the use of frequent-flyer programmes had become more widespread and their revenue benefits marginal. By the 1990s, most major airlines had developed programmes, yielding little advantage from this tool (Gilbert and Karabeyekian, 1995). Frequent-flyer programmes

had become part of many business travellers' expectations, resulting in heavy costs for airlines. Meanwhile, many 'low-frills' airlines, such as Ryanair, who offer no loyalty programme have achieved rapid growth and higher levels of profitability than their full-service competitors who offer a frequent-flyer loyalty programme.

- Programmes to develop loyalty may motivate those customers who qualify for loyalty rewards, but may demotivate others who do not qualify. It has been suggested that grocery retailers have considered adding fast checkouts with shorter queues for their high-profit customers, similar to the dedicated check-in areas used by airlines for their business class passengers. However, the negative effects on grocery shoppers who did not qualify for the fast checkout might have had a demotivational effect greater than the motivational effect on those who did.

### 5.5.3 Relationship breakdown

Buyer–seller relationships may break down for a variety of reasons. It was noted earlier that in some cases the service supplier may actively seek to break off a relationship where a customer is judged to offer no long-term profit potential. At other times, it is the customer who drifts away. Sometimes there are good extraneous reasons for this defection. For example, a customer of an airline may break off their relationship if the airline ceases to serve their local airport, or if the customer moves home to an area not served by the airline. For some categories of product, relationships may end when a customer no longer needs that product and the supplier does not have any new service propositions that might satisfy the customer's changing needs. Many relationships fail when a customer dies or a company goes out of business.

Of more concern to marketers is where a breakdown in a buyer's commitment to a relationship is associated with greater competition and the availability of alternative suppliers. Competition tests the true loyalty of a customer. A further challenge to loyalty arises from service failures. Service encounters can result in failure as perceived by customers in a number of ways, including the unavailability of a service, slow service and errors in delivery (Bitner et al., 1990). When a supplier fails to deliver on its promises, the trust that goes to the foundation of a relationship is undermined. Through a recovery process, service failure can be transformed into a positive act that creates increasingly strong attitudes of customers towards a supplier (Hart et al., 1990). A service failure can occur at any stage of a customer's relationship with a supplier. It has been argued that a failure occurring early in the customer's relationship with a supplier will be perceived more adversely than one that occurs later in a relationship, because the customer has less experience of successful service experiences to counterbalance the failure (Boulding et al., 1993). Drawing on literature of conflict resolution, the existence of a relationship has been shown to moderate the effects of disputes on attitudes towards relationship partners (Kaufmann and Stern, 1992).

Companies often put a lot of effort into finding out the reasons why customers defect, but getting to the real reasons for defection calls for a wide range of research methods. In one study of bank customers in Australia and New Zealand, the reasons for switching banks were classified into three main problem areas: service failures, pricing problems and denied services. Results indicated that problems with pricing had the most important impact on switching behaviour. In contrast, customers tended to complain more often about service failures prior to exiting the firm. This finding suggested that customers were staying silent about the problems that were most important in their decision to leave the bank (Colgate and Hedge, 2001). This highlights the point made in Chapter 2 that services organizations should pay a lot of attention to gathering complaints about service delivery while they are still in a position to rectify the situation, rather than allowing profitable customers to leave.

## 5.6 Managing customer information

Whatever the reason for a relationship developing, an important part in creating and sustaining that relationship is likely to be made by information held about customers. A small-business owner, such as a small shopkeeper or guest-house owner, may have the ability to keep in their head all the information that they need in order to deliver a high quality of relationship. But in a large service organization, information about individual customers must be shared, so that, for example, a customer of a hotel chain will find their personal details readily available every time they deal with one of the chain's hotels or the reservations office. They should not need to explain each time that their preference is for a non-smoking room, or be asked for their loyalty programme each time.

We are probably all familiar with companies where knowledge seems to be very poor – the hotel reservation that is mixed up, the delivery that does not happen as specified or junk mail that is of no interest at all. On the other hand, customers may revel in a company that delivers the right service at the right time and clearly demonstrates that it is knowledgeable about all aspects of the transaction. The small-business owner may have been able to achieve all of this in his or her head, but, in large organizations, the task of managing knowledge becomes much more complex. Where it is done well, it can be a significant contributor to a firm's sustainable competitive advantage.

Managing information about customers has become an increasingly complex task as service organizations have grown in size and customers' expectations of seamless service delivery have become greater. Unfortunately, it is not uncommon to find firms that have invested heavily in IT systems to handle customer information, only to find that the information may actually hinder, rather than help, the task of creating more effective customer relationships. In too many organizations, numerous databases and customer service systems exist, which are not linked to each other. A customer may make an initial enquiry to a free telephone line and place a subsequent order with another system within the company that is not connected to the initial enquiry line. The rapid growth of some companies, changes in corporate information technology policy and mergers and de-mergers have resulted in disconnected information systems being a not uncommon phenomenon.

Customer relationship management (CRM) has become a generic term to describe processes that essentially seek to join up a company's customer-focused information systems and to track dealings with individual customers throughout the relationship life cycle. Many companies offer technological solutions that promise integrated information management. However, technology is of little value if management does not give the leadership and create a culture that is conducive to integrated systems.

There are many definitions of customer relationship management that reflect the varying scope of CRM within different companies. It is defined here as:

> The systems and processes used by an organization to integrate all sources of information about a customer so that the organization can meet individual customers' needs more effectively and efficiently.

One reason for variation in definitions is that organizations may pay differing levels of attention to the components of CRM (Figure 5.10). The basic components can be described as:

- data collection and management;
- customer analysis and profiling;
- computer-aided sales support;
- customer information and service.

These are not mutually exclusive components, but form the basis for the following discussion.

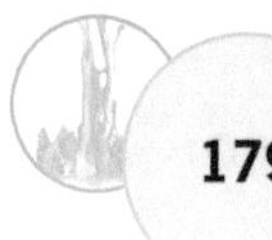



Figure 5.10 The components of customer relationship management (CRM)

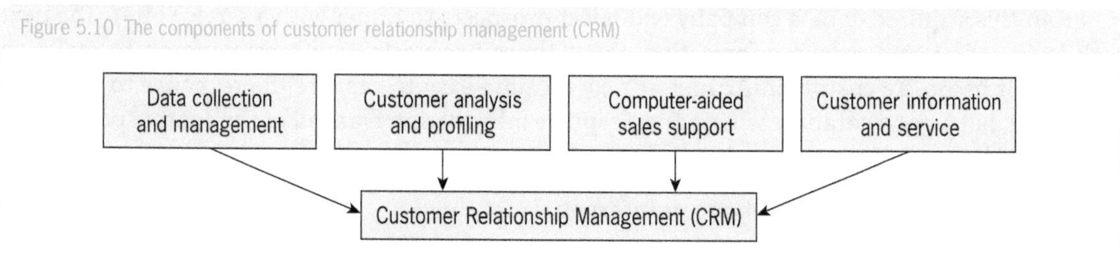



## 5.6.1 Data collection and management

Two different types of knowledge about customers can be identified:

- 'Explicit' knowledge can be easily quantified and passed between individuals in the form of words and numbers. Because it is easily communicated, it is relatively easy to manage within a customer relationship management system.
- 'Tacit' knowledge is not easy to see or express; it is highly personal and is rooted in an individual's experiences, attitudes, values and behaviour patterns. Tacit knowledge can be much more difficult to formalize and disseminate within an organization. If tacit knowledge can be captured, mobilized and turned into explicit knowledge, it will then be accessible to others in the organization and enable the organization to progress, rather than have individuals within it continually relearning from the same point. The owner of a small business could have all of this information readily available to him in his head. The challenge taken on by many large corporations is to emulate the knowledge management of the small-business owner. Inevitably, the focus of attention has started with explicit data, and has sometimes struggled to incorporate tacit knowledge.

A company's database is likely to be constructed from a number of sources, including its own trading records and bought-in lists from specialized database providers.

A customer is likely to have started life with an organization as a *prospect*. Although CRM is essentially about maintaining ongoing relationships with customers, it must be remembered that customers have to be acquired in the first place. To build up a database of prospects, a company will often buy in the services of specialist companies that offer database management services. One supplier of database management services is Experian, which has compiled a database of UK consumers and businesses from, among other sources:

- the Electoral Roll, listing over 42 million adults;
- investor data from 630 company share registers, comprising 8.5 million individuals;
- lifestyle data from ongoing and ad hoc surveys, which establish lifestyle and product purchasing data;
- home data, including details on residential properties such as value, location, size etc;
- telephone data, matching telephone numbers and addresses for 14 million individuals;
- county court judgments.

A client company can purge and merge these lists to form its own database. It is crucial for a company to maintain its list by removing duplicated names and the names of those who do not want to be, or should not be, contacted.

From this acquired data, a company will select prospects to target with a service offer. The next task is to collect and record information about those prospects who have gone on to make an enquiry, or become a customer. At first, it may be quite easy to capture the response to an initial sales offer, but a good database will go on to capture information from all of the contact points that a customer has with the organization. Information may typically come from:

- orders received by mail, telephone or Internet;
- payments received by cheque, standing order or credit card;
- enquiries made by mail, phone and Internet for further services;
- comments and complaints received from the customer;
- information from survey questionnaires that the customer may have completed.

At the same time as the company is collecting information directly from its customers, it may also be buying in supplementary data about them. At the least, it would hope to acquire additional demographic data (for example, the customer might not have stated at the time of first order their newspaper reading habits and whether they had children – this information may be obtained either directly from the customer, or bought in from another company). The company is also likely to periodically buy in creditworthiness data and other lifestyle data.

How much data should a company collect about its customers? A trade-off has to be made between the cost and inconvenience of collecting information and the associated benefits to the company. Is it really worthwhile for a company to ask questions of prospective customers the first time that they call? Will this be regarded as too intrusive? Will it add to costs by slowing up the process of taking customers' orders? Will the information actually be used to profitably improve sales and service delivery? Or is the information crucial to ensure that the prospective customer's needs – crucial for the long-term development of a relationship – are correctly diagnosed?

Merging and updating databases can be a very complex task, especially where a company has multiple points of access by customers. It is quite common to find telephone sales and Internet sales databases, for example, not linked to each other. The problem of linkages is particularly great where companies have merged or been acquired, and the resulting 'legacy' systems do not interface easily with each other. It is reported that when Lloyds Bank merged with Trustee Savings Bank (TSB), it took over two years for both banks' customer databases to be effectively integrated.

### 5.6.2 Customer analysis and profiling

A clear understanding of the needs of individual customers is essential if their needs are to be catered for effectively and efficiently. A key to successful customer relationship management is the analysis of data to produce models of buyer behaviour. A well-developed database can have a huge number of pieces of information available about each customer. According to the research company Gartner, a bank may typically have 1000 pieces of information on each of its customers. Having amassed a lot of data from previous sales, a company can identify the variables that are associated with sales success and profitable customer relationships. Analysts are no longer constrained by simple correlation and regression techniques to identify causative factors. Data mining using techniques such as 'fuzzy logic' can look for patterns in the data that might not have been expected at the outset.

Where a company has a large database of customers, it could further refine its model by conducting experiments. It would typically offer a number of different service propositions to two or more subsamples of the database, who are otherwise similar in terms of demographics etc. The company would monitor the response to each offer that was put to the groups. It would typically measure a number of response indicators, from short term to long term. At the very least, it would record whether the customer made an enquiry in response to the service offer. It would then record whether an order was made, and might, as part of its experimental framework, go on to record whether the customer went on to buy further services from the company. On the basis of an experiment with a subsample of its database, the company might then roll out the most successful service offer to everybody in its database who satisfies some specified criteria.

Profiling is about more than just generating sales leads or cross-selling additional services to existing customers. Profiling is commonly used to analyse:

- *The current profitability of individual customers, or groups of customers*. Many service companies divide their customers into categories based on their profitability (for example, UK banks have been known to refer to segments of 'lemons', who are of little long-term value, and 'peaches' and 'plums', who offer better prospects for profit).
- *The expected lifetime value of each customer, based on models developed of customer longevity*. Models can sometimes only build up a very general picture of future profitability, for example in the way that banks have identified that student customers in general, and medical students in particular, are likely to go on to become their most profitable customers. Where there is evidence of future lifetime profits, a service company may consider it worthwhile incurring a loss in the short term (as banks frequently do with student bank accounts).
- *Sources of service failure*. These can be identified and an analysis undertaken to see whether failures are associated with particular types of customer in particular service contexts.
- *Early warning signs that a customer is about to defect from the company*. A model can be developed to identify these. Has a bank customer suddenly started using a rival bank's ATMs? Have they initiated new direct debits to a rival financial services provider? These may be signals that a customer is likely to defect and, if they are spotted in time, the bank may take action (e.g. a promotional offer to reward loyalty) that may reduce the chances of defection actually occurring.
- *Which customers should be 'exited'*. Based on a profitability analysis, a company can identify these. Many companies have a segment of customers who incur costs to service, but may generate insufficient revenue to allow a profit. However, care must be taken to avoid exiting customers who have potential to become profitable, but for whom this potential has not yet been realized. Again, a well-developed model should allow improved multivariate predictions of which customers have long-term profit potential.

### 5.6.3 Computer-aided sales support

When the customer database is made accessible to a company's sales teams, it has the potential to enhance their performance substantially. For companies involved in business-to-business services, the database may hold company information such as product listings, specifications, availability and pricing details. Customer and potential customer details may include buyer details, contact details, quotations outstanding, order status, previous purchases, installed equipment and purchases from competitors. It is also possible to store information about competitors on the database, thereby making it directly available to the field sales force where it is most needed, rather than being hidden away in inaccessible, centrally held files. As well as improving the productivity of sales personnel, a database can improve the quality of sales leads generated.

### 5.6.4 Customer information and service (CIS)

There are many reasons why customers and potential customers may wish to contact a supplier of services. Companies may need to respond to enquiries about any of the following: a bill (public utilities); statements (banks); amount outstanding on a loan (finance company); adjusting monthly investment (pension company); technical questions (Internet service providers); availability (package holidays); or schedules (flights). Provision of advice and information is now expected by customers immediately, by telephone, fax or Internet. Increasingly, customers expect a supplier to have all of the information available at one contact point, without being passed around from department to department and from one nameless person to another only to be left with a vague promise of a call back.

#### Thinking around the subject: CRM = citizen relationship management!

CRM is not just for private-sector service providers – in the public sector, CRM has come to mean 'citizen relationship management'. In the UK, central government has provided funding for the CRM National Programme, to promote best practice in CRM by local government. By 2004, it was estimated that around 170 of the 388 local authorities in England had implemented some form of CRM (Moran, 2004).

The public sector is drawing on the experience of the private sector to help manage its own relationships, but with local authorities typically providing around 700 different services, far more than most companies, any CRM project is likely to be very complex and costly. One of the lessons learnt from CRM in the private sector was that 'big bang' implementations could be extremely problematic. As a result, many local authorities have favoured a step-by-step approach and recognized a need to introduce the tools of CRM gradually. Local authorities have tended to adopt one of two basic approaches in implementing CRM, either broad and thin or narrow and deep. With the first approach, a contact centre provides a single point of access to connect callers to all the services that the local authority provides. By analysing all incoming calls, an authority can learn about the types of enquiries it is getting and allocate resources accordingly. This also helps planning of the future roll-out of the CRM system by identifying prime candidates for integration. In the 'narrow and deep' approach, local authorities start with a narrow range of services and expand the range one by one as each process is adapted to the CRM system.

The London Borough of Tower Hamlets was an early showcase of local authority CRM and has seen benefits from integration. As an example, by connecting the borough's refuse collection contractor to the CRM system, Tower Hamlets claims to have increased the volume of special collections by 20 per cent, resulting in less dumping and fly tipping. The council claims that, since beginning its CRM project, the number of people who say they are satisfied with council services has risen considerably, and in 2004 Tower Hamlets was among the top-performing councils in terms of customer satisfaction.

However, as private-sector companies have found, call centres not only increase demand; they can also raise users' expectations. For these expectations to be met, there must be effective integration with back-office systems. Many private-sector companies found this to be a difficult task, with integration and process change accounting for 30 to 50 per cent of the total cost of CRM implementation. In the public sector, the range of services is typically much more diverse, and therefore the costs of integrating 'legacy' systems and updating processes can be much greater. One of the most ambitious integration projects was undertaken by Liverpool Direct, a joint venture between Liverpool City Council and BT. This project involved bringing together 500 databases into a centralized system, providing a single source of information for staff in a 225-seat call centre handling 160,000 calls a month. After implementation, the council claimed to resolve 90 per cent of enquiries with a single contact.

With around three-quarters of CRM systems in the private sector reportedly failing, how can local authorities hope to achieve anything better? Governments have been associated with many cost overruns in computerization projects – why should local authority CRM projects be different? And how many local authority chief executives have the energy to cut across traditional departmental boundaries to create a centralized resource for citizens – and remain accountable to elected members for expenditure on a system that is good value and meets citizens' expectations?

Customer helplines are an important feature offered by many services companies. A database and computerized telephone system now provide the opportunity for companies to deal directly with their customers in a speedy and informed manner. Companies often use helplines to understand the causes of service failure and to enable them to put things right before a dissatisfied customer tells their friends about the failure.

Creation of call centres has become a major service activity in its own right, with call-centre operators, large and small, providing outsourced support to banks, airlines, insurance companies and telephone operators, among others. Specialist companies have the ability to understand and invest in the latest call-centre technology and can meet clients' need for flexibility. At the UK Call Centre Expo held in London in October 2012, over 150 suppliers of call-centre services promoted these.

### 5.6.5 Challenges for customer relationship management

Customer relationship management is a good idea in theory, but unfortunately it too often fails in practice to be effective. There have been many reports of CRM systems that have failed to deliver their promised benefits (e.g. King and Burgess 2008), with suggestions that typically three-quarters of CRM systems fail. It has even been noted that companies' use of CRM and relationship development strategies in general can actually damage customer relationships and can lead to a deterioration of consumers' trust. O'Malley and Prothero noted three main areas of concern: the relational rhetoric employed by firms; the motives behind customer care and loyalty programmes; and the use of marketing techniques considered to be intrusive and unacceptable. Consequently, relationship marketing was seen to have the unintended consequence of making consumers more distrustful of organizations than before such strategies were adopted (O'Malley and Prothero, 2004). These authors suggested that customer relationship management can get in the way of consumers enjoying a brand, rather than facilitating it.

The evident failings of many CRM systems remind us that CRM is not just a technological solution provided by installing software in the company. CRM is really about an entire change of mindset, in which the organization as a whole becomes customer orientated and focuses on the ongoing needs of customers, just as the small shopkeeper was able to do. Even integration of the technology of CRM fails in many companies, with a failure to bring together otherwise free-standing applications such as sales automation, data-mining tools and business applications. Without such integration, CRM is likely to be ineffective (not providing what customers want) and inefficient (providing a given level of customer service at a higher cost to the company than is necessary).

The activities of CRM have been increasingly constrained by legislation. European regulations limit the ability of a company to use information that it has collected in a different area of business. So, if a solicitor had built up a database of clients buying its legal services, it cannot then use the data to try to sell unrelated financial services, unless the client had specifically agreed. This has limited the database-building activities of many large services organizations, whose ability to 'cross-sell' services is made difficult. Furthermore, the domestic and EU legislation makes it difficult for companies who are dominant in one market to use customer information collected in that market to promote services in other markets, even if they are related markets. In the UK, British Telecom is a dominant provider of domestic telephone services. It has been held against the public interest that the company should use its database to cross-sell security alarm systems that are connected through the telephone network.

A challenge to CRM comes from the opposite perspective of *customer-managed relationships*. So far, CRM has been presented as something that is done by sellers to manipulate buyers, even if the use of the word 'relationship' might suggest some sense of mutuality or equality in the relationship. The idea of buyers managing their suppliers is nothing new in business-to-business markets. The relationship between large UK grocery supermarket buyers and grocery manufacturers is not typically supplier managed. The size of the top five retailers has given them considerable power to determine the nature of the relationships that they have with their suppliers, including terms of delivery, the range of products bought and returned-goods policy.

### 5.6.6 From customer relationship management to customer experience management

To overcome the observed problems of customer relationship management, increasing numbers of companies have appointed 'customer experience managers'. As we saw in Chapter 3, there has been growing academic interest in customer experience management as an intellectual integrator of service quality, relationships and brands (Grewal et al., 2009; Palmer, 2010; Tynan and McKechnie, 2009). Initially, they have appeared in high-value sectors associated with high levels of emotional involvement by consumers. As in the case of relationship marketing, the concept appears to have subsequently disseminated to relatively mass-market and low-involvement contexts. But will customer experience managers succeed where customer experience managers often fail? Customer experience managers also require great inter-functional skills and authority in order to deliver customer value in the form of a superior customer experience. Similar by to the way in which everybody in an organization may be described as a part-time relationship-builder with customers, everybody in an organization potentially contributes towards the customer experience. The problem remains of how customer experience managers will succeed as integrators, when there is widespread evidence of the failure of customer relationship managers as integrators. Given the broader domain of experience compared with relationships, why should the more complex management environment of customer experience be expected to lead to greater rather than less success?

## Case study

### Points mean prizes, and a goldmine of data for companies

Steve Worthington, Monash University, Melbourne, Australia

Jane is 53 years old and lives with her cat in a northern suburb of Melbourne. She works full-time on the other side of town, so she prefers to drive rather than catch public transport. On the weekend Jane likes to do some gardening, and she is also fond of red wine. In fact, she drinks so much that it makes financial sense for her to buy her wine by the carton. Jane's daughter lives a few kilometres away and has an 18-month-old girl. Jane likes to buy clothes and toys for her granddaughter, even though she has more than enough already.

How do we know all these things? Because some time ago Jane applied for a loyalty card at her local supermarket so that she could earn frequent-flyer points every time she goes shopping. She now hands over her card whenever she is at the checkout. Although her identity is kept confidential by the supermarket chain, Jane would probably recognize herself from the 'profile' that it has built from its database. The supermarket knows that she is a *pet owner*, because she buys cat food. It knows that she *drives to work*, because she buys fuel at a petrol station owned by the same company. From her regular purchases it also knows that she is a *gardener* and a *wine drinker*. From her occasional purchases of baby products, it has even deduced that there is a baby in the family, but that it is not hers. Given her age, it has assumed that Jane is a *new grandmother*.

Jane now receives regular mail from the supermarket chain (and affiliated companies) with advertising and promotions that are specially designed to appeal to her. After doing extensive survey and focus group research with people like Jane, the supermarket chain has developed a sophisticated segmentation that allows it to target different kinds of customers with different messages. Like Jane, many people who hold a loyalty card do not realize just how valuable their personal information can be, even when it is aggregated with that of their fellow customers.

Loyalty programmes take a number of forms. The simplest comprise cards which are stamped each time that a customer makes a purchase, then after so many stamps are obtained, a reward is given. This is popular with simple low-value purchases, for example many coffee-shop chains give their customers cards to earn a free cup of coffee after they have purchased six coffees. More usually, the customer is given a credit-card-style plastic card with a magnetic strip, chip or barcode containing a unique member identification number and perhaps the name of the customer. There is usually no payment facility associated with a loyalty card; its sole purpose is to monitor transactions in order to reward customers in proportion to their spending. Whenever a purchase is made, information about the purchase (such as the price, product, place of purchase and date) is recorded alongside the customer's number. Over time, therefore, the information about consumer behaviour gathered through loyalty card data can be substantial.

Loyalty programmes have often been confined within an organization, so that the company that a customer spends their money with is the company that gives the rewards. In many cases, however, loyalty programmes incorporate more than one company. Airlines that belong to one of the global alliances such as Oneworld or Star Alliance have for some time allowed customers of one airline to accumulate points when travelling with another airline, and also allow them to take rewards on another airline or service provider. Airline programmes have also been extended to cover related businesses, for example car rental and hotels. There are many other examples of collaborative loyalty programmes; for example, in the UK the Nectar card combines, among others, the supermarket chain Sainsbury's, car rental company Hertz, travel company Expedia.co.uk, electricity supply company EDF and opticians Dolland and Atchison.

Increased customer fidelity is just one benefit of setting up a loyalty programme; in addition, such programmes can generate a wealth of commercially valuable information about purchasing behaviour. In fact, this aspect of a loyalty programme can be just as important for a company as any increase in sales due to customers spending to earn reward points. For this reason, 'loyalty programme' is something of a misnomer; a better term would be 'rewards and information exchange programme', because that is a more accurate description of the transaction between customer and company. In return for providing information about themselves and their spending patterns, members of a loyalty programme receive rewards in proportion to their spending. The company operating the programme can then use the information that these programmes generate to more accurately target offers to customers, refine their marketing approaches, and potentially to also then sell aggregated information and 'insights' about consumer behaviour to their suppliers.

The costs of running a loyalty programme can be substantial when spread across millions of members. For instance, it has been estimated that the cost to the Australian retailer Woolworths of purchasing Qantas frequent-flyer points, accrued through its Everyday Rewards scheme, is between A$60 and A$80 million per year and 'lift the cost of customer loyalty by 0.4c to 3c for every dollar spent by customers'.

There are a number of ways that retailers can recoup these costs. The first and most obvious is to raise prices. If a retailer with a loyalty programme did this, it would mean that members of the loyalty programme, who receive benefits in the form of reward points, are being cross-subsidized by customers who are not members, and therefore do not receive any rewards.

Another way to recover the costs of running a loyalty programme is to generate more revenue by increasing sales volumes. This is the ostensible purpose of a 'loyalty' scheme – to encourage people to spend their money at one store rather than another so as to earn reward points. But an even more effective way to increase sales is to turn the purchasing data from a loyalty programme into commercially valuable information. Such information might be used to refine the range of products sold to match customers' habits, or to develop offers or deals targeted at particular types of shoppers. For example, it has been reported that in Australia, Woolworths uses postcode data from its Everyday Rewards members to evaluate possible locations for new supermarkets and petrol outlets.

In addition, programme operators can partially offset the cost of their loyalty programme by aggregating member data and selling this in de-identified form to suppliers or other corporate entities. UK retailer Tesco provides a telling example of how this can be done; its customer database is based on the behaviour of the 13 million households that hold a Tesco Clubcard. Information on who buys which products, when and where they buy them and how much they spend can be seen at the level of individual products. This information can help manufacturers and suppliers to understand the purchasing decisions and habits of customers and to design products and marketing campaigns accordingly. The information that suppliers purchase from Tesco is aggregated, so there are no breaches of privacy law. By 'collaborating' with the retailer in this way, partners also strive to reach or retain a position as a preferred supplier, further strengthening Tesco's market power.

Customers may not realize how much information they are giving away about themselves. Some may not care, but others may be so concerned about privacy issues that they would not use a loyalty card. It would be a significant problem for companies if a large group of customers who were hard to reach through conventional market research techniques also became hard to reach through their lack of participation in loyalty programmes.

In order to better understand how loyalty programmes are perceived by customers, a study was undertaken in Australia during July 2009 by The Australia Institute, in collaboration with the Department of Marketing at Monash University, and involved an online survey of 1000 people. Some of the findings are summarized below.

Four in five survey respondents (83 per cent) reported having at least one loyalty card; this figure is probably higher than for the population as a whole because of the nature of the survey sample. When looking at the average number of loyalty cards (up to a maximum of five in this survey), it is possible to see distinct differences between men and women and between people of various ages. Women held an average of 2.02 loyalty cards, while for men this was only 1.29. Average numbers of loyalty cards increase more or less consistently with increases in age. Whereas 18–24-year-olds had only 1.55 cards, those over 60 reported having 1.76 cards.

Around two in three loyalty card holders surveyed (70 per cent) said they had redeemed awards or points from a loyalty card scheme. By far the most common type of redemption was for vouchers to spend at a particular store or group of stores. Three in four of those who had made a redemption (73 per cent) estimated its value at A$100 or less, while just under half (46 per cent) made redemptions worth A$50 or less. The mean value of redemptions was A$113.

The survey asked which aspect of a loyalty card scheme was most important to respondents – keeping their personal information confidential or getting more rewards. Around half of respondents (49 per cent) said privacy was more important, while 45 per cent preferred getting more rewards (with another 6 per cent not sure about this question). Women were slightly more concerned about privacy compared to men. However, there were major differences in attitudes to privacy across the age spectrum. People aged between 18 and 24 years were much more likely to regard rewards (63 per cent) as more important than privacy (28 per cent). Respondents aged between 35 and 44 years were divided roughly evenly between preferring privacy (50 per cent) and preferring rewards (48 per cent). Among the oldest age group (65 years and over) there was an overwhelming preference for privacy (58 per cent) over rewards (35 per cent). In other words, concerns about privacy are associated with increasing age, and to a smaller extent with women. This finding is notable, given that women and older people tend to have more loyalty cards on average than men and younger people.

A minority of respondents said they had opted out of receiving marketing materials from their loyalty card schemes – between 15 and 20 per cent depending on the type of programme. Those who had opted out almost invariably did this when they were joining the scheme, by ticking a box on the application form; there were very few who had made a request by phone or in writing after they had joined. The number of people opting out of receiving information, or allowing the information to be shared with other companies, has been a growing concern for companies keen to get the maximum value out of their database. But are people showing unreasonable concern for privacy? The study suggested that someone who is not a member of a loyalty programme would typically forgo A$123 per year in loyalty benefits to shop at a retail outlet that offers a loyalty programme, but not actually take part in it.

*Source*: based on Worthington (2000, pp. 222–34).

## Case study review questions

1 Discuss the methods by which the operator of a loyalty programme can assess its effectiveness.

2 What practical issues are likely to arise where a company seeks to extend a company-specific loyalty programme to embrace other collaborating service providers?

3 How should service companies seek to overcome the reluctance of some groups to share their personal information?

## Summary and links to other chapters

Most services involve networks of suppliers who, together with the customer, co-create value. Ongoing relationships between a service provider and its customers are often a key point of differentiation, and according to service dominant logic, the relationship can create value in use for manufactured goods.

An ongoing relationship is one basis on which the service offer can be defined and distinguished from its competitors (Chapter 1). A relationship can improve the quality of the service encounter (Chapter 9), for example by configuring the service to meet the recorded preferences of each customer. The process of choosing between competing suppliers is facilitated by an ongoing relationship, which can reduce perceived risk (Chapter 6). Service quality is a prerequisite for the development of an ongoing buyer–seller relationship and can often only be provided with appropriate selection, training and monitoring of employees (Chapter 10). To be effective, relationship marketing needs to embrace intermediaries (Chapter 5).

### Chapter review questions

1 Discuss the theoretical reasons underlying a phone company's decision about whether to outsource some of its customer-facing tasks, and identify the likely advantages and disadvantages of a decision to outsource.

2 Critically assess methods used by banks to develop ongoing relationships with their personal customers.

3 Using a service company's loyalty scheme of your choice, critically assess its overall value to the company in developing profitable business.

### Activities

1 Go to the Internet or pick up brochures to find information about mobile-phone service providers. Compare the service offer for a 'pay as you go' phone with that for a monthly contract phone. What benefits does a monthly contract give to the consumer and to the company compared to a 'pay as you go' phone? Why do you think a large market still exists for 'pay as you go' phones? What evidence do you see of mobile-phone service providers seeking to move 'pay as you go' customers to an ongoing relationship with the company?

2 If you hold a loyalty card for a service provider, such as a retailer or airline, reflect on the extent to which this has affected your buying behaviour. Has your relationship with the service provider caused you to spend more money with that provider, compared to what might have been the case had you not been a member of its loyalty programme? Do you feel a true sense of relationship with the service provider? If you have made repeat purchases from the company, why is this? Finally, consider the benefits that the service provider may be getting from its relationship with you. Who do you think gains most benefit from the relationship, you or the service provider?

3 If you are studying at a college or university, identify all of the contacts that you have had with your college/university. Critically assess how effectively this information was used to take you through the stages of being a prospective student to being an actual student. What steps, if any, would you recommend to improve the university/college's information handling process?

## Key terms

**Customer loyalty** The tendency of a customer to choose one business or product over another for a particular need. It shows the preference of a customer to buy from or visit a business more often. Loyalty is demonstrated by the actions of the customer and is also defined by their attitudes.

**Customer relationship management (CRM)** An operational procedure for understanding customers' needs and enabling the firm to build better relationships and increase sales. It creates a comprehensive picture of customer needs, expectations and behaviours by analysing information from every customer transaction. Customer relationship management creates the customer intelligence necessary to develop customer relationships.

**Data mining** (also called knowledge discovery in databases (KDD) or knowledge discovery and data mining) An analytic process designed to explore data (usually large amounts of data – typically business or market related) in search of consistent patterns and/or systematic relationships between variables, and then to validate the findings by applying the emerged patterns to new subsets of data.

**Just-in-time (JIT)** A strategy to deliver goods and services at the time that they are required for consumption or for incorporation into a further production process.

**Loyalty programmes** Structured marketing efforts that reward, and therefore encourage, loyal buying behaviour.

**Outsource** To delegate non-core operations from internal production to an external entity specializing in the management of that operation.

**Private Finance Initiative (PFI)** A method, developed initially by the UK government, to provide financial support for Public–Private Partnerships (PPPs) between the public and private sectors.

**Profiling** A means of generating prospects from within a large population; it involves inferring a set of characteristics of a particular class of person from past experience, then searching databases for individuals with a close fit to that set of characteristics.

**Public–Private Partnerships (PPP)** A method by which a public service is funded and operated through a partnership between government and one or more private-sector companies.

**Relationship marketing** An approach to marketing in which emphasis is placed on building longer-term relationships with customers rather than on individual transactions. It involves understanding the customer's needs as they go through their life cycle and providing a range of products or services to existing customers as they need them.

**Structural bonds** Economic, legal and social practices that tie two or more business parties to each other through increased costs of transferring their dealings to another partner.

**Web 2.20** A term often used to describe an Internet environment in which peer-to-peer communication is just as important as business-to-consumer communication.

## Selected further reading

*For an introduction to the general principles of relationship marketing and its role in turning buyers into regular customers, the following are useful:*

**Buttle, F.D.** (2008) *Relationship Marketing*, 2nd edn, Butterworth-Heinemann, London.

**Das, K.** (2009) 'Relationship marketing research (1994–2006): an academic literature review and classification', *Marketing Intelligence & Planning*, 27 (3), 326–63.

**Egan, J.** (2011) *Relationship Marketing – Exploring relational strategies in marketing*, 4th edn, Pearson Education, Harlow.

**Grönroos, C.** (2009) 'Marketing as promise management: regaining customer management for marketing', *Journal of Business & Industrial Marketing*, 24 (5/6), 351–59.

**Hansen, S.** (2008) 'The global diffusion of relationship marketing', *European Journal of Marketing*, 42 (11/12), 1156–61.

*For a more thorough understanding of the theoretical underpinnings of buyer–seller relationships, the following are useful:*

**Palmatier, R.W., Houston, M.B., Dant, R.P. and Grewal, D.** (2013) 'Relationship velocity: toward a theory of relationship dynamics', *Journal of Marketing*, 77 (1), 13–30.

**Duncan, T. and Moriarty, S.E.** (1998) 'A communication-based marketing model for managing relationships', *Journal of Marketing*, 62 (2), 1–14.

**Healy, M., Hastings, K., Brown, L. and Gardiner, M.** (2001) 'The old, the new and the complicated: a trilogy of marketing relationships', *European Journal of Marketing*, 35 (1/2), 182–93.

**Morgan, R.M. and Hunt, S.D.** (1994) 'The commitment–trust theory of relationship marketing', *Journal of Marketing*, 58 (3), 20–38.

**Palmer, A.** (2000) 'Relationship marketing: a Darwinian synthesis', *European Journal of Marketing*, 35 (5), 687–704.

*Business-to-business relationships and networks are explored in the following:*

**Cain, R.** (2009) 'Outsourcing without fear', *World Trade*, Troy, 22 (1), 47–8.

**Laing, A.W. and Lian, P.C.S.** (2005) 'Inter-organisational relationships in professional services: towards a typology of service relationships', *Journal of Services Marketing*, 19 (2), 114–28.

**Mattsson, L.-G. and Johanson, J.** (2006) 'Discovering market networks', *European Journal of Marketing*, 40 (3/4), 259–74.

**Prenkert, F. and Hallén, L.** (2006) 'Conceptualising, delineating and analysing business networks', *European Journal of Marketing*, 40 (3/4), 384–407.

**Rauyruen, P., Miller, K.E. and Groth, M.** (2009) 'B2B services: linking service loyalty and brand equity', *Journal of Services Marketing*, 23 (3), 175–86.

*Operationalization of relationship marketing through customer relationship management is discussed in the following:*

**Boulding, W., Staelin, R., Ehret, M. and Johnston, W.J.** (2005) 'A customer relationship management roadmap: what is known, potential pitfalls, and where to go', *Journal of Marketing*, 69 (4), 155–66.

**Mitussi, D., O'Malley, L. and Patterson, M.** (2006) 'Mapping the re-engagement of CRM with relationship marketing', *European Journal of Marketing*, 40 (5/6), 572–89.

**Payne, A. and Frow, P.** (2005) 'A strategic framework for customer relationship management', *Journal of Marketing*, 69 (4), 167–76.

**Ryals, L. and Knox, S.** (2001) 'Cross-functional issues in the implementation of relationship marketing through customer relationship management', *European Management Journal*, 19 (5), 534–42.

*A number of critical articles have sought to identify limits to the concepts of relationship marketing, highlighting the fact that it is often adopted cynically by many companies at the same time as the quality of relationships deteriorates:*

**O'Malley, L. and Tynan, C.** (2000) 'Relationship marketing in consumer markets: rhetoric or reality?', *European Journal of Marketing*, 34 (7), 797–815.

**Zolkiewski, J.** (2004) 'Relationships are not ubiquitous in marketing', *European Journal of Marketing*, 38 (1), 24–9.

*Finally, customer loyalty is an important outcome of relationship marketing and the following provide useful references, and a caution that loyalty to a service provider is about more than merely repetitious purchasing:*

**Ang, L. and Buttle, F.** (2006) 'Customer retention management process: a quantitative study', *European Journal of Marketing*, 40 (1/2), 83–99.

**Dick, A.S. and Basu, K.** (1994) 'Customer loyalty: toward an integrated conceptual framework', *Journal of the Academy of Marketing Science*, 22 (2), 99–113.

**Jones, T. and Taylor, S.F.** (2007) 'The conceptual domain of service loyalty: how many dimensions?', *Journal of Services Marketing*, 21 (1), 36–51.

**Reichheld, F.** (2006) *The Ultimate Question: Driving Good Profits and True Growth*, Harvard Business School Press, Cambridge, MA.

*The emerging trend from customer relationship management to customer experience management is discussed in the following:*

**Palmer, A.** (2010) 'Customer experience management: a critical review of an emerging idea', *Journal of Services Marketing*, 24 (3), 196–208.

**Tynan, C. and McKechnie, S.** (2009) 'Experience marketing: a review and reassessment', *Journal of Marketing Management*, 25 (5/6), 501–17.

## References

**Araujo, L. and Easton, G.** (1986) 'Networks, bonding and relationships in industrial markets', *Industrial Marketing and Purchasing*, 1 (1), 8–25.

**Arnett, D.B., German, S.D. and Hunt, S.D.** (2003) 'The identity salience model of relationship marketing success: the case of nonprofit marketing', *Journal of Marketing*, 67 (2), 89–105.

**Bagozzi, R.P.** (1995) 'Reflections on relationship marketing in consumer markets', *Journal of the Academy of Marketing Science*, 23 (4), 272–7.

**Baker, W.E.** (1994) *Networking Smart: How to Build Relationships for Personal and Organisational Success*, McGraw-Hill, New York.

**Barnes, J.G.** (1994) 'Close to the customer: but is it really a relationship?', *Journal of Marketing Management*, 10 (7), 561–70.

**Barry, H., Bacon, M.K. and Child, K.L.** (1957) 'A cross-cultural survey of some sex differences in socialization', *Journal of Abnormal and Social Psychology*, 55 (3), 327–32.

**Becker, L.C.** (1990) *Reciprocity*, University of Chicago Press, Chicago, IL.

**Berry, L.L.** (2002) 'Relationship marketing of services: perspectives from 1983 and 2000', *Journal of Relationship Marketing*, 1 (1), 59–77.

**Bitner, M.J., Booms, B.H. and Tetreault, M.S.** (1990) 'The service encounter: diagnosing favorable and unfavorable incidents', *Journal of Marketing*, 54 (1), 71–84.

**Boulding, W., Kalra, A., Staelin, R. and Zeithaml, V.A.** (1993) 'A dynamic process model of service quality: from expectations to behavioral intentions', *Journal of Marketing Research*, 30 (February), 7–27.

**Burt, R.** (1992) *Structural Holes: The Social Structure Of Competition*, Harvard University Press, Cambridge, MA.

**Cain, R.** (2009) 'Outsourcing without fear', *World Trade*, 22 (1), 47–8.

**Christopher, M., Payne, A. and Ballantyne, D.** (1991) *Relationship Marketing*, Butterworth-Heinemann, Oxford.

**Colgate, M. and Hedge, R.** (2001) 'An investigation into the switching process in retail banking services', *International Journal of Bank Marketing*, 19 (5), 201–12.

**Constantinides, E. and Fountain, S.J.** (2008) 'Web 2.0: conceptual foundations and marketing issues', *Journal of Direct, Data, and Digital Marketing Practice*, 9 (3), 231–44.

**Cova, B. and Cova, V.** (2002) 'Tribal marketing: the tribalisation of society and its impact on the conduct of marketing', *European Journal of Marketing*, 36 (5/6), 595–620.

**Crosby, L.A., Evans, K.R. and Cowles, D.** (1990) 'Relationship quality in services selling: an interpersonal influence perspective', *Journal of Marketing*, 54 (3), 68–81.

**Cutts, R.L.** (1992) 'Capitalism in Japan: cartels and keiretsu', *Harvard Business Review*, 70 (4), 48–55.

**Day, G.S. and Wensley, R.** (1983) 'Marketing theory with a strategic orientation', *Journal of Marketing*, 47 (4), 79–89.

**Dick, A.S. and Basu, K.** (1994) 'Customer loyalty: toward an integrated conceptual framework', *Journal of the Academy of Marketing Science*, 22 (2), 99–113.

**Dwyer, F.R., Schurr, P.H. and OH, S.** (1987) 'Developing buyer and seller relationships', *Journal of Marketing*, 51 (2), 11–27.

**Financial Times** (2006) 'SkyTeam members charged with violating rules on cartels', *Financial Times*, 20 June, 31.

**Gilbert, D.C. and Karabeyekian, V.** (1995) 'The frequent flyer mess – a comparison of programmes in the USA and Europe', *Journal of Vacation Marketing*, 1 (3), 248–56.

**Goodwin, C. and Ross, I.** (1992) 'Consumer responses to service failures: influence of procedural and interactional fairness perceptions', *Journal of Business Research*, 25 (2), 149–63.

**Grewal, D., Levy, M. and Kumar, V.** (2009) 'Customer experience management in retailing: an organizing framework', *Journal of Retailing*, 85 (1), 1–14.

**Grönroos, C.** (1989) 'Defining marketing: a market-oriented approach', *European Journal of Marketing*, 23 (1), 52–60.

**Grönroos, C.** (1994) 'From marketing mix to relationship marketing', *Management Decision*, 32 (1), 4–20.

**Gummesson, E.** (2006) 'Many-to-many marketing as grand theory: a Nordic School contribution', in R.F. Lusch and S.L. Vargo (eds), *Toward a Service-Dominant Logic of Marketing: Dialog, Debate, and Directions*, Sharpe, New York.

**Hakansson, H. and Snehota, I.** (1995) *Developing Relationships in Business Networks*, Routledge, London.

**Hamel, G., Doz, Y. and Prahalad, C.K.** (1989) 'Collaborate with your competitors – and win', *Harvard Business Review*, 67 (1), 133–9.

**Han, S.L., Wilson, D.T. and Dant, S.P.** (1993) 'Buyer–supplier relationships today', *Industrial Marketing Management*, 22 (4), 331–8.

**Hart, C., Heskett, J.L. and Sasser, W.E. Jr** (1990) 'The profitable art of service recovery', *Harvard Business Review*, 68 (4), 148–56.

**Helgesen, O.** (2006) 'Are loyal customers profitable? Customer satisfaction, customer loyalty and customer profitability at the individual level', *Journal of Marketing Management*, 22 (3), 245–66.

**Kaufmann, P.J. and Stern, L.W.** (1992) 'Relational exchange, contracting norms and conflict in industrial exchange', in G.L. Frazier (ed.), *Advances in Distribution Channel Research*, vol. 1, JAI Press, Greenwich, CT.

**Kelley, S.W. and Davis, M.A.** (1994) 'Antecedents to customer expectations for service recovery', *Journal of the Academy of Marketing Science*, 22 (1), 52–61.

**Ketter, P.** (2008) 'Companies need to manage outsourcing risks', *T&D Alexandria*, 62 (3), 14.

**King, S.F. and Burgess, T.F.** (2008) 'Understanding success and failure in customer relationship management', *Industrial Marketing Management*, 37 (4), 421–31.

**McNeil, I.R.** (1980) *The New Social Contract: An Inquiry into Modern Contractual Relations*, Yale University Press, New Haven, CT.

**Meyers-Levy, J. and Sternthal, B.** (1991) 'Gender differences in the use of message cues and judgements', *Journal of Marketing Research*, 28 (1), 84–96.

**Miller, K.D., Fabian, F. and Lin, S.J.** (2009) 'Strategies for online communities', *Strategic Management Journal*, 30 (3), 305–22.

**Moran, N.** (2004) 'CRM for the citizen', *Financial Times*, 2 March, 14.

**Morgan, R. and Hunt, S.** (1994) 'The commitment–trust theory of relationship marketing', *Journal of Marketing*, 58 (3), 20–38.

**Narver, J.C. and Slater, S.F.** (1990) 'The effect of a market orientation on business profitability', *Journal of Marketing*, 54 (4), 20–35.

**Ndubisi, N.O.** (2006) 'Effect of gender on customer loyalty: a relationship marketing approach', *Marketing Intelligence & Planning*, 24 (1), 48–61.

**O'Brien, L. and Jones, C.** (1995) 'Do rewards really create loyalty?', *Harvard Business Review*, 73 (3), 75–82.

**Office of Fair Trading (OFT)** (2003) *UK Payment Systems: An OFT Market Study of Clearing Systems and Review of Plastic Card Networks*, Office of Fair Trading, London.

**Ohmae, K.** (1989) 'Managing in a borderless world', *Harvard Business Review*, 67 (3), 152–61.

**O'Malley, L. and Prothero, A.** (2004) 'Beyond the frills of relationship marketing', *Journal of Business Research*, 57 (11), 1286–94.

**Palmatier, R.W., Houston, M.B., Dant, R.P. and Grewal, D.** (2013) 'Relationship velocity: toward a theory of relationship dynamics', *Journal of Marketing*, 77 (1), 13–30.

**Palmer, A.** (2010) 'Customer experience management: a critical review of an emerging idea', *Journal of Services Marketing*, 24 (3), 196–208.

**Palmer, A. and Bejou, D.** (1994) 'Buyer–seller relationships: a conceptual model and empirical investigation', *Journal of Marketing Management*, 6 (10), 495–512.

**Palmer, A. and Bejou, D.** (1995) 'The role of gender in the development of buyer–seller relationships', *International Journal of Bank Marketing*, 13 (3), 18–27.

**Palmer, A. and Gallagher, D.** (2007) 'Religiosity, relationships and consumption: a study of church going in Ireland', *Consumption, Markets and Culture*, 10 (1), 31–49.

**Patterson, P.G.** (2007) 'Demographic correlates of loyalty in a service context', *Journal of Services Marketing*, 21 (2), 112–21.

**Payne, A., Ballantyne, D. and Christopher, M.** (2005) 'A stakeholder approach to relationship marketing strategy: the development and use of the "six markets" model', *European Journal of Marketing*, 39 (7/8), 855–71.

**Perry, C., Cavaye, A. and Coote, L.** (2002) 'Technical and social bonds within business-to-business relationships', *Journal of Business and Industrial Marketing*, 17 (1), 75–88.

**Pfeffer, J. and Salanick, G.R.** (1978) *The External Control of Organizations*, Harper and Row, New York.

**Reichheld, F.F.** (1993) 'Loyalty based management', *Harvard Business Review*, 71 (2), 64–73.

**Reichheld, F.F. and Sasser, W.E. JR** (1990) 'Zero defections', *Harvard Business Review*, 68 (5), 105–11.

**Reinartz, W. and Kumar, V.** (2003) 'The impact of customer relationship characteristics on profitable lifetime duration', *Journal of Marketing*, 67 (1), 77–99.

**Sheth, J. and Parvatiyar, A.** (2002) 'Evolving relationship marketing into a discipline', *Journal of Relationship Marketing*, 1 (1), 3–16.

**Sierra, J.J. and McQuitty, S.** (2005) 'Service providers and customers: social exchange theory and service loyalty', *Journal of Services Marketing*, 19 (6), 392–400.

**Turnbull, P.W. and Wilson, D.T.** (1989) 'Developing and protecting profitable customer relationships', *Industrial Marketing Management*, 18 (3), 233–8.

**Tynan, C. and McKechnie, S.** (2009) 'Experience marketing: a review and reassessment', *Journal of Marketing Management*, 25 (5/6), 501–17.

**Vogt, P.** (2009) 'Brands under attack: marketers can learn from Domino's video disaster', *Forbes*, available at www.forbes.com/2009/04/24/dominos-youtube-twitter-leadership-cmo-network-marketing.html (accessed 8 July 2013).

**Webster, F.E.** (1992) 'The changing role of marketing in the corporation', *Journal of Marketing*, 56 (4), 1–17.

**Williamson, O.E.** (1975) *Markets and Hierarchies: Analysis and Antitrust Implications*, Free Press, New York.

**Williamson, O.E.** (1985) *The Economic Institutions of Capitalism*, Free Press, New York.

**Williamson, O.E.** (1993) 'Calculativeness, trust, and economic organization', *Journal of Law and Economics*, 36 (1), 453–86.

**Worthington, S.** (2000) 'A classic example of a misnomer: the loyalty card', *Journal of Targeting, Measurement and Analysis for Marketing*, 8 (3), 222–34.

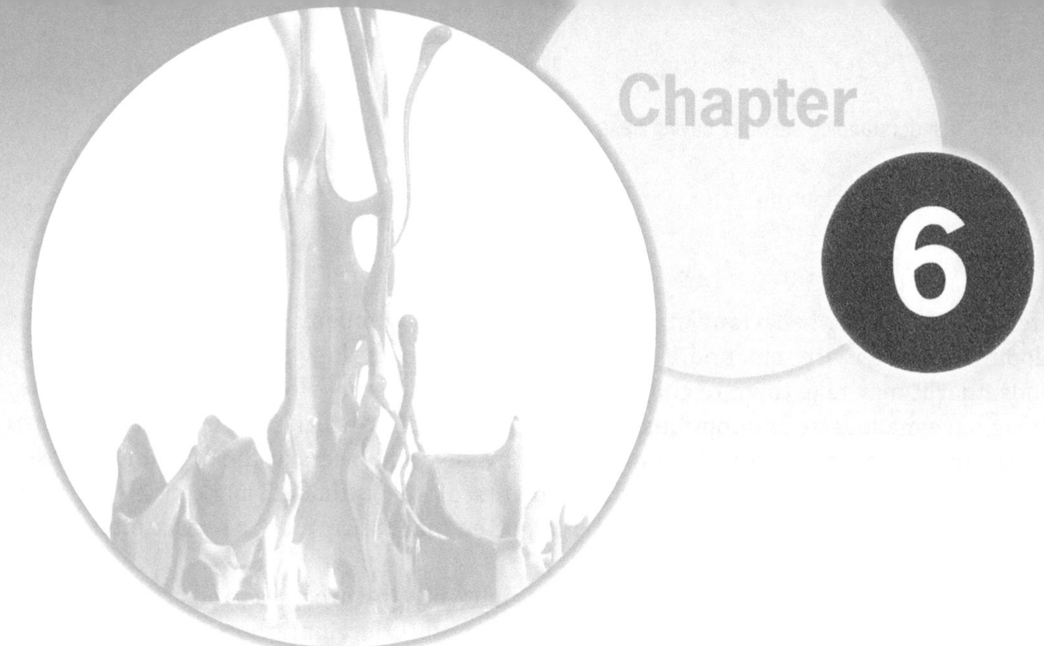


# Understanding services buying behaviour

*Think about the last time that you decided to go on holiday to somewhere that you had never been to before. What motivated you to take that holiday? How did you go about the process of searching for information about the alternatives available? Did you have feelings of uncertainty and risk in buying something that you could not evaluate before purchase and which you had no previous experience of buying? Whom did you consult when it came to making your choice? Which sources of information did you trust? If you think you had a hard time choosing between the alternatives, spare a thought for the service provider who had to work hard to convince you – and probably thousands of others – that their holidays are to be trusted and are the best choice for you. In this chapter we explore how services companies address the complexity of services buying processes.*

## Learning objectives

After reading this chapter, you should understand:

- Processes by which consumers initiate, carry out and conclude the purchase of services
- The effects of service intangibility on perceptions of risk in the buying process
- The effects on behaviour of post-consumption dissonance
- Decision-making units and their effects on services buying
- Differences between personal and business buying of services
- Bases for segmenting services markets

## 6.1 Introduction

This chapter explores buyer behaviour in a services context. A company can put years of effort into developing a new service, but find it rejected by buyers in the few minutes, or sometimes even seconds, that it may take them to choose between the competing alternatives available. The company may have made false assumptions about the processes by which purchase decisions are made, for example by underestimating the role played by key influencers in the decision process. Although the chapters of this book break the elements of the extended marketing mix into separate sections for discussion, it should never be forgotten that buyers judge a service offer much more holistically.

It is important for services marketers to gain an insight into the processes and critical factors involved in an individual's purchase decision. Organizations must develop a thorough understanding of a number of aspects of their customers' buying processes, in particular:

- Who is involved in making the purchase decision?
- How long does the process of making a decision take?
- What is the set of competing services from which consumers make their choice?
- What is the relative importance attached by decision-makers to each of the elements of the service offer?
- What sources of information are used in evaluating competing service offers?

Although this chapter tries to identify some general principles of buyer behaviour, the application of the principles can vary between different contexts. The buying behaviour of a private individual can be quite different from the behaviour of individuals buying for a commercial or government organization. With commerce becoming increasingly globalized, assumptions made about buying behaviour in the home market can be quite different in a foreign market.

## 6.2 Models of buyer behaviour

There is now a considerable amount of literature that describes and empirically validates models of buyer behaviour. A model is a means of simplifying reality by demonstrating links between different parts of a system. Buyer behaviour models typically describe various stages in what can be a complex process, typically comprising: the parameters that are considered important in the evaluation process; the sources of information consulted; and the people involved in influencing or making a decision. We look through each of these features of buyer behaviour models in turn.

Figure 6.1 Simplified stages in the buyer decision process

The basic processes involved in purchase decisions are illustrated in Figure 6.1. Simple models of buyer behaviour usually see some underlying need triggering a search for need-satisfying solutions. When possible solutions have been identified, these are evaluated according to some criteria. The eventual purchase decision is a consequence of the interaction between the final decision-maker and a range of influencers. Finally, after purchase and consumption, the consumer develops feelings about their purchase that influence future decisions. In reality, service purchase

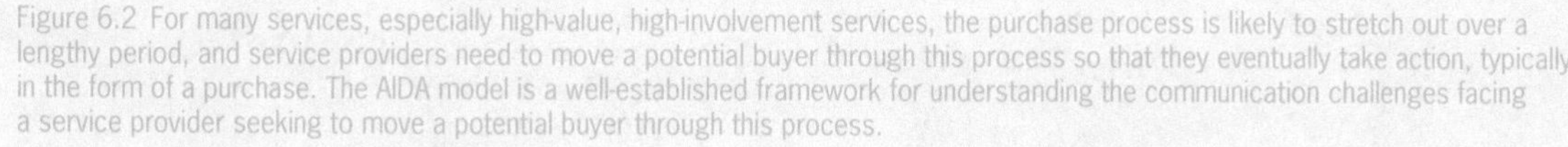

Figure 6.2 For many services, especially high-value, high-involvement services, the purchase process is likely to stretch out over a lengthy period, and service providers need to move a potential buyer through this process so that they eventually take action, typically in the form of a purchase. The AIDA model is a well-established framework for understanding the communication challenges facing a service provider seeking to move a potential buyer through this process.

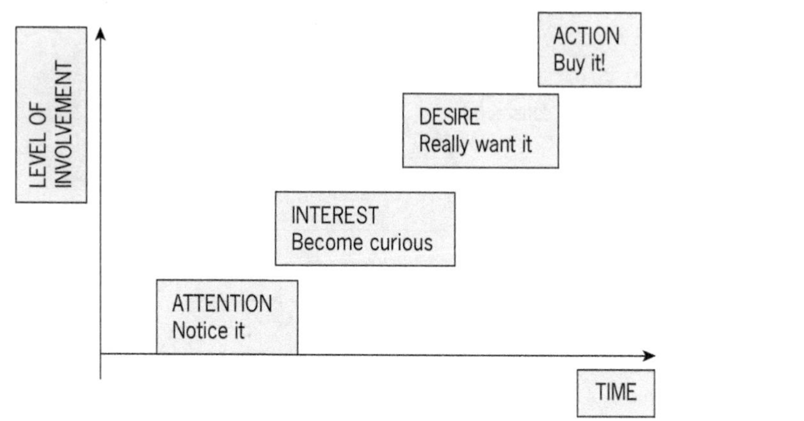


decision processes can be complex iterative processes involving large numbers of influencers and diverse decision criteria. Needs can themselves be difficult to understand and should be distinguished from expectations. The intangible nature of services and the general inability of buyers to check the quality or nature of a service until after it has been consumed adds to the importance of understanding the sources of information which are used in the process of evaluation. In this process, a service provider has to understand what buying state an individual is currently in; for example, they may be 'just looking', or about to commit themselves to a purchase. This is the basis for the 'AIDA' model, which recognizes that a company must first capture the **A**ttention of a potential buyer, then generate **I**nterest in the company's service, leading to a **D**esire by the individual to purchase this service specifically, and finally **A**ction needs to be taken in the form of an actual purchase (Figure 6.2).

## 6.2.1 Need recognition

The buying process is triggered by an underlying need. That need motivates us to seek a solution that will restore a sense of physiological and psychological balance that was previously absent. Needs can be extremely complex and are no longer dominated by basic physiological needs. The service sector has benefited from the tendency for societies to climb to higher levels of Maslow's 'hierarchy of needs' (Maslow, 1943). Among consumer services, many high-growth sectors would appear to be catering to individuals' 'higher-order' social and self-actualization needs. Multichannel television services, flower-delivery services and long-haul travel are all a long way from satisfying our basic physiological needs, but are typical of the sectors that have expanded rapidly in recent years by satisfying consumers' higher-order needs. Figure 6.3 offers an illustration of how changing needs have influenced the type of food we buy. In less developed societies, consumers are driven primarily by the basic nutritional content of food in order to satisfy a basic need for body maintenance. In more developed societies we are increasingly likely to base our search for food on the basis of a need for social togetherness or curiosity. Hence the great growth in social eating out, and in particular the variety of ethnic restaurants that can now be found in most towns.

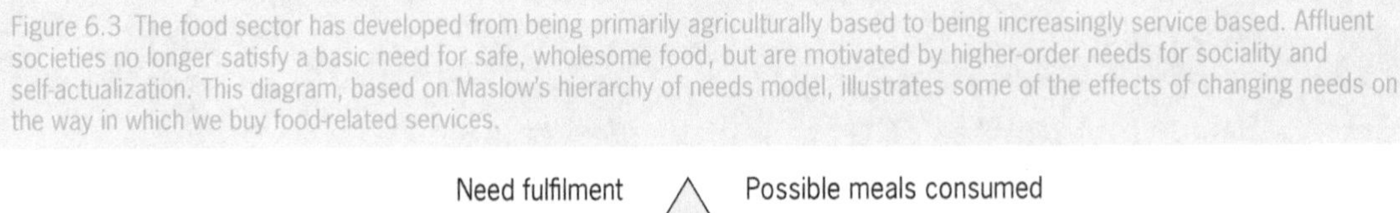
Figure 6.3 The food sector has developed from being primarily agriculturally based to being increasingly service based. Affluent societies no longer satisfy a basic need for safe, wholesome food, but are motivated by higher-order needs for sociality and self-actualization. This diagram, based on Maslow's hierarchy of needs model, illustrates some of the effects of changing needs on the way in which we buy food-related services.

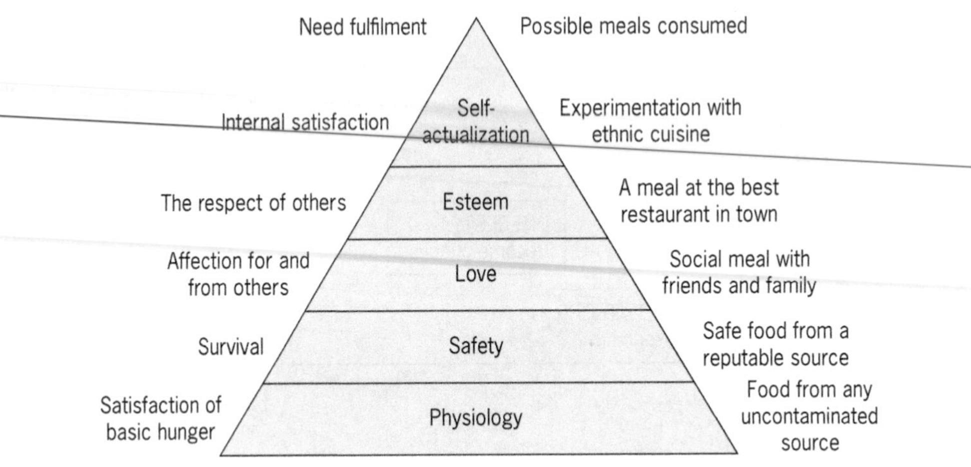


Maslow's hierarchy provides a basis for understanding the needs that underlie demand for services, but the hierarchy is no more than a conceptual model. In practice, it is difficult to measure where an individual actually is on the hierarchy of needs. Furthermore, it is essentially based on Western values of motivation and there is a lot of evidence of cultural influences on needs (e.g. Jai-Ok et al., 2002). How, for example, would you explain religious sacrifice and penance, which are an important motivator for many services associated with religious rituals, especially in non-Western consumers?

In addition to our inherent physiological and psychological needs, our needs are influenced by the situation in which we currently find ourselves. The subjects of age and socio-economic status can have profound effects on buying behaviour. The stage that an individual has reached in the 'family life cycle' also has a significant influence on needs (Figure 6.4).

So far, needs have been discussed in the context of a stimulus–response model in which the stimulus of a need leads to action being taken. However, it has been suggested that stimulus–response models are too simplistic in the way that needs are portrayed as being something conscious. While this criticism may be true of products in general, it has particular relevance to services. As well as being physically intangible, many services may be mentally intangible. Few young people, for example, recognize an underlying need for old-age security that a pension will provide. Such people may only purchase a pension policy if they become aware of the product. Prior to this, they may not have been aware of the underlying need that a pension policy seeks to satisfy.

## Thinking around the subject: The worldwide rise of the middle-class service consumer?

According to Maslow's hierarchy of needs, individuals satisfy their lowest level of needs with basic agricultural products and later with manufactured goods. It is only when they become more prosperous that they can think about becoming large-scale consumers of services. Refer to Figure 6.3 for an example of how this thinking can be applied to food consumption. Just look around in your own town and it is likely that a lot of the fancy restaurants, kindergartens and financial services providers will be found in 'middle class' areas of towns.

Service providers are interested in the middle classes because of their willingness and ability to consume services, especially those aspirational services provided through market mechanisms (rather than intervention services provided by the state as a necessity, such as law enforcement and social care services). But for Western-based companies, it is not just their domestic middle classes that are of interest, but those in emerging economies.

The OECD has defined 'middle class' as comprising those earning 10 to 100 dollars per day at purchasing power parity. By this measure, the Brookings Institute has forecast that by 2022, over half of the world's middle-class people will be living in the Asia Pacific region, double the figure in that part of the world in 2012.

In China, less than 20 per cent of people belonged to the middle classes in 2012, but despite this low percentage, they were estimated in a report by HSBC to account for about $1.5 trillion of spending, third only to the USA and Japan. By 2020, the number of middle-class people in China and their spending per head were expected to increase to a point where the value of their combined spending tripled, exceeding that of Japan, and just below the USA (HSBC, 2012).

What services will the growing number of middle-class Chinese consumers buy? China is already the world's biggest market for mobile phone services. The Chinese middle classes have for some time sent their children to good schools and colleges, and universities around the world have eyed up the sheer size of the education market. Leisure is likely to become an increasing part of middle-class Chinese consumers' lifestyle, as they eat out more and travel the world as tourists.

But what does it mean to be middle class in China? The consultancy firm McKinsey reported in 2012 that in the eastern coastal towns of China, being middle class has led to consumption patterns quite similar to those of a Westerner, with communications and leisure services featuring strongly in their expenditure. But McKinsey also noted diversity in China, with middle classes in more rural parts of China not being so readily drawn into a Western lifestyle, with expenditure instead directed to preserving social status and cultural values, for example through investment in land and property.

There has been debate within China about whether Western services companies seeking to enter the Chinese market are failing to understand the Chinese middle classes, by defining them in Western terms. Recent discussion on a Chinese blog (www.sina.com) suggested that being middle class in China was indicated by: annual income over 200,000 RMB (£20,000); above-average education level, and with professional and technical qualifications; being engaged in 'mental' rather than manual occupations; holding stocks or options in markets in the hope of future gain; having power and influence at work and dressing in a 'designer' casual style; having rich spiritual and cultural needs, such as enjoying opera, ballet and concerts; and owning at least one house or apartment and a car.

Even crude income figures are a misleading way of describing the middle classes, as living in China is much less expensive than living in most Western countries. For instance, a person earning $1000 a month can live a good life in China, but not in the USA, and some have suggested a golden rule in defining the middle class – that they should have one-third of their income available for discretional expenditure on things such as holidays and entertainment.

Will cultural convergence inevitably mean that middle-class consumers will consume essentially the same services in Beijing, Birmingham and Brisbane? Or is being middle class about more than income, and should take account of individuals' need for identity in the cultural context of their time?

## In practice: New baby, new markets

An individual's need for different types of service typically changes through their lifetime, and certain 'trigger' events may bring about a new set of needs. Lifecycle Marketing (Mother & Baby) Ltd has understood the radically changed needs of mothers-to-be and publishes the magazine *Emma's Diary* and website www.emmasdiary.co.uk to guide them through the stages of pregnancy and childbirth. On registering with the company, individuals receive further information and offers appropriate to their needs at the different stages of their pregnancy. The company has built up a valuable database of customers who have come to trust the advice given in *Emma's Diary*. Advertisers in the magazine and on the website realize that the birth of a child, especially the first one, is a significant trigger to new patterns of expenditure. Targeted individuals are likely to be highly receptive to the firms' messages.

Figure 6.4 *Emma's Diary*. (Reproduced courtesy of Lifecycle Marketing (Mother & Baby) Ltd)

## 6.2.2 Information search

In the classic model of buyer behaviour, the next stage in the process is to collect information about services that are capable of satisfying the underlying need. But where do buyers look for information when making purchases? In the case of the routine repurchase of a familiar service, probably very little additional information is sought. But where there is a greater element of novelty or risk, buyers are likely to seek out more comprehensive information about the alternative ways in which they can satisfy their needs. The following information sources are likely to be used:

- Personal experience will be a starting point, so if a buyer has already used a company's services, the suitability of the proposed purchase may be assessed in the light of the previous purchases.
- Word-of-mouth recommendation from friends is important for many categories of services where an individual may have had no previous need to make a purchase. When looking for a plumber or a solicitor, for example, many people will initially seek the advice of friends or seek out the views of other users of social network sites. There is evidence that, within the travel sector, consumers undertake extensive 'surfing' of the Web to establish information about a resort and the alternative means of getting there, even if the Internet is not subsequently used as the medium for making a purchase.
- Rather than being guided by other individuals directly, we may be indirectly influenced by the choices of 'reference groups'. What restaurant is it considered fashionable to eat in at the moment? What bar in town is currently the coolest place to be seen in by your peer group?
- Newspaper editorial content and review sites such as Trip Advisor may be consulted as a relatively objective source of information.
- Advertising and promotion in all of its forms is studied, sometimes being specifically sought and at other times being casually seen without any search activity involved.

The greater the perceived risk of a purchase, the longer and more widespread the search for information. Of course, individuals differ in the extent to which they are prepared to methodically collect information. Some may have a type of personality that leads them to make a purchase more impulsively than for more calculating individuals. Relatively impulsive decisions may also reflect their lower risk threshold, lower level of involvement or greater familiarity with that type of purchase. In the case of some high-involvement services, such as the choice of a healthcare professional, there is evidence that some segments of consumers use a prior information search to empower them in their subsequent negotiations with the provider (Newholm et al., 2006).

## Thinking around the subject: Can you believe online gossip?

Word-of-mouth recommendation can be an important way of influencing buyers' choices, but it has traditionally been a fairly slow means of spreading recommendation about a product. Now, the Internet allows the whole process to be speeded up and has widened its impact. From word of mouth, companies now talk about word of mouse, leading to 'viral marketing' in which a purchase recommendation can spread very quickly as one person passes on a message to half a dozen friends, each of whom in turn passes on the message to another half dozen friends.

While readership of printed newspapers continues to fall, usage of online social networking platforms such as Facebook, Twitter and LinkedIn continues to rise. Online communication appears increasingly important as more websites offer user-generated content, such as blogs, video and photo sharing opportunities. Service companies have adapted to these trends by shifting their budgets from 'above-the-line' (traditional mass media advertising) to 'below-the-line' (e.g. direct mail and viral marketing activities).

Because social media campaigns leave the dispersion of marketing messages to consumers, they tend to be more cost-efficient than traditional mass media advertising. For example, one of the earliest successful viral campaigns saw the online mail service Hotmail recruit 12 million subscribers in just 18 months with a tiny marketing budget of only $50,000. Similarly, Google's Gmail succeeded in its early days entirely through a 'recruit a friend' approach with very little mass media support.

To achieve best results, a review by Hinz et al. (2011) noted that firms must consider four critical factors: (1) content, in that the attractiveness of a message makes it memorable (Berger and Milkman, 2010); (2) the structure of the social network (Bampo et al., 2008); (3) the behavioural characteristics of the recipients and their incentives for sharing a message; and (4) the seeding strategy, which determines the initial set of targeted consumers chosen by the initiator of the viral marketing campaign (Bampo et al., 2008).

However, with a lot of gossip being spread through viral channels, which ones should a user trust? In a face-to-face context, a user may be able to form a view about the trustworthiness of the person they are listening to, but in the much bigger online social media environment, this can be quite difficult. Although Ipsos MORI reported in 2012 that people are more likely to trust messages derived through social media than through conventional media, this has been challenged by reports of bogus comments and reviews posted by companies who act using false identities to praise their own service while criticizing their competitors. In 2013 Samsung admitted that it had been posting anonymous comments praising its own products and criticising rival HTC on Taiwanese gadget sites. Samsung's strategy was uncovered when a blog, TaiwanSamsungLeaks.org, revealed that Samsung's marketing team had paid students to post claims on forums, with comments such as 'The HTC One X repeatedly crashes', 'The Galaxy S3 benchmarks better than the HTC One X' and 'The Galaxy Note is way better than the HTC Sensation XL'.

Social media is not a static concept and firms seeking to use it must recognize and respond to its emerging challenges and opportunities. As fraudulent postings become an issue, a challenge has been to establish verification of posters, for example by limiting access to blogs to those customers who have actually paid a company to buy the product being reviewed. But does this not highlight a major paradox of social media – in principle it should be open to all, so does some form of control stifle the whole concept of social media, or make it more workable?

### 6.2.3 Evaluation and decision

A lot of effort has gone into trying to understand the processes that consumers use to evaluate competing services. By the time that all possible competing alternatives have been reduced to a smaller shortlist (or 'choice set'), many possibilities will have been discarded on the way. This may be simply due to poor awareness of a product's existence, or an inability to acquire sufficient information about it. Even allowing for services of which a consumer has not become aware, they will probably be left with too many choices to evaluate each one individually in detail. It is usual, therefore, to base evaluation on a 'choice set' of a small number of alternatives, which will be subjected to a more detailed comparative analysis.

There is increasing interest in the role of consumers' emotional states in the evaluation process (O'Shaughnessy and O'Shaughnessy, 2003). Many low-involvement service purchasers can be evaluated in a fairly rational way using methods such as those described below. However, high-involvement services may involve strong emotions, which are more difficult to model. As an example, the evaluation process for selecting a garage to carry out a planned and routine replacement of a tyre is likely to be quite different from the evaluation process to repair a broken-down car that is urgently needed to get the person to an important appointment. The emotional significance of having a car to get to that appointment is likely to impact on the evaluation process and the final decision.

A private buyer seeking to buy a low-involvement service, such as a car insurance policy, may have narrowed down the set to a choice of four. Analysts of buyer behaviour have developed a number of frameworks for trying to understand how a consumer chooses between these competing alternatives. One approach is for the consumer to use a sense of intuition as to what feels best. Such non-systematic methods of evaluation may be quite appropriate where the service in question involves low levels of cost, risk and involvement.

Even apparently intuitive bases of evaluation can be reduced to a series of rules, implying some systematic basis. One framework is a multiple-attribute choice matrix, which holds that consumers refer to a number of component attributes of a product to evaluate the overall suitability of the product. Figure 6.5 shows a typical matrix in which four competing car insurance policies are compared in terms of five important attributes. In this matrix, the four short-listed alternatives in

Figure 6.5 A hypothetical choice set for motor insurance: a multiple attribute matrix

| Importance | Weights | A | B | C | D |
|---|---|---|---|---|---|
| Location of branch | 10 | 10 | 7 | 8 | 10 |
| Friendliness of staff | 9 | 10 | 9 | 8 | 8 |
| Reputation of lender | 8 | 10 | 10 | 9 | 9 |
| Overall cost | 7 | 10 | 10 | 10 | 5 |
| Short-term incentives | 6 | 4 | 10 | 10 | 4 |
| Overall rating | | 44 | 46 | 45 | 36 |
| Weighted rating | | 7.3 | 7.2 | 7.0 | 6.1 |
| Choice using unweighted approach | | | √ | | |
| Choice using linear compensatory approach | | √ | | | |
| Choice using lexicographic approach | | √ | | | |

the choice set are shown by the column headings A, B, C and D. The left-hand column shows five attributes on which buyers base their purchase decision. The second column shows the importance that the consumer attaches to each attribute of the service (with maximum importance being given a score of 10 and a completely unimportant attribute a score of zero). The remaining four columns show how each service scores against each of the five evaluation attributes. Consumers' perceptions of attributes and the importance they attach to them can only be found out through a programme of market research. Conjoint analysis has been widely used in the analysis of components of service offers.

If it is assumed that a consumer evaluates each service provider without weighting each attribute, service provider B will be the preferred supplier, as it has the highest overall rating. It is more realistic to expect that some factors will be weighted as being more important than others, therefore the alternative *linear compensatory* approach is based on consumers creating weighted scores for each service provider. The importance of each attribute is multiplied by the score for each attribute, so, in this case, provider A is preferred as the attributes that consumers rank most highly are also those that are considered to be the most important. A third approach to evaluation is sometimes described as a lexicographic approach. This involves the buyer in starting their evaluation by looking at the most important attribute and ruling out those suppliers that do not meet a minimum standard. Evaluation is then based on the second most important attribute, with service providers that do not meet their standard being eliminated. This continues until only one option is left. In Figure 6.5, branch location is given as the most important attribute, so the initial evaluation may have reduced the choice set to A and D (these score highest on location). In the second round, friendliness of staff becomes the most important decision criterion. Only A and D remain in the choice set, and as A has the highest score for friendliness of staff, it will be chosen in preference to D.

However, it can be one thing for a buyer to express a preference for a particular service, or even an intention to purchase it, but they may nevertheless make their purchase with another service provider. In a study of restaurant patrons, it was found that the patrons who expressed strong purchase intent and made a subsequent purchase demonstrated distinct attitudes when compared to those patrons who also expressed strong purchase intent but failed to make a subsequent purchase. The results suggest that the service manager could be misled, and therefore could make costly mistakes, by planning for the future simply on the basis of what consumers say they will do (Newberry et al., 2003).

Can we have too much choice? Making decisions involves effort and the psychological anxiety that we might have made the wrong decision. Limiting the range of services that we choose from is therefore a natural reaction. Ideally, we would like to be presented with just one choice that reflects our needs perfectly. Good sales personnel realize that most buyers cannot handle more than a shortlist of five or six alternatives and have developed the skill of probing a buyer's key preferences and then presenting a simple choice set of just three or four alternatives. More than this, and the buyer may just walk away confused and defer a purchase. But if the three or four alternatives offered are poorly selected, the buyer may walk away anyway.

Increasingly, with the use of databases, companies are able to understand the preferences of customers and present choices based on this understanding. An ongoing buyer–seller relationship (discussed in more detail in Chapter 5) is often used to provide a better-informed choice set. Indeed, summing up developments in relationship marketing, Sheth and Parvatiyar have described firms' motivation to develop ongoing relationships as being based primarily on 'choice reduction' (Sheth and Parvatiyar, 2002).

The more choice is offered to a buyer, the greater the probability that they will regret the choice that they actually made. We will return to the notion of regret in the next section.

## Thinking around the subject: A confusing design or designed to confuse?

The term 'confusion marketing' has been used to describe the practices of some service providers. Even staff working for some companies have been heard to use the term, off the record. In an ideal world, we should all be able to evaluate the options open to us and make a rational choice from the available options. Classical economic theory is based on an assumption of informed decision-making. But how do you go about the task of evaluation when there is enormous choice and service providers appear to go out of their way to confuse buyers with excessive, missing or inappropriate information?

Many buyers of mobile phone services have been overwhelmed at the choices available to them – in the UK the final purchase decision has to be made from a permutation of five basic network operators, dozens of different tariffs for each network, hundreds of different handsets and thousands of retail outlets. To many people, the tariff plans offered by the phone companies seem unbelievably complex, with an array of peak/off-peak price plans, 'free' inclusive minutes and discounts for loyalty. Comparing a few 'headline' prices may be difficult enough, but the task becomes even harder when account is taken of extras, which are often hidden in the small print; for example, the charges made for itemized billing and multimedia messages or for using a phone abroad. One professor of mathematics calculated that it would take a buyer over a year to evaluate the costs and benefits of all permutations of networks, tariffs and handsets.

Is the approach of mobile phone companies an attempt to confuse buyers with low 'headline' prices, but a confusing range of supplementary prices? Or does the approach reflect a genuine concern to segment markets so finely that every buyer's preferences are catered to?

### 6.2.4 Post-consumption evaluation

The buying process does not end once a service has been purchased and consumed. Completion of consumption often marks the beginning of the process of making a follow-up purchase. We can only truly evaluate a service after we have consumed it, and at this point we develop attitudes towards the service. If we are entirely happy with the service, we may become an advocate of it and tell our friends about it, as well as putting the service provider at the top of our shortlist the next time we seek that type of service. Where we are unhappy with some aspect of the service, we may experience cognitive dissonance. Festinger (1957) first defined dissonance as the psychologically uncomfortable state following the act of choosing between a set of alternatives, which motivates an individual to do something to eliminate the inconsistency between thoughts and behaviour, thereby reducing the dissonant state. It has been noted that dissonance may result when 'an opinion is formed or a decision taken when cognition and opinions direct us in different directions' (Sweeney et al., 2000, p. 369).

We can reduce dissonance in a number of ways, including: trying to filter out of our minds bad aspects of the service and concentrating on the good aspects so that we believe we made the right choice; downplaying the expectations that we thought we had about the service; and initiating some form of complaining behaviour. For goods that had caused us dissonance, we might return the goods to the seller. However, this is not possible in the case of service processes that have already been consumed. We may be able to claim against a service provider's guarantee of satisfaction, and it is to reduce the prospect of dissonance that some service providers offer to refund the cost of a service if the customer is not completely satisfied.

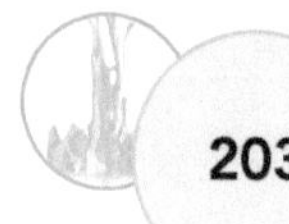



## In practice: Are you confused (.com)?

In the UK domestic gas and electricity supply market, consumers are faced with a sometimes bewildering and confusing choice of suppliers, all offering a basic commodity product, which by law cannot be differentiated. Evaluation is made more difficult because the different companies choose different bases for pricing, with many companies offering several different price plans. Some give introductory discounts, some give high-user or low-user discounts and many give discounts for payment by direct debit. The website confused.com has become a popular choice for many consumers seeking comparative information on a novel purchase. This calculator for gas and electricity guides consumers through the choices available and identifies which supplier and price plan is best for them. It is claimed that an average family that switches suppliers on a comparison website could save up to £200 on their annual energy bills.

Figure 6.6 A typical price comparison website. (Reproduced with permission of Confused.com)



It was noted in the previous section that too much choice can result in a psychologically costly decision-making process. Too much choice can also increase post-purchase levels of dissonance. 'Regret theory' contends that, the more choices we have forgone, the greater the likelihood that we will regret the choice that we actually made (Herrmann et al., 1999). If there was only one hotel in a resort where we could stay, we could not be unhappy when we subsequently saw another hotel that looked better. If we had, in fact, been offered a choice of hotels in the resort, we might subsequently regret not choosing those hotels that were not our first choice.

## 6.3 The effects of intangibility and risk on the buying process

Think back to the simple model of buyer behaviour in Figure 6.1, showing a continuous process from a need triggering a search for information, analysis which led to a decision and then feelings after the purchase. This may be generally true, but there are problems in applying this linear model to services. Pure services cannot be fully evaluated until after consumption, therefore it may be unrealistic to conceptualize evaluation as being completed before the decision is made, when full evaluation can only occur after the service has been consumed. You cannot, for example, evaluate a restaurant in the way that you can evaluate a television by testing it before making a purchase. You can only really evaluate the restaurant after you have eaten there.

Recognizing the difficulty of evaluating services before consumption, an alternative buyer behaviour model was proposed by Fisk (1981) and is shown diagrammatically in Figure 6.7. The model sees the purchase process as being divided into three stages – pre-consumption, consumption and post-consumption. The pre-consumption stage comprises the range of activities that commonly

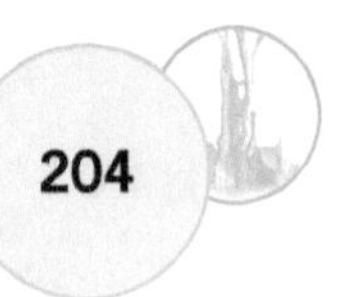

Figure 6.7 A multi-stage conceptualization of the consumption/evaluation process for services. (Based on Fisk, 1981)

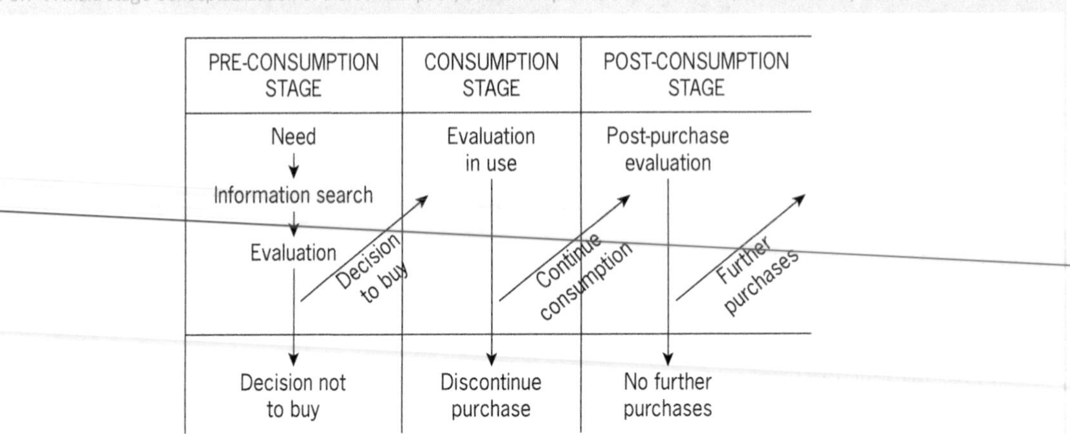


take place before a purchase decision is made, beginning with the initial problem recognition, collection of information and identification of the choice set. At this stage, consumers identify what they expect to be the best solution. In the following consumption stage, the consumer actually decides through experience what they consider to be the best choice. During this phase, expectations raised during the pre-consumption phase are compared with actual service delivery. A gap between the two results in attempts to reduce dissonance; for example, dissatisfaction resulting from failure to meet expectations may be resolved by complaining. In the post-consumption phase, the whole service encounter is evaluated and this determines whether the consumer will be motivated to purchase the service again.

All purchasing decisions are likely to involve some degree of risk and uncertainty, and this is generally greater for services than goods where there is less tangible evidence on which to base a pre-purchase evaluation. There is evidence that intangibility often leads to a consumer's evaluation of a service being based on tangible evidence and price rather than the core service offer (Zeithaml, 1981).

A number of factors influence the perception of risk and uncertainty experienced by a consumer when approaching a service purchase:

- *The level of tangible evidence that is available to support evidence of the service process and outcomes.* Service providers often go to great lengths to demonstrate service benefits using tangible cues, e.g. an airline that seeks to charge a premium price for its Business Class seats may demonstrate the benefits of its seats with a replica seat in travel agents' offices or a virtual guide on its website.
- *The level of the buyer's involvement in the service.* Where involvement levels are high (as in the case of many personal healthcare services), the perceived risk of a decision is likely to be greater than a low-involvement service such as the rental of a video.
- *The novelty of the purchase.* If a particular type of purchase is new to us, we are more likely to experience high levels of risk than if we are a repeat buyer. A first-time mortgage buyer will most likely perceive much higher levels of risk than somebody who has arranged many mortgages during their life.
- *The purchaser's individual risk threshold.* Just as some people are more prepared to take risks in the way they gamble money or drive their car, so some buyers will be more prepared to take risks when choosing between competing services. A cheap holiday with an unknown foreign airline may appeal to some, but be perceived as too risky by others.

- *Situational factors affect perceptions of risk.* If we are desperate to use a service, we may lower our risk threshold. If we have just missed the last bus home, we may be more prepared to risk a taxi ride in a 'dubious' car which is perceived as being more risky than the taxi that we might choose in more relaxed conditions.
- *There may be a perception of safeguards available to consumers that reduce perceptions of risk.* In many cases, legislation protects consumers from non-delivery of a service, so consumers may be more prepared to take a risk. Within the financial services sector, for example, there is an extensive protection mechanism that prevents small savers losing deposits paid to regulated banks. Most UK investors do not therefore perceive a risk of losing their money when putting their savings in a UK-based bank, but perceptions of risk would be much higher if the bank was 'offshore' and unregulated.
- *Loss of reputation for commercial buyers.* In the case of purchases made by an individual for their organization, the individual may perceive risk to their personal reputation of making a wrong choice. It is often said that 'nobody got fired for choosing IBM'. An individual buyer may fear that this may not be true if they choose an unknown service brand.

## In practice: Try before you buy?

Figure 6.8 An Internet trial offer (Reproduced with permission of Orange Broadband)

The market for Internet service providers (ISPs) in many countries is fiercely competitive, but buyers have few bases for evaluating competing service providers. If I sign up for a 12-month contract for this provider, can I be sure of a reliable connection? Will it be fast? How good are the information sources provided by the site? If I have a technical problem, will I get good advice speedily? The possibility of failure in any of these areas may pose a risk to purchasers, who may just prefer to carry on with their existing ISP, or not bother buying at all. Freeserve (now known as Orange Broadband) established itself as a leading UK ISP but appreciated the risks its potential customers may have perceived. Like many of its competitors, it offered a free trial period, during which customers can test the company's service claims with little or no risk to themselves. The company's experience was that a high proportion of trial users went on to sign up for a one-year service contract.

### 6.3.1 Search, experience and credence bases for buying

In an attempt to distinguish between different kinds of buying situations, services have often been divided into three groups according to the type of buying behaviour associated with them: search, experience and credence services.

Search services are those for which it is generally easy to define the service in terms of known and measurable characteristics, and a buyer could be reasonably confident that the service they select will provide benefits as defined in the service description. Such services are essentially commoditized products in which points of commonality between service offers are relatively high and points of difference relatively low. As an example, airline tickets between two points may be evaluated on their search characteristics, typically the price of the ticket, the number of changes involved and the journey time. For short journeys in particular, intrinsic qualities such as the comfort of the airline and the quality of its customer services may be relatively unimportant. Most airlines would be quite generic in the service they provide – safe transport between the two points. Many online search facilities, such as those of expedia.com and opodo.com, allow customers to search for flights and for these to be ranked according to the customers' criteria, typically price and convenience of the timing.

Experience products can only be evaluated through consumption, because they are likely to be quite individual and incapable of being reduced to standardized, generic searchable characteristics. This type of service is likely to emphasize **hedonistic benefits** rather than **utilitarian benefits**, typical of theatre performances and many health and caring services. Risk is likely to be perceived as quite high for experience-based services, and buyers will seek to reduce this risk by seeking the opinions of friends and contributors to customer review sites.

Credence products are very difficult or impossible to assess prior to purchase. Evaluation is therefore likely to be based upon the credibility of the supplier and its reputation for delivering its promises. If we are planning to buy a service for which we have no previous purchasing experience, we may base our evaluation on the credibility of a service provider, which may be gained through personal experience of buying other types of service from the company, media reports about the company, or word-of-mouth recommendation from our friends. Many financial services companies promote themselves on credence values by stressing their long history and good past performance.

In general, goods are more likely to be evaluated on the basis of search qualities, whereas services are more likely to be evaluated on credence qualities, with most hybrid products being based on a combination of search, credence and experience qualities. Figure 6.9 illustrates schematically a model showing the dominance of each characteristic.

Figure 6.9 A model of services buying behaviour based on search, credence and experience qualities. Goods are more likely than services to be evaluated on the basis of their search criteria because it is generally easier to specify the product using criteria which are easy for everybody in a market to understand (although there are many goods such as fashion clothing for which experience of the product is an important part of evaluation, and others such as ethically produced food for which credence is important). Some commodified services, such as an airline ticket between two points, may be evaluated on the basis of search criteria (e.g. price, timing). However, many high-involvement service processes (e.g. hairdressing and fitness training) can only be evaluated through experience, and many services which entail a high level of trust in the service provider, such as investment management services, may be evaluated primarily on the credence of the service provider. (Based on Mitra et al., 1999)

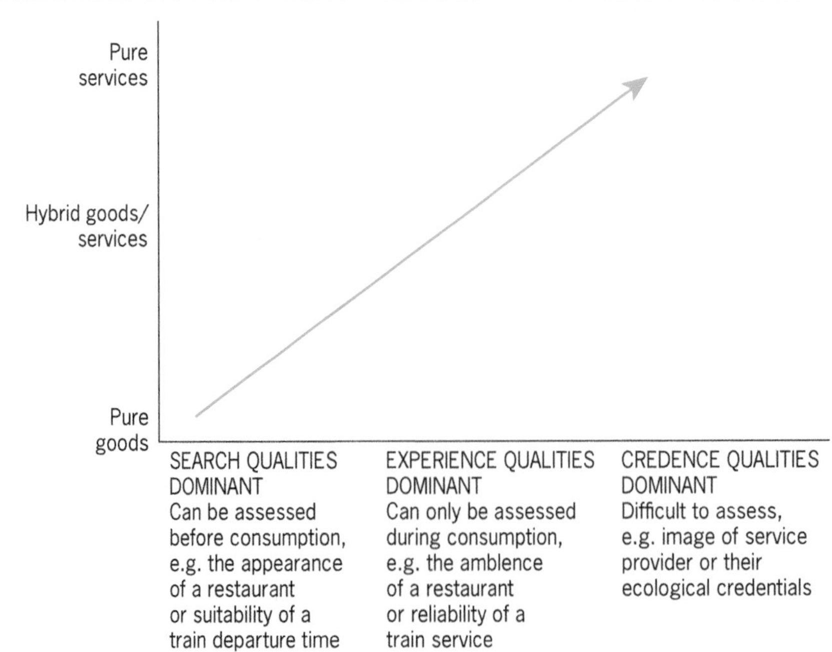

## 6.4 The decision-making unit

Few service purchase decisions are made by an individual in total isolation from other people. Usually other people are involved in some role and have a bearing on the final decision. It is important to recognize who the key players in this process are, in order that the service format can be configured to meet these people's needs, and that promotional messages can be adapted and directed at the key individuals involved in the purchase decision. A number of roles can be identified among people involved in the decision process:

- *Influencers* are people or groups of people to whom the decision-maker refers in the process of making a decision. Reference groups can be primary (e.g. friends, acquaintances and work colleagues) or secondary in the form of remote personalities with whom there is no two-way interaction. Where research indicates that the primary reference group exerts major influence on purchase decisions, this could indicate the need to facilitate word-of-mouth communication, for example giving established customers rewards in return for the introduction of new customers. An analysis of secondary reference groups used by consumers in the decision process can be used in a number of ways. It will indicate possible personalities to be approached who may be used to endorse a product in the company's advertising. It will also indicate which opinion leaders an organization should target as part of its communication programme in order to achieve the maximum 'trickle down' effect. The media can be included within this secondary reference group – what a newspaper writes in its columns can have an important influence on purchase decisions.

Figure 6.10 The buying process does not end with a purchase. In this advertisement, BT encouraged its UK phone customers who had recently switched to a rival company to reflect on their feelings towards their new supplier. As well as encouraging former customers to return, this advertisement made existing BT customers feel more comfortable with their current supplier, by reducing the temptation to search for alternatives. (Reproduced courtesy of British Telecommunications plc)

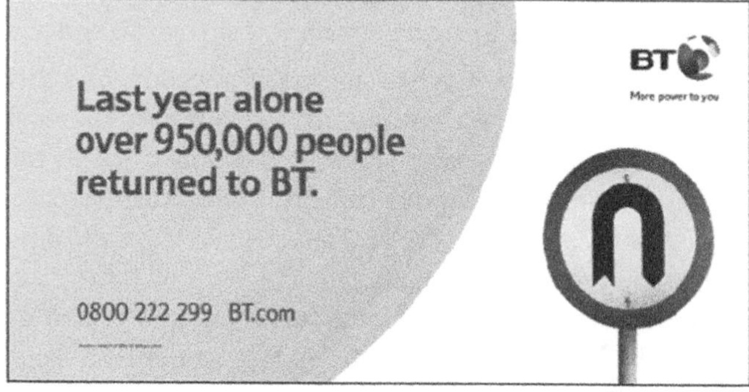


- *Gatekeepers* are most commonly found among commercial buyers. Their main effect is to act as a filter on the range of services that enter the decision choice set. Gatekeepers can take a number of forms – a secretary barring calls from sales representatives to the decision-maker has the effect of screening out a number of possible choices. In many organizations, it can be difficult to establish just who is acting as a gatekeeper. Identifying a marketing strategy that gains acceptance by the gatekeeper, or by-passes them completely, is therefore made difficult. In larger organizations and the public sector in particular, a select list of suppliers who are invited to submit tenders for work may exist. Without being on this list, a provider of services is unable to enter the decision set.

  Although gatekeepers are most commonly associated with the purchase of services by business organizations, they can also have application to private consumer purchases. In the case of many household services, an early part of the decision process may be the collection of information or telephoning to invite quotations for a service. While the final decision may be the subject of joint discussion and action, the initial stage of collecting information is more likely to be left to one person. In this way, a family member picking up holiday brochures or identifying suitable websites acts as a gatekeeper for their family, restricting subsequent choice to the holidays of those companies whose brochures or websites appealed to him or her.

- In some cases, ordering a service may be reduced to a routine task and be delegated to a *buyer*. In the case of business-to-business services, low-budget items that are not novel may be left to the discretion of a buyer. In this way, casual window-cleaning may be contracted by a buying clerk within the organization without immediate reference to anybody else. In the case of modified rebuys, or novel purchases, the decision-making unit is likely to be larger.
- The *users* of a service may not be the people responsible for making the actual purchase decision. This is particularly the case with many business-to-business service purchases. Nevertheless, research should be undertaken to reveal the extent to which users are important influencers in the decision process. In the case of the business airtravel market, it is important to understand the pressure that the actual traveller can exert on their choice of airline, as opposed to the influence of a company buyer (who may have arranged a long-term contract with one particular airline), a gatekeeper (who may discard promotional material relating to new airlines) or other influencers within the organization (e.g. cost-centre managers, who may be more concerned with the cost of using a service, in contrast to the user's overriding concern with its quality).
- The *decision-maker* is the person (or group of individuals) who makes the final decision to purchase, whether they execute the purchase themselves or instruct others to do so. With many family-based consumer services, it can be difficult to identify just who within the family carries most weight in making the final decision. Research into family service purchases that are purchased jointly has suggested that, in the case of package holidays, wives dominate in making the final decision, whereas, in the case of joint mortgages, it is the husband who dominates. Within any particular service sector, an analysis of how a decision is made can only realistically be achieved by means of qualitative in-depth research. In the case of decisions made by commercial buyers, the task of identifying the individuals responsible for making a final decision – and their level within the organizational hierarchy – becomes even more difficult.

## Thinking around the subject: Profiting from pester power?

What role do children play in the purchase of services which they consume? There has been a lot of debate about the extent of 'pester power', where parents apparently give in to the demands of their children. Increasingly, advertisers are aiming their promotional messages over the heads of adults and straight at children. The ethics of doing this have been questioned by many, and some countries have imposed restrictions on television advertising of children's products. However, even with advertising restrictions, companies have managed to get through to children in more subtle ways, for example by sponsoring educational materials used in schools and paying celebrities to endorse their products.

For fast-food restaurants, gaining the minds of children can be crucial to getting parents along. In the minds of many young children, having a birthday party at the local McDonald's has become highly desirable. How has this come about? There is little doubt that the basic service format appeals to young children – brightly coloured internal decor, play facilities and the food itself are clearly attractive to the young consumer. In addition, like many fast-food restaurants, McDonald's has developed a programme of educational support materials, which it takes to schools. Its materials promote the identity of McDonald's in an apparently educational manner, while at the same time generating desire among pupils. Having access to these materials may help cash-strapped teachers by providing much-needed resources, but is it ethical to target young children in this way? Does it make it harder for parents to encourage their children to eat a healthy diet?

Figure 6.11 Typical members of the buying decision-making unit for a family package holiday

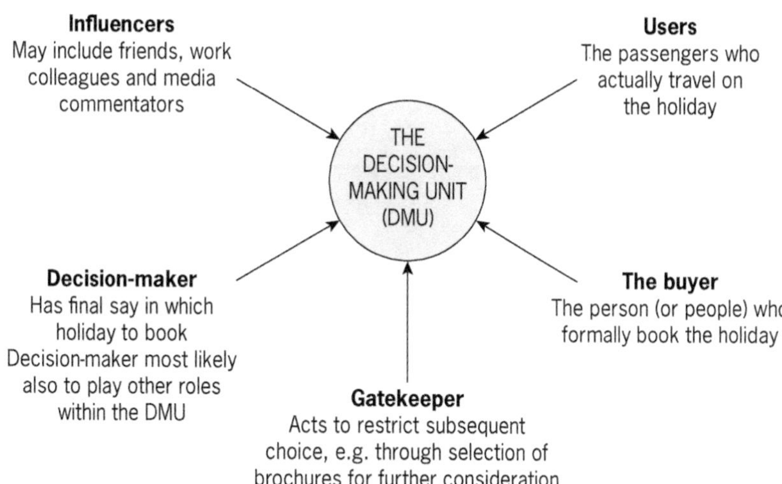


In reality, people play multiple roles in this process, sometimes switching between roles. An illustration of the roles with reference to the purchase of a package holiday is shown in Figure 6.11.

### 6.4.1 Personal and organizational buyer behaviour compared

The processes by which private consumers purchase services can differ from the way in which organizations buy services. A number of reasons can be identified for this:

- Two sets of needs are being met when an organization buys services – the formal needs of the organization and the needs of the individuals who make up the organization. While the former might be thought of as being the more economically rational, the needs that individuals in an organization seek to satisfy are influenced by their own perceptual and behavioural environment, very much in the same way as would be the case with private consumer purchases. Individuals may be more risk averse when buying on behalf of their organization. Would an individual within an organization want to run the risk of being blamed for hiring an unknown firm of management consultants, rather than a firm with a good international reputation?
- More people are typically involved in organizational purchases. High-value services purchases may require evaluation and approval at a number of levels of an organization's management hierarchy. An attempt should be made to find out where in an organization the final decision-making power lies. An analysis of the decision-making unit (see above) might also reveal a wide range of influencers who are present in the decision-making process.
- Organizational purchases are more likely to be made according to formalized routines. At their simplest, this may involve delegating to a junior buyer the task of making repeat orders for services that have previously been evaluated. At the other extreme, many high-value service purchases may only be made after a formal process of bidding and evaluation has been undertaken.
- The greater number of people involved in organizational buying often results in the whole process taking longer. A desire to minimize risk is inherent in many formal organizational motives and informally present in many individuals' motives, often resulting in lengthy feasibility studies

being undertaken. In some new markets, especially overseas markets, trust in service suppliers might be an important factor used by purchasers when evaluating competing suppliers and it may take time to build up a trusting relationship before any purchase commitment is secured.

Figure 6.12 If a domestic telephone breaks down, it may cause no more than annoyance and inconvenience to the customer. However, for business users, the consequences of a failure can be much more serious, possibly leading to lost sales, delayed orders and missed production. Few members of the organizational decision-making unit would want to carry the blame for selecting a phone provider that subsequently lets the company down. For business customers, telephone providers must appeal to all members of the decision-making unit by stressing that their services are reliable and have benefits in use that will be good value to the company. BT, the largest provider in the UK telecoms market, offers numerous packages for its domestic market. This advertisement aimed at the business sector stresses a particular concern of business buyers – the need to get a faulty phone repaired quickly so that business is not interrupted. (Reproduced courtesy of British Telecommunications plc)

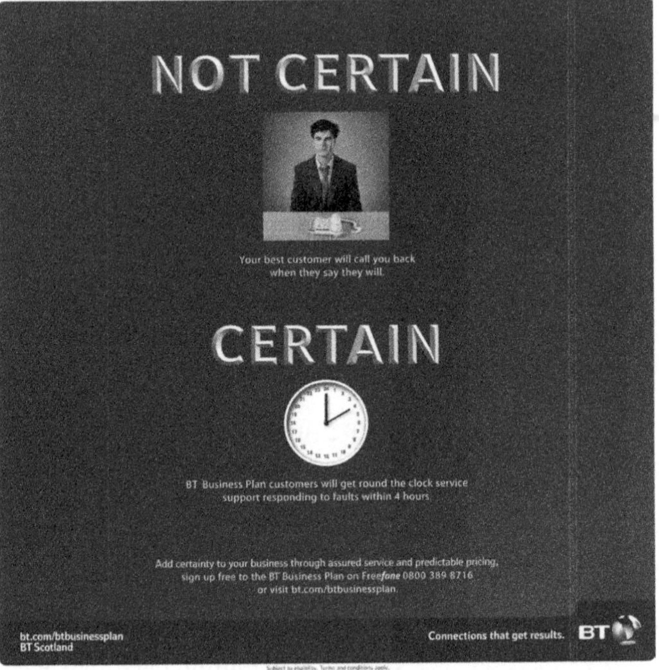


- The elements of the service offer that are considered critical in the evaluation process are likely to differ. For many services, the emphasis placed on price by many private buyers is replaced by reliability and performance characteristics by the organizational buyer. In many cases, poor performance of a service can have direct financial consequences for an organization – a poor parcel delivery service might merely cause annoyance to a private buyer, but might lead to lost production output or lost sales for an organizational buyer.
- The need for organizational buyers' risks to be reduced and their desire to seek the active co-operation of suppliers in tackling shared problems have resulted in greater attention being paid to the development of organizational buyer–seller relationships over time, rather than seeing individual purchases in isolation. The importance of mutual trust in the relationship between a service organization and its commercial buyers has been shown in a number of studies. It has been pointed out by Grönroos (1990) that, as the complexity of service offerings increases, the organizational buying unit perceives a greater need for confidence and trust in its services suppliers. The subject of ongoing buyer–seller relationships is considered in more detail in Chapter 5.

## 6.5 Learning about buyer behaviour

How do services organizations find out about how buyers actually make choices between competing services? Marketing research is essentially about the managers of a business *keeping in touch* with their markets. The small business owner may have been able to do marketing research quite intuitively and adapted his or her product offer according to buyers' preferences. Larger organizations operating in competitive and changing environments need more formal methods of collecting, analysing and disseminating information about their markets. It is frequently said that information is a source of a firm's competitive advantage and there are many examples of firms who have used a detailed knowledge of their customers' needs to develop better service offers that have given the firm a competitive advantage. A recent trend has been for market researchers to rename themselves as customer insight departments. This is recognition that marketers value insights above *everything else*; above being objective, above data collection, above classic methodology, even above validity and reliability.

The range of techniques used by companies to collect information about buyer behaviour is continually increasing. Indeed, companies often find themselves with more information than they can sensibly use. The great advances in electronic point of sale (EPOS) technology have, for example, given retailers a wealth of new data, of which not all companies have managed to make full use. More recently, many companies have developed techniques for 'mining' the vast amount of 'free' data left by users of blogs, with a view to making sense out of this data. As new techniques for data collection appear, it is important to maintain a balance between techniques so that a good overall picture is obtained. Reliance on just one technique may save costs in the short term, but only at the long-term cost of not having a good holistic view of market characteristics.

Research techniques need to be varied and appropriate, incorporating qualitative and quantitative approaches. Although quantitative and qualitative research are often seen as opposite ends of a research techniques spectrum, their methods overlap. Market researchers need to feel comfortable 'operating in all slices of the information map' (Smith and Dexter, 2001), incorporating harder, more scientific objective data with softer, anecdotal, qualitative data.

Conjoint analysis is a versatile marketing research technique that can provide valuable information to analyse the real-life trade-offs that consumers make when evaluating a range of features or attributes that are present in competing service offers. Once data are collected about consumers' preferences for particular attributes and features, the researcher can conduct a number of 'choice simulations'. This can improve the researcher's ability to predict which formulation of a service will be successful before a service is launched to the market. A limitation of this technique is that consumers' evaluation of individual attributes of a service may be quite meaningless on its own, and it is the creative combining of attributes that determines their final choice.

Observational techniques may be used to describe buying behaviour, but they do not in themselves provide explanation. For this, other techniques need to be used. Experimental observational research may provide insights into how consumers interact with a service, for example by observing how and in what order an individual reads an advertisement. The Internet has created new opportunities for observing how individuals move around a company's website. Which hyperlinks were most productive in bringing visitors to the company's site? Which combination of pages did they visit? In what order were they visited? How long did they spend on each page? Companies often use alternative page designs, which are randomly allocated to visitors; then the results (e.g. an order, further enquiry etc.) are compared. A number of specialist information intermediaries have emerged to carry out mass observation of website users using cookies and sell the data back to companies. From this, a company can build up a picture of individuals' behaviour and preferences, which can be valuable information for website developers and for companies, which can target their customers more accurately.

Observational techniques can raise ethical questions where those being observed are not aware that they are being studied. Many people may be unhappy at the thought that closed-circuit television (CCTV) footage of them walking round a store is being used in a study of how they make choices. The use of unseen cookies to observe Internet usage has been challenged by many on ethical and legal grounds.

Quantitative surveys may give the appearance of a rigorous, scientific approach, and many marketers may delude themselves (and others) into thinking that you 'can't argue with the figures'.

However, quantitative analysis techniques can suffer from a number of weaknesses, including poor sampling, invalid measurement techniques, poor analysis and inappropriate interpretation. Simply asking a potential consumer whether they would buy a new service is likely to result in answers that are intentionally or unintentionally dishonest. The failure to use techniques that are more probing than a simple questionnaire may explain why many forecasts of new service take-up are inaccurate (we will return to demand forecasting in Chapter 7).

## Thinking around the subject: Snooping or learning?

Finding out about how people actually go about choosing and using a service can be a daunting task because there are so many barriers that get in the way between what people actually do, what they say they do and what researchers subsequently interpret they do. Where researchers are far removed from the subjects that they are interested in, a very false picture of consumer behaviour can be the basis for marketing decisions. Observing behaviour is not new to marketers who have often preferred to know about the reality of what people actually do, rather than individuals' expressed attitudes, which may never be manifested in actual purchasing behaviour.

In a nation that has been gripped by voyeuristic 'reality' television programmes such as *Big Brother*, it is not surprising that marketers should also try to gain a better insight into behaviour that might previously have been considered private. How far should marketers legitimately be able to go in their pursuit of these better insights? And at what point does it become intrusive?

In recent years, researchers have paid increasing attention to the use of ethnography in the study of consumer behaviour. A typical study might involve asking participants to use a web-based service and watching their interactions with it and with their friends. But what if consumers are observed in a non-consensual manner? In one widely reported study, ethnographic researchers travelled on London's number 73 bus to observe how passengers used their mobile phones, and revealed a variety of behaviours that were not affected by respondents' need to conform. A mobile phone is more than a mere technology-based service, and it became quite apparent that the pattern of needs satisfied by a mobile phone was very complex.

More recently, marketers have used technology to probe individuals' behaviour, but critics have argued that 'Big Brother' techniques may be exploiting consumers without their agreement. Many users of the Internet may be unaware that cookies lodged in their computer are spying on them, trying to understand their buying behaviour. So when an Internet service provider flashes a banner advert for car rental on your screen, it may not have been by chance, but an analysis of your previous search behaviour that led the system to deduce that you were in the process of looking for a car rental service. Closed-circuit television has been used by researchers to study how people move around a supermarket and the processes used in searching for products. Would you be happy in the knowledge that all of your indecisions, strained facial expressions and bad tempers were being recorded to be replayed over and over again by researchers?

Qualitative techniques can offer deeper insights into buyers' thought processes as they choose between competing service offers. A range of ethnographic approaches seek to understand often apparently simple phenomena from the perspective of the buyer (see Thinking around the subject). A commonly used approach is the focus group. Groups normally consist of about eight people, plus a trained moderator who leads the discussion. Focus groups do not claim to be statistically representative of the population that they come from, but nevertheless there would be little value in recruiting a group which was not typical of the target population as a whole. Many focus groups are now undertaken online or through video conferencing. Virtual ethnography (or 'webnography') has emerged as a powerful source of learning in which a researcher participates in an online community (Kozinets, 2006).

Despite the range of research techniques available, many of the great services marketing developments of recent times have come about from individuals taking inspired decisions, based on casual observation of buyer behaviour. Many small businesses catering for niches have started in this way. Many Internet-based service providers launched in the early days of the dot.com boom, such as Lastminute.com and Screwfix.com, were essentially based on small entrepreneurs' intuitive assessment of what they thought customers would want from the Internet.

It must always be remembered that information cannot in itself give answers. Indeed, too much information about buyers can lead to a 'paralysis by analysis'. In a turbulent marketing environment, it is the quality and timeliness of interpretation of data that gives a firm a competitive advantage. In markets where risks are low and consumers' tastes change rapidly, inspired decisions may win out over the more analytical approaches needed where high risks and capital commitments are involved.

## 6.6 Market segmentation and buyer behaviour

The purpose of studying buyer behaviour is to develop a company's marketing mix so that a desired response is achieved from targeted buyers. Naturally, individuals differ in the way they respond to marketing stimuli, implying differences in individuals' processing determinants. Some buyers will be relatively innovative and represent an important market segment for new services. Some may be concerned about the ethical standards of a service provider, while others could not care less, and just focus on price. Service providers need to understand individual differences and fine-tune their marketing mix so that it achieves a desired response from each member of the target market. In a diverse society, it is unlikely that one formulation of the marketing mix will bring about a desired response from everybody. Just as a carpenter needs to adjust his hammers and drills to suit the job in hand, so too the marketer needs to adjust the marketing mix to the needs of individual buyers.

**Market segmentation** is a fundamental principle of marketing and its advantages are well documented, as are the conditions that are necessary for its successful implementation. This section provides a brief overview of segmentation issues relevant to the services sector, and further information on segmentation theory and practice can be found in the suggested further reading at the end of the chapter. In the service industries there is a clear understanding of the benefits that may accrue from successful market segmentation and it is therefore used extensively throughout the sector. Many services organizations are at the forefront of the development of segmentation methods within the UK, with banks, building societies, insurance companies and the travel and hospitality sectors, among others, having well-defined approaches to the segmentation of their markets.

It can be argued that segmentation is a much more important tool for the services marketer than for the goods marketer. The inseparability of services production and consumption results in service suppliers being able to define their segments in such a way that only individuals within a specified segment benefit from a particular marketing mix. This is an advantage not available to most goods marketers. Because goods production can be separated from their consumption, it is usually possible for a consumer to buy in one market and then to sell on to another market segment. It is very difficult for the manufacturer of soft drinks or training shoes, for example, to ensure that only a targeted segment of, say, students or citizens of a particular country can buy its product at a concessionary price. It is quite likely that goods will be transferred from a market with a low price to a segment that is charged a higher price. This is routinely seen in the way that cheap alcohol and tobacco products are transported around the world from low-price to high-price countries. By contrast, services organizations can generally insist on proof of an individual's membership of a segment in order to benefit from a preferential marketing mix. So, a train company can ensure that only students, who may be considered to be a more price-sensitive segment, can benefit from a lower-price offer, by requiring proof of student status each time that they travel at a concessionary price.

The development of segmentation and target marketing reflects the movement away from production orientation towards marketing orientation. When the supply of services is scarce relative to supply, organizations may seek to minimize production costs by producing one homogeneous product that satisfies the needs of the whole population. Over time, increasing affluence has increased buyers' expectations. Affluent customers are no longer satisfied with the basic package holiday, but instead are able to demand one that satisfies an increasingly wide range of needs – not just for relaxation, but for activity, adventure and status associations. Furthermore, society has become much more fragmented. The 'average' consumer has become much more of a myth, as incomes, attitudes and lifestyles have diverged.

Alongside the greater fragmentation of society, technology is increasingly allowing highly specialized services to be tailored to ever-smaller market segments. Using computerized databases, insurance policies need no longer be aimed at broad market segments, but can cater to very small groups who have distinctive needs and buying history.

Different buyers within a market can behave very differently when evaluating alternative services. To be fully marketing oriented, a company would have to adapt its offer to meet the needs of each individual. In fact, very few firms can justify aiming to meet the needs of each specific individual. Instead, they aim to meet the needs of small subgroups within the market. With developments in technology and the fragmentation of society, these segments have tended to become smaller over time, in a process that has sometimes been referred to as '**mass customization**'. This exploits the cost advantages of large-scale production with the flexibility of systems to adapt services to each individual buyer.

## Thinking around the subject: Segmentation or discrimination?

Segmentation and targeting are central to the marketer's task of profitably meeting consumers' needs. But, to some social commentators, the practices of segmentation and targeting may appear to be more like discrimination, with all the connotations of social divisiveness that have been associated with various forms of social discrimination. Admittedly, marketers seldom find themselves practising the kind of blatant discrimination that typified South Africa during its years of apartheid, but there can be a thin line between the desirable aims of segmentation and the undesirable consequences of social discrimination. The issue is particularly great for services marketers, because the inseparability of services allows segmentation strategies to be implemented much more effectively than for goods, which can generally be traded freely between segments.

Legislation in most Western countries is gradually squeezing out the opportunities for marketers to blatantly sell their services to one group but not to another. The days when the owner of a bar could admit customers on the basis of their colour are now thankfully long gone. Nightclubs in the UK, which once advertised different prices for men and women, would now most likely find themselves breaking the Sex Discrimination Act. However, marketers have sometimes found subtle ways of pursuing their segmentation strategies anyway. A bar may subtly make its atmosphere more conducive to one ethnic group and seemingly inaccessible to others. Nightclubs have learnt that discriminating on the basis of gender may be illegal, but a differential pricing policy based on whether a customer is wearing trousers or a skirt may come close to achieving the nightclub's objectives legally.

Despite a growing volume of legislation in developed countries to protect clearly identifiable groups based on sex, race, disability and, increasingly, age, many people remain concerned that the processes of segmentation and targeting are leaving pockets of individuals who are denied access to many basic

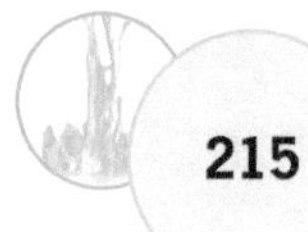



services. This is seen in the way that mainstream banks in most Western countries have targeted relatively affluent individuals with a steady source of income. In the UK, a sizeable group of people find it difficult to borrow money from these banks, or even to open a basic bank account. Without a bank account, many life opportunities are closed to individuals; for example, without a credit or debit card, it can be difficult to buy goods and services online. In the USA, banks have been suspected of 'redlining' certain areas of towns, from which the banks will not take new customers. Many states have responded with legislation making illegal such a geographically generalized basis for selection. In the UK, geodemographics remains an important basis for banks' segmentation and targeting, but, although there is no legislation to prevent geodemographic targeting, the government has shown its impatience with banks' reluctance to target poorer groups, even with basic bank accounts. One initiative in response to this apparent problem was the creation of a 'basic bank account' based on collaboration between the main banks and local post offices, making banking facilities available to poorer people with a bad credit history. In many service sectors providing essential public services, such as electricity, water and telephones, regulatory agencies ensure that private-sector companies do not unduly disadvantage poorer groups in their pursuit of profits.

When does segmentation become discrimination? To what extent should commercial organizations be expected to do business with individuals who on a narrow commercial basis are unlikely to be profitable? How far will companies' shrewd analysis of their social and political environment – and a visible response to problems of emerging discrimination – allow these issues to be resolved? Or will it take further government legislation to protect the interests of disadvantaged groups, who may be further marginalized in society by commercial firms' segmentation and targeting policies?

## 6.6.1 Bases for market segmentation

If the segmentation methods used by services organizations are examined closely, it becomes apparent that demographic variables tend to be the most widely used segmentation bases. In this respect service industries are no exception – the same tends to be true in goods marketing. Age, sex and socio-economic analyses, along with geographic location, provide useful information for building up a profile of users of a service. This can be used for targeting purposes in media planning, assisting in new service development, and can contribute to pricing policy and service outlet location decisions. Some indication of the importance of demographic bases for segmentation can be seen in the choice of magazines in which American Express advertises, the range of accounts offered by Citibank, the pricing practices of British Airways and the location of Lidl supermarkets.

In all of these applications of segmentation methods there is a heavy reliance on the availability of accurate and timely market data. Geodemographic segmentation, for example, require sources of information that provide details of customers' demographics and their geographical location and can involve secondary data acquisition or primary investigations undertaken on behalf of an organization. The sophistication of segmentation methods has developed enormously as a result of innovations in information technology. Three developments should be mentioned:

- A number of firms offer a geodemographic segmentation analysis that allows the identification of small geographical pockets of households according to a combination of their demographic characteristics and their buying behaviour. These computerized data systems – such as Mosaic (see Figure 6.13) – are of considerable value in the planning of direct mail campaigns, store location, and merchandising.
- The wealth of data provided by the operation of electronic point of sale systems means that services firms can study in detail the buying behaviour of individuals or groups of individuals. How often does an individual visit their store? What goods and services tend to be bought as complementary products to each other? How responsive are individuals to price reductions or coupon offers? EPOS offers insights into buying behaviour of different market segments.

Figure 6.13 Mosaic™ is a widely used method of geodemographic segmentation. Many companies are in the business of providing customer analysis services to help firms' segmentation, targeting and positioning strategies. One of the most widely used is Experian's Mosaic™ consumer classification system. This gathers information about individuals from multiple sources under a number of headings shown in the diagram, and uses this to build up a picture of every household in the UK. From this information, each person has been assigned to one of 155 Mosaic™ person types, aggregated into 67 household types (further aggregated into 15 broad groups). Each type has been given a distinctive and sometimes glib title, such as B05 'Mid-career climbers', D16 'Side street singles' and I41 'Stressed borrowers'. For a company planning a mailshot, or deciding on the best location for new service outlets, such information about consumer behaviour at the individual and household level can avoid waste by targeting the company's efforts at those groups who are most likely to respond to a proposition.

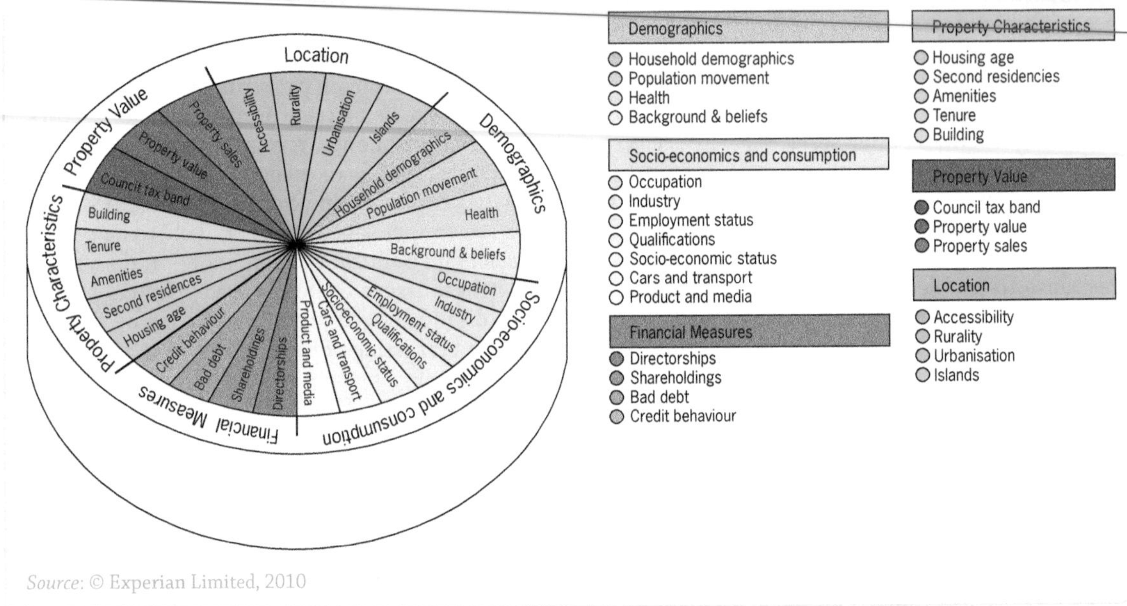


*Source*: © Experian Limited, 2010

- As services have migrated to the Internet, opportunities for tracking customers have increased, with many services such as Google Analytics available to provide companies with data about the buying behaviour of a visitor before they reach a company's website. Some have challenged the ethics of using 'cookies' which can send information back to a third-party company for analysis, especially when they can be used to segment visitors who are charged different prices, depending on their previous browsing history.

For most practical marketing purposes, services organizations tend to rely upon demographic and geographic data. Yet there is a real conflict between the theoretical and practical aspects of market segmentation. In practice, the established bases are employed, at least in part, because the data are readily available in this format and targeting is therefore reasonably straightforward. However, although the bases do have this practical value, they do not really explain *why* there are differences in the buying behaviour of consumers. There are therefore a number of other approaches to segmentation that are seen to be more theoretically sound, such as psychographics (based upon personality, attitudes, opinions and interests) and self-concept (how customers perceive themselves). Many companies in the tourism sector, for example, have been observed to base their segmentation and targeting on lifestyle factors (see for example Gonzalez and Bello, 2002). Such approaches rely on attitude measurement techniques in order to elicit the necessary information from customers. These segmentation bases provide a useful supplementary set of tools for the subdivision of markets, generally used in conjunction with demographic profiles for targeting purposes.

## Thinking around the subject: Any excuse for a pint?

Companies are able to capture ever-increasing amounts of information in order to build up a better picture of their customers' buying behaviour. The retailer Tesco is one of many companies that gather large volumes of data from till receipts, loyalty-card data and other bought-in data, to give previously unimaginable insights into consumer behaviour. The story has frequently been told of an exercise undertaken by the company using data-mining techniques, which apparently discovered a correlation between sales of beer and sales of nappies. The two products were not in any way complementary to each other, so why should their sales appear to be associated? Was this just another spurious correlation, to be binned along with other gems of information such as a previously reported correlation between an individual's shoe size and their propensity to use a gym? The company did not give up, and refined its analysis to study the correlation for different categories of store and by different times of day. Where it also had details of customers' demographic characteristics (gathered through its Club Card loyalty programme), it was able to probe for further insights. The company was edging towards a better understanding of why the sales of these two products should be closely correlated, but it took further qualitative analysis techniques to provide a fuller explanation. It appeared that men were offering to run a household errand to the shops in order to buy babies' nappies. This was an excuse to leave the family home in order to buy more beer for their own consumption. The company is claimed to have learnt from this exercise and subsequently positioned the two products closer together in selected stores.

The story of Tesco's analysis of beer and nappy sales may have become distorted with telling, and may even come close to being an urban myth. But should it take data mining to reveal these insights to buyers' behaviour? The landlord of the traditional Irish pub spotted this type of behaviour long ago, with pubs doubling up as the local post office, bookseller or grocer, giving the Irish drinker plenty of good excuses for visiting the pub. He would have had none of the technology available to today's businesses, just a good set of ears and eyes. Do we sometimes look for complex technological solutions to understand buyer behaviour, when the answer might be much easier to find using more traditional judgements?

## Case study

### Coffee to go is no go for Israeli consumers

Michael Etgar, College of Management, Tel Aviv, Israel

The ways in which people from different countries buy cups of tea or coffee have been steeped in tradition. The English tearoom has been quintessentially English, usually providing homely surroundings in a very traditional atmosphere. Other regions, by contrast, have traditionally drunk coffee and have taken great delight in pavement cafés. The Viennese coffee-house has become a cultural institution in itself. With growing globalization of service industries and evidence of cultural convergence, these traditional drinking places have been facing challenges and opportunities. So, many British people are now quite happy to patronize trendy coffee bars in preference to a traditional English tearoom. Café culture has spread from the warm climates of the Mediterranean to the streets of Watford and Woking.

Many service companies have spotted changing habits in a nation's pattern of drinking, and have extended their established service format to new markets where they are considered novel. But this can be a very risky process and a good understanding of buyer behaviour is essential to ensure success. Who will be the early adopters for the new service format? What factors will it take for there to be a trickle-down effect to other groups who are maybe more traditional in their buying behaviour? How can a company avoid being ridiculed as being totally alien to the culture from which it seeks custom?

Starbucks has become a household name among coffee drinkers in the 37 countries where it operates. It was established in 1971 and by 2012 had a worldwide network of over 17,000 outlets, roughly half of these managed directly by Starbucks and half operated by franchisees. But the failure of its launch in Israel illustrates how important it is to understand the processes by which people buy and consume coffee.

Starbucks joined a long list of foreign services companies that have entered the Israeli market. In the 1995–2000 period over 30 different global retailing chains entered the country, among them Burger King, McDonald's, Zara, Max Mara, Ace, Mothercare, Blockbuster and Toys R Us. With just a few exceptions, foreign chains failed to understand buyer behaviour, lost money and stopped operating, with heavy losses. During this period, the coffee-house sector grew rapidly and, despite Starbucks' failure, several coffee-house chains both local and international survived and prospered.

Starbucks decided not to set up its own branches in Israel but to operate through a local company – Israel Coffee Partners (ICP). Starbucks International had a 20 per cent stake in the venture. ICP received a master franchisee licence to open and operate Starbucks branches in Israel. The first Starbucks coffee shop opened in Israel in 2000 and the company aimed to establish 80 branches within five years. Yet within three years it had opened just six branches, in urban areas in and around Tel Aviv and Herzeliya Pituach. In 2003, Starbucks' Israeli venture had accumulated debts of over US$6 million and it was closed. At the same time, another US-based coffee-house chain – Coffee Bean – entered the Israeli market and appeared to prosper. What went wrong for Starbucks?

One possible reason for the company's failure may be its insistence on standardizing its service offer, which required that all the components of the retailing format in the USA were copied identically in Israel. A major innovation of Starbucks to the Israeli market was the concept of 'coffee to go', whereby customers bought their coffee in order to drink it elsewhere. The original US-based Starbucks concept was coffee only without any fresh foods, while local tradition demanded having a light snack with coffee. As a result, consumers had to queue up, pay and then receive their cups of coffee in Styrofoam cups, easy for carrying them out in the streets. Customers were expected to leave and not to delay and consume their coffee on the premises. All on-the-premises consumption was expected to be fast and efficient. Places for sitting down were limited and the décor was simple.

However, this type of coffee consumption did not fit the local style of consumption. While the Starbucks concept provided a real added value to consumers in countries without a tradition of good-quality coffee (such as Canada and Japan), its value proposition was lost on the Israelis. Unlike the USA or Japan, when Starbucks arrived in Israel the country had already been exposed to quality Italian-style espresso coffee and several local chains serving quality coffee had already been operating in this market. The Israelis, like other Mediterranean people, like to sit down in their coffee-houses for discussions, meals and even business meetings. The concept of buying cups of coffee in Styrofoam cups and taking them somewhere else was not a part of the local culture. A factor that contributed to the failure of the chain was faulty or insufficient market intelligence about local culture, customer behaviour and the competitive situation. Better understanding of the local coffee-house scene and the directions of its development might have avoided some of these pitfalls.

The company had also underestimated the price premium that customers were prepared to pay for a globally promoted brand. In many markets that Starbucks had entered, such as South Korea and Turkey, drinking a skinny latte at Starbucks became a symbol of new-found middle-class status for some socially mobile groups. Starbucks had greatly underestimated the power of established operators to keep their custom and greatly overestimated the power of its brand to attract customers. This belief led the local operator to set high prices (relative to the market prices in corresponding coffee-house chains). Similarly, the arrival of the chain was not supported by advertising and, later on, the brand was not maintained by advertising effort. In reality, brand awareness was not as high as expected and it did not translate into usage rates. The Starbucks brand equity was greatly reduced in the fight with other brands and consumers were not willing to pay premium prices.

## Case study review questions

1. Critically evaluate methods that Starbucks could use to study buyer behaviour when it is considering entering a new foreign market.
2. If you were opening a coffee-house, discuss the most important aspects of buyer behaviour that you would seek to understand before proceeding.
3. Discuss the possible effects of peer-group influence on the process of choosing between competing coffee-houses.

## Summary and links to other chapters

The intangibility of services and their perceived riskiness makes the buyer's task of choosing between competing products more complex than is the case for manufactured goods. Consumers cannot properly evaluate a service until after it has been consumed; therefore the bases for prior evaluation are limited. Tangible cues are vital to give some indication of subsequent service quality. Brands and ongoing relationships with a service provider can help to reduce the riskiness of a service purchase. Very often, the image of the service provider is more important in evaluation than the image of individual service offers, and this image is increasingly being influenced by its perceived ethical standards.

The development of ongoing buyer–seller relationships as a means of simplifying service purchase decisions is discussed further in Chapter 5. The role of brands in appealing to specific target markets will be discussed at more length in Chapter 8. Methods of judging the quality of a service, and hence influencing repurchase intention, are discussed in Chapter 9. Attempts to influence buyer behaviour through promotional activities are discussed in Chapter 13. Methods used to turn one-off purchases into an ongoing relationship were explored in Chapter 5.

### Chapter review questions

1. Identify the causes and consequences of risk in the services purchasing process. Critically assess methods that an Internet service provider can use to overcome problems of buyers' perceived risk.
2. Critically examine how the methods and effectiveness of market segmentation differ between a seller of pre-recorded videos and the operator of a cinema.
3. To what extent do you think that buyer behaviour can be reduced to 'rules'-based models applicable to a variety of service buying situations?

### Activities

1. Consider a recent case where you took part in some type of service activity with a group of friends. This might include going out for a meal at a restaurant, going to a bar or going to the cinema. Critically examine the processes involved in deciding between the alternatives available. Ask yourself: How long did the whole process take from having the initial idea to making the final decision? Who initiated the process? Who were involved as influencers? What sources of information did you consult? How important was word-of-mouth recommendation? How was the final decision arrived at? After you had made your decision and consumed the service, what thoughts did you have? Did these subsequently affect your repurchase intention? Did you make any recommendation to friends?
2. Refer to the buyer evaluation matrix shown in Figure 6.5. Now apply this to the decision-making process that you and your friends might go through if you were evaluating competing service offers from a fitness club or a mobile phone service provider.
3. Review consumer magazines containing adverts for telecommunication/Internet services. Now review professional/trade magazines containing adverts for telecommunication/Internet service providers. Critically evaluate the ways in which the messages differ between the two types of magazine. What do the differences – if any – say about differences in the buying process between private buyers and business-to-business buyers?

## Key terms

**Cognitive dissonance** Mental discomfort that occurs following a purchase decision that the buyer may subsequently believe to have been a poor decision.

**Geodemographic segmentation** Segmentation of markets using a combination of geographic and demographic information.

**Hedonistic benefits** A service provides essentially pleasurable rather than practical benefits.

**Market segmentation** A process of identifying groups of customers within a broad product market who share similar needs and respond similarly to a given marketing mix formulation.

**Mass customization** Combining mass production techniques with individualized design.

**Needs** The underlying forces that drive an individual to make a purchase and thereby satisfy their needs.

**Utilitarian benefits** A service provides essentially functional and practical benefits.

**Word of mouth** The act of recommendation by existing customers to their friends and colleagues.

## Selected further reading

*For a general review of buyer behaviour, numerous books are available that deal with products in general, including:*

**Solomon, M., Bamossy, G., Askegaard, S. and Hogg, M.** (2009) *Consumer Behaviour: A European Perspective*, 4th edn, FT Prentice Hall, Harlow.

**Blythe, J.** (2013) *Consumer Behaviour*, 2nd edn, Sage London.

*The following two classic papers review the general differences between goods and services in the way consumers make purchase decisions:*

**Gabbott, M. and Hogg, G.** (1994) 'Consumer behaviour and services: a review', *Journal of Marketing Management*, 10 (4), 311–24.

**Zeithaml, V.A.** (1981) 'How consumers' evaluation processes differ between goods and services', in J.H. Donnelly and W.R. George (eds), *Marketing of Services*, American Marketing Association, Chicago, IL.

*For an update of services buying behaviour in the context of the Internet, consult the following:*

**Aljukhadar, M. and Senecal, S.** (2011) 'Segmenting the online consumer market', *Marketing Intelligence & Planning*, 29 (4), 421–35.

**Dennis, C., Merrilees, B., Jayawardhena, C. and Wright, L.T.** (2009) 'E-consumer behaviour', *European Journal of Marketing*, 43 (9/10), 1121–39.

**Eccleston, D. and Griseri, L.** (2008) 'How does Web 2.0 stretch traditional influencing patterns?', *International Journal of Market Research*, 50 (5), Web 2.0 special issue.

## References

**Bampo, M., Ewing, M.T., Mather, D.R., Stewart, D. and Wallace, M.** (2008) The effects of the social structure of digital networks on viral marketing performance. *Information Systems Research*, 19 (3), 273–290.

**Berger, J. and Milkman, K.L.** (2010) 'Social transmission, emotion, and the virality of online content', working paper, Marketing Science Institute.

**Festinger, L.** (1957) *A Theory of Cognitive Dissonance*, Stanford University Press, Palo Alto, CA.

**Fisk, R.P.** (1981) 'Toward a consumption/evaluation process model for services', in J.H. Donnelly and W.R. George (eds), *Marketing of Services*, American Marketing Association, Chicago, IL.

**Gonzalez, A.M. and Bello, L.** (2002) 'The construct "lifestyle" in market segmentation: the behaviour of tourist consumers', *European Journal of Marketing*, 36 (1/2), 51–85.

**Grönroos, C.** (1990) 'Relationship approach to marketing in service contexts: the marketing and organisational interface', *Journal of Business Research*, 20 (1), 3–11.

**Herrmann, A., Huber, F. and Braunstein, C.** (1999) 'A regret theory approach to assessing customer satisfaction when alternatives are considered', *European Advances in Consumer Research*, 4, 82–8.

**Hinz, O., Skiera, B., Barrot, C. and Becker, J.U.** (2011) 'Seeding strategies for viral marketing: an empirical comparison', *Journal of Marketing*, 75 (6), 55–71.

**HSBC** (2012) *Consumer in 2012; The rise of the EM middle class*, New York, HSBC, available online at: http://www.us.hsbc.com/1/PA_1_083Q9FJ08A002FBP5S00000000/content/new_usshared/unique_fragments/HSBC%20Home/Premier/pdf/The_Consumer_in_2050.pdf (accessed 12 April 2013).

**Ipsos MORI** (2012) Ipsos MediaCT Tech Tracker, Ipsos MORI, London.

**Jai-Ok, K., Forsythe, S., Qingliang, G. and Sook, J.M.** (2002) 'Cross-cultural values, needs and purchase behaviour', *Journal of Consumer Marketing*, 19 (6), 481–502.

**Kozinets, R.V.** (2006) 'Netnography 2.0', in R.W. Belk (ed.), *Handbook of Qualitative Research Methods in Marketing*. Cheltenham, UK: Edward Elgar.

**Maslow, A.** (1943) 'A theory of human motivation', *Psychological Review*, 50 (4), 370–96.

**Mitra, K., Reiss, M.C. and Capella, M.C.** (1999) 'An examination of perceived risk, information search and behavioral intentions in search, experience and credence services', *Journal of Services Marketing*, 13 (3), 208–28.

**Newberry, C.R.F., Klemz, B.R. and Boshoff, C.** (2003) 'Managerial implications of predicting purchase behavior from purchase intentions: a retail patronage case study', *Journal of Services Marketing*, 17 (6), 609–20.

**Newholm, T., Laing, A. and Hogg, G.** (2006) 'Assumed empowerment: consuming professional services in the knowledge economy', *European Journal of Marketing*, 40 (9/10), 994–1012.

**O'Shaughnessy, J. and O'Shaughnessy, N.J.** (2003) *The Marketing Power of Emotion*, Oxford University Press, Oxford.

**Sheth, J. and Parvatiyar, A.** (2002) 'Evolving relationship marketing into a discipline', *Journal of Relationship Marketing*, 1 (1), 3–16.

**Smith, D. and Dexter, A.** (2001) 'Whenever I hear the word paradigm I reach for my gun: how to stop talking and start walking', *International Journal of Market Research*, 43 (3), 321–40.

**Sweeney, J.C., Hausknecht, D. and Soutar, G.N.** (2000) 'Measuring cognitive dissonance: a multidimensional scale', *Psychology and Marketing*, 17 (5), 369–86.

**Zeithaml, V.A.** (1981) 'How consumers' evaluation processes differ between goods and services', in J.H. Donnelly and W.R. George (eds), *Marketing of Services*, American Marketing Association, Chicago, IL.

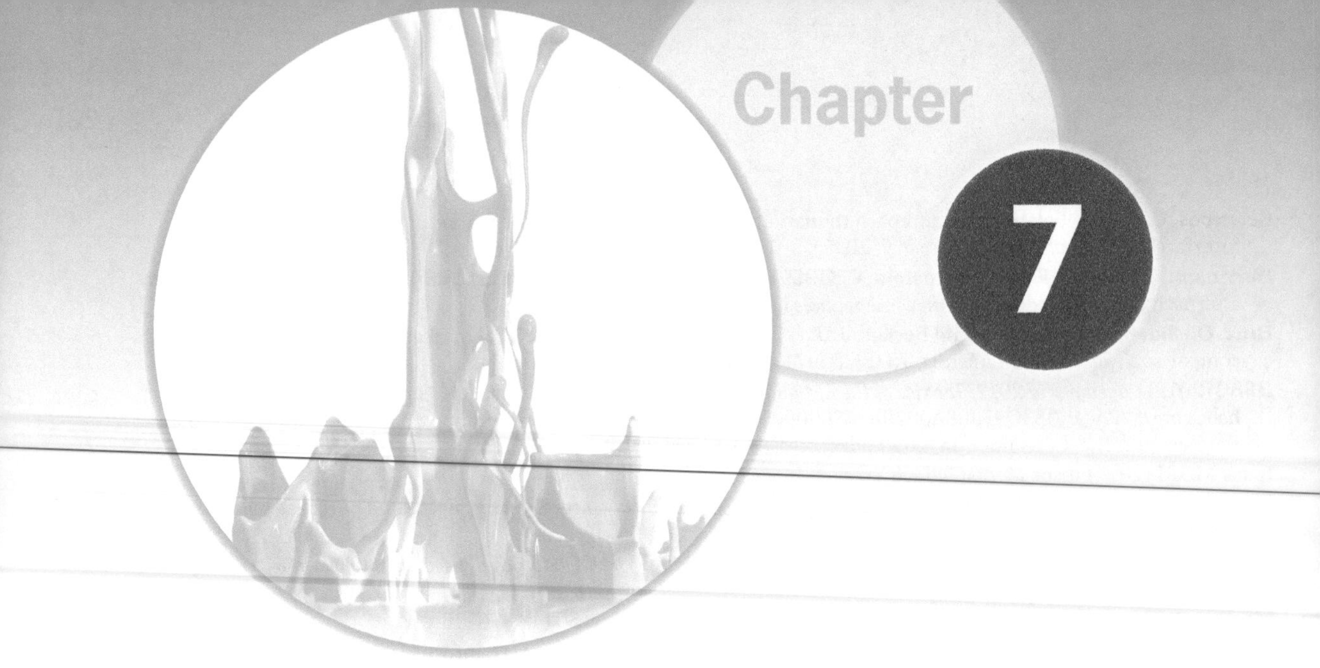


# Innovation and new service development

*You probably take for granted that you can book a cheap airline flight at 2 o'clock in the morning from the comfort of your home, and pay no more than the cost of a pair of jeans to fly away to somewhere exciting. Just 20 or 30 years ago, this might have seemed an impossible dream, but by innovating in the way they produce their service and make it available to customers, airlines have allowed the dream to become a profitable reality. But airlines cannot stand still, and need to be thinking about what the next generation will want to buy in 20 or 30 years' time. What about trips into outer space, a dream today, but like previous dreams of cheap transatlantic travel, could this dream become an everyday affordable reality? Or will issues of climate change and the depletion of natural resources make travel an unaffordable luxury, fuelling further innovation to make 'virtual' tourism an acceptable and enjoyable treat for all? Services companies cannot afford to stand still, but the future is invariably uncertain. It is easy to look back at successful service innovations, but much more difficult to predict the future. This chapter will explore the foundations for successful service development.*

## Learning objectives

After reading this chapter, you should understand:

- Reasons why innovation can be crucially important to services organizations
- Life cycles that services typically go through, from launch, through growth, to eventual maturity and decline
- Processes for developing and evaluating new services and deleting old ones
- Methods used to forecast demand for new services

## 7.1 Introduction

In previous chapters, we have seen how the business environment for most services firms is continually changing. Just consider the following examples of external changes that have occurred in most European countries:

- a growing number of active elderly people in the population;
- increased cultural diversity, with new groups of immigrants requiring non-traditional types of services;
- new technologies that allow new types of services to be developed and distributed;
- deregulation of many service sectors, which allow new opportunities to compete in previously restricted markets;
- greater concern among consumers and legislators about climate change and the impacts of consumption and production activities.

These are examples of just some of the changes that call for services companies to continually assess whether the services they currently provide are the ones that customers really want. Smarter organizations go one step further by trying to understand not just what customers want today, but what they are likely to want tomorrow. Consider the case of climate change, which has become an important issue in the business environment of many services organizations, with airlines being one of the service sectors at the forefront of this debate. How can a service provider adapt to a system of service delivery with lower carbon emissions? Is there a significant preference from customers for 'green' services? Should a company wait for legislation to change its production methods? Should it be more proactive, and thereby have a competitive cost advantage when regulation is eventually introduced? How does it promote to buyers its environmentally friendly credentials?

History is full of examples of organizations that have failed to understand their business environment, or simply failed to respond to change in the environment. The result has been a gradual decline in their profitability, and eventually they may cease to exist as a viable business unit. Theodore Levitt called this 'marketing myopia' and cited the example of railway companies that focused their vision on providing railway services, rather than transport more generally, and therefore failed to take account of the innovations in road transport (Levitt, 1960). Consider these more recent examples:

- The profits of music retailers such as HMV were hit badly by the growth of downloadable music sites, and the slowness of the companies to respond to changes in consumers' preferences for the way they buy music.
- Healthy eating became an important issue in the early twenty-first century. The profits of the fast-food company McDonald's fell and the company was forced to close branches in some countries as consumers sought more healthy convenience food, before the company belatedly responded to change with healthier menu items.
- Newspapers' revenues have continued to decline, and this decline has only been offset by those newspapers such as the *Financial Times* which developed a far-sighted strategy to embrace rather than ignore competing online media.

On the other hand, there have been many spectacular successes where organizations have spotted emerging trends in their business environment and capitalized on these with innovative new services, or new ways of operating their business, in order to meet the new opportunities presented. Consider these examples:

- In the airline market, companies such as Ryanair and easyJet spotted the opportunities presented by government deregulation and offered profitable low-cost 'no frills' air services, often aimed at people who would not previously have flown.
- Many supermarkets have noted consumers' concern for the purity of the food that we eat, and this, combined with rising incomes, has led them to successfully promote ranges of organic foods.
- Many of the UK's pub operators have identified changing social behaviour, with fewer people using pubs as a regular venue primarily for beer drinking, but much greater dining out for social purposes. This has led pubs to increase their profits by reconfiguring as restaurants.

There is every indication that the pace of change in most organizations' business environment is speeding up and it is therefore increasingly important for organizations to have in place systems for monitoring their environment and, just as importantly, for responding to such change. Successful organizations are not so much those that deliver value to customers today, but those that understand how customers' definitions of value are likely to change in the future. In the language of service dominant logic, innovation can be critical to creating value in use, both by manufacturing and service-based companies (Michel et al., 2008). Think back to Chapter 1 and you may recall the example of car manufacturers that have created value in use by the addition of innovative ancillary services.

Of course, it is much more difficult to predict the future than to describe the past. A stark indication of the rewards of looking forwards rather than backwards is provided by an analyst who studied stock market performance. If a cumulative investment of $1 had been invested from 1900 on 1 January each year in the stock that had performed best in the *previous year*, and then reinvested the following year, the accumulated value in 2000 would have been just $250. However, if it had been invested each year in the stock that performed best in the *year ahead*, the accumulated value would be over $1 billion. Successful companies have often been those that understand their business environment and have invested in growth areas, while cutting back in areas that are most likely to go into decline. Being first to market when trends are changing can be much more profitable than simply reacting to a market trend. However, predicting future trends can be very difficult and can involve a lot of risk.

This chapter begins by looking at the concept of a service life cycle, which leads companies to identify failing service offers and to replace these with new ones. We then look at the process of new service development, and the steps necessary to achieve a successful launch.

For a launch to be successful, an organization must have developed a very good understanding of its customers' needs, and the relative strength of its competitors. From this, it should develop robust forecasts for the future. Such forecasts become particularly important for new services that involve high capital commitments and long development times. We explore methods used by services companies to make better predictions about likely demand for a new service.

## 7.2 The service life-cycle concept

Most services go through some form of life cycle, necessitating changes in marketing strategy as the service passes from one stage in the cycle to the next. There is evidence that service life cycles are becoming shorter, especially where the service offer has a high-technology base. Within the mobile phone sector, a top of the range service offer of just 10 years ago might today look quite old-fashioned, as newer facilities such as GPS navigation and email become incorporated into services provided with smartphones.

Figure 7.1 Five stages in the product/service life cycle: an application to Internet cafés

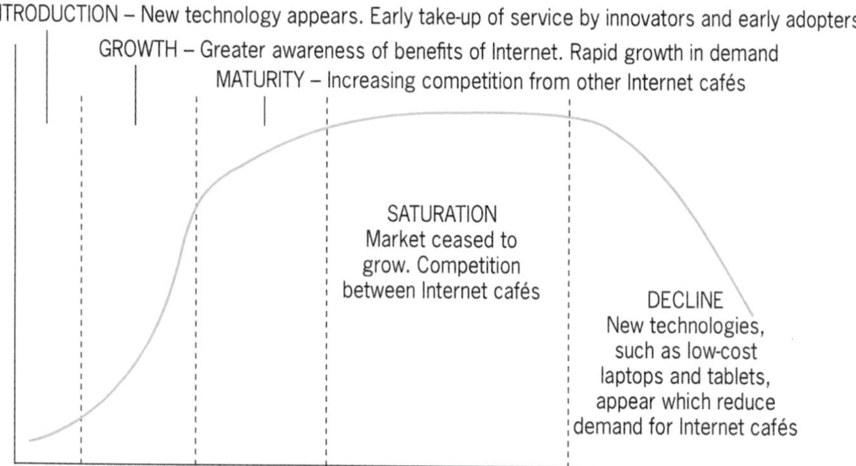
INTRODUCTION – New technology appears. Early take-up of service by innovators and early adopters
GROWTH – Greater awareness of benefits of Internet. Rapid growth in demand
MATURITY – Increasing competition from other Internet cafés
SATURATION
Market ceased to grow. Competition between Internet cafés
DECLINE
New technologies, such as low-cost laptops and tablets, appear which reduce demand for Internet cafés

The product/service life cycle graphically depicts the changing fortunes of a service, or groups of services, within an organization's portfolio. Services typically go through a number of stages between entering the portfolio and leaving, each calling for adjustments to marketing activities. Five stages are identified in Figure 7.1:

1 *Introduction*. New services are often costly to develop and launch, and may have teething problems. People may be wary of trying something new, especially a new service whose intangibility prevents prior evaluation. Sales therefore tend to be slow and are restricted to those who like trying out new products or who believe they can gain status or benefit by having such a product.
2 *Growth*. By this time, the service has been tested and any problems have been resolved. The service is now more reliable and more readily available. Buyers now start to see the benefits that can be gained by using the service. Sales start to increase greatly and this is a signal for competitors to start entering the market.
3 *Maturity*. Almost everyone who wants to buy the service has now done so, which is a particular problem for services that are bought as a one-off rather than a recurrent purchase. The number of competitors in the market has risen.
4 *Saturation*. Here there are too many competitors and there is no further growth in the market. Competitors tend to compete with each other on the basis of price.
5 *Decline*. With falling demand and new substitute products appearing, organizations drop out of the market.

The usefulness of the life-cycle concept lies in the recognition that marketing activity for a service is closely related to the stage in the life cycle that a service has reached. In this way, promotional planning in the launch phase may emphasize raising awareness through public-relations activity. Later, in the growth phase the emphasis may shift to more advertising, resorting to sales promotion incentives as the market matures and becomes more competitive. Finally, as the service goes into decline, all promotional activity may be cut. The message used at each stage may position the service offer quite differently, beginning for example as a 'latest technology' message, through 'most reliable' and perhaps, in the saturation stage, to 'lowest price'. In a similar way, accessibility and pricing decisions can also often be related to the stage that a service has reached in its life cycle.

Although the idea of service life cycles is appealing and seems to be validated by research, it is important to be aware of the possible failings with this conceptual approach in terms of both goods and services. It can be argued that the product/service life-cycle concept is probably more useful for strategic planning and control purposes than for developing short-term forecasts and costed marketing programmes. In reality, life-cycle patterns are far too variable in both shape and duration for any realistic predictions to be made. Some products have been in the maturity/saturation stage for many years (e.g. bank current accounts), whereas others disappear very soon after introduction (e.g. some trendy clothing retailers). Evidence also seems to suggest a variety of life-cycle modifications and mutations.

A further difficulty in applying the life-cycle concept lies in the inability of marketers to accurately ascertain where in the life cycle a service actually is at any time. A stabilization of sales may be a movement into maturity or simply a temporary plateau due to external causes, for example. In fact, it is possible that the shape of the life cycle is a result of an organization's marketing activity rather than being an indication of environmental factors that the organization should respond to – in other words, it could in fact lead to a self-fulfilling prophecy.

Another criticism of the concept is that the duration of the stages will depend upon whether it is a product class, form or brand that is being considered. For example, the life cycle for holidays is probably quite flat, whereas life cycles for particular types of holidays and for specific holiday operators' brands become progressively more cyclical.

With these points taken into consideration, the life-cycle concept may still be helpful in guiding a firm in its marketing-mix decisions. Although life cycles may be unpredictable for services in terms of the length of time a service may remain at a particular stage, the understanding that services are likely to change in their sales and profit performance over a period of time implies a need for proactive service-mix management.

## 7.3 Refining the service portfolio

Decisions about the range of services offered by an organization are of strategic importance. In order to remain competitive in the face of declining demand for its principal service line, a service company may need to widen its **service portfolio**. For example, increasing diversity in food tastes has forced many specialized fast-food outlets to widen their menus and to offer home delivery. At the same time, decisions may need to be made to delete services from the mix in cases where consumer tastes have changed or competitive pressures have made the continuing provision of a service uneconomic. Service-mix extension and deletion decisions are continually made in order that organizations can provide services more effectively (providing the right services in response to consumers' changing needs) and more efficiently (providing those services for which the organization is able to make most efficient use of its resources).

For any service organization, its service offering will be constrained by the capabilities, facilities and resources at its disposal. It is therefore important for service firms to constantly examine their capabilities and their objectives to ensure that the range of services provided meets the needs of the consumer as well as the capabilities of the organization. Through a process sometimes referred to as a service product audit, an organization can get an understanding of whether it is continuing to provide the right services to the right target groups. Key questions for an audit are:

- What benefits do customers seek from the company's services?
- What is the current and continuing availability of the resources required to provide the service?
- What skills and technical know-how are required?
- What benefits are offered over and above the competition?
- Are competitor advantages causing the organization to lose revenue?
- Does each service provided still give a sufficient financial return?
- Do the company's services meet the targets that justify continued funding?

The answers to these questions form the basis of service-mix development strategy.

## 7.4 New service development

The following are typical circumstances where it may be particularly important for a company to develop new services:

- If a major service has reached the maturity stage of its life cycle and may be moving towards decline, new services may be sought to preserve sales levels.
- New services may be developed as a means of utilizing spare capacity, for example unoccupied rooms during off-peak periods may lead a hotel operator to develop new services designed to fill the empty rooms.
- New services can help to balance an organization's existing sales portfolio and thereby reduce risks of dependency on only a few services offered within a range.
- In order to retain and develop a relationship with its customers, an organization may be forced to introduce new products to allow it to cater to customers' diverse needs.
- An opportunity may arise for an organization to satisfy unmet needs with a new service as a result of a competitor leaving the market.

Although the underlying principles of innovation and the new product development process are essentially similar for goods and services, a number of differences between the two have been noted, including differences in key success factors (Henard and Szymanski, 2001; Johne and Storey, 1998), the range of activities undertaken (Edgett, 1994; Johne and Storey, 1998), managerial pressures, the types of strategies pursued (Venkatraman and Prescott, 1990) and the role of front-line staff (Papastathopoulou et al., 2006).

### Thinking around the subject: Speech recognition in cyberspace

Putting the spoken word into print has seen a quickening pace in the technologies available that can do the job speedily and accurately. Historically, hardwiring of documents gave way after several centuries to the typewriter, which eventually gave way to the word processor and keyboard. From the 1990s voice recognition appeared as a new means of getting voice into print. But the quickening pace of technological change demonstrates the opportunities as well as challenges for service-based companies which seek to embrace new technology.

A UK company called Speech Machines *spotted* the opportunities presented by emerging technologies of voice recognition in the 1990s to offer an innovative service. It used its computers to receive dictation over the telephone or as voice messages sent through the Internet by email. The dictation was transcribed automatically by the company's computers with a claimed 95 per cent accuracy. Specially written software managed the incoming dictation and automatically sent the transcribed document to one of the contract typists the company used for checking and correction of the final manuscript. It was then sent back to the customer through the Internet. The service found a useful niche in the USA with the legal and medical professions, offering a speedy and efficient alternative to employing a secretary in-house.

But developments in voice recognition which were the basis for the company's innovative service also came to be its biggest challenge. Before long, affordable computers incorporating high-quality voice recognition were allowing its customers to transcribe their voice in-house, rather than relying on the company's central computers.

The life cycle for basic service-based speech recognition might have been going into decline, but the broader life cycle for document management services was still growing, as companies continued to outsource many of their administration tasks. The company, which was subsequently taken over by the American company MedQuist (now part of Mmodal), has focused on a number of key market segments. The company continues to innovate and in 2013 its biggest hopes for innovation were being placed on the emerging technology of 'voice analytics' – not just transcribing what people are saying, but trying to understand the meaning of what they say and transforming this into managerially useful and actionable data.

### 7.4.1 What is meant by a 'new service'?

The intangible nature of services means that it is often quite easy to produce slight variants of an existing service, with the result that the term '**new service**' can mean anything from a minor style change to a major innovation. A number of attempts have been made to classify types of new services (e.g. Toivonen and Tuominen, 2009). In fact, the term 'new service' could be applied to any of the following:

- *Process changes*. These include redesign of the service encounter, for example a sandwich bar offering a new ordering facility via its website.
- *Outcome changes*. These may be considered important where a service is evaluated primarily on the basis of outcomes; for example, a financial services company may offer a new form of equity-based investment that guarantees a specified return at the end of a five-year period.
- *Changes to associated 'tangibles'*. The use of new tangible materials can create the impression of a new service; for example, an airline's website may be redesigned, but nevertheless offer very much the same processes and outcomes as previously.
- *Service line extensions*. These are additions to the existing service product range – a university offering a new part-time MBA programme, for example. However, although the programme may be new to the university, it is not genuinely a new service if it is already offered by other universities.
- *Major innovations*. These are entirely new services for new markets – the provision of diagnostic tele-medicine services, for example.

## In practice: From burgers to bananas?

Fast food was a great marketing success story of the 1980s and 1990s. Chains developed in response to changes in the pattern of family meal eating, growing levels of disposable income (especially among younger adults), a growing desire for variety seeking and increasing concern with value for money. McDonald's has a long record in innovation with the development of new menus and new service formats in new countries. However, by the end of the 1990s, there was growing concern in many Western countries about problems of obesity caused by eating too much high-fat food. McDonald's has continued its pattern of innovation with products that address the changed needs of the early twenty-first century, including McCafés and, here, a fruit bag that is aimed at making fresh fruit more appealing to children (and their parents).

Figure 7.2 Not just burgers from McDonald's

## Thinking around the subject: Service innovation in the slums of India

Service innovation is not exclusively the domain of high-tech service providers in Western countries. Service innovation can occur in the poorest of communities, spurred on by the old adage that 'necessity is the mother of invention'. In their book *Poor Economics*, Banerjee and Duflo describe levels of ingenuity in poverty-stricken areas which might put to shame a Western service development manager, surrounded by piles of quantitative and qualitative data (Banerjee and Duflo, 2011).

Consider some of the cases of ingenuity among the poor that the authors noted:

- A small tailor's shop in Dakar, built in a tree house a few feet off the ground, with a wooden ladder that the tailor would throw down so his clients did not have to step through the garbage surrounding his shop and which would then quickly be pulled up to leave the pavement unobstructed.
- The slum dwellers of Mumbai who innovated with new ways of collecting and sorting garbage into the categories that modern recycling plants demanded.

The authors ask why the individuals behind these innovations put up with the conditions in which they operated. Why, for example, did the tailor not move to a prosperous suburb, but instead operate out of a rubbish-infested street in a poor part of town? It seemed that necessity led to innovation – the rubbish-infested street was presumably the only place where the business would be visible, and at the same time cheap enough to make the business viable. The rental charge of a retail unit in a pleasanter location would probably make his services unaffordable to most of his poor clients. The owner also probably could not raise the finance to operate out of better premises. Many families in India are too poor to afford to pay for their children to attend high school, so children are often forced to earn their living from a very early age. It has been claimed that the Indian government does little to protect young people from such economic challenges.

Such harsh environments for service development have spurred further innovation in the form of micro-credit – small loans given by lenders to individuals whom the mainstream banks would not look at. Micro lenders have themselves adopted low-cost business models which adapt to the needs of their small-scale, asset-poor clients.

Some innovators from poor economies have gone on to create major service businesses when the opportunities arose. Could surviving and prospering in the face of adversity be the greatest mark of a great service innovator? Even in Western developed economies, do we spend too much time concentrating on innovations of large corporations while overlooking the small-scale innovations made out of necessity by some of the poorer members of a community?

## 7.4.2 The new service development processes

A systematic process of development can help to reduce the risk of failure when new services are launched. In reality, there is evidence that most firms do not have a formal new service development (NSD) strategy. A study by Kelly and Storey (2000) showed that:

- Only half of a sample of firms in banking, telecommunications, insurance and transportation had a formal NSD strategy.
- Only a quarter had a culture in which ideas were continually generated.
- Only a third had an idea-search methodology.

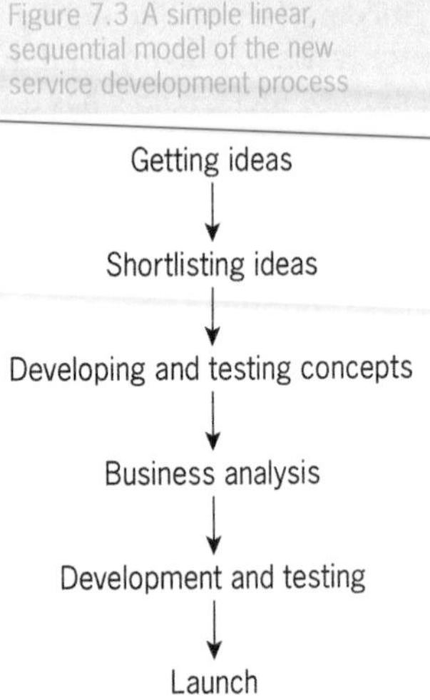

Figure 7.3 A simple linear, sequential model of the new service development process

Although a variety of different procedures have been proposed and implemented, they all tend to have the common themes of beginning with as many new ideas as possible and having the end objective of producing a tested service ready for launch. One common sequence is shown in Figure 7.3, although in practice, many of the sequential stages shown are compressed so that their timing overlaps with earlier and later stages.

Although, in principle, the new-product development process is similar for goods and services, differences arise because of the intangibility, inseparability, variability and perishability of services. The differences are discussed below in the context of each stage of the development process.

### Getting ideas

The process of generating ideas should be easier for services compared with goods. The inseparability of services presents multiple opportunities for customers to communicate ideas for new service developments to the organization. Goods manufacturers generally need to rely on proceduralized approaches such as focus groups, customer panels and written suggestion schemes, because they do not normally have any direct contact with the customers who buy their products. However, the front-line staff of service organizations typically have many direct encounters with their customers, so in principle, the task of collecting customers' ideas for new service development should be easier. With the development of Web 2.0 technologies, many services companies have sought to embrace customers as co-creators of new service ideas (Blazevic and Lievens, 2008; Kristensson et al., 2008; Cheng et al., 2012).

A key challenge is not just capturing ideas, but passing them on to people in the organization who can act on them. Internally, a study of new service development found that the most common source of new service ideas was the marketing function rather than the operational function. The marketing function had constant contact with both customers and competitors and thus had market information 'on tap'. Operations staff may have given more weight to the perceived problems of developing new services (Seegy et al., 2008), and there is a danger that front-line staff may be reluctant to pass on ideas if they perceive that one consequence would be an increased workload for themselves.

### Shortlisting ideas

This stage involves evaluating the ideas generated and rejecting those that do not justify the organization's resources. Criteria are usually established so that comparisons between ideas can be made but, because each firm exists in its own particular environment, there is no standard set of evaluative criteria that fits all. Easingwood found a variety of screening practices, and noted that screening processes for financial services were particularly rigorous. Within this sector, each new idea would be evaluated by customer discussion groups, feedback on proposed features and advertising would be collected and financial projections would be calculated in some detail. It was suggested that this rigour is partly due to the difficulties in withdrawing a financial service once it is being provided. Intangibility makes services difficult to assess and therefore 'image' is an important means by which customers reassure themselves about the credibility of a service provider. Easingwood (1986) found that enhancement or support of an organization's image was an important criterion used by firms in the screening process.

### Developing and testing concepts

Ideas that survive the short-listing stage need to be translated into service concepts. These concepts are then tested with a sample of target users to assess their reactions to them. A challenge for pure services is to convey the concepts without the help of the diagrams or artists' impressions that are available when a new concept for a manufactured product is presented. It may be very difficult to build up a mental picture of a new service concept when nothing similar could have been experienced previously.

### Business analysis

The proposed idea is now translated into a business proposal. The likelihood of success/failure is analysed, including resource requirements in terms of manpower, extra physical resources etc. At this stage, many of the factors that will determine the financial success of the proposed new service remain speculative. The activities of competitors' new-product development processes could have a crucial effect on the firm's eventual market share, as well as the price that it is able to sustain for its service.

### Development and testing

This is the translation of the idea into an actual service that is capable of delivery to customers. The tangible elements, as well as the service delivery systems that make up the whole service offering, all have to be designed and tested. One possibility is to test a new service with a sample of existing customers with no external promotion. Many banks have tested their new online banking facilities on existing customers, who were invited to try the new service and give their feedback, ahead of a full launch. Most companies balance the need for rigorous development and testing against the need to get to market quickly. This is particularly important for high-technology companies, where there are likely to be important 'first mover' advantages. At the height of the dot.com boom, many new online services were launched with only minimal research either into consumers' likely adoption of the service or into the underlying technology needed to support the service.

### Launch

The organization now makes decisions on when to introduce the new service, where, to whom and how. Timing is a key issue. The longer a new service takes to go through the various developmental stages, the greater the chance that competitors will enter the market first. The firm can be a pioneer and enter the market first or be a follower and reduce the risks considerably. In the UK, there was a race in 2003 to launch the first 'Third Generation' mobile phone network. The new operator '3' created publicity for being the first to launch a network (on 03/03/2003), despite the fact that no handsets were available until some time afterwards. If there are still some uncertainties about how a new service will work, or if there are doubts about the capacity of the new service to cope, a service provider may go for a 'soft launch'. This involves opening the service to selected customers, who are advised that some aspects of the service process may not be completely finalized. By offering a special price, customers can obtain a bargain and the company obtains feedback, which it can use to fine-tune the service before a full public launch. The hotel and cruise-ship industries frequently use soft launches; for example, the Cunard Line invited employees' families on the inaugural cruise of its new flagship *Queen Mary 2*, prior to the ship's first advertised transatlantic crossing. For companies operating globally, timing of the launch in different national markets can be critical, as markets are likely to be at different stages of development and a global rollout may be inefficient for a company to manage (Wong, 2002). A staggered rollout allows a company to exploit profits from one market before moving on to progressively less attractive markets, thereby maintaining a portfolio of services at different stages of market development.

So far, the stages of new product development have been presented as if they are steps that necessarily have to be tackled in a sequential order. In fact, the time taken to go through this process can be considerable, allowing competitors to gain a lead. There have therefore been many attempts to carry out some of the steps simultaneously. Virtual reality systems, for example, are allowing customers to get a feel of the final service process at a very early stage, allowing this to take place at the same time as concept testing and avoiding the need to wait while all steps of the process are progressed (Dahan and Hauser, 2002).

The new-service development process can be extremely complex, with many examples of cost overruns and delayed results (Kim and Wilemon, 2003). A key to more effective new-service development activity is close working relationships between marketing and operational functions. Even simple administrative matters, such as rapid communication following the results of one stage, can help to speed up the new-product development process. One study by Papastathopoulou et al. (2006) observed significant differences between marketing and operations functions in their involvement in the stages of business analysis, technical development, testing and launching. In the case of new-to-the-market projects, the involvement of marketing and sales was seen to influence outcomes positively, whereas in the case of 'me-too' retail financial services a more positive effect derived from the involvement of the technical and operations-related functions.

The complexity of the new-service development process has often led to companies outsourcing the whole process to specialist companies who have developed an expertise in product development and market testing (Howley, 2002). The use of an outside consultancy can also be useful where a company's ethos is production orientated and it seeks to bring on board broader marketing skills. It has been noted that brilliant inventors do not necessarily make good marketers of a new product (Little, 2002).

## 7.5 Demand forecasting

A good forecast of demand is vital, in order that a company can be prepared for the future more efficiently and effectively than its competitors, by having the right services, in the right place, at the right time and with the right capacity.

There have been many examples of spectacular failures to accurately forecast demand for new services:

- London's Millennium Dome (now known as The $O_2$ Arena), open to the public for just one year in 2000, proved to be a disappointment in terms of visitor numbers. Against forecasts of 12 million paying visitors, only about half this figure actually visited. Forecasts were made difficult because of the absence of comparable previous projects that might have given some idea of the likely take-up. Many uncertainties remained during the forecasting process, including the effects of competing millennium attractions, the impact of press reviews, the state of the national economy and the capacity of the local transport infrastructure.

- When Carphone Warehouse launched its new free broadband service in the UK in 2006, it experienced an unexpectedly high level of take-up, resulting in delays and frustration for potential customers.
- When Apple's iTunes service was launched in 2001, few people would have predicted that it would go on to become the world's leading music download site, achieving a total of 25 billion songs downloaded by February 2013.

## Thinking around the subject: Fly me to the moon

For many, space represents the final frontier for tourism. In 2001, the world's first space tourist, Dennis Tito, paid a reported $20 million for a visit to the International Space Station. Already a number of companies are looking at the possibilities for mass-market space tourism. Although the price of travelling into space may still appear prohibitive, analogies have been drawn with the early days of transatlantic air travel. In 1939, it cost the equivalent of £79,000 in today's inflation-adjusted money to make a return flight from Britain to the USA, something which can be routinely done today for around £400. Sir Richard Branson's Virgin Galactic plans to begin commercial passenger flights into space from a purpose-built spaceport in New Mexico, USA. The flights will allow the public to experience the thrill of weightlessness outside the Earth's atmosphere at a cost of £120,000 per ticket. Would space tourism go the same way as transatlantic air travel by eventually becoming mass-market? What would be the price at which space tourism really begins to grow? Who would be the innovators, and just how many people in the later adopter groups would really want to experience weightlessness? A greater uncertainty in planning for the future is the effect of aircraft emissions on global warming, which could lead to prohibitively high taxes on operations, or a feeling of guilt by potential passengers about the effects on climate change of their travel into space.

Figure 7.4 Richard Branson – space tourism pioneer.

*Source*: www.virgingalactic.com

**Demand forecasting** often begins by trying to predict general changes in the macromarketing environment. This in itself can be very difficult; for example, economists frequently disagree in their forecasts of economic growth during the year ahead. When it comes to predicting macro-environmental change, larger companies often retain expert consultants, such as the Future Foundation (www.futurefoundation.net), and Trendspotting (www.trendspotting.com) which employs economists, sociologists and psychologists, among others, to try to build a picture of the world as it will evolve. Such macro-level forecasts can inform more detailed forecasts about market size, growth rates, market share etc.

When it comes to forecasting demand for completely new services, simply asking potential buyers whether they would buy the service can be fraught with difficulties. Because services are intangible, it can be difficult to present potential customers with a mock-up of the product in a way that manufacturing companies often do to test likely reaction to a new product. There has been a lot of discussion, for example, about just what features and benefits customers will use when high-speed fourth-generation mobile Internet services become widely available and affordable. Simply asking somebody what they would use such a service for is likely to be limited to the scope of respondents' imagination. In the context of developing a low-cost car, Henry Ford once famously commented that if he had asked people what they wanted, they would have simply replied 'faster horses', rather than being able to imagine ever owning a car. For intangible services, the problem of consumers' limited vision can be even greater, requiring more sophisticated research methods that seek to understand deep-seated needs and motivators. Where possible, companies have sought to experiment with new service formats targeted at trial groups, before committing themselves to large-scale provision. This may be a valid approach where capital commitments are high and the market is relatively stable, but in fast-moving markets, too much time spent understanding consumer behaviour may allow competitors to gain a lead in an emerging new service sector. In the early days of the Internet, many new online services were developed with very little research; indeed, in those days, the problem of Henry Ford's horses was ever more present, with most consumers having little idea of how they might use the Internet. So, in order to be first to market and have a 'first mover' advantage, the process of understanding customers and forecasting demand was often based more on intuition and judgement than on a rigorous analysis.

A number of approaches to demand forecasting are available. Qualitative and quantitative techniques may be used as appropriate. In looking at the future, facts are hard to come by. What matters is that senior management is in a position to make better-informed judgements about the future in order to aid strategic marketing planning.

A starting point for a demand forecast is to examine historical trends. At its simplest, a firm identifies a historic and consistent long-term change in demand for a product over time and seeks to explain this in terms of change in some underlying variables, such as household income levels or price levels. Correlation and regression techniques can be used to assess the significance of historical relationships between variables. However, a simple extrapolation of past trends has a number of weaknesses. One variable, or even a small number of variables, is seldom adequate to predict future demand for a product, yet it can be difficult to identify the full set of variables that have an influence. New variables may emerge over time. There can be no certainty that the trends identified from historical data are likely to continue in the future and they will be of diminishing value as the length of time over which they are used to forecast increases.

Models have become increasingly sophisticated in their ability to forecast consumer demand. This can be partly explained by a growing amount of readily available data that can be used to build and validate a model. Reliability is improved by increasing the volume of data on which a model is based and the number of variables that are used for prediction.

Inevitably, models, no matter how sophisticated, need interpretation. This is where the creative side of marketing management is called for, especially in combining market intelligence with harder economic approaches. In interpreting quantitative demand forecasts, management must use its judgement based on a holistic overview of the market situation.

## In practice: When I'm 64

Ageing of the population should be a major opportunity for many services organizations. In 2005, the European Commission published a Green Paper on Demographic Change, which predicted that from 2005 to 2030, the number of EU citizens aged over 80 would almost double, from 18.8 million to 34.7 million. Between 1960 and 2005 average life expectancy has risen by five years for women and nearly four years for men. Nursing homes may expect a boom in demand as the population ages, spurred on by increased wealth of elderly people, who are retiring with occupational pensions, and by the gradual breakdown in extended families – a traditional source of caring for elderly relatives. However, the link between growth in size of the elderly population and demand for a company's services can be complex. During the period 1995–2004, the number of elderly people in residential care homes in the UK actually fell and many care homes and their operators went out of business, despite growth in the number of elderly people during this period. With the number of people in the UK aged over 80 expected to rise from 2.6 million in 2010 to 4.8 million in 2030, this would equate to an increase of 630,000 (or 82 per cent) in the number of care home places required by 2030, assuming current patterns of take-up. But for care home operators contemplating investment ahead of this potential increase in demand, many uncertainties remain. Trying to forecast future demand for care homes is complicated by uncertainty over the future health needs of elderly people – will elderly people of the future be healthier and be able to look after themselves for longer? Will they make greater efforts to live in their own homes, rather than in a residential care home? Some care homes, such as the one in Figure 7.5, have spotted this trend and now offer an outreach service to care for people in their own homes. Costs of operating residential care homes are likely to increase, fuelled by increasing government regulations and by wages rising in real terms, reflecting a scarcity of people of working age relative to the number of elderly people. How much will elderly people and their relatives be able or willing to pay for residential care-home accommodation? How much will the government be prepared to pay towards care?

Figure 7.5 A growth industry?

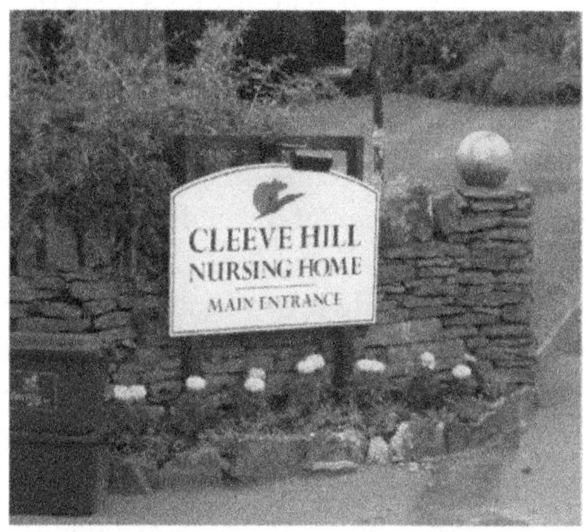


How sophisticated should a firm's demand forecasting efforts be? The amount of time and expense incurred in undertaking research must be compared with the benefits that will result from it in terms of making a better-informed decision. Very often, the issue is how harmful a badly informed decision could be to a firm. Where the capital costs involved in developing a new service are low, and the market is changing rapidly, it may make sense to do very little research and go straight to the market with a new product. This is true of many mobile catering businesses, which can set up their facilities quickly and easily, and move on if demand fails to materialize. In such a case, little will have been lost, but had the business owner taken time to carry out lengthy market research, they could have been beaten to the market by a more intuitive competitor. Contrast this with the marketing research needed for a much more risky major infrastructure investment such as an airport, which will have a high capital cost and a long lifespan. The research process here would typically take several years and take many forms (Figure 7.6).

Figure 7.6 Balancing the costs and benefits of undertaking detailed demand forecasts

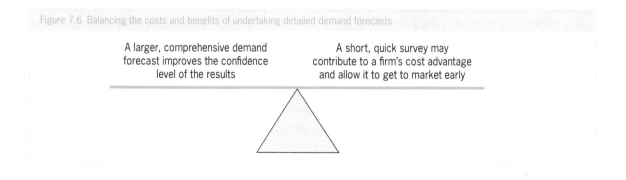

A larger, comprehensive demand forecast improves the confidence level of the results

A short, quick survey may contribute to a firm's cost advantage and allow it to get to market early

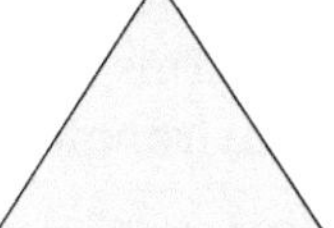

### 7.5.1 Trend extrapolation

At its simplest, a firm identifies a historic and consistent long-term change in demand for a product over time and seeks to explain this in terms of change in some underlying variables. Marketing planning then seeks to predict changes in these underlying variables and therefore – on the basis of the long-term relationship between variables – the likely future size and nature of a market.

While correlation techniques can be used to identify the significance of historical relationships between a number of variables, extrapolation methods suffer from a number of shortcomings. First, one variable is seldom adequate to predict future demand for a product, yet it can be difficult to identify the full set of variables that have an influence. Second, there can be no certainty that the trends identified from historical data are likely to continue in the future. Trend extrapolation takes no account of discontinuous environmental change, as was brought about by the banking crisis which affected many markets from 2008. Third, trend extrapolation is of diminishing value as the length of time over which it is used to forecast increases – the longer the time horizon, the more chance there is of historical relationships changing and new variables emerging. Fourth, it can be difficult to gather information on which to base an analysis of trends – indeed, a large part of the problem in designing a marketing information system is in identifying the type of information that may be of relevance at some time in the future.

At best, trend extrapolation can be used where planning horizons are short, the number of dependent variables relatively limited and the risk level relatively low.

### 7.5.2 Qualitative research techniques

As the example of Henry Ford above indicated, it can be very difficult to carry out any form of structured, quantitative research about likely take-up of a product whose characteristics are very difficult to envisage. Companies therefore often use qualitative approaches founded in the social sciences in an attempt to understand issues of deeper symbolic significance of a proposed new service in the lives of potential adopters. Many Internet service providers, for example, have employed anthropologists to probe deeply into the significance to individuals of social network sites. Rather than focusing on the hard technology of Web 2.0 technologies, more insight into likely future uptake may be gained by understanding individuals' needs for a sense of community and belonging to a 'tribe' and how this may be better achieved through social network sites rather than traditional face-to-face communities.

### 7.5.3 Expert opinion

Trend analysis is commonly used to predict demand where the state of the dependent variables is given. In practice, it can be very difficult to predict what will happen to these variables. One solution is to consult expert opinion to obtain the best possible forecast of what will happen to them. Expert opinion can vary in the level of its speciality, from an economist being consulted for a general forecast about the state of the national economy, to industry-specific experts. Expert opinion may be unstructured and come either from a few individuals inside the organization or from external advisers or consultants. Paid and unpaid advisers may be used to keep abreast of a whole range of issues, such as technological developments, environmental issues, government thinking and intended legislation. Consultancy firms may be employed to brief the company on specific issues or to continuously monitor the environment.

### 7.5.4 Scenario building

Scenario building is an attempt to paint a picture of what the future may look like, based on differing assumptions about the business environment. This qualitative approach is a means of handling environmental issues that are hard to quantify because they are less structured, more uncertain and may involve very complex relationships.

In the real world, many unpredictable environmental factors can interact with each other, resulting in a seemingly endless permutation of scenarios. One method of analysing the relationship between environmental factors is cross-impact analysis, which presents a framework within which the combined effects of changes in a number of factors can be assessed. A number of permutations are shown in Figure 7.7, where the interaction of the distinct possibility of oil prices rising to $200 per barrel with the 'wild card' event of cancer being linked to flying can be noted. For an airline, a development option if this scenario came true might be to rapidly downsize its passenger-carrying capacity and to concentrate on business and freight traffic.

Figure 7.7 In planning for the future, companies often like to ask 'what if'-type questions. Cross-impact analysis uses combinations of events to develop specific scenarios for the future. These allow the company to consider the likelihood of a particular scenario occurring and the likely consequences, negative and positive, for the company if it does. In this diagram, an airline may consider not only the consequences of oil prices rising to $200 a barrel, but the combined effects of this happening with a scare linking flying to increased risk of cancer. What contingency plan should the airline develop, just in case this scenario turns out to be true? Should it immediately reduce its capacity, until oil prices stabilize and people's fear of flying reduces? Should it instead focus more on investments in modification to its aircraft so that they operate more efficiently, and with a reduced risk of cancer?

| Wild cards \ Possible events | OPEC forces price of oil to $200 per barrel | OPEC cartel collapses: oil drops to $12 per barrel | Economic downturn becomes a slump and lasts for 5 years | Government introduces heavy fossil-fuel taxes |
|---|---|---|---|---|
| New hydrogen-powered engine cuts costs and pollution | | | | |
| Development of 'virtual reality' allows people to gain experience of travel without actually travelling | ↑ | | | |
| Possible link between flying and cancer causes fear of flying | Contingency plans... | → | | |
| New wave of aircraft terrorism | ↓ | | | |
| | | | | |

The use of scenarios can allow a company to come to a view as to which is the most likely outcome, and plan accordingly, while still being able to develop contingency plans that could be rapidly implemented if any of the alternative foreseen scenarios came true.

### 7.5.5 Marketing intelligence

Business owners have for a long time developed the art of 'keeping their ear close to the ground' through informal networks of contacts. With the growing sophistication of the business environment, these informal methods of gathering intelligence often need to be supplemented. In contrast to market research, intelligence gathering concentrates on picking up relatively intangible ideas and trends, especially about competitors' developments. A number of studies (e.g. Fleisher et al., 2008; Qiu, 2008) have noted the ways in which businesses informally gather information as a form of 'competitive intelligence'. Sources typically include:

- Newspapers, printed and online, especially trade newspapers, should be scanned regularly and from these a company can learn about competitors' planned new product launches.
- There are many specialized media-cutting services, which will regularly review published material and alert a company to items that fall within predetermined criteria.
- Employees can be a valuable source of marketing intelligence, especially sales personnel who can act as the ears as well as the mouth for an organization. Staff suggestion schemes and quality circles are often used to gain market intelligence.
- Similarly, intermediaries are close to customers and their observations are often encouraged through seminars, consultation meetings and informal communication methods.
- Informal networks developed through trade and professional associations allow business owners to share information with people who could be competitors.

Market intelligence is a valuable contributor to the development of corporate knowledge. One outcome of a knowledge-based organization has often been referred to as the 'learning organization', in which the challenge is to learn at the corporate level from what is known by the individuals who make up the organization.

### Thinking around the subject: Finding true knowledge on the shop floor?

Information is often described as management's window on the world, but what happens if management work in a large corporate head office, far removed from customers and day-to-day operations? It is sadly all too familiar for senior management to become cut off from the service operations that they manage. A BBC television series *Back to the Floor* invited chief executives to spend a few days changing their role to that of a front-line employee. In one case, the chief executive of the grocery retailer Sainsbury's seemed to be oblivious to customers' annoyance with shopping trolley design and availability. Why had the need for a new design of trolley not been picked up through the company's internal channels of communication? In another case, the chief executive of Pickfords Removals could not understand why the company was so inflexible when minor changes in customers' requirements occurred. Of course, the managers of small businesses do not generally have such problems as they are in regular contact with their customers and do not need structured information management systems to give them a window on the world. Their success in keeping in touch with customers has led many larger businesses to emulate some of their practices. 'Management by walking about' has become a popular way in which senior executives try to gain information about their marketing environment that is not immediately apparent from structured reporting systems. Some companies have adopted a formal system of role exchanges where senior executives spend a period at the sharp end of their business.

## 7.6 Competitor analysis

Any plan to develop a competitive advantage must be based on a sound analysis of just who a company's competitors are. At first, it may seem obvious who the competitors are, but, as Theodore Levitt pointed out, a myopic view may focus on the immediate and direct competitors while overlooking the more serious threat posed by indirect and less obvious sources of competition. When railway companies in the 1930s saw their main competitors as other railway companies, they overlooked the fact that the most serious competition would derive from road-based transport operators (Levitt, 1960). More recently, banks have been made to realize that their competitors are not just other banks, or even other financial services organizations, but any organization that has a strong brand reputation and customer base. Through these, supermarkets, airlines and car companies have all developed banking services that now compete with mainstream banks.

Even without considering the possibility of new market entrants appearing, it is possible to identify direct and indirect competitors. Direct competitors are generally similar in form and satisfy customers' needs in a similar way. Indirect competitors may appear different in form, but satisfy a fundamentally similar need. Consider the examples of services in Figure 7.8, the underlying needs which they satisfy and their direct and indirect competitors.

Taking this bigger picture to consider indirect competitors is important because consumers essentially seek to satisfy their underlying need, which can be met in a number of ways. Most customers do not need a bank – they may simply need a cash withdrawal service that can be provided just as well by a supermarket or a petrol station. The precise form of a new competitor may appear quite unlike the established service format, but in terms of positioning within consumers' minds the new service can rank just as highly. If all that a customer needs a bank for is to withdraw cash, a supermarket may have a superior position in their mind in terms of accessibility, trust and ease of use.

Michael Porter identified five forces that determine the competitive intensity and attractiveness of a market. Attractiveness refers to the overall profitability of an industry sector, with the least attractive being one that is dominated by fierce price-based competition between essentially generic products, allowing little opportunity for profits (Porter, 1980).

The five forces are:

- the threat of new entrants;
- the threat of substitute products;
- the intensity of rivalry between existing firms;
- the power of suppliers;
- the power of buyers.

Figure 7.8 Examples of services, the needs they satisfy and their direct and indirect competitors

| Product | Typical underlying need | Direct competitors | Indirect competitors |
|---|---|---|---|
| Overseas holiday | Relaxation | Rival tour operators | Garden conservatories |
| Restaurant meal | Social gathering | Other restaurants | Ready-prepared gourmet meals for home entertaining |
| Television programme | Entertainment | Other television programmes | Internet service provider |

The first three of these forces constitute 'horizontal' competition within a company's macro-environment, while the last two are about the bargaining power of a company in its 'vertical' supply chain comprising its micro-environment of suppliers and customers. A change in any of the five forces would generally require an organization to reassess its position in a marketplace.

The overall attractiveness of an industry sector does not mean that every firm in the sector will achieve the same levels of profitability. Differences will be apparent because of differences in firms' core competencies, allowing some to achieve profitability above the industry average. As an example, the environment of the airline industry has changed greatly in the past 20 years, and some airlines have been better able than others to adapt to change, with the result that they have achieved profitability while others have sustained losses. A tool for reconciling the external and internal environments is SWOT analysis, which matches an organization's internal **S**trengths and **W**eaknesses with the external **O**pportunities and **T**hreats that it faces. An external opportunity is only an opportunity if an organization has the internal strengths to take advantage of it.

## 7.7 Service deletion

As well as maintaining successful services and investing in new ones, services organizations must also have the courage to eliminate services that are no longer likely to benefit the organization as a whole. Good portfolio management depends upon reliable marketing information to show when a product is failing to achieve its objectives.

In general, there is a tendency to 'add on' rather than subtract and thus many service offers do not die but merely fade away, consuming resources of an organization that could be better used elsewhere. 'Old' services may not even cover overheads. In addition, there are a number of hidden costs of supporting dying services that need to be taken into consideration:

- A disproportionate amount of management time may be spent on them, and this may delay the search for new services.
- Economies of scale may be lost as smaller numbers of customers become uneconomic to process.
- They often require frequent price adjustments (and stock adjustments where tangible components are involved).

Firms should therefore have a marketing planning system that incorporates service deletion decisions. However, in reality, there are a number of reasons why logical deletion procedures are not readily followed:

- Often firms do not have the information that they need to identify whether a service needs to be considered for deletion. Even if an organization is aware of a potential deletion candidate, the reasons for its failure may not be known and management may just leave things as they are and hope that a short-term problem will be self-correcting.
- Managers often become sentimental about services, hoping that sales will pick up when the market improves. Sometimes, particular elements of marketing strategy will be blamed for lack of success and there could be a belief that a change in advertising or pricing, for example, will improve the situation.
- Within organizations, there may be political difficulties in seeking to delete a service. Some individuals will have vested interests in a service and may fight elimination efforts. In fact, some individuals may seek to distort the facts of a service's performance to ensure that deletion is not considered at all.

- Finally, there is sometimes the fear that the sales of other products and services are tied into the service being deleted. As an example, a car dealer that closes its new car sales department may subsequently lose business in its servicing and repairs department. Furthermore, some candidates for elimination may be sold to a small number of important customers, leading to fears that deletion could cause the loss of an entire business relationship to other service providers who still provide the eliminated service.

Many companies tackle service deletion in a piecemeal fashion, only considering the matter once a service is seen to be losing money, or when there is some crisis leading to a cutback. There is, therefore, a need for a systematic approach. At regular intervals, every service should be reviewed in terms of its sales, profitability, average cost, market share, competitor share, competitor prices etc.

Having acquired the relevant information, an organization can identify 'weak' elements of its service portfolio using a number of metrics. Some of these relate to poor sales performance, some to poor profit performance and others to more general danger signals such as new competitor introductions or increasing amounts of management time being spent on one service. Identification of a 'weak' service does not automatically mean that deletion is required.

One possible method of deciding which products to delete is the development and implementation of a product/service retention index. This can include a number of factors, each of these being individually weighted according to the importance attached to them by a particular firm. Each service is then ranked according to each factor, and the resulting product retention index is equal to the sum of the products of the weighted indices. An illustration of a product retention index is shown in Figure 7.9.

As an alternative to deletion, a company may consider revitalization approaches, by making adjustments to the marketing programme, including:

- modifying the service format/market position;
- increasing the price (may be a good idea if demand is fairly inelastic);

Figure 7.9 An example of a product retention index

| Factor weighting (FWi) (10 = high; 1 = low) | Factor | Product/service score (SRi) (10 = high; 1 = low) |
|---|---|---|
| 7 | Future market potential for product/service? | 4 |
| 7 | How much could be gained from modification? | 6 |
| 6 | How much could be gained from marketing strategy modification? | 5 |
| 6 | How much useful executive time could be released by abandoning product/service? | 8 |
| 5 | How good are the firm's alternative opportunities? | 7 |
| 4 | How much is the product/service contributing beyond its direct costs? | 3 |
| 4 | How much is the product/service contributing to the sale of other products/services? | 5 |
| The product/service retention index SRI = the sum of FWi Sri | | |

- decreasing the price (may be useful if demand is elastic);
- increasing promotional expenditure to stimulate sales;
- decreasing promotional expenditure to cut costs;
- revising the promotional mix;
- increasing sales-force effort to boost sales;
- decreasing sales-force effort to reduce costs;
- changing the channels of distribution;
- franchising service provision to another company that is better suited to providing the service.

If, on the other hand, deletion is the chosen alternative, decisions must be made about how this should be implemented. This is not always a simple task and a number of options can be identified:

- *Ruthlessly eliminate 'overnight'.* The potential problem here is that there are still likely to be customers some of whom may still be in the service process for a long time to come. How will they respond? Will they take their business to competitors? Will they take their business for other services in the mix with them?
- *Increase the price and let demand fade away.* This could mean that the firm makes good profits on the service while demand lasts.
- *Reduce promotion or even stop it altogether.* Again this could increase profitability while demand lasts.

Whichever decision is made, an organization has to consider the timing of such a decision, by taking the following factors into account:

- *Inventory level.* Where these are significant tangible components of a service offer, stock levels should be considered in order to avoid having excess stocks that cannot later be sold.
- *Notification of consumers.* It is generally better for firms to inform consumers that service deletion is imminent. Such a policy allows customers time to make alternative arrangements and this may also have the added advantage of promoting the firm's 'caring' image. Some announcements of deletion have even had the effect of raising awareness of the service, which has helped to build a long-term sustainable demand (e.g. announcement of the proposed withdrawal of London–Scotland sleeper trains led to a surge in demand).
- *Resources.* Management should move freed-up resources, particularly labour, to other services as soon as possible. This not only eliminates the possibility of idle resources, but can motivate staff who might otherwise suffer a drop in morale.
- *Legal implications.* Service elimination may bring with it legal liabilities. In the case of suppliers, an organization may be committed to take supplies regardless of a deletion strategy (for example, a holiday tour operator may be contractually committed to buying aircraft seats for the remainder of a season). In the case of customers, it may not be possible to delete services provided under a long-term contract until that contract comes to an end. This can be particularly important for the financial services sector where mortgages and pension plans usually allow no facility for a unilateral withdrawal of supply by the service producer, even though a pension policy may still have over 30 years to run.

Service deletion decisions are often forced on management by circumstances beyond its control. However, one study found evidence that the adoption of a systematic approach, using interdisciplinary teams to deal with the decision and keeping the time between the making and the implementation of the decision short, are all important dimensions of 'successful deletion' (Gounaris et al.,

2006). By reading market climate and assessing the fit between their current offering, the market and future possibilities, managers are afforded greater time to consider, plan and execute the deletion for minimum disruption to revenue.

## Case study

### Mobile banking: hot new service in Mombasa, but why a cooler reception in Manchester?

Nicole Koenig-Lewis, Swansea University and Alexander Moll, Virtual Identity AG

Internet banking is now taken for granted by many people, who may be relieved at not having to visit a bank branch or use a telephone call centre to undertake many banking transactions. Mobile banking (m-banking) is probably ten years behind Internet banking in its development. In ten years' time, will we be taking mobile banking similarly for granted? Whenever any new banking technology comes along, there are sceptics who doubt that the new technology will catch on with the public. When ATMs first appeared, many people thought they would never be popular because people liked to go into a branch and deal with a human being. In the late 1990s when the Internet was only beginning to catch the public's imagination, doubters expressed major concerns about privacy, security, download speeds and access to the Internet. When Egg bank launched its then revolutionary online banking service in 1998, even Egg itself turned out to have been unduly cautious as prospective customers appeared in unexpectedly high numbers, crashing its servers and swamping its telephone lines.

Mobile phones have become an essential part of our lives. We use our mobile phone to check e-mails, get news updates, browse the Internet and connect with friends via social networks, as well as using it as a personal organizer, as a camera and as a music player to consume and share music, pictures, games, ringtones etc. A number of people keep their mobile phones with them at all times, even in the bathroom, and are unable to ever turn it off. A study by SecureEnvoy found that in 2012, 66 per cent of the UK population admitted the fear of being without their mobile phone – called 'nomophobia'. Especially, young adults between 18 and 24 years tend to be most addicted, with just over three-quarters unable to stay separate from their phones for more than a few minutes (SecureEnvoy, 2012).

But what is happening with mobile banking?

More recently, high hopes have been held for m-banking, following the more general development of mobile commerce, which in turn has been helped by the appearance of sophisticated, easy-to-use smartphones such as the iPhone. M-banking enables customers to access their bank accounts through mobile devices to check their balance or to conduct financial transactions. The range of services that can be undertaken while mobile is likely to increase, and many have suggested that mobile phones are likely to evolve as ubiquitous payment devices, allowing a mobile phone to be used in a similar way to a credit card (Wilcox, 2009).

But will the growth of m-banking be as swift as the previous growth of online banking? And can we assume that the West will lead, while the less developed emerging economies catch up later? Some critics have argued that banks in the West have less to gain from promoting m-banking than they had from promoting the first generation of Internet banking. It has been claimed that m-banking does not provide significant cost-saving benefits for banks in comparison to those that can be achieved by migrating customers from traditional banking methods to online banking (Laukkanen et al., 2007). If consumers do not see advantages in m-banking, will banks significantly increase the allocation of resources to support it?

Forecasting the likely uptake of new technologies is vital for the rapidly changing communication sector where new applications/services appear daily. However, these forecasts are very difficult and there are many cases of inaccurate forecasts. For example, in the 1980s many experts failed to predict the rapid adoption of mobile phones. Also the uptake of texting was completely unexpected. On the other hand, picture phones and video-calling has been much slower to take off than originally predicted. In making predictions, analysts have tried to draw comparisons with previous adoption patterns for new technology, which have typically got off to a slow start as they target relatively high-income, innovative segments and eventually become affordable to all.

In an attempt to improve forecasts, models of consumer adoption have been applied, most notably the technology acceptance model (TAM) and innovation diffusion theory (IDT). These models are not without their problems; for example, it has been pointed out that the TAM typically only explains about 40 per cent of variance in purchase intention (Venkatesh and Davis, 2000). As an extension to TAM, the unified theory of acceptance and use of technology (UTAUT and UTAUT2) was proposed by Venkatesh et al. in 2003 and 2012, respectively. These models produced a significant improvement in the variance explained in behavioural intention (56 and 74 per cent, respectively) and technology use (40 and 52 per cent, respectively). However, it has been suggested that other factors such as trust, perceived risk, and convenience also influence mobile banking adoption behaviour.

A study by the Mobile Marketing Association in 2010 revealed that while m-banking was gaining popularity, it was still far away from becoming mainstream in Western European countries, as only 14 per cent of UK adult consumers and 9 per cent of French and German consumers use mobile phones for banking, with SMS being the most popular medium for viewing account balances (Mobile Marketing Association and Lightspeed Research, 2010). However, these figures are higher for young consumers between 18 and 34, with 24 per cent of UK young people and 20 per cent of German young people already engaging in m-banking (Mobile Marketing Association and Lightspeed Research, 2010). It seems that young people are more predisposed to adopt m-commerce services in general than other Internet users because these services are usually low-cost entertainment services (e.g. ringtones, songs) which fit with their lifestyle (Bigne et al., 2005). A report from Juniper Research (2013) predicted that by the end of 2017 there will be over 1 billion mobile banking users, compared to just over 590 million in 2012. While this forecast appears to be substantial, it still only represents 15 per cent of the mobile phone subscribers worldwide.

In Western countries, where m-banking adoption has been moving quite slowly, it might at first sight seem surprising that mobile banking has been powering ahead in emerging economies. A survey carried out by GMSA in 2012 indicated that nearly 70 per cent of the world's registered 81.8 million mobile money customers were located in sub-Saharan Africa. This represented 56.9 million people, more than twice the number of Facebook users in the region. Owing to limited access to traditional financial services in these countries, it is not surprising that TNS's annual Mobile Life study (2012) found that 36 per cent of Ugandans already use their phone as a wallet, compared with just 9 per cent globally. Security concerns are the key barrier in adopting mobile payments in Europe and the UK. While using a mobile wallet is perceived to be a safer option than carrying cash in Indonesia (71 per cent) and Uganda (43 per cent), only 9 per cent in Denmark share this view (TNSGlobal, 2012).

In Kenya, the M-Pesa service ('M' for mobile, 'Pesa' for 'money' in Swahili) was launched by Safaricom in partnership with Vodafone in 2007 and allows customers to use their mobile phone to pay bills, deposit cash and send cash to other mobile phone users. The adoption of the M-Pesa service was speedy, with 11,000 new registrations per day during 2009. By 2010, Kenya's Central Bank reported that there were more M-Pesa subscribers than bank accounts in the country. By 2013, Safaricom claimed it had 15 million users conducting more than 2 million transactions daily. The World Bank has estimated the value of these transfers to be about $10 billion a year, equivalent to a third of Kenya's GDP.

This rapid adoption of the M-Pesa service in Kenya can be largely explained by the lack of a land-line telephone network and a poorly developed banking infrastructure. The Financial Access Survey 2009 showed that only 23 per cent of the Kenyan adult population had a bank account but 48 per cent owned a mobile phone, with the rate of ownership rising to 72.8 per cent in urban areas and 80.4 per cent in Nairobi (FSD Kenya and Central Bank of Kenya, 2009). Furthermore, Kenyans with bank accounts have to pay high charges for moving cash around, whereas M-Pesa provides a service which allows transferring cash safely without facing high costs. Setting up an account is straightforward and very easy.

But not all developing economies of Africa are similar in terms of adoption of m-banking; for example, the GSMA survey found that in 2012, Nigeria, with a population of 162.5 million (four times that of Kenya) and GDP of $244 billon (seven times larger than Kenya's $33.6 billion according to World Bank figures) was well behind Kenya in mobile banking adoption. According to the World Bank, 60 per cent of Kenyans aged 15 had used a mobile phone to send money, compared to 9.9 per cent of Nigerians. Similarly, 66.7 per cent of Kenyans had received mobile payments, much more than the figure for Nigerians (11.2 per cent).

Why should there be such a difference in take-up? One reason may simply be that Kenya started the process of adoption and reached a critical mass earlier – the Nigerian government only began issuing mobile banking licences in 2011, four years after M-Pesa started. But a report in 2012 by the Brookings Institution recognized that 'replication [of M-Pesa] in many cases has proven harder and slower [than in Kenya]' (Brookings Institution, 2012). It referred to a 2011 study by the International Finance Corporation which listed 50 factors that affected the successful development of mobile banking in any given country. One important factor is the regulatory environment, which in Kenya is much more liberal than in Nigeria. In Kenya, the mobile phone company Safaricom was able to develop a mobile banking platform alone, without the involvement of banks. This would not have been possible in Nigeria, where regulations prohibited mobile phone companies from applying for mobile banking licences.

In Europe the situation is different, with fewer incentives to use m-banking services as a range of digitized payment methods are already accessible for bank customers. Furthermore, there is a tendency for most people to have access to bank accounts, and in some countries, including the UK, making simple bank transfers or payments can be free or inexpensive. Thus there has been a trend for European banks to offer services which are unique to m-banking customers. NatWest, for example, launched a mobile banking service where Polish workers in the UK can send money home (Montia, 2008). According to one survey, other m-banking services of interest to customers are geo-location, which leads customers to the nearest ATM or bank branch, and the use of the mobile phone to make in-store payments and receive deposit and withdrawal notices (Mobile Marketing Association and Lightspeed Research, 2010).

The mobile phone is one piece of technology that is now widely owned. Technology providers and financial institutions believe that m-banking will one day reach a critical tipping point in Western markets, after which it will become mainstream. But what will it take to reach this tipping point? Will it be the availability of even more sophisticated smartphones? Will it occur when consumers overcome fears about the security of mobile banking and recognize a new generation of phones as really easy to use? Will widespread adoption only occur when mobile phones become widely used as easy payment devices, making it easy for a customer to use their phone to pay for a bus ticket or a drink in a bar? Or will the tipping point only occur when banks put serious resources into the further development of m-banking? And can the West learn anything from Kenya which is more advanced in consumer adoption, or does Kenya's progress simply reflect that the new service offer provided by m-banking had much less effective competition from established banking methods?

### Case study review questions

1 Discuss the causes of uncertainty in forecasts of levels of consumer adoption of new-technology based services such as m-banking.

2 Identify methods by which a bank could seek to improve the accuracy of its forecasts of take-up of m-banking.

3 Discuss the concept of a 'tipping point' in the adoption of new technology-based services. What factors do you consider would contribute to a tipping point for m-banking? How is this likely to differ between Western and non-Western countries?

## Summary and links to other chapters

The business environment of most services organizations is becoming increasingly turbulent, with changes in the economic, social, political and technological environments leading to yesterday's highly sought-after services sometimes becoming unwanted tomorrow. Companies that do not adapt their range of service offers to meet the changing needs of customers and the changing technocrat production possibilities are likely to lose out to companies that are more flexible and nimble. Successful new service development calls for systematic processes, and the resources devoted to the task vary between service sectors. As well as having a strategy for developing new services, companies should have a strategy for deleting services that have become unprofitable.

The focus of new service development is often the service encounter itself (Chapter 2), or making it more easily accessible to consumers (Chapter 4), and we have seen how the Internet has allowed for the development of a wide range of new services (Chapter 3). New service development is often designed around a company's relationship-building strategy – what new services should it develop to get a greater share of its customers' total expenditure (Chapter 5)? Finally, companies need to promote the distinguishing benefits of new services, and we will return to this subject in Chapter 13.

## Chapter review questions

1. Service employees are close to customers and should therefore be a good source of ideas for new service development. Critically discuss how the benefits of this input to the new service development process can be maximized.
2. Critically discuss the view that innovation and new service development are easier tasks for service-based organizations, compared with manufactured-goods companies.
3. Critically evaluate possible methods that may be used by an airline for predicting demand for travel on a proposed new long-haul route.

## Activities

1. Take a look inside your local post office. Post offices have been undergoing a transformation in many countries, as governments deregulate mail services, and many of the functions traditionally undertaken by post offices have migrated online. Identify ideas for new services that the post office might be able to provide. Which services would you consider deleting? Consider the economic, political, social and technological factors that might influence your new service/deletion decisions.
2. Consider a poorly performing service that you are familiar with, such as a bus service that seems to run empty, or a university course that has a falling number of students. Consider the merit of deleting the selected service. If you consider that the service justifies deletion, identify the most cost-effective strategy for deleting it, so that the reputation of the service provider is maintained and as many customers as possible are retained.
3. If you are following a course of study at a college or university, list your ideas for new services or service improvements offered by the college or university. Explore how your ideas could be most effectively communicated to senior decision-makers, and identify possible barriers to actually implementing your ideas.

## Key terms

**Business environment** The social, technological, economic and political factors external to an organization that are likely to have an impact on its activities, either directly or indirectly.

**Demand forecasting** An attempt to obtain the best estimate of the number of people who are able and willing to buy a product at some time in the future.

**New service** An additional service offered by a company, ranging from a completely new service that is unlike anything previously offered in the market, to minor modification of existing services.

**Scenario** A picture of possible internal and external environments that are likely to be relevant to an organization in the future.

**Service life cycle** A hypothetical description of the stages that a service passes through between its development and deletion.

**Service portfolio** The total range of services offered by an organization.

## Selected further reading

*The methods used by service organizations to search for new service ideas are discussed in the following:*

**Blazevic, V. and Lievens, A.** (2008) 'Managing innovation through customer coproduced knowledge in electronic services: an exploratory study', *Journal of the Academy of Marketing Science*, 36, 138–51.

**Füller, J., Matzler, K. and Hoppe, M.** (2008) 'Brand community members as a source of innovation', *The Journal of Product Innovation Management*, 25, 608–19.

**Olsen, N.V. and Sallis, J.** (2006) 'Market scanning for new service development', *European Journal of Marketing*, 40 (5/6), 466–84.

**Toivonen, M. and Tuominen, T.** (2009) 'Emergence of innovations in services', *The Service Industries Journal*, 29 (7), 887–902.

*The management of the new service development process is explored further in the following articles:*

**Smith, A.M. and Fischbacher, M.** (2005) 'New service development: a stakeholder perspective', *European Journal of Marketing*, 39 (9/10), 1025–48.

**Stevens, E. and Dimitriadis, S.** (2005) 'Managing the new service development process: toward a systematic model', *European Journal of Marketing*, 39 (1/2), 175–98.

**Cheng, C.C., Chen, J.-S. and Tsou, H.T.** (2012) 'Market-creating service innovation: verification and its associations with new service development and customer involvement', *Journal of Services Marketing*, 26 (6), 444–57.

*Consumer adoption processes for innovative services are discussed in the following:*

**Berry, L.L., Shankar, V., Turner, P., Cadwallader, S. and Dotzel, T.** (2006) 'Creating new markets through service innovation', *MIT Sloan Management Review*, 47 (2), 56–63.

**Hossain, L. and de Silva, A.** (2009) 'Exploring user acceptance of technology using social networks', *Journal of High Technology Management Research*, 20, 1–18.

**Vlachos, P.A. and Vrechopoulos, A.P.** (2008) 'Determinants of behavioral intentions in the mobile internet services market', *Journal of Services Marketing*, 22 (4), 280–91.

**Walker, R.H. and Johnson, L.W.** (2006) 'Why consumers use and do not use technology enabled services', *Journal of Services Marketing*, 20 (2), 126–35.

*Service deletion is discussed in the following articles:*

**Argouslidis, P.C.** (2007) 'The evaluation stage in the service elimination decision-making process: evidence from the UK financial services sector', *Journal of Services Marketing*, 21 (2), 122–36.

**Argouslidis, P.C. and McLean, F.** (2004) 'Service elimination decision-making: the identification of financial services as candidates for elimination', *European Journal of Marketing*, 38 (11/12), 1355–81.

**Gounaris, S.P., Avlonitis, G.J. and Papastathopoulou, P.G.** (2006) 'Uncovering the keys to successful service elimination: "Project ServDrop"', *Journal of Services Marketing*, 20 (1), 24–36.

## References


**Brookings Institution** (2012) 'How replicable is M-Pesa?', Brookings Institution, Washington, DC.

**Banerjee, A.V. and Duflo, E.** (2011) *Poor Economics: Rethinking Poverty and the Ways to End It*, Random House, India.

**Bigne, E., Ruiz, C. and Sanz, S.** (2005) 'The impact of internet user shopping patterns and demographics on consumer mobile buying behaviour', *Journal of Electronic Commerce Research*, 6 (3), 193–209.

**Blazevic, V. and Lievens, A.** (2008) 'Managing innovation through customer coproduced knowledge in electronic services: an exploratory study', *Journal of the Academy of Marketing Science*, 36 (1), 138–51.

**Cheng, C.C., Chen, J.-S. and Tsou, H.T.** (2012) 'Market-creating service innovation: verification and its associations with new service development and customer involvement', *Journal of Services Marketing*, 26 (6), 444–57.

**Dahan, E. and Hauser, J.R.** (2002) 'The virtual customer', *Journal of Product Innovation Management*, 19 (5), 332–51.

**Easingwood, C.J.** (1986) 'New product development for service companies', *Journal of Product Innovation Management*, 3 (4), 264–75.

**Edgett, S.** (1994) 'The traits of successful new service development', *Journal of Services Marketing*, 8 (3), 40–9.

**Fleisher, C.S., Wright, S. and Allard, H.T.** (2008) 'The role of insight teams in integrating diverse marketing information management techniques', *European Journal of Marketing*, 42 (7/8), 836–51.

**FSD Kenya and Central Bank of Kenya** (2009) 'Results of the FinAccess National Survey: dynamics of Kenya's changing financial landscape', available at http://www.fsdkenya.org/finaccess/documents/09-06-10%20FinAccess%20FA09%20Brochure.pdf (accessed 8 July 2013).

**Gounaris, S.P., Avlonitis, G.J. and Papastathopoulou, P.G.** (2006) 'Uncovering the keys to successful service elimination: "Project ServDrop"', *Journal of Services Marketing*, 20 (1), 24–36.

**Henard, D.H. and Szymanski, D.M.** (2001) 'Why some new products are more successful than others', *Journal of Marketing Research*, 38 (3), 362–75.

**Howley, M.** (2002) 'The role of consultancies in new product development', *Journal of Product & Brand Management*, 11 (6/7), 447–58.

**Johne, A. and Storey, C.** (1998) 'New service development: a review of the literature and annotated bibliography', *European Journal of Marketing*, 32 (3/4), 184–251.

**Juniper Research** (2013) Press release: 'Mobile banking users to exceed 1 billion in 2017, representing 15 per cent of global mobile subscribers', available at https://www.juniperresearch.com/viewpressrelease.php?pr=356 (accessed 13 May 2013).

**Kelly, D. and Storey, C.** (2000) 'New service development: initiation strategies', *International Journal of Service Industry Management*, 11 (1), 45–65.

**Kim, J. and Wilemon, D.** (2003) 'Sources and assessment of complexity in NPD projects', *R & D Management*, 33 (1), 16–30.

**Kristensson, P., Matthing, J. and Johansson, N.** (2008) 'Key strategies for the successful involvement of customers in the co-creation of new technology-based services', *International Journal of Service Industry Management*, 19 (4), 474–91.

**Laukkanen, T., Sinkkonen, S., Kivijärvi, M. and Laukkanen, P.** (2007) 'Innovation resistance among mature consumers', *Journal of Consumer Marketing*, 24 (7), 419–27.

**Levitt, T.** (1960) 'Marketing myopia', *Harvard Business Review*, 38 (4), 45–56.

**Little, G.** (2002) 'Inventors don't always make great marketers', *Design Week*, 17 (27), 15.

**Michel, S., Brown, S.W. and Gallan, A.S.** (2008) 'An expanded and strategic view of discontinuous innovations: deploying a service-dominant logic', *Journal of the Academy of Marketing Science*, 36 (1), 54–66.

**Mobile Marketing Association and Lightspeed Research** (2010) 'Europeans opt for mobile banking in increasing numbers', available at www.mmaglobal.com/news/europeans-opt-mobile-banking-increasing-numbers (accessed 8 July 2013).

**Montia, G.** (2008) 'NatWest launches Polish mobile money transfer service', available at http://www.bankingtimes.co.uk/2008/12/23/natwest-launches-polish-mobile-money-transfer-service/ (accessed 8 July 2013).

**Papastathopoulou, P.G., Gounaris, S.P. and Avlonitis, G.J.** (2006) 'Successful new-to-the-market versus "me-too" retail financial services: the influential role of marketing, sales, EDP/systems and operations', *International Journal of Bank Marketing*, 24 (1), 53–70.

**Porter, M.E.** (1980) *Competitive Strategy*, Free Press, New York.

**Qiu, T.** (2008) 'Scanning for competitive intelligence: a managerial perspective', *European Journal of Marketing*, 42 (7/8), 814–35.

**SecureEnvoy** (2012) '66% of the population suffer from Nomophobia the fear of being without their phone', available at http://www.securenvoy.com/blog/2012/02/16/66-of-the-population-suffer-from-nomophobia-the-fear-of-being-without-their-phone/ (accessed 12 May 2013).

**Seegy, U., Gleich, R., Wald, A., Mudde, P. and Motwani, J.** (2008) 'The management of service innovation: an empirical investigation', *International Journal of Services and Operations Management*, 4 (6), 672–86.

**TNSGlobal** (2012) 'Asian consumers lead the world into banking and buying via mobile', available at http://www.tnsglobal.com/press-release/asian-consumers-lead-world-banking-and-buying-mobile (accessed 13 May 2013).

**Toivonen, M. and Tuominen, T.** (2009) 'Emergence of innovations in services', *The Service Industries Journal*, 29 (7), 887–902.

**Venkatesh, V., Morris, M.G., Davis, G.B. and Davis, F.D.** (2003) 'User acceptance of information technology: toward a unified view', *MIS Quarterly*, 27 (3), 425–78.

**Venkatesh, V., Thong, J.Y.L. and Xin, X.** (2012) 'Consumer acceptance and use of information technology: extending the unified theory of acceptance and use of technology', *MIS Quarterly*, 36 (1), 157–78.

**Venkatesh, V. and Davis, F.D.** (2000) 'A theoretical extension of the technology acceptance model: four longitudinal field studies', *Management Science*, 46 (2), 186–204.

**Venkatraman, N. and Prescott, J.** (1990) 'Environment–strategy coalignment: an empirical test of its performance implications', *Strategy Management Journal*, 11 (1), 1–23.

**Wilcox, H.** (2009) Press release: 'Mobile banking users to exceed 150m globally by 2011 according to Juniper Research', *Juniper Research*, available at http://juniperresearch.com/shop/viewpressrelease.php?pr=120 (accessed 8 July 2013).

**Wong, V.** (2002) 'Antecedents of international new product rollout timeliness', *International Marketing Review*, 19 (2/3), 120–32.

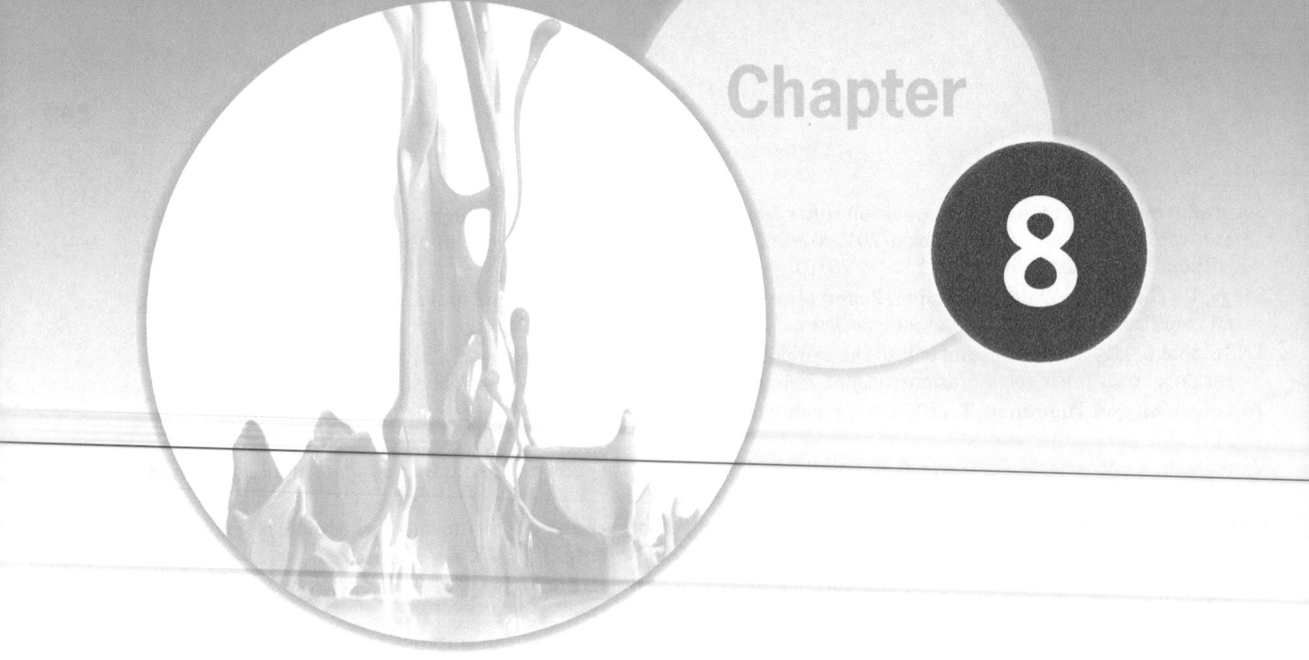


# Developing service brands

*You are about to book a hotel on a travel website where you come across a range of familiar and not so familiar hotel brand names. Some of the hotels do not even appear to have a brand name. You have never visited any of the hotels in person, so you need to use your judgement to assess whether a particular hotel will be to your liking. You might have previously stayed in one of the branded chain hotels and had a wonderful time, or it may have been a nightmare stay. How will the reputation of the brand influence your choice? And what about the small unbranded hotels that you see listed? Without a brand name, what is the basis for their competitive advantage? This chapter explores the theories and practices of branding in the services sector.*

## Learning objectives

After reading this chapter, you should understand:

- The role of branding in service organizations
- Strategies to develop strong service brands
- Reasons for the coexistence of branded service providers with small reputation-based providers

## 8.1 Introduction

One of the central challenges for marketing managers – for goods as well as services – is to develop a strong brand. Without a strong brand, a supplier of services is essentially supplying a generic type of product to a market that cannot really tell the difference between one supplier and another. In this type of situation, price is likely to be the key point of difference between suppliers, and fierce price-based competition is generally bad for companies who cannot raise their selling price.

The services sector has been relatively slow in developing strong brands, compared with the manufacturing sector, where many brands can trace their history back for well over a century.

There is mixed evidence on the relative importance of brands for goods and services-based organizations (see Krishnan and Hartline, 2001). On the one hand, there is evidence that intangibility increases the importance to buyers of a brand, helping them to reduce perceived risk (Brady et al., 2005). On the other, compared to the manufacturing sector, brands have been relatively slow to develop in the services sector. To get some idea of the apparent relative absence of strong brands within the services sector, consider the data presented in Figure 8.1, which shows the results of the annual *BusinessWeek*/Interbrand survey of the world's top 100 brands. Most notably, although services typically account for around three-quarters of GDP in modern economies, service brands account for less than one-quarter of the top 20 brands. Of the top brands, McDonald's, Disney, Google and American Express would be recognized as essentially service-based businesses. Over half of the brands in the top 20 – Coca-Cola, Nokia, Toyota, Intel, Hewlett Packard, Mercedes-Benz, Gillette, BMW, Louis Vuitton, Samsung and Apple – are essentially manufactured goods brands

Figure 8.1 The world's top 20 global brands.

| Rank 2012 | Brand | 2012 Brand value ($m) | Country of ownership |
|---|---|---|---|
| 1 | Coca-Cola | 77 839 | U.S. |
| 2 | Apple | 76 568 | U.S. |
| 3 | IBM | 75 532 | U.S. |
| 4 | Google | 69 726 | U.S. |
| 5 | Microsoft | 57 853 | U.S. |
| 6 | GE | 43 682 | U.S. |
| 7 | McDonald's | 40 062 | U.S. |
| 8 | Intel | 39 385 | U.S. |
| 9 | Samsung | 32 893 | S.Korea |
| 10 | Toyota | 30 280 | Japan |
| 11 | Mercedes-Benz | 30 097 | Germany |
| 12 | BMW | 29 052 | Germany |
| 13 | Disney | 27 438 | U.S. |
| 14 | Cisco | 27 197 | U.S. |
| 15 | Hewlett-Packard | 26 087 | U.S. |
| 16 | Gillette | 24 898 | U.S. |
| 17 | Louis Vuitton | 23 577 | France |
| 18 | Oracle | 22 126 | U.S. |
| 19 | Nokia | 21 009 | Finland |
| 20 | Amazon | 18 625 | U.S. |

*Note*: The brand valuations draw upon publicly available information, assessed by Interbrand.
*Source*: Interbrand Best Global Brands Annual Report, 2012

(although many of these have added significant service elements to their products). The remainder are best described as a combination of goods and services organizations.

Why should brands be apparently so relatively undeveloped in the services sector to the extent that the list of top brands is dominated by manufacturing companies? These are some possible reasons:

1 We have seen that services are generally much more variable compared with manufactured goods. Very few people will have encountered a faulty bottle of Coca-Cola, because of the multiple opportunities that the manufacturer has for quality control before the finished product reaches the consumer. However, the same cannot be said about a train journey or the encounter at a bank, which are produced live in front of the customer, with few opportunities for quality control. Strong brands are all about a consistent reputation, and the chances of consistency in encounters with a live service are much lower than for a soft drink.
2 Big brands demand big investments, not only in procedures for quality control, but also to promote the values that the brand stands for. Small firms have fewer resources to develop global brands; and this is a particular problem for the services sector, which tends to be dominated by small businesses.
3 Global brands are based on global trade. We saw in Chapter 1 that services have been relatively slow to develop international trade, on account of the inseparability of services (which generally requires the producer or consumer to cross international boundaries in order that they can meet and the service be produced/consumed), and the generally slower rate at which barriers to trade in services have been removed.
4 Many service sectors such as postal services and energy supply have until recently been dominated by government-owned suppliers. Where such services are provided in a monopolistic or regulated market, the service provider may have little need or inclination to develop strong brands.

Despite these issues, it is apparent that services businesses are increasingly developing strong brands, often taking market share from small, family-owned businesses which develop their business on the basis of their personal reputation rather than a heavily promoted brand. In the following sections, we will explore the basis for developing strong service brands, and then ask why so many small businesses continue to exist in the services sector, often with very little attempt made at developing a strong brand.

## 8.2 The development of service brands

As a service business grows, brands are likely to become an increasingly important part of its marketing strategy. Branding is essentially about the reputation of a seller. Even the smallest part-time, self-employed service provider earns a reputation over time. This is often without the help of any formal marketing strategy – the service provider's name is effectively a brand. As a brand, this may be easy to manage when the individual and brand are synonymous. So, a local plumber, John Smith, has all the tools of branding in his own hands, and the strength of his brand is as good as the level of service he personally delivers. But, if John Smith sought to grow by employing additional people, possibly in different regions, the task of developing a strong brand would be much more complex. A customer calling on the services of John Smith could not be sure that it would actually be John Smith who delivered the service, so John Smith must ensure that his employees deliver a standard and style of service that is consistent with what he would have delivered himself.

Historically, branding first became important with the development of industrialization and mass production. In an age of mass production, producers were no longer able to have a direct and individual relationship with their growing number of customers, and therefore could not provide personal reassurance of product quality. A brand acted as a substitute for a personal relationship in managing buyers' exposure to risk. Branding became important when purchasers of goods such as clothing, processed food and cosmetics became industrialized. The same process is repeating itself with services. In Chapter 2, we saw how many service sectors have adopted the principles of industrialization – mass production, standardization and mechanization, to reduce the variability of their services.

### 8.2.1 How do brands work?

A brand identity provides a shorthand reference to the whole bundle of attributes provided by a service offer or service provider, and in particular emphasizes benefits of the service relative to competitors. Brands are important in guiding buyers when choosing between otherwise seemingly similar competing services. Consider the following cases:

- Buyers of pension plans are typically not very knowledgeable about pensions, yet several tens of thousands of British people have entrusted their pension provision to the Virgin group, largely on the strength of its brand reputation for honesty and openness, and despite the company being a relative newcomer to the pensions industry with no proven track record.
- When booking an overseas hotel, many travellers will choose from a shortlist of hotel brand names with which they are familiar, despite the existence of locally run hotels that would probably offer better quality at a lower price.
- Buyers of package holidays in the UK are often prepared to pay a premium for the Thomson brand name, in preference to less well-known competitor brands that offer lower prices for an apparently identical holiday.

Branding has been found to simplify the decision-making process by providing a sense of security and consistency that may be absent outside of a relationship with a supplier. Risk levels are perceived as being higher for products that fulfil important needs and values, so in these situations the value of brands can be higher.

The use of brands in the services sector is becoming increasingly important as a means of limiting the search activities of potential buyers. Rather than considering all possible options, a brand encourages buyers not to consider other products that do not come with the statement of values that a brand stands for. As we will see later, many service organizations such as Virgin and Tesco have used this relationship-based brand strategy to extend their activities to services which are not operationally related to their core activities.

There have been many conceptualizations of the unique attributes of a brand and how these affect buying decision processes. These usually distinguish between elements that can be objectively measured (such as the reported reliability of an airline) and the subjective values that can only be defined in the minds of consumers (such as the perceived personality of the Virgin airline brand). In early work, Gardner and Levy (1955) distinguished between the 'functional' dimensions of a brand and its 'personality', while other dimensions have been identified as utilitarianism versus value expressive (Munson and Spivey, 1981), need satisfaction versus impression management (Solomon, 1983), and functional versus representational (de Chernatony et al., 2010). The functional dimensions of a brand serve to reassure buyers that important elements of a service offer will be delivered as promised, for example an airline can be trusted to operate reliably, a tour operator not to overbook its hotels and a savings institution to return its investors' money promptly when required.

## In practice: Taxi!

Figure 8.2 A London cab

London's famous black taxis come close to being a generic, unbranded service. London taxis are highly regulated in terms of the standards of drivers, the vehicle itself and prices charged. Drivers must pass a 'knowledge' test before being allowed to operate, and cannot refuse to carry a passenger, except in clearly specified cases. Few people would bother spending much effort in selecting one cab from another – they have been reduced to a commodity whose consistent standards are rigorously maintained by the licensing body, the Public Carriage Office.

Contrast this with the situation in towns where regulations are fewer and buyers may have little idea about the integrity of the car that they are getting into or the reliability of its driver. This is the classic opportunity for the development of brands by taxi operators to give them a distinctive position in the marketplace, and thereby simplify buyers' choice processes. While many local authorities control the fares that all taxi operators must charge, it is open to individual operators to develop a brand that is associated with reliability, safety and courteousness. Next time a customer seeks a taxi, they may know which taxi companies to avoid and which to go for out of preference.

With increasing affluence, the non-functional expectations of brands have become more important. While there are many companies offering bank accounts and credit cards, individual companies such as Virgin and American Express have created emotional brands that guide customers in a market dominated by otherwise generic products. There is extensive literature on the emotional relationship consumers develop between a brand and their own perceived or sought personality. Brands are chosen when the image that they create matches the needs, values and lifestyles of the buyer. Through socialization processes, individuals form perceptions of their self, which they attempt to reinforce or alter by relating with specific groups, products and brands. There is evidence that branding plays a particularly important role in purchase decisions where the product is conspicuous in its use and purchase and in situations where group social acceptance is a strong motivator (Miniard and Cohen, 1983; Moschis, 1976). While conspicuous consumption is most commonly associated with manufactured goods (for example, brands of training shoes, designer clothes labels and makes of car), the concept of a conspicuous brand also has meaning in a services context. An individual may use their membership of an upmarket gym or their possession of a 'gold' credit card to make statements about themselves in much the same way as they use a Rolex watch or Nike trainers.

Some authors have suggested that brands have become increasingly important in the development of shared community values. Social groups that once identified with shared values relating to the church, work or geographic location find these sources of identity more difficult in an increasingly individualistic and mobile world, and instead brands may be a source of shared community values (Cova, 1997). Some have talked of a 'Brandscape' as an increasingly important type of community, in which consumers feel emotionally linked to one another, either formally or informally (Sherry, 1998). Members of a gym or upmarket fashion retailer may feel this sense of linking, and increasingly the Internet has been used to develop online branded communities, such as YouTube and Facebook.

A brand can also be important by appealing to employees of an organization. The brand values that appeal to customers should be the same as those with which employees identify, and there has been a lot of talk among labour-intensive services organizations about delivering their 'brand promise' through employees (Knox and Freeman, 2006).

### Thinking around the subject: A brand new university, or just a new brand?

Brands seem to be encroaching into product areas where the language of brand management has until now appeared alien. But what about promoting a university as a brand? 'Good' universities have known for some time that they have their reputation to preserve, but the language today in many universities is about managing brand values. Research among applicants to UK universities has often shown a low level of knowledge about the standards of provision of such items as accommodation, library facilities and the quality of teaching. However, certain universities have come to be rated more highly than others, often on the basis of quite incidental information, such as their sports teams or the nightlife in town. For many 'modern' universities, developing a strong brand image with which to challenge the established universities has been seen as a priority. Even students felt it was important to belong to a university which had a 'good' name, however irrational the basis for its good name. De Montfort University has been one of the pioneers in university brand-building, supporting its efforts with television advertising. It undertook research among current students, which showed, perhaps surprisingly, that many preferred limited university funds to be spent on a brand-building advertising campaign, rather than improvements to the library facilities. Going to a known rather than an unknown university was seen as an important part of a university education. Cynics have been quick to criticize such efforts. How can a brand be sustained over the long term if the physical and intellectual capacity of a university is crumbling all around?

### 8.2.2 Brand vision

It has become popular to talk about the idea of a 'brand vision'. There have been many definitions of what this term means, but essentially it describes the company's perception of the values and qualities that its brand represents. A brand vision gives a clear statement about the 'soul' of the brand and provides a sense of direction to customers, and all of those employees and intermediaries who have responsibilities for delivering it. If a brand is to thrive, there must be a vision about what the brand will look like way into the future, in an environment that may be very challenging. A brand vision statement should be complementary to the company's corporate vision statement and sometimes can be combined with it. In fact, what is important is not what the statement is called, or the formalized procedures for developing it, but whether there is a shared sense of brand vision within an organization.

A brand vision should encapsulate the core values of the brand. There has been some discussion about how many values should be associated with a brand, and in what level of detail they should be described. There seems to be a consensus that the number of core values should be limited, ideally to four or five. As the number of brand values increases, confusion can set in about what are the most important values, and the opportunities for conflicts between core values can increase. In the case of people-intensive service businesses, staff become an important part of the brand promise, and therefore it is particularly important that they understand the values of the brand. If the values of a brand which are promoted to customers are not shared by staff, dissonance may result when customers do not receive the brand promise. Many people-intensive service organizations base their staff recruitment on matching the values of the brand with the values of potential employees.

Recall from the case study in Chapter 3 that the restaurant chain T.G.I. Friday's used an auditioning process as part of its recruitment procedure, providing an opportunity for the selection panel to observe the match between the values of the brand and values of the individual. Some employers have taken the view that technical skills are relatively unimportant in the recruitment process, and instead it is more important that new recruits share core values. For example, it has been suggested that banks recruit to their call centre individuals who have values of honesty and integrity, rather than technical knowledge about banking skills.

There have been some notable entrepreneurs and CEOs who have had a passionate belief in their brand vision to the point of being evangelical. It is easy for bureaucratic, procedures-driven organizations to assemble a committee to write down brand vision statements, but this can easily fall into a trap of saying more and doing less. An example of a visionary brand evangelist is Sir Richard Branson who has had a consistent and passionate belief in the Virgin brand, which has been applied to a wide range of services, including air travel, music retailing, mobile phones, personal finance and train services.

The brand vision is based on a number of key values:

- fun – enjoyment and humour, not offensive and incompetent;
- value for money – simple, not cheap;
- quality – attention to detail, not expensive for the sake of it;
- innovation – challenging convention, not different for the sake of being different;
- competitive challenge – responding to consumer needs, not being irrelevant;
- brilliant customer service – empowered, not unprofessional people.

## 8.3 Services branding strategy

As services organizations grow, their brand may become their greatest asset. Where consumers perceive that risks are high and physical evidence is low, the reputation encapsulated by a brand may be critical in recruiting new customers, and retaining existing ones. But how should a service company go about developing its brand? Indeed, how many brands should it develop? The branding literature has identified a number of branding strategies, but we will focus here on just two important strategies: first, individual service branding, where each product or group of products has a separate brand identity; and second, strong corporate branding, where everything that an organization produces is sold under the same brand name. In between is a range of branding permutations, such as family brands that group related services together under the umbrella of a strong corporate brand.

Individual brands linked to specific service offers, or groups of service offers, tend to be relatively undeveloped in the services sector and are more likely to be used by companies that have separate operating units serving quite distinct market segments (for example, the UK restaurant operator Gondola operates three branded restaurant chains, Pizza Express, Ask and Zizi, each with a distinctive market positioning in terms of the range of food offered, ambience of the restaurants and price levels charged). Sometimes, sub-brands are used by services companies in the way that McDonald's has developed 'Big Mac' as a sub-brand. In the case of such brands, there is usually a significant tangible component that helps to establish a distinctive identity (although there are also cases of very intangible sub-brands, for example banks and credit card companies that offer branded premium accounts).

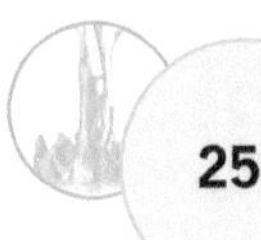

## In practice: What's in a brand?

Faced with an intangible product that cannot be assessed prior to consumption, many buyers of services rely on brands as an indicator of the standard of service that they should expect from a service provider. In the manufacturing sector, brands generally indicate a consistent standard of output; for example, one bar of Cadbury's chocolate will taste very much like the next one, and different ranges of Cadbury's chocolates will be consistent in their overall quality. However, for services, brands tend to indicate consistency of process, rather than outcomes. One company that has applied this consistency of process across a number of services activities is Virgin Group. Originally founded as a music business, the Virgin style of handling customers has subsequently been applied to air travel, rail services, Internet access and mobile phones, among others. Although these service sectors may appear quite different in terms of the technical characteristics of their service processes, Virgin Group has come to stand for a consistent style of service, characterized by honest communication, slightly cutting-edge, entertaining and sometimes just a bit quirky. Many people would consider the Virgin brand to be the group's most important asset, and it has been carefully managed. In some situations the brand is used by units in which Virgin Group is only a minority shareholder; for example, consistency of brand values is maintained between air and rail travel, even though Virgin Atlantic is partly owned by Delta Airlines and Virgin Trains is jointly owned with Stagecoach Group.

Figure 8.3 Virgin promotes its broadband package

Single, strong corporate brand strategies have been widely developed in the services sector and have allowed companies to diversify into new service areas. The brand essentially becomes a corporate brand and sends a message to buyers that, if the company can be trusted to provide one service, then it should be trusted to provide additional, and possibly completely unrelated, services. Corporate reputation can be very important in simplifying the choice for buyers, who may have little knowledge about a complex service that is new to them and may be unwilling to trust a relatively unknown company. There are many examples of companies in the services sector that have used a strong corporate reputation to extend their brand into completely new service areas. Virgin

Group has used its brand to expand from music to airlines, financial services and mobile phones. The Boots Company, another trusted corporate brand, has expanded into optician and dentistry services. To be successful, the single corporate branding strategy adopted by companies such as Virgin and Boots demands a relentless maintenance of the organization's reputation. Unethical business practices or poor reliability in one aspect of the organization's service provision could undermine general trust in the company and affect sales of services that may have had no operational connection with the service that gave rise to problems. In the case of Virgin Group, does the frequently reported unreliability of its UK train services (or at least perceptions of unreliability) undermine consumers' perceptions of the reliability of its financial services?

A strategic need that sometimes has to be addressed is 'debranding'. Developing just one strong corporate brand which is applied to every activity of the organization makes sense for companies who can expand their relationship with customers by applying their corporate brand name to a new type of service. But often, a service organization may seek to dispose of some of its service activities to another company, for strategic or legal reasons. What happens to the brand name if the company behind the corporate brand name is no longer actually providing the service? One solution is to come to an agreement with the new owner of the service operations to allow them to continue to use the brand. The Virgin Group has made extensive use of this approach – in fact many Virgin branded service companies are not actually owned by the Virgin Group, or at least have only a minority ownership by Virgin. This entails complex agreements about how the brand should be managed in order to preserve the core brand values. Some of the complexity involved was seen in Virgin Radio, which the Virgin Group had sold to Absolute radio, with an agreement for the latter to use the Virgin brand name. However, the agreement did not allow Absolute Radio to sell the brand on to a new third-party owner who might compete with the Virgin Group, so in 2008 when the radio station was sold to a subsidiary of *The Times* of India, the Virgin brand name was changed to Absolute Radio.

On other occasions, a service organization seeks to dissociate itself from an activity which it is disposing of. Where once it used its corporate brand name on everything it did, it must now subtly remove this and rely on a weaker branding of the particular service offer. A practical example of this is the airport operator BAA, which in 2008 was ordered by the UK Competition Commission to sell off London's Gatwick Airport because of concerns about the effects of concentrated airport ownership on competition. The company had previously applied BAA branding to all of its airports, but in 2009 began a process of removing its branding, in preparation for a sale.

### 8.3.1 Delivering a consistent brand

By far the most important element of branding is delivering a consistent standard of service. But what does a consistent standard of service mean in practice? It does not generally mean uniform output in the way that manufacturing companies can produce bottles of soft drinks or DVD players that are consistent in their reliability, because we have already noted that services are often concerned with processes rather than outputs. Also, the customization of services often requires one service process for one customer to be different from an essentially similar process for another customer.

The concept of brand consistency in the context of services can be taken to imply consistency of positioning in a consumer's mind. Therefore, consistency focuses on relatively abstract concepts such as integrity, honesty and reliability. It is these brand qualities that have allowed the Marks and Spencer brand to develop trust from customers as a clothes retailer, and to use the brand to move into financial services, while trust in the Sainsbury's brand has allowed the grocery retailer to move into banking and energy supply. Many financial services companies have recognized the limits on the development of functional aspects of branding by concentrating on the emotional aspects. Virgin Group has been successful in this respect by appealing to groups who value its 'no-nonsense' approach to doing business, while the investment management company Schroders has stressed its long-established history and comprehensive range of facilities.

We saw in Chapter 2 how consistency of service delivery can be facilitated by the process of industrialization. By simplifying service processes, companies can reduce the possibilities of failure in complex, multi-stage processes. Staff training has further helped to ensure that front-line staff are familiar with the promises of a brand and have the capability to meet brand promises in the eyes of customers. In Chapter 9, we will return to the subject of service quality, and how organizations seek to understand customers' expectations, which act as a benchmark against which service delivery is assessed. A brand that over-promises and under-delivers may lead to a perception of poor service quality, and ultimately mistrust of the brand.

Brand reputation can be destroyed following a serious service failure, such as an airline suffering a plane crash or a food poisoning outbreak at a restaurant. Of course, companies should try to ensure that a serious service failure does not occur, but when it does, they should have in place strategies to recover their reputation. This typically includes proactive public relations activity to try to convince customers and other stakeholders that the company acted with integrity. In many cases a failure can actually earn sympathy for the company and its brand reputation may be restored. But if badly handled, deep mistrust in the brand may be difficult to recover from. We will return to the subject of communication in a crisis in Chapter 13.

### 8.3.2 Positioning the brand

Positioning strategy distinguishes a brand from competing brands in order to give the owner of the brand a competitive advantage within the market. Positioning puts a firm in a sub-segment of its chosen market, so a firm that adopts a product positioning based on 'high reliability/high cost' will appeal to a sub-segment that has a desire for reliability and a willingness to pay for it. For some marketers, positioning has been seen essentially as a communications issue where the nature of a service is given and the objective is to manipulate consumer perceptions of it. However, we need to bear in mind that positioning goes to the heart of what a brand stands for, comprising both the functional and emotional elements that were described earlier.

Services organizations must examine the opportunities for their brand and take a position within the marketplace. A position can be defined by reference to a number of scales. The level of service quality provided to customers and the price that is charged are two very basic dimensions of positioning strategy that are relevant to service industries. Figure 8.4 shows these two dimensions applied to European supermarket retailing, in which both the price and quality scales are conceptualized as running from high to low. Quality in this case can be considered as a composite of product range, speed of service, quality of personnel, quality of the shopping environment etc. Price can be a general indication of price levels charged relative to competitors. The position of a number of European grocery retailers is shown on the map. This shows that most supermarkets lie on a diagonal line between the high-quality/high-price position adopted by Marks and Spencer and the low-price/low-quality position adopted by Netto. Points along this diagonal represent feasible positioning strategies for supermarket operators. A strategy in the upper left quadrant (high price/low quality) can be described as a 'cowboy' strategy and generally is not sustainable, although it may be an attractive position in some instances – for example, some tourism-related activities where tourists are unlikely to return to the area. A position in the lower right quadrant

Figure 8.4 A simplified service positioning map for UK supermarkets, showing two simplified dimensions of positioning – perceived price and perceived quality

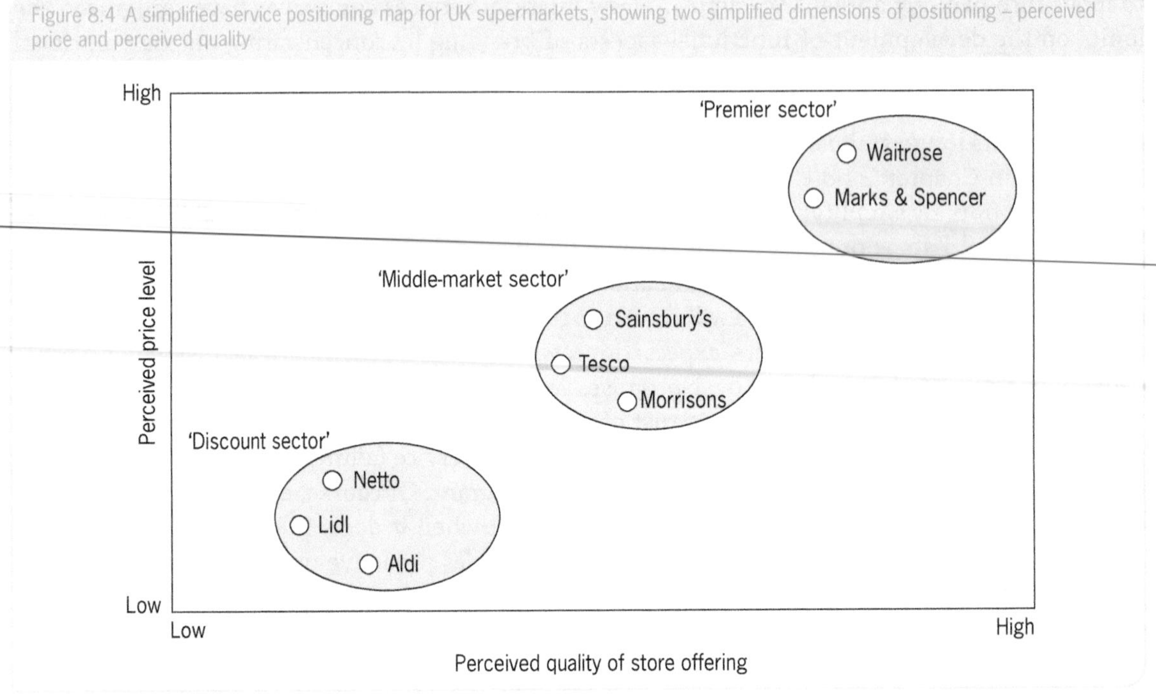


(high quality/low price) may indicate that an organization is failing to achieve a fair exchange of value for itself.

Service brands can be positioned either on a stand-alone basis or as part of a service organization's overall brand – in effect, it is the service organization that adopts a position, rather than the individual service. The fact that consumers are likely to evaluate the service provider at least as much as a particular service makes this approach to position analysis attractive. Shostack (1987) suggests that, within a range of services provided by an organization (or 'service family'), a marketer can consider positioning strategies based on the complexity and variability of a service. Complexity refers to the number of steps that make up a service production process and variability the extent to which service output and processes deviate from a norm. In this way, a doctor's service is highly complex in terms of the number of processes involved in a consultation or operation. It is also highly variable, for service outcomes can be diverse in terms of both planned and unplanned deviations in outcomes. Some processes can be high in complexity but may be considered low in variability. Hotels, for example, can offer a complete range of processes but are able to establish relatively low levels of diversity. A singer provides an example of a service that may be considered low in complexity but high in variability. The process of service industrialization has led to a tendency for service companies to position themselves as less complex and less diverse, meaning that they produce a relatively narrow range of services, which achieve relatively high levels of consistency. In this way, solicitors have developed strong brands around specialist house-conveyancing businesses, offering one service line with little scope for variability. By developing expertise and reducing overheads, such companies can satisfy customers who do not have the need for the more complex, but also more variable, services of full-service solicitors.

An example of Shostack's framework is a dental practice that could make its overall brand position more divergent by adding general counselling on health matters or reduce it by undertaking only diagnostic work. Complexity could be increased by adding retailing of supplies, or reduced by

Figure 8.5 This figure shows the positioning options that may be available to a dentistry service. As an alternative to simplifying its services by moving to the bottom left-hand area, it could offer a range of more diverse services, which may also entail more complex processes and move it up the diagram. If the business were to position itself in the upper right-hand area of the diagram, the task of brand building would probably be more difficult, because of the increased variability of outcomes and the difficulty of managing complex processes to a consistent standard. (Based on Shostack, 1987)

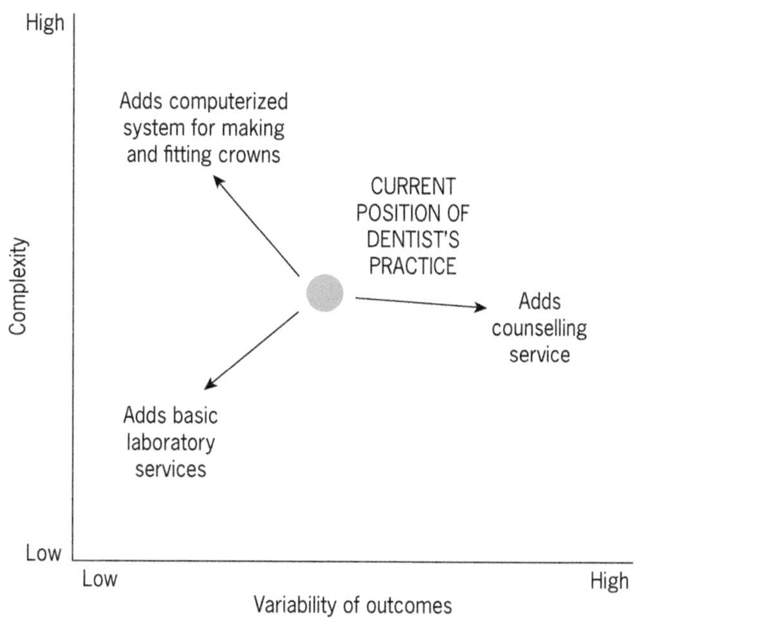


offering only a limited range of dental treatments. These options are shown diagrammatically in Figure 8.5. The position adopted by an organization will be influenced by its strengths and weaknesses relative to the market that it seeks to address. A large dental practice may be better placed to position itself as a provider of complex services, but would need to ensure that diversity in outcomes was minimized in order not to affect its brand reputation adversely. A small dentist may find the most achievable service position to be the provision of relatively simple services with divergent outcomes.

Services organizations can position themselves according to the complexity of their processes and the variability of outcomes. A common trend among services companies has been to simplify their processes, and to produce more consistent outcomes. This is represented by a move downwards and to the left in Figure 8.5 and is commonly associated with service industrialization and the development of strong brands.

### 8.3.3 Repositioning

Over time, an organization may need to reposition a brand. This could come about for a number of reasons:

- The original positioning strategy was inappropriate. Overestimation of an organization's competitive advantage or of the size of the sub-segment to which the positioning was intended to appeal could force a re-evaluation of positioning strategy.
- The nature of customer demand may have changed. As an example, many full-service airline brands faced challenges from the late 1990s from no-frills airlines. Some airlines, such as British Airways and KLM, set up their own separate brands (Go and Buzz, respectively) with a relatively

low-price/low-features position, while other airlines, including Aer Lingus and Jersey European (now Flybe), repositioned their brand to meet the needs of customers for relatively low prices and fewer additional benefits.

- Service providers seek to build upon their growing brand reputation to reposition towards meeting the needs of more profitable sub-segments. In many service industries, organizations start life as simple, no-frills, low-price operations, subsequently gaining a favourable image that they use to 'trade up' to relatively high-quality/high-price positions. This phenomenon is well established in the field of retailing, in which McNair (1958) identified what has become known as the 'Wheel of Retailing'. This contends that retail businesses start life as cut-price, low-cost, narrow-margin operations that subsequently 'trade up' with improvements in display, more prestigious premises, increased advertising, delivery and the provision of many other customer services, which serve to drive up expenses, prices and margins. Eventually, retailers mature as high-cost, conservative and 'top-heavy' institutions with a sales policy based on quality goods and services rather than price appeal. This in turn opens the way for the next generation of low-cost innovatory retailers to find a position that maturing firms have vacated.

### 8.3.4 Brand name strategy

Given the importance of a strong centralized brand for deepening and extending customer relationships, it is important that growth-oriented services organizations adopt a brand name that can be applied to new markets. So what makes a good service brand name? For very small services businesses, the owner's name may provide the strongest reassurance to customers. Many large services organizations have successfully grown and kept their founder's name – examples include McDonald's restaurants, Sainsbury's supermarkets and Barclays Bank. But a family name can also become a limiting factor. To use a family name for a newly launched bank, airline or telecommunications company may give the appearance of parochialism and country-of-origin effects may be a limitation. Increasingly, a brand name must work in overseas markets and a foreign name may be perceived as alien (although, of course, a foreign family name may have a positive country-of-origin effect by improving perceptions of the brand – a pizza chain may sound more authentic in foreign markets if it has an Italian name).

As organizations grow, their original brand name may become perceived as too limiting in the scope of services provided. A company called Radio Rentals, for example, survived long after it had ceased dealing in radios, and most of the televisions that it supplied were sold rather than rented. The company gradually declined before disappearing. Services organizations have often chosen to change their name to reflect the broader range of services that they now provide, but the danger of this approach is that customers who have been loyal to a brand may not identify with the new brand name. One approach adopted by many services companies is to abbreviate their previous brand name as a series of initials. In this way, British Airports Authority had become too limiting as a brand. It was not particularly British (it owns airports outside Britain and is itself owned by a Spanish company); it has interests beyond airports (it has operated hotels and the Heathrow Express train service); and since privatization it has not been an authority, but a private, market-led company. Sometimes, services organizations have been forced to change a brand name where its good reputation has been lost. The accountancy and consultancy firm Arthur Andersen was harmed by a series of scandals in the early 2000s and decided to rename parts of the remaining business Accenture.

Mergers and acquisitions often raise the question of whether an acquired brand name should be retained or replaced with that of the acquirer. Conventional thinking has been that, if a service operates at a global level (quite likely in the case of airlines, hotels and telecommunications companies, for example), then there will be benefits from operating with a global brand name that is readily available throughout the world (as examples, HSBC Bank and T-mobile have applied their brand names to most of their acquired brands). More recently, observers have noticed a tendency to favour more local identity. This often combines a globally uniform visual identity with familiar local names. The German-based tour operator TUI has done this with brands that it has acquired in different countries, for example Thomson in the UK and Hapag-Lloyd in Germany.

It was noted earlier that there can be a case for using separate brand names where different market segments need to be addressed with quite distinct service offers, including a distinct brand identity. In sectors where fashionability is important, a brand strategy could be to launch new brands that are seen as exciting, but which gradually mature over time and are killed off when they are replaced by a new brand. This effect is visible in restaurant chains; for example, Whitbread plc in the UK has developed new brand formats, or acquired established high-growth brands (such as Costa Coffee), while at the same time allowing the relatively mature brand of Beefeater to die. In this market, the cost of developing an exciting new brand was perceived as less than the cost of reinvigorating a brand with an old, tired image.

### 8.3.5 Global service brands

With the development of industrialized, mass-produced services, described in Chapter 2, the possibilities for developing consistent brands with international appeal have increased. We will see in Chapter 14 that many market segments have become more homogenized in terms of their similarity between countries, so that when buyers' preferences for fitness centres, for example, are explored, a 25-year-old aspirational male student living in Manchester may have more in common with another 25-year-old aspirational male student living in Munich than somebody of their age group but a different lifestyle living in their home city. Because of the dual forces of industrialization and cultural convergence, globalized brands have become prominent in a number of services sectors, such as hotels, car rental and fast food.

For services companies seeking to give their brands global coverage, there are a number of additional important considerations, for example understanding the consistency of brand values and expectations between different cultures, delivering consistent performance in many different operating environments, recruiting front-line staff who may share cultural values different from the core values of the brand, and choosing a brand name which will translate well into foreign markets. We will return to the issues raised by globalization of brands in Chapter 14.

Mindful of research suggesting that important segments of consumers may be weary of big global brands, some multinational organizations have developed small brands which are not closely associated with the parent organization, while retaining a globally promoted brand which targets buyers who appreciate the security and emotional attachments that a global brand can give them (Oliver, 2000). This has been linked to the notion of 'glocalization' – combining the worldwide strength of a large organization with a smaller-scale national or regional brand identity.

### 8.3.6 Branding in the age of Web 2.0

**Web 2.0**, comprising social network media and blogs etc., has become an important part of many firms' brand development strategy. Although social network media have effects on both goods and services marketing, they can be particularly important for services which are perceived as more risky, and for which a potential buyer seeks the views of other customers. Some strong service brands have been built almost entirely through 'word-of-mouse' recommendation, with very little paid-for advertising. Skype, for example, is now a widely recognized Internet telecommunications service provider, but developed its brand with very little paid-for advertising. However, while word-of-mouth recommendation through the Internet can help to build a brand, the opposite can also occur and the values of a brand become rapidly undermined.

There has been a lot of recent discussion of 'brand communities', formed when individuals become interdependent because of collective identity, shared rituals and moral responsibility to members (Muniz and O'Guinn, 2001). A brand community is capable of collective action over time, notably sharing information, perpetuating the history and culture of the brand, providing assistance to new members and exerting pressure on members to remain loyal to the brand. In one study, 62 per cent of 'Generation Y' users had visited a brand or fan page on a social network site, and 48 per cent actually joined such a network, citing reasons that included: getting news/product updates, viewing promotions, viewing/downloading music/videos, posting opinions and connecting with other customers (O'Malley, 2009).

It was noted in Chapter 6 that companies would generally love their brand to be at the heart of a community, and many companies have developed their own blogs and online forums for this purpose. The power of social media for brand development is indicated by the research organization The Group's FTSE100 social media index, which measures how FTSE100 companies use social media and reported that of the most talked about companies in social media, 14 out of the top 20 were essentially service-based companies during January 2013 (The Group, 2013). Although use of social media is becoming much more widespread with the growing use of mobile devices, patterns of usage differ. Forrester Research has reflected diversity of usage in its Mobile Mind Shift Index (MMSI), which segments people into six categories: Disconnecteds, Dabblers, Roamers, Adapters, Immersers and Perpetuals. The last three groups are particularly important for companies to address, as social media are likely to influence subsequent buying behaviour by the individuals themselves and of their social networks. Other groups are more likely to be passive spectators. The company had previously reported that typically 70 per cent of social media users could be described as 'spectators' – those who actively read blogs, tweets, customer reviews and content in forums as part of their regular online activity. Twenty-four per cent created their own content online, while 33 per cent regularly engaged in conversation; these have the ability to live on indefinitely on the Internet (Forrester, 2013).

However, there is a dilemma faced by companies planning to use online social media to develop their brands. On the one hand, they may seek to control the communication environment within the network, in an effort to make sure that their brand message comes through clearly. They may also be attracted by the availability of demographic and lifestyle information available to improve their targeting to individual members of the network. But, on the other hand, a true social network implies members feeling a sense of ownership of the community, and there is evidence that individuals may be resentful of corporate intrusion into what is perceived to be their own community space (Croft, 2008; Hitwise, 2008). If online brand communities are perceived by users as not being trustworthy, open, interesting, relevant and engaging with the target audience, they can rapidly harm a company's reputation. There have been reported cases of companies disguising their involvement in a community by falsely posting messages that purported to come from a member of the public, praising the company. While the company might have thought that it could influence opinion by manipulating the community, the subsequent uncovering of its covert actions generated bad publicity that undermined trust in the company. Online social networks can rapidly devalue a brand, and examples were noted in Chapter 6 where viral campaigns have drawn attention to bad practice by a brand.

## Thinking around the subject: Big Mac, big business, big problem?

Television images of young people joining protest marches against world capitalism have featured on our television screens recently. To protesters who trashed an RBS bank in London during the G20 talks in 2009, big banks were seen as the cause of gross inequalities in wealth throughout the world, and big fast-food chains contribute to obesity in the developed world while millions in poorer countries suffer malnutrition. Some have come to resent the way in which Microsoft has dominated software sales, and increasingly also Internet-based services. Large, successful companies, it seems, just have to accept that they will never please some people who hold large corporate organizations responsible for all of the world's problems. But just how hostile is the environment to large, apparently faceless business organizations?

A report by the Future Foundation appears to challenge the idea that young people are becoming more hostile towards big business. According to a 2001 study by the organization, 16- to 24-year-olds had more positive feelings towards multinationals than their parents, with the original protest generation, those who came of age in the 1960s, least likely of all to trust multinationals. In 2013, the death of Steve Jobs – boss and founder of Apple – was viewed by young people with sadness, rather than being seen as the end of a capitalist who had made a fortune of billions of dollars.

In the wake of violent protests surrounding recent World Trade Organization meetings, the Future Foundation found that younger generations are less inclined towards direct action than their parents and grandparents. Nearly half of all 16- to 34-year-olds claimed they would not demonstrate if a multinational company had done something wrong. Further confounding the myth of young people wanting to change the world was the statistic that fewer than one in 20 strongly agreed that they 'would not buy the products of a large multinational company that had done something wrong'. This was evident in 2013 when strong public feelings were aroused following reports that the Starbucks coffee shop chain was making large profits in the UK, but avoiding paying corporation tax by using legal but morally questionable accounting techniques to shift its profits to low-tax countries. Although some groups planned boycotts of Starbucks shops, *The Independent* newspaper reported that young people soon returned to the chain's shops to enjoy its free wifi and the experience of their skinny latte.

Does this all indicate the ultimate supremacy for big business where the golden arches of McDonald's and the Microsoft logo are symbols of its global sovereignty? Should big businesses feel safe in the knowledge of this study, or do they still need to be alert to possible trouble in the future? And even if a high proportion of young people support the idea of capitalism and big business, can large services organizations – whose processes are so visible to the public – afford to ignore the vociferous and extreme minority whose direct action and boycotts can do costly and long-lasting harm to their image?

## 8.4 Small businesses and brand development

The services sector is dominated by small businesses, at least when measured by the number of business units. Think about the last time that you had your hair cut, travelled in a taxi or consulted a solicitor, and the chances are that you would have been dealing with a small business. The theories and practices of brand building described so far in this chapter might appear to be quite alien to many small businesses which survive and prosper without grand branding strategies, and often even without a brand name. Instead of talking about the brand, it may be more appropriate to talk about the reputation of a small service provider.

By far the majority of business organizations in most countries are small, and this is especially true of the services sector. The term 'small business' (**small and medium-sized enterprise (SME)**) is difficult to define. In an industry such as railway operation, a firm with 100 employees would be considered very small, whereas among solicitors, a practice of that size would be considered large.

The term 'small business' is therefore a relative one, based typically on some measure of numbers of employees or capital employed.

In the UK, Department for Business Innovation and Skills statistics for 2012 indicated that out of an estimated 4.8 million private-sector businesses, almost all of these (99.2 per cent) were small (0 to 49 employees). Only 30,000 (0.6 per cent) were medium-sized (50 to 249 employees) and 6000 (0.1 per cent) were large (250 or more employees). (The proportion of businesses employing fewer than 50 people was relatively high in the hotel sector (47.0 per cent) and low in financial services (14.7 per cent) (BIS, 2013).)

Small services businesses are often created to satisfy a variety of personal objectives. This was illustrated by the results of a survey undertaken by Barclays Bank and ACCA (Association of Chartered Certified Accountants) into the reasons why individuals set up their own business. It was claimed by 34 per cent of respondents that their main reason was a desire for independence, while 17 per cent were motivated mainly to 'make money' and 13 per cent were incited by 'a family tradition' or 'to create a better future'. About 9 per cent of respondents were prompted to become entrepreneurs in order to 'work by themselves' and 8 per cent because they have 'no alternative/to avoid unemployment'. The survey also showed that despite a challenging economic environment, the most common small business growth target over the next three years is to expand moderately (36 per cent). A further 8 per cent aim to expand significantly. Almost one-third of all responding firms want to remain at their present size and 11 per cent of all small businesses have no growth targets (Barclays Bank, 2013). Developing a strong brand may be low on the list of priorities for many small businesses.

Many small service businesses are set up by individuals using a capital lump sum that they have received (such as an inheritance or a redundancy payment) to invest in what they perceive to be relatively pleasant and enjoyable businesses such as antique shops, tearooms and restaurants. Many fail in a competitive environment where personal objectives cannot be achieved without undue sacrifice. Many fail because they underestimate the boring, time-consuming backroom activities that have to be undertaken when their hobby becomes a business. As a result of these two pressures, it has been estimated that around three-quarters of new restaurants fail within two years of opening (Parsa et al., 2005).

Many small services businesses remain that way – single-outlet providers with small numbers of local and loyal customers. The owner may not have the inclination or ability to grow their business beyond this small local scale and may have little role for marketing and brand development where the business is essentially a lifestyle activity. However, many small businesses have successfully made the transition to become multi-outlet organizations employing often several thousand staff, with customers around the world. Many of the largest services organizations, such as McDonald's restaurants, Starbucks coffee shops and Google, started life as small businesses.

Making the transition from a small single-outlet service business to a multi-outlet branded chain can be a big challenge. The challenge is generally much greater for an expanding service business than for the expanding manufacturing business. A labour-intensive service business that provides inseparable face-to-face services, and which promotes its personal service, may be difficult to replicate in a larger organization. Manufacturers have used various control systems to achieve high levels of consistency, but the inseparability and variability of services make this a much more difficult task for growth-oriented services providers. Using a variety of quality control measures, a beverage manufacturer can be reasonably confident that bottles of soft drink are consistent in taste and composition at all factories where the product is made. However, for a service provider such as a restaurant, it can be much more difficult to ensure that a service encounter will be the same on all occasions at all times. Many professional or craft-based service businesses have failed to manage the transition from a small, personalized unit to a large managed unit, and it is this difficulty in managing multiple service encounters to a consistent standard that goes a long way to explaining the domination of small businesses in many service sectors.

### 8.4.1 Marketing advantages of small services businesses

Customers often associate small businesses with a bundle of positive attributes such as friendliness, flexibility, originality and individuality, whereas 'big' may be associated with negative connotations such as impersonal, inflexible, standardized and lacking a human dimension. The term 'small is beautiful' is commonly attributed to Schumacher who challenged conventional economic thinking for failing to consider the most appropriate scale for an activity (Schumacher, 1999). Although his original work challenged the notion that 'bigger is better' in the context of developing economies, the concept of an appropriate scale has attracted continuing debate in Western developed economies. While considerable research has been undertaken to investigate links between size of production units and indices of efficiency, effectiveness and profitability (e.g. Reijnders and Verstappen, 2003), there has been relatively little research into the consequences of size on consumers' evaluations of service outcomes and processes. Among the limited research into consumers' perceptions of small businesses, Uusitalo (2001) found in a study of Finnish grocery shoppers that respondents particularly appreciated personal contacts with staff, which were stronger in smaller stores than larger stores. A related line of enquiry has approached consumers' attitudes to small businesses from an opposite perspective by analysing attitudes towards 'big business'. Some authors have noted a subculture in many societies which holds an attitude against big businesses, which are associated with a range of problems, including increasing world inequality, favouring of the interests of capital over the interests of labour, lack of democratic accountability and a cultural uniformity of output (Klein, 2001; Notes From Nowhere Collective, 2003; Wall, 2005). By implication, small businesses are seen to be less bad.

Small businesses survive and prosper where they are able to exploit the marketing advantages of being small. The following are often cited as key competitive advantages:

- Small businesses generally offer much greater adaptability than larger firms. With less bureaucracy and fewer channels of communications, decisions can be taken rapidly. A larger organization may be burdened with constraints that tend to slow the decision-making process, such as the need to negotiate new working practices with trade union representatives or the need to obtain board of directors' approval for major decisions. As organizations grow, there is an inherent tendency for them to become more risk averse by building in systems of control that make them slower to adapt to changes in their business environment.
- In many service sectors, there are very few economies of scale available to allow larger organizations to become more efficient and dominate a market through lower prices which derive from greater efficiency. Hairdressing and general household decorating services, for example, are likely to lose a lot of their competitive advantage as they grow, for example through higher levels of overheads and lower flexibility, which may put them at a competitive disadvantage in some markets.
- It is also argued that small businesses tend to be good innovators. This comes about through greater adaptability, especially where large amounts of capital are not required. The Internet opened many opportunities for small entrepreneurs to establish novel business formats, and this effect can be seen in the travel agency sector, where it was small businesses that innovated with Web-based sales facilities, and the larger travel agency chains took some time to set up

their own Internet facilities. Small firms can be good innovators where they operate in markets dominated by a small number of larger companies and the only way in which a small business can gain entry to the market is to develop an innovatory service aimed at a small niche.

## In practice: Be my guest

In many sectors, the public perception of large, dominant organizations is contrasted by the reality of domination by a large number of small businesses. This is true of the hospitality and accommodation sector, where, for every large Hilton or Holiday Inn chain, there are probably hundreds of small guest-house owners, bed and breakfast businesses and operators of self-catering accommodation. Small businesses, such as this guest house, manage to hold their own against competition from larger hotel chains for a number of reasons. They generally offer a much more personal and friendly welcome than large chains, especially to guests who tire of the same format of the branded chains. Guest houses have lower overheads, because the owners often do not typically employ any staff and this saving can be passed on as lower prices. Many owners of guest houses would probably not see themselves as being business people at all, but simply earning additional income by taking people into what is, after all, their home. Nevertheless, guest houses cannot afford to be complacent. The growth of low-cost 'budget' hotel chains, such as Premier Inn, has attracted many guests who would otherwise have chosen a guest house on the basis of price. Guest-house owners must also be alert to changing expectations of customers, for example in the range of in-room entertainment equipment.

Figure 8.6 The traditional guest house

## 8.4.2 Small firms' brand strategy

So, should small services businesses even attempt to develop their own brand and, if so, how should they go about doing so? In fact, the term 'brand' may not be recognized by many small businesses who are doing many of the things that brand managers in larger organizations are doing. Even the smallest self-employed plumber would aim to provide a consistent standard of service, seeking repeat business on the basis of the quality of his work, and taking a particular position in his market with respect to such factors as price, types of work undertaken, level of sophistication, area covered, etc. The main difference is that instead of talking about developing a strong brand, he would be developing his personal reputation, expressed through his consistency and association with particular types of services.

Small businesses which have developed low-profile brands may appeal to segments of buyers that seek the experience of surprise, rather than the monotony of standardized branded chain output. An example of this can be seen in the hotel sector, where Albazzaz et al. (2003) described a shift from traditional large hotel chains to small hotels. They noted that 'a small but growing contingent of travellers, grown tired of staying in large personality-free hotels geared towards a mass audience, has begun to migrate towards a new, more intimate breed of hotel' (2003, p. 4), and that such consumers are looking for something new and 'seek out properties that are noticeably different in look and feel from branded hotels, choosing an element of surprise over the more straightforward values of consistency, comfort and convenience' (2003, p. 4). One consequence of

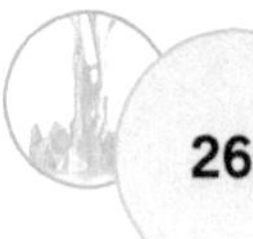



this has been the development and popularity of two formats of small hotel – 'boutique' hotels and 'town house' hotels. Boutique hotels have been defined as having individual design and being smaller than 50 rooms (Drewer, 2005, p. 6) and having unique character; a personal touch; homely feel and high quality standards (McIntosh and Siggs, 2005). The growth in popularity of these hotels has been attributed to growth in the segment of consumers 'searching for authenticity and personalised experiences, rather than simply viewing the hotel as accommodation' (Drewer, 2005, p. 6).

Such apparent risk-taking behaviour by consumers may appear to be contrary to an important function of branding which is to improve consistency of a product or service process, and thereby increase the predictability of what a consumer will actually receive (de Chernatony et al., 2010). The literature on small hotels implies that consumers may gain benefit through the surprise of idiosyncratic features that do not conform to a tightly specified brand blueprint.

Whether a buyer chooses a small rather than a large hotel may be based on differences in evaluation criteria. A branded hotel gives a buyer security and familiarity (Freund de Klumbis and Munsters, 2005). However, Sasse and Harwood-Richardson note that while hotel buyers may have confidence in 'predictable branded hotel products offered by larger hotel chains', they are more likely to rely on 'reputation shaped by customers' satisfaction and word-of-mouth communication' in the case of smaller independent hotels (Sasse and Harwood-Richardson, 1996, p. 31).

Another issue is that small businesses can survive and prosper not by using their own brand, but by linking it to the brand of a franchise or a voluntary consortium. The principles of franchising were discussed in Chapter 4 where it was noted that franchising allowed a franchisor to expand rapidly using the enthusiasm and capital of franchisees, who are often (but certainly not always) small businesses. This is an attractive route for an entrepreneur seeking to set up in business, because the failure rate for franchisees is much lower than for small businesses in general. An important reason for this relatively low failure rate is the existence of a previously proven brand which an entrepreneur is buying into, rather than risking their investment in a new and previously unknown brand.

Returning to the example of the hotel sector, many of the world's major hotel brands are effectively series of small (and sometimes not so small) businesses operating under a franchise owner's brand name. US hotel brands and international hotel brands headquartered in the USA have increasingly evolved away from being hotel-operating companies to being brand management and franchise administration organizations. A hotel consortium is another variation on the idea of a small business operating under the umbrella of a bigger brand, although in this case control of the brand is in the hands of co-operating consortium members rather than a single brand owner. Many European hotels are too small, idiosyncratic in their design, or in the wrong location to be accepted as a franchise, therefore membership of a hotel consortium may be a more appropriate option. As an example, in Switzerland, it is reported that whereas only 8 per cent of hotels belong to corporate or franchised chains, 27 per cent are affiliated to a collaborative brand (Marvel, 2003).

## Case study

### How far can the Tesco brand be stretched?

Tesco is widely recognized as a very successful brand. In 2012, it was estimated by Verdict Research that Tesco accounted for £1 in every £8 of all consumers' retail spending in the UK, derived not just from its core supermarkets, but also through sales of insurance, personal finance, telephone and energy services. Having achieved success in the UK, it had turned its attention to world markets, with retail operations stretching from Eastern Europe to the Far East and the USA. Part of the explanation for the company's continued successful growth has been the development of a strong trusted brand, and an ability to apply this to emerging service sectors. But its brand has not worked in all markets it has entered, most notably the United States where in 2013 it was forced to write off £1.3 billion in its failed 'Fresh and Easy' convenience store development.

Like most large and successful service-based organizations, Tesco started small, being founded shortly after the First World War when Jack Cohen left the Flying Corps with just £30 of capital available to him. He invested most of this in the bulk purchase of tins of surplus war rations, which he then sold from a barrow in the street markets of London. At first, he was selling a generic commodity product and branding had no significant role to play. Over time, Cohen appreciated the need to differentiate his tea from that of his competitors and adopted the name Tesco – derived by taking the first two letters of his own surname and prefixing it with the initials of the owner of the tea-importing business from which he bought his tea – T E Stockwell.

The Tesco brand name became particularly important to Cohen when he expanded beyond his single market barrow. He initially acted as a wholesaler to other traders, then opened his first shop in Tooting, London, before going on to open further shops. In 1947, Tesco became a public company and the money provided by the sale of shares was used to develop larger stores, in particular the new style of self-service store that was modelled on the American example, and which proved increasingly successful for Tesco. The company had developed its own brand in a number of product areas, such as tea and dairy products, but still relied on selling other manufacturers' products. In the 1950s, the power of a retailer to influence the decision of customers was being reduced with the development of mass media aimed at the final consumer, particularly following the introduction of commercial television. Retailers increasingly became dispensers of manufacturers' branded goods, which buyers specifically sought out, rather than relying on the persuasion of the retailer.

In this environment, Tesco aimed to make manufacturers' branded goods available to consumers at the lowest possible price and its brand message became 'pile it high and sell it cheap'. The main constraint on offering lower prices was the existence of Resale Price Maintenance, which allowed manufacturers to control the price at which their products were sold to the public by retailers. The abolition of Resale Price Maintenance in 1964 was to be extremely beneficial to Tesco's business strategy, in which low prices were a key element of its marketing. It was only from the 1980s that the power of UK retailer brands really came to match the power of manufacturers, with the emergence of five very large retailers in the grocery sector. It then became more important to manufacturers that they should have access to Tesco's shelf space than for Tesco to have access to a particular manufacturer's branded products. Throughout the 1990s, Tesco carefully nurtured its brand, increasingly identifying with a number of good causes, for example lead-free petrol and educational charities. The company also had a comprehensive corporate social responsibility agenda, and went out of its way to present itself as a good citizen.

By 1997, Tesco PLC had overtaken Sainsbury's for the distinction of being the largest grocery retailer in the UK, and by the year ending April 2013 operated 6700 stores in 12 countries worldwide, with total profits of £3.5 billion. In order to grow, the Tesco brand had to offer some unique advantage over its competitors. In the early days this was based on low price, and this price orientation was emphasized above all else as late as 1977, when Tesco initiated a price-cutting war among the major supermarkets. More recently, Tesco has additionally sought to differentiate its brand by offering a better quality of service, in terms of the facilities available instore, the products sold and the relationships it builds with customers.

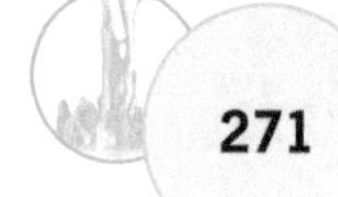



It seemed that the Tesco brand had become an unstoppable juggernaut, as the company developed new store formats with separate sub-brands – Tesco Extra for very large out-of-town stores selling a wide range of non-food items and Tesco Metro stores for convenience shopping in town centres. Tesco Online was launched in 2001 and soon became one of the biggest online retail operation in Britain. Tesco realized that customers who trust its brand for their weekly shopping are also likely to trust it with a wide range of other services. It has therefore developed a range of banking, insurance, telephone and energy services that appeal to customers who trust the Tesco brand and who, when faced with a confusing range of service providers, look first to those organizations that they know and trust. To facilitate the task of encouraging customers to spend more of their total expenditure with the company, Tesco has developed various communication vehicles that allow it to understand individual customers' needs better, so that customers receive well-targeted offers that are of immediate relevance. The company was a trailblazer with its 'Club Card' loyalty programme, which gives customers rewards proportionate to their expenditure, but, more importantly, gives Tesco valuable information about individual customers' demographics and spending patterns. It has also developed narrowly targeted services aimed at particular groups, for example a mother and baby club for young mothers and an online dietary advice service.

The company has realized that although having 12 per cent of overall consumer expenditure in the UK is impressive, there are clearly limits to growth at home. It has therefore been active in extending its brand to overseas countries, through a combination of new start-up businesses, joint ventures and acquisitions. By 2013, the company had operations in 12 overseas markets, including the USA, six countries in Europe, and five in Asia. In India, the company had been thwarted in its attempts to open conventional retail stores because of government restrictions on foreign ownership of retailers, but demonstrated its resolve to serve the Indian market by opening its first wholesale cash and carry store in 2010, and developing a franchise agreement with the retail arm of Tata to help Tata develop its Star Bazaar hypermarkets. The company has often had to fight to get access to foreign markets and when it has entered its brand has not always been as well received as back home. In some markets, it has had to start with very little or no brand recognition, and in the highly competitive American market, Tesco developed a new 'Fresh and Easy' brand, but ultimately the resources of Tesco and its understanding of the US market were not enough to bring about a successful development and its American venture was abandoned in 2013.

Back in the UK, could Tesco become too powerful and the brand suffer because of negative connotations that market dominators often attract? When Tesco announced record profits of £3.8 billion in 2011, the company talked down its profit prospects for the year ahead and seemed to go out of its way to avoid antagonizing the apparently growing number of people who resented the 'Tescoization' of Britain. The company had already had skirmishes with farmers' groups over the low price that Tesco was accused of paying farmers for their milk and the large mark-up that Tesco applied when it resold that same milk to customers. Environmental campaigners had protested that the company's trucks unnecessarily transported goods around the country, so that potatoes grown by a farmer just a few miles away from a Tesco store could travel hundreds of miles between distribution centres before they ended up in that store. There were suspicions that Tesco was trying to distort competition by holding large 'land banks', which prevented new store developments by competitors. The company had upset small shopkeepers, who felt threatened by Tesco's move into the convenience store sector, following its acquisition of the One Stop chain and the development of its Tesco 'Express' format. Even government agencies seemed apparently resigned to being 'bullied' by Tesco. It was reported that in one town in northern England, the company built a new store that was larger than it had been given planning permission for, but the local authority baulked at the prospect of spending large amounts of local taxpayers' money fighting the best lawyers that Tesco could afford. At the same time, the authority apparently felt no such qualms about coming down heavily on a small retailer which had installed shutters on the front of its store without permission. It also seemed that Tesco's customers in its UK market were questioning its supremacy. In 2012, a survey of 11,292 people by the consumer magazine *Which?* gave the store low marks for its pricing, store environment, quality of fresh produce and customer service, and *Which* believed the supermarket was not doing enough to help shoppers on tight budgets (*Which?*, 2013).

One of the problems for companies that have reached a dominant position is that there may be nothing in their history that has prepared their senior management for it. Nowadays, it seems that when a company becomes market leader, it not only has to worry about being resented because of its size – it also stands a good chance of being targeted by anti-globalization protesters, the green lobby and labour activists, as well as government regulators, among others. Tesco has caught the attention of the UK Competition Commission, reflecting growing government concern about companies with dominant market positions. Senior managers, who have spent their working lives learning how to manage and grow their business, are increasingly required to become politicians, a role requiring a different set of skills and for which they may be ill-suited. Faced with the 'curse of growth', companies can throw money at the problem by hiring armies of PR people, reputation management consultancies who may try to defuse criticism and protect the brand through a corporate social responsibility agenda. But, better still, they could avoid such problems in the first place by acting as 'good citizens' in the eyes of key stakeholder groups.

### Case study review questions

1 Critically assess the factors that explain the successful development of the Tesco brand.
2 If large dominant companies such as Tesco really are seen as bullying, manipulative operators, how do you explain their continuing popularity with customers in a fiercely competitive market environment? Is it in the public interest that successful companies should be able to grow to a point where they dominate a market?
3 Discuss the different challenges and opportunities for brand building that Tesco is likely to face as it enters new overseas markets.

## Summary and links to other chapters

Brand development goes to the heart of marketing strategy, and services organizations' decisions concerning many different aspects of their marketing strategy have effects on brand development and maintenance. We saw in Chapter 6 how a strong brand helps buyers choose between what might seem to be otherwise similar service offers, and can help to reduce their perceptions of risk. Providing a consistent standard of service is a key element of a brand, and in Chapter 9 we will define service quality and discuss how firms use consistent standards of quality to develop a brand position. Brand values must be communicated to both current and potential customers and, in Chapter 13, we will explore communication aspects of a brand, including crisis management, where a catastrophic service failure threatens to undermine the perception of a brand. Finally, in Chapter 14 we will look at the additional challenges and opportunities facing service companies when they seek to take their brands to overseas markets.

### Chapter review questions

1 Critically assess the role of brands for services organizations, using examples from a service sector of your choice.
2 Discuss the factors that might influence the positioning strategy of a regional chain of bars.
3 Critically examine the marketing advantages and disadvantages of small- and large-scale service providers in either the hospitality sector or the provision of local bus services.

## Activities

1 Examine the branding strategy used by banks or financial services organizations with which you are familiar. Critically examine the message that is communicated by the brand. Which market segments is a brand particularly addressing? Are there any important segments that may be alienated by the brand message? To what extent has a service provider used brands and sub-brands to segment its market?

2 Examine the restaurants in your area. What criteria would you use to define the market position of a restaurant? Now try using a position map to define the brand position of restaurants in your area.

3 Take one of the following service sectors: hotels/guest houses; solicitors; coffee shops/snack bars; opticians. Undertake an audit of all service providers in your area, noting whether they are independent businesses or part of a larger chain. Critically assess the strengths and weaknesses of different sizes of organization in terms of their marketing capabilities.

## Key terms

**Brand** A distinctive identity comprising a name, logo, slogan and/or design scheme that distinguishes a service from other services and conveys expectations about the service.

**Economies of scale** Unit costs decrease as output/throughput increases.

**Position in the marketplace** How one service compares in its marketplace in terms of relevant customer-focused criteria.

**Small and medium-sized enterprise (SME)** There are various criteria for size (relative and absolute) used to define 'small and medium'.

**Web 2.0** A term often used to describe an Internet environment in which peer-to-peer communication is just as important as business-to-consumer communication.

## Selected further reading

*The following provide a general and authoritative introduction to the principles of branding and how brands work:*

**Aaker, D.** (2010) *Building Strong Brands*, Simon and Schuster, New York.

**Brakus, J.J., Schmitt, B.H. and Zarantonello, L.** (2009) 'Brand experience: what is it? How is it measured? Does it affect loyalty?', *Journal of Marketing*, 73, 52–68.

**De Chernatony, L.** (2010) *From Brand Vision to Brand Evaluation*, 3rd edn, Elsevier, Oxford.

**Kapferer, J.-N.** (2008) *The New Strategic Brand Management: Creating and Sustaining Brand Equity Long Term*, Kogan Page, London.

*For further discussion of the application of general branding principles to services in particular, refer to the following:*

**Brodie, R.J., Whittome, J.R.M. and Brush, G.J.** (2009) 'Investigating the service brand: a customer value perspective', *Journal of Business Research*, 62, 345–55.

**De Chernatony, L. and Cottam, S.** (2006) 'Why are all financial services brands not great?', *Journal of Product and Brand Management*, 15 (2), 88–97.

**Pina, J.M., Martinez, E., Chernatony, L. de and Drury, S.** (2006) 'The effect of service brand extensions on corporate image: an empirical model', *European Journal of Marketing*, 40 (1/2), 174–97.

**Stride, H. and Lee, S.** (2007) 'No logo? No way: branding in the not-for-profit sector', *Journal of Marketing Management*, 23 (1/2), 107–22.

*The following provide a useful review of the role of small businesses and their marketing advantages and challenges in the services sector:*

**Bridge, S., O'Neill, K. and Martin, F.** (2012) *Understanding Enterprise, Entrepreneurship and Small Business*, 4th edn, Palgrave Macmillan, Basingstoke.

**Down, S.** (2010) *Enterprise, Entrepreneurship and Small Business*, Sage, London.

**Joyner, M.** (2009) *Integration Marketing: How Small Businesses Become Big Businesses and Big Businesses Become Empires*, John Wiley, London.

*The role of brands in motivating internal employee audiences within services organizations is explored in the following:*

**De Chernatony, L. and Cottam, S.** (2006) 'Internal brand factors driving successful financial services brands', *European Journal of Marketing*, 40 (5/6), 611–33.

## References

**Albazzaz, A., Birnbaum, B., Brachfeld, D., Danilov, D., Kets de Vries, O. and Moed, J.** (2003) *Lifestyles of the Rich and Almost Famous: The Boutique Hotel Phenomenon in the United States*, High Tech Entrepreneurship and Strategy Group Project, Insead Business School, Fontainebleau.

**Barclays Bank** (2013) 'Entrepreneurs in numbers', available at http://www.barclays.co.uk/BusinessBankAccounts/Entrepreneursinnumbers/P1242621930322 (accessed 18 July 2013).

**BIS** (2013) *Small Business Survey*, Department for Business, Innovation and Skills, London.

**Brady, M.K., Bourdeau, B.L. and Heskel, J.** (2005) 'The importance of brand cues in intangible service industries: an application to investment services', *Journal of Services Marketing*, 19 (6), 401–10.

**Cova, B.** (1997) 'Community and consumption – towards a definition of the "linking value" of product or services', *European Journal of Marketing*, 31 (3/4), 297–316.

**Croft, M.** (2008) 'Consumers in control', *Marketing Week*, 31 (14), 29–30.

**De Chernatony, L., Mcdonald, M. and Wallace, E.** (2010) *Creating Powerful Brands*, 4th edn, Butterworth-Heinemann, Oxford.

**Drewer, P.** (2005) *Key Note Market Report Plus, 2005: Hotels*, 20th edn., Key Note, Hampton, available at www.keynote.co.uk (accessed November 2005).

**Forrester** (2013) *The Mobile Mind Shift Index*, Forrester Research, Cambridge, MA.

**Freund de Klumbis, D. and Munsters, W.** (2005) 'Developments in the hotel industry: design meets historic properties', available at http://fama2.us.es:8080/turismo/turismonet1/economia%20del%20turismo/hosteleria/development%20in%20the%20hotel%20industry.pdf (accessed 8 July 2013).

**Gardner, B.B. and Levy, S.J.** (1955) 'The product and the brand', *Harvard Business Review*, 33 (2), 33–9.

**Hitwise** (2008) 'The impact of social networking in the UK', available at www.bergenmediaby.no/admin/ressurser/QCetFnO$_11_Social_Networking_Report_2008.pdf (accessed 2 April 2009).

**Interbrand** (2012) *Best Global Brands Annual Report 2012*, Interbrand, New York.

**Klein, N.** (2001) *No Logo*, Flamingo, London.

**Knox, S. and Freeman, C.** (2006) 'Measuring and managing employer brand image in the service industry', *Journal of Marketing Management*, 22 (7), 695–716.

**Krishnan, B.C. and Hartline, M.D.** (2001) 'Brand equity: is it more important in services?', *Journal of Services Marketing*, 15 (5), 328–42.

**Marvel, M.** (2003) 'Hotel chain penetration in Europe: understanding the European Hotel Market', *EHLITE*, 4, 12–14.

**McIntosh, A.J. and Siggs, A.** (2005) 'An exploration of the experiential nature of "boutique accommodation"', *Journal of Travel Research*, 44 (1), 74–81.

**McNair, M.P.** (1958) 'Significant trends and developments in the post-war period', in A.B. Smith (ed.), *Competitive Distribution in a Free High Level Economy and its Implications for the University*, University of Pittsburgh Press, Pittsburgh, PA.

**Miniard, P.W. and Cohen, J.B.** (1983) 'Modeling personal and normative influences on behavior', *The Journal of Consumer Research*, 10 (2), 169–80.

**Moschis, G.P.** (1976) 'Social comparison and informal group influence', *Journal of Marketing Research*, 13 (3), 237–44.

**Muniz, A.M. and O'Guinn, T.C.** (2001) 'Brand community', *Journal of Consumer Research*, 27 (4), 412–32.

**Munson, J.M. and Spivey, W.** (1981) 'Product and brand-user stereotypes among social classes', *Journal of Advertising Research*, 21 (4), 37–46.

**Notes From Nowhere Collective** (2003) *We Are Everywhere: The Irresistible Rise of Global Anticapitalism*, Verso, London.

**Oliver, R.W.** (2000) 'New rules for global markets', *Journal of Business Strategy*, 21 (3), 7–9.

**O'Malley, G.** (2009) 'Study: Gen Y notices social net ads, but claim irrelevance', *Online Media Daily*, available at www.mediapost.com/publications/article/101409/#axzz2Yj8rkX9m (accessed 8 July 2013).

**Parsa, H.G., Self, J.T., Njite, D. and King, T.** (2005) 'Why restaurants fail', *Cornell Hotel and Restaurant Administration Quarterly*, 46 (3), 304–22.

**Reijnders, W. and Verstappen, P.** (2003) *SME en Marketing*, Kluwer, Amsterdam.

**Sasse, M. and Harwood-Richardson, S.** (1996) 'Influencing hotel productivity', in N. Johns (ed.), *Productivity Management in Hospitality and Tourism*, Cassell, London.

**Schumacher, E.F.** (1999) *Small Is Beautiful: A Study of Economics as if People Mattered*, Point Roberts, Wash, Hartley and Marks Publishers, Vancouver.

**Sherry, J.F.** (1998) 'The soul of the company store: Nike Town Chicago and the emplaced brandscape', in J.F. Sherrry (ed.), *Servicescapes: The Concept of Place in Contemporary Markets*, NTC Business Books, Lincolnwood, IL.

**Shostack, G.L.** (1987) 'Service positioning through structural change', *Journal of Marketing*, 51 (1), 34–43.

**Solomon, M.** (1983) 'The role of products in social stimuli: a symbolic interactionism perspective', *Journal of Consumer Research*, 10 (Dec.), 319–29.

**The Group** (2013) *FTSE 100 Social Media Index*, available at http://www.the-group.net/336-resources-:-social-media-index (accessed 18 July 2013).

**Uusitalo, O.** (2001) 'Consumer perceptions of grocery retail formats and brands', *International Journal of Retail & Distribution Management*, 29 (5), 214–25.

**Wall, D.** (2005) *Babylon and Beyond: The Economics of Anti-Capitalist, Anti-Globalist and Radical Green Movements*, Pluto Press, London.

**Which?** (2013) *Best and Worst Supermarkets*, Which?, London.

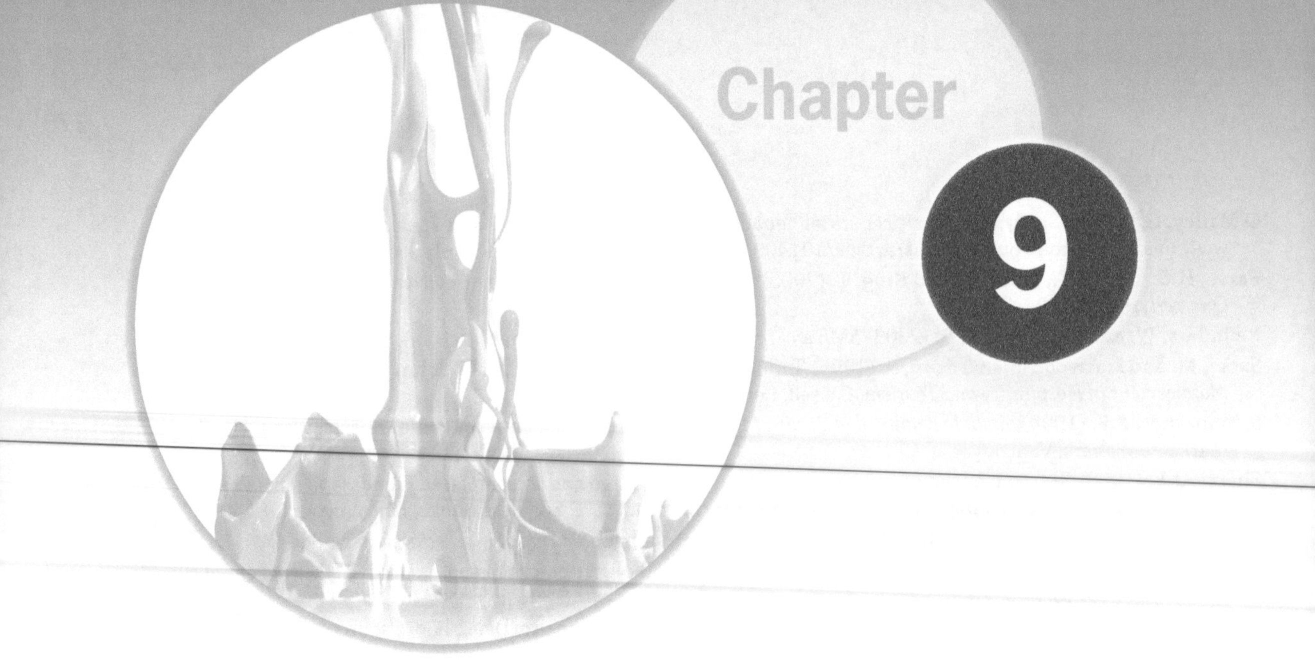


# Service quality

*You may have looked through one of the many 'league tables' of university rankings to choose where to study. But you may have come away very confused when you find that the same university has different positions in different tables. Then you begin to wonder what the league tables are measuring anyway. What does quality mean in this context? Who measured it? How was it measured? Do these measures specifically have any relevance to me? You have started your journey into the complex world of understanding service quality, which is explored in this chapter.*

## Learning objectives

After reading this chapter, you should understand:

- The importance of service quality in the service–profit chain
- Linkages between the concepts of service quality, satisfaction and value
- Major paradigms for the study of service quality – performance-only measures, disconfirmation models and importance–performance approaches
- Methods used to research consumers' expectations of service quality and to monitor the quality of service performance
- Methods used to set standards of service quality

## 9.1 Introduction

The subject of service quality has aroused considerable recent interest among business people and academics. Of course, buyers have always been concerned with quality, but the increasingly competitive market for many services has led consumers to become more selective in the services they choose. Conceptualizing quality for services is more complex than for goods and this chapter reviews conceptual frameworks for evaluating service quality. Because of the absence of tangible manifestations, measuring service quality can be difficult and this chapter discusses possible research approaches. Comprehensive models of service quality are discussed and their limitations noted. Understanding just what dimensions of quality are important to customers in their evaluation process can be more difficult than is usually the case with goods – services can be mentally as well as physically intangible, making it more difficult for companies to understand the expectations against which consumers evaluate a service. A further problem in defining service quality lies in the importance that customers often attach to the quality of the service provider as distinct from its service offers – the two cannot be separated as easily as in the case of goods. As well as discussing conceptual issues about the measurement of service quality, this chapter explores how companies set quality standards and implement programmes of quality management.

## 9.2 Defining service quality

Quality is an extremely difficult concept to define in a few words. In fact, the term has only become widely used in a business context in the past 50 years or so. That is not to say that the underlying concept of quality has not been of historic importance – instead, the term 'value' was more likely to have encompassed what we now describe as 'quality'. A product that provides a high level of consumption benefits relative to costs could be said to be of relatively high value. Discussion of quality as a significant business concept in its own right really began in the early post-Second World War period in the context of manufacturing processes, with advocates such as Deming focusing attention on the need to measure, monitor and rectify deviations from predetermined levels of process performance. Discussion of quality was influenced by a philosophy of 'conforming to requirements' (Crosby, 1984). This implies that organizations must establish requirements and specifications and, once these have been established, the quality goal of the various functions of an organization is to comply strictly with these specifications. However, the questions remain: whose requirements and whose specifications? A second series of definitions therefore state that quality is all about fitness for use (Juran, 1982), a definition based primarily on satisfying customers' needs. These two definitions can be united in the concept of customer-perceived quality – quality can only be defined by customers and occurs where an organization supplies goods or services to a specification that satisfies their needs. Goods and services share much of the conceptual underpinning of quality. However, services tend to pose much greater problems in understanding customers' needs and expectations, which form the basis for evaluation. Inseparability implies consumer–producer co-production of a service and, therefore, consumers must often assume some responsibility for the quality of the service that they receive through a process of co-creation – something that is unusual for manufacturing companies. Finally, the intangibility and complexity of many service processes can make measurement of quality much more difficult than for manufactured goods.

Many analyses of service quality have attempted to distinguish between objective measures of quality (often derived from manufacturing-sector approaches) and measures that are based on the more subjective perceptions of customers (a significant contribution of the services quality literature). Grönroos (1984a) distinguished between 'technical' and 'functional' quality. Technical quality refers to the relatively quantifiable aspects of a service that consumers receive in their interactions with a service firm. Because it can easily be measured by both customer and supplier, it forms an important basis for judging service quality. Examples of technical quality include the waiting time at a supermarket checkout and the reliability of train services. This, however, is not the only element that makes up perceived service quality. Because services involve direct consumer–producer interaction, consumers are also influenced by *how* the technical quality is delivered to

Figure 9.1 Consumers' perception of technical and functional quality applied to an optician's practice. (Based on Grönroos, 1984b)

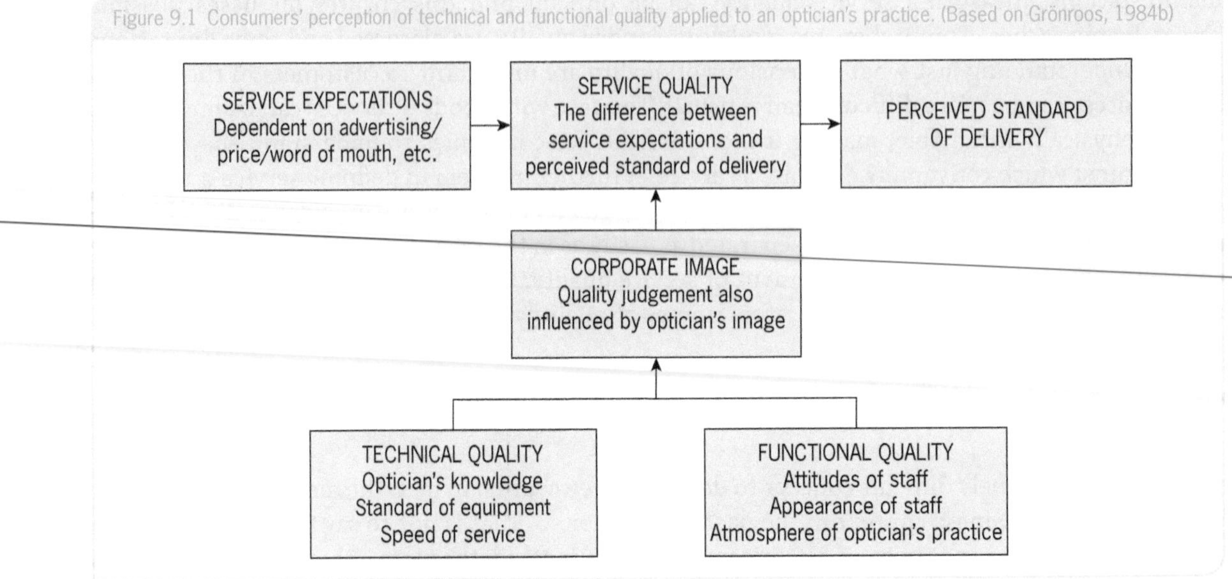


them. This is what Grönroos describes as **functional quality** and cannot be measured as objectively as the elements of technical quality. In the case of the queue at a supermarket checkout, functional quality is influenced by such factors as the environment in which queuing takes place and consumers' perceptions of the manner in which queues are handled by the supermarket's staff. Grönroos also sees an important role for a service firm's corporate image in defining customers' perceptions of quality, with corporate image being based on both technical and functional quality. Figure 9.1 illustrates diagrammatically Grönroos's conceptualization of service quality as applied to an optician's practice.

If quality is defined as the extent to which a service meets customers' requirements, the problem remains of identifying just what those requirements are. The general absence of easily understood criteria for assessing quality makes articulation of customers' requirements and communication of the quality level on offer much more difficult than is the case for goods. Service quality is a highly abstract construct, in contrast to goods where technical aspects of quality predominate. Many conceptualizations of service quality therefore begin by addressing the abstract expectations that consumers hold in respect of quality. Consumers subsequently judge service quality as the extent to which perceived service delivery matches up to these initial expectations. In this way, a service that is perceived as being of mediocre standard may be considered of high quality when compared against low expectations, but of low quality when assessed against high expectations. Much research remains to be done to understand the processes by which expectations of service quality are formed, and this is discussed later in this chapter.

Analysis of service quality is complicated by the fact that production and consumption of a service generally occur simultaneously, with the process of service production often being just as important as the service outcomes. Traditional goods-dominant views of marketing saw production and consumption as quite separate activities, but more recent interest in service dominant logic (Lusch and Vargo, 2006) and customer co-creation emphasizes customers' involvement in the service production process, so what was hidden from view in manufacturing contexts becomes an important basis for assessing quality in services.

A further problem in understanding and managing service quality flows from the intangibility, variability and inseparability of most services, which result in a series of unique buyer–seller exchanges with no two services being provided in exactly the same way. It has been noted that intangibility and perceived risk affect expectations and, in one study of a long-distance phone service, a bookstore and a pizza-shop service, it was concluded that intangibility had some role in service quality expectations (Bebko, 2000). Managing customers' expectations can be facilitated by means of managing the risks a consumer perceives when buying a particular service.

## 9.2.1 Quality and satisfaction

A review of the literature will reveal that the terms 'quality' and 'satisfaction' are quite often used in a seemingly interchangeable manner. However, while the two concepts are related and appear to merge, there are still gaps in our understanding of them, their relationship to each other and their antecedents and consequences (Gwynne et al., 1999). According to Cronin and Taylor (1992):

> *"the distinction between quality and satisfaction is important to both managers and researchers alike, because service providers need to know whether their objective should be to have consumers who are satisfied with their performance or to deliver the maximum level of perceived service quality."*

Oliver (1997) took the view that satisfaction is 'the emotional reaction following a disconfirmation experience'. Getty and Thompson (1994) defined satisfaction as a 'summary psychological state experienced by the consumer when confirmed or disconfirmed expectations exist with respect to a specific service transaction or experience'. Rust and Oliver (1994) suggested that customer satisfaction or dissatisfaction – a 'cognitive or affective reaction' – emerges as a response to a single or prolonged set of service encounters. Satisfaction is a 'post-consumption' experience that compares perceived quality with expected quality, whereas service quality refers to a global evaluation of a firm's service delivery system (Anderson and Fornell, 1994; Parasuraman et al., 1985). Perceived quality, on the other hand, may be viewed as a global attitudinal judgement associated with the superiority of the service experience over time (Getty and Thompson, 1994). As such, it is dynamic in nature and less transaction specific (Parasuraman et al., 1988).

Not surprisingly, there has been considerable debate concerning the nature of the relationship between the constructs of satisfaction and quality. While the majority of research suggests that service quality is a vital antecedent to customer satisfaction (Cronin and Taylor, 1992; Parasuraman et al., 1985), there is also evidence to suggest that satisfaction may be a vital antecedent of service quality (Bitner, 1990). Regardless of which view is taken, the relationship between satisfaction and service quality is strong when examined from either direction. Satisfaction affects assessments of service quality and assessments of service quality affect satisfaction (McAlexander et al., 1994). In turn, both are vital in helping buyers develop their future purchase intentions. In an empirical study of the relationship between quality and satisfaction, Iacobucci et al. (1995) concluded that the key difference between the two constructs is that quality relates to managerial delivery of the service while satisfaction reflects customers' experiences with that service. They argued that quality improvements that are not based on customer needs will not lead to improved customer satisfaction.

There is a suggestion that consumers are indifferent to levels of quality that fall within their **zone of tolerance** and are motivated by unexpectedly high levels of service quality, which in turn produce 'delight'. There is also evidence that satisfied customers may nevertheless not return to a service provider (Brady and Cronin, 2001). There has been discussion whether some characteristics of a service generate satisfaction in customers while others generate dissatisfaction (Galloway, 1999). The general argument is that the achievement of some standard, or improvement, in an element will generate satisfaction, but its absence, or reduction, will not generate dissatisfaction.

Conversely, the failure to achieve a standard in another element may generate dissatisfaction in the customer, though its presence will not necessarily generate satisfaction and repeat purchase. Traditional survey methodologies are based on assumptions of linearity; that is, they assume consistent returns across all responses. There is, however, some research evidence that indicates that the impact of poor performance may carry a greater consequence than the benefit of excellent performance (or 'customer delight'). Suggestions that word-of-mouth effects from poor performance are many times greater than those resulting from positive performance represents evidence of a possible non-linear effect (Cronin, 2003).

Customers typically judge a service on the basis of only a limited range of attributes, some of which are important in determining satisfaction, while others are not critical to satisfaction but may be sources of dissatisfaction. For a bank, increasing the number of branches may not be a satisfier that encourages a customer to spend more of their budget with that bank. However, a reduction in the number of branches may be a dissatisfier that reduces behavioural intention. In one study of the retail banking sector, it was found that integrity and, to a lesser extent, reliability were dissatisfiers. Consumers behaved as if these were assumed standards that all banks will achieve, and were dissatisfied where a bank failed to achieve them (Johnston, 2001).

## Thinking around the subject: Top of the league table for health service quality – but which league?

Most people might agree that Nike shoes are better quality than Tesco 'Value' shoes, or that Belgian chocolate is better quality than a budget range of chocolate found in a local newsagent's store. But trying to rate the quality of a service can lead to much more diversity of views, and quite alarmingly, even apparently objective methods of evaluation can result in quite different results.

We live in an age of quality league tables which are used to measure everything from the reliability of Internet connection to the performance of schools and hospitals. So how can it be that league tables of quality often give quite different results for the same service?

A spat broke out in the UK health sector in 2009 when 12 NHS hospital trusts in England were described as 'significantly underperforming' according to one report, despite nine of these hospitals recently having been rated as good or excellent by government regulators. The failing hospitals received the lowest score in the annual *Dr Foster Hospital Guide*, which is based on a range of indicators including death rates, infection rates and staffing levels. However, the Care Quality Commission had in the previous month given nine of those trusts 'good' or 'excellent' ratings for their overall performance. Why the difference in ratings?

One cause of variance is the way that composite league tables are made up. There are many bases for evaluating the quality of a hospital, including a wide range of outcomes and processes. These outcomes and processes are not of equal importance, and some people will consider one element of their care to be relatively unimportant, while other people will regard that element as being crucial. So, by taking a standard set of data, different league tables of quality can arrive at very different results just by applying different weightings to the standard data.

A further problem arises where data are based on self-reports by managers themselves. For example, at Alder Hey Children's Hospital, it was reported that hospital managers awarded themselves the maximum score for cleanliness using a self-assessment audit tool. When all of its scores were added up, it was awarded an overall rating of 'excellent' and proceeded to issue a press release describing the hospital as nationally the best in its class. However, just a few weeks later, inspectors from the government's Care Quality Commission arrived unannounced and are reported to have found filthy conditions, with brown running water from taps, mouldy bathrooms and soiled furniture and equipment.

The NHS has focused its efforts on quality-of-service issues and routinely monitors a number of service indicators, for example the waiting time to see a consultant or to have elective surgery undertaken. But even such apparently simple indicators can hide a lot of issues. What does it mean when one consultant has a longer waiting time than another consultant? To many people, a long waiting list may be a sign of a top-rated consultant who is very popular with patients, rather than a failing professional who cannot keep up with the demands put on them. And figures for waiting time can often be manipulated, scrupulously or unscrupulously. For example, some ambulance services have been reprimanded for trying to make their response times appear better than they actually were, by measuring the response time from when an ambulance set out, rather than from when a call for help was received.

Attempts to measure doctors' medical performance are much less developed, with debate about the most appropriate methodologies for assessing the efficacy of an operation or clinical diagnosis. Many medical outcomes cannot be assessed simply on the basis of success/failure, but require more subjective quality-of-life assessments to be taken into account. And even if doctors' performance were to be measured by their medical success, could there be a danger that they would 'cherry pick' patients with good prospects of success, and refuse to treat those more problematic cases where there is less chance of recovery?

Some have argued that putting a lot of quality of service data into the public domain helps politicians to allocate funding and users to make informed choices. But could disaggregated data leave open too many opportunities for quite legitimate manipulation, so that every organization can come top of its own chosen league table?

## 9.3 The service–profit chain

What is the effect on a company's profitability of providing a high quality of service? This is an important question, and has led to extensive research into the financial returns from improving all aspects of an organization's value-creating processes. The idea of improvements in service quality feeding through to increased profitability is best portrayed through the concept of a service–profit chain (Figure 9.2). A number of studies have sought to establish the contribution to profitability made by groups of employees, who trade services internally between each other during the process of delivering a service to external customers (e.g. Paraskevas, 2001).

There is considerable support for a link between improvements in service quality and improvements in financial performance. One study found that customer satisfaction, as measured by the American Customer Satisfaction Index (ACSI), was significantly related to firms' stock market values (Fornell et al., 2006). In a large and wide-ranging empirical study undertaken in the UK, it was found that service providers associated with higher customer satisfaction had a significantly better return on equity than the poorer providers, and this appeared to apply to both small and large organizations (Bates et al., 2003).

A number of studies have sought to establish a link between satisfaction and loyalty. Dick and Basu (1994), in a conceptual paper on loyalty, viewed satisfaction as an antecedent of relative attitude because, without satisfaction, consumers will not hold a favourable attitude towards a brand as compared to other alternatives available, and will therefore not be predisposed to repurchase (Dick and Basu, 1994). The link between customer satisfaction and loyalty has been widely replicated (e.g. Fornell et al., 1996). It was noted in Chapter 6 that it can be much more profitable for companies to retain loyal customers than to recruit new ones to replace lapsed customers.

The opposite of satisfaction – dissatisfaction – has been seen as a primary reason for customer defection or discontinuation of purchase. Zeithaml et al. (1996) suggested that a customer's relationship with a company is strengthened when a customer makes a favourable assessment of the company's service quality and weakened when a customer makes negative assessments. They argued that favourable assessment of service quality leads to favourable behavioural intentions such as 'praise for the company' and expressions of preference for the company over other

Figure 9.2 The service–profit chain. (Adapted from Heskett et al., 1997)

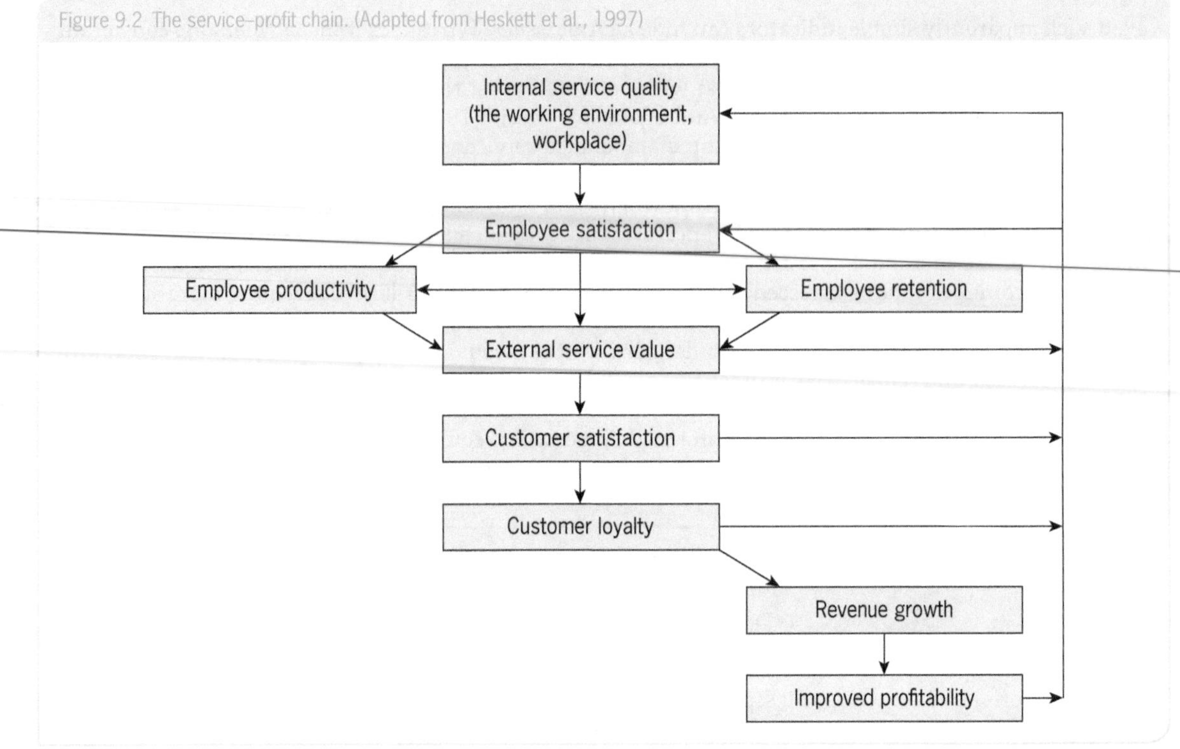


companies. In an earlier study Zeithaml et al. (1990) had reported a positive relationship between service quality and willingness to pay a premium price and to remain loyal even when prices go up.

Much of the research into the outcomes of satisfaction has measured behavioural intentions, for example the likelihood of recommending a service or repurchasing it. However, the dangers of predicting actual behaviour on the basis of intention have been noted (e.g. Newberry et al., 2003). In the light of increasing levels of competition in most services markets, behavioural intention based on loyalty generated through good service can easily be broken. This has been attributed to a number of factors, including greater choice and information available to customers, the 'commoditization' of many categories of services and increased levels of competition. Customers may be 'captive' and therefore repeat purchasing behaviour is unlikely to be influenced in the short term by levels of satisfaction. Any observed loyalty may be what Dick and Basu have described as 'spurious' loyalty. For many buyers, the psychological cost of switching may be perceived as too high and they may therefore be prepared to tolerate high levels of dissatisfaction before a trigger point is reached and they switch. Individuals' perceptions of equity in service encounters have been shown to influence repeat service purchase (Bolton and Lemon, 1999).

Some researchers have pointed out that much of the evidence to support a link between quality and financial performance is anecdotal in nature and refuted by analysis of corporate performance. It is suggested that there is widespread evidence of managers' frustration with the inability of quality improvements to improve organizational performance (Anderson et al., 1994). In a study by Cronin and Taylor (1992) service quality did not appear to have a significant positive effect on intentions to purchase again. Passikoff (1997) cites a Juran Institute study that indicated that fewer than a third of top managers of the USA's largest corporations believed that their customer satisfaction programmes yield any economic benefit. It has been suggested that if firms are not able to demonstrate a link between customer satisfaction and financial performance, then they may abandon the focus on customer satisfaction measurement (Ambler, 2003).

Developments in information technology are offering new insights into the link between quality and financial performance. Large multiple-outlet services organizations are increasingly able to experiment with elements of service quality in test sites and to judge financial performance over time. A fast-food restaurant, for example, may implement a new staff payment system or training programme in a number of 'experimental' sites and be able to identify changes in performance relative to other 'control' branches. Some service providers have disaggregated their information even further by linking service quality questionnaires to features of the service that a respondent actually received. In this way, individual employees or groups of employees can be linked to measures of quality. While information technology, and the use of 'balanced scorecards' (discussed in Chapter 10), is opening up new possibilities for correlating data about inputs and perceived outcomes, the problem of analysing cross-sectional data remains. It is very difficult within a research framework to isolate all of the contributors to customers' perceptions of quality except those in which the researcher is interested. We will return to the issue of rewarding staff in return for performance in Chapter 10.

We saw in Chapter 2 how service providers have often been keen to transfer many traditional face-to-face encounters online, giving rise to issues about the quality of online service. A number of studies have sought to develop frameworks for measuring online service quality, but there is some evidence that overall quality remains strongly affected by face-to-face encounters that are associated with many online transactions (Beatson et al., 2006).

## Thinking around the subject: Customer service cut as credit crunch bites

Does high quality of service pay dividends? According to one study, it does not help to pay bills which urgently need to be paid, and there is evidence that when the business environment gets tough, quality of service is one of the first things to be cut.

A survey carried out in the UK in 2009 by the Institute of Customer Service (ICS) provided gloomy reading. The survey was undertaken at the depths of the 'credit crunch' when many services companies, especially in the retail and financial services sectors, were seeing their profitability severely squeezed. The ICS found that 30 per cent of organizations surveyed had cut investment in customer service training and 21 per cent had laid off customer-facing staff during the previous year. Much of this was incremental, for example cutting the number of checkout staff employed at a supermarket, which might have saved one job out of a rota involving 20 people. The hope might have been that customers would not really notice, but invariarably with less slack in the system, delays are more likely to occur, especially at peak times.

The ICS claimed that cutting back on service standards was counter-productive and pointed to its previous research indicating that companies with a reputation for service excellence and committed front-line staff have a 24 per cent higher net profit margin than same-sector rivals who do not enjoy a similar standing. The ICS also claimed that this translated into the achievement of 71 per cent more profit per employee.

Interestingly, the ICS's survey found that a far smaller proportion of companies – just 6 per cent – had cut their investment in technology. There was evidence that many companies were saving money on staff while redirecting customers to automated services. So instead of making it easy for a customer to speak to a customer service representative on the phone, they might instead be directed to a website and a list of 'frequently asked questions'. There might still be a customer service line, now charged at a 'premium rate' which additionally earned money for the company. Of course technology has a role in improving service quality. But should it be a replacement, or something that runs in parallel with face-to-face contact? More fundamentally, how does a company assess the impact on profitability of changes in its standards of service?

ICS continues to monitor customer satisfaction and its report of July 2013 highlighted big differences between the best sector – retailing – and the worst – utility services (ICS, 2013).

## 9.4 Frameworks for understanding and measuring service quality

Given the complex nature of service quality, it is not surprising that there have been divergent views about the best way to conceptualize and measure it. There are essentially three approaches to conceptualizing and measuring service quality:

- performance-only measures;
- disconfirmation models;
- importance–performance approaches.

These approaches are not mutually exclusive and, in practice, organizations' use of quality measurement methodologies combines elements of more than one approach. Nevertheless, the three approaches provide useful headings for discussing the literature.

### 9.4.1 Performance-only measures

The simplest approach to measuring service quality is to ask customers to rate the performance of a service. In reality, most simple survey forms handed out to customers to provide feedback on service quality ask just a small number of performance-based questions.

Performance-only measures of service quality have their philosophical roots in the quality literature derived from the manufacturing sector. For most manufactured goods, it is possible to define quality in terms of easily measurable criteria, such as the reliability of a car or the quality of gold from which a gold ring is made. It can be argued in this approach that services are not unique in being shaped in consumers' minds by abstract notions of expectations, when many manufactured goods promote an image and hence an expectation against which performance is based. So, by this argument, if performance-only measures are good for the manufacturing sector, they should also be good for the services sector.

Performance-only measures avoid the need to measure customers' expectations of a service. While the idea of defining a service in terms of its expectations may sound good in principle, actually measuring expectations can be difficult. There are conceptual difficulties in defining just what is meant by expectations, with a number of possible levels of expectations. These conceptual problems are discussed in the following section. There is also the practical difficulty of measuring a customer's expectations. Ideally, expectations should be measured before a service has been consumed. However, in reality, this is often not practical, so researchers are likely to record expectations retrospectively. The danger here is that stated expectations may be influenced by subsequent performance of service delivery, making the retrospective measure of expectations fairly meaningless.

Difficulties with conceptualizing expectations led to the development and application of a more direct form of measurement technique in the form of SERVPERF. This approach requires the customer to rate a provider's performance, extending from 1 (strongly disagree) to 5 (strongly agree). The instrument requires the consumer to rate only the performance of a particular service encounter. This eliminates the need to measure expectations, on the grounds that customer expectations change when they experience a service and the inclusion of an expectations measure reduces the content and discriminant validity of the measures (Cronin and Taylor, 1992; McAlexander et al., 1994). Studies conducted using this performance-based measure have found that SERVPERF explains more of the variance in an overall measure of service quality than measures that incorporate expectations. Cronin and Taylor (1994) acknowledged that it is possible for researchers to infer consumers' disconfirmation through arithmetic means (the P 2 E gap) but that 'consumer perceptions, not calculations, govern behaviour'.

## 9.4.2 Disconfirmation approaches

By this approach, a service is deemed to be of high quality when consumers' expectations are confirmed by subsequent service delivery. Because of the emphasis on differences between expectations and perceptions, this type of model is often referred to as a disconfirmation model. Pre-eminent among these is the work of Parasuraman, Zeithaml and Berry, who have been strong advocates of the need for services organizations to learn more about their customers through a rigorous marketing-research-oriented approach that focuses on the expectations and perceptions of customers. They make the point that only customers can judge quality – all other judgements are considered to be essentially irrelevant. They set out to determine what customers expect from services and what the characteristics are which define these services (effectively what is the service in the mind of the customer?). Quality is determined by the difference between what a customer expects and the perceived level of actual performance. These findings have evolved from a set of qualitative marketing research procedures, culminating in the quantitative technique for measuring service quality that is known as SERVQUAL (Parasuraman et al., 1988). The SERVQUAL model has been widely applied.

The SERVQUAL technique can be used by companies to better understand the expectations and perceptions of their customers. It is applicable across a broad range of services industries and can be easily modified to take account of the specific requirements of a company. In effect it provides a skeleton for an investigatory instrument, which can be adapted or added to as needed.

SERVQUAL is based on a generic 22-item questionnaire, which is designed to cover five broad dimensions of service quality that the research team consolidated from their original qualitative investigations. The five dimensions covered, with some description of each and the respective numbers of statements associated with them, is as follows:

- tangibles (appearance of physical elements) 1 to 4
- reliability (dependability, accurate performance) 5 to 9
- responsiveness (promptness and helpfulness) 10 to 13
- assurance (competence, courtesy, credibility, security) 14 to 17
- empathy (easy access, good communications, customer understanding) 18 to 22

Customers are asked to rate the 22 statements relating to their expectations and a perceptions section consisting of a matching set of company-specific statements about service delivery. They are asked in each instance to rate, on a Likert scale from 1 (strongly agree) to 7 (strongly disagree), whether or not they agree with each statement. In addition, the survey asks for any comments that they wish to make about their experiences of the service, and their overall impression of it. Customers are also asked for supplementary demographic data. The contents of a typical questionnaire are shown in Figure 9.3.

Measures of service quality can be derived quite simply by subtracting expectation scores from perception scores. These scores can subsequently be weighted to reflect the relative importance of each aspect of service quality. The outcome from a one-off study is a measure that tells the company whether its customers' expectations are exceeded or not. SERVQUAL results can be used to identify which components of a service the company is particularly good or bad at. It can be used to monitor service quality over time, to compare performance with that of competitors, to compare performance between different branches within a company or to measure general customer satisfaction with a particular service industry.

An organization or industry group can use the information collected in this way to improve its position by acting upon the results and seeking to surpass customers' expectations on a continuous

Figure 9.3 A typical application of the SERVQUAL survey questionnaire, applied here to the hotel sector. This part of the questionnaire records respondents' ratings of service performance. A corresponding section records respondents' expectations for each of these items. (Based on Gabbie and O'Neill, 1997)

| PART B – PERFORMANCE | Strongly disagree ☻ Strongly agree ☺ |
|---|---|
| (1) The hotel has modern-looking equipment | 1...2...3...4...5...6...7 |
| (2) The physical facilities at the local hotel are visually appealing | 1...2...3...4...5...6...7 |
| (3) Staff at the hotel appear neat | 1...2...3...4...5...6...7 |
| (4) Materials associated with the service are visually appealing | 1...2...3...4...5...6...7 |
| (5) When the hotel promised to do something by a certain time, it did it | 1...2...3...4...5...6...7 |
| (6) When patrons have problems, the hotel shows a genuine interest in solving them | 1...2...3...4...5...6...7 |
| (7) The hotel performs the service right the first time | 1...2...3...4...5...6...7 |
| (8) The hotel provides its services at the time it promises to do so | 1...2...3...4...5...6...7 |
| (9) The hotel insists on error-free service | 1...2...3...4...5...6...7 |
| (10) Staff at the hotel were able to tell patrons exactly when services would be performed | 1...2...3...4...5...6...7 |
| (11) Staff at the hotel give prompt service to the patrons | 1...2...3...4...5...6...7 |
| (12) Staff at the hotel are always willing to help patrons | 1...2...3...4...5...6...7 |
| (13) Staff of the hotel are never too busy to respond to patrons | 1...2...3...4...5...6...7 |
| (14) Behaviour of staff at the hotel instils patrons with confidence | 1...2...3...4...5...6...7 |
| (15) Patrons of the hotel feel safe in their transactions | 1...2...3...4...5...6...7 |
| (16) Staff of the hotel are consistently courteous with patrons | 1...2...3...4...5...6...7 |
| (17) Staff of the hotel have the knowledge to answer patrons | 1...2...3...4...5...6...7 |
| (18) The hotel gives patrons individualized attention | 1...2...3...4...5...6...7 |
| (19) The hotel has opening hours convenient to all of its patrons | 1...2...3...4...5...6...7 |
| (20) The hotel has staff who give its patrons personalized attention | 1...2...3...4...5...6...7 |
| (21) The hotel has the patrons' best interest at heart | 1...2...3...4...5...6...7 |
| (22) The staff of the hotel understand the specific needs of its patrons | 1...2...3...4...5...6...7 |

basis. Additionally, the perceptions–expectations results, along with the demographic data, may facilitate effective customer segmentation.

The SERVQUAL methodology identifies five gaps where there may be a shortfall between expectations and perceptions of actual service delivery:

1 *Gap between consumer expectations and management perception.* Management may think that they know what consumers expect and proceed to deliver this, when in fact consumers may expect something quite different.

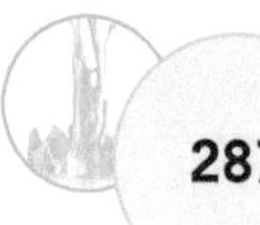



2 *Gap between management perception and service quality specification.* Management may understand what customers expect, but fail to set appropriate quality specifications or may not set them clearly. Alternatively, management may set clear quality specifications but these may not be achievable.

3 *Gap between service quality specifications and service delivery.* Unforeseen problems or poor management can lead to a service provider failing to meet service quality specifications. This may be due to human error but also to mechanical breakdown of facilitating or support goods.

4 *Gap between service delivery and external communications.* There may be dissatisfaction with a service due to the excessively heightened expectations developed through the service provider's communications efforts. Dissatisfaction occurs where actual delivery does not meet up with expectations held out in a company's communications.

5 *Gap between perceived service and expected service.* This gap occurs as a result of one or more of the previous gaps. The way in which customers perceive actual service delivery does not match up with their initial expectations.

The five gaps are illustrated in Figure 9.4, where a hypothetical application to a restaurant is shown.

The gaps model is useful as it allows management to make an analytical assessment of the causes of poor service quality. If the first gaps are great, the task of bridging the subsequent gaps becomes greater, and indeed it could be said that in such circumstances quality service can only be achieved by good luck rather than good management.

Much attention has been given to the processes by which customers' expectations of service quality are formed. Two main standards of expectations emerge. One standard represents the expectation as a *prediction* of future events (Swan and Trawick, 1981). This is the standard typically used in the satisfaction literature. The other standard is a normative expectation of future events, operationalized as either *desired* or ideal expectations. This is the standard typically used in the service-quality literature (Parasuraman et al., 1988).

Zeithaml et al. (1993) have proposed that three levels of expectations can be defined against which quality is assessed:

- the *desired* level of service, reflecting what the customer wants;
- the *adequate* service level, defined as the standard that customers are willing to accept;
- the *predicted* service level – that which they believe is most likely to actually occur.

This has led to the idea that *zones of tolerance* may exist in consumers' perceptions of service quality. If perceptions fall below the desired level of service, this may still be acceptable as long as they do not fall below expectations based on an adequate level of service. In other words, rather than a service either meeting or failing a consumer's quality expectations, there is an intermediate zone of tolerance (see Figure 9.5).

A further problem of using expectations as a benchmark occurs where expectations, as well as being an antecedent comparative benchmark, may also be part of the event that a respondent is assessing. Anticipation of an event has often been recognized as an important consumption benefit, for example in the way that some organizations use queues and waiting time to generate emotions of excitement and anticipation for the main event. For many people, anticipation of Christmas or summer holidays can become just as important as the holidays themselves (Cowley et al., 2005). Expectations can become synonymous with anticipation and excitement, and become part of the perceived service quality.

Disconfirmation models of service quality have been challenged on a number of grounds. One stream of objections holds that absolute measures of performance provide a more appropriate

Figure 9.4 The gaps model: sources of divergence between service quality expectation and delivery. (Modified from Parasuraman et al., 1985)

New restaurant is recommended + Hunger + Pleasant meal at similar restaurant previously

leads to

Expected service of good standard with particular emphasis on relaxing environment

GAP 1 Failure to understand customers' expectations

Management assume that customers require speed of service

GAP 2 Failure to specify appropriate service standard

Management set unachievable target of all food being delivered within 3 minutes of order

GAP 3 Failure to deliver specified service standard

Cold food delivered after 10 minutes

GAP 4 Failure to communicate appropriate service standard

Advertising and publicity imply top-quality food and service

General perception of poor quality of service

GAP 5

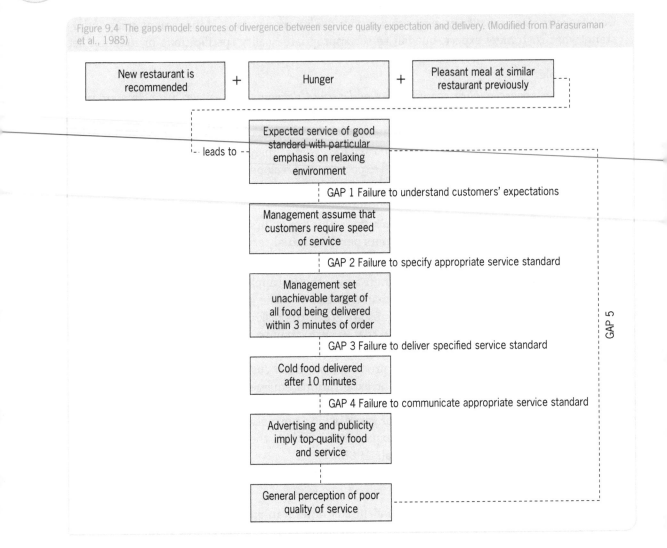

Figure 9.5 Consumers' zones of tolerance for service quality

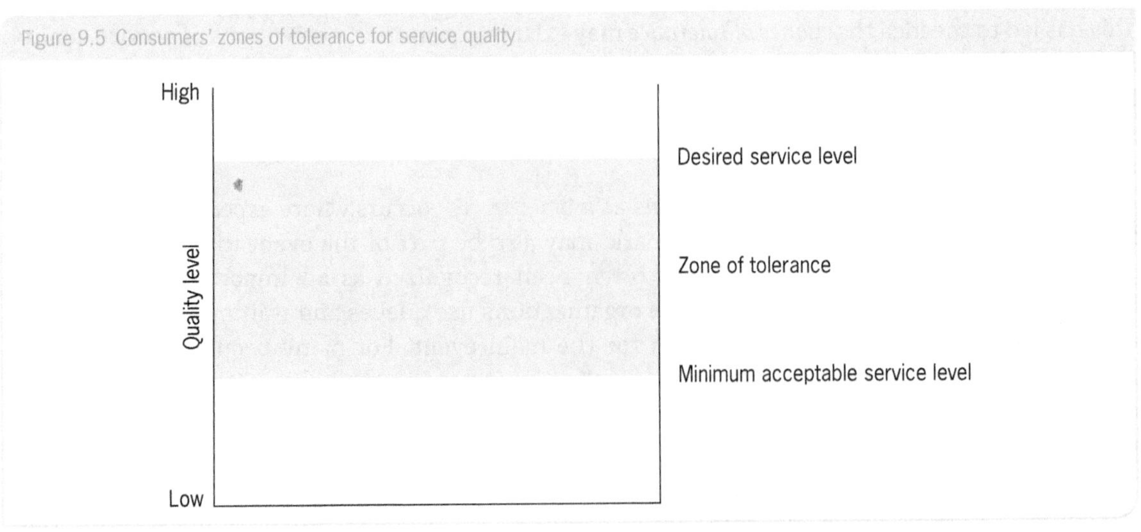

measure of quality than explanations based on disconfirmation models (Cronin and Taylor, 1994). Researchers have asked whether the calculated difference scores (the difference between expectations and evaluation) are appropriate from measurement and theoretical perspectives. Invariably, customers' expectations are measured after consumption of a service, at the same time as they are asked about their perceptions of a service. Should not expectations be based on a respondent's state of mind before consumption, free of influence from actual consumption? There has been debate about whether it is practical to ask consumers about their expectations of a service immediately before consumption and their perceptions of performance immediately after. It has also been suggested that expectations may not exist or be clear enough in respondents' minds to act as a benchmark against which perceptions are assessed (Iacobucci et al., 1995). Furthermore, expectations are only formed as a result of previous service encounters, that is, perceptions feed directly into expectations (Kahneman and Miller, 1986).

From a measurement perspective, there are three psychometric problems associated with the use of difference scores: reliability, discriminant validity and variance restriction problems. A study by Brown et al. (1993) found evidence that these psychometric problems indeed arise with the use of SERVQUAL; they recommend instead use of non-difference score measures, which display better discriminant and nomological validity. However, Parasuraman, Zeithaml and Berry respond by arguing that the alleged psychometric deficiencies of the difference-score formulation are less severe than those suggested by critics. Despite their argument that the difference scores offer researchers better diagnostics than separate measurement of perceptions and expectations, some would argue that there is little evidence to support the relevance of the expectations–performance gap as the basis for measuring service quality and, instead, that there is greater validity in measuring service quality on the basis of simple performance-based measures (Bolton and Drew, 1991; Cronin and Taylor, 1994).

It has been claimed by Parasuraman, Zeithaml and Berry that the five dimensions of quality that form the basis of the SERVQUAL scale items are transferable to most service sectors. However, many studies have failed to replicate the five-factor model. Buttle (1996) questioned the dimensionality of the SERVQUAL construct and argued that the dimensions of SERVQUAL are context specific. This reflects the results of many researchers who have used the SERVQUAL scale and have failed to produce a five-factor solution similar to the universal solution initially proposed by Parasuraman, Zeithaml and Berry. Babakus and Boller (1992) noted that service quality might be complex and multidimensional for some services, but unidimensional for others.

Critics of SERVQUAL have argued that the approach concentrates on service-process dimensions, but not the perceived quality of the service outcomes. While the framework may be useful for measuring quality in a high-involvement, inseparable service such as retail banking, it may be less appropriate to investment management, where customers are likely to be more concerned about investment performance (an outcome) rather than about process issues relating to the items measured by SERVQUAL.

Relatively little attention has been devoted to an understanding of how perceptions are formed and remain stable after consumption. It can be argued that disconfirmation models are flawed because *when* a respondent gives a response relating to their perception of service delivery can be just as important as the actual recorded score, or the level of expectations against which perceptions are compared. For example, a person may have a very negative attitude about a haircut immediately after leaving a hairdresser, but their perceptions of the haircut may become more favourable over time as they get used to it (O'Neill et al., 1998). It could be argued that in terms of understanding behavioural intention, it is the later measure of perceptions that is most useful to management.

Finally, disconfirmation models do not in themselves indicate the importance to a consumer of individual items of quality, although the SERVQUAL methodology has been adapted to incorporate an additional question asking respondents to rate the importance to them of each item. We now turn to importance–performance frameworks.

### 9.4.3 Importance–performance analysis

A weakness of disconfirmation approaches to service quality is their failure to explicitly recognize which items are particularly important to consumers. So, although an individual item of the SERVQUAL scale may show a high level of dissatisfaction, a manager does not have a clear idea whether this failing represents a particularly important aspect of the service offer. Should the manager concentrate on rectifying an item that is showing a high level of dissatisfaction, but which may be quite unimportant to the consumer, or on rectifying an item that shows only marginal levels of dissatisfaction, but may be absolutely crucial to consumers?

Importance–performance analysis (IPA) is a simple and easy-to-use approach that compares the performance of elements of a service with the importance of each of these elements to the consumer (Arbore and Busacca, 2011). The elements that are used to define measurement scales can be derived through exploratory research. In practice, some researchers have used scale items that are very similar to those used in a typical SERVQUAL study. The difference is in the treatment of scores. Instead of calculating a perceptions minus expectations (P – E) score, IPA analysis calculates a performance minus importance (P – I) score. High performance of a relatively important aspect of the service could indicate that management is 'over-delivering' on this aspect of service quality. On the other hand, poor performance of an important item indicates a priority area for management action. The resulting scores for importance and performance can be plotted on a grid (Figure 9.6), with each cell in the grid representing a different course of management action. Particular attention should be given to the extreme observations on the grid since they indicate the greatest disparity between importance and performance.

Importance–performance analysis has been applied within many service sectors, including banking (Joseph et al., 1999), healthcare (Hawes and Rao, 1985), tourism (Murdy and Pike 2012; O'Neill et al., 2002), and education (Wright and O'Neill, 2002; Pike, 2003).

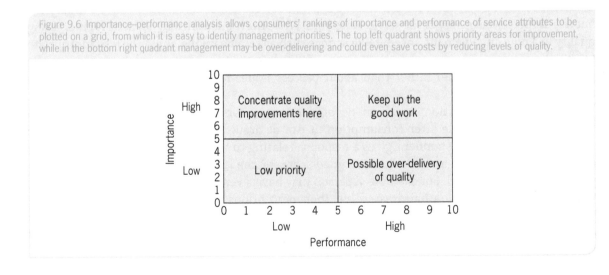

Figure 9.6 Importance–performance analysis allows consumers' rankings of importance and performance of service attributes to be plotted on a grid, from which it is easy to identify management priorities. The top left quadrant shows priority areas for improvement, while in the bottom right quadrant management may be over-delivering and could even save costs by reducing levels of quality.

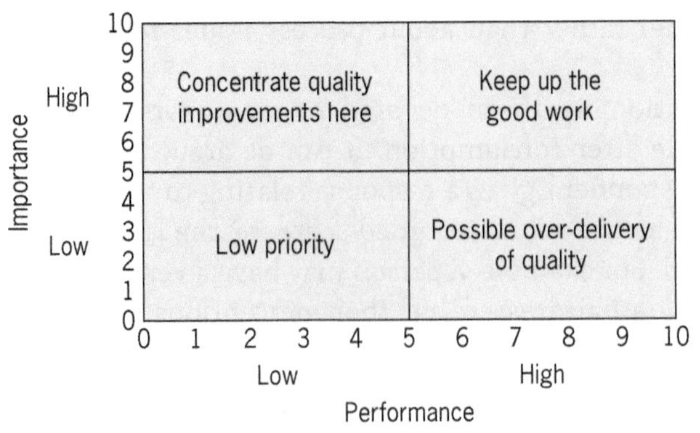

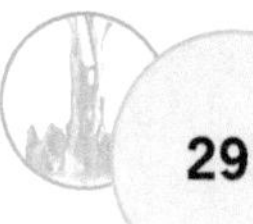



Importance–performance scores are simple to calculate, but their theoretical credibility has been challenged. Bacon (2003) suggested that importance and performance are essentially different constructs and that any measures of difference between them using the same scales 'reflects a "rule of thumb" . . .' guide for action and that attributes that score close to the cross-point on the grid may be overlooked or misinterpreted in terms of an appropriate managerial response for action.

### 9.4.4 Composite models of satisfaction

It should be evident from the previous discussion that there is a diversity of approaches to measuring service quality, and whether a service is deemed to be of good quality or not may be sensitive to the type of framework employed. The fragmentation of approaches has led some to develop integrated frameworks that incorporate a number of the theoretical underpinnings and practical applications described above.

One attempt to integrate various streams was made by Brady and Cronin (2001). Their hierarchical service-quality model comprises three main dimensions: interaction quality; physical environment quality; and outcome quality. Each of these primary dimensions is further divided into a number of sub-dimensions (Figure 9.7). Their model is based on the work of Dabholkar et al. (1996) and derived from qualitative insights and empirical tests. It has the benefit of integrating outcomes

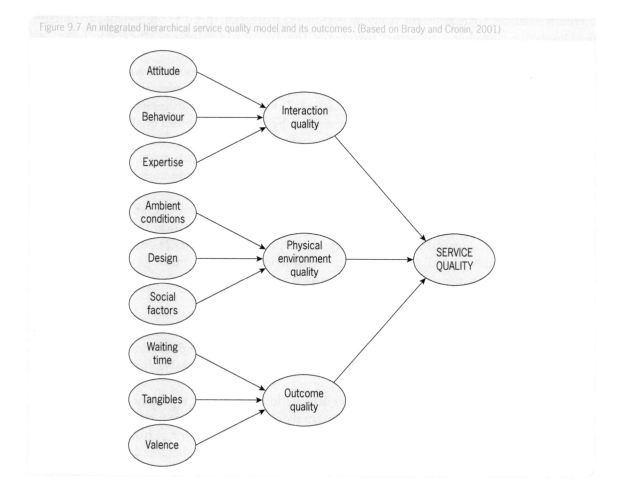

Figure 9.7 An integrated hierarchical service quality model and its outcomes. (Based on Brady and Cronin, 2001)

Figure 9.8 The European Consumer Satisfaction Index (ECSI) model

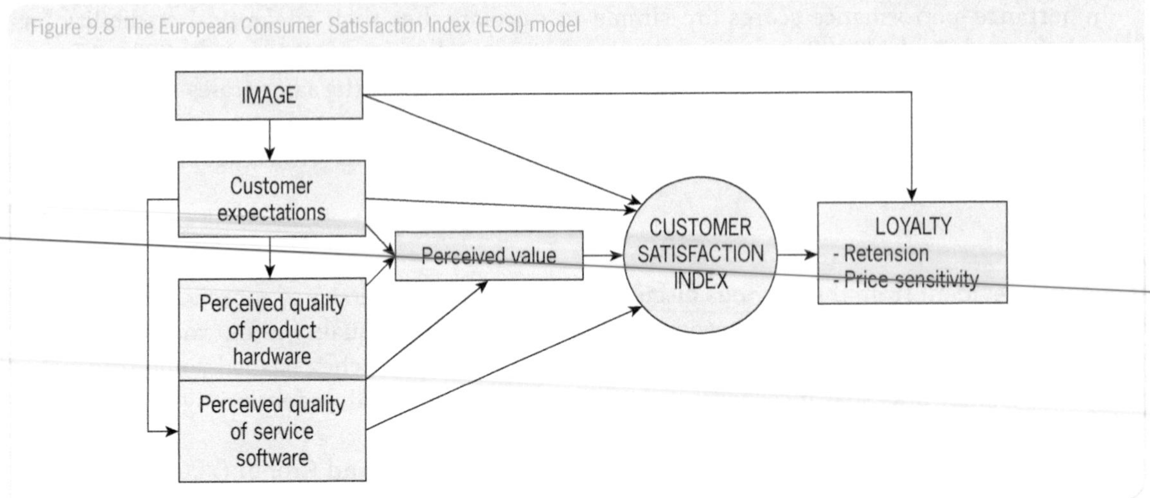


and processes and takes into account not just the actions involved in service processes, but also the general atmosphere in which they take place.

A number of attempts have been made to try to measure customer satisfaction at a national level, to provide a baseline when customer satisfaction is tracked over time. The large number of currently available approaches for studying customer satisfaction includes the Swedish barometer, the Norwegian customer satisfaction barometer, the American Customer Satisfaction Index and more recently the European Customer Satisfaction Index.

The theoretical model for the European Consumer Satisfaction Index (see Figure 9.8) introduces seven interrelated latent variables. The model links image, customer expectations, perceptions of quality and perceived value to customer satisfaction. The model distinguishes between the tangible and intangible contributors to customer satisfaction by dividing perceived quality into two parts – 'software' and 'hardware'. The 'hardware' component refers to the quality of tangible elements of a product, while 'software' relates to associated service such as guarantees given, after-sales service provision, conditions of product display and assortment, documentation and descriptions, opening hours, friendliness of the personnel, etc.

The variables on the left-hand side of the model are causative factors that explain customer satisfaction and those on the right-hand side are indicators of performance. The model shows the main causal relationships, although, in reality, there may exist many more points of dependence between the variables, as well as bi-directional interactions. The theoretical ECSI model used is a structural model, employing a probabilistic approach and using simultaneous-equation estimation techniques.

The ECSI model is much less detailed and elaborate than many standard company-specific approaches to measuring customer satisfaction. This follows from the fact that it has to be equally applicable for a number of different industry sectors. Numerous simplifications and reductions have been introduced in the specification in order to make it as comparable and useful as possible from sector to sector.

Although composite measures of customer satisfaction such as that represented by ECSI may be too general for many services organizations' internal quality-management purposes, these indexes provide an important complement to traditional measures of economic performance, providing useful information not only to the firms themselves, but also to shareholders and investors, government regulators and buyers.

## 9.4.5 From service quality to experience?

The concept of 'customer experience', discussed in Chapter 3, may be seen as a further development in the literature on service quality. You may recall from Chapter 3 that service experience is essentially about consumers' perceptions of the combination of a wide range of cues presented by a service, which may typically comprise:

- the physical environment;
- service-delivery process design;
- relationships between customers and the firm's employees;
- brand associations.

The true benefit of a customer experience may lie in attitudinal outcomes of 'surprise', 'delight' or 'excitement'. The first encounter with a stimulus may be valued more highly because of its novelty, but the stimulus is less likely to be subsequently sought because of its lack of novelty value. Does this imply that service quality will be perceived as lower on subsequent occasions, simply because the hedonistic novelty value is now lower? You may recall from Chapter 3 that the value of customer experience may also derive from the sequencing of different elements of a service process. In the theatre, a musical cannot be assessed by judging the quality of each individual chord, but only by the way that all pieces come together. Similarly, measures of service quality that focus on, say, speed of service and quality of food in a restaurant as two separate measurable dimensions of service quality may overlook a possible perception by customers, for example that waiting may raise a sense of excitement, which is rewarded with a meal that was so good because it took a long time to prepare. Waiting time may be perceived quite differently at different stages of the service process. It is the holistic experience that counts, rather than evaluations of individual components of a service (Chase and Dasu, 2001).

You will recall that a crucial aspect of defining customer experience lies in understanding individuals' emotional states, before, during and after a service process. Narrow, technical measures of service quality may reflect differences in consumers' emotional states as much as differences in the technical performance of a company's service processes. An individual eating in a restaurant for a celebration meal may bring a high level of emotions to their evaluation of service quality, compared with the casual lunchtime diner. Emotions of the celebration diner may be focused on the ambience of the meal, while the lunchtime diner's emotions may be more focused on the consequences of being late for a subsequent meeting, should their meal be delayed.

Is customer experience a measurable phenomenon that can become a managerially useful tool for planning and control purposes? Probably the greatest problem in developing a simple and operationally acceptable measure of customer experience is the complexity of context-specific variables. The discussion above indicated that experience is conditioned by differences between individuals, differences over time in an individual's emotional state and a variety of situation-specific factors. To be of use to managers, a measure of experience must take account of these moderating influences.

A second problem derives from the non-linearity of customer experience. Models of service quality and satisfaction implicitly assume that consumers will prefer outcomes with higher scores on these scales. However, experience is more complex and non-linearity may imply lower cut-off points at which an experience is not recognized, and a higher point beyond which 'more' experience may actually be associated with negative benefits (think of music in a restaurant, which at first is a pleasant experience, but, as the volume goes up, a pleasant experience becomes a negative one). The effects of non-linearity have also been observed in attempts to measure 'flow', defined by

Csikszentmihalyi (1988) as an experiential state 'so desirable that one wishes to replicate it as often as possible'.

A third practical problem in measuring and managing experience derives from the need to incorporate not only contextual parameters, but also the sequencing of events and their retention in the memory in the form of an attitude some time after an event occurred. The standard questionnaire approach, even one using multiple-item scales for measuring underlying constructs, may be inadequate to measure effectively the composition of customer experience. Issues of lengthy questionnaires leading to survey fatigue and unreliable results are well documented (Lee et al., 2000). The effects of attitude change over time, resulting from selective perception, and retention of cues may imply that the timing of administration of a research instrument may be as important as the measurement scales themselves.

Is it worth developing a multidimensional scale for customer experience in the first place? In principle, managers would benefit by being able to see which components of a total customer experience contribute most significantly to profitable customer retention and recommendation. An alternative approach may be to use a quasi-experimental approach in which two or more experience 'treatments' are compared by measuring consumers' emotions and repurchase intentions/actual repurchase behaviour at the next point in their buying cycle. By taking a large cross-section of consumers, and the use of a paired comparison sample, the effects of individual and situational differences may be reduced, leaving the measurement of emotions and the purchase intention to be accounted for by differences in the experience treatments. As an example of this approach, a restaurant chain may seek to measure the effect of a new experience design featuring a changed environment, service processes, personnel behaviours and brand messages. The sample of customers of a control restaurant would be matched with a similar sample at the experimental restaurant in terms of demographics and usage behaviour. By focusing on a specific meal occasion (for example, evening dining rather than lunchtime), motivation as a source of the motion should be held relatively constant. In order to measure long-term effects of the experience on repurchase/repurchase intention, survey research should be undertaken a week after the service encounter, or at a point of time that previous research had suggested corresponds to a key future decision point in the buying cycle. Of course, even this relatively controlled cross-sectional approach will not fully account for the non-linearity of customer experience over time, nor for the fact that the experimental treatment may arouse high emotions when it is new, but these effects will be likely to wear off with repeated exposure.

Given the difficulty of measuring customer experience in a linear manner and in a way that takes account of contextual differences, many researchers have argued that qualitative techniques are the only way to really understand experience from the perspective of the consumer. It has been noted by Holbrook that a decision-oriented, information-processing-perspective approach makes assumptions about consumption decisions that are economically rational, but which may be at variance with hedonistic models of customer experience, especially where the novelty value of an experience is difficult to model in a rational manner, or at best can only be quantified as a likelihood of an event occurring (Holbrook, 2006).

## 9.5 Setting quality standards

We now move from the conceptualization and measurement of service quality to its management and implementation. A starting point for quality management is to determine the level of quality that a company should provide. A casual observation of most service sectors would indicate that there is a range of quality standards on offer, for example in airlines (compare Lufthansa with Ryanair) and hotels (compare Travelodge with Marriott).

The evidence of a wide range of quality standards occurs despite many services being committed to a total quality management (TQM) approach. In fact, the idea of total quality in the services sector can be quite misleading, for a number of reasons:

- Total quality may be a valid concept in the manufacturing sector, where checking and rechecking of components and the finished product can filter out almost all defective products before they reach the customer. How many times have you bought a defective bottle of soft drink or chocolate bar? Even complex manufactured products such as cars can have a TQM approach applied to the many components and sub-assemblies that make up a car, which explains why reliability levels for cars are typically very high. Contrast this situation with that of many services, where the production process is conducted live, much of it in the presence of the customer. The possibilities for filtering out poor performance before the effects reach the consumer are much fewer. While service companies can aim to improve performance through better training and simplification of service processes, among other things, the achievement of total quality is much less realistic than is the case with manufactured goods.
- Total quality implies that a company has a very deep insight into the mindset of customers. Given the argument that service quality can only be defined in the minds of consumers, the concept of TQM implies that the target 'total quality' aimed for will vary between customers and may vary with individual customers over the course of time.

It is more realistic to talk about a *return on quality* rather than total quality as an end in itself. It was noted earlier in this chapter that evidence linking high levels of quality with improved profitability is fairly ambiguous. Increased profitability for a company can be achieved by cutting costs or raising revenue, or by a combination of the two. In practice, it is difficult for service companies to do both simultaneously. Lower costs invariably (but by no means always) result in lower quality, and vice versa. It has been noted that, during 2009, the no-frills, low-cost airline Ryanair was more profitable than British Airways in total profits and made considerably more profit per passenger carried. Yet this was despite a poorer reliability record, the use of smaller, less convenient airports, providing minimal customer services (e.g. no in-flight meals and no individual seat allocations) and charging for many ancillary services that are taken for granted with British Airways (e.g. in-flight drinks). A similar picture emerged in many European retail sectors, with some of the more profitable operators being no-frills chains such as Primark and Matalan. Are customers prepared to pay for additional quality? The profitable growth of many no-frills airlines suggests that in this sector, at least, a large number of customers are prepared to sacrifice standards of quality in return for a lower price. So how far should a company go in improving its levels of quality? The simple answer is, as far as customers are prepared to pay for the enhanced level of quality. To return to the airline example, an operator can invest in additional aircraft to keep in reserve and bring out only when it suffers operating problems (such as bad weather, emergency maintenance, strikes at airports, etc.). This will certainly increase one dimension of quality – reliability – as customers will not have to wait until a defective aircraft is repaired before they can proceed with their journey. However, keeping additional aircraft in reserve can be very expensive, and the improvement in reliability may not be reflected in customers' willingness to pay a higher price, which covers the additional costs.

## Thinking around the subject: What price quality?

What level of service quality should an organization provide for its customers? Figure 9.9 shows schematically a cut-off point at which a service provider should cease investing in service quality improvements. Too high and the customers may love the service, but the costs of providing it may lead to a financial loss by the company. Too low and the company may get insufficient custom at a high enough price to cover even its fixed costs. Management should have a sound understanding of the dynamics of its market, and the willingness of customers to pay extra in return for improved quality levels (or conversely, the opportunities for cutting quality levels and gaining market share through lower prices). Figure 9.9 shows the principles of an ideal level of quality. As a company raises its level of service from a notional 50 per cent to a notional 100 per cent, its costs per customer climb too and these are indicated by the cost-per-customer line. However, higher levels of quality can be expected to increase the amount that customers are prepared to pay for the service. It can be seen that at above a notional 88 per cent quality, the costs of provision become greater than the price that customers are willing to pay. This is a simplification of reality and measuring quality for this purpose is likely to be complex and multifaceted. Costs can also be difficult to measure. Nevertheless, the diagram illustrates the principle that 'total quality' is not necessarily the most profitable level of quality for a company and that a sound understanding of costs and markets is needed before determining the ideal level of quality to provide.

Figure 9.9 Plotting the cost benefit of quality improvements

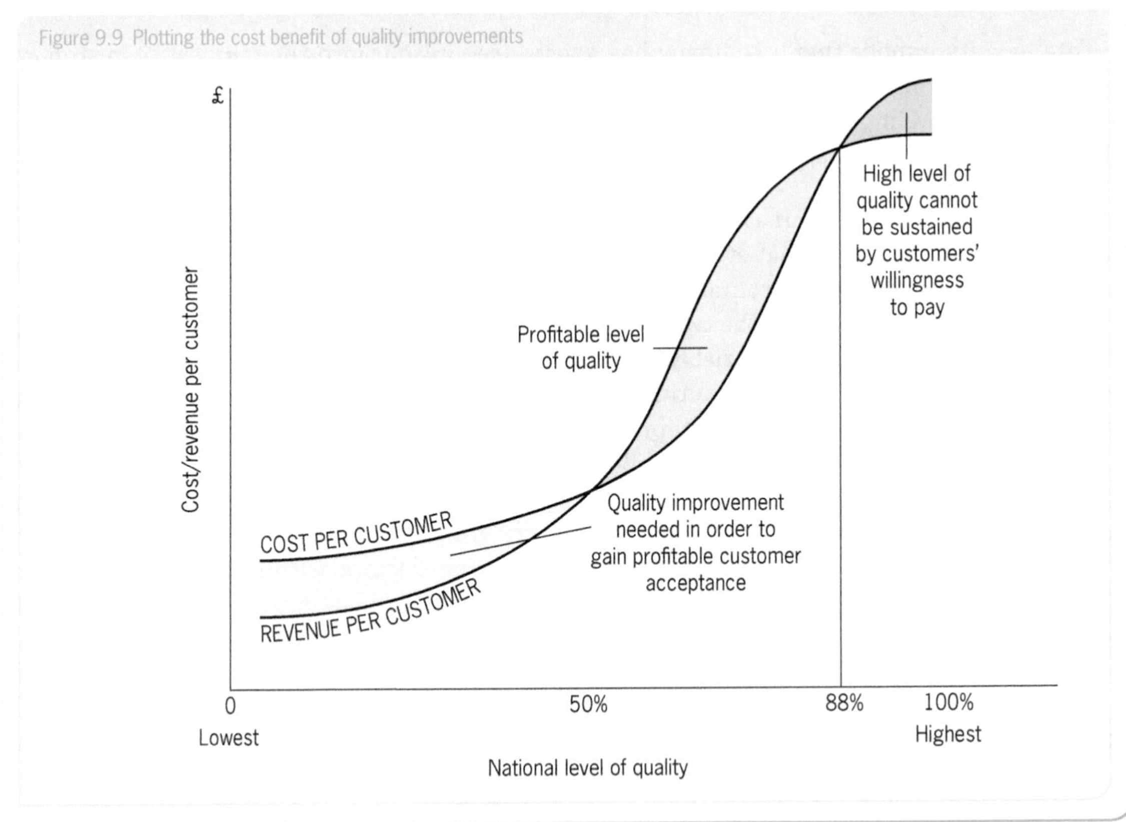


A precise specification of service standards serves a valuable function in communicating the standard of quality that consumers can expect to receive. It also serves to communicate the standards that are expected of employees. While the general manner in which an organization goes about promoting itself may give a general impression as to the level of quality it seeks to deliver, more specific standards can be stated in a number of ways, which are considered below:

- At its most basic, an organization can rely on its terms of business as a basis for determining the level of service to be delivered to customers. These generally act to protect customers against excessively poor service rather than being used to proactively promote high standards of excellence. The booking conditions of tour operators, for example, make very few promises about service quality, other than offers of compensation if delays exceed a specified standard or if accommodation arrangements are changed at short notice.
- Generally worded customer charters go beyond the minimum levels of business terms by stating in a general manner the standards of performance that the organization aims to achieve in its dealings with customers. In this way, banks publish charters that specify in general terms the manner in which accounts will be conducted and complaints handled and typically include general promises to discuss the price to be charged for any special services; to inform customers in writing of any special conditions attached to loans; and to investigate any dissatisfaction with service through a formalized complaints procedure.
- Specific guarantees of service performance are sometimes offered, especially in respect of service outcomes. As an example, parcel delivery companies often guarantee to deliver a parcel within a specified time and agree to pay compensation if they fall below this standard. Many of the public utilities now offer compensation payments if certain specified services are not delivered correctly, for example a missed appointment or loss of service. Increasingly, service organizations set their service guarantees with reference to benchmarks established by best-practice companies within their sector, or in a completely different sector. Sometimes, guarantees concentrate on the manner in which a service is produced rather than specifically on final outcomes. In this way, building societies set standards for the time that it will take to give a decision on a mortgage application and to subsequently process it. While there can be great benefits from publicizing specific guaranteed performance standards to customers, failure to perform could result in heavy compensation claims, or claims for misleading advertising. Many highly specific targets are therefore restricted to internal use, where their function is to motivate and control staff rather than to provide guarantees to potential customers. While the major banks give their branch managers targets for such quality standards as queuing time for counter staff and availability of working ATMs, these do not guarantee a specified level of service to their customers.
- Many services companies belong to a trade or professional association and incorporate the association's code of conduct into their own service offering. Codes of conduct adopted by members of professional associations as diverse as car repairers, undertakers and solicitors specify minimum standards below which service provision should not fall. The code of conduct provides both a reassurance to potential customers and a statement to employees about the minimum standards that are expected of them.
- Of more general applicability is the adoption of ISO quality accreditation. Contrary to popular belief, a company operating in accordance with the ISO 9000 series does not guarantee a high level of quality for its service. Instead, ISO accreditation is granted to organizations that can show that they have in place management systems for ensuring a consistent standard of quality – whether this itself is high or low is largely a subjective judgement. Although this standard was initially adopted by manufacturing industries, it has subsequently found significant use among service companies, including education providers, leisure centres and building contractors. Increasingly, industrial purchasers of services are seeking the reassurance that their suppliers are ISO registered.
- For some basic utility services, which operate in a monopolistic environment, quality standards are sometimes imposed from outside. In the case of privately owned utilities in the UK, the

relevant regulating authority has the power to set specific service targets – for example, the water supply watchdog Ofwat sets standards for the quality and availability of household water supply. In the case of publicly owned services, governments issue customer charters setting out the standards of service that users of the service can expect – for example, the period of time that a hospital patient has to wait for an operation. Critics of such charters would argue that they provide little – if any – practical compensation for users of a service who suffer from poor standards of quality. Worse still, they may unrealistically raise users' expectations without providing resources that would allow the organization to meet these expectations.

In complex and/or recurring business-to-business transactions, the level of service quality is likely to be specified in a **service level agreement (SLA)**. The growth of outsourcing within the services sector has resulted in specialist service providers delivering complex services to their clients' customers. We saw in Chapter 5 how an airline such as Air France delivers many of its services through outsourced contracts for catering, baggage handling and maintenance, etc. Each of these contracts is likely to specify in great detail the level of quality to be achieved by the supplier, and failure to achieve this standard may automatically trigger penalty payments. A dilemma often occurs in deciding what level of detail to include in a service level agreement. One argument is that a company outsourcing a key business process should specify quality standards in as much detail as it would if it was providing the service itself directly to its customers. Only if this is done will consistent standards be maintained through a network of outlets. An alternative view is that one reason for outsourcing customer-facing processes is to bring in the specialist skills of the outsource provider, who may have learnt a lot about customer expectations from its contracts with the customers of its other clients. It follows that it should be in a better position than its clients to determine the standards of quality that are most appropriate for the types of customer that it has experience of dealing with. It is therefore better to set quality standards at a fairly general level in terms of overall customer satisfaction, rather than trying to 'micro-manage' the outsourced supplier with a series of tightly specified technical quality-performance standards.

## In practice: Satisfaction guaranteed?

Figure 9.10 The Premier Inn good night guarantee

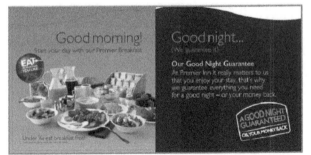

Many services organizations offer guarantees of service standards and customer satisfaction, failing which some form of compensation or refund will be provided. At first sight, allowing customers to define satisfaction may seem like an invitation for niggling complaints brought by customers to justify payment of the compensation on offer. But against this, guarantees can give important benefits to a service provider. When evaluating competing hotels, a guarantee may be a decisive choice criterion for some customers, who may consider that they have nothing to lose by trying a previously unknown hotel. For the service provider, the offer of an incentive may encourage some customers to voice their complaints, rather than going away dissatisfied, never to return and, worse still, telling their friends about their bad experience. To be workable, a guarantee scheme should allow the service provider an opportunity to put things right before the guarantee is invoked; this can act as a powerful motivator for front-line staff.

### 9.5.1 Benchmarking studies

Customers' quality expectations in other similar service industries can be a useful source of information for managers. Often, customers' needs may be similar between different industries, even though the service product on offer is ostensibly quite different. Many common dimensions cut across the boundaries of industries and apply to services in general – for example, courteous and competent staff, a pleasant environment and helpfulness, to name but a few. It can therefore be beneficial to investigate the nature of service provision in closely related service areas, and draw upon the findings of any research that has been made available. In particular, it is worthwhile investigating what is known in those service sectors that have a good track record of analysing and responding to customers' needs and identifying whether it is applicable to an industry that has only recently adopted a customer-led approach. For example, it is possible to learn a lot about certain aspects of hospital service from what hotel and catering establishments have been researching and practising for some considerable time. Continuing with this theme, many services organizations that have been operating for many years in a non-market-based environment can benefit from an understanding of the operations of their counterparts in other countries that have openly marketed their services in a freely competitive market. In this way, managers within European state-run health systems may learn something from US healthcare providers about customer service (although critics of the US healthcare system may point out that their apparent wasteful insurance administration processes should not be copied).

The term 'benchmarking' is frequently used to describe the process by which companies set standards for themselves, based on a study of best practice elsewhere (Dattakumar and Jagadeesh, 2003). Best practice can be defined in terms of firms within the same sector, or in completely different sectors that share similar processes (e.g. benchmarks for waiting time in a bank could be based on benchmarks established within the convenience retail sector).

Benchmarking can be undertaken at a number of levels, based on what is compared and what the comparison is being made against:

- performance benchmarking – essentially based on outcome measures (e.g. throughput per hour, profit per customer);
- process benchmarking – for example the efficiency and effectiveness of customer-handling procedures;
- strategic benchmarking – for example comparing the integrity of a company's strategic plan with best practice in the industry;
- internal benchmarking – which involves comparing internal processes and structures;
- competitive benchmarking – which may be with respect to market share, selling price, etc.;
- functional benchmarking – sometimes the task will be to assess the performance of a company's functions (e.g. advertising or sales) with best practice.

Benchmarking involves a five-step continuous process: plan the study; form the benchmarking team; identify potential benchmarking partners; collect and analyse the information; and adapt and improve. While benchmarking produces a standard against which improvement can be made, these improvements are continuous and benchmarks can go out of date very quickly.

## 9.6 Researching service quality

So far, we have looked in general at conceptual frameworks for understanding service quality. We will now turn our attention to specific research methods that services organizations use to learn more about customers' expectations and perceptions of service quality. A clear, sustained and continuous quality improvement is not possible without some indication of quality performance. To know the real effect of changes over time, managers need measures against which to compare the quality performance of the service.

There are three principal types of measures that a company must be concerned with in its efforts to manage service quality:

- service performance measures that are internally focused and evaluate the current performance of the service and ensure that it is continuing to reliably meet the design specifications;
- customer measures, which are both internal and externally focused and aimed at assessing the impact of the service performance on customers;
- financial measures, which are indicators of the financial health of the organization.

The correlation between financial and customer measures will determine the revenue-generating potential of the service, while the relationship between service performance measures and customer measures will give some indication as to how the service is performing in customers' eyes. In turn, this will have a direct bearing on a company's financial performance and overall market share.

Before discussing methods of researching service quality, it should be recognized that companies generally need to learn about standards of quality for two principal purposes – planning and control. Insights from customers can be invaluable for improving service provision, and may typically probe into a lot of detail about what customers find particularly satisfying or dissatisfying about a service. However, a lot of service quality measurement is carried out primarily for control purposes, typically involving the identification of deviation from standards of performance and rewarding employees in recognition of their achievement of high standards. For such measures, a simple score might be sufficient in order to distinguish between employees who justify a bonus and those who don't. Very often, data can be used for both planning and control purposes.

A number of methods for researching customers' expectations and perceptions are available and these are examined below. However, as a set of general principles for the effective measurement of service quality, Zeithaml et al. (1990) stress the need for a marketing research programme to be:

- *Varied*. Every research method has its limitations and in order to overcome this and to achieve a comprehensive insight into a problem, a combination of qualitative and quantitative research techniques should be used.
- *Ongoing*. The expectations and perceptions of customers are constantly changing, as is the nature of the service offer provided by companies and their competitors. It is therefore important that a service research process is administered on a continuous basis so that any changes can be picked up quickly and acted upon if necessary.
- *Undertaken with employees*. The closeness of staff to customers within the services sector makes it important that they are asked about problems and possible improvements as well as their personal motivations and requirements.
- *Shared with employees*. Employees' performance in delivering service quality may be improved if they are made aware of the results of studies of customer expectations, complaint analysis, etc.

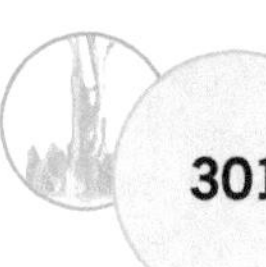

## 9.6.1 Regular questionnaire surveys

The assumption that most people make is that data from such surveys will be used to take corrective action where expectations are not reached. However, many of these surveys are of dubious quality and therefore of limited value.

Questionnaires are often used as a relatively low-cost method of gathering the opinions of a large representative sample of service users. Typical applications include filling in a questionnaire on the aeroplane after a holiday, or being asked by the local council to fill in a customer satisfaction card. Such surveys usually ask recipients to detail any complaints that they may have about the services provided and provide any comments/suggestions for improving them. They can range in depth from a small card containing no more than three or four questions and completed by the respondent, through to a multi-page in-depth questionnaire administered by a professional researcher. In addition to the traditional self-completion questionnaire, customer surveys are increasingly carried out by telephone and online. Online surveys can allow for rapid analysis and dissemination of results.

Although questionnaires may be a relatively low-cost method of gathering information about quality performance, they are subject to a number of limitations. First, a typical questionnaire does

Figure 9.11 Like many services companies, this hotel routinely monitors its customers' level of satisfaction. This simple comment card combines responses that can be measured quantitatively with an opportunity for customers to express comments in an unstructured manner. Analysis of these responses allows a hotel chain to identify differences in performance between its hotels, and to monitor changes in performance over time. Many companies link survey results to bonuses paid to their employees. Like most self-completion surveys, a company must be alert to the representativeness of its respondents, with evidence that very happy and very unhappy customers are more likely to provide comments than customers holding average views.

M

Merton Dene Hotel

*PLEASE ☑ TO INDICATE YOUR RATING FOR EACH OF THE FOLLOWING*

| | Excellent | Good | Poor |
|---|---|---|---|
| Speed and friendliness of check-in............ | ☐ | ☐ | ☐ |
| The comfort of your room.......................... | ☐ | ☐ | ☐ |
| The cleanliness of your room...................... | ☐ | ☐ | ☐ |
| The service in the restaurant...................... | ☐ | ☐ | ☐ |
| The service provided by our staff................ | ☐ | ☐ | ☐ |
| The enjoyment of your breakfast................ | ☐ | ☐ | ☐ |
| Value for money......................................... | ☐ | ☐ | ☐ |
| Will you stay in this hotel again.................. | ☐ | Yes ☐ | No ☐ |

Any general comments which you have time to make will be greatly appreciated

..................................................................................................

..................................................................................................

..................................................................................................

..................................................................................................

not allow for great depth in probing respondents' attitudes towards quality. Most questionnaires tend to focus on the technical aspects of quality rather than the functional aspects. In the case of self-completion questionnaires, it can be difficult to ensure that replies are obtained from a representative sample of service users. There is a suggestion, for example, that customers who are particularly satisfied or particularly dissatisfied are more likely to take part in a questionnaire survey than the broad group of customers who would typically be neither very satisfied nor dissatisfied.

The timing of the questionnaire can be quite crucial. It was noted above that perceptions of quality can lead to attitude change, which can have an important effect at the time that the next purchase decision is made. Typically, service quality questionnaires are administered immediately after consumption of the service, but there is evidence that quality ratings can change over time (Palmer and O'Neill, 2003). Gestalt analysis, for example, has been used to show how a small element of the service offer that gives dissatisfaction can affect perceptions of quality at the time that it occurs, but over time fades into the background and does not affect attitude to the service over the long term.

## In practice: Curl up and die of embarassment?

When should you ask a customer about their perceptions of service quality? Many services organizations find that the most convenient time is immediately after consumption of the service. Details of the service are fresh in customers' memories, and the service provider does not have the trouble and expense of trying to contact customers later by mail or telephone. However, service providers should be interested in the long-term attitude change that results from the perceived quality of the service encounter. It is this longer-term attitude change that is likely to influence whether a customer returns and recommends the service provider to their friends. Sometimes the difference between immediate perceptions of quality and more long-term considered attitudes can be quite great. Hairdressing provides a good example of this. Many people who have been to a hairdresser to have their hair restyled leave the hairdresser with a sense of doubt about their new-look image. At this stage, the hairdresser may score very poorly in any survey of quality. However, given the passage of time, the customer may become used to their haircut and, after a few weeks, probably cannot imagine themselves looking any different. A few complimentary comments from friends and, after a few weeks, the score of the hairdresser will be much higher.

Figure 9.12 Hairdressers face particular problems with customer perceptions

### 9.6.2 Qualitative research techniques

Qualitative techniques are often used by companies to complement their questionnaire-based approaches. The use of qualitative techniques in general has been growing rapidly in recent years, as companies try to gain a much deeper insight into consumers' needs and the nature of individuals' motivators. Qualitative techniques are often used as a precursor to a questionnaire survey.

In order to develop meaningful questions in a questionnaire survey, more unstructured qualitative techniques can be useful for generating a list of relevant questions to ask. On other occasions, qualitative research is used to try to interpret the findings of a questionnaire survey, especially where a company has discovered a correlation between a service quality score and some aspects of service delivery, and the company wishes to learn more about the causal relationship.

The focus group is a widely used technique for learning about service quality, although many focus groups are assembled to discuss a number of aspects of a company's activities, for example its image and range of services. Another commonly used technique is a one-to-one unstructured interview with a sample of customers or with selected key customers. In all of these cases, a company cannot hope to gain a representative sample of customer attitudes towards service quality; however, it makes up for this through depth of understanding. A key role is played by the individual who leads the research, although many techniques are available for analysing qualitative data in an apparently more objective manner.

### 9.6.3 Webnography

The Internet is becoming a valuable source of customer comments as people post reviews and share comments on blogs and various online social media. The analysis of online comments has been variously called 'webnography', 'virtual ethnography' and 'netnography' and a spectrum of webnographic approaches exist from purely observational to full participatory (Kozinets, 2006). Technology is increasingly allowing masses of qualitative information left online to be collated and sense made out of it.

It has been suggested that webnographic approaches are particularly suitable for conducting research about hi-tech services among 'leading edge' and technology-savvy consumers (Puri, 2007). Furthermore, an anonymous Internet environment can encourage contribution of impulsive comments without contributors fearing reprisals, creating a source of data which may be more expressive and potentially more credible than if comments were moderated by the need to conform to social norms and the prospect of retribution for breaching those norms (Puri, 2007). Against this, it has been suggested that the presence of dishonest and intentionally malicious comments in online fora has led many to question the validity of this source of data (Keller and Berry, 2006).

The difficulty of obtaining representative samples using webnographic techniques has been noted (Kozinets, 2006). Against this, it can be objected that qualitative research is essentially about discovering meanings attributed by people who are engaged in the topic of the study, and what counts is depth of understanding rather than representativeness of those being studied.

### 9.6.4 Customer panels

Customer panels can provide a continuous source of information on customer expectations. Groups of customers, who are generally frequent users, are consulted by a company on a regular basis so that their opinions about the quality of service provided can be studied. On other occasions they may be employed to monitor the introduction of a new or revised service – for example, a panel could be brought together by a bank following the experimental introduction of a new branch design format. Research methods used with customer panels can be a combination of qualitative and quantitative.

The use of continuous panels can offer organizations a means of anticipating problems and may act as an early warning system for emerging issues of importance. Retailers have been involved in the operation of continuous panels to monitor their level of service provision, as well as letting panels contribute to new-product-development research. The validity of this research method is quite dependent on how well the panel represents consumers as a whole. Careful selection should therefore be undertaken to ensure that the panel possesses the same social, economic, demographic, behavioural and lifestyle characteristics as the population of customers being analysed. There has been a suggestion that the number of people prepared to become members of panels is not rising as quickly as firms' appetite for information. The result has been the emergence of 'professional' panel members who may not be representative of target users as a whole.

### 9.6.5 Transaction analysis

A popular method of evaluative research involves tracking the satisfaction of individuals with particular transactions in which they have recently been involved. This type of research enables management to judge current performance, particularly customers' satisfaction with the contact personnel with whom they have interacted, as well as their overall satisfaction with the service.

The research effort normally involves a mail-out questionnaire survey, a telephone call or, increasingly, an email to individual customers immediately after a transaction has been completed. A wide range of services organizations use this approach. For example, the UK's Automobile Association surveys customers who have recently been served by its breakdown service and many banks invite customers who have just used their mortgage services to use a structured questionnaire to express their views on the service received. An additional benefit of this research is its ability to associate service-quality performance with individual contact personnel and to link this to reward systems.

### 9.6.6 Mystery customers

The use of '**mystery customers**' is a method of auditing the standard of service provision, particularly the staff involvement in such provision. A major difficulty in ensuring service quality is overcoming the non-conformance of staff with performance guidelines. This so-called service–performance gap is the result of employees being unable and/or unwilling to perform the service at the desired level. An important function of mystery-customer surveys is therefore to monitor the extent to which specified quality standards are actually being met by staff.

This method of researching actual service provision involves the use of trained assessors, who visit services organizations and report back their observations. Audits tend to be tailored to the specific needs of an organization and focus on an issue that it wishes to evaluate. The format of the enquiry is therefore something that is determined jointly by the client and research organization.

The constructive nature of this research technique has to be stressed, as the mystery customer can easily be mistakenly perceived by staff as an undercover agent spying on them on behalf of the management. However, if the techniques are applied correctly, they can allow management to know what is really happening at the sharp end of their business. To be effective, mystery-shopping surveys need to be undertaken independently, should be objective and must be consistent. The training of assessors is critical to the effective use of this research method and should include, for example, training in observation techniques that allow them to distinguish between a greeting and an acknowledgement.

## Thinking around the subject: Would you want to be a mystery student?

Mystery customers have for some time been part of the quality management process at restaurants and shops, among many other service sectors, but could they have a role in higher education? The idea of a 'mystery student' would be met with horror by many teaching staff, who may feel more comfortable with quality being measured using a paper trail of course documentation, rather than live assessment of their teaching abilities, especially if they did not know which of their students was 'spying' on them.

But, if the prospect of mystery customers in the classroom is still some way off, there is evidence that universities are beginning to use mystery customers to assess the quality of their support functions. A mystery shopping exercise was carried out by Sheffield University in December 2005 and involved 169 telephone calls and 109 email requests being made to the university by researchers posing as students. The results, reported by the *Times Higher Education Supplement*, indicated that the university's processes were falling short of expected standards of customer care. It was reported that one in five telephone callers who asked for information received nothing; one in six telephone inquirers felt that the person they spoke to failed to convey a positive impression of the university; and one in three callers who left a voice-mail message asking to be called back did not actually receive the call back. Seven departments took more than a month to send requested material and one department took three months to reply. The mystery callers also picked up on points of detail, for example a quarter of all voicemail 'greeting' messages were not personalized and the covering letters received from the university appeared impersonal, often with no dates or signature. Many were poorly photocopied.

With the introduction of tuition fees, UK students had raised their expectations for 'customer care'. Although the idea of mystery shoppers may have appeared alien to educational values, which have stressed professional responsibility, there has been a growing recognition that universities must increasingly look at themselves and ask the hard question whether they are delivering what students (potential and actual) expect.

How far should mystery shopping in universities go? Would the standards of lectures delivered to students improve if staff could expect to be rated by a 'mystery student'? Would this be better than a paper-based exercise in which the reality of service delivery can be very different from that described on paper? Or is education a professional service in which the 'customer' often does not know what is best for them, and teaching staff, like doctors and other professionals, should be judged by their peers for fundamental aspects of quality that may not be immediately apparent in relatively superficial, peer-based evaluation? If mystery customers are not to be formally incorporated into universities' quality assessment programmes, is there a danger that savvy students will use new media technology to do their own 'mystery shopping' and report the results on peer-to-peer websites such as ratemyprofessors.com? Many universities have become alarmed at the power of such sites to portray examples of poor quality, often supported by covert video images posted on YouTube.

### 9.6.7 Analysis of complaints

Dissatisfaction of customers is most clearly voiced through the complaints that they make about service provision. For some service providers, this may be the sole method of keeping in touch with customers. Complaints can be made directly to the provider or perhaps indirectly through an intermediary or a watchdog body. Complaints by customers, if treated constructively, provide a rich source of data on which to base policies for improving service quality. However, customer complaints are at best an inadequate source of information. Most customers do not bother to complain, remain dissatisfied and tell others about their dissatisfaction. Others simply change to another supplier and do not offer potentially valuable information to the service provider about what factors were wrong and caused them to leave.

In market-orientated organizations, complaints analysis can form a useful pointer to where the process of service delivery is breaking down. As part of an overall programme for keeping in touch with customers, the analysis of complaints can have an important role to play. The continuous tracking of complaints is a relatively inexpensive source of data, which enables a company to review the major concerns of customers on an ongoing basis and hopefully rectify any evident problems. In addition, the receipt of complaints by the firm enables staff to enter into direct contact with customers and provides an opportunity to interact with them over their matters of concern. As well as providing customers' views on these issues in particular, complainants can also contribute views about customer service in general. Many companies have gone to great lengths to make it easy for customers to complain, for example by creating freephone telephone lines and making comment cards readily available.

### In practice: How much is a complaint worth?

How far should a company go in encouraging its customers to complain? Of course, cultures differ greatly in their willingness to complain about bad service. The traditional reserve of the British may seem like a gift to the average duty manager of a restaurant who does not have to put up with the rough ride that more demanding Australian or American customers may give. In principle, the idea of collecting feedback from customers is good because of the opportunities that it gives to put things right, both immediately in terms of the complainant's satisfaction and strategically in terms of designing more effective processes. But could this lead to a culture among some clients of always complaining, just to see what they can get back? Many tour operators can recount stories of customers who routinely submit complaints about trivial matters, in an effort to get some compensation, which will be put towards the cost of their next holiday. How does a company strike a balance between listening to customer complaints and keeping its costs of compensation down, especially when it is positioning itself as a low-cost provider and operating in an environment where things are quite likely to go wrong?

### 9.6.8 Employee research

Research undertaken among employees can enable their views about the way that services are provided and their perceptions of how they are received by customers to be taken into account. Data gathered from staff training seminars and development exercises, feedback from quality circles, job appraisal and performance evaluation reports, etc. can all provide valuable information for planning service-quality improvements. One way in which formal feedback from staff can be built into a systematic research programme is the operation of a staff suggestion scheme. The proposals that staff may make about how services could be provided more efficiently and/or effectively can have an important role to play in improving service quality.

Research into employees' needs can also allow identification of policies that improve their motivation to deliver a high quality of service. Many of the techniques employed to elicit the views of employees as internal customers are in principle the same as those used in studies of external customers. Interviews and focus groups may be used in the collection of qualitative data on employee needs, wants, motivations and attitudes towards working conditions, benefits and policies.

In Chapter 10 the issue of obtaining the engagement of employees is considered in some detail. In this respect, involving employees in the research process and its findings, for example by using them to gather data, showing them videotapes of group discussions and interviews with customers and circulating them with the findings of research reports, can help to improve their understanding of service quality issues throughout their organization. This is particularly the case in high-contact, people-intensive service sectors.

There are, however, many barriers to the flow of information from employees to managers, especially in organizations where there is no culture of listening to staff. Having clearly identified means of listening, acting on the results and having a shared commitment to improving quality can greatly improve employees' perceptions. There is a problem of possible conflict between control and planning functions concerning information given by staff. If employees are aware of problems mentioned to them by customers, should they keep quiet for fear of losing a bonus, or maybe a prospect of promotion? And, if employees have ideas for improving service quality, they may be reluctant to mention their ideas to management, for fear of being asked to do more work themselves to help overcome any problem. As an example, on-board personnel of a train company may perceive that customers are confused when they get on a train because they are not sure exactly where the train will stop, and the announcement given over the public announcement system comes only after the train has left the station. Should employees suggest that an announcement should always be made two minutes before departure? Would they willingly want to give themselves an additional task to perform?

### 9.6.9 Intermediary research

Intermediaries often perform a valuable function in the process of service delivery, acting as a co-producer in a manner that is quite different from the role performed by goods intermediaries. Research into intermediaries focuses on two principal concerns:

1. Where intermediaries form an important part of a service delivery process, the quality perceived by customers is to a large extent determined by the performance of intermediaries. In this way, the perceived quality of an airline may be tarnished if its ticket agents are perceived as being slow or unhelpful to customers. Research through such techniques as mystery-customer surveys can be used to monitor the standard of quality delivered by intermediaries.
2. Intermediaries as co-producers of a service are further down the channel of distribution and hence closer to customers. They are therefore in a position to provide valuable feedback to the service principal about consumers' expectations and perceptions. As well as conducting structured research investigations of intermediaries, many service principals find it possible to learn more about the needs and expectations of their final customers during the process of providing intermediary support services such as training. But, as in the case of employees, there can be a potential conflict of research where intermediaries may avoid giving honest answers if this may prejudice their performance bonuses.

### 9.6.10 Management by walking about

All of the techniques described above are essentially involved in providing senior management with insights into service quality as it is perceived by customers at the point of delivery. A small service provider, such as a self-employed decorator or builder, is in a good position to understand customers' perceptions of quality, from the comments that they receive back directly from customers and from customer referrals and repeat business. In the large multi-outlet corporation, this opportunity of customer feedback is not available to key corporate decision-makers on a regular basis. Many large organizations therefore use formal or informal methods for getting their senior staff to the front line in order that they can understand at first hand the expectations of customers and the delivery performance of the company.

'Management by walking about' (MBWA) has become a popular way in which senior executives try to gain knowledge about aspects of their operations that is not immediately apparent from structured reporting systems. This has been linked to the idea of 'trading places', whereby employees see their organization through the lens of a customer (Bowers and Martin, 2007). Some companies have adopted a formal system of role exchanges where senior executives spend a period at the sharp end of their business. Even the vice-chancellors of some universities have taken the bold step of trying to live the student life for a day or a week, and experiencing classrooms and lectures at first hand. Many have hoped that this would give vice-chancellors a better understanding of the day-to-day issues that are of greatest concern to students. Although many services organizations have developed similar programmes for their senior management, others have been critical of the idea. To some, management by walking about is no more than a gimmick, while others adopt the arguments of the scientific management approach by claiming that the time of a highly paid executive is more cost-effectively spent in the boardroom rather than doing relatively unskilled work on the shop floor.

## 9.7 Managing and monitoring service performance

As a service organization grows in size and complexity, reliance on informal, judgement-based approaches to measuring service quality and acting on the results becomes more difficult. Instead, large services organizations need institutionalized systems for measuring and managing services quality. It is sometimes said that

*'what gets measured gets done; what gets rewarded gets repeated'.*

If service quality is to be maintained at a desired level, it is important that a firm has in place systems for measuring it and incorporating the results, formally or informally, into employees' rewards. In this section we explore the main elements of a service performance monitoring system, which would typically begin by specifying targets, collecting performance data, analysing it and reporting to the individuals who can then act on the information.

### 9.7.1 Targets

A clear statement of service-quality targets provides a benchmark against which results can be assessed and a standard set for employees to achieve. In general, the greater the level of disaggregation of targets, the greater the degree of control that will be possible. To be effective in service quality management, targets should be specified and communicated that achieve the following:

- They should give individuals a clear indication of the standards of performance that are expected of them.
- They should distinguish between controllable aspects of quality that can be managed by an individual and those that are uncontrollable and should therefore be excluded from their standards for performance.
- They should show which performance targets are to take priority, for example should a train operating manager prioritize the need to keep delays to a minimum or cancellations to a minimum? By cancelling a train, this indicator may suffer, but it may improve indicators for delay elsewhere in the system. In any event, targets should not be mutually incompatible.
- They should be sufficiently flexible to allow for changes in the organization's environment that were not foreseen at the time when the targets were set.

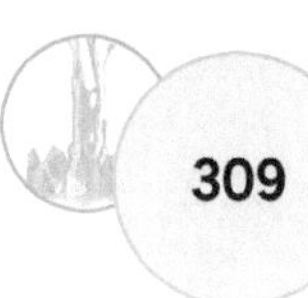

Quantitative performance targets are generally preferred to qualitative ones. We have seen in this chapter how firms have used methodologies such as SERVQUAL to measure essentially intangible attitudes of customers. There is a danger, however, in setting purely quantified targets that they may be represented by a series of relatively simple indicators. Staff seeking to achieve these targets may concentrate their attention on meeting these, possibly at the expense of other more important qualitative aspects of their performance. A telephone enquiry office with a target of answering calls within a specified time may lose sight of the quality of information given during the call if its attention is primarily focused on responding within the target time.

### 9.7.2 Performance monitoring

Technical measures of service quality are the most frequently collected information, for example a bank may record the percentage availability of its ATMs. It is the qualitative aspects of service delivery that have been less likely to be measured. While the bank may have a daily report of its ATM availability across its entire network, it may rely on a small annual survey of customers to measure customers' attitudes to the bank.

There have been a number of attempts to develop improved performance measures. One approach that has attracted considerable interest from academics and practitioners in recent years is the balanced scorecard (BSC). The balanced scorecard is a framework for describing value-creating strategies that link tangible and intangible assets (Speckbacher et al., 2003). This is done by formulating strategic objectives with respect to four types of assets: financial, customer, internal business process, and learning and growth (see Kaplan and Norton, 2001a; Malmi, 2001). However, it has been noted that organizations using the BSC often start with only a very simple scorecard, and subsequently enhance its functions and its scope step by step (see Kaplan and Norton, 2001b). It is claimed that the true potential of the BSC approach can only be achieved if its measures are linked to employees' reward systems (Kaplan and Norton, 1996; Malmi, 2001; Otley, 1999).

### 9.7.3 Reporting and control action

As services organizations grow, there is a tendency for quality control systems to become increasingly formalized and bureaucratic. Quality control in a small family-run service business may rely on a variety of informal social pressure to bring about change, but such methods may break down in larger organizations where claims of unfair treatment or victimization of staff can land an employer in the law courts. The sheer amount of information used for control purposes demands a structured approach to control.

The key to effective control is to give the right information to the right people at the right time. Providing too much information can be costly in terms of the effort required to assemble and disseminate it and can also reduce effective control where the valuable information is hidden among information of secondary importance. Also, the level of reporting will be determined by the level of tolerance allowed for compliance to target.

Many quality control systems fail because employees within an organization have been given inappropriate or unrealistic targets, and they simply become discredited. Even where achievable targets are set, and appropriate data are collected, control systems may still fail because of a failure by management to act on the information available. Control information should identify variances from target and should be able to indicate whether the variance is within or beyond the control of the person responsible for meeting the target. If it is beyond their control, the issue should become one of revising the target, or changing service processes, so that the target becomes once more achievable.

## 9.8 Creating a service quality culture

Service quality does not come about by chance – organizations need to develop strategies for ensuring that they deliver consistent and high-quality services. If numerous studies are brought together (e.g. Evans and Lindsay, 2005), key factors emerge from the literature which describe the characteristics of organizations that have successfully developed high standards of service quality:

- a history of top-management commitment to quality, in which measures of service quality are seen to be as important as financial indicators;
- a customer-focused philosophy within the organization and a culture that rewards good, customer-centric actions by employees;
- satisfying employees as well as customers, on the basis that satisfied employees are likely to lead to satisfied customers – we will explore this further in Chapter 10;
- appropriate systems for monitoring service quality.

Responsibility for developing a culture of quality rests with senior management. In addition to introducing reward systems linked to performance, successful services organizations have introduced participative cultures in which knowledge is shared and a commitment made to continually improve performance. One widely used approach is the '**quality circle**' (QC). This consists of a small group of employees who meet together with a supervisor or group leader to discuss their work in terms of production and delivery standards. Quality circles are especially suited to high-contact services where there is considerable interaction between employees and consumers. Front-line service staff who are in a position to identify quality shortcomings as they impact on customers are brought together with operational staff who may not interact directly with customers but can significantly affect service quality. By sitting down and talking together, employees have an opportunity to jointly recognize and suggest solutions to problems. In this way, a QC run by a car repair garage would bring together reception staff who interact with the public and mechanics who produce the substantive service. By analysing a quality problem identified by the receptionists (e.g. delays in collecting completed jobs), the mechanics might be able to suggest solutions (e.g. rescheduling some work procedures).

To be successful, the quality circle leader has to be willing to listen to and act upon issues raised by QC members. This is essential if the QC is to be sustained. Circle members must feel that their participation is real and effective; thus the communication process within the QC must be two-way. Consent can be real or perfunctory. In the latter case, if the QC appears to become only a routinized listening session, circle members may consider it to be just another form of managerial control. While circle members might consent to such control, their active participation in processes to improve service quality may be absent.

Quality circle members need speedy and real feedback on ideas they come up with to solve operational problems. Where a QC has successfully identified reasons why marketing objectives are not being attained, its suggestions should be commented on in a constructive manner.

## 9.9 Managing the extended marketing mix for quality

Quality of service is dependent upon a wide range of strategic and tactical decisions made by managers, and in this final section we will link the integrating subject of service quality with other elements of the extended marketing mix, which was introduced in Chapter 1. Quality affects all

Figure 9.13 It is not good enough for services to simply maintain their existing level of quality, because consumers' expectations are likely to have moved on. Even a company that strives to improve its performance may find its quality ratings falling if its customers' expectations have moved ahead faster than its improvement in performance.

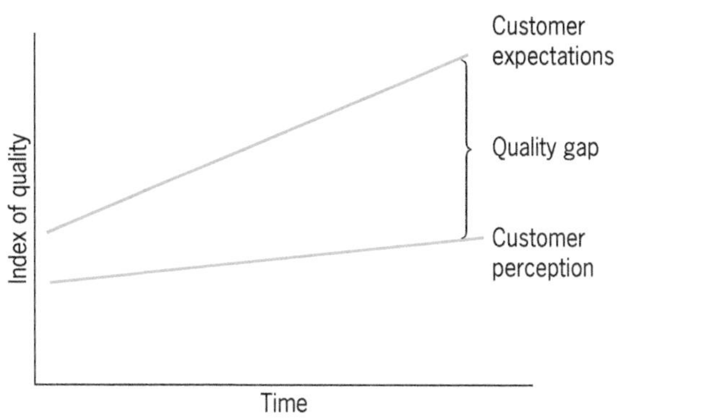


aspects of the marketing mix – decisions about service specification cannot be taken in isolation from decisions concerning other elements of the mix. In this task, service companies must recognize that the relationship between customers' perceptions and expectations is dynamic. Merely maintaining customers' level of perceived quality is insufficient if their expectations have been raised over time. Marketing-mix management is therefore concerned with closing the quality gap over time, either by improving the service offer or by restraining customers' expectations (see Figure 9.13).

## 9.9.1 Promotion

Promotion decisions have the effect of developing consumers' expectations of service quality. Where marketer-dominated sources of promotion are the main basis for evaluating and selecting competing services, the message as well as the medium of communication can contribute in a significant way towards customers' quality expectations. Too often, promotion sets expectations that organizations struggle to meet.

On some occasions, however, the image created by promotion may actually add to the perceived quality of the service. This is quite common for goods of conspicuous consumption, where the intangible image added to products such as beer can actually lead to consumers believing that the beer is of higher quality than another beer of identical technical quality that has been promoted in a different way. The possibility for achieving this with services is generally less, on account of the greater involvement of customers in the production/consumption process and the many opportunities that occur for judging quality. It is, however, possible in the case of some publicly consumed services, where high-profile advertising may actually add to the perceived quality of the service. In this way, the promotion of an exclusive gym may add to a customer's feeling that they belong to an exclusive and prestigious group. Without the advertising, the prestigious value of the gym would not be recognized by others.

## 9.9.2 Price

Price decisions affect both customers' expectations and their perceptions of service quality, as well as the service organization's ability to produce quality services. In cases where all other factors are equal, price can be used by potential customers as a basis for judging service quality. If two outwardly similar restaurants charge different prices for a similar meal, the presumption may be made that the higher-priced restaurant must offer a higher standard of quality, which the customer will subsequently expect to be delivered. It will be against this benchmark that service quality will be assessed.

The price charged can influence the level of quality that a service organization can build into its offering. The concept of price positioning is discussed in Chapter 11, where it is noted that, while any position along a line from high price/high quality to low price/low quality may be feasible, high-price/low-quality and low-price/high-quality positions are not generally sustainable over the long term.

### 9.9.3 Accessibility

Accessibility decisions can affect customers' expectations of quality as well as actual performance. A poor-quality service sold through a high-quality agent may give heightened expectations of quality. Poor delivery may subsequently harm the image of the agent itself, which partly explains why many travel agents are reluctant to continue to act as intermediaries for tour operators with poor service-quality records. The manner in which an intermediary initiates, processes and follows up the service delivery process can often affect perceived quality received by the customer – an agent who incorrectly fills out the departure time for a coach ticket harms the quality of the service that the customer receives. For these reasons, an important element of quality management involves the recruitment and monitoring of a network of intermediaries who are able to share the service principal's commitment to quality standards. You may recall from Chapter 4 that accessibility decisions also involved questions of where and when to make a service available to consumers. Quality may be perceived to be higher where access becomes more locally available and for longer periods of time.

### 9.9.4 People

People, and especially front-line contact personnel, are important elements of consumers' perceptions of functional quality, and therefore the nature of the buyer–seller interaction becomes crucial in the management of service quality. Recruitment, training, motivation and control of personnel are therefore important elements of the marketing mix that impact on quality standards. Front-line employees have the best possible vantage point for observing quality standards and are the most able to identify any problems. Whether these contact personnel have the ability or channels to articulate these failings can be another matter.

## Case study

### 'Satisfaction guaranteed' – service customers' dream or service providers' nightmare?

Rod McColl, ESC Rennes School of Business, France

A quick scan of any business telephone directory or an Internet search would reveal an interesting trend occurring in the marketing of service businesses. It is the idea of service companies providing a written guarantee of their service performance. Product guarantees are nothing new, dating back to the 1850s in the USA. Today, most consumers would not even consider buying a new car, washing machine or mobile phone without checking the terms and conditions of the guarantee or warranty.

Until recently, it had been considered too difficult and inherently risky to guarantee a service. As services are essentially about processes, they are fundamentally more difficult to deliver at a consistently high standard. For example, tradespeople do not always arrive at the time they say they will (sometimes not even on the day promised), insurance companies are sometimes elusive when clients make a claim and their policies are often riddled with fine-print written in legal jargon. Banks often have long queues at their branches, trains and planes often fail to run to schedule and retail staff can often be unfriendly and unhelpful. Each of these service failures may result in reduced customer satisfaction, possibly a complaint, negative word of mouth or lost loyalty.

Despite the challenges of managing quality in a service business, many organizations around the world are addressing service delivery challenges and providing a guarantee of their service performance. Current examples of service guarantees may be found across many service sectors, such as retailing, public utilities including electricity and gas, financial services, insurance, transport, fast food, video rental and hotels.

It is not just in the prosperous, demanding Western world that service guarantees have been used. Demonstrating that service guarantees are attracting global interest in developing countries, Standard Chartered Bank (Vietnam) Ltd has recently launched three service guarantees including promises that a customer will have to wait no longer than 8 minutes for teller service, 30 minutes for opening a new account and 24 hours for a decision on a personal loan. And when it hosted the 2010 FIFA football World Cup, the government of South Africa was required to make 17 guarantees of service performance, covering safety and security, healthcare services, transport and a guaranteed level of telecommunication services.

The *conditional or specific guarantee* spells out certain elements of the service offering that an organization chooses to stand behind. In the hotel sector, IBIS, the French-based international hotel chain, guarantees that 'any problems caused by the hotel will be rectified within 15 minutes'. Radisson Hotels, on the other hand, offers an *unconditional* 100 per cent satisfaction guarantee across its hotels worldwide. Unconditional guarantees offer compensation when the customer is less than 100 per cent satisfied – they are simple to understand and usually have no hidden clauses or conditions. With an unconditional guarantee the customer is the ultimate judge of quality.

Service guarantees are implemented for three main reasons – as a marketing tool, as a quality tool or as a customer service device. From a marketing perspective, a service guarantee can differentiate a firm from the competition. For marketers, a service guarantee can encourage trial and help reduce buyers' perceived risk, particularly when a highly intangible service is purchased. It also potentially generates positive word of mouth from satisfied customers by reducing 'referral fear'.

A comprehensive case of a company using a service guarantee as a quality tool may be found at AAMI, a medium-sized Australian insurance company. Its guarantee was introduced as a strategic tool to drive its internal quality programme and to give an operational focus to the way in which claims were handled, so that service standards met customers' expectations. AAMI executives claimed that the guarantee process helped the company's quality initiatives in a number of ways:

- It defined and focused on customers' most important needs and concentrated resources on those needs. In doing so, it created a sense of urgency about service priorities.
- It helped to understand the service-delivery process, including the controllable and uncontrollable variables and possible weaknesses or failure points such as human resources or outside-supplier quality.
- It helped to establish customer-satisfaction measures as key performance indicators.
- It allowed errors to be tracked rather than rely on customer complaints.
- The process established a feedback loop for continuous improvement.

AAMI claimed that its guarantee gave their total quality management initiative a 'fresh focus' as previous attempts to improve customer service had been quite disparate. Despite the fact that the Australian general insurance industry code of practice required a minimum standard of performance, AAMI launched its more demanding guarantee requirements to pre-empt and exceed any efforts by competitors to move beyond the minimum requirements of the code of practice. As part of its continuous improvement process, ideas for new service guarantees are generated from customers' complaints, market research and staff research. A guarantee committee evaluates the potential for including new promises in the guarantee. For example, research identified that customers making insurance claims were unhappy about the delay between the agreement of a settlement and actually receiving their cheque. Customers expected a delay of no more than five working days but the average for the company was more than 15 days. The company's operations were modified to deliver against the customer's expectation and so this promise was added to the guarantee.

Other companies were using service guarantees not as a marketing or quality tool, but as a customer service device to encourage dissatisfied customers to complain. Complaints were then tracked as a monitor of the service level.

Practitioners agree that an effective service guarantee should be easy to understand and well communicated, meaningful to the customer, easy for the customer to invoke and easy for a customer to receive a payout. Guarantee design issues are therefore very important and go beyond just choosing the type of guarantee and stating any conditions. Strong service guarantees are enhanced by the promise of compensation should the service guarantee be invoked. In the case of AAMI, this penalty was established at a level where it could hurt the company and the effort of complaining for the customer was warranted. According to AAMI, '$25 isn't very much if you have a major disagreement with the company but for something minor like not having a decision-maker on hand at the time of your call, it is quite high'. AAMI's service guarantee (described by the company as a charter) outlines 18 specific service standards that customers can expect from the company. Any breaches of the guaranteed conditions are independently audited by a national accounting and audit firm. AAMI's performance against each service promise is made publicly available in an annual report.

Many other Australian service providers have followed the example of AAMI, and some of their guarantees are summarized in Figure 9.14. Australia Post offers a postal pack that is guaranteed to arrive by 10.00 a.m. the next day. It promises to supply a free replacement courier bag as compensation in the event of the original parcel not arriving by the specified time. The company claims that it meets its published deadlines 99 times out of 100, as audited by an independent accounting firm. This translated to around 30,000 parcels per year that failed to meet the promised delivery times. One manager noted that 'even if we had to compensate every one of those 30,000 customers with a replacement courier bag, it is such a small cost compared with the benefits of customer satisfaction'.

Figure 9.14 Overview of a range of service guarantees introduced by Australian service providers

| Case/industry | Guarantee type | Conditions | Invoking authority | Compensation |
|---|---|---|---|---|
| Communications – Telstra | Conditional | $25 of rental reduction per month for each day phone is out of order. | Customer and/or company | Monetary $25 |
| Video rental – Home Video | Conditional | If you don't like the movie you can return the video at no charge. | Customer | Monetary (Refund) |
| Postal services – Australia Post | Conditional | Express Post Pack – If the package does not reach destination by next day, you receive a free bag. | Customer | Monetary (Replacement) |
| Insurance – AAMI | Conditional/ Service Charter | Service Charter includes 17 service promises. | Customer and/or company | Monetary $25 |
| Real Estate – Hayden Real Estate | Conditional | No fees unless the property is sold. | Customer and/or company | Monetary (No charge) |
| Hotel – Radisson Hotels | Unconditional | 100% satisfaction or money refunded. | Customer | Monetary (Refund) |
| Plumbing – ABC Plumbing | Conditional | On-time arrival for all appointments. | Customer | Monetary (Refund) |

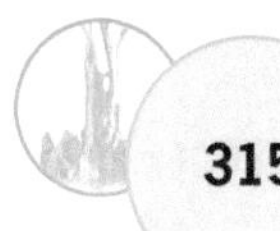

Another key consideration in the design of a service guarantee is deciding who has the authority or responsibility for invoking the service guarantee should the need arise: the customer, the company or either party. By virtue of its design, the unconditional guarantee implies that authority and responsibility for invoking the guarantee rest with the customer.

Australia Post requires a disgruntled customer to contact their local post office or to call the customer service department on a free 1300 number and quote their parcel's barcode number in order to invoke the guarantee. At AAMI insurance, between 70 and 80 per cent of the penalties paid under their guarantee were initiated by employees, rather than customers.

Industry experts suggest that any service guarantee that is entirely dependent upon the customer initiating a claim is less powerful than one that could be activated by either party, or by the service company only. However, for the company-invoked guarantee, there may be concerns that employees are under pressure not to invoke the guarantee if it reflects poorly on them personally or on their department. For example, if the housekeeping department of a hotel was more frequently cited for causing guests to activate the guarantee, housekeeping staff might become discouraged from initiating further payouts. The company-invoked guarantee may on the other hand act as a pleasant surprise to a guest in the service recovery process, particularly if the guest had been unaware of the existence of the service guarantee.

At Australia Post, experience showed that some customers would demand compensation for late deliveries beyond a replacement courier bag, which was the offer stated in the service guarantee. This was the case for misplacing important documents such as job applications that did not arrive at the destination on time. The response of Australia Post has been to 'judge each claim individually on its merit'. In one instance, when football final tickets went astray, the company arranged for replacement tickets.

Examples of poor guarantee designs exist. Some years ago, Lufthansa Airlines guaranteed a number of conditions to passengers, including that they would receive a seat in the class in which they booked and that their luggage would arrive with them at the destination. These promises were considered so fundamental to passengers that they weakened the impact of the guarantee and raised doubts in their minds that these promises might not be fulfilled. Another airline in the USA suffered from implementing a 100 per cent satisfaction guarantee, as customers claimed for all sorts of minor disputes such as the ice-cream served during the in-flight meal being too soft.

ANZ bank discontinued its service guarantee of 'more than 5 minutes in a queue or receive $5', claiming it had enabled the bank to demonstrate successfully its commitment to better customer service. Some observers argued that the service guarantee was discontinued because it conflicted with the bank's policy of discouraging branch banking in favour of Internet, telephone and automatic teller machine banking. A guarantee of not spending more than 5 minutes in a queue may have actually encouraged customers to visit the branches.

Implementing a service guarantee presents a number of possible benefits, but also potential risks. In designing an effective service guarantee, a company would need to identify which type of guarantee would work best.

## Case study review questions

1. Based on the information in the case and from your own ideas, develop a model depicting the possible benefits of a service guarantee for customers and the service provider.
2. Should a business school offer a service guarantee to its students? If so, what might it include? Are there any potential problems in implementing such a guarantee?
3. In what industries or circumstances would it not be sensible to offer a service guarantee?
4. Two potential benefits of offering a service guarantee are that it will increase the number of legitimate complaints and motivate employees to deliver better service. If you were the manager of a hotel that offered a 100 per cent unconditional service guarantee, how would you determine if your guarantee was working?
5. Think of a service (not one covered in the case study) that could benefit from a conditional service guarantee. Try to identify what aspects of the service could be included in a service promise to its customers.

## Summary and links to other chapters

Quality is a complex concept when applied to services and this chapter has reviewed some of the difficulties in seeking to measure a concept that can only be defined in consumers' minds. Much of what passes for service-quality measurement is ad hoc and misleading. However, there is disagreement over more comprehensive approaches to service-quality measurement and the role of expectations in influencing quality evaluations. Quality measurement alone is of little value if management does nothing to set standards for quality and to successfully implement these standards. This chapter has reviewed issues involved in the management of quality, which will be returned to in Chapter 10 in the context of human resource management.

A large part of this chapter's discussion on quality can be related back to the chapter discussing service encounters – blueprinting can be a valuable tool for designing services processes that consistently meet customers' expectations (Chapter 2). Increasingly, quality is assessed by customers on the basis of experiential values (Chapter 3). Quality of service is a prerequisite to the development of strong brands (Chapter 8) and stable long-term buyer–seller relationships (Chapter 5). Quality often results from co-creation of value with intermediaries (Chapter 4). Pricing (Chapter 11) can be used by potential buyers to evaluate the likely quality of a service, and a firm's communication efforts (Chapter 13) may act to raise or lower expectations of quality standards.

## Chapter review questions

1. Analyse the reasons why the assessment of service quality can be conceptually and practically much more difficult than the measurement of quality for manufactured goods.
2. Critically assess the role of expectations in defining and measuring service quality.
3. Discuss the factors that a consumer service organization should take into account when deciding on the level of service quality to provide. Would the factors be different in a business-to-business context?

## Activities

1. Gather together a sample of questionnaires from services companies that are designed to give the company an indication of its service-quality performance. Then critically assess the contribution that you think each of the questionnaires will make in giving the company a good indication of its performance. What, if any, changes would you recommend making to the questionnaire? What additional sources of information would you recommend in order to better inform the company's service-quality management?
2. Consider a selection of restaurants in an area with which you are familiar. What criteria are most important for defining their level of quality? Attempt to draw a positioning map showing the relative quality level of each restaurant.
3. Review a sample of websites belonging to courier/parcel delivery companies. Examine the promises made by each company with respect to reliability of delivery. Note what, if any, guarantees are provided to customers. Do you think the companies' promises and guarantees reassure potential customers? Where guarantees are offered, how easy are these to invoke?

## Key terms

**Benchmark** To set performance standards by reference to best practice elsewhere.

**Code of conduct** A code outlining the responsibilities of, or best practice for, an individual or organization.

**Customer charter** A statement by a service organization to its customers of the standards of service that it pledges to achieve.

**Customer delight** A service that exceeds a customer's expectations.

**Customer experience** Customers' perception of, and emotional response to, the totality of processes and outcomes that comprise a service offer.

**Disconfirmation model** Customers' prior expectations of a service are confirmed/disconfirmed by subsequent delivery of the service.

**Expectations** The standard of service against which actual service delivery is assessed.

**Focus group** A form of qualitative research in which a group of people are asked about their attitude towards a product, service, concept, advertisement or idea.

**Functional quality** Customers' subjective judgements of the quality of service delivery.

**Gaps model** An analysis of the causes of difference in quality between what customers expect and what they get.

**Management by walking about (MBWA)** A process by which key decision-makers in an organization keep in touch with issues at the point of service production and delivery.

**Mystery customers** A person employed by an organization to systematically record the standard of its service delivery.

**Quality circles** Groups of employees formed to discuss methods of better meeting customers' expectations of quality.

**Service level agreement (SLA)** A formal negotiated agreement between two parties specifying expected levels of service to be provided.

**Service–profit chain** The linkage between service production processes, value creation in the eyes of customers and, ultimately, the level of profitability achieved by an organization.

**SERVPERF** A method of measuring service quality using only performance measures.

**SERVQUAL** A method of measuring service quality, based on the gaps between the expectations of customers and their perceptions of actual service delivery.

**Technical quality** Objective measures of quality, not necessarily the measures that consumers consider to be the most important.

**Total quality management (TQM)** A management strategy aimed at embedding awareness of quality in all organizational processes.

**Webnography** The collection and analysis of comments posted on open access Internet fora.

**Zone of tolerance** The area between minimally acceptable and desired service quality levels.

## Selected further reading

*The following articles provide background discussion on the subjects of quality and satisfaction, and the effects of service intangibility:*

**Bebko, C.P.** (2000) 'Service intangibility and its impact on consumer expectations of service quality', *Journal of Services Marketing*, 14 (1), 9–26.

**Brady, M.K. and Cronin, J.J.** (2001) 'Some new thoughts on conceptualizing perceived service quality: a hierarchical approach', *Journal of Marketing*, 65 (3), 34–49.

**Etgar, M. and Fuchs, G.** (2009) 'Why and how service quality perceptions impact consumer responses', *Managing Service Quality*, 19 (4), 474–85.

**Grace, D. and O'Cass, A.** (2004) 'Examining service experiences and post-consumption evaluations', *Journal of Services Marketing*, 18 (6), 450–61.

**Parasuraman, A., Zeithaml, V.A. and Berry, L.L.** (1988) 'SERVQUAL: a multiple-item scale for measuring consumer perceptions of service quality', *Journal of Retailing*, 64 (1), 12–40.

*The link between service quality, customer loyalty and profitability is explored in the following papers:*

**Ferguson, R.J., Paulin, M. and Bergeron, J.** (2010) 'Customer sociability and the total service experience: antecedents of positive word-of-mouth intentions', *Journal of Service Management*, 21 (1), 25–44.

**Gruca, T.S. and Rego, L.L.** (2005) 'Customer satisfaction, cash flow and shareholder value', *Journal of Marketing*, 69 (3), 115–30.

**Piercy, N. and Rich, N.** (2009) 'High quality and low cost: the lean service centre', *European Journal of Marketing*, 43 (11/12), 1477–97.

**Rust, R.R., Lemon, K.N. and Zeithaml, V.A.** (2004) 'Return on marketing: using customer equity to focus marketing strategy', *Journal of Marketing*, 68 (1), 109–27.

*The complex role played by expectations in consumers' evaluation of service quality is further explored in the following articles:*

**Boulding, W., Kalra, A., Staelin, R. and Zeithaml, V.A.** (1993) 'A dynamic process model of service quality: from expectations to behavioural intentions', *Journal of Marketing Research*, 30 (1), 7–27.

**Cowley, E., Farrell, C. and Edwardson, M.** (2005) 'The role of affective expectations in memory for a service encounter', *Journal of Business Research*, 58 (10), 1419–25.

**Yap, K.B. and Sweeney, J.C.** (2007) 'Zone-of-tolerance moderates the service quality–outcome relationship', *Journal of Services Marketing*, 21 (2), 137–48.

**Palmer, A. and Koenig-Lewis, N.** (2011) 'The effects of pre-enrolment emotions and peer group interaction on students' satisfaction', *Journal of Marketing Management*, 27 (11), 1208–31.

*Discussion of service quality through electronic channels is brought up to date in the following articles:*

**Carlson, J. and O'Cass, A.** (2010) 'Exploring the relationships between e-service quality, satisfaction, attitudes and behaviours in content-driven e-service web sites', *Journal of Services Marketing*, 24 (2), 112–27.

**O'Cass, A. and Carlson, J.** (2012) 'An empirical assessment of consumers' evaluations of web site service quality: conceptualizing and testing a formative model', *Journal of Services Marketing*, 26 (6), 419–34.

**Parasuraman, A., Zeithaml, V.A. and Malhotra, A.** (2005) 'E-S-Qual: a multiple-item scale for assessing electronic service quality', *Journal of Service Research*, 7 (3), 213–33.

*Benchmarking is explored further in the following:*

**Koller, M. and Salzberger, T.** (2009) 'Benchmarking in service marketing – a longitudinal analysis of the customer', *Benchmarking: An International Journal*, 16 (3), 401–14.

**Merrill, P.** (2009) *Do It Right the Second Time: Benchmarking Best Practices in the Quality Change Process*, 2nd edn, American Society for Quality, Milwaukee, WI.

## References

**Ambler, T** (2003), *Marketing and the Bottom Line*, 2nd edn, FT Prentice Hall London.

**Arbore, A. and Busacca, B.** (2011) 'Rejuvenating importance-performance analysis', *Journal of Service Management*, 22 (3), 409–29.

**Anderson, E.W. and Fornell, C.** (1994) 'A customer satisfaction research prospectus', in R.T. Rust and R.L. Oliver (eds), *Service Quality: New Directions in Theory and Practice*, Sage, Thousand Oaks, CA.

**Anderson, E.W., Fornell, C. and Lehmann, D.R.** (1994) 'Customer satisfaction, market share and profitability', *Journal of Marketing*, 58 (3), 53–66.

**Babakus, E. and Boller, G.W.** (1992) 'An empirical assessment of the SERVQUAL scale', *Journal of Business Research*, 24 (3), 253–368.

**Bacon, D.R.** (2003) 'A comparison of approaches to importance–performance analysis', *International Journal of Market Research*, 45 (1), 55–71.

**Bates, K., Bates, H. and Johnston, R.** (2003) 'Linking service to profit: the business case for service excellence', *International Journal of Service Industry Management*, 14 (2), 173–83.

**Beatson, A., Coote, L. and Rudd, J.M.** (2006) 'Determining consumer satisfaction and commitment through self-service technology and personal service usage', *Journal of Marketing Management*, 22 (7), 853–82.

**Bebko, C.P.** (2000) 'Service intangibility and its impact on consumer expectations of service quality', *Journal of Services Marketing*, 14 (1), 9–26.

**Bitner, M.** (1990) 'Evaluating service encounters: the effects of physical surroundings and employee responses', *Journal of Marketing*, 54 (2), 69–82.

**Bolton, R. and Drew, J.** (1991) 'A multistage model of customers' assessments of service quality and value', *Journal of Consumer Research*, 17 (4), 375–84.

**Bolton, R.N. and Lemon, K.N.** (1999) 'A dynamic model of customers' usage of services: usage as an antecedent and consequence of satisfaction', *Journal of Marketing Research*, 36 (2), 171–86.

**Bowers, M.R. and Martin, C.L.** (2007) 'Trading places redux: employees as customers, customers as employees', *Journal of Services Marketing*, 21 (2), 88–98.

**Brady, M.K. and Cronin, J.J. Jr** (2001) 'Some new thoughts on conceptualizing perceived service quality: a hierarchical approach', *Journal of Marketing*, 65 (3), 34–49.

**Brown, T.J., Churchill, G.A. and Peter, J.P.** (1993) 'Improving the measurement of service quality', *Journal of Retailing*, 69 (1), 127–39.

**Buttle, F.** (1996) 'SERVQUAL: review, critique, research agenda', *European Journal of Marketing*, 30 (1), 8–32.

**Chase, R.B. and Dasu, S.** (2001) 'Want to perfect your company's service? Use behavioral science', *Harvard Business Review*, 79 (6), 78–84.

**Cowley, E., Farrell, C. and Edwardson, M.** (2005) 'The role of affective expectations in memory for a service encounter', *Journal of Business Research*, 58 (10), 1419–25.

**Cronin, J.J.** (2003) 'Looking back to see forward in services marketing: some ideas to consider', *Managing Service Quality*, 13 (5), 332–7.

**Cronin, J.J. and Taylor, S.A.** (1992) 'Measuring service quality: a re-examination and extension', *Journal of Marketing*, 56 (3), 55–68.

**Cronin, J.J. and Taylor, S.A.** (1994) 'SERVPERF versus SERVQUAL: reconciling performance-based and perceptions-minus-expectations measurement of service quality', *Journal of Marketing*, 58 (1), 125–31.

**Crosby, P.B.** (1984) *Quality Without Tears*, New American Library, New York.

**Csikszentmihalyi, M.** (1988) 'The flow experience and its significance for human psychology', in M. Csikszentmihalyi and I.S. Csikszentmihalyi (eds), *Optimal Experience: Psychological Studies of Flow in Consciousness*, Cambridge University Press, Cambridge.

**Dabholkar, P.A., Thorpe, D.I. and Rentz, J.O.** (1996) 'A measure of service quality for retail stores scale development and validation', *Journal of the Academy of Marketing Science*, 24 (1), 3–16.

**Dattakumar, R. and Jagadeesh, R.** (2003) 'A review of literature on benchmarking', *Benchmarking: An International Journal*, 10 (3), 176–209.

**Dick, A.S. and Basu, K.** (1994) 'Customer loyalty: toward an integrated conceptual framework', *Journal of the Academy of Marketing Science*, 22 (2), 99–113.

**Evans, J.R. and Lindsay, W.M.** (2005) *The Management and Control of Quality*, 6th edn, Thomson South-Western, Mason, OH.

**Fornell, C., Johnson, M.D., Anderson, E.W., Cha, J. and Bryant, B.E.** (1996) 'The American Customer Satisfaction Index: nature, purpose, and findings', *Journal of Marketing*, 60 (4), 7–18.

**Fornell, C., Mithas, S., Morgeson, F.V. III and Krishnan, M.S.** (2006) 'Customer satisfaction and stock prices: high returns, low risk', *Journal of Marketing*, 70 (1), 3–14.

**Gabbie, O. and O'Neill, M.** (1997) 'SERVQUAL and the Northern Ireland hotel sector: a comparative study – part 2', *Managing Service Quality*, 7 (1), 43–9.

**Galloway, L.** (1999) 'Hysteresis: a model of consumer behaviour?', *Managing Service Quality*, 9 (5), 360–70.

**Getty, J.M. and Thompson, K.N.** (1994) 'The relationship between quality, satisfaction and recommending behaviour in lodging decisions', *Journal of Hospitality and Leisure Marketing*, 2 (3), 3–22.

**Grönroos, C.** (1984a) 'A service quality model and its marketing implications', *European Journal of Marketing*, 18 (4), 36–44.

**Grönroos C.** (1984b) *Strategic Management and Marketing in the Service Sector*, Chartwell-Bratt, Bromley.

**Gwynne, A., Ennew, C. and Devlin, J.** (1999) 'Service quality and customer satisfaction: a longitudinal analysis', *Proceedings of the 28th European Marketing Academy Conference*, 25.

**Hawes, J.M. and Rao, C.P.** (1985) 'Using importance–performance analysis to develop health care marketing strategies', *Journal of Health Care Marketing*, 5 (4), 19–25.

**Heskett, J.L., Sasser, W.E. and Schlesinger, L.A.** (1997) *The Service Profit Chain*, Free Press, New York.

**Holbrook, M.B.** (2006) 'Consumption experience, customer value, and subjective personal introspection: an illustrative photographic essay', *Journal of Business Research*, 59 (6), 147–60.

**Iacobucci, D., Ostrom, A. and Grayson, K.** (1995) 'Distinguishing service quality and customer satisfaction: the voice of the consumer', *Journal of Consumer Psychology*, 4 (3), 277–303.

**ICS** (2013) *UKCSI July 2013, The State of Customer Satisfaction in the UK*, Institute of Customer Service, London.

**Johnston, R.** (2001) 'Linking complaint management to profit', *International Journal of Service Industry Management*, 12 ( 1), 60–9.

**Joseph, M., McClure, C. and Joseph, B.** (1999) 'Service quality in the banking sector: the impact of technology on service delivery', *International Journal of Bank Marketing*, 17 (4), 182–91.

**Juran, J.M.** (1982) *Upper Management and Quality*, Juran Institute, New York.

**Kahneman, D. and Miller, D.T.** (1986) 'Norm theory: comparing reality to its alternatives', *Psychological Review*, 93 (2), 136–53.

**Kaplan, R.S. and Norton, D.P.** (1996) 'Using the balanced scorecard as a strategic management system', *Harvard Business Review*, 74 (1), 75–85.

**Kaplan, R.S. and Norton, D.P.** (2001a) 'Transforming the balanced scorecard from performance measurement to strategic management, *Accounting Horizons*, Part I, 15 (1), 87–104 and Part II, 15 (2), 147–60.

**Kaplan, R.S. and Norton, D.P.** (2001b) *The Strategy-Focused Oganization: How Balanced Scorecard Companies Thrive in the New Business Environment*, Harvard Business School Press, Boston, MA.

**Keller, E. and Berry, J.** (2006) 'Word-of-mouth: the real action is offline', *Advertising Age*, 77 (49), 20.

**Kozinets, R.V.** (2006) 'Netnography 2.0', in R.W. Belk (ed.), *Handbook of Qualitative Research Methods in Marketing* (129–42), Edward Elgar, Cheltenham, UK.

**Lee, E., Hu, M.Y. and Toh, R.S.** (2000) 'Are consumer survey results distorted? Systematic impact of behavioral frequency and duration on survey response errors', *Journal of Marketing Research*, 37 (1), 125–33.

**Lusch, R.F. and Vargo, S.L.** (2006) 'Service-dominant logic: reactions, reflections and refinements', *Marketing Theory*, 6 (3), 281–88.

**Malmi, T.** (2001) 'Balanced scorecards in Finnish companies: a research note', *Management Accounting Research*, 12 (2), 207–20.

**McAlexander, J.H., Kaldenberg, D.O and Koenig, H.** (1994) 'Service quality measurement', *Journal of Health Care Marketing*, 14 (3), 34–9.

**Murdy, S. and Pike, S.** (2012) 'Perceptions of visitor relationship marketing opportunities by destination marketers: an importance-performance analysis', *Tourism Management*, 33 (5), October, 1281–5.

**Newberry, C.R.F., Klemz, B.R. and Boshoff, C.** (2003) 'Managerial implications of predicting purchase behavior from purchase intentions: a retail patronage case study', *Journal of Services Marketing*, 17 (6), 609–20.

**Oliver, R.** (1997) *Satisfaction: A Behavioral Perspective of the Consumer*, McGraw-Hill, New York.

**O'Neill, M., Palmer, A. and Beggs, R.** (1998), 'The effects of survey timing on perceptions of service quality', *Managing Service Quality*, 8 (2), 126–32.

**O'Neill, M., Palmer, A. and Charters, S.** (2002) 'Wine production as a service experience – the effects of service quality on wine sales', *Journal of Services Marketing*, 6 (4), 342–60.

**Otley, D.** (1999) 'Performance management: a framework for management control systems research', *Management Accounting Research*, 10 (4), 363–82.

**Palmer, A. and O'Neill, M.** (2003) 'The effects of perceptual processes on the measurement of service quality', *Journal of Services Marketing*, 17 (3), 252–74.

**Paraskevas, A.** (2001) 'Exploring hotel internal service chains: a theoretical approach', *International Journal of Contemporary Hospitality Management*, 13 (5), 251–8.

**Parasuraman, A., Zeithaml, V.A. and Berry, L.L.** (1985) 'A conceptual model of service quality and its implications for future research', *Journal of Marketing*, 49 (4), 41–50.

**Parasuraman, A., Zeithaml, V.A. and Berry, L.L.** (1988) 'SERVQUAL: A multiple-item scale for measuring consumer perceptions of service quality', *Journal of Retailing*, 64 (1), 12–40.

**Passikoff, R.** (1997) 'The limits of customer satisfaction', *Brandweek*, 38, 17.

**Pike, S.** (2003) 'Hot chicks', 'better parties' or academic stuff – perceptions of a regional university campus using repertory grid analysis and importance–performance analysis, *Australia and New Zealand Marketing Academy Conference (ANZMAC)* Proceedings, Adelaide, 1–3 December, pp. 1288–95.

**Puri, A.** (2007) 'The web of insights: the art and practice of webnography', *International Journal of Market Research*, 49 (3), 387–408.

**Rust, R.T. and Oliver, R.L.** (eds) (1994) *Service Quality: New Directions in Theory and Practice*, Sage, Thousand Oaks, CA.

**Speckbacher, G., Bischof, J. and Pfeiffer, T.** (2003) 'A descriptive analysis on the implementation of balanced scorecards in German-speaking countries', *Management Accounting Research*, 14 (4), 361–87.

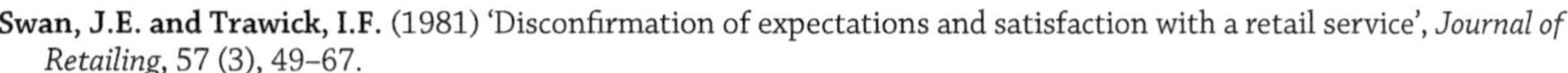

**Swan, J.E. and Trawick, I.F.** (1981) 'Disconfirmation of expectations and satisfaction with a retail service', *Journal of Retailing*, 57 (3), 49–67.

**Wright, C. and O'Neill, M.** (2002) 'Service quality evaluation in the higher education sector: an empirical investigation of students' perceptions', *Higher Education Research & Development*, 21 (1), 23–39.

**Zeithaml, V.A., Berry, L.L. and Parasuraman, A.** (1993) 'The nature and determinants of customer expectations of service', *Journal of the Academy of Marketing Science*, 21 (1), 1–12.

**Zeithaml, V.A., Berry, L.L. and Parasuraman, A.** (1996) 'The behavioral consequences of service quality', *Journal of Marketing*, 60 (2), 31–46.

**Zeithaml, V.A., Parasuraman, A. and Berry, L.** (1990) *Delivering Service Quality: Balancing Customer Perceptions and Expectations*, Free Press, New York.

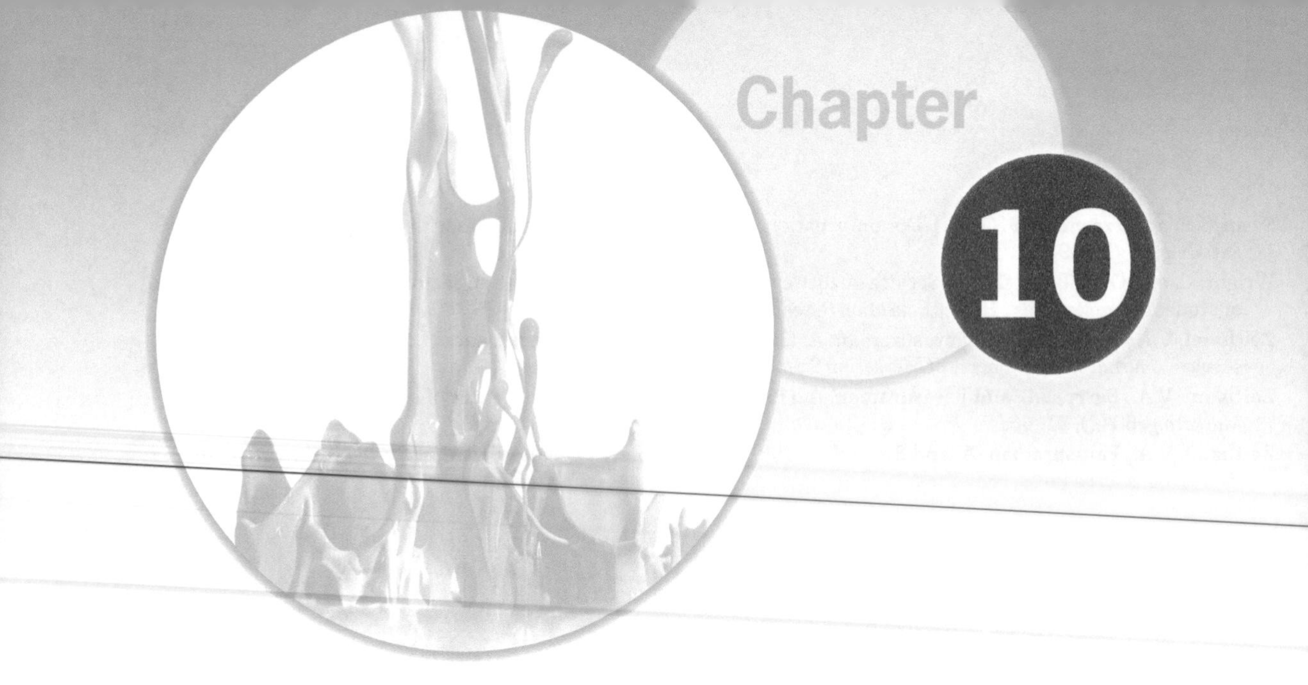


# Engaging employees in service delivery

*Consider a weekend leisure break in a hotel and the things which typically are most likely to go wrong: the checking-in procedure is slow and unfriendly; facilities in the room are not as promised and the hotel is slow to put things right; or the bill is wrongly made up and it takes a lot of effort by the customer to put it right. All of these instances illustrate the importance of employees in meeting customers' expectations. Appropriate actions by front-line employees, and effective management of these employees, could have avoided many of these problems. Of course, employees can also be responsible for particularly good service encounters. But how do you get the best out of employees so that they feel engaged with their job and instinctively do what is best for the customer? That is the subject of this chapter.*

## Learning objectives

After reading this chapter, you should understand:

- The interrelationship of marketing, human resource management and operations management
- The contribution of employee performance to customer satisfaction and subsequently to an organization's profitability
- Key issues involved in the recruitment, motivation, training and control of staff employed in the services sector, especially those involved in front-line service encounters

## 10.1 Introduction

The importance of people as a component of the service offer has been stressed on many occasions in previous chapters of this book. Most service production processes require the service organization's personnel to provide significant inputs to the service production process, both at the front-line point of delivery and in those parts of the production process that are relatively removed from the final consumer. In the case of many one-to-one personal services, the service provider's personnel constitute by far the most important element of the total service offering. The management of this input, in terms of recruiting the best personnel and training, motivating, rewarding and controlling them, becomes crucial in influencing the quality of service that customers experience.

Services management has often been described as the bringing together of the principles of marketing, operations management and human resource management, in which it can sometimes be difficult – and undesirable – to draw distinctions between the three approaches (Figure 10.1). In this way, methods to improve the service provided by staff of a fast-food restaurant can be seen as a marketing problem (e.g. the need to analyse and respond to customer needs for such items as speed, variety and cleanliness), as an operations management problem (scheduling work in a manner that reduces bottlenecks and allows a flexible response to patterns of demand) or as a **human resource management (HRM)** problem (selecting and motivating staff in such a way that maximizes their ability to deliver a specified standard of service). There has been debate about whether organizations need a separate human resource (HR) department, or whether their functions should be located within teams responsible for operations and marketing (Martins and Grahl, 2010).

It can be almost a cliché to say that for some businesses, the employees are the business – if these are taken away, the organization is left with very few assets with which it can seek to gain competitive advantage in meeting customers' needs. Numerous studies have demonstrated the effects of employees' customer orientation on service performance (e.g. Donavan et al., 2004).

Figure 10.1 The interfaces between marketing management, operations management and human resource management

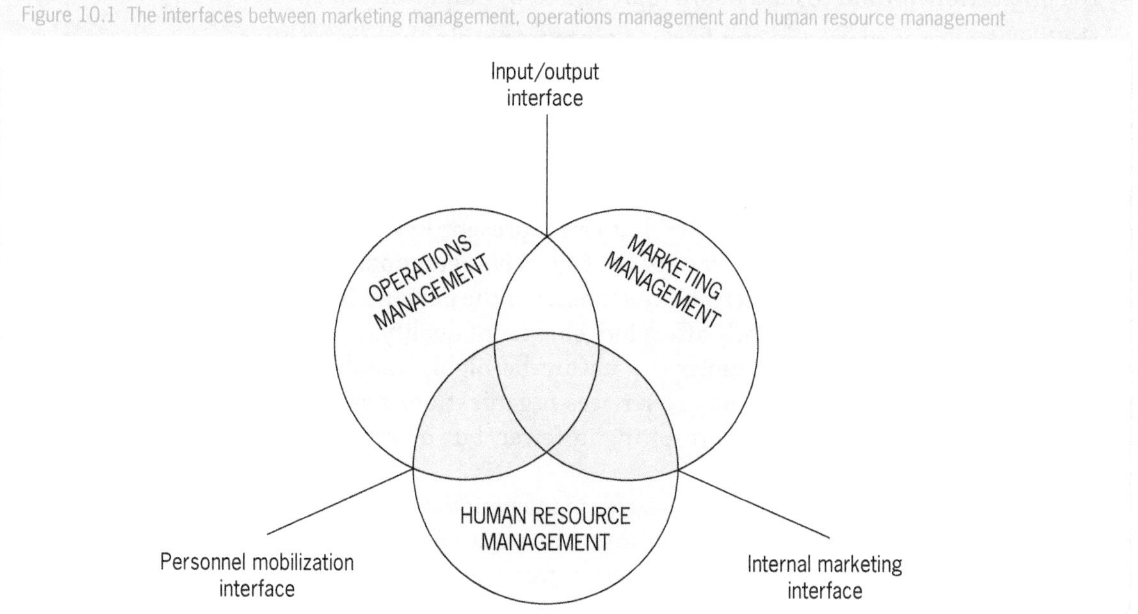

Figure 10.2 The importance of personnel within the service offer. The challenge of internal marketing is particularly great where employees account for a high proportion of an organization's total costs, and where employees have a high level of interaction with customers.

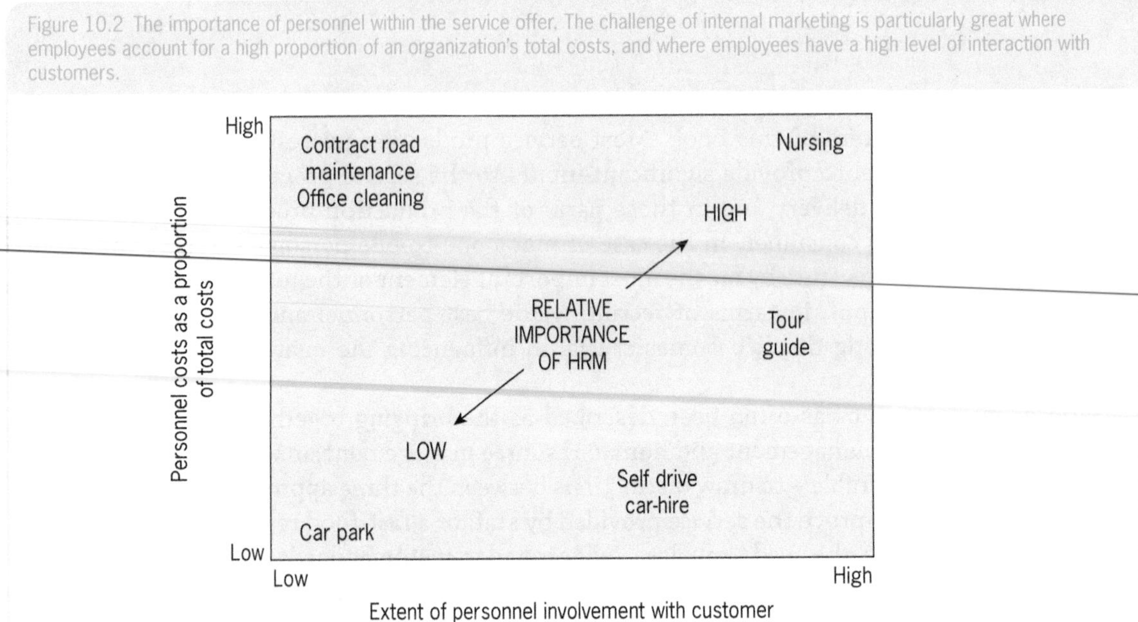


It has also been suggested that the concept of a service brand personality is inextricably linked to the personality of the individuals who work for the organization (Harris and Fleming, 2005).

While for some organizations the management of personnel can be seen as just one other asset to be managed, for others human resource management is so central to the activities of the organization that it cannot be seen as a separate activity. Some indication of the importance attached to human resource management within any organization can be gained by examining two aspects of personnel:

- the proportion of total costs that are represented by employee costs;
- the importance of customer–employee encounters within the service offer.

In Figure 10.2 these two dimensions are shown in a matrix form with examples. For human resource management, the most critical group of services is found where employees account for a high proportion of total costs and form an important part of the service offering perceived by the consumer. Many personal services such as hairdressing fall into this category. In other cases, employee costs may be a small proportion of total costs, but can represent key individuals who can significantly affect consumers' perceptions of a service. In this way, personnel costs are typically a relatively small proportion of the costs of a telephone service, yet the performance of key front-line staff such as service engineers can significantly affect judgements of quality.

The human input to services can by its nature be highly variable, resulting in variability in perceived quality. For this reason, many services organizations have sought to replace personnel with equipment-based inputs, often resulting in fewer, but more highly trained, personnel being required.

The importance attached to human resource management is also a reflection of the competitiveness of the environment in which an organization operates. At one extreme, the highly competitive environment that faces most Western European fast-food restaurants requires organizations to ensure that their staff meet customers' needs for speed, friendliness and accuracy more effectively

than their competitors. On the other hand, organizations with relatively protected markets (for example some public-sector services) can afford to be less customer-led in the manner in which their human resources are managed.

### Thinking around the subject: Customers before employees?

Many companies have developed a philosophy of putting their employees first. This at first might sound contradictory to the marketing philosophy that puts customers at the centre of a firm's thinking, but there are many examples of companies who have made this proud claim and achieved credible results. The American South Western Airlines has frequently been cited as an advocate of this approach, and has expanded rapidly and profitably. The airline has argued that employees are such a major part of its service offer that, if they are not happy, it is unlikely that the airline's customers will be happy. Being a relatively new airline with no history of poor industrial relations undoubtedly helped employees to identify with the company's mission. Having staff incentive schemes that encourage employees to perform to their best in a highly competitive market also helps. But can this approach work in all situations? If employees do not share a company's mission, management's attempts to put employees first may not be reciprocated in the form of employees' enthusiastic contribution to the business. And, if there is very little external competition to spur them on, captive customers may come second best by a long way.

In reality, it is difficult to talk about employees coming first if by implication customers come second. They should both be seen as part of a virtuous circle in which attention given to one reinforces attention given to the other. One approach advocated by Bowers and Martin (2007) is for a company to improve the interface by treating employees as customers and customers as employees.

## 10.2 Internal marketing

The term '**internal marketing**' has come to be widely used to describe the practice of turning many of the established techniques of marketing inward by focusing on employees. Of course, services marketers have a lot to learn from human resource management. The role of marketing is to achieve organizational goals by satisfying customers' needs. Human resource management is concerned with achieving organizational goals. It therefore follows that HRM must itself be concerned with satisfying the needs of external customers. Human resource management can be contrasted with the more traditional personnel management, which is often seen as being isolated and separate from the business aims of firms. Personnel management has frequently been oriented towards control and administrative activities rather than the alignment of human resources towards achieving strategic organizational goals. In so doing, personnel management has often become too concerned about achieving its own set of sub-goals, which are not necessarily related to the marketing needs of an organization. In this way, the maintenance of a uniform pay structure may have been seen as a desirable objective in its own right by personnel managers, despite the fact that the marketing needs of an organization may require more flexibility in the manner in which staff are paid.

## In practice: The world's favourite airline?

Established airlines have faced increasing competition as a result of deregulation and the emergence of budget, 'no-frills' airlines such as easyJet and Air Berlin. While these new airlines have been particularly successful in attracting price-sensitive travellers, a large part of the market still prefers to travel with a 'full service' airline and is prepared to pay more than the rock-bottom prices sometimes advertised by budget airlines. British Airways promotes the fact that it has achieved high customer satisfaction ratings through the actions of its employees. Its reputation for good staff is based not just on smiling at customers, but on being able to empathize with customers and to solve their problems. Operating aircraft is subject to all sorts of uncertainties, such as aircraft failure, bad weather and overbooking, all of which can have an immediate and profound impact on customers. An important role of employees is to ameliorate the effects of such uncertainties and to use initiative to solve customers' problems.

Figure 10.3 Appreciating your staff – a classic BA advert. (Reproduced courtesy of British Airways)

We're not the best airline because of our awards. We're the best airline because of our people.

Thanks to everyone who works for British Airways, we've been voted 'Best Airline of the Year' for the 10th year running by the readers of Business Traveller Magazine.

The term 'internal marketing' came to prominence from the 1980s and an early definition of internal marketing provided by Berry was:

> *"the means of applying the philosophy and practices of marketing to people who serve the external customers so that (i) the best possible people can be employed and retained and (ii) they will do the best possible work."*
>
> (Berry, 1980)

In an attempt to refine the concept, Varey and Lewis (1999) conceptualized a number of dimensions:

- *Internal marketing as a metaphor*. Jobs in an organization are 'products' to be marketed and managers should think like a marketer when dealing with people. However, the employer is both a buyer and consumer in the employment relationship.
- *Internal marketing as a philosophy*. Managers may hold a conviction that HRM requires 'marketing-like' activities. However, this does not address employees' divergent needs and interests, which may themselves be quite different from those of the organization. This is especially the case if the 'marketing' activities are actually promotional advertising and selling of management requirements. Employees may merely be seen as the manipulable subject of managerial programmes.
- *Internal marketing as a set of techniques*. Human resource management may adopt market research, segmentation and promotional techniques in order to inform and persuade employees. But internal marketing as the manipulation of the '4Ps' imposes management's point of view on employees and cannot be said to be employee (customer) centred. Therefore, it is employees who must change their needs or must understand the position of the employer as they respond to the market.

- *Internal marketing as an approach.* There is an explicit symbolic dimension to HRM practices, such as employee involvement and participation and statements about the role of employees within the organization. These are used to bring about indirect control of employees. Nevertheless, the symbolism of internal marketing may reveal many contradictions. For example, individualism contradicts team working, and the service culture as defined by management may contradict attitudes towards employee flexibility and responsibility. The complexities of managing people and their actions and knowledge may be reduced to mere 'techniques' of symbolic communication.

Much debate surrounds just how internal marketing fits within traditional HRM structures and processes. Hales (1994), for example, is critical of the 'managerialist' perspective on internal marketing and of the literature on internal marketing as an approach to HRM. Viewed as an activity in isolation, internal marketing is unlikely to succeed. For that to happen, the full support of top management is required.

Finally, it should be noted that, although academics (especially marketing academics) may use the term 'internal marketing' excitedly, practitioners are more likely to use terms such as 'employee engagement' to describe an essentially similar phenomenon (discussed later in this chapter).

### 10.2.1 Employees as internal customers

Every organization can be considered to be a marketplace consisting of a diverse group of employees, who engage in exchanges with each other. In order to have their needs met, employees are often dependent upon internal services provided by other departments or individuals within their organization. These internal encounters include relationships between customer-contact staff and the backroom staff, managers and the customer-contact staff, managers and the backroom staff and, for large organizations, between the head office and each branch. In the most general sense, employees have been seen by some as 'consumers' of services provided by their employer, such as a pleasant working environment, provision of a pension scheme and good facilities for performing their tasks.

Increasingly, organizations are asking internal service departments, such as information technology, human resources, accounting and media services, to be more accountable. In many cases, organizations have outsourced the services traditionally provided by such internal departments, resulting in extended 'network' or 'virtual' organizations. This has resulted in employees effectively trading services with other employees within their organization.

This view of different internal suppliers and customers, some of whom deal directly within the service delivery process and others who provide support services to the service delivery process, appears to be closely related to the concept of the value chain (Porter, 1980). A modified value chain in terms of internal suppliers is shown in Figure 10.4. This idea of a value chain and internal trading of services is closely related to the idea developed in the total quality management literature of 'Next operation as customer' (NOAC) (Denton, 1990). 'Next operation as customer' is based on the idea that each group within an organization should treat the recipients of their output as an internal customer and strive to provide high-quality outputs for them. Through this approach, quality will be built into the service delivered to the final customer.

There are, however, problems in drawing analogies between internal and external markets for services. External customers can usually take their business elsewhere if they are not satisfied with the service provided, while internal customers may be required to use a designated service unit within their organization. Consequently, the internal customer is frequently a captive customer

Figure 10.4 A modified value chain for internally produced services

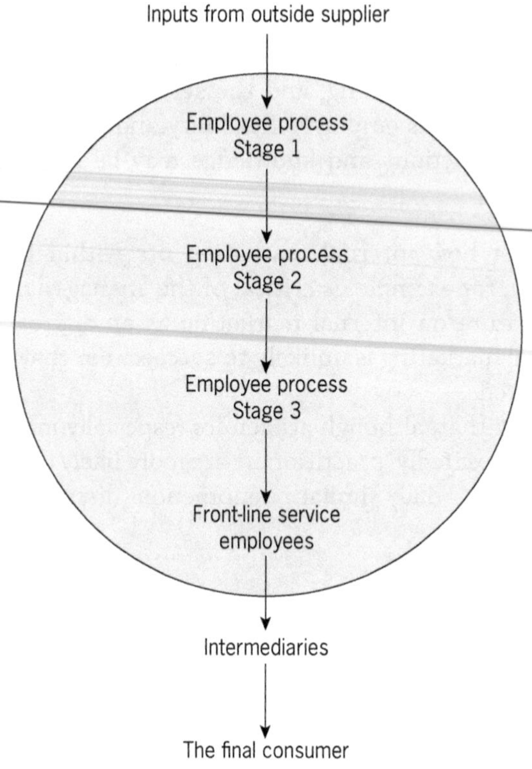

Inputs from outside supplier

Employee process Stage 1

Employee process Stage 2

Employee process Stage 3

Front-line service employees

Intermediaries

The final consumer

(Albrecht, 1990). Employees as customers may be tied to employment contracts with little short-term prospect of 'buying' employment elsewhere.

Many studies of internal marketing, which focus on internal customers and suppliers, have not differentiated between the different types of internal customers that may exist within the firm and their differing internal service expectations. This would appear to be no more marketing oriented than a marketing plan that treats all external customers as homogeneous. There is a need to explore the service expectations of different internal customer segments within the internal market and to identify any differences between these segments. This knowledge can then be applied to the internal marketing programme to maximize its effectiveness.

There is a widely held view that, if employees are not happy with their jobs, external customers will never be uppermost in their minds (Gounaris and Boukis, 2013). Researchers have tended to agree that satisfied internal customers are a critical prerequisite to the satisfaction of external customers. For example, in one study of 223 financial advisers and their clients, participants' enjoyment had a significant effect on satisfaction evaluations (Kin et al., 2012).

From an internal marketing perspective, there is an argument that, by satisfying the needs of their internal customers, firms enhance their ability to satisfy the needs of their external customers. Nevertheless, it has also been recognized that service encounters are a three-way fight between the firm, the contact personnel and the customer. The service encounter is thus a 'compromise between partially conflicting parties' (Bateson, 1989). To give an example, it may sound like a good idea to give employees longer rest breaks because this satisfies their needs as internal 'customers'. But longer rest breaks may result in greater waiting time for external customers as fewer staff are now available to serve them. A fine balance has to be drawn and there is no conclusive proof that in all situations happier employees necessarily result in happier external customers and a more profitable service operation (see Silvestro, 2002).

### Thinking around the subject: 'Theory of business' used to evaluate employees' contribution

Trying to understand the process of value creation within an organization can be very difficult, involving many linkages between different elements of an internal value chain. Just how much is each individual employee, or group of employees, worth to a company? Bruhn et al. (2004) reported the case of the German bank Direkt Anlage Bank AG (DAB), which used the 'balanced scorecard' (BSC) approach to try to make such estimates. DAB used the balanced scorecard to record information down to the lowest level of the command structure, that is, every employee had a personal BSC derived from divisional BSCs, which were in turn derived from the corporate BSC. In 1999 the management of DAB developed a 'theory of business', portrayed as a diagram of supposed cause-and-effect linkages among key performance indicators, including qualitative and quantitative indicators.

To test the theory, DAB developed a monitoring system to collect the necessary data. From January 2000, DAB measured all the BSC indicators on a monthly basis. These indicators comprised the four perspectives of the BSC:

- human resources (global employee satisfaction, recommendation rate of DAB as employer, employee turnover, employee fluctuation, job performance such as number of failures and absence);
- customers (global customer satisfaction, satisfaction with dimensions and items, intention to remain loyal, recommendation rate of DAB, market share, number of new customers, name recognition rate);
- processes (cycle time, capacity, number of failures, service level, productivity);
- finance (profitability, revenue, cost, shareholder value).

DAB used longitudinal data to develop and estimate a structural equation model of its 'theory of business', enabling the estimation of the direction and strength of the relationships. The model allowed DAB to simulate the effects of changes across linkages, for example how an increase in employee satisfaction would lead to better processes, how this might influence customer satisfaction and, ultimately, the effect on profitability. The development of such a model might seem a remarkable achievement, given the complexity of large organizations. Can quantitative models of employees' contribution to a business ever really hope to capture the more qualitative contributions that can make all the difference in the eyes of customers?

## 10.3 Controlling and empowering staff

There are two basic approaches to managing service employees. On the one hand, staff can be supervised closely and corrective action taken where they fail to perform to standard. On the other hand, staff can be made responsible for controlling their own actions. The latter approach is often referred to as 'empowering' employees.

Should employees of service organizations be closely controlled, or should they be empowered to act in the best way they see fit? There is an argument that because many services are carried out on a one-to-one basis with little possibility of management intervention, day-to-day control by management is impossible. In such circumstances, controlling staff can be problematic as it is usually not possible to remove the results of poor personnel performance before their effects are felt by customers. While the effects of a poorly performing car maker can be concealed from customers by checking his or her tangible output, the inseparability of the service production/consumption process makes quality control difficult to achieve. Nevertheless, many companies that use industrialized service processes rely on control powers with varying degrees of formality.

Empowerment may be crucial for delivering services that are tailored to the needs of individual customers and may help turn service failures into effective recovery. The degree of empowerment given to employees, or the control exercised over them, depends on the format of a service delivery system. For low-contact, standardized services, employees can be controlled by mechanistic means such as rules and regulations. For high-contact, highly divergent services, high levels of empowerment may be more appropriate.

Empowerment essentially involves giving employees discretion over the way they carry out their tasks. Kelley (1993) distinguished between three types of employee discretion:

- *Routine discretion* occurs where employees are allowed to select an alternative from a prescribed list of possible actions in order to do their job (e.g. a service engineer having a choice of three sub-systems to install in order to rectify a specified problem).
- *Creative discretion* is exercised where employees are required to develop alternative methods of performing a task (e.g. an interior design consultant may have complete freedom to choose their own designs).
- *Deviant discretion* is negatively regarded by the employer as it involves behaviours that are not part of the employee's formal job description and are outside their area of authority.

Discussion of empowerment frequently stresses the need to share information, so that employees understand the context in which they work. Empowerment also implies a culture that encourages employees to experiment with new ideas and can tolerate them making mistakes and learning from them. Such a culture would be more in line with the image of the 'learning organization' (Garvin, 1993). Empowered employees need to be rewarded in a timely fashion and their initiatives, triumphs and achievements acknowledged.

The reasons for empowering employees can be divided into the mutually supportive dimensions of those that improve the motivation and productivity of employees and those that improve service delivery for consumers.

On the motivational side, empowerment of front-line service employees can lead to both attitudinal and behavioural changes in employees. Attitudinal changes resulting from empowerment include increased job satisfaction and reduced role stress. A consequence of increased job satisfaction is greater enthusiasm for their job, which can be reflected in better interaction with customers.

Behaviourally, empowerment can lead to quicker response by employees to the needs of customers, as less time is wasted in referring customers' requests to line managers. In situations where customer needs are highly variable, empowerment can be crucial in allowing employees to customize service delivery. In the event of a service failure, empowerment can facilitate a rapid recovery – if failures are not rectified quickly and satisfactorily, customers may lose trust and confidence in a service provider.

Advocates of tighter control mechanisms point to the disadvantages of empowerment. One of the consequences of empowerment is that it increases the scope of employees' jobs, requiring employees to be properly trained to cope with the wider range of tasks that they are expected to undertake. It also impacts on recruitment, because it is necessary to ensure that employees recruited have the requisite attitudinal characteristics and skills to cope with empowerment. Hartline and Ferrell (1996) found that, while empowered employees gained confidence in their abilities, they also experienced increased frustration and ambiguity through role conflict. Additionally, because empowered workers are expected to have a broader range of skills and to perform a greater number of tasks, they are likely to be more expensive to employ because of their ability to command higher rates of pay.

Far from improving the efficiency of service delivery processes, empowerment can actually lead to inefficiencies. An employee who is empowered to customize each service to individuals' specific requirements will be less efficient than one who is quite strictly controlled as to how much customization is to be carried out. Of course, it is another matter whether the empowered employee is more effective at satisfying customers' needs, but if the service blueprint is based on a no-frills, low-cost proposition, excessive empowerment and customization by employees may not be viable for a company. The company could, in the short term, cause delays to waiting customers who seek a standard service and, in the long term, find itself delivering excessive value to customers. Customization of service could also be perceived by some customers as unfair in situations where employees are observed to be favouring some customers rather than others. It has been pointed out by Martin (1996) that employees may consciously or unconsciously discriminate to give better service to friends or people who are similar to themselves in terms of age, gender or ethnicity.

Finally, empowering employees can cost actual money in the short term, which has to be balanced against possible revenue gains in the long term. Faced with a service failure, an empowered employee may over-compensate customers, not only incurring immediate costs for the company, but raising expectations for compensation next time that a service failure occurs.

Even with highly empowered employees, some residual forms of control are necessary. Control systems are closely related to reward systems in that pay can be used to control performance, for example bonuses forfeited in the event of performance falling below a specified standard. In addition, warnings or ultimately dismissal form part of a control system. In an ideal service organization that has a well-developed HRM policy, employees' involvement in their work should lead to considerable self-control or informal control from their peer group. Where such policies are less well developed, three principal types of control are used:

- *Simple controls* are typified by direct personal supervision of personnel – for example, a head waiter can maintain a constant watch over junior waiters and directly influence performance when this deviates from standard.
- *Technical controls* can be built into the service production process in order to monitor individuals' performance – for example, a supermarket checkout can measure the speed of individual operators and control action (e.g. training or redeployment) taken in respect of those shown to be falling below standard.
- *Bureaucratic controls* require employees to document their performance – for example, the completion of work sheets by a service engineer of visits made and jobs completed. Control action can be initiated in respect of employees who on paper appear to be underperforming.

In addition to these internal controls, the relationship that many front-line service personnel develop with their customers allows customers to exercise a degree of informal control. College lecturers teaching a class would in most cases wish to avoid hostility from their class, which might result from consistently delivering a poor standard of performance – in other words, the class can exercise a type of informal control.

So, in what situations should a service provider decide to empower its employees, rather than to tightly control them? A number of authors have suggested a contingency approach to empowerment. Ahmed and Rafiq (2003) have built on the work of Bowen and Lawler (1992) to develop a model of five factors that influence whether a control or empowerment approach is most appropriate:

- *Business strategy.* Firms undertaking a differentiation business strategy, or a strategy that involves high degrees of customization and personalization of services, should empower their employees. However, firms pursuing a low-cost, high-volume strategy should use a production-line approach to controlling employees.
- *Tie to the customer.* Where service delivery involves managing long-term relationships with customers rather than just performing a simple one-off transaction, empowerment is vital. Employees should be able to identify and respond flexibly to customers' changing needs over time, something that may be inhibited by a tightly scripted control approach.
- *Technology.* If the technology involved in service delivery simplifies and industrializes the tasks of employees, a controlled, production-line approach is more appropriate than empowerment. However, where the technology is non-routine or complex, empowerment is more appropriate.
- *Business environment.* Some environments are more variable than others; for example, an employee of a building repair contractor is likely to face variability caused by diversity of tasks, diversity of locations and diversity of weather conditions which will not allow the same level of control as a similar craftsman working within a factory environment.
- *Types of employees.* Bowen and Lawler (1992) recognized that empowerment and control approaches require different types of employees. Employees most likely to be effectively empowered are those who have high growth needs and who need to have their abilities tested at work. Where empowerment requires teamwork, employees should have strong social and affiliative needs and good interpersonal and group skills. Empowerment requires 'Theory Y'-type managers who allow employees to work independently to the benefit of the organization and its customers. The control approach requires 'Theory X'-type managers who believe in close supervision of employees (McGregor, 1960).

## Thinking around the subject: Can you control a doctor?

Many service sector employees have highly specialized technical skills, and find themselves managed by managers who know very little about the skills of the people they manage. How can managers control such people? Is empowering specialist staff to do what they think best a professional necessity, or something that goes against the principles of consumer sovereignty?

Health services present an interesting case study. In most developed countries, health service providers have seen an increase in the number of managers who have no clinical background. Increasingly, marketing managers are being appointed, mindful that in an increasingly market-driven health sector, understanding and responding to patients' needs becomes increasingly important. Indeed, the language of some hospital managers now talks about 'customers' rather than 'patients'.

Although the chief executive of a hospital in principle has ultimate authority over all employees, many people would recognize that it is the medical consultants who have the real power in a hospital. If they do not like a change that is proposed by the chief executive, they can point to their professional codes of conduct and years of training that have given them knowledge-based power. Consultants may argue that they have patients' long-term interests at heart, because they have invested heavily in their specialized training and will be around for many years to pick up the consequences of their actions. By contrast, managers are perceived as having relatively simple training, and move on to another job with no professional responsibility to see through the consequences of their actions. Managers with a non-clinical background may become too focused on relatively superficial quality-of-service issues, such as car parking and food, while consultants could argue that only they can judge the true quality of the core service of a hospital, namely the outcome of medical and surgical procedures. They point out that a typical patient is incapable of assessing clinical performance, owing to their limited knowledge and the fact that the outcomes of many clinical procedures will not fully present themselves for many months or even years into the future.

For a chief executive, the professional knowledge-based power of consultants may be seen as a source of frustration which is difficult to control. As an example, it has been claimed that many UK NHS hospitals' operating theatres are under-utilized on Friday afternoons. For a chief executive, one method of increasing the number of patient admissions would be to use these very expensive facilities on Friday afternoons, rather than to leave them idle. Consultants would argue that it is bad professional practice to commence operations just before the weekend, when there is only limited cover available in a hospital to rectify any clinical complications. Cynics may argue that consultants are using professional arguments as a smokescreen for giving themselves a long weekend, and a chance to get away early to play golf. Some have pointed out that consultants may nevertheless use Friday afternoons to undertake profitable private surgery elsewhere. How can a chief executive with a non-clinical background argue with the knowledge and professional responsibilities of a consultant? Should consultants be empowered to use their skills in the way that they consider best? After all, non-technical management may have practical difficulties in controlling such specialists. Or is health too important to be left to a group of people who, although they have specialist skills, may treat empowerment as an opportunity to put their own interests first?

## 10.4 Creating engagement by employees

Strategies to empower employees to make more effective service encounters are less likely to be successful if employees do not feel engaged in their job. Motivation, consent, participation and communication form essential focal points for an organization's HRM strategy for bringing about the sense of engagement that underlies empowerment. Human resource management stresses the individual employee and their importance to the organization and this importance cannot be made real if employees do not feel motivated to share organizational goals. Research has shown that service employee perceptions of how they are treated by their organization are associated with more effective service delivery and enhanced customer perceptions of service quality (Bienstock et al., 2003).

Motivation concerns the choices that employees make between alternative forms of behaviour in order that they as employees attain their own personal goals. The task of management is to equate the individual's personal goals with those of the organization – that is, getting employees morally involved with the service that they help to produce. This in turn requires employees to consent to the management of their work activity. Where this consent is obtained, employees can be motivated by some form of participation in the organization. Such participation gives the employee a small stake in the organization, be it financial or in the form of discretionary control over the performance of their work function.

## In practice: Service with a smile

How does this chain of coffee shops put a smile on his face, even when he is feeling down and facing customers who may be having a bad day? A number of issues are explored in this chapter, including making him feel a valued part of a team and matching the rewards on offer – financial and non-financial – to his needs and expectations. People earning a minimum wage level can be happier than those on high salaries, suggesting that the design of the job can result in marketing benefits by having happy, motivated staff facing customers. And there can be a virtuous circle, with happy staff leading to happy customers, which can itself lead to a pleasant working environment which adds to the happiness of staff.

Figure 10.5 A cheerful barista. (Reproduced by permission of i-Stock)

### 10.4.1 Consent

The term 'consent' covers a variety of management-led initiatives and strategies, which seek to give authority to management without actively emphasizing its coercive power. For many services provided on a one-to-one basis, direct monitoring and supervision of employees by management may be impossible to achieve anyway. Active consent is therefore of great use to the management of services organizations.

There have been various forms of employee participation and involvement designed to help management in the generation of consent. Such initiatives have included scientific management, paternalism and the 'human relations' approach. Each initiative has its own prescription for the generation of consent.

*Scientific management* approaches seek co-operation between employer and employee in terms of the division of labour, whereby individual employees work in pre-defined ways as directed by management. Advocates of scientific management saw mutual benefits for the employee and employer. For employees, specializing in one work activity would give the opportunity to earn more, especially through piece-rate pay systems, while management would benefit through greater work control and higher productivity. What Taylor (1911), the leading advocate of scientific management, did not expect was the hostility of employees to what is often described as the process of deskilling. We saw in Chapter 2 how the process of industrialization of services has resulted in many jobs being deskilled in accordance with the scientific-management prescription. However, it is necessary to balance the benefits of specialization and improved efficiency against employees' sense of alienation from their job, which occurs where they are involved in only a very small part of a service delivery process. In this way, scientific management may suggest that a visitor attraction employs guides who each conduct tours of just a part of the attraction, before passing visitors on to another guide who specializes in another area. However, a much greater sense of involvement from employees will probably occur if guides are trained to be able to deliver a complete guided tour of the attraction from beginning to end, although this may call for additional training.

*Paternalism* is often associated with Quaker employers such as Cadbury or Rowntree, who attempted to show that they were interested in their workforce at home as well as at work. Within

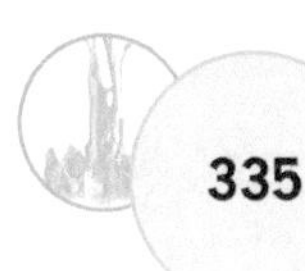



the services sector, many retail employers, such as Marks and Spencer, have traditionally taken a paternalistic attitude towards their employees by providing benefits such as on-site leisure services or temporary accommodation. This and other benefits, such as subsidized social clubs, are often designed to encourage employee identification with the company and therefore loyalty, which legitimizes managerial authority and hence consent to it.

*Human relations* approaches look at man as a social animal. Mayo (1933), in his study of General Electric in the USA, argued that productivity was unrelated to work organization and economic rewards as suggested by scientific management. Mayo emphasized the importance of atmosphere and social attitudes, group feelings and the sense of identification that employees had. He suggested that the separation of employees that scientific management had created prevented them from experiencing the sense of identification and involvement that is essential for all humans. Hence, one solution was to design group structures into production processes. Such processes were thought to assist in the generation of employees' loyalty to their organization via the work group. Mayo's work is similar in focus to that of Herzberg (1966) and Maslow (1943). Maslow suggested that humans have psychological needs as well as economic needs. To Herzberg, humans have lower- and higher-order needs. The former are the basic economic needs of food and shelter, whereas the latter are more psychologically based in terms of recognition and contribution to the group and the organization.

Some authors have pointed to an 'us and them' barrier between managers and employees as a reason for dissatisfaction at work, and it has been observed that employees who have a stake in the management of their organization are likely to be more highly motivated. In his book *Joy at Work*, Bakke has argued that everyone in an organization should be put in charge and the 'higher ups' should function as support for those on the front line. The distinction between 'management' and 'employees' too often serves to create resentment based on poor communication and feelings of powerlessness (Bakke, 2006).

### 10.4.2 Motivation

Motivation concerns goals and rewards. Maslow (1943) argued that motivation is based on individuals' desire to satisfy various levels of need. These levels range from the need to realize potential and self-development down to the satisfaction of basic needs such as hunger and thirst. Rewards for reaching goals can be tangible, for example money, or can be intangible (e.g. commendations or awards, which add to status or self-esteem). An organization has to bring about congruence between its own goals and those of its employees. This is the basis for designing an appropriate motivation package. Within the tourist attractions sector, a comparison can be made between many commercial operations (e.g. DisneyLand and Warwick Castle), where financial incentives are an important motivator, and volunteer-based organizations, such as the UK's National Trust, which attracts many unpaid volunteers, motivated by a desire to share in the preservation of historic buildings. Employees' attitudes and opinions about their colleagues and the work environment may make all the difference between workers merely doing a good job and delivering exceptional service (Arnett et al., 2002).

### 10.4.3 Communication

To many people, internal marketing is essentially about improving communication between a company and its employees. Many services organizations consider effective communication to be based on a one-way channel of information from managers to employees through such media as staff newsletters, but this is no more a definition of internal marketing than advertising is a definition of marketing. As in the case of marketing to external customers, communication to employees needs to be based on a sound understanding of the needs of individual segments within the workforce. There should also be some facility for feedback from employees.

Communication as an element of internal marketing is most notable when it is absent. Rumours about revised working arrangements, reductions in the workforce and changes to the terms of employment often circulate around companies, breeding a feeling of distrust by employees in their management. Some managers may take a conscious decision to give employees as little information as possible, perhaps on the basis that knowledge is power. There are sometimes strategic reasons for not disseminating information to employees (for example, business strategy may be a closely guarded secret in order to keep competitors guessing). However, in too many services organizations information is unnecessarily withheld from employees, creating a feeling of an underclass in terms of access to information. Such practices do not help to generate consent and moral involvement by employees.

Communication should be in a format that appeals to employees, rather than the convenience of management, in much the same way as external communications must begin by addressing the needs and media habits of the target audience. Do employees actually bother to read a boring-looking newsletter? Could the message be more effectively communicated through brightly coloured posters, a staff social event or even hiring a celebrity to make an announcement? In short, which form of communication will be most effective at eliciting the desired response from employees? In good-practice organizations, information can be communicated through a number of channels:

- The staff newsletter is a well-tried medium, but in many instances these are seen as being too little, too late and with inadequate discussion of the issues involved.
- Many organizations use team briefings (see below) to cascade information down through an organization and to communicate back upwards again.
- Company intranets, email and internal blogs have developed new opportunities for communicating information to a company's employees, allowing much greater personalization to the specific needs of individual employees, and also facilitating feedback. Open blogs to which any employee can contribute may be good for generating an engaged audience, but can be challenging to management where messages of dissent are posted by employees. If too much control is exerted by management, disaffected employees may instead turn to external open access blogs to air their grievances.
- Returning to the point that communication should be in a format that employees are likely to be receptive to, some organizations arrange social events to get a message across. A reception at a high-profile venue with a celebrity making an announcement about a new service offer may be listened to and the message retained longer than the same message received through an email.
- As with external communication, messages placed in unexpected places can attract attention, for example the values of a company can be restated in messages on coffee cups or by the water cooler.

Finally, external advertising should regard the internal labour force as a secondary target market. The appearance of advertisements on television can have the effect of inspiring confidence of employees in their management and pride in their company.

### 10.4.4 Strategies to increase employee engagement

The methods that an organization uses to encourage engagement by its employees are likely to be influenced by the type of person it employs and the extent to which their jobs present opportunities to exercise autonomy (that is, the extent to which employees are able to control their own work processes) and discretion (the degree of independent thinking they can exercise in performing their work).

This section considers various strategies to increase employees' engagement and comments on the suitability of such strategies for services organizations. In practice, organizations are more likely to be concerned with securing greater engagement by making individual employee objectives more congruent with those of the whole organization rather than through what could be described as collective participation. This type of engagement may be available to all employees, but the extent to which their actual participation is real and effective may well depend on where they are positioned in the employment hierarchy, that is, whether they are within the core or the peripheral groups of workers. Increased engagement is brought about by a combination of consultation and communication methods:

- *'Open door' policies* encourage employees to air their grievances and to make suggestions directly to their superiors. The aim of this approach is to make management accessible and 'employee friendly'. To be effective, the human relations approach would require employees to feel that they do, in fact, have a real say in managerial matters. As a consequence, management must appear to be open and interested in employee relations. It is likely that this approach to managerial style and strategy will emphasize open management through some of the methods described below.
- *Team briefings* are a system of communication within the organization where the leader of a group provides group members (up to about 20) with management-derived information. The rationale behind team briefings is to encourage commitment to and identification with the organization. Team briefings are particularly useful in times of organizational change, although they can be held regularly to cover such items as competitive progress, changes in policy and points of future action. Ideally, they should result in information 'cascading' down through an organization.
- *Quality circles* (QCs) are small groups of employees who meet together with a supervisor or group leader in an attempt to discuss their work in terms of production quality and service delivery. As such, they are a more focused form of team briefing. To be successful, the QC leader has to be willing to listen to and act upon issues raised by QC members. This is essential if the QC is to be sustained. Circle members must feel their participation is real and effective, and therefore the communication process within the QC must be two-way. If a quality circle appears to become only a routinized listening session, members may consider it to be just another form of managerial control.
- The *type of ownership* of an organization can influence the level of consent and participation. Where the workforce own a significant share of

Figure 10.6 Many successful service providers operate 'employee of the month' schemes to recognize excellent service by staff. This employee is obviously happy about winning the award, and it may reinforce his good performance. However, invariably one downside of such schemes can be a feeling of disillusionment by employees who are not selected for an award but who may feel equally deserving.

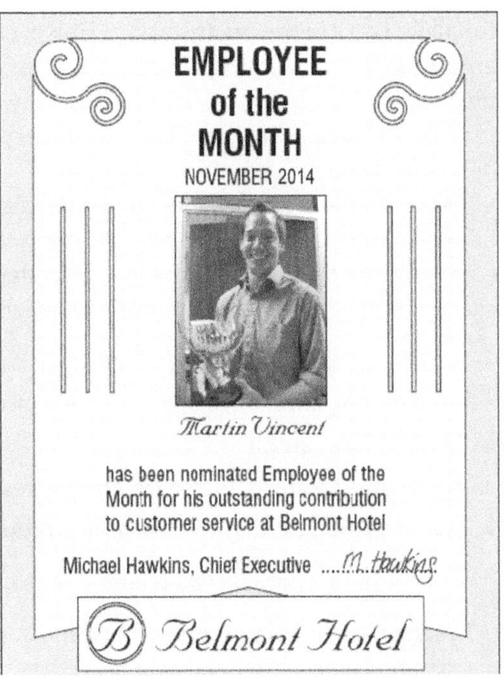
EMPLOYEE
of the
MONTH
NOVEMBER 2014
Martin Vincent
has been nominated Employee of the
Month for his outstanding contribution
to customer service at Belmont Hotel
Michael Hawkins, Chief Executive
Belmont Hotel

a business, there should in principle be less cause for 'us and them' attitudes to develop between management and the workforce. For this reason, many labour-intensive service organizations have significant worker shareholders and there is evidence that such companies can outperform more conventionally owned organizations (Rosen et al., 2005).

- **Mission statements** are used by services organizations in an attempt to create a shared vision for all employees. A corporate mission statement is a means of reminding everybody within the organization of its essential purpose. In the services sector, where the interface between the consumer and production personnel is often critical, communication of the values contained within the mission statement assumes great importance. The statement is frequently repeated by organizations in staff newsletters and in notices at their place of work. Is a mission statement a valuable guiding principle for all of a firm's employees, or just more management fudge? Too often, mission statements are ridiculed by employees (and customers) because of the vacuous nature of the language that is used, or because they are regarded as very unrealistic.

## 10.5 Leadership

Many of the most successful services companies, including Virgin Group, Federal Express and McDonald's, attribute their success in part to the quality of leadership within their organizations. The results of poor leadership are evident in many failing service organizations, especially within the public sector.

The principles of human resource management need to be implemented with effective leadership. What is good leadership for one organization need not necessarily be so for another. Organizations operating in relatively stable environments may be best suited to a leadership style that places a lot of power in a hierarchical chain of command. In the UK, many banks and insurance companies until recently had leadership styles that had been drawn from models developed in the armed forces, evidenced by some managers having titles such as superintendent and inspector. Such rigid, hierarchical patterns of leadership may be robust and provide a sense of certainty and continuity for all workers in the organization. However, they are likely to be less effective where the marketing environment is changing rapidly and a flexible response is called for (as has happened in the banking sector). The literature has developed two typologies of leadership – transactional and transformational – which broadly correspond respectively to the control and empowerment approaches described above.

What makes a good leader of people? And are leaders born, or can individuals acquire the skills of leadership? On the latter point there is little doubt that development is possible, and successful companies have invested heavily in leadership development programmes. As for what makes a successful leader of people, there have been many suggestions of desirable traits, including:

- setting clear expectations of staff;
- recognizing excellence appropriately and facilitating staff in overcoming their weaknesses;
- leading by example;
- being able to empathize with employees;
- showing adaptability to changing circumstances.

In too many companies, bad leadership is characterized by:

- 'management by confusion' in which expectations of staff are ambiguously stated and management actions are guided by a secretive 'hidden agenda';

- reward systems that are not based on performance and are perceived as being unfair;
- the deliberate or inadvertent creation of an 'us and them' attitude;
- failing to understand the aspirations of employees;
- failing to take the initiative where environmental change calls for adaptation.

For services organizations that involve the management of highly skilled professionals, such as hospital consultants, airline pilots and solicitors, a leader who is trained in business skills but has no primary knowledge of the professionals whom they are managing must take a facilitating role to leadership of such professionals, whose knowledge power can be great (see Goffee and Jones, 2007, and 'Thinking around the subject' on page 332 'Can you control a doctor?').

## 10.6 Recruiting, training and rewarding employees

Attention is now given to the application of a number of the important principles of human resource management referred to above. Emphasis is placed on the impact of such personnel practices on the marketing activities of services organizations through methods of recruiting, selecting, training and rewarding staff.

### Thinking around the subject: Managers told to get packing their bags

Beginning with a small shop in Dundalk in 1960, the Irish grocery retailer SuperQuinn has grown to a successful chain of 12 shops and seven shopping centres employing over 2000 people throughout Ireland. A large part of this success has been attributed to the leadership style of the company's founder, Feargal Quinn, and the emphasis on linking employees' activities to excellence in service quality. But what makes such leadership style distinctive?

An important principle is that managers should lead by example and never lose contact with the most important person in the organization – the customer. It is the task of a leader to set the tone for customer-focused excellence. To prevent managers losing sight of customers' needs, Quinn uses every opportunity to move them closer to customers, including locating their offices not in a comfortable room upstairs, but in the middle of the sales floor. Managers regularly take part in customer panels, where customers talk about their expectations and perceptions of SuperQuinn. Subcontracting this task entirely to a market research agency is seen as alien to the leadership culture of the company. The company requires its managers to spend periods doing routine front-line jobs (such as packing customers' bags), a practice that has become commonplace in many successful services organizations. This keeps managers close to the company and improves their ability to empathize with junior employees.

Does this leadership style work? Given the company's level of growth, profits and rate of repeat business, it must be doing something right, contradicting much of the scientific-management theories that management is a specialist task, which can be separated from routine dealings with customers and employees.

### 10.6.1 Recruitment and selection

Recruitment is the process by which an organization secures its human resources. Traditionally, the recruitment function has been performed by personnel specialists who, as functional specialists, are removed from line management. Current HRM practice favours the integration of the recruitment function into the line areas where a potential employee will be working.

The focus of recruitment activity is to attract, and hopefully retain, the right employee for the right job within the organization. The recruitment process is closely linked to that of selection (described below), which is concerned with how potential recruits are tested in terms of the job and person specifications.

In order to recruit the right personnel, services organizations must carefully consider just what they want from particular employees. As an example, tour operators seeking to recruit representatives to work in overseas resorts recognize that academic qualifications are not in themselves an important characteristic that should be possessed by new recruits. Instead, the ability to work under pressure, to empathize with clients, to work in groups and to be able to survive for long periods without sleep may from previous experience be identified as characteristics that allow representatives to perform their tasks in a manner that meets customers' expectations.

There are five key elements of the recruitment process:

- development of recruitment policies;
- establishment of routine recruitment procedures;
- establishment of job descriptions;
- development of a person specification;
- advertising of job vacancies.

The process of selection is concerned with identifying and hopefully employing the most suitable candidate and involves six principal tasks:

- examining candidates' CVs or application forms;
- short-listing candidates;
- inviting candidates for interview;
- interviewing and testing candidates;
- choosing a candidate for employment;
- offering and confirming the employment.

Traditionally, all of these areas have been considered to be the preserve of the personnel department. However, there are many examples of how customers' expectations have influenced the recruitment and selection process. One example is the use of a 'service predisposition instrument' (SPI) to identify attitudes of applicants, and this provides measures of service elements, cognitive expressions and a personal service outcome (Lee-Ross, 2000).

## Thinking around the subject: No staff, no service

In many prosperous towns and regions, it has been quite common to find shops and restaurants advertising for staff, sometimes, it seems, putting as much effort into this as they put into advertising for customers. Service businesses operating on very tight profit margins cannot afford to pay premium wage rates and still remain competitive in attracting price-sensitive customers. But many service sectors require staff to work long, antisocial hours, and many jobs themselves are not particularly pleasant. It is not surprising, therefore, that many services businesses find their growth constrained by the availability of staff, rather than the availability of customers. Service organizations around the world have benefited from immigrants filling the jobs that cannot be filled by local people. The wave of immigrants from Eastern Europe to the UK, which occurred following the removal of immigration restrictions in May

2004, saw an estimated 600,000 East Europeans finding employment in the UK, especially in the services sector, driving buses, serving in restaurants and working in a range of labour-intensive care services for the young and elderly.

But it is not just unfilled low-wage jobs that have held back the development of services organizations. Many sectors have faced acute specific skills shortages. Companies involved in computer maintenance, for example, have developed innovative schemes to recruit and retain staff, with some companies having 'talent retention programmes'. Companies have been known to give bonuses to existing employees who recommend a friend who is subsequently recruited as an employee.

Nor is it just in the prosperous countries of the Western developed world where staff shortages occur. Many people associate China with being a country of labour surplus, and having an economy that has grown rapidly on the basis of the availability of cheap labour. Nevertheless, many services organizations in China have reported skills shortages holding back their development. In 2007, HSBC bank claimed that a lack of skilled staff, trained in the financial services sector, was holding back its growth in China. Gradual liberalization of the financial services sector in China, and the appearance of international banks in China, had squeezed the pool of available staff, making it harder for companies to hire and retain qualified staff. To give some indication of the size of the problem, the *Financial Times* reported that, in 2007, HSBC sought to hire 1000 additional people, in addition to its existing 3000 staff. Citigroup planned a similar increase, and Standard Chartered increased its number of employees from 1200 to 2200 in the previous year (*Financial Times*, 2007).

Would paying staff a higher wage solve a company's recruitment problems and allow it to grow, or would that growth simply be unprofitable if customers were not prepared to pay more than the going price for its services? Would greater investment by a company in staff training help, or would newly trained staff simply complete their training, then leave to find a better wage elsewhere?

### 10.6.2 Training and development

Training refers to the acquisition of specific knowledge and skills, which enable employees to perform their job effectively. The focus of staff training is the job. In contrast to this, staff development concerns activities that are directed to the future needs of the employee, which may themselves be derived from the future needs of the organization. For example, workers may need to become familiar with personal computers, electronic mail and other aspects of information technology, which as yet may not be elements within their own specific job requirements.

If a service organization wishes to turn all of its employees who interface with the public into 'part-time marketers', it must include such an objective within its overall corporate plan and identify the required training and development needs. This is essential if any process of change is to be actively consented to by the workforce. Initially this may be merely an awareness training programme whereby the process of change is communicated to the workforce as a precursor to the actual changes. It may involve making employees aware of the competitive market pressures that the organization faces and how the organization proposes to address them. This initial process may also involve giving employees the opportunity to make their views known and to air any concerns they may have. This can help to generate some moral involvement in the process of change and could itself be the precursor to an effective participation forum.

If marketing as a function is to become integrated into the jobs of all employees, marketing managers cannot merely state this need at strategic HRM meetings – it is also essential that programmes are developed by which such strategies can be operationalized. In many cases, it may be possible to specify these needs in terms of the levels of competence required in performing particular tasks. For example, in the case of bank counter staff, personnel might be required to be aware of a number of specific financial services offered by the bank and be able to evaluate customers and make appropriate suggestions for service offers. Failure to develop general sales skills and to disseminate knowledge of specific services available could result in lost opportunities for the organization.

A practical problem facing many services organizations that allocate large budgets to staff training is that many other organizations in their sector may spend very little, relying on staff being poached from the company doing the training. This occurs, for example, within the banking sector, where many market entrants have set up online banking operations using the skills of staff attracted from established banks. The problem also occurs in many construction-related industries and in the car repair business.

## In practice: If the shoe fits . . .

Figure 10.7 Labour-intensive service industries have long realized that recruiting, training and motivating the right staff is an important basis for delivering value to customers. In conditions of full employment, companies must sell themselves as a good employer so that they can recruit the people who will ultimately deliver marketers' promises to customers. The *Sunday Times* conducts an annual survey of Britain's best companies to work for, and the shoe-repair and key-cutting chain Timpson has scored highly for a number of years. Employee benefits include at least 16 weeks' maternity leave on full pay (compared to the statutory minimum of six weeks at 90 per cent pay) and/or at least four weeks' maternity leave above the statutory minimum of 40 weeks. One sign of the company's success is a low level of staff turnover – at least 40 per cent of its staff have worked at the company for more than five years. Managers are given considerable discretion in how they run their branches, for example in setting the prices that they charge. Customers have come to trust the chain and rewarded it with sustainable long-term profits. (Reproduced courtesy of Timpson)

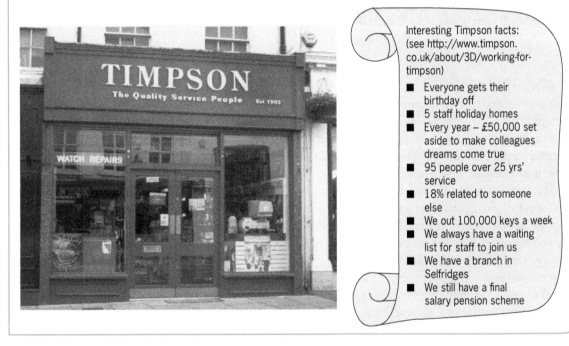

Interesting Timpson facts: (see http://www.timpson.co.uk/about/3D/working-for-timpson)

- Everyone gets their birthday off
- 5 staff holiday homes
- Every year – £50,000 set aside to make colleagues dreams come true
- 95 people over 25 yrs' service
- 18% related to someone else
- We out 100,000 keys a week
- We always have a waiting list for staff to join us
- We have a branch in Selfridges
- We still have a final salary pension scheme

While the ease with which an organization can lose trained staff may be one reason to explain many companies' generally low level of spending on training and development, a number of policies can be adopted to maximize the benefits of such expenditure to the organization. Above all else, training and development should be linked to broader HRM policies, which will have the effect of generating longer-term loyalty by employees. Judged by narrow criteria, training can be seen as a short-term risky activity that adds relatively little to the long-term profitability of an organization.

Where involvement-generating HRM policies alone are insufficient to retain trained staff, an organization may seek to tie an individual to it by seeking reimbursement of any expenditure if the employee leaves the organization within a specified time period. Reimbursement is most likely to be sought in the case of expenditure aimed at developing the general abilities of an individual as opposed to their ability to perform a functional and organizational specific task. Thus, an organization might seek to recover the cost of supporting an individual to undertake a general university degree, but not a product-specific sales training course. In some instances, government initiatives exist to support staff training and development.

Where an organization is a market leader, it may have no alternative but to accept a certain level of wastage in return for maintaining a constant competitive advantage over other organizations, and hence achieving higher levels of profitability. In this way, the travel agency chain Thomas Cook provides a level of training that many have considered to be one of the best in the sector. A travel clerk who is Thomas Cook trained can readily find employment with one of its competitors. Against such potential loss – which itself is offset by the HRM policies adopted by the company – Thomas Cook enjoys a very high reputation with the travel-buying public. This in turn has allowed it to position itself as a high-quality service provider, removing some of the need for heavy price discounting that has harmed many of its rivals.

### 10.6.3 Career development

Another mechanism that can assist an organization in its goals of recruiting and retaining staff is a clearly defined career progression pathway, referring to a mechanism that enables employees to visualize how their working life might develop within an organization. During periods of scarcity among the skilled labour force, offers of defined career paths may become essential if staff of the right calibre are to be recruited and retained. However, some have argued that the opportunities for career development within organizations have become increasingly constrained by the trend towards outsourcing, which was discussed in Chapter 5. Legendary stories of staff who started working for a bank as a cleaner or driver and rose through a combination of career development and good luck to become a senior executive are now harder to achieve where the bank's cleaners and drivers are outsourced to a completely different company with its own career paths.

### 10.6.4 Rewarding staff

The process of staff recruitment and retention are directly influenced by the quality of reward on offer. The central purpose of a reward system is to improve the standard of staff performance by giving employees something that they consider to be of value in return for good performance. What employees consider to be good rewards is influenced by the nature of the motivators that drive each individual. For this reason, one standardized reward system is unlikely to achieve maximum motivation among a large and diverse workforce.

Reward systems have been seen by many as an essential tool to link corporate goals, such as customer orientation, with individual and organizational performance (e.g. Milkovich and Newman, 2002). While some studies have demonstrated positive effects of incorporating non-financial performance measures into employees' reward schemes (e.g. Widmier, 2002), many companies have encountered problems in linking pay to customer satisfaction. Reasons for this can be attributed to the difficulties of measuring customer satisfaction as well as to the missing link between customer satisfaction and customer retention.

In principle, the balanced scorecard (BSC) approach should offer a way forward for linking performance measures with employees' rewards. The BSC framework can be used for describing value-creating strategies that link tangible and intangible assets (Speckbacher et al., 2003). This is done by formulating strategic objectives with respect to assets in four perspectives: financial; customer internal business process; learning; and growth (Kaplan and Norton, 2001; Malmi, 2001). Although a great strength of the BSC concept is its potential link with an organization's reward system (Kaplan and Norton, 1996; Malmi, 2001; Otley, 1999), very few organizations appear to have actually made this link successfully. Research by Speckbacher et al. (2003) showed that, while 27 of a sample of 38 companies (more than 70 per cent) had linked incentives to the BSC, only half were actually able to formulate cause-and-effect relationships among the different objectives and measures. Of these, just under half had linked incentives to BSC measures.

Rewards to employees can be divided into two categories – non-monetary and monetary. Non-monetary rewards cover a wide range of benefits, some of which will be a formal part of the reward system, such as subsidized housing or sports facilities and public recognition for work achievement (for example where staff are given diplomas signifying their level of achievement). At other times, non-monetary rewards can be informal and represent something of a hidden agenda for management. In this way, a loyal, long-standing restaurant waiter may be rewarded by being given a relatively easy schedule of work, allowing unpopular Saturday nights to be removed from their duty rota. However, many HRM professionals would not recognize these non-monetary benefits as being part of a narrowly defined reward system. Instead, they are seen as going to the root of the relationship between staff and employer. Subsidized sports facilities are not merely a reward, but part of the total work environment, which encourages consent, moral involvement and participation by the workforce. In the case of the hidden agenda of informal non-monetary rewards, these would be seen as being potentially harmful to the employment relationship by reducing the level of consent from the workforce at large.

Monetary rewards are a more direct method of improving the performance of employees and form an important element of a traditional 'hard' HRM policy. In the absence of well-developed HRM policies to promote involvement, monetary rewards can form the principal motivator for employees. A number of methods are commonly used in the services sector to reward employees financially:

- Basic hourly wages are used to reward large numbers of employees, implying payment according to their inputs rather than outputs. Compared with the manufactured-goods sector, it is generally more difficult to measure service outcomes and to use these as a basis for payment, but, nevertheless, this sometimes occurs. Delivery drivers employed by a courier firm may, for instance, be paid a fixed amount for each parcel delivered. In some cases, strict payment by output could have potentially harmful effects on customers – the delivery driver may concentrate on delivering as many parcels as quickly as possible, but with little regard for courtesies when dealing with people. If a performance metric is not included in an employee's reward calculation, it may simply be ignored by the employee, in favour of the metrics that are measured and included.
- A fixed salary is more commonly paid to the core workers of an organization. Sometimes the fixed salary is related to length of service – for example, many public-sector service workers have traditionally received automatic annual increments not related to performance. As well as being administratively simple, a fixed salary avoids the problems of trying to assess individuals' eligibility for bonuses, which can be especially difficult where employees work in teams. A fixed salary can be useful to a firm where long-term development of relationships with customers is important and staff are evaluated qualitatively for their ability in this respect rather than quantitatively on the basis of short-term sales achievements. Many financial services companies have adopted fixed salaries to avoid possible unethical conduct by employees, who may be

tempted to sell commission-based services to customers whose needs have not been properly assessed.

- A fixed annual salary plus a variable commission is commonly paid to service personnel who are actively involved in selling, as a direct reward for their efforts. Commission payments paid by services firms have come in for a lot of critics recently, especially within the financial services sector where employees have received bonuses for selling financial products which were not suitable for the customer in the long term, and some have blamed the banking crisis of 2008 on a bonus culture within banks (see vignette below). Where sales people are in fact involved in service delivery (e.g. many restaurant waiting staff selling additional side orders), this form of payment can be a motivator to good service delivery as well as increasing sales.
- Performance-related pay (PRP) has become increasingly important within the services sector. Performance-related pay links some percentage of an employee's pay directly to their work performance. It was noted above that rewarding employees according to their performance may sound fine in principle, but can be difficult to achieve in practice. For some workers, outputs can be quantified relatively easily; for example, the level of new accounts opened forms part of most bank managers' PRP. More qualitative aspects of job performance are much more difficult to appraise, for example the quality of advice given by doctors or dentists. Qualitative assessment raises problems about which dimensions of job performance are to be considered important in the exercise and who is to undertake the appraisal. If appraisal is not handled sensitively, it can be viewed by employees with suspicion as a means of rewarding some individuals according to a hidden agenda. There is also the problem in many service industries that service outcomes are the result of joint activity by a number of employees and therefore the team may be a more appropriate unit for appraisal than the individual employee. Of course, appraisals should be carried out for reasons other than just determining employees' pay. Well-managed services organizations routinely appraise staff to assess their career development and training needs. Without a transparent system of assessment, suspicions can be raised within an organization about perceived favouritism that is not linked to performance.
- Profit-sharing schemes can operate as a supplement to the basic wage or salary and can assist in the generation of employee loyalty through greater commitment. Employees can be made members of a trust fund set up by their employer where a percentage of profits is held in trust on behalf of employees, subject to agreed eligibility criteria. Profit-sharing schemes have the advantage of encouraging staff involvement in their organization. Such schemes do, however, have a major disadvantage when, despite employees' most committed efforts, profits fall as a result of some external factor such as an economic recession. There is also debate about whether profit sharing really does act as a motivator to better performance in large companies, or merely becomes part of basic pay expectations.
- In many services organizations, an important element of the financial reward comes directly from customers in the form of tipping in return for good service. The acknowledgement of tipping puts greater pressure on front-line service staff to perform well and, in principle, puts the burden of appraisal directly on the consumer. It can also reduce the level of basic wage that may be expected by employees. Against this, reliance on tipping poses a number of problems. Support personnel may be important contributors to the quality of service received by customers but may receive none of the benefits of tipping received by front-line staff. A chef may be an important element of the benefit received by a restaurant customer, but tipping systems tend to emphasize the quality of the final delivery. Attempts to institutionalize tipping by levying service charges and sharing proceeds among all staff may, on the other hand, reduce individual

motivation. A fixed service charge also reduces the ability of consumers to make payments based on perceived quality. A further problem of relying on tipping is that customers may be put off by the prospect of feeling obliged to pay a tip and, for this reason, many service providers prohibit their employees from receiving tips. While customers from some countries – such as the USA – readily accept the principle of tipping, others – including the British – are more ambivalent. In the public sector, attempts at tipping may be viewed as a form of bribery.

## Thinking around the subject: Bonuses may be good news for employees, but are they bad news for everybody else?

One aftermath of the 'credit crunch' of 2008 was the vilification of employees who earned large bonuses, especially senior employees working in the banking sector. For many years, bonuses had been presented as a means of improving the performance of employees, who, through a process of Pavlovian operant conditioning, responded to the promise of a bonus by working harder and smarter. It seemed that the bonus was now the cause of so many problems in many service sectors, and not their solution.

During 2009 a report published in the UK by the House of Commons Treasury Select Committee said that the banking crisis had 'exposed serious flaws and shortcomings' in remuneration policies. The report specifically criticized bonus schemes for encouraging risk-taking at the expense of shareholders' interests and the long-term health of the banks themselves. The report highlighted practices such as cash bonuses paid immediately regardless of the long-term impact of a deal or transaction. Bonuses might have been earned for hitting targets for new lending, but this may have resulted in staff making loans to individuals and companies who were quite likely not going to be able to pay back the loan. For the bank employee, one more loan might have resulted in a bigger bonus, and for the bank, it could report higher levels of lending, to the delight of shareholders, at least in the short term. But many of these loans would come back to haunt the banks, when customers could not repay their loans. Further criticism of the bonus culture came from the Financial Services Authority's Turner Report, which found a 'strong prima facie' case that inappropriate bonus policies had contributed to the financial crisis of the credit crunch. Bonuses seemed to be out of control, and Members of Parliament (MPs) on the Treasury Select Committee found evidence that 'remuneration consultants' had an effect of ratcheting up bonuses paid throughout the sector by recommending the payment of increasing levels of bonuses.

But can you realistically run a complex service business without the use of bonuses? After all, they had been introduced to avoid staff becoming complacent in their jobs. Without bonuses, would staff be motivated to go that extra mile to generate new business, or provide a higher level of customer service? And what about junior banking staff who may be motivated to work even harder to improve the quality of service they provide? A junior bank manager may be far removed from the bonus culture of high finance in the City, but is it not reasonable to expect that they would smile more at their customers, or put more effort into making sure their ATMs were not out of order, if they thought that a bonus would result for providing better service? Even the MPs 'wholeheartedly' supported continued bonus payouts for RBS staff on modest salaries, who they said should 'not be penalised for failures at the top of the organization'.

Debate about the bonus culture initially focused on bankers, whose greed was blamed in the eyes of many people for the problems of the credit crunch. But it seemed that a bonus culture was raising issues in many other service sectors where critics accused a bonus mentality of leading employees to put their own interests before the interests of customers, the company or the economy generally. In the education sector, it emerged that many head teachers were being paid large performance bonuses. In 2009, the Association of Teachers and Lecturers said a banking-style 'bonus culture' was creeping into UK state schools. It claimed that heads running chains of schools could earn £200,000 a year, and some senior staff in schools were earning bonuses of more than £50,000 on top of their normal salary. The union claimed that while the vast majority of school leaders still saw education as a public service, a few had been seduced into seeing it as a chance to make money. The debate in the education sector seemed to be similar to the debate in banking – could bonuses actually hinder the process of providing services which met the needs of users and society generally in the long term?

### 10.6.5 Industrial relations

For services organizations employing large numbers of staff, successful management of industrial relations can be crucial for preventing disruptive forms of collective actions, such as strikes or 'work to rule' practices by trade unions. The existence of trade unions within an organization may emphasize a divergence of interests between the employer and employees. Where divergence is great, a result may be overtime bans, 'go slows' and strikes, which may be used in order to pursue employees' interests. Such actions only occur where negotiation has failed. Nevertheless, many service sectors such as railways and airlines have periodically suffered bad disruption as a result of failures in industrial relations. Because services cannot be stored, the effects of withdrawal of labour can be felt by customers immediately.

Services organizations that do not feel secure with trades unions sometimes try to marginalize their impact by refusing to recognize them and by developing organization-specific employee relations policies described below. Within the service sector, many organizations have moved on from the traditional view of industrial relations to the situation where they speak of 'employee relations'. Employee relations focus on fostering identification with the employing organization and its business aims. It therefore concerns itself with direct relations between employees and management – that is, independently of any collective representation by trades unions.

## 10.7 Reducing dependency on human resources

Employees represent an expensive and difficult asset to manage and, furthermore, the quality of employees' contribution to the total service offer can often be seen by final consumers as being highly variable. Services organizations therefore frequently pursue strategies to reduce the human element of their production process, and we saw some examples of this in Chapter 2. The aim of employee replacement schemes can be to reduce service variability, to reduce costs, or both. Cost cutting could be important where an organization is pursuing a cost-leadership strategy, allowing it to gain a competitive advantage.

To summarize some of the points made in Chapter 2, services organizations use a number of strategies to reduce dependency on employees:

- At one extreme, the human element in a service production and delivery process can be almost completely replaced by automatic machinery. Examples include bank ATMs, vending machines and automatic car washes. Constraints on employee replacement come from the limitations of technology (for example, completely automatic car washes can seldom achieve such high standards of cleanliness as those where an operator is present to perform some operations inaccessible to machinery); from the cost of replacement equipment (it is only within the past few years that self-service checkout equipment has made it economically feasible for supermarkets to consider replacing checkout staff with automated self-service machines); and from the attitudes of consumers towards automated service delivery (some segments of the population are still reluctant to use Internet banking services, preferring the reassurance provided by human contact).
- Equipment can be used alongside employees to assist them in their task. This often has the effect of deskilling their task by reducing the scope they have for exercising discretion, thereby reducing the variability in quality perceived by customers. Thus, in-car satellite navigation systems have reduced taxi drivers' need to have a detailed knowledge of the streets in the area where they work.

- The inseparability of the service offer means that consumers of a service are usually involved in some way as co-producers of the service. The involvement of the service provider's personnel can be reduced by shifting a greater part of the production process to the consumer through various self-service methods that were explored in Chapter 2.

## Case study

### A 24/7 society may be good for customers, but can employees cope with the stress?

What happens when a company's customers want access to its services 24 hours a day, and they want immediate availability, not a promise of availability tomorrow or sometime in the future? One consequence is often stress at work for those who are charged with responding to the promises companies must make if they are to stay alive in a competitive business environment.

The perishability and inseparability of services have put many service sectors such as catering and retailing at the forefront of discussion about the 24/7 society. The 24/7 culture has had a big impact on service employees' lifestyles, with many individuals having to adjust to varying and often unsocial shift patterns. Employees often have to accept that Saturdays and Sundays are part of their normal working week, and this trend is set to continue. A Future Foundation report, published in 2006, indicated that, by 2020, over 13 million people in the UK will be operating in an out-of-hours economy (outside the traditional Monday-to-Friday hours of 9 a.m. to 6 p.m.), compared with the 7 million who did so in 2003.

While flexibility serves the interests of those who can afford to enjoy the benefits of the 24/7 society, the supporting workforce may see little reward for the unsociable hours they put in. Managers and supervisors, under pressure to meet targets and boost sales, are also hard-hit, often working extended hours as unpaid overtime. It is not just the highly visible retail sector where staff are expected to be flexible – many backroom jobs in other service sectors have become more stressful. The entertainment sector, for example, increasingly employs casual contract workers to meet its needs. The BBC has struggled to compete against satellite and cable television services, all intent on meeting viewers' demand for entertainment 24/7. It now employs a large number of freelancers, who give it greater flexibility at lower cost.

Evidence of increasing levels of stress at work is mounting. In the UK, the 2010/11 Labour Force Survey showed that the total number of cases of stress was 400,000 out of a total of 1,152,000 for all work-related illnesses. The sectors that reported the highest rates of work-related stress in the last three years were health, social work, education and public administration (ONS 2013). A report by the mental health charity Mind provided further evidence of the extent of stress in the workplace. It noted that in a survey of 2000 workers, 19 per cent had taken a day off sick because of stress, but 90 per cent of those people cited a different reason for their absence, afraid to tell their boss that they were suffering stress. Over half of managers (56 per cent) said they would like to do more to improve staff mental well-being but they needed more training and/or guidance and 46 per cent said they would like to do more but it is not a priority in their organization. Respondents cited problems of juggling home with work demands and unrealistic deadlines and constant time pressures (Mind 2013).

Employers are increasingly having to recognize the sometimes hidden costs to their business of having high levels of stress in their workforce. Moreover, the law is now requiring them to take some responsibility for employees' stress at work. In the UK, the Management of Health and Safety at Work Regulations 1999 (specifically Regulations 3, 4, 13 and 19) explicitly state that employers must assess the risk of their employees developing stress-related illness because of work.

Although stress is all around us today, some would argue that the harmful consequences of the 24/7 society have been exaggerated. People may remember the stress for customers of having to get to their bank before it closed at 3.30 in the afternoon – good for the banks' employees, but possibly stressful for its customers. Or the rush to stock up with food from supermarkets just before a public holiday, in the knowledge that they would be closed for a number of days over the holiday period.

One advantage of the 24/7 society is that there is not as much pressure to have to buy something from the shops before they close, or to drink up in a pub before a rigidly enforced closing time. Another benefit is that it can offer the opportunity for people to choose the times they want to work, a great benefit for families with young children. And Sunday, previously held out as a day of rest for the family to spend together, is now a shared leisure day in which shopping as a family unit has replaced the previously solo shopping trips in which housewives typically took on the biggest burden.

Businesses, employees and consumers are all perpetuating the move towards a 24/7 economy, and inevitably there are winners and losers. The Future Foundation research found that it was the affluent who benefit most. A third of consumers who consumed services between the hours of 6 p.m. and 9 a.m. had a household income of £46,000 or more. Only a fifth of those with an income of £10,430 or less participated. But the flip side of a vibrant night-time economy is an army of low-paid staff, many working for little above the minimum wage, often trying to juggle multiple part-time jobs with study or looking after children.

Who benefits from the 24/7 economy? To some critics, it is in the interests of neither the economically disadvantaged, who pick up the jobs that nobody else wants to do, nor the employed, who have little to do other than work harder to spend more money achieving their desired lifestyle. Or are we in danger of over-romanticizing the 'good old days' when Sunday was Sunday and everybody lived a happier, less stressful life?

### Case study review questions

1. What factors should influence the extent to which services organizations aim to satisfy customers' desire for 24/7 access to services?
2. Critically assess methods that services organizations can use to reduce the harmful effects, and promote the beneficial effects, of 24/7 service provision for their employees.
3. 24/7 access to services has been accused of leading to a wide range of social problems, including employee stress and damage to family life. Critically evaluate these effects and the extent to which you consider the services sector to be a contributor to these alleged problems.

## Summary and links to other chapters

Human resource management is not something that should be considered as separate from marketing management. For services that involve a high level of contact between employees and customers, high levels of service quality may only be achieved with appropriate human resource management. There has been much debate about the nature of internal marketing and its relationship to theories of human resource management. Control and empowerment are two important issues that have a long history of debate within the HRM literature, and have a close relationship with service process design.

The close relationship between this chapter and Chapter 2 on the service encounter and Chapter 9 on service quality should be evident. Reducing staff inputs is often a key feature of service firms' efforts to industrialize service processes (Chapter 2). Issues of human resource management are central to many organizations' attempts to develop relationship marketing strategies (Chapter 5). Without appropriately trained staff, relationships can degenerate to little more than data stored on a computer.

## Chapter review questions

1 Critically assess the concept of 'internal marketing' in the context of the services sector. Do you think that marketers have made a useful contribution to the issue of how to engage employees in order to deliver the standards of services that their customers expect?

2 The perishability of services and variability of customer demand call for flexible working practices by front-line employees in the services sector. Identify methods of improving employee flexibility and critically evaluate their effects on customer satisfaction.

3 The service–profit chain portrays a linkage between employee and customer satisfaction. Critically discuss the nature of this linkage and the problems of trying to quantify it.

## Activities

1 Consult the jobs section of your local newspaper and examine jobs that are advertised by local services organizations. To what extent is the organization's communication through its job advertisements consistent with its communication to customers? What do stated job requirements say about service standards offered by the organization? Do you notice any difference in job requirements between staff required for front-line roles and those required for behind-the-scenes functions? Does the marketing environment of an organization influence the way it seeks new staff? For example, is there a difference between private-sector, public-sector and not-for-profit-sector organizations?

2 Look at one of the annual listings of 'top companies to work for' – for example *The Sunday Times* list of 'The 100 best companies to work for in the UK' (features.thesundaytimes.co.uk/public/best100 companies/live/template). What, if any, association do you see between the names on this list and the quality of service provided by those service companies listed with which you are familiar?

3 Carry out a survey of colleagues who have casual, part-time jobs with service providers. Try to understand what motivates each individual to perform better in his or her job. Does being treated as a casual worker act as a demotivator, or does it keep them 'on their toes' in case they are not called to work again? Does a pattern of motivation emerge, based either on the individual involved or on the nature of the employment offered?

## Key terms

**Balanced scorecard (BSC)** A tool for reporting the activities of employees using diverse and predetermined criteria.

**Empowerment** Giving employees authority to act using their own initiative, without reference to senior management.

**Employee engagement** Employees' feeling of involvement in their job.

**Human resource management (HRM)** Strategies and practices to improve the effectiveness and efficiency of an organization's human resources.

**Internal marketing** The application of the principles and practices of marketing to an organization's dealings with its employees.

**Mission statement** A means of reminding everyone within an organization of the essential purpose of the organization.

## Selected further reading

*This chapter has discussed very briefly some of the basic principles of human resource management as they apply to services organizations. For a fuller discussion of these principles, the following texts are recommended:*

**Beardwell, J. and Claydon, T.** (2010) *Human Resource Management: A Contemporary Approach*, 6th edn, FT Prentice Hall, Harlow.

**Torrington, D., Hall, L., Taylor, S. and Atkinson, C.** (2012) *Human Resource Management*, 8th edn, FT Prentice Hall, London.

*The following references provide further insight into the role of internal marketing in services organizations:*

**Ahmed, P. and Rafiq, M.** (2003) 'Internal marketing issues and challenges', *European Journal of Marketing*, 37 (9), 1177–86.

**Ballantyne, D.** (2003) 'A relationship-mediated theory of internal marketing', *European Journal of Marketing*, 37 (9), 1242–60.

**Vasconcelos, A.F.** (2008) 'Broadening even more the internal marketing concept', *European Journal of Marketing*, 42 (11/12), 1246–64.

*The marketing role of front-line employees is explored in the following articles:*

**Bowers, M.R. and Martin, C.L.** (2007) 'Trading places: employees as customers, customers as employees', *Journal of Services Marketing*, 21 (2), 88–98.

**Gummesson, E.** (1991) 'Marketing-orientation revisited: the crucial role of the part-time marketer', *European Journal of Marketing*, 25 (2), 60-75.

**Kong, M. and Jogaratnam, G.** (2007) 'The influence of culture on perceptions of service employee behavior', *Managing Service Quality*, 17 (3), 275–97.

*Leadership and empowerment in the context of service industries are discussed in the following:*

**Lindgreen, A., Palmer, R., Wetzels, M. and Antioco, M.** (2009) 'Do different marketing practices require different leadership styles? An exploratory study', *Journal of Business & Industrial Marketing*, 24 (1), 14–26.

**Melhem, Y.** (2003) 'The antecedents of customer-contact employees' empowerment', *Employee Relations*, 26 (1), 72–93.

**Prabhu, V. and Robson, A.** (2000) 'Achieving service excellence – measuring the impact of leadership and senior management commitment', *Managing Service Quality*, 10 (5), 307–17.

## References

**Ahmed, P. and Rafiq, M.** (2003) 'Internal marketing issues and challenges', *European Journal of Marketing*, 37 (9), 1177–86.

**Albrecht, K.** (1990) *Service Within*, Dow Jones-Irwin, Homewood, IL.

**Arnett, D.B., Laverie, D.A. and McLane, C.** (2002) 'Using job satisfaction and pride as internal marketing tools', *Cornell Hotel and Restaurant Administration Quarterly*, 43 (2), 87–96.

**Bakke, D.W.** (2006) *Joy at Work: A Revolutionary Approach to Fun on the Job*, PVG, Seattle, WA.

**Bateson, J.E.G.** (1989) *Managing Services Marketing – Text and Readings*, 2nd edn, Dryden Press, Forth Worth, TX.

**Berry, L.L.** (1980) 'Services marketing is different', *Business*, 30 (3), 24–9.

**Bienstock, C.C., DeMoranville, C.W. and Smith, R.K.** (2003) 'Organizational citizenship behaviour and service quality', *Journal of Services Marketing*, 17 (4), 357–78.

**Bowen, D.E. and Lawler, E.E. III** (1992) 'The empowerment of service workers: what, why, when, and how', *Sloan Management Review*, 33 (3), 31–9.

**Bowers, M.R. and Martin, C.L.** (2007) 'Trading places: employees as customers, customers as employees', *Journal of Services Marketing*, 21(2), 88–98.

**Bruhn, M., Kudernatsch, D. and Tuzovic, S.** (2004) 'Integrating the balanced scorecard approach with the concept of customer-oriented compensation systems: the need for causality', working paper presented at the 6th Australasian Research Workshop, February, University of Otago, Dunedin, NZ.

**Denton, D.K.** (1990) 'Customer focused management', *HR Magazine*, 35 (8), 62–7.

**Donavan, D.T., Brown, T.J. and Mowen, J.C.** (2004) 'Internal benefits of service-worker customer orientation: job satisfaction, commitment, and organizational citizenship behaviours', *Journal of Marketing*, 68 (1), 128–46.

**Financial Times** (2007) 'HSBC highlights China staffing woes', *Financial Times*, 3 April, 15.

**Garvin, D.A.** (1993) 'Building a learning organization', *Harvard Business Review*, 71 (4), 78–92.

**Goffee, R. and Jones, G.** (2007) 'Leading clever people', *Harvard Business Review*, 85 (3), 72–9.

**Gounaris, S. and Boukis, A.** (2013) 'The role of employee job satisfaction in strengthening customer repurchase intentions', *Journal of Services Marketing*, 27 (4), 322–33.

**Hales, C.** (1994) 'Internal marketing as an approach to human resource management: a new perspective or a metaphor too far?', *Human Resource Management Journal*, 5 (1), 50–71.

**Harris, E.G. and Fleming, D.E.** (2005) 'Assessing the human element in service personality formation: personality congruency and the Five Factor Model', *Journal of Services Marketing*, 19 (4), 187–98.

**Hartline, M.D. and Ferrell, O.C.** (1996) 'The management of customer contact service employees: an empirical investigation', *Journal of Marketing*, 60 (4), 52–70.

**Herzberg, F.** (1966) *Work and the Nature of Man*, World Books, Cleveland, OH.

**House of Commons** (2009) *Treasury Committee: Banking Crisis*, Stationery Office, London.

**Industrial Society** (2001) *Managing Best Practice*, no. 83, Occupational Stress, Industrial Society, London.

**Kaplan, R.S. and Norton, D.P.** (1996) *The Balanced Scorecard: Translating Strategy into Action*, Harvard Business School Press, Boston, MA.

**Kaplan, R.S. and Norton, D.P.** (2001) 'Transforming the balanced scorecard from performance measurement to strategic management', *Accounting Horizons*, 15 (1), 87–104.

**Kelley, S.W.** (1993) 'Discretion and the service employee', *Journal of Retailing*, 69 (1), 104–26.

**Kin, C., Kimmy, Y., Chan, W. and Lam, S.K.** (2012) 'Do customers and employees enjoy service participation? Synergistic effects of self- and other-efficacy', *Journal of Marketing*, 76 (6), 121–40.

**Lee-Ross, D.** (2000) 'Development of the service predisposition instrument', *Journal of Managerial Psychology*, 15 (2), 148–57.

**Malmi, T.** (2001) 'Balanced scorecards in Finnish companies: a research note', *Management Accounting Research*, 12 (2), 207–20.

**Martin, C.L.** (1996) 'How powerful is empowerment?', *The Journal of Services Marketing*, 10 (6), 4–5.

**Martins, L.-P. and Grahl, J.** (2010) 'Customer relations and HRM restructuring: theory and some new evidence', *Human Resource Management Journal*, in press.

**Maslow, A.** (1943) 'A theory of human motivation', *Psychological Review*, 50 (4), 370–96.

**Mayo, E.** (1933) *The Human Problems of an Industrial Civilization*, Macmillan, New York.

**McGregor, D.** (1960) *The Human Side of Enterprise*, McGraw-Hill, New York.

**Milkovich, G.T. and Newman, J.M.** (2002) *Compensation*, 7th edn, McGraw-Hill, New York.

**Mind** (2013) Work is biggest cause of stress in people's lives, Mind, available at http://www.mind.org.uk/news/8566_work_is_biggest_cause_of_stress_in_peoples_lives (accessed 18 July 2013).

**ONS** (2013) *Labour Market*, Office for National Statistics, available at http://www.statistics.gov.uk/hub/labour-market/index.html (accessed 18 July 2013).

**Otley, D.** (1999) 'Performance management: a framework for management control systems research', *Management Accounting Research*, 10 (4), 363–82.

**Porter, M.E.** (1980) *Competitive Strategy: Techniques for Analyzing Industries and Competitors*, Free Press, New York.

**Rosen, C.M., Case, J. and Staubus, M.** (2005) *Equity: Why Employee Ownership is Good for Business*, Harvard Business School Press, Boston, MA.

**Silvestro, R.** (2002) 'Dispelling the modern myth: employee satisfaction and loyalty drive service profitability', *International Journal of Operations & Production Management*, 22 (1), 30–49.

**Speckbacher, G., Bischof, J. and Pfeiffer, T.** (2003) 'A descriptive analysis on the implementation of balanced scorecards in German-speaking countries', *Management Accounting Research*, 14 (1), 361–87.

**Taylor, F.W.** (1911) *The Principles of Scientific Management*, Harper and Row, New York.

**Varey, R.J. and Lewis, B.R.** (1999) 'A broadened conception of internal marketing', *European Journal of Marketing*, 33 (9/10), 926–44.

**Widmier, S.** (2002) 'The effects of incentives and personality on salesperson's customer orientation', *Industrial Marketing Management*, 31 (7), 609–15.

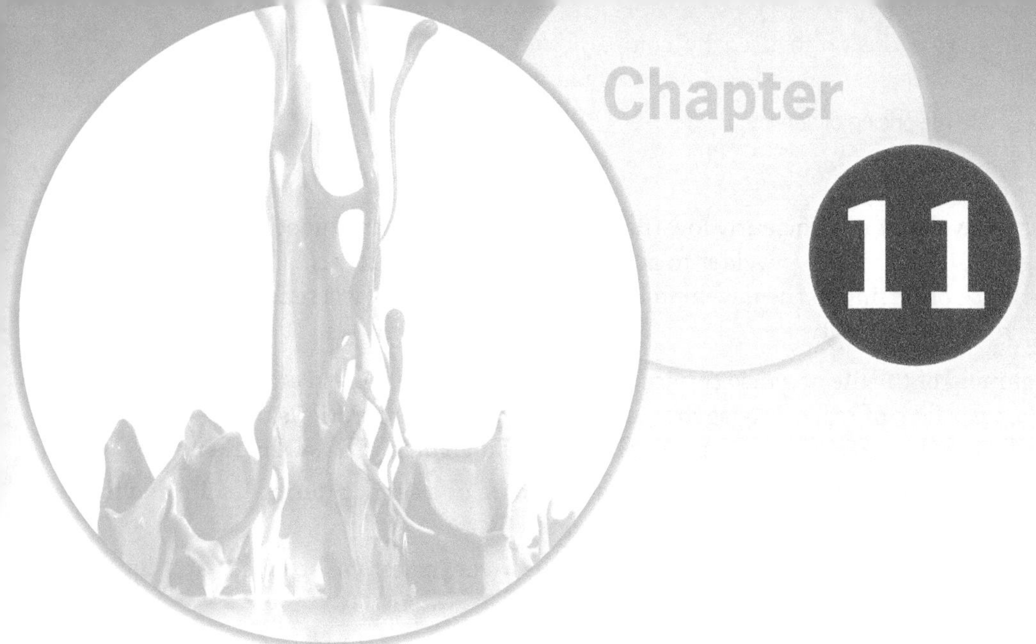


# The pricing of services

*You might have been searching for a new mobile phone service and become bewildered by seemingly endless choice and confusing prices. Some prices you might have expected to be higher than average because the contract would provide a very high level of benefits. But then you start looking at the small print and you find that some things included as standard in one offer are charged extra by other companies. Then you get even more confused by a plethora of 'special offers' and 'loyalty' discounts. Look on the Internet and the prices that you previously saw in the shop on Saturday afternoon are different again. This chapter explores the reasoning underlying what might at first seem to be confusing pricing.*

## Learning objectives

After reading this chapter, you should understand:

- Factors influencing services organizations' price decisions, including organizational objectives, cost levels, strength of demand and level of competition
- Pricing strategy and tactics used by services organizations
- The effects of inseparability on service firms' ability to offer finely segmented prices
- Price bundling of complex, interdependent service offers
- Pricing constraints and opportunities facing not-for-profit services

## 11.1 Introduction

Within the services sector, the term price often passes under a number of names, sometimes reflecting the nature of the relationship between customer and provider within which exchange takes place. Professional services companies therefore talk about fees, while other organizations use terms such as fares, tolls, rates, charges and subscriptions. The art of successful pricing is to establish a price level that is sufficiently low that an exchange represents good value to buyers, yet is high enough to allow a service provider to achieve its financial objectives.

The importance of pricing to the development of marketing strategy is reflected in the range of strategic uses to which it is put:

- At the beginning of the life of a new service, pricing is often used to gain entry to a new market. As an example, a firm of real estate agents seeking to extend its operations to a new region may offer initially very low commission rates in order to build volume in a new market.
- Price is used as a means of maintaining the market share of a service during its life and is used tactically to defend its position against competitors.
- Ultimately, for organizations working to profit objectives, prices must be set at a level that allows them to meet their financial objectives.
- Because of their intangibility, the quality of services can be more difficult to evaluate than for goods, therefore price often becomes an indicator of quality.
- The perishability of services results in price being used as a strategic and tactical tool for matching supply and demand. We will look at the subject of flexible pricing as a tool of demand management in the next chapter.

Pricing is clearly linked to the other elements of the marketing mix, and price is used to establish a position in the market for a service. A high price, for example, may only be sustainable if it is matched by a high level of service quality or accessibility to the service. Some services may be positioned as low price, with low levels of investment in staff training and only limited additional service features.

The points above may be true of commercially provided services, but what about public services? Many public and not-for-profit sector services are provided to the end consumer at either no charge or at a charge that bears little relation to the value of a service to the consumer or producer. Public services, such as museums and schools, that have sought to adopt marketing principles often do not have any control over the price element of the marketing mix. The reward for attracting more visitors to a museum or pupils to a school may be additional centrally derived grants, rather than income received directly from the users of the service.

## 11.2 Organizational influences on pricing decisions

Organizations show a wide variation in the objectives that they seek to achieve. An analysis of corporate objectives is a useful starting point for understanding the factors that underlie price decisions. Some commonly found organizational objectives and their implications for price decisions are analysed below:

- *Profit maximization.* It is often assumed that all private-sector organizations exist primarily to maximize their profits and that this will therefore influence their pricing policies. In fact, the notion of profit maximization needs to be qualified with a time dimension, for marketing strategies that maximize profits over the short run may be detrimental to achieving long-term profits. An organization charging high prices in a new market may make that market seem very attractive to new entrants, thereby having the effect of increasing the level of competition in subsequent years and so reducing long-term profitability. Also, the time frame over which profitability is sought can affect pricing decisions. If an innovative service is given an objective to break even after just one year, prices may be set at a low level in order to capture as large a share of the market as quickly as possible, whereas a longer-term profit objective may have allowed the organization to tap relatively small, but high-value, segments of its market in the first year and save the exploitation of lower-value segments until subsequent years. The notion of profit maximization has a further weakness in the services sector, where it can be difficult to establish clear relationships between costs, revenue and profits (see below).

- *Market-share maximization.* It has been argued frequently (e.g. Cyert and March, 1963) that it is unrealistic to expect the managers of a business to put all of their efforts into maximizing profits. To begin with, there can be practical difficulties in establishing relationships between marketing strategy decisions and the resulting change in profitability. Second, management often does not directly receive any reward for increasing its organization's profits – its main concern is to achieve a satisfactory level of profits rather than the maximum possible. Managers may be more likely to benefit from decisions that increase the market share of their organization (e.g. through improved career opportunities and job security). An objective to maximize market share may be very important to service industries where it is necessary to achieve a critical mass in order to achieve economies of scale, and therefore a competitive advantage. The price competition that accompanied the emerging market for Internet service providers in the late 1990s was based on the desire of the main competitors to achieve a critical size that made them consumers' first choice for Internet-related activities.
- *Survival.* Sometimes, the idea of maximizing profits or market share is a luxury to a service provider whose main objective is simply to survive and to avoid the possibility of going into receivership. Most businesses fail when they run out of cash flow at a critical moment as debts become due for payment. In these circumstances, prices may be set at a very low level simply to get sufficient cash into the organization to tide it over its short-term problems. Following the banking crisis of 2008, many retailers faced great difficulty in obtaining credit to keep their business going. In a bid to stay alive, many retailers were forced to lower their prices dramatically simply in order to keep cash flowing into the business until business conditions got better. For many retailers, conditions did not get better and even the additional business generated by low prices could not save them.
- *Social considerations.* Profit-related objectives can have little meaning to many public-sector services. At one extreme, the price of many public services represents a tax levied by government based on wider considerations of the ability of users to pay for the service and the public benefits of providing that service (e.g. fixed charges for National Health Service dental work in the UK, with exemptions for disadvantaged groups). Where public services are provided in a more market-mediated environment, pricing decisions may nevertheless be influenced by wider social considerations. For example, non-vocational educational classes run by local authorities may charge a nominal fee for an adult literacy class, but a much higher fee for a golf tuition class. Although social objectives are normally associated with public-sector services, they can sometimes be found within the private sector. Services provided by employers for their staff are often provided at a price that does not reflect their true value; instead they contribute towards the staff's total benefit package – examples include staff restaurants and sports clubs, which are often priced at much lower levels than their normal market value.
- *Personal objectives.* It was noted in Chapter 1 that most services organizations are very small scale and the objectives of the business can be indistinguishable from the personal objectives of the owner. Pricing may be used by the small-business owner to achieve personal lifestyle objectives; for example, a decorator quoting for a job may quote a very high price if the job looks uninteresting or unpleasant.

In practice, organizations work towards a number of objectives simultaneously – for example, a market-share objective over the short term may be seen as a means towards achieving a long-term profit-maximizing objective.

## 11.3 Factors influencing pricing decisions

An organization's objectives determine the desired results of pricing policies. Strategies are the means by which these objectives are achieved. Before discussing pricing strategy, it is useful to lay the groundwork by analysing the underlying factors that influence price decisions. Four important bases for price determination can be identified:

- what it costs to produce a service;
- the amount that consumers are prepared to pay for it;
- the price that competitors are charging;
- the constraints on pricing that are imposed by regulatory bodies.

The cost of producing a service represents the minimum price that a commercial organization would be prepared to accept over the long term for providing the service. The maximum price achievable is that which customers are prepared to pay for the service. This will itself be influenced by the level of competition available to customers to satisfy their needs elsewhere. Government regulation may intervene to prevent organizations charging the maximum price that consumers would theoretically be prepared to pay. These principles are illustrated in Figure 11.1.

Figure 11.1 The key influences on price decisions

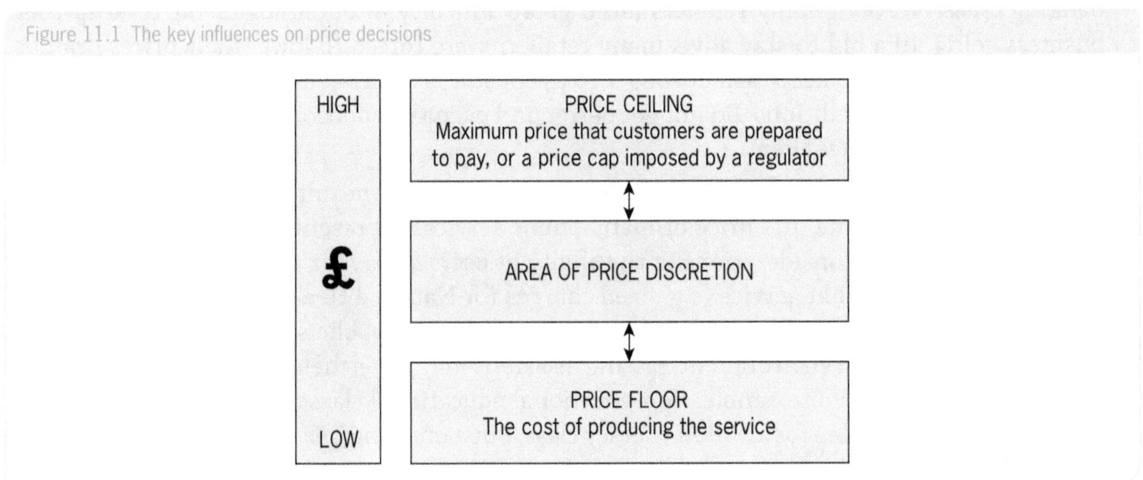


## 11.4 Costs as a basis for pricing

Many empirical studies have shown the importance of costs as a basis for determining prices within the service sector. For example, Zeithaml et al. (1985) in their study of service firms in the USA found that it was the dominant basis for price determination.

At its simplest, a 'cost-plus' pricing system works by using historical cost information to calculate a unit cost for each type of input used in a service production process. Subsequent price

Figure 11.2 'Cost plus' method of price setting for a bus operator

| **Cost information for most recent trading year:** | | |
|---|---|---|
| Total drivers' employment cost | £250 000 | |
| Total drivers' hours worked | 20 000 | |
| Cost per drivers' hour | | £12.50 |
| Total vehicle running costs | £150 000 | |
| Total mileage operated | 250 000 | |
| Vehicle operating costs per mile | | £0.60 |
| Total other overhead costs | £40 000 | |
| Overhead per mile operated | | £0.16 |
| Required return on sales turnover | 15% | |
| For a price quotation based on a 200-mile journey requiring 12 hours of driver's time: | | |
| Total price = | | |
| 200 miles × £0.60 = | £120.00 | |
| 12 hours × £12.50 = | £150.00 | |
| Overheads (based on mileage): | | |
| 200 miles × £0.16 = | £32.00 | |
| Total = | £302.00 | |
| Add 15% margin = | £45.30 | |
| TOTAL PRICE = | £347.30 | |

decisions for specific service outcomes are based on the number of units of inputs used, multiplied by the cost per unit, plus a profit margin. This method of setting prices is widely used in service industries as diverse as catering, building, accountancy and vehicle servicing. An example of how a bus operator might calculate its prices on this basis is shown in Figure 11.2.

There are many reasons why 'cost-plus'-type pricing methods are so widely used in the services sector:

- Prices are easy to calculate and allow the delegation of price decisions for services that have to be tailored to the individual needs of customers. For example, every building job, vehicle repair or landscaped gardening job is likely to be unique and a price for each job can be calculated by junior staff using standard unit costs for the inputs required to complete the job and a predetermined profit margin.
- Where an agreement is made to provide a service, but the precise nature of the service that will actually be provided is unknown at the outset, a contract may stipulate that the final price will be based in some way on costs incurred. A garage agreeing to repair a car brought in by a customer with an unidentified engine noise could not realistically give a price quotation before

undertaking the job and examining the nature of the problem. In these circumstances, the customer may agree to pay an agreed amount per hour for labour, plus the cost of any parts that the garage buys in.
- Trade and professional associations often include codes of conduct that allow a service provider only to increase prices beyond those originally agreed in an estimate on the basis of the actual costs incurred. Solicitors and accountants, for example, who need to commit more resources to complete a job than was originally allowed for in their quotation are bound by their professional bodies to pass on only their reasonable additional costs.

Against these attractions, pricing services on the basis of historical costs presents a number of problems:

- In itself, cost-based pricing does not take account of the competition that a particular service faces at any given time, nor of the fact that some customers may value the same service more highly than others.
- Calculating the costs of a service can in fact be very difficult, and often more difficult than in the case of goods. One reason for this is the structure of costs facing many services businesses (discussed below).
- While it may be possible to determine costs for previous accounting periods, it can be difficult to predict what these costs will be in the future. This is a particular problem for services that are contracted to be provided at some time in the future. Unlike goods, it is not possible to produce the service at known cost levels in the current period and to store it for consumption in some future period. Historical cost information is often adjusted by an inflation factor where service delivery is to be made some time in the future, but it can be difficult to decide what is the most appropriate inflation factor to use for a specific input. Where input costs are highly volatile (e.g. aviation fuel), one solution is for a service producer to pass on part of the risk of unpredictable inflation to customers. Charter airlines frequently do this by requiring customers to pay for any increase in fuel costs beyond a specified amount.

### 11.4.1 Cost structures

The costs of producing a service can be divided into those that are variable and those that are fixed. **Variable costs** increase as service production increases, whereas **fixed costs** remain unchanged if an additional unit of service is produced. Fixed costs therefore cannot be attributed to any particular unit of output. In between these two extremes of costs are semi-fixed costs, which remain constant until a certain level of output is reached, when expenditure on additional units of productive capacity is needed. The particular problem of many services industries is that fixed costs represent a very high proportion of total costs, resulting in great difficulty in calculating the cost of any particular unit of service.

The importance of fixed costs for a number of service industries is illustrated in Figure 11.3, where variable costs are defined as any cost that varies directly as a result of one extra customer consuming a service for which there is currently spare capacity. Thus one more passenger on a domestic flight from London to Moscow will probably only result in nominal additional variable costs of additional in-flight catering and airport departure and security charges, which have to be paid for each passenger. The cost of cabin crews and aircraft depreciation would not change, nor would those more remote fixed costs such as head-office administration and promotion.

It can be argued that over the long term, all costs borne by a business are variable. In the case of the airline, if the unit of analysis is a particular flight rather one individual passenger, the

Figure 11.3 Examples of fixed and variable costs in selected service industries

| Service | Fixed costs | Variable |
|---|---|---|
| Restaurant | Building maintenance<br>Rent and rates | Food<br>Waiters and cooks |
| Bank mortgage | Staff time<br>Building maintenance | Sales commission<br>Corporate advertising<br>Paper and postage |
| Domestic air journey | Aircraft maintenance and depreciation<br>Head office administrative costs | Airport departure tax<br>In-flight meal |
| Hairdresser | Building maintenance<br>Rent and rates | Shampoos used |

proportion of costs that are variable increases. So, if the airline withdrew just one return journey between the two points, it would save fuel costs, making fuel a variable cost. It would probably also save some staff costs, but may still have to incur aircraft depreciation costs and the more remote head-office administration costs. If the whole route were closed, even more costs would become variable – staff employed at the terminal could be cut, as could the flight crews. It may be possible for the airline to avoid some of its aircraft depreciation costs by reducing the size of its fleet. Even promotional costs would become variable, as part of the airline's advertising would no longer need to be incurred if the service were closed completely.

High levels of fixed costs are associated with high levels of interdependency between the services that make use of the fixed-cost elements. To illustrate this, the cost of maintaining a retail-bank branch network is fixed over the short to medium term, yet the network provides facilities for a wide range of different service activities – current accounts, mortgages, business loans and foreign-currency business, to name but a few. Staff may be involved in handling each of these activities in the course of a working day and it is likely that no special space is reserved exclusively for each activity. For many of these activities, the short-term direct costs are quite negligible – for example, the additional cost of one order to change sterling into dollars is little more than the cost of a receipt slip. But users of this service would be expected to contribute towards the overhead costs of staff and space. There is frequently no obvious method by which these fixed costs can be attributed to specific units of output, nor even to particular types of service. The fixed costs for money exchange could, for example, be allocated on the basis of the proportion of floor space occupied, proportion of staff time used and proportion of total turnover, or some combination of these bases. Allocation bases are often the result of judgement and political in-fighting. They can change as a result of argument between cost-centre managers, who invariably feel that their product is contributing excessively to fixed costs and may put forward an argument why their pricing base is putting them at a disadvantage in the marketplace against competitors who have a simpler cost structure. In the end, cost allocation is a combination of scientific analysis and bargaining.

### 11.4.2 Marginal cost pricing

A special kind of cost-based pricing occurs where firms choose to ignore their fixed costs. The price that any individual customer is charged is based not on the total unit cost of producing it, but only

Figure 11.4 Travel companies have for a long time used marginal cost pricing, mindful that some revenue is better than an empty plane seat or hotel room. They have realized that some people could be tempted by low-price offers to fill spare capacity at very short notice. The online travel intermediary lastminute.com has successfully made use of marginal cost pricing by bringing together companies that have spare capacity with buyers who are looking for a last-minute bargain. (Reproduced courtesy of lastminute.com)

lastminute.com

the additional costs that will result directly from servicing that additional customer. The principle here is that the company would be better off just so long as the marginal revenue obtained from catering for one additional customer is greater than the marginal cost of servicing that customer. It is used where the bulk of a company's output has been sold at a full price that recovers its fixed costs, but, in order to fill remaining capacity, the company brings its prices down to a level that at least covers its variable, or avoidable, costs. Marginal cost pricing is widely used in service industries with low short-term supply elasticity and high fixed costs. It is common in the airline industry, where the perishability of a seat makes it unsaleable after departure. The Internet has seen the development of a number of companies which specialize in selling surplus capacity at low rates (Figure 11.4).

Against the attraction of filling spare capacity and getting a contribution towards fixed costs where otherwise there would have been none, marginal cost pricing does have its problems. The biggest danger of pricing on this basis is that it can be taken too far, allowing too high a proportion of customers to be carried at marginal cost, with insufficient customers charged at full price to cover the fixed costs. Many airlines and holiday tour operators have fallen into the trap of selling holidays on this basis, only to find that their fixed costs have not been fully covered. Another problem is that it may devalue customers' perception of a service. If a service promoted for its prestige value can be sold for a fraction of its original price, it may leave potential customers wondering just what the true value of the service is. It may also cause resentment among customers who had committed themselves to a service well in advance, only to find that their fellow consumers obtained a lower price by booking later (and thereby also making marketing planning much more difficult for many service operators). Companies can try to overcome problems of marginal cost pricing by differentiating the marginally costed product from that which is purchased at full price. Holiday tour operators, for example, reduce the price of last-minute stand-by holidays, but offer no guarantee of the precise accommodation to be used – or even the precise resort, unlike the full price holiday, where this is clearly specified.

## 11.5 Demand-based pricing

The upper limit to the price of a service is generally determined by what customers are prepared to pay. In fact, different customers often put differing ceilings on the price that they are prepared to pay for a service. Successful demand-based pricing therefore segments markets to achieve the

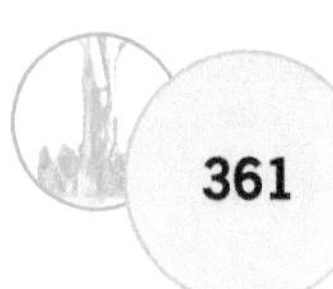



maximum price from each segment. Price discrimination, as it is often called, can be carried out on the basis of:

- discrimination between different groups of users;
- discrimination between different points of use;
- discrimination between different times of use.

### 11.5.1 Price discrimination between different groups of users

Effective price discrimination requires groups of consumers to be segmented in such a way that maximum value is obtained from each segment. Sometimes this can be achieved by simply offering the same service to each segment, but charging a different price. In this way, a hairdresser can offer students or senior citizens a haircut that is identical to the service offered to all other customer groups in all respects except price. The rationale could be that these segments are more price sensitive than other segments, and therefore additional profitable business can only be gained by sacrificing some element of margin. By performing more haircuts, even at a lower price, a hairdresser may end up having increased total revenue from this segment, while still preserving the higher prices charged to other segments.

On other occasions, the service offering is slightly differentiated and targeted to those in segments who are prepared to pay a price that reflects its differential advantages. This is particularly important where it is impossible or undesirable to restrict availability of a lower price to certain pre-defined groups. Thus airlines operating between London and New York offer a variety of fare and service combinations to suit the needs of a number of segments. One segment requires to travel at short notice and typically is travelling on business. For the employer, the cost of not being able to travel at short notice may be high, so this group is prepared to pay a relatively high price in return for ready availability. A sub-segment of this market may wish to arrive refreshed ready for a day's work and be prepared to pay more for the differentiated business or first-class accommodation. For non-business travellers, one segment may be happy to accept a lower price in return for committing themselves to a non-changeable ticket for a particular flight several weeks before departure. Another segment may seek more flexibility and be prepared to pay a higher price for this.

The intangible and inseparable nature of services makes the possibilities for price discrimination between different groups of users much greater than is usually the case with manufactured goods. Goods can easily be purchased by one person, stored and sold to another person. Because services are produced at the point of consumption, it is possible to control the availability of services to different segments. Therefore, a hairdresser who offers a discounted price for a student segment is able to ensure that only students are charged the lower price, for example by requiring to see a Student Union identity card. A student cannot go into the hairdressers to buy a haircut and sell it on to somebody whom the hairdresser deemed to be in a less price sensitive segment.

Charging different prices to different groups can raise ethical issues where a group associates price discrimination with discrimination on the basis of clearly identified social or demographic characteristics. As an example, gas and electricity companies have been accused of offering better prices to affluent consumers who can afford to shop around, while poorer households are given less favourable tariffs. Discriminatory pricing may also be perceived as unfair by customers where it is carried out covertly and they perceive that they are disadvantaged as a result (see 'Thinking around the subject: Cookies allow price discrimination at Amazon' on page 000).

## In practice: Sun, sea and savings

Budget airlines discovered a segment of travellers who were highly responsive to lower air fares. These airlines have simplified their operations, for example by using cheaper but less accessible airports, cutting out free in-flight catering and not paying travel agents commission. The result has been a lower-cost structure, which has been passed on in lower prices, with the price of a return fare from London to Glasgow falling in some cases to less than the price of a pair of jeans. Low prices have tempted many customers to fly with 'budget' airlines. Some of these customers would have transferred from other full-service airlines, on the basis that a low price is a fair trade-off for the loss of some of the additional facilities offered by full-service airlines. For some people, low prices by air meant that they switched from competing rail and road services, while, for others, new possibilities for taking short holidays or visiting friends were opened up that had previously not been affordable.

Figure 11.5 A discount travel website. (Reproduced courtesy of Jet2.com)

## Thinking around the subject: Price discrimination by supermarket backfires

Many service-sector companies have offered reduced prices for segments of senior citizens, calculating that these segments are more price sensitive than others and could usefully fill spare capacity at a profit, even at the lower prices charged. Service marketers are more fortunate than marketers of goods, where price discrimination can backfire. With services, a supplier can insist that only the senior citizen receives the benefit of the service they have paid for (for example, by insisting on seeing proof of age during a train journey). But goods can be bought by a low-price segment and sold on to a relatively high-price one. The pitfalls of this approach to market segmentation were learnt by a German grocery retailer that offered 20 per cent off the price of all purchases made by senior citizens at selected times of the week. Entrepreneurial senior citizens were then seen lining up outside the supermarket offering to do other customers' shopping for them. The 20 per cent price saving was split between the senior citizen and the person needing the goods, saving effort for the latter and making additional income for the former, but making a mockery of the retailer's attempts at price discrimination. Had it been haircuts that were being offered at 20 per cent discount to senior citizens, it would have been impossible for these to be sold on to other market segments.

### 11.5.2 Price discrimination between different points of consumption

Services organizations frequently charge different prices at different service locations. The inseparability of service production and consumption results in service organizations being able to define their price segments on the basis of the point of consumption. This is something that is generally much more difficult for a goods manufacturer to achieve; for example, branded fashion clothes may be sold at premium prices in Western Europe, supported by extensive promotion. However, without such promotion, the price of identical clothes may be much lower in some Far Eastern countries. Such price differences present opportunities for entrepreneurs to buy in the cheap market and to sell them in the higher-price market. This cannot generally happen with services. Services are inseparable, so trading between locations is much more of a problem; for example, cheap dental services in Eastern Europe cannot be easily made available to customers in London in the way that cheap manufactured goods could be moved between the two countries.

Some service locations offer unique advantages to consumers. Hotels fall into this category, with high premiums charged by chains for those hotels located in 'honeypot' areas. A hotel room in the centre of Stratford-upon-Avon offers great benefit to the consumer who wishes to visit the theatre without a long drive back to their accommodation. Hotel prices for comparable standards of hotel therefore fall as distance from the town increases.

Travel services present an interesting example of price discrimination by location, as operators frequently charge different prices at each end of a route. The New York to London air-travel market is quite different from the London to New York market. The state of the respective local economies, levels of competition and customers' buying behaviour differ between the two markets, resulting in different pricing policies in each. Because of the personal nature of an airline ticket and the fact that discounted return tickets specify the outward and return dates of travel, airlines are able to avoid tickets being purchased in the lower-priced area and used by passengers originating from the higher-priced area.

### 11.5.3 Price discrimination by channels of access

Price discrimination is frequently based on the channel of access, so for example an intermediary may be offered a preferential price to stimulate recommendation by the intermediary to its clients. Services are increasingly distributed through Internet-based intermediaries, and the issue of differential pricing by channel is becoming increasingly complex. An airline, for example, may sell a ticket on its own website at one price, but may have negotiated special rates with intermediaries who can often sell the same ticket on their own website for a lower price. It is not uncommon to find the same air ticket being simultaneously offered by many intermediaries at different prices.

For the service provider, charging different prices for different points of access may make sense because of the different competitive environment of each point of access. A loyal customer of an airline may be less inclined to search for a lower price, especially if they are travelling on business and they feel tied to the airline because of a frequent-flyer programme they belong to. A bargain-hunting leisure traveller visiting the site of an intermediary such as Expedia or Opodo will be in a competitive environment where prices are compared with other airlines, and to have any hope of gaining a sale, the airline must offer prices which are competitive with comparable airline offers. For the customer, different prices between intermediaries may be sustainable where different levels of service are offered, for example good after-sales service without the need to use a premium-rate telephone number.

Discriminatory pricing online is becoming more complex as channels of distribution for many services multiply. The airline's intermediaries, for example, are increasingly likely to work through

intermediaries of their own, and these can take many forms, such as price comparison sites. Some intermediaries described generically as 'cashback' sites (e.g. www.topcashback.co.uk) offer part of the payment that they receive for a 'click through' back to the customer, effectively lowering the final price.

### 11.5.4 Price discrimination by time of production

Goods produced in one period can usually be stored and consumed in subsequent periods. Charging different prices in each period could result in customers buying goods for storage when prices are low, and running down their stockpiles when prices are high. Because services are instantly perishable, much greater price discrimination by time is possible.

Services often face uneven demand, which follows a daily, weekly, annual, seasonal, cyclical or random pattern. At the height of each peak, pricing is usually a reflection of:

- the greater willingness of customers to pay higher prices when demand is strong;
- the greater cost, which often results from service operators trying to cater for short peaks in demand.

The greater strength of demand that occurs at some points in a daily cycle can occur for a number of reasons. In the case of rail services into the major conurbations, workers must generally arrive at work at a specified time and may have few realistic alternative means of getting to work. A railway operator can therefore sustain a higher level of fares during the daily commuter peak period. Similarly, the higher rate charged for telephone calls during the daytime is a reflection of the greater strength of demand from the business sector during the daytime. As well as price discrimination between different periods of the day, it can also occur between different periods of the week (e.g. higher fares for using many train services on a Friday evening), or between different seasons of the year (holiday charter flights over public-holiday periods).

Price discrimination by time can be effective in inducing new business at what would otherwise be a quiet period. Hotels in holiday resorts frequently lower their prices in the off-peak season to try to tempt additional custom. Many of the public utilities lower their charges during off-peak periods in a bid to stimulate demand. Lower electricity tariffs are available during the night in order to appeal to a price-sensitive market, which is able and willing to programme washing machines to operate at night-time.

In most cases of price discrimination by time, there is also some relationship to production costs. An argument of telephone operators and electricity generators is that the marginal cost of producing additional output during off-peak periods is relatively low – as long as peak demand has covered the fixed costs of providing equipment, off-peak output can be supplied on a marginal cost basis (see above).

Figure 11.6 Although the costs of serving different groups of individuals may not vary much, this university sports centre practises price discrimination by charging different prices for different groups of users. Sometimes, lower prices are offered to fill capacity at quiet times when the marginal cost of providing facilities is particularly low (for example, many sports centres have low-priced membership schemes that are only available for use during off-peak periods). However, in the absence of clear product differentiation, the reputation of a service provider may be harmed by a feeling of unfairness by those groups who fail to qualify for a lower price.

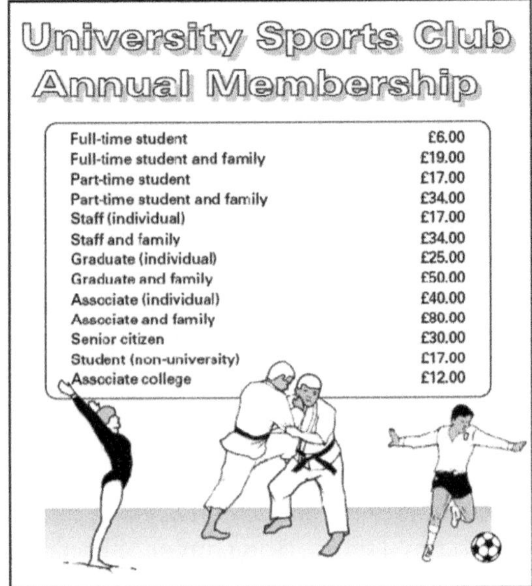

University Sports Club
Annual Membership
Full-time student £6.00
Full-time student and family £19.00
Part-time student £17.00
Part-time student and family £34.00
Staff (individual) £17.00
Staff and family £34.00
Graduate (individual) £25.00
Graduate and family £50.00
Associate (individual) £40.00
Associate and family £80.00
Senior citizen £30.00
Student (non-university) £17.00
Associate college £12.00

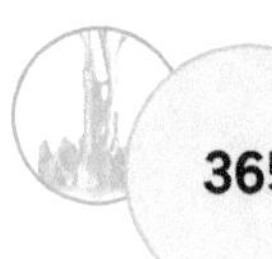



## Thinking around the subject: Cookies allow price discrimination at Amazon

The Internet and electronic databases have opened up vast new possibilities for companies to practise price discrimination between different groups of customers. Airlines and hotels have for some time practised revenue management techniques, designed to get the highest price possible for each unit of output. We are now all familiar with the idea that the price of a ticket for a plane journey on a specific route on a specific date at a specific time may vary – you may see it on an airline's website at one price today, but by tomorrow it may have gone up or down.

There are dangers in practising price discrimination too avidly, as the online retailer Amazon.com found to its cost. In September 2002, the company attempted to implement a differential pricing structure by tracking customers' online purchasing behaviour, in order to charge loyal customers higher prices for its DVDs. Consumers were quick to discover the price differences and complaints followed. Amazon customers on DVDTalk.com, an online forum, reported that certain DVDs had three different prices, depending on the so-called cookie a customer received from Amazon. Cookies are small files that websites transfer to customers' hard drives through the browsers they use. These files allow sites to recognize customers and track their purchase patterns. Depending on previous purchases, a DVD such as *Men in Black* could cost $33.97, $25.97 or $27.97. The list price was $39.95. One customer is reported to have ordered the DVD of Julie Taymour's *Titus*, paying $24.49. The next week he went back to Amazon and saw the price had jumped to $26.24. As an experiment, he stripped his computer of the electronic tags that identified him to Amazon as a regular visitor and the price fell to $22.74. One angry message posted on DVDTalk. com stated, 'Amazon apparently offers good discounts to new users, then once they get the person hooked and coming back to their site again and again, they play with the prices to make more money' (cited in Bicknell, 2000). Loyal, repeat customers were particularly incensed.

Amazon.com quickly issued reports claiming that it had been presenting different prices to different customers but denied that it had done so on the basis of any past purchasing behaviour at Amazon. A spokesman stated that the company had just been carrying out a simple price test and were not discriminating against loyal customers. However, the company later admitted that it had been carrying out discriminatory pricing, justifying its use by the fact that the practice was commonplace among both Internet and bricks-and-mortar companies. Faced with vociferous criticism from its loyal customers, the company quickly ended its use of cookies to discriminate between customers and refunded the difference to customers who had paid the higher prices. Amazon.com may have had to retreat on this occasion, but the case emphasizes that traditional methods used to calculate prices are sledgehammers compared with the Internet's sharp scalpel. The Web provides a continuous feedback loop in that the more a customer buys from a website, the more the site knows about him or her and the weaker his or her bargaining position is. As one commentator put it, 'It's as if the corner drugstore could see you coming down the sidewalk, clutching your fevered brow, and then doubled the price of aspirin.' Is the use of cookies to determine prices charged to individuals an ethical practice?

*Source*: Based on Streitfeld (2002).

### 11.5.5 Auctions and one-to-one pricing

Price discrimination between groups of buyers may sound fine in theory, but there can be problems in actually implementing it. First, it can be very difficult to identify homogeneous segments in terms of individuals' responsiveness to price changes. Second, it can be very difficult to predict just what level of price will be acceptable to that group, and much trial and error may be necessary to establish the most appropriate price. One alternative adopted by some companies is to leave price determination to a process of individual negotiation between buyer and seller. For high-value commercial goods and services, individual negotiation of prices has always been quite commonplace. However, in the case of mass-market services, the existence of a published price list has simplified the process of exchange for buyer and seller, who do not need to spend time negotiating a price on each occasion that a relatively low-value service is sought. In developed economies, it has been quite rare for relatively low-value consumer sales to be individually negotiated. However, auctions provide an opportunity for a seller to get the highest price possible for an individual consumer product. Internet-based auction sites have offered new opportunities for service providers to set their prices on the basis of what the highest bidder is prepared to pay.

Auction sites such as ebay.com essentially put the onus of pricing on the buyer by allowing customers to disclose the price at which they would be prepared to purchase. Faced with surplus aircraft seats, hotel rooms or theatre seats, service providers can make them available on a website and sell them to bidders who bid the highest amount, as long as this is above a minimum reserve price. If the system is working effectively, the service provider can be reasonably sure that it has secured the maximum achievable price for the services on offer.

While auctioning of services to the highest bidder has numerous attractions, there are also problems. An auction may be good in the short term for clearing spare capacity, but in itself does nothing to develop strong brand values. In fact, auctions may treat a service like a commodity in which the only distinguishing feature is price. Auctions can be administratively difficult to administer, even with the use of the Internet. It can be difficult to control auction sites to ensure that bidders actually pay for the service that they successfully bid for and that suppliers deliver their promises. Many consumers would prefer the certainty of fixed prices rather than taking a chance with an auction where neither the availability of a specific service nor its price can be guaranteed.

As well as consumer sales, Internet auctions have found a valuable role for business-to-business procurement (Timmins, 2003). A company can put out a tender and invite suppliers to bid, following which it would choose the lowest-price bidder.

### Thinking around the subject: Haggling by computer?

What is there in common between the haggling over prices that takes place in many Eastern markets and modern direct marketing? At first sight the two would appear to be worlds apart, but in fact they can both be processes by which the seller seeks to establish the maximum amount that a buyer is prepared to pay. In the Eastern bazaar, the seller will learn that some buyers are more price sensitive than others, resulting in each transaction being uniquely priced. This is exactly what modern direct-marketing firms often seek to achieve, except that they are likely to have a mass of information on each potential customer to initiate a price or a level of purchase incentive. And, if this price is too high, the company may try again with a lower price or better incentive, knowing what the likely reaction of a particular market segment will be to the lower price. Credit-card companies, mortgage lenders and banks have used such techniques and are becoming increasingly sophisticated in their use. Can a centralized database do a better job than one-to-one haggling in a marketplace?

### 11.5.6 Customer lifetime pricing

It will be recalled from Chapter 5 that the development of ongoing buyer–seller relationships is becoming a much more important part of marketing strategy for many organizations. Rather than seeing each transaction in isolation, companies are trying to view each transaction with a customer in the context of those that have gone before, and those that they hope will occur in the future. Information technology is increasingly allowing companies to track individual customers and to charge a price that is appropriate to their position in the relationship life cycle.

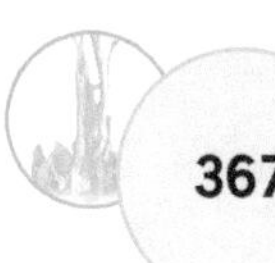



A very low price may be needed to tempt a customer to try a supplier in the first place (for example, satellite television companies and Internet service providers often offer free, or reduced-price, trials of their services). With repeated transactions, a company can build up a picture of a customer's price sensitivity with regard to different types of services. As the relationship develops, the nature of the service may become tailored to the precise needs of the customer, such that the customer will be happy to pay a higher price in return for the benefit received. To switch to a lower-cost provider would involve the psychological cost of searching and explaining their needs to a new supplier and possibly having to understand a new service production system. A customer who has found a reliable car-repair garage may come to be happy paying a little bit over the odds if they can trust the garage to understand their needs and to satisfy them effectively.

Sometimes, there may be financial as well as psychological switching costs when a relationship develops into some form of structural tie between buyer and seller. Customers frequently sign service supply agreements that bind them to a supplier for a specified period of time (e.g. a 12-month contract for a mobile phone). At other times the structural bonds may be more subtle, as when a commercial customer has invested heavily in a computer software system and switching to another company for service support or upgrades may be very expensive.

Sometimes, inertia sets in and a supplier may try to raise its prices in the expectation that a buyer will not be bothered to shop around. Many private customers of telephone companies do not switch to cheaper alternatives because the psychological cost of doing so is seen as too great in relation to the likely financial benefits.

## 11.6 Competitor-based pricing

There are very few situations where a commercial organization can set its prices without taking account of the activities of its competitors. Just who the competition is, against which prices are to be compared, needs to be carefully considered, for competition can be defined in terms of the similarity of the service offered, or merely of the similarity of the underlying needs that a product satisfies. For example, a chain of video rental shops can see its competition purely in terms of other rental chains or, more widely, it can include cinema and satellite television services or, even more widely still, it can include any form of entertainment.

Having established what market it is in and who the competition is, an organization must establish what price position it seeks to adopt relative to its competitors. This position will reflect the service's wider marketing-mix strategy, so, if the company has invested in providing a relatively high-quality service, the benefits of which have been effectively promoted to target users, it can justifiably pitch its price level at a higher level than its competitors.

For services targeting similar sub-segments of a market, the pricing decisions of competitors can have a direct bearing on an organization's own pricing decisions. Price in these circumstances can be used as a tactical weapon to gain short-term competitive advantage over rivals. However, in a market where competitors have broadly similar cost structures, price cutting can be destabilizing and result in costly price wars with no sustainable increase in sales or profitability. An example of price being used to gain short-term competitive advantage is provided by the decision of Midland Bank (now part of HSBC bank) to offer free banking for customers who kept their accounts in credit. While the Midland's market share increased in the short term, it was neutralized during the following year when competing banks offered free banking to match that originally offered by Midland. The market eventually stabilized with all of the main competitors offering free banking and all lost revenue as a result of the continuance of free banking.

### 11.6.1 Going-rate pricing

In some services markets which are characterized by a fairly homogeneous service offering, demand is so sensitive to price that a firm would risk losing most of its business if it charged just a small amount more than its competitors. On the other hand, charging any lower would result in immediate retaliation from competitors.

Where cost levels are difficult to establish, charging a going rate can avoid the problems of trying to calculate costs. As an example, it may be very difficult to calculate the cost of renting out a video film, as the figure will be very dependent upon assumptions made about the number of uses over which the initial purchase cost can be spread. It is much easier to make price decisions on the basis of the going rate amongst nearby competitors.

Many service providers face '**price points**', around which customers expect to pay for a service. The UK market for Internet service providers (ISPs), for example, has developed a number of price points, and customer evaluation processes may begin with the question 'How much do I want to spend?' and comparison is then based on what level of service (e.g. connection speed, download limits, free telephone calls, helpline availability, etc.) they can obtain within this price. The service provider's task then becomes one of designing a profitable service around the price point, rather than designing the service and then fixing a price.

### 11.6.2 Sealed-bid pricing

Many business-to-business services are provided by means of a sealed-bid tendering process, where interested parties are invited to submit a bid for supplying services on the basis of a predetermined specification. In the case of some government contracts, the organization inviting tenders may be legally obliged to accept the lowest-priced tender, unless exceptional circumstances can be proved. Price, therefore, becomes a crucial concern for bidders, regardless of their efforts to build up long-term brand values, which in other markets might have allowed them to charge a premium price. The first task of a bidding company is to establish a minimum bid price based on its costs and required rate of return, below which it would not be prepared to bid. The more difficult task is to try to put a maximum figure on what it can bid. This will be formed on expectations of what its competitors will bid, based on an analysis of their strengths and weaknesses.

In Britain, the requirement for compulsory competitive tendering of government contracts

Figure 11.7 An example of going-rate pricing is often found in areas where a number of restaurants cluster closely together, all offering a basically similar service at a similar price. For the price-sensitive diner, the 'Dish of the Day' may be set at the going rate, while more specialized dishes for which there is less direct competition are priced at a premium rate. Where a 'going rate' is clearly recognized by consumers, the task of the service provider may be to design a service around the price point. Just what menu can the restaurant include in a going rate price of £6 and still make a profit? If it is forced to offer a low 'going-rate' price to tempt customers in, can it increase its margin by selling additional items (e.g. drinks) that are not included in the going-rate price?

has been replaced by a more general requirement of local authorities to obtain 'best value', although tendering remains important for many high-value government service contracts.

## 11.7 Distortions to market-led pricing decisions

Services are more likely than goods to be supplied in non-competitive environments. The high fixed costs associated with many public-utility services means that it is unrealistic to expect two companies to compete (can you imagine two competing sets of water-supply pipes running down each road?). More importantly, much investment in services infrastructure is fixed and cannot be moved to where market opportunities are greatest. While a car manufacturer can quite easily redirect its new cars for sale from a declining market to an expanding one, a railway operator cannot easily transfer its track and stations from one area to another. The immobility of many services can encourage the development of local monopoly power. The nature and consequences of such market distortions, and government responses to them, are discussed below.

In most Western countries there is a presumption that competition is necessary as a means of minimizing prices charged to consumers. However, while price competition may appear to act in the short-term interests of consumers, this normally restrains the combined profits of competitors. It is common, therefore, for competing organizations to seek to come to some sort of agreement (formal or informal) among themselves about prices to be charged, in order to avoid costly price competition.

Anti-competitive pricing occurs not just at a national level between large organizations, but also locally for services where the possibility of newcomers entering a market is limited by technical, economic or institutional barriers. Many local services providers have understandings – if not outright agreements – that have the effect of limiting price competition. In this way, local estate agents and building contractors have sometimes been accused of covert collusion to not engage in price competition, although obtaining evidence of such collusion can be very difficult.

To counter market imperfections, most Western governments have actively sought to eliminate anti-competitive pricing practices. Government regulation of prices charged by private-sector services providers can be divided into two broad categories:

- direct government controls to regulate monopoly power;
- government controls on price representations.

### 11.7.1 Direct government controls to regulate monopoly power

There is generally a presumption by governments that restrictive practices among companies have the effect of raising prices higher than they would be in a competitive market environment. Governments throughout the world have therefore passed legislation to prevent prices being inflated by monopolies and restrictive practices.

Within the European Union, Article 81 of the Treaty of Rome has the effect of voiding any restrictive practices between firms such as price fixing or market sharing. Article 82 deals with firms who abuse a dominant market position, for example through price discrimination and exclusive dealing rights.

In the UK, the Enterprise Act 2002 strengthens the Competition Act 1998 by including provision for a Competition Appeal Tribunal (CAT) and its supporting body, the Competition Service. The Act introduced criminal sanctions with a maximum penalty of five years in prison for the directors of companies that operate agreements to fix prices, share markets, limit production and rig bids. The voice of consumers was strengthened with designated consumer bodies able to make 'super-complaints' to the Office of Fair Trading (OFT).

The Competition Commission has power to investigate alleged anti-competitive pricing practices referred to it by a number of designated bodies, including the Secretary of State for Business, Innovation and Skills, the Office of Fair Trading and industry regulatory bodies. The following are examples of previous investigations by the Competition Commission:

- In 2010 an OFT investigation found that individuals in Royal Bank of Scotland's (RBS's) Professional Practices Coverage Team had disclosed confidential future pricing information to their counterparts at Barclays Bank. The OFT found evidence that the information was taken into account by Barclays in determining its own pricing. RBS agreed to pay a fine of £28.6 million after admitting breaches of competition law between October 2007 and February 2008.
- In 2006, the OFT found that an agreement between 50 of the UK's fee-paying independent schools to exchange detailed fee information was in breach of the Competition Act, and imposed penalties totalling just under £500,000 on the schools. The schools concerned had exchanged confidential information relating to their intended fee levels for boarding and day pupils through a survey known as the 'Sevenoaks Survey'.
- In a 2003 report, the Competition Commission concluded that a monopoly situation existed for the supply of extended warranties for electrical goods. This had resulted in a lack of choice, excessive prices, insufficient information and lack of competition at the point of sale, leaving customers unduly pressurized to agree to disadvantageous terms. The Commission estimated that the top five UK providers of extended warranties – Dixons Group, Comet, Powerhouse, Littlewoods and Argos – had collectively made between £116 million and £152 million more profit each year than they would have done had they been operating in a competitive market environment. The Commission accordingly recommended a series of actions to overcome this market imperfection, including making prices clearer at the outset, providing written quotations and allowing cancellation within 30 days.

The Competition Commission does not just involve itself with national organizations; it also investigates local abuse of monopoly power. In 2009, the OFT referred UK local bus services, excluding London and Northern Ireland, to the Competition Commission. This followed consultation on the results of an OFT market study which found evidence that limited competition between bus operators tended to result in higher prices and lower quality for bus users. In the case of bus services subsidized by the government, the lack of competition appeared to result in poorer value for taxpayers.

During the 1980s and 1990s, the privatization of many UK public-sector utilities resulted in the creation of new private-sector monopolies. To protect the users of these services from exploitation, the government's response has been twofold. First, it has sought to increase competition, in the hope that this in itself will be instrumental in moderating price increases. In this way, the electricity generating industry was divided into a number of competing private suppliers (National Power, Powergen, Nuclear Electric, Scottish Power and Scottish Hydro), while conditions were made easier for new generators to enter the market. In some cases, there have been only very limited opportunities to increase competition, as in the case of privatized water-supply companies.

For many of the newly privatized monopolies, effective competition proved to be an unrealistic possibility and the companies retained a dominant market position. The result has been the creation of a series of regulatory bodies, which can determine the level and structure of many of the charges made by these companies. Even within the apparently competitive telecommunications sector, the regulator has frequently intervened with instructions to operators to reduce specific categories of prices. In 2003, Ofcom published the result of an investigation by the Competition Commission into the 'termination charges' levied by mobile phone operators for calls coming in from other networks. The regulator found evidence of overcharging and ordered termination costs to be cut. In 2006, Ofcom – with the European Regulators Group (ERG), a body of EU telecoms regulators – turned its attention to investigating mobile-phone roaming charges throughout Europe and was instrumental in the development of an EU directive to regulate these charges throughout Europe.

### 11.7.2 Government controls on price representations

In addition to controlling or influencing the actual level of prices, government regulations often specify the manner in which price information is communicated to potential customers. This is particularly important for services that are complex and infrequently purchased, and for which many customers would be ill-equipped to make valid comparisons between competing suppliers. In the UK, the Competition Act 1998 requires that all prices shown should conform to a code of practice on pricing. Misleading price representations that relegate details of supplementary charges to small print or give attractive low lead-in prices for services that are not in fact available are made illegal by this Act. There are other regulations that affect specific industries. The Consumer Credit Act 1974 requires that the charge made for credit must include a statement of the annual percentage rate (APR) of interest. Also within the financial services sector, the Financial Services Act 1986 resulted in quite specific requirements in the manner in which charges for certain insurance-related services are presented to potential customers.

The Office of Fair Trading has power to investigate cases of misleading price representations. In 2009, it received complaints from local trading standards offices about alleged misleading price representations made on the website of the UK-based airline Jet2. com. The OFT investigated whether the airline was complying with the 2008 Consumer Protection from Unfair Trading Regulations. The OFT found evidence of misleading price information and the airline subsequently agreed to amend its pricing, in particular by ensuring that consumers are made aware of any fixed non-optional costs early in the booking process and by clearly displaying in the website's running total price the inclusion of costs which are not taxes (for example, airport charges).

## 11.8 Pricing strategy

The fundamental economic, organizational and legal factors that underpin pricing decisions have been described. This section now moves on to analyse how organizations give strategic direction to pricing policy in order that organizational objectives can be met. The challenge here is to make pricing work as an effective element of the marketing mix, combining with the other mix elements to give a service provider a profitable market position. An effective strategy must identify how the role of price is to function as a service goes through different stages in its life from the launch stage through growth to maturity.

This analysis of pricing strategy considers first the development of a strategy for a new service launch and, second, price adjustments to established services. In practice, of course, it is often not easy to distinguish the two situations, as where an existing service is modified or relaunched.

### 11.8.1 New-service pricing strategy

In developing a price strategy for a new service, two key issues need to be addressed:

- What price position is sought for the service?
- How novel is the service offering?

The choice of price position cannot be separated from other elements of the marketing mix. For many consumer services, the price element can reinforce a perceived quality position. This is especially important where consumers have difficulty in distinguishing between competing services before consumption, and the price charged is one of the few – or only – indicators of likely service quality. Private consumers choosing a painter or decorator with no knowledge of their previous work record may be cautious about accepting the cheapest quotation on the basis that it may reflect an inexperienced decorator with a poor quality record. Similarly, an expensive restaurant may be presumed to be better than a cheaper one.

The novelty of a new service offer can be analysed in terms of whether it is completely new to the market or merely new to the company providing it, but already available from other sources. In the case of completely new innovative services, the company will have some degree of monopoly power in its early years. On the other hand, the launch of a 'me too' service to compete with established services is likely to face heavy price competition from its launch stage. The distinction between innovative services and copycat services is the basis of two distinct pricing strategies – 'price skimming' and 'saturation pricing', which are now examined.

### 11.8.2 Price-skimming strategy

Most completely new product launches are aimed initially at the segment of buyers who can be labelled 'innovators'. These are buyers who have the resources and inclination to be the trendsetters in purchasing new goods and services. This group includes the first people to buy innovative services such as downloadable music services. Following these will be a group of early adopters, followed by a larger group often described as the 'early majority'. The subsequent 'late majority' group may only take up the new service once the market itself has reached maturity. Laggards are the last group to adopt a new service and only do so when the product has become a social norm and/or its price has fallen sufficiently.

Price-skimming strategies seek to gain the highest possible price from the early adopters. When sales to this segment appear to be approaching saturation level, the price level is lowered in order to appeal to the early-adopter segment, which has a lower price threshold at which it is prepared to purchase the service. This process is repeated for the subsequent adoption categories.

The art of effective pricing of innovative services is to identify who the early adopters are, how much they are prepared to pay and how long this price can be sustained before competitors come on the scene with imitation services at a lower price. A price-skimming strategy works by gradually lowering prices to gain access to new segments and to protect market share against new market entrants. Pricing strategy is therefore closely related to the concept of the service life cycle and a typical price-skimming strategy showing price levels through time is shown in Figure 11.8(a).

While the above analysis may be true of services bought by private consumers, is the same effect likely to be true for services bought by businesses? A business buyer is less likely to want to be a trendsetter for its own sake, although individuals within an organization may gain status by being the first to have an innovative service. Sometimes, using a new service ahead of competitors can give a forward-thinking firm a price advantage over its competitors (e.g. the first courier delivery

Figure 11.8 Pricing strategies compared: (a) price skimming; (b) saturation pricing

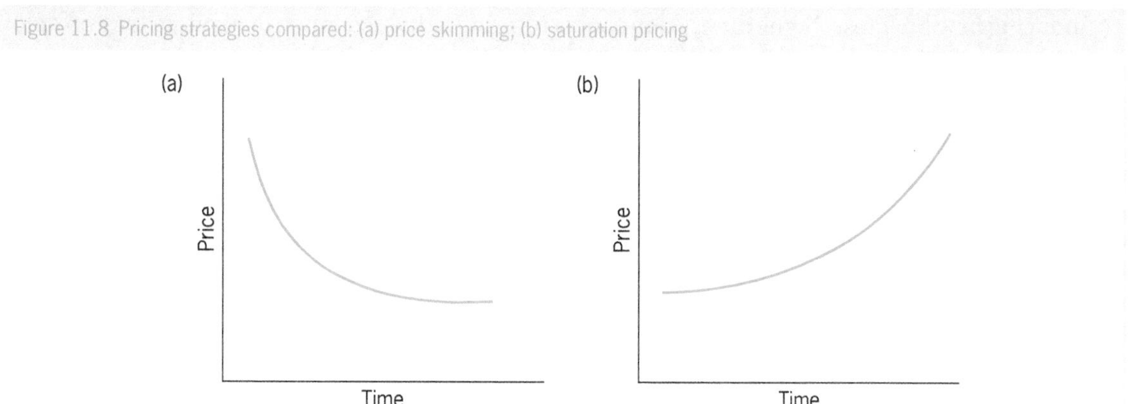


companies to equip their fleets of vehicles with GPS-based navigation systems gained cost advantages over their competitors and were able to offer a better service to customers).

For many innovative services, the trend of falling prices may be further enhanced by falling costs. Lower costs can occur as a result of economies of scale (e.g. the cost per customer of providing the technical support for a home shopping service declines as fixed costs are spread over more volume of throughput) and as a result of the experience effect. The latter refers to the process by which costs fall as experience in production is gained. This is of particular strategic significance to service industries, since, by pursuing a strategy to gain experience faster than its competitors, an organization lowers its cost base and has a greater scope for adopting an aggressive pricing strategy. The combined effects of these two factors can be seen in the mobile phone market, where high initial prices have been brought down by the ability of network operators to spread their capital costs over increasing numbers of users. Also, operators have learnt from experience how a given level of service can be provided more efficiently, for example through adjusting transmitter locations.

### 11.8.3 Saturation pricing strategy

Many 'new' services are launched as copies of existing competitors' services. In the absence of unique features, a low initial price can be used to encourage people who show little brand loyalty to switch service suppliers. Once an initial trial has been made, a service provider would seek to develop increased loyalty from its customers, as a result of which they may be prepared to pay progressively higher prices. A saturation pricing strategy is shown diagrammatically in Figure 11.8(b).

The success of a saturation pricing strategy is dependent upon a sound understanding of the buying behaviour of the target market, in particular:

- *The level of knowledge that consumers have about prices.* For some services, such as the rate of interest charged on credit cards, consumers typically have little idea of the charge that they are currently paying, or indeed of the 'going rate' for such charges. There is now considerable research showing the effects of consumers' knowledge of prices on their buying behaviour (e.g. Aalto-Setala and Raijas, 2003; Wakefield and Inman, 1993). Any attempt to attract new customers on the basis of a differential price advantage may be unsuccessful if knowledge of prices is low. Other incentives (e.g. free gifts or money-off vouchers) may be more effective at inducing new business. Sometimes, companies offering a diverse range of services may offer low prices on services where price comparisons are commonly made, but charge higher prices on other related services where consumer knowledge is lower. Customers of solicitors may shop around for a standard service such as house conveyancing, but may be more reluctant to do so when faced with a non-routine purchase such as civil litigation.

- *The extent to which the service supplier can increase prices on the basis of perceived added value of the service offering.* The purpose of a low initial price is to encourage new users of a service to try a service and return later, paying progressively higher prices. If the new competitor's service is perceived to offer no better value than is offered by the existing supplier, the disloyalty that caused the initial switching could result in a switching back at a later date in response to a competitor's tactical pricing. Worse still, a new service could be launched and experience teething troubles in its early days, doing nothing to generate a perception of added value.
- *The extent to which the service supplier can turn a casually gained relationship into a long-term committed relationship.* Incentives are frequently offered to lessen the attractiveness of switching away from the brand. This can take the form of a subscription rate for regular purchase of a service, or offering an ever-increasing range of services, which together raise the cost to the consumer of transferring their business elsewhere. Banks may offer easy transfers between various savings and investment accounts and, in doing so, aim to reduce the attractiveness of moving one element of the customer's business elsewhere. A loyalty programme can have the effect of tying a customer to a seller.

In some cases, a high initial uptake of a new service may itself add value to the service offering. This can be true where co-production of benefits among consumers is important. For example, a social networking website will be able to offer a more valuable service if large numbers of users are connected to its service, thereby offering more communications possibilities for potential new users. In the same way, airport landing slots become increasingly valuable to an airline as an airport becomes progressively busier, as each airline is able to offer a more comprehensive and valuable set of potential connections to customers. In both cases, a low initial price may be critical to gain entry to a market, while raising prices is consistent with increasing value to the users of the service.

### 11.8.4 Evaluating strategic pricing options

In practice, pricing strategies often contain elements of skimming and saturation strategies. The fact that most new services are in fact adaptations and are easy to copy often prevents a straightforward choice of strategy. Even when a price strategy has been adopted and implemented, it may run off target for a number of reasons:

- Poor market research may have misjudged potential customers' willingness to pay for a new service. As an example, NatWest Bank sought to charge personal customers £30 for using its then innovative Internet-based banking service, 'NatWest Online'. Take-up was reported to be less than expected, with the result that the charge was abolished soon after launch. A service provider may have misjudged the effect of price competition from other services, which, although different in form, satisfied the same basic needs.
- Competitors may emerge sooner or later than expected. The fact that new services can often be easily and quickly copied can result in a curtailment of the period during which an organization can expect to achieve relatively high prices. As an example, an optician opening the first eye-care

centre in an expanding market town may expect to enjoy a few years of higher price levels before competitors drive down price levels, only to find another optician had a similar idea and opens a second eye-care centre shortly afterwards.

- The effects of government regulation may be to extend or reduce the period during which a company enjoys a price advantage. For mobile phone companies that have invested in 3G phone networks, how long can they earn premium prices before licences for a new generation of mobile phone services or mobile Internet are granted by the government?

### 11.8.5 Price leader or follower?

Many services markets are characterized by a small number of dominant suppliers and a large number of smaller ones. Perfect competition and pure monopoly are two extremes, which rarely occur in practice. In markets that show some signs of interdependency among suppliers, firms can often be described as price makers or price followers. Price makers tend to be those who, as a result of their size and power within a market, are able to determine the levels and patterns of prices, which other suppliers then follow. Within the UK insurance industry, the largest firms in the market often lead changes in rate structures. Price takers, on the other hand, tend to have a relatively low size and market share and may lack product differentiation, resources or management drive to adopt a proactive pricing strategy. Smaller estate agents in a local area may find it convenient simply to respond to pricing policies adopted by the dominant firms – to take a proactive role themselves may bring about a reaction from the dominant firms, which they would be unable to counter on account of their size and standing in the market.

## 11.9 Service portfolio pricing

Multi-output service providers usually set the price of a new service in relation to the prices charged for other services within their portfolio. A number of product relationships within a product portfolio can be identified for pricing purposes:

- The *core service* is the focus for pricing and represents the core benefit that a buyer seeks from a service, for example an insurance policy or a plane ticket.
- *Optional additional services* are those that a consumer chooses whether or not to add to the core service purchase, often at the time that the core service is purchased. As a matter of strategy, an organization could seek to charge a low lead-in price for its core service, but to recoup a higher margin from the additional optional services. Simply breaking a service into core and optional components may allow for the presentation of lower price indicators, which through a process of rationalization may be more acceptable to buyers. Research may show that the price of the core service is in fact the only factor that buyers take into account when choosing between alternative services (see Palmer and Boissy, 2009). In this way, many travel agents and tour operators cut their margins on the core holiday that they sell, but make up some of their margin by charging higher mark-ups for optional extras such as travel insurance policies and car hire.
- *Captive services occur* where the core service has been purchased and the provision of additional services can only be provided by the original provider of the core service. Where these are not specified at the outset of purchasing the core service, or are left up to the discretion of the service provider, the latter is in a strong position to charge a high price. Against this, the company must consider the effect that the perception of high exploitative prices charged for these

captive services will have on customer loyalty when a service contract comes due for renewal. An example of captive service pricing is provided by many car insurance companies who, after selling the core insurance policy, can treat the sale of a 'green card' (which extends cover beyond the geographical limits defined in the policy) as a captive sale.

- *Competing services* within a company's portfolio occur where a new service targets a segment of the population that overlaps the segments served by other products within the portfolio. By a process of 'cannibalization', a service provider could find that it is competing with itself. In this way, an airline offering a low-priced direct service from Glasgow to Frankfurt may find that the low price – in addition to generating completely new business – has an important side effect in abstracting traffic from its connecting services from Glasgow to London and from London to Frankfurt.

Deciding what elements of a price should be described as optional can cause legal and ethical problems where a customer has no real choice about whether to buy the optional part of the service. Low-cost airlines have often managed to get their core price down to very low levels, sometimes just one penny, but then add a long list of optional extras. Customers may understand that pricing baggage as an optional extra is legitimate, but many airlines make a charge for using a credit card which is not shown in the headline price for the ticket. They may respond that credit card charges are optional because there is always one type of payment card that does not attract a charge. But is this an ethical practice where the chosen free card-payment option involves an obscure card which very few people have access to?

### 11.9.1 Pricing models

The previous discussion of core, optional, captive and competing services implies that there are often different ways of achieving a given level of revenue, involving different emphasis on prices charged for each of the components. A pricing model describes the way that an organization uses pricing of its total service offer to maximize its overall revenue. So, one element of the total service offer may be charged at a very low price, on the assumption that this will bring in business, which is then prepared to pay relatively high prices for related services. Many restaurants, for example, advertise a main course at a low price, or through promotional pricing such as 'buy one get one free' or 'two for £10'. Such prices may barely cover production costs, but the restaurant may estimate that it will then earn a reasonable profit when customers buy drinks and desserts at full price. If the restaurant wanted to refine the application of its pricing model further, it might use specifically targeted voucher offers given to customers (or types of customer) who from previous experience gave the greatest return on the 'loss leader' main meal by purchasing more optional services than the average customer.

In some sectors, a number of different pricing models coexist. For example, in the emerging multi-channel television broadcasting market, some channels are provided free of charge to users, but make revenue from selling advertising space, while others charge a subscription to users, either on a monthly/annual basis, or a 'pay-to-view' basis. In the UK, the BBC provides a further model, where most services are provided without charge to users or advertising revenue. Instead, government provides funding.

The concept of **price bundling** works within the context of a pricing model. Price bundling is the practice of marketing two or more services in a single package for a single price. Bundling is particularly important for services on account of two common characteristics of services. First, the high ratio of fixed to variable costs that characterizes many services organizations makes the allocation of costs between different services difficult and sometimes arbitrary. Second, there is often a high level of interdependency between different types of service output from an organization. In this way, the provision of an ATM card becomes an interdependent part of the bank current-account offering, for which most UK banks do not charge separately. For some services, the administrative cost of charging for individual elements of a service offer may cost as much as the provision of the service itself (for example, Internet service providers realized from an early stage that it would not be practical to charge for each individual email message that is sent, because the amount of information that would have to be transmitted to create a bill may be more than the amount of information transmitted by the email message itself).

Price bundling of diverse services from an organization's service portfolio is frequently used as a means of building relationships with customers. In this way, a mortgage could be bundled with a household contents insurance policy or a legal protection policy. Where the bundle of service represents ease of administration to the consumer, the service organization may be able to achieve a price for the bundle that is greater than the combined price of the bundle's components.

A service provider may feel compelled to bundle services in accordance with consumers' expectations, leading to the development of a dominant pricing model. Expectations often differ between countries, for example buying a mobile phone handset separately from a mobile service contract may be considered normal in some markets, whereas in other markets the expectation would be that the handset is included in a bundled package.

Sometimes, a dominant pricing model is challenged by a disruptive model which threatens to become the standard model. The effect of dominant pricing models can be seen in the development of dial-up Internet access in the UK. Until 1998, the dominant pricing model for ISPs serving the private consumer market was a monthly fee giving entitlement to a specified number of hours online. In 1998, Freeserve challenged this pricing model by making its service free to consumers, but made up the income loss by selling advertising banner space and recouping a percentage of the amount consumers paid in telephone calls. Shortly afterwards, the majority of ISPs were forced to respond by copying Freeserve's pricing model.

Although price bundling may appear attractive to many service organizations, there are dangers that they may fall foul of competition legislation. In the UK, the Office of Fair Trading has investigated the anti-competitive effects of mortgage lenders bundling household insurance with their core offer and of travel agents bundling insurance with package holidays. In both cases, firms were held to be abusing their position in the way that they sold these additional services.

## 11.10 Tactical pricing

In practice, manoeuvrability around the central pricing strategy will be needed to allow detailed, local application of the overall strategy. This is the role of **tactical pricing**. The distinction between strategic and tactical pricing can sometimes be difficult to draw. In highly competitive, undifferentiated services markets, the development of tactical plans can be all important and assume much greater importance than for a service where an organization has more opportunity for developing a distinctive strategic price position. Some of the tactical uses of pricing are analysed below:

- Tactical pricing can provide short-term competitive advantage. Periodic price reductions can be a means of inducing potential customers to try a service, whether it is new or established. The price cut can be a general, across-the-board reduction or it can be targeted (e.g. by the use of voucher codes). The extent of the uptake will be dependent on the importance of price comparisons, the extent to which consumers of that type of service typically make casual purchases and are not tied to a relationship with another supplier (e.g. lower single bus fares may result in little additional demand if a large proportion of travellers are tied to a season ticket with another operator) and consumers' perceptions of the price offer. Economic rationality may expect that sales of a service will increase as its price is reduced. However, the price reduction may reduce the perceived value of a service, leading to a feeling that its quality has been eroded. Subsequent price increases may lead to the feeling that the service is overpriced if it could be offered previously at a lower price. There may also be significant price points at which a service is perceived as being of good value. A transatlantic air ticket priced at £399 may be perceived as offering much better value than a ticket priced at £400. Even if economic rationality is assumed on the part of consumers, it can be difficult to predict the effects of a price change. Comparison with previous occasions when price was adjusted assumes that all other factors are the same, whereas, in reality, many factors, such as the availability of competitors' services and general macro-environmental considerations, require some judgement to be made about how a similar price change might perform this time around.

- Tactical pricing can be used to remove unplanned excess supply. The strategic price position sought by an organization may be incapable of achievement on account of excess supply, both within the organization and within the market generally. A temporary price cut can be used to bring demand and supply back into balance. Pricing can also be used to capitalize on excess

## Thinking around the subject: A small penny – a big price difference?

Many service sectors have been accused of deliberately confusing customers in the way prices are presented, and the 'no frills' airline sector has attracted particular criticism from government agencies and consumer groups for the way prices are advertised. Many of the 'tricks of the trade' used by the sector go back a long way, for example the use of '99' pricing rather than whole-pound pricing to make a buyer feel that the price is below a psychologically important price barrier (Bray and Harris, 2006). Airlines have been fined for advertising low 'lead-in' prices in bold print, but, when customers have tried to find such prices, they have not been available. Airlines may have had an excuse for non-availability when printed price lists became out of date, but how could they excuse misleading lead-in prices for web-based adverts that can be automatically updated in real time from a database?

The practice of some airlines of showing a low basic price in large figures, while hiding compulsory additional costs in small print, has been widely criticized. For many budget-airline tickets, taxes and security charges may amount to more than the basic price of the ticket, but the total cost of the ticket may only be found at the point where a potential buyer is about to complete their purchase. One critic has likened airlines' practice of making separate charges for taxes and security charges as being similar to car manufacturers making an additional charge for the steering wheel.

Does confusion pricing work? There is some evidence that consumers may make irrational choices, evidenced by paying a higher price for a ticket with a low basic price than for a similar ticket for which total price is expressed upfront (Palmer and Boissy, 2009). Should governments intervene to stop such practices? Or should the old maxim apply that a buyer should beware, and study the small print before committing to a purchase? Do most buyers have the time or inclination to go through every company's small print with a fine-tooth comb? One sign of governments' impatience with airlines' pricing practices was a statement in 2006 by the EU Transport Commissioner, Jacques Barrot, that the EU would press ahead with proposals to make fares easily comparable between airlines.

demand relative to supply. In addition to removing discounts and increasing prices, firms can remove low-margin elements from their service portfolio in order to maximize their returns from high-margin lines.

- Short-term tactical pricing can be used to protect markets against new entrants. Where a new entrant threatens the existing market of an established supplier, the latter may react with short-term price reductions where price comparisons are commonly made. If the new entrant is a small opportunist company seeking to make inroads into the larger dominant firm's market, a low price may force the new company to respond with low prices, putting strain on its initial cash flow and possibly resulting in its withdrawal from the market, if not ceasing to trade completely. Many established operators of bus routes have responded to new market entrants by lowering their prices or even running free buses, in the hope that they can drive the new competitor out of the market. However, such pricing may be deemed to be anti-competitive by regulatory agencies.
- Differential pricing with respect to time, which may have been part of the strategic pricing plan, can be implemented by a number of tactical programmes. Off-peak discounts are frequently used in industries such as rail travel, telecommunications and hotels. The opposite – peak surcharges – can also be used. Other options include offering added-value price bundles at certain periods (e.g. free shopping vouchers for off-peak passengers) and subtly altering a service offering and making it available only at certain times (e.g. a restaurant may slightly differentiate lunch from dinner and charge more for the latter on account of the willingness of customers to pay more for an evening social meal).
- Similarly, differential pricing with respect to place must be translated from a strategic plan to a tactical programme. Implementing differential pricing by area is relatively easy for services on account of the difficulty in transferring service consumption. Hotels and shops, among others, often use different price lists for different locations, depending upon the local competitive position and such lists are often adjusted at short notice to respond to local competitive pressure. Sometimes a common base price is offered at all of an organization's service outlets, and tactical objectives are achieved by means of discounts, which are only available at certain locations. Reduced-price vouchers offered by a national hotel chain may have their validity restricted to those locations where demand is relatively weak. In some cases, companies advertise a number of core services nationally at a fixed rate, while related services are priced according to local market conditions.
- For differential pricing between different consumer segments, the problem of turning a strategy into a tactical programme hinges on the ease with which segments can be isolated and charged different prices. Because services are consumed at the point of production, it is often easy to confine price differences within small segments of a market. In this way, cinemas are able to ensure that only students are able to use reduced-price student tickets by asking for identification as the service process is being undertaken. Sometimes, the implementation of a highly segmented pricing programme can cause problems for service providers where compromise needs to be made between the desire for small, homogeneous segments and the need for segments that are of a worthwhile size to service. As an example, UK train operators place all elderly people in one segment, which is offered a low-price Senior Citizen Railcard. However, the simplicity of this large homogeneous segment is offset by the fact that many people in it are well off and less price-sensitive, and may even be travelling on business. There is also the problem with this form of price segmentation that goodwill can be harmed where arguments develop over a customer's eligibility to a particular price offer.

- Tactical pricing programmes are used to motivate intermediaries. Where a service is provided through an intermediary, the difference between the price that a customer pays and the amount that the service principal receives represents the intermediary's margin. In some cases, price sensitivity of the final consumer is low, but awareness of margins by the intermediary is high, requiring tactical pricing to be directed at maintaining intermediaries' margins relative to those offered by competitors. An example is provided by holiday insurance offered by travel agents – customers do not typically shop around for this ancillary item of a package holiday, but travel agents themselves decide which policy to recommend to their clients, largely on the basis of the commission level that they can earn. The price charged to the final consumer can also affect an intermediary's motivation to sell a principal's service – if the agent perceives the selling price to be too high, they may give up trying to promote it in favour of a more realistic and attractive competitor. On the other hand, if the price is too low, intermediaries working on a percentage commission basis may consider that the reward for them is not worth their effort.

Figure 11.9 It is not just large services organizations that practise price discrimination. Many smaller businesses, such as this hairdressing salon, charge different prices for different groups, typically offering discounts for students and senior citizens. Price discrimination would work for a haircut (unlike most goods), because one person cannot buy a cheap haircut and sell it on to another person who is not eligible for a lower price. However, even small businesses must ensure that discriminatory pricing does not create feelings of resentment from those who pay a higher price for an essentially similar service.

*Julia's Salon*

***PRICE LIST***

| | | |
|---|---|---|
| Cut | Ladies | £25 |
| | Gentleman | £17 |
| Cut and blow dry | Ladies | £32 |
| | Gentlemen | £25 |
| Permanent waving | from | £42 |
| Colouring | | by quotation |
| Highlights | | by quotation |

***SPECIAL RATES***

| | |
|---|---|
| Senior citizens | 10% off all prices Monday–Thursday only |
| Students | 20% off on Wednesday afternoon |
| Children | 25% off all prices |

## 11.11 Pricing strategies for not-for-profit services

It was noted at the beginning of this chapter that price is often a very constrained element of the marketing mix for public services, where there is much less freedom to implement the strategies and tactics of pricing described above. At one extreme, some publicly provided services can operate in a market-mediated environment where pricing policies do not differ significantly from the private sector – indeed, legislation frequently requires such services to act as though they were a market-orientated, private-sector operator. In the UK, local authorities that still run their own bus services are expected to run them as profit-making businesses. At the other extreme, some public services can only sensibly be distributed by centrally planned methods where price loses its role as a means of exchange of value.

Services that, by their very nature, require a high degree of central planning, but which are expected to exhibit some degree of marketing orientation, present particular pricing challenges for marketers. It may be difficult or undesirable to implement a straightforward price–value relationship with individual service users for a number of reasons:

- External benefits that are difficult or impossible for the service provider to appropriate from individual users may be generated by a service. For example, road users within the UK have not generally been charged directly for the benefits that they receive from the road system. This reflects the technical difficulties in appropriating charges from users and the political problem that access to road space is deemed to be a 'birthright', which should not be restricted by direct charging. Nevertheless, the London 'congestion charge' (Figure 11.10) shows how change in the technical and political environment has allowed governments to charge more directly for road space used.

## In practice: Charging for congestion

Road users within the UK have not generally been charged directly for the benefits that they receive from the road system, largely because of the impracticality of road pricing and issues of equity between users. Instead, users have paid for the use of roads through direct and indirect taxation. However, with improved technology and growing realization of the social and economic costs of traffic congestion, there has been a move towards pricing the use of roads. The London congestion charge, introduced in 2003, provides evidence that pricing a public service can change consumers' behaviour, with traffic volumes reported to have fallen by 16 per cent in the months following the introduction of the charge.

Figure 11.10 The London congestion charge

- The benefits to society at large may be as significant as the benefits received by the individual who is the immediate recipient of a public service. An early argument for the free provision of doctors' services was that society as a whole benefited from an individual being cured of a disease, and therefore not spreading it to other members of the community. Similarly, education and training courses may be provided at below cost in order to add to the level of skills available within an economy generally.
- Pricing can be actively used as a means of social policy. Subsidized prices are often used to favour particular groups, for example prescription charges for medicines are related to consumers' ability to pay, with exemption for the very ill and unemployed, among others. Communication programmes are often used by public services to make the public aware of the preferential prices for which they may be eligible. Sometimes, the interests of marketing orientation and social policy can overlap. For example, reduced admission prices to museums for the unemployed may at the same time help a disadvantaged group within society while generating additional overall revenue through segmenting the market in terms of ability to pay.

Problems can occur in public services that have been given a largely financial, market-oriented brief, but in which social policy objectives are superimposed, possibly in conflict. Museums, leisure centres and car-park charges have frequently been at the centre of debate about the relative importance of economic and social objectives. One solution that has sometimes been adopted is to split a service into two distinct components, one part being an essentially public service, which is provided for the benefit of society at large, and the other part comprising those elements that are indistinguishable from commercially provided services. In this way, museums have often retained free or nominally priced admission charges for the serious, scholarly elements of their exhibits, while offering special exhibitions that match the private sector in the standard of production and the prices charged.

## Thinking around the subject: Free hospital treatment: just pay through the phone?

In the public sector, pricing models are increasingly being discussed and developed for services that have previously been considered a vital service available freely to all. The UK's National Health Service (NHS) has a long and proud tradition of providing health services to all, according to an individual's need, paid for out of general taxation, according to an individual's means. Both socialist and right-wing Conservative governments have encountered opposition when they suggested an American-style market-based approach to charging for National Health Service provision. But the need to increase revenue became a priority for cash-strapped NHS trusts from the 1990s, at a time when increasing demand for services was not fully matched by increased government funding. Could NHS trusts copy some of the ideas of pricing models from the private sector?

Although the principle of a health service free at the point of use has been firmly enshrined in the minds of politicians and users, a number of charges have been introduced over the years, for example for prescriptions. However, these tended to be centrally determined with exemptions for those in greatest need. But, from the mid-1990s, individual NHS trusts began exploiting charges for ancillary services as a means of boosting their revenue. One of the first targets for charging was users of hospitals' car parks. Trusts argued that providing car parks was not central to the mission of National Health Service Trusts and, conveniently, government was encouraging more people to use public transport and leave their cars at home. Critics argued that patients were essentially captive and public transport was not a realistic alternative for most people. What began for most hospitals as a small charge soon became a cash cow for hospital finance directors, mindful of the lack of alternatives available to patients. A House of Commons Health Select Committee investigation in 2006 found evidence that some patients did not go to hospital for treatment because of the cost of parking. It showed that, at one hospital in London, a patient who attended the Accident and Emergency department (A&E) on the advice of her general practitioner (GP) was charged £3.75 for the first two hours' use of the hospital car park and £7.50 thereafter. She was 10 minutes over the two-hour period and therefore had to pay the higher charge. She also questioned the fact that charges were reduced to £1 per hour after 6 p.m., when many hospital departments were closed.

Another source of revenue exploited by many hospital trusts comes from the use of bedside telephones by patients. Many trusts entered agreements with private telephone service providers that allowed incoming and outgoing patient calls only through the officially appointed system, which used a premium-rate number. A proportion of the revenue was retained by the hospital. Conveniently, hospital trusts pointed to evidence that mobile phones could harm sensitive medical equipment, and therefore used this to eliminate competitive pressure from patients' mobile phones, forcing them to use the hospital's own telephone system. The ethics of hospital telephone pricing were challenged by the House of Commons Health Select Committee, which accused some trusts of using excessively long recorded messages at the beginning of each incoming and outgoing call, adding to patients' costs and boosting hospitals revenues. It cited a hospital in Essex where people wishing to telephone patients were being charged 49p per minute at peak time and 39p off-peak. By comparison, a typical household rate for a long-distance phone call was around 7p in the peak and 2p in the off-peak. One relative of a patient in a Gloucester hospital claimed to have run up a bill of nearly £1200 for phoning a disabled patient in hospital. The select committee also expressed doubts about whether a ban on mobile phones in hospitals was actually a result of possible interference with medical equipment and recommended that visitors should be able to use mobile phones within certain areas of hospitals.

Summing up, the Select Committee on Health described the system of NHS charges as a mess, with Lord Lipsey of the Social Market Foundation describing it as 'a dog's dinner'. Successive governments had shied away from an overt market-based framework for pricing services provided by the National Health Service. However, it appeared that pricing was coming in through the back door, raising issues about the ethics of charging apparently exploitative prices that reflect patients' captivity. Or were managers of NHS trusts simply being realistic and pragmatic, charging as much as they could for ancillary services so that they could invest more in what a hospital is essentially all about – providing better health treatments?

## 11.12 Internal market pricing

Within large organizations, services may be provided in a quasi-market environment in which it is necessary to determine an internal price that a supplying department charges a receiving department. Setting transfer prices can raise a number of issues for an organization, even where external market prices can be readily ascertained. Allowing users of resources to purchase their services from the cheapest source – internal or external – could result in the in-house supplier losing volume to a point where it ceases to be viable. This could result in the loss of an internal facility to perform specialized jobs that cannot easily be handled by outside contractors. By allowing part of its requirements to be bought in from outside, an organization may increase the loss incurred by its internal supplier, while adding to the profits of outside companies. The internal pricing of services therefore needs to reconcile the possibly conflicting requirements of the in-house production unit to make profits and maintain some capacity and of the resource users to minimize their total expenditure.

A number of possible solutions to the problem of internal pricing can be identified:

- If an external market exists, a 'shadow' price can be imputed to the transfer, reflecting what the transaction would have cost if it had been bought in from outside.
- Where no external market exists, bargaining between divisional managers can take place, although the final outcome may be a reflection of the relative bargaining strength of each manager.
- Corporate management could instruct all divisions to trade on an agreed full-cost pricing basis.
- A system of dual pricing can be adopted where selling divisions receive a market price (where this can be identified), while the buying division pays the full cost of production. Any difference is transferred to corporate accounts.
- A proportion of the internal service producer's fixed costs can be spread over all resource users as a standing charge, regardless of whether they actually use the services of the unit. This would enable the internal supplier to compete on price relatively easily while still allowing resource users, for whom a higher standard of service is worth paying a premium, to buy their requirements in from outside.

Public services that are provided free of charge to users are nevertheless often traded within the public sector on the basis of price. During the 1990s, the UK National Health Service moved from being a centrally planned organization to one that was based on negotiated contracts between hospitals who provide care services and the health authorities and fund-holding general practitioners, who buy services on behalf of their patients. The fund-holding health authorities and GPs clearly wanted their funds to buy the best available care for their patients at the lowest possible price. The early days of internal trade within the National Health Service saw many of the pricing problems commonly associated with internal trading. The wide discrepancies in prices quoted by different hospitals for the same operation reflected a lack of costing information on which prices were based, and the high level of overhead costs associated with many medical facilities. The prospect emerged of whole hospitals being suddenly closed because of their lack of price competitiveness, undoing the benefits of centralized planning, which had sought to balance supply and demand for specialized facilities at a regional level. The problems of effectively managing an internal price-led market for health services subsequently resulted in greater resort to centralized planning and resource allocation through primary care groups.

## Case study

### UK rail fares move to market-based pricing

The pricing of train fares in Britain has evolved over the past 40 years in response to changes in the operating environment of railways. As it has evolved from a centrally planned public service to a more competitive private sector industry, new forms of pricing have emerged.

Gone are the days when there were just a handful of tickets available between any two points – typically full price single and return fares, a cheap off-peak day return fare, a child fare and a season ticket fare for commuters. One constant theme in the development of railway pricing has been the proliferation of different types of fares. For a return journey from Manchester to London, no fewer than 21 different fares were available in July 2013. The pricing of train tickets is complicated by the existence of 'regulated' and 'unregulated' fares.

A number of market segments have been identified by train operators. The business traveller typically has a need for the flexibility of travelling at any time of the day and, because an employer is often picking up the bill, this segment tends to be relatively insensitive to the price charged. Some segments of the business market demand higher standards of quality and are prepared to pay a price of £399 for a flexible first-class ticket from Manchester to London. Some rail companies have added dedicated car-parking facilities and business lounges to their offer aimed at business people. Leisure segments are on the whole more price-sensitive and prepared to accept a lower level of flexibility. Those who are able to book their ticket one week in advance can pay just £23 for the same journey.

A keen eye is kept on the competition in determining prices. Students are more likely than business travellers to accept the coach as an alternative and therefore the Manchester to London student Saver rail fare of £28.30 is pitched against the equivalent student coach fare of £22.10, the higher rail fare being justified on the basis of a superior service offering. For the business traveller, the comparison is with the cost of running a car, parking in London and, more importantly, the cost of an employed person's time. Against these costs, the flexible first class fare of £399 may be perceived as good value. For the family market, the most serious competition is presented by the family car, so a family discount rail-card allows the family as a unit to travel for the price of little more than two adults.

The political environment has had an important effect on rail pricing policies. Before the 1960s, railways were seen as essentially a public service and fares were charged on a seemingly equitable cost per mile basis, with a distinction between first and second class, and a system of cheap same-day returns, which existed largely through tradition. From the 1960s, the state-owned British Rail moved away from social objectives with the introduction of business objectives. With this came recognition that pricing must also be used to maximize revenue rather than to provide social equality. However, government intervention occasionally came into conflict with British Rail's business objectives – for example, British Rail was instructed to curtail fare increases during the 1980s as part of the government's anti-inflation policy and again, in the autumn of 1991, it was instructed to reduce some proposed Inter-City fare increases on account of the poor quality of service on some routes.

The underlying cost of a train journey is difficult to determine as a basis for pricing. Fixed costs have to be paid by train operating companies to Network Rail for the use of the track and terminals. In addition, trains and staff represent a fixed cost, although many companies have sought to make these more flexible. Companies recognize that trains operating in the morning and evening peak periods cost more to operate as fixed costs of vehicles used solely for the peak period cannot be spread over other off-peak periods. The underlying cost of running commuter trains has been publicly cited by train operating companies as the reason for increasing season ticket prices by greater than the rate of inflation during recent years.

The privatization of British Rail in the mid-1990s led to further developments in pricing. In principle, the government sought to facilitate competition which would have the effect of reducing prices charged to passengers. Other service sectors such as buses, electricity supply and telecommunications had been privatized and deregulated, and price-based competition had followed, so why should not the same happen with railways? Train operators have had some success in attracting passengers away from other modes of transport, especially the car and coach, by offering cheap, advance booking fares.

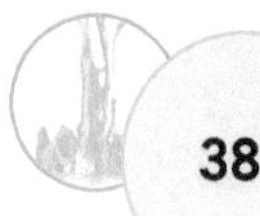


In some cases, completely new demand has been generated among people who could now afford to go away for the weekend, because a previously expensive fare was now affordable. Some competition between railway companies has occurred, for example Chiltern Railways has competed with Virgin Trains between Birmingham and London. But competition between rail operators has generally been limited to a small number of busy routes where there are either two different lines or two operators running over the same line.

For most passengers, the prospect of competition leading to lower prices has been no more than a dream based on idealistic principles of economic theory. Competition between rail operators has been the exception rather than the rule, and many passengers have effectively been captive, with no realistic alternative form of competition, and for whom making their journey to work in the first place is absolutely essential. Commuters into the main cities of Britain would probably feel that competition is fine in theory, but cannot benefit them in practice. For this reason the government has retained some regulation of fares where competitive pressures alone cannot be relied upon to protect the interests of passengers.

Certain standard-class rail tickets are regulated by the government, including standard-class weekly season fares and most commuter fares in and around London. The amount by which an individual regulated ticket can be increased by a rail company is usually capped at the Retail Price Index (RPI) plus a maximum of 1 per cent. In January 2010, rail operators were forced to reduce many regulated fares because inflation (measured by the RPI) in the previous year was minus 1.4 per cent so the maximum average increase was –0.4 per cent, Fares charged by the rail operators Southeastern and Northern Rail in the West Yorkshire Passenger Transport Executive area were exceptions, as they are allowed to raise individual fares by up to RPI plus 3 per cent, in recognition of those operators' commitments to additional investment.

Regulation has also been necessary to ensure a national network of ticket prices that allows a passenger to buy just one ticket for use on the trains of multiple operators who may be involved in a journey; for example, a journey from Cardiff to Newquay would involve a minimum of two train operators, and it would be unreasonable to expect passengers to buy separate tickets for each part of their journey. Furthermore, many sections of route are shared by two or more operators, and the rail network becomes more attractive to passengers if they can travel on the trains of any operator, rather than the operator which issued a ticket. A complex system exists to allocate revenue to operators where the tickets can be used on the trains of more than one company.

Interchangeability of tickets between train operators has been a key element in retention of an integrated national rail network. However, there has been a proliferation of tickets issued by operators for use only on their services. For the issuing train operator, there are a number of advantages arising from selling these restricted tickets. They are easy to implement, because they do not require negotiation with other rail operators, or the government's rail regulator. The operator gets to keep all of the revenue for such restricted tickets, rather than sharing it with other operators, as happens with tickets available on the trains of any operator. Many train operators that are part of larger transport networks have introduced restricted tickets which also allow use on the company's local bus services (for example, the 'First South Wales Bus Railcard' is restricted to trains and buses operated by First Group within South Wales). Inevitably, the ever finer segmentation of markets with specialized tickets has led to more confusion among customers, and even staff. A discussion thread on the website 'railUKforums' discussed the subject of 'tickets you would never want to buy' and identified a number of apparently special offer, restricted tickets that were actually more expensive than comparable, unrestricted tickets.

Many critics have argued that the move to market-based pricing on Britain's railways has not served users or the country well. They point out that train fares are still among the highest in Europe, despite the level of subsidy given by government increasing steadily since privatization – in 2011/12, the railway industry received a total of £3.9 billion in government subidies. As an example, the first-class fully flexible ticket price of £399 for a return journey between London and Manchester compares very unfavourably with a fare of €163 (about £143) for a first-class flexible ticket between Paris and Dijon, a similar distance, but faster journey. Critics argue that fiddling about with price-based competition is relatively unimportant in ensuring competitive advantage for railways, compared with investment in new infrastructure.

At a time of increasing ecological concerns, railways should be seen as good for the environment, but critics have argued that market-based pricing has at best been of only marginal benefit. Competitive fares might have attracted a lot of young and elderly people from competing coach services, and Britain's coach network has suffered as a result. However, coaches could also claim to be good for the environment. Outside the main urban areas, a frequent complaint is that peak-hour train fares work out very expensive compared with driving to work, and many people may find the high fare too much of a barrier to forgoing the convenience of their car. Another common complaint is that railway pricing has done nothing to stop the growth of travel by air. Since privatization, the network of UK domestic air services has grown rapidly, with low-cost airlines such as Ryanair and easyJet selling tickets which are often much less than a comparable train journey. On some routes, such as London–Scotland, the market share of airlines has been increasing, and reached a peak of 85 per cent of the rail/air traffic total in 2009 before falling back as the recession set in and fuel prices rose sharply (DfT, 2010). For a person travelling on business at peak periods, flying is often a cheaper option than using the train. Can pricing get such people back onto the ecologically more friendly train, or are market forces fundamentally incapable of making resource allocation decisions that really require long-term, centralized planning?

### Case study review questions

1. Critically assess the case for government regulation of rail fares.
2. Evaluate the financial benefits to rail operators of offering reduced fares to students.
3. Discuss the limitations of ever-finer segmentation of markets as train companies seek to offer a wider range of fares to meet the requirements of more market segments.

## Summary and links to other chapters

The prices charged by an organization are the result of a range of factors, including the organization's objectives, the nature of the service and the competitiveness of the market in which it operates. Very big differences frequently exist in the price charged for two identical services. This reflects the ability of many services firms to practise price discrimination between different groups of customers and a high level of fixed costs, which allows services to be charged at low marginal costs. The perishability of services further encourages wide variation in prices charged for a service.

Price is just one aspect of the positioning of an organization and its service offers and the price position adopted must be consistent with positions adopted with respect to accessibility, quality and promotion (Chapters 4, 9 and 13). In circumstances where it is difficult to evaluate a service prior to consumption, customers use price as an indicator of the expected quality of a service (Chapter 9). Pricing is a crucial tool in the management of peaks and troughs in demand (Chapter 12). Pricing is also an important part of many service organizations' relationship marketing strategies and Chapter 5 discussed the concept of lifetime relationship pricing.

## Chapter review questions

1 Discuss the problems facing a company seeking to set a launch price for an innovative new service that it has developed. Identify the problems and, using examples, suggest methods by which it could seek to reduce uncertainty surrounding its pricing decisions.

2 Give examples to illustrate situations where price competitiveness may be largely absent in services markets. Critically evaluate the effects of a lack of price competition and what measures, if any, governments should adopt to improve price competitiveness.

3 Identify the reasons why marketers have become increasingly involved in the pricing of public-sector services. Discuss the social and ethical issues involved in public-sector pricing of services.

## Activities

1 Gather together price lists from a selection of any of the following services organizations in your area: sports centres; cinemas/theatres; restaurants. Analyse their pricing and the extent to which cost-based, customer-based and competitor-based pricing is being applied.

2 Examine prices charged by a selection of public-sector organizations with which you are familiar, for example swimming pools, museums and universities. Assess the extent to which prices are influenced by market forces as distinct from government social policy considerations.

3 Study the sports-club price list shown in Figure 11.6. What if any changes in pricing practice would you suggest, based on a sports facility with which you are familiar?

## Key terms

**Contribution** Sales revenue less variable costs. It is the amount available to pay for fixed costs and provide any profit after variable costs have been paid.

**Cookie** A message given to a web browser by a web server, which is stored by the browser in a text file. The message is then sent back to the server each time the browser requests a page from the server.

**Cost-plus pricing** A pricing method in which a percentage mark-up is added to the costs of producing a service.

**Customer lifetime pricing** An approach to pricing that is based on developing a profitable long-term relationship with customers.

**Fixed costs** Costs that do not increase as total output increases.

**Marginal cost pricing** The addition to total cost resulting from the production of one additional unit of output.

**Price bundling** The practice of charging a combined price for a number of service elements, rather than setting prices for each individual element.

**Price discrimination** The practice of selling a product at two or more prices, where the difference in prices is not based on differences in costs.

**Price points** Prices at which demand can suddenly increase/decrease.

**Price skimming** Pricing strategy in which a marketer sets a relatively high price for a product or service at first, then lowers the price over time.

**Tactical pricing** Short-term price variation aimed at thwarting competition or gaining market entry.

**Variable costs** Costs that change in proportion to the activity of a business.

## Selected further reading

*For a general overview of the principles of pricing, applied to the services sector, the following provide useful overviews:*

**Avlonitis, G.J. and Indounas, K.A.** (2005) 'Pricing objectives and pricing methods in the services sector', *Journal of Services Marketing*, 19 (1), 47–57.

**Docters, R., Reopel, M., Sun, J.-M. and Tanny, S.** (2004) 'Capturing the unique value of services: why pricing of services is different', *Journal of Business Strategy*, 25 (2), 23–8.

**Indounas, K.** (2009) 'Successful industrial service pricing', *Journal of Business & Industrial Marketing*, 24 (2), 86–97.

*Tactical pricing in the services sector is discussed in the following articles:*

**Bray, J. and Harris, C.** (2006) 'The effect of 9-ending prices on retail sales: a quantitative UK based field study', *Journal of Marketing Management*, 22 (5/6), 601–7.

**Naylor, G. and Frank, K.E.** (2001) 'The effect of price bundling on consumer perceptions of value', *Journal of Services Marketing*, 15 (4), 270–81.

**Palmer, A. and Boissy, S.** (2009) 'The effects of airline price presentations on buyers' choice', *Journal of Vacation Marketing*, 15 (1), 39–52.

*Pricing in the context of ongoing buyer–seller relationships is explored in the following article:*

**Ryals, L.** (2006) 'Profitable relationships with key customers: how suppliers manage pricing and customer risk', *Journal of Strategic Marketing*, 14 (2), 101–13.

## References

**Aalto-Setala, V. and Raijas, A.** (2003) 'Actual market prices and consumer price knowledge', *Journal of Product & Brand Management*, 12 (2), 180–92.

**Bicknell, C.** (2000) 'The Amazon Story', *Wired News*, July, available at http://www.wired.com/techbiz/media/news/2000/07/37792 (accessed 8 July 2013).

**Bray, J. and Harris, C.** (2006) 'The effect of 9-ending prices on retail sales: a quantitative UK based field study', *Journal of Marketing Management*, 22 (5/6), 601–7.

**Cyert, R.M. and March, J.G.** (1963) *A Behavioural Theory of the Firm*, Prentice-Hall, Englewood Cliffs, NJ.

**Department for Transport (DfT)** (2010) *Regional Transport Statistics*, Department for Transport, available at http://www.dft.gov.uk/pgr/statistics (accessed 18 May 2010).

**Palmer, A. and Boissy, S.** (2009) 'The effects of airline price presentations on buyers' choice', *Journal of Vacation Marketing*, 15 (1), 39–52.

**Streitfeld, D.** (2002) 'Ads on Web don't click', *Washington Post*, 29 October, 1.

**Timmins, N.** (2003) 'A bid to save money for the government: online auctions', *Financial Times*, 29 January, 12.

**Wakefield, K.L. and Inman, J.J.** (1993) 'Who are the price vigilantes? An investigation of differentiating characteristics influencing price information processing', *Journal of Retailing*, 69 (2), 216–33.

**Zeithaml, V.A., Parasuraman, A. and Berry, L.L.** (1985) 'Problems and strategies in services marketing', *Journal of Marketing*, 49 (2), 33–46.

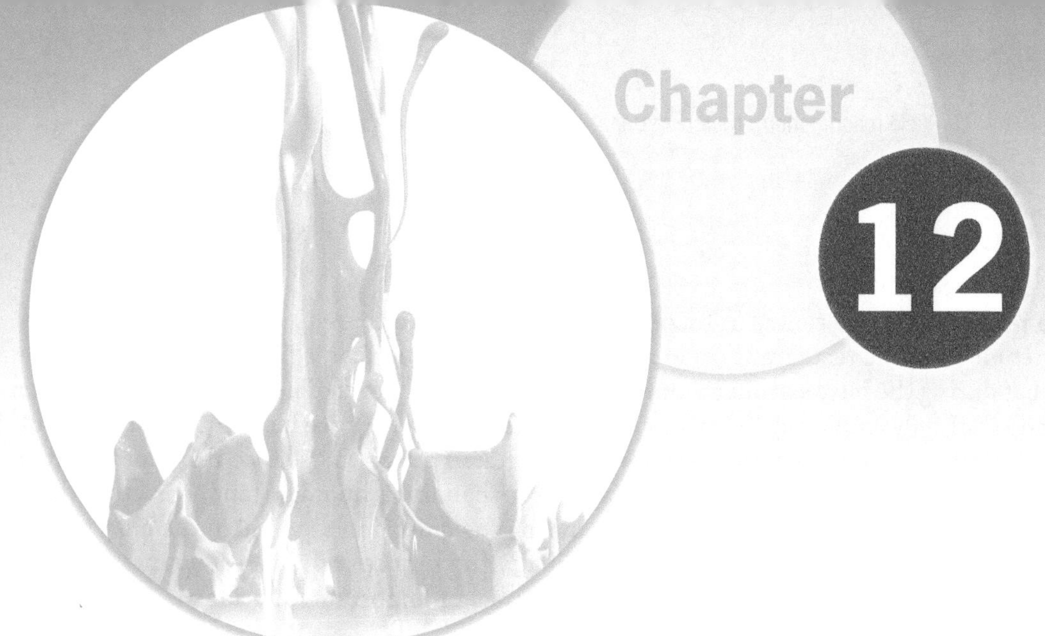


# Yield management: matching capacity with demand

*You are staying at a hotel and get chatting to another guest at breakfast. She delights in telling you about the bargain she got – just £45 for the night. You choke on your croissant when you realize that this is just half the price that you paid for an identical room. Do you feel unfairly treated? Or are you savvy enough to realize that hotels have to match their available rooms with people who are willing to pay the highest price for them? Maybe you realize that if you had left booking your room until the last minute you could have got a bargain as the hotel desperately lowered its prices to earn some revenue rather than no revenue from an unsold room. But perhaps you had to be sure of getting a room because of an important business meeting that you were attending, so could not leave your booking to the last minute. And if all other hotels in the area were sold out, you would expect to pay a very high last-minute price. For many service industries facing fluctuating patterns of demand, the fixed price list is a thing of the past. This chapter explores how services organizations seek to profitably reconcile supply and demand using price and non-price mechanisms.*

## Learning objectives

After reading this chapter, you should understand:

- The effects of service perishability on a service organization's ability to supply a service at the time and place that customers require it
- The nature of variable customer demand
- Techniques used to match service supply to demand
- Queuing and reservation systems
- Yield management techniques, which allow companies to maximize their returns on fixed capacity where demand is variable

## 12.1 Introduction

Imagine a restaurant in the centre of town which is popular with tourists in summer. During the quiet winter months, the restaurant could manage with a building that is half the size it currently occupies, but during the busy summer months it faces a very high level of demand, which keeps its facilities and staff fully employed. This situation is typical of many service industries whose output is perishable, but whose customers' preferred time for consuming the service may not coincide with the company's preferred time for producing it. Perishability is an important characteristic of services, and the possibility of producing output during the quiet period to sell in the busy period – common among manufacturing firms – is not possible with a service such as a restaurant. Strategic marketing planning for such organizations raises a number of important questions:

- What level of demand should the business aim to cater for at its peak? It may not be viable for the company simply to invest in larger facilities if these are only going to be used for a few weeks or even days during the year.
- How should the business maximize its revenue through flexible pricing during the busy periods without alienating the core business that will be needed to sustain it during the quieter periods?
- How can demand be stimulated to fill spare capacity during quiet periods?
- How are problems of congestion to be handled at times of peak demand?

Managing the relationship between supply and demand challenges the strategic and tactical skills of the services marketer. This chapter begins by gaining an understanding of the causes and consequences of fluctuating demand for services. It then looks at methods of changing patterns of demand on the one hand and changing the pattern of supply on the other. Reservation and queuing systems aim to reconcile differences between supply and demand at any one time. **Yield management** has emerged as a technique for turning fluctuating demand from a problem to an opportunity whereby service organizations can make the maximum revenue for the available level of demand.

## 12.2 Causes and consequences of fluctuating demand

Irregular patterns of demand can cause major problems for services organizations. Manufacturing companies also often face irregular patterns of demand, but they are generally better able to cope with such a pattern. Because goods manufacturers are able to separate production from consumption, they have the ability to hold stocks of goods, which can be built up in order to cater for any peaks in demand that occur. As an example, lawnmower manufacturers can work during the winter months making lawnmowers to store in order to meet the sudden surge in demand that occurs each spring. Those lawnmowers that are not sold in that spring can be sold later in the year at a lower clearance price, or put back into stock for the following year. In contrast, the perishability and inseparability of the service offer means that it is not sufficient to broadly match supply and demand over the longer term within a broadly defined geographical market. Instead, supply and demand must be matched for each specific time and each specific place. An excess of production capacity in one time period cannot be transferred to another period when there is a shortage, nor can excess demand in one area normally be met by excess supply located in another area.

The fact that services cannot be stored does not generally cause a problem where demand levels are stable and predictable. However, most services experience demand that shows significant temporal variation. Peaks in demand can take a number of forms:

- daily variation (commuter train services in the morning and evening peaks, leisure centres during evenings);
- weekly variation (night clubs on Saturday nights, trains on Friday evenings);
- seasonal variation (air services to the Mediterranean in summer, department stores in the run-up to Christmas);
- cyclical variation (the demand for mortgages and architectural services);
- unpredictable variation (the demand for building repairs following storm damage).

In practice, many services experience demand patterns that follow a number of these peaks – a restaurant, for example, may have a daily peak (at midday), a weekly peak (Fridays) and a seasonal peak (e.g. December).

Financial success for organizations in competitive markets facing uneven demand comes from being able to match supply to demand at a cost that is lower than its competitors, or with a standard of service that is higher, or both. In free markets, a service organization must take a strategic view as to what level of demand it seeks to cater for. In particular, it must decide to what extent it should even attempt to meet peak demands, rather than turn business away. The precise cut-off point is influenced by a number of factors:

- Infrequently occurring peaks in demand may be very expensive to provide for where they require the organization to provide a high level of equipment or personnel that cannot be laid off or found alternative uses during quiet periods. Commuter rail operators often do not stimulate peak-period demand – or may even try to reduce it – because they would be required to purchase and maintain additional rolling stock for which the entire overhead cost would be carried by those few journeys during the peak when they operate. Similarly, enlarged platforms at terminals may be required in order to cater for just a few additional peak trains each day.
- Peaks in demand may bring in a high level of poor-quality custom. Restaurants in tourist areas may regard the once-only demand brought by Bank Holiday day-trippers to be of less long-term value than catering for the relatively stable all-year-round trade from local residents.
- Quality of service may suffer when a service organization expands its output beyond optimal levels. For example, waiting time in a restaurant may become unacceptable if it seeks to cater for additional customers in the peak period, without investing in additional kitchen facilities.
- On the other hand, some organizations may lose valuable core business if they do not cater for peaks. A bank that frequently suffers lunchtime queues for cash-handling transactions may risk losing an entire relationship with a customer if they transfer not only their cheque facility to a competing bank, but also their mortgage and insurance business.

An indication of the financial implications for organizations of uneven patterns of demand is shown in Figure 12.1, where two levels of capacity are indicated. The *optimum* capacity is notionally defined as that for which a facility was designed – any additional demand is likely to result in queues or discomfort. The *maximum available* capacity is the upper technical limit of a service to handle customers (e.g. a 70-seat railway carriage can in practice carry up to 200 people in crush conditions). At the peak, business is lost; when demand is satisfied above the optimum capacity level, customer service suffers; while in the slack period, resources are wasted.

Figure 12.1 Implications of uneven service demand relative to capacity. The shaded area A represents lost revenue opportunities, as the company is unable at this time of day to satisfy customers who are able and willing to pay. The shaded area B represents a waste of resources for the company. At these times, the company has capacity available, but no revenue is earned. In area C, the service is operating with more than its designed throughput, resulting in loss of quality to customers.

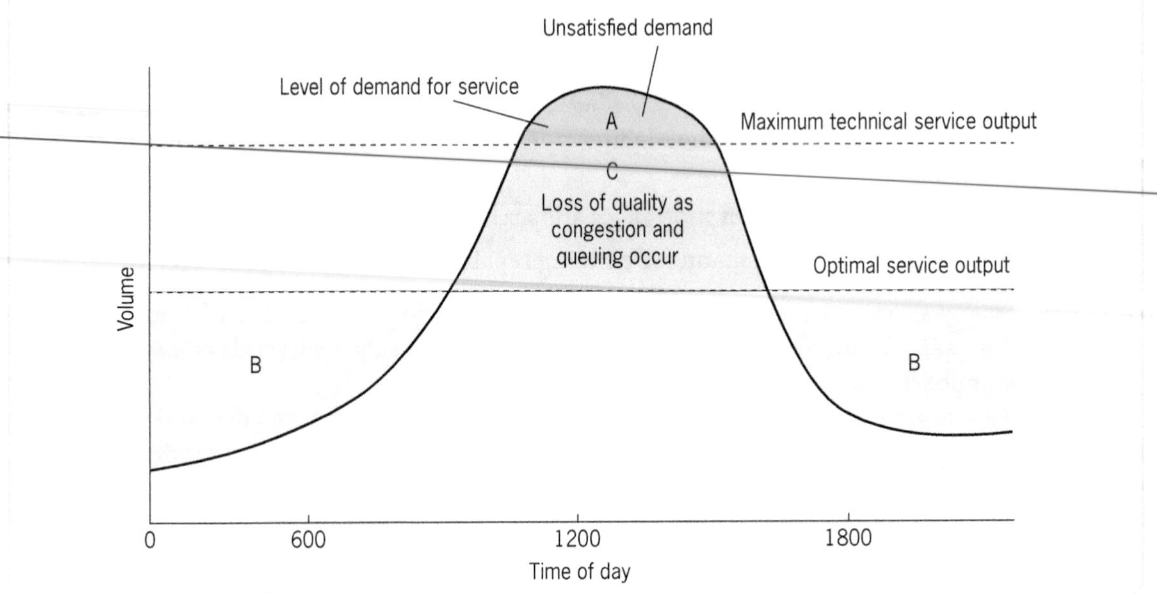


Once a strategic decision has been made about the level of demand that it is desirable to meet, tactics must be developed to bring about a match between supply and demand for each time period. The task of marketing management can conceptually be broken down into two components:

- managing the pattern of demand, in order to even out peaks and troughs;
- managing the supply of service, in order to match the pattern of customer demand.

### 12.2.1 Managing the pattern of customer demand

Where demand is highly peaked, an organization could simply do nothing and allow queues to develop for its service. This is a bad strategy, which could harm the long-term development of relationships with customers, and may deny short-term opportunities that peaks and troughs can present. A simple queuing strategy is most typical of services operating in non-competitive environments, for example some elective surgery undertaken by the National Health Service. In competitive markets, a more proactive market-oriented strategy is needed to manage the pattern of demand and the methods most commonly used are described below:

- Demand is frequently stimulated during the off-peak periods using all of the elements of the marketing mix. Prices are often reduced during slack periods in a number of tactical forms (e.g. 'off-peak' train tickets, the 'happy hour' in pubs and money-off vouchers valid only during slack periods). The product offering can itself be reformulated during the off-peak period by bundling with other services or goods (e.g. activity breaks offered at weekends in business hotels to fill spare room capacity). Distribution of a service could be made more favourable to customers during slack periods – for example, during quiet times of the day or season, a takeaway restaurant may offer a free home-delivery service. Promotion for many service companies is concentrated on

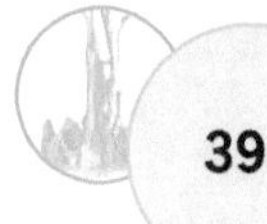

stimulating demand during slack periods. For some services where consumption takes place in public, stimulating demand in quiet periods may be important as a means of improving the quality of the service itself. In the case of theatres, having more customers not only results in increased income, but also a greater ambience for all customers as a result of the atmosphere that the interaction of a live performer and audience creates.

- Similarly, demand is suppressed during peak periods using a reformulation of the marketing mix. Prices are often increased tactically, either directly (e.g. surcharges for rail travel on Friday evenings, higher package-holiday prices in August) or indirectly (e.g. removing discounting during peak periods). Promotion of services associated with peak demand is often reduced (e.g. train operators in the London area concentrate most of their advertising on leisure travel rather than on the highly peaked journey to work). Distribution and the product offering are often simplified at peak periods (e.g. restaurants and cafés frequently turn away low-value business during peak periods).

Figure 12.2 This restaurant has a novel idea for stimulating demand during the quiet early evening period. To encourage early diners (when there is surplus capacity), it charges customers individually according to the time that their order is taken. As the evening gets busier, the price goes up.

## Thinking around the subject: A new date for Valentine's Day?

Holidays and festivities create great opportunities and problems for services organizations. In much of Western Europe, Christmas has a major impact on the operations and finances of many service providers. Retailers, bars and restaurants often make the majority of their profits in the run-up to Christmas and may wish it was Christmas all year long. Indeed, in an attempt to spread the pressure on their stores, some retailers begin displaying Christmas merchandise from September in an attempt to get customers spending earlier, rather than in the hectic scramble in the final weeks before Christmas.

For restaurants, Valentine's Day presents a golden opportunity to develop business at a traditionally quiet time of year for many restaurants. It seems that Valentine's Day is following a similar pattern to Christmas Day in the strategic plans of many restaurants – start advertising early and try to encourage people to consume earlier rather than leave it to the day itself. But is not Valentine's Day unique, and would a Valentine's Day meal on any day other than 14 February seem as unattractive as Christmas lunch on 18 December or 3 January? Not to miss an opportunity, restaurants have developed special Valentine's Day menus that are available not just on 14 February – which has become a day of excessive demand for restaurants – but in the week or so before and after. In a seemingly bizarre attempt to shift demand from Valentine's Day to the two weeks before and two weeks after, one restaurant in North Yorkshire is reported to have advertised a special Valentine's meal package, comprising a three-course meal, champagne and chocolates – £25 for two. The quirk in the marketing strategy? The small print describing the terms of the offer stated 'Valentine's meal package available 1–23 February 2006, except February 14'!

## 12.3 Managing service capacity

There is a limit to how far it is desirable or practical to change the pattern of demand that a company faces. Instead, a service provider must look to manage its capacity more effectively so that the capacity more closely follows the pattern of demand that the company faces.

The extent to which an organization is able to adjust its capacity to meet changes in demand is a reflection of the flexibility of its production processes. Capacity is said to be completely inflexible where it is impossible to produce additional capacity. It is not possible, for example, to enlarge a historic stately home to cater for a demand peak that occurs on summer Sunday afternoons. Capacity is said to be flexible where supply can be adjusted in response to demand. Highly flexible supply allows an organization to meet very short-term variations in demand by introducing additional capacity at short notice. Sometimes, capacity can be flexible up to a certain point, but inflexible beyond that. A railway operator can provide additional trains to meet morning commuter peaks until it runs out of spare rolling stock and terminal facilities, when supply becomes very inflexible. Any discussion of the concept of flexibility of supply requires a time frame to be defined – supply may be inflexible to very sudden changes in demand, but it may be possible to supply additional capacity with sufficient advance planning.

In the area of capacity management, marketing management cannot be seen in isolation from operations management and human resource management. Typical strategies that are used within service industries for making capacity more responsive to demand include the following:

- Equipment and personnel can be scheduled to switch between alternative uses to reflect differing patterns of demand for different services. A hotel can switch a large hall from meeting a peak demand for banquets and parties – which occurs in the evenings – to meeting a peak demand for conferences, which occurs during the working day. Similarly, personnel can be trained to allow different jobs to be performed at different peak periods. Tour operators often train staff to be resort representatives in Mediterranean resorts during the summer peak for beach holidays, and skiing representatives in the Alps during the winter skiing peak.
- Efforts are often made to switch resources between alternative uses at very short notice. For example, a store assistant engaged in restocking shelves can be summoned at short notice to perform much more perishable and inseparable service functions, such as operating a checkout desk to reduce queues.
- Capacity can be bought in on a part-time basis at periods of peak demand. This can involve both personnel resources (e.g. bar staff hired in the evenings only, tour guides hired for the summer only) and equipment (aircraft chartered for the summer season only, shops rented on short leases for the run-up to Christmas).
- Operations can be organized so that as much back-up work as possible is carried out during slack periods of demand. This particularly affects the tangible component of the service offering. In this way, equipment can be serviced during the quiet periods (e.g. winter overhaul programmes carried out on a holiday charter operator's fleet of aircraft) and personnel can do as much preparation as possible in the run-up to a peak (a theatre bar taking orders for interval drinks before a performance and preparing them ready to serve during the interval).

Although it is desirable that the supply of service components should be made as flexible as possible, these components must not be looked at in isolation. The benefits of flexibility in one component can be cancelled out if they are not matched by flexibility in other complementary components of a service. For example, a strategy that allows an inclusive-holiday tour operator to increase the carrying capacity of its aircraft at short notice will be of only limited value if it cannot also increase the availability of additional hotel accommodation.

A strategy to carry out routine aircraft maintenance work during the quieter winter season may simply create an additional peak problem for the airline's maintenance facility which becomes underutilized in the summer and overstretched in winter. Capacity management must therefore identify critical bottlenecks that prevent customers' demands being satisfied cost-effectively.

### Thinking around the subject: Can full buses lose money?

The accountants came into a large bus company and worked out the cost of running school buses during the peak period. Sadly, although the buses were full and even overcrowded, the accountants calculated that they were not making any profit, as they were tying up assets with no alternative use during the rest of the day. The accountants decided that the school bus journeys should in future bear all of the fixed costs of assets used, with the result that, on paper, they then became loss making. So, one morning and evening journey a day had to be able to cover all of the capital, depreciation and maintenance costs of the vehicle, as well as the direct operating costs of wages and fuel. The marketing people of the bus company were exhorted to choke off demand for the school buses and to encourage more use of buses during the off-peak period. The new costing base encouraged them to run more off-peak services, which could make a profit with even small numbers of customers. Bus utilization improved markedly, with fewer peak-hour-only buses sitting around in the garage for most of the day and the remaining buses working almost continuously from early morning until the evening. Unfortunately, solving one problem created another one. The engineers employed during the day to maintain the buses when they came into the depot between the morning and afternoon peaks now found they had no buses to work on. Instead, they had to service the buses at night-time, which involved higher overtime rates of pay. The marketing department had got rid of one peak, but had seemingly created a new maintenance peak for the engineers. This example emphasizes the importance of taking a broad view on demand management to avoid creating further bottlenecks.

## 12.3.1 Flexible employees

We saw in Chapter 10 that, for many services organizations, employees are the biggest item of cost and potentially the biggest cause of bottlenecks in service delivery systems. Having the right staff in the right place at the right time can demand a lot of flexibility on the part of employees. Too often, customers are delayed because, although staff are available, they are not trained to perform the task that currently needs performing urgently. At other times, employees may go about a backroom task oblivious of the fact that delays are occurring elsewhere in the front-line delivery system. Worse still, employees can have a negative attitude towards their job, which sees a customer's problem as nothing to do with them, and take no interest in finding staff who may be able to help. Many service industries have been notorious in the past for rigid demarcation between jobs, which were organization-focused rather than customer-focused. In Britain, train drivers and guards for a long while existed as two separate groups that were not able to stand in for each other.

To improve their flexibility, many service providers have sought to develop multiple skills among their employees so that they can be switched between tasks at short notice. Within the hotel sector, for example, it is quite usual to find staff multi-skilled in reception duties, food and beverage service and room service. If staff shortages occur within one area, staff can be rapidly transferred from less urgent tasks where there may be sufficient staff coverage.

An effective multi-tasking strategy must be backed up by adequate training so that employees can effectively perform all the functions that are expected of them. Transferring a poorly trained employee to a task with which they are not familiar may actually make service delivery worse, not better. Multi-skilling is closely related to the development of empowerment discussed in Chapter 10. This implies that employees become problem solvers on behalf of customers and use their initiative to resolve an issue, either by direct action themselves or by referral to others who are capable of resolving the issue.

Flexibility in working also applies to the rostering of employees' duties. Where patterns of demand are unpredictable, it is useful to have a pool of suitably trained staff who can be called up at short notice. Many service providers therefore operate 'stand-by' or 'call-out' rotas, where staff are expected to be available to go into work at short notice.

A flexible workforce sounds attractive in principle, but there are some drawbacks. Training in multiple skills would appear to be against the principles of scientific management (discussed in Chapter 10), wherein employees specialize in one task and perform this as efficiently as possible. Multiple skill training represents an investment for firms, and in service sectors with high turnover, such as the hospitality sector, the benefits of this training may be short-lived. Recruiting staff may become more expensive, with staff capable of performing numerous tasks able to command higher salaries than somebody whose background only allows them to perform a narrower range of tasks. Finally, there is also the problem that requiring staff to work flexible hours may make their working conditions less attractive than those in a job where they have certainty over the days and times that they will be working. Expecting excessive flexibility may be contrary to the principles of staff engagement discussed in Chapter 10, exacerbating problems where there is a shortage of skilled staff. Service industries must compete with other sectors for good employees and, if a job is perceived as offering too much uncertainty, staff may prefer to work elsewhere where working conditions are more predictable.

As well as being able to achieve short-term flexibility, service organizations must also have the flexibility over the longer term to shift their employees from areas in decline to those where there is a prospect of future growth. For example, in order to retain its profitability, a bank must have the ability to move personnel away from relatively static activities such as cash handling and current-account chequeing towards the more profitable growth area of financial services.

Flexibility within a service organization can be achieved by segmenting the workforce into core and peripheral components. Core workers have greater job security and have defined career opportunities within an internal labour market. In return for this job security, core workers may have to accept what Atkinson (1984) described as 'functional flexibility', whereby they become responsible for a variety of job tasks. Peripheral employees, on the other hand, have less job security and limited career opportunity. In terms of Atkinson's prescription they are 'numerically flexible', while financial flexibility is brought about through such processes as short-term employment contracts, subcontracting and outsourcing. The principal characteristics of the flexible firm are illustrated in Figure 12.3.

As a strategic tool, the model of the flexible firm has important implications for services organizations that experience fluctuating demand. However, critics of the concept have suggested that the strategic role attributed to the flexibility model is often illusory, with many organizations introducing 'flexibility' in very much an opportunistic manner. It has been suggested in one study of the hospitality sector that the distinction between core and peripheral employees is not as great as has been commonly portrayed (Deery and Jago, 2002).

Figure 12.3 Components of the flexible firm

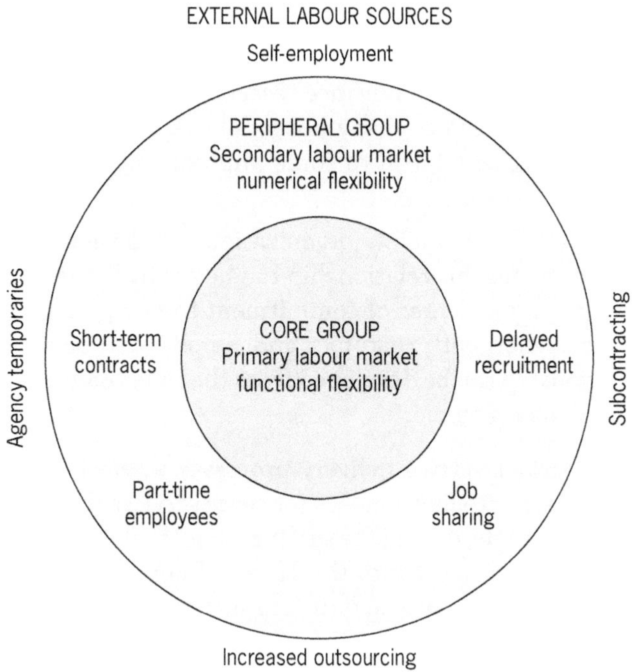


## Thinking around the subject: Too much flexibility for staff?

The conventional wisdom is that services organizations need highly flexible employment practices so that they can effectively and efficiently meet customers' demands when and where they occur. But how far should a company go in pursuit of flexibility? Stories abound of services companies who pay young people the basic minimum wage and provide very insecure employment. Some fast-food chains have been accused of making it a habit to lay staff off at short notice if there is not the level of demand to keep them busy.

To some people, this may sound like exploitation, but, to others, young people were at least being given an opportunity to work and customers benefited by lower prices and service when they needed it. But, apart from the ethics of such practices, there is the question whether too much flexibility makes good business sense. If staff can be laid off at very short notice, will they show such concern to customers as an employee who has more secure employment? Or will the insecurity keep employees on their toes to perform well at all times? Many casual workers in bars, restaurants and call centres have portfolios of part-time jobs that they juggle about, and a good employee should be in demand to do additional work for a number of employers, giving the employee power to choose whom they should work for. If an employee is not performing to standard, their phone is less likely to ring with offers of work. Can flexibility be applied to complex service processes, or is it realistically limited to jobs that have been highly industrialized and deskilled?

## 12.4 Queuing and reservation systems

Where demand exceeds the supply capacity of a service and demand and supply management measures have failed to match the two, some form of queuing or reservation system is often desirable. A formal queuing or reservation system is preferable to a random free-for-all for a number of reasons:

- From an operational viewpoint, advance reservation systems allow an organization to identify when peaks in demand will occur. Where there is reasonable mid- to short-term supply flexibility, supply can be adjusted to meet demand, either by bringing in additional capacity to meet an unexpected surge in demand or by laying off capacity where demand looks like falling below the expected level. In this way, advance reservations for a charter airline can help it to schedule its fleet to accommodate as many potential passengers as possible. Similarly, a low level of advance reservations could lead to some unpromising-looking flights being cancelled or 'consolidated'.
- Reservation and queuing systems allow organizations to develop a relationship with their customers from an early stage. This relationship can be formed at the simplest level by using a telephone enquiry to gain some degree of commitment from a potential customer and to offer them a service at a time when both customer and supplier can be assured of achieving their objectives. Or the relationship can be developed from the time when a potential customer walks into a service outlet and joins a queue.

Queues are an inevitable part of service delivery processes where it is not possible to manage supply or demand to bring them into line. Queues for some services that cannot easily be expanded have become legendary; for example, during the summer months it is not uncommon to find queues of several hundred people waiting to get into the Tower of London. Long waits have been shown to be a major source of customer dissatisfaction (see Bitner et al., 1990). There is also evidence indicating that customers' dissatisfaction with long waits affects both their overall satisfaction with the service and their future intentions to use those providers (Taylor, 1994). Where queues are inevitable, a number of approaches to dealing with them are possible:

- *Understand customers' expectations of waiting time.* Individuals differ in their expectations of waiting time and, even for a particular individual, expectations may be situation-specific. A rail passenger travelling on a business journey may regard minor delay as a failure, but be more prepared to accept a longer delay for a leisure journey. An attempt should be made to understand the psychological world of consumers when they enter the service process. With younger people expecting instant gratification in a wide range of goods and services, their expectations of delay may be quite different from those of an older consumer who has long memories of waiting for goods and services.
- *Reduce actual waiting time.* The most direct approach to dealing with queuing is to decrease actual waiting time. Operational methods to accomplish this goal include various forecasting techniques and the use of staffing and resource allocation models to meet the demand. If demand can be forecast accurately, then in some instances resource allocation can be modified to deal with fluctuating demand patterns. However, it was noted above that capacity may not always be sufficiently flexible to avoid queuing situations.
- *Don't over-promise on waiting time.* Organizations should be careful about the promises they make with regard to queuing time. Where expectations of a short wait are held out, any lengthening of the waiting time will be perceived as a service failure. This could have serious implications for customers' perception of subsequent stages in the service that they are about to receive. It may be better to warn customers to expect a long delay; then, if the actual delay is subsequently shorter, customers will perceive this as exceeding their expectations. They will then enter the next stage of the service process with a more positive mind. Many airline customers have felt relieved when their plane departed 'only' 15 minutes late instead of the 30 minutes that was previously announced by the airline.

- *Reduce perceptions of waiting time*. If the actual waiting time cannot be reduced, customers' subjective perceptions of the length of the delay might be managed. This is especially important in that there is evidence showing that customers tend to overestimate the actual length of their wait time (Hornik, 1984; Katz et al., 1991). By offering activities to fill up waiting time or by providing various distractions, service providers may reduce customers' perceptions of waiting-time length. As an example, customers waiting to collect their car from servicing may have their mind taken off their wait by the provision of a comfortable television lounge. Waiting time will appear to pass by more quickly where the customer can perceive that progress is being made – for example, by seeing that a queue is moving steadily. Uncertainty about the length of waiting time left causes anxiety and makes perceived time longer. Customers should also be able to perceive that the queue is being processed fairly. Where a delay is of uncertain duration, regular communication to customers makes time appear to pass by more quickly – the hardship caused by delay in waiting for a train can be lessened with appropriate communication to customers explaining the cause of the delay. Good communication skills by front-line employees can transform the impact of waiting time.
- *Manage the impact of waiting time*. Service providers should be able to recognize where excessive waiting time has amounted to a service failure and take actions to bring about an equitable resolution to the consequences of failure. Employees' actions, such as apologizing for a delay, may provide some immediate help. Other actions, such as making compensation payments, may also be considered.

A queue presents opportunities for service providers as well as problems. During the waiting process, an organization can make its customers more familiar with other services that may be of interest to them at some other time. Diners waiting for a meal may have the time and interest to read about a programme of special events that associated hotels within the chain are offering. Sometimes, the organization may be able to use a queue for one service to try to cross-sell a higher-value service. In this way, a potential customer for an economy-class air ticket may be persuaded to buy an upgraded class of ticket rather than wait for the next available economy-class seat. Having a queue can also make a company's operations more efficient, as there is no slack time between customers. These efficiency gains may be passed on in the form of lower prices, thereby strengthening an organization's competitive position in a price-sensitive market.

## Thinking around the subject: Can a queue be part of the treat?

Ask anybody who has visited a popular theme park about their worst experience and they will probably mention the queues for the popular rides. However, researchers at Alton Towers theme park in Staffordshire, UK, found that queuing could actually enhance the enjoyment of a visit. They noted that queuing systems seemed to be so successful that visitors could wait for up to an hour for the popular Nemesis ride and hardly seemed to notice the wait. A number of techniques were used to bring this about. Queues were designed to twist in multiple directions, making it difficult for visitors to estimate their length. By exposing those in the queue to those who have just come off a ride, the level of anticipation was raised. Astonishingly, Alton Towers researchers found that on quiet days when there was very little queuing, visitors were scoring lower levels of enjoyment than on busy days. Why could this be? One theory, proposed by Cowley et al. (2005), is that expectations could actually be part of the enjoyment of a service, rather than simply a benchmark against which performance is measured. Could a queue actually heighten visitors' sense of anticipation and achievement? Interestingly, are there other services for which queuing might actually improve customers' perceived level of satisfaction?

## 12.5 Yield management and flexible pricing

Many service industries struggle to match a probabilistic demand pattern to a finite set of resources in order to optimize profits. It is quite intuitive that when demand is strong a company should seek to charge the highest price achievable for the use of its finite resources, while at less busy times it will be prepared to accept a lower price. This is the basis of yield management (YM) – sometimes also referred to as revenue management – which has become an increasingly widespread management technique throughout the services sector.

One of the principles of yield management is to exploit as much as possible of individual buyers' '**consumer surplus**'. This is the value of a product that an individual places on it above the price that they actually paid. If a consumer's perceived value of a product exceeds the price they actually paid, they will consider that they have achieved a 'bargain'. If the valuation is below the price level offered, the consumer will not buy. Yield management seeks to appropriate excess value in the first case and to lower the price charged in the second case to the point where a purchase would represent value to the buyer, and – as long as the price is above marginal production cost – profitable new business for the supplier.

There is nothing new in the principles of yield management. The process of maximizing returns on assets can be traced back to the routine bargaining for goods and services by traders in many less developed economies. Industrialization of many service processes has often had the effect of simplifying pricing structures in order that they can be administered and implemented by relatively junior employees. However, recent developments in information technology have enabled computers to do what the trader in an Eastern bazaar was able to do in his head – estimate the maximum value that could be extracted from each potential customer and sell to those customers who are prepared to offer the best price.

Yield management has gained widespread acceptance within the airline and hotel sectors. The term originated in the airline industry to mean yield per available seat mile but has since been applied to other industries by altering it to yield per available inventory unit. Simply put, YM is the process of allocating the right type of capacity or inventory unit to the right kind of customer at the right price so as to maximize revenue or yield. Highlighting its link with marketing, yield management has been defined as a 'revenue technique which aims to increase net yield through the predicted allocation of available capacity to predetermined market segments at optimum price' (McMahon-Beattie and Yeoman, 2004).

Yield management suits service organizations where the capacity is fixed, where demand is unstable and where the market can be segmented. Analysing these features further, Kimes identified a number of preconditions for the success of YM and suggested a number of factors that are prerequisites for the effective operation of a YM system (Kimes, 1997). Preconditions include fixed capacity, high fixed and low variable costs, and variable demand through time. This means that organizations such as hotels can benefit from controlling capacity when demand is high and relaxing that control when demand is low. Utilization of reservation systems can assist in managing demand because such systems can log requests for inventory units in advance of consumption.

Managers who are familiar with their organization's booking and demand patterns will be more confident in their decision about which reservations to accept or deny. A detailed knowledge of sales and booking data is essential to help managers forecast peaks and troughs in demand, thereby allowing them to align demand with supply more effectively.

It has been noted by Kimes that 'Yield Management is essentially a form of price discrimination'. In reality, hotels and airlines operate YM systems that rely on opening and closing rate bands. During low periods of demand a service provider can offer discount prices. At high-demand periods, discounts can be closed off. Also, by offering multiple rates, the service manager will, hopefully, profitably align price, service and buyer and increase net yield. Service firms should have the ability to divide their customer base into distinct market segments, such as business and leisure, to which they can apply the principles of differential pricing. Airlines typically segment their passengers by their willingness to pay. Low fares are offered to passengers who are willing to accept restrictions on travel. Business people or time-sensitive travellers are usually willing to pay higher fares to travel at peak times with no restrictions.

Overbooking is a common feature of yield management. By overbooking, service firms risk not being able to accommodate customers who have made a reservation, thereby creating a service failure in the eyes of the customer. So why is deliberate overbooking a feature of yield management? In an ideal world, a company would achieve 100 per cent utilization of its resources at all times. In some cases, the conditions of an advance booking by a customer result in the customer forfeiting payment for the service if they do not show for the service at the allotted time. However, in many markets, competitive pressures mean that customers would be deterred from making a binding commitment in advance, and therefore the market works on the basis of verbal, no-commitment reservations. This is typical, for example, within the car rental sector, where rental companies must presume that a certain proportion of bookings will be 'no-shows'. Where the scale of an operation is large and there is a lot of historical data to work from, a company should be able to predict the proportion of no-shows at any particular time and overbook on the assumption that this proportion of bookings will not materialize. Where there is a rapid turnaround in resources (typical of car rental businesses), the effects of an under-assumption of no-shows (i.e. more customers turn up than there is capacity) may simply be a delay (e.g. a wait while returning cars are prepared for a new customer). Sometimes, a company can overcome an overbooking situation by offering customers a free upgrade to a higher grade of facility (e.g. an overbooked airline economy cabin may be overcome if selected economy passengers are upgraded to business class). At other times, the consequences of overbooking may be difficult to handle. An airline may have overbooked a flight on a route where the next flight may not be until the following day, or even the following week. Attempts are therefore made to 'buy back' a booking from customers who have turned up. Incentives such as free tickets for future use and cash bonuses are offered to try to tempt customers to wait for a later flight. Many customers are happy to accept these incentives in return for the inconvenience that has been caused. For the service provider, the cost of these incentives must be assessed against the benefits of getting closer to full utilization of resources. In the case of air travel within Europe, an EU directive requires airlines to pay compensation on a graduated scale if a passenger is denied boarding because of overbooking.

At times of extreme demand (for example, hotels located close to where a major sporting event is due to take place), service providers may seek non-refundable deposits. This is necessary because there may be no history of no-shows for that specific event. Also, the service provider may be much more constrained in its options for resolving an overbooked situation. Offering an incentive for a customer to come back later may be irrelevant where the whole purpose of consuming the service is to take part in a specific event.

It should also be noted that the level of overbooking is part of a company's marketing-mix positioning. A service provider may undertake less overbooking than its rivals and thereby reduce inconvenience to its customers. This should be reflected in its pricing and promotional strategy.

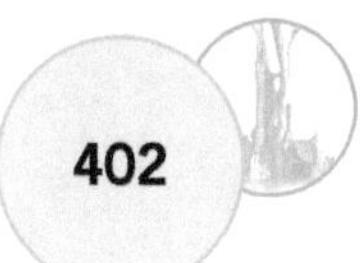

## In practice: How much for a room?

Yield management systems can comprise complex computer programs, with algorithms capable of pricing individual units of capacity in specific places on specific dates, and updating this information in real time. The principles of yield management can be illustrated by comparison with a manual entry journal, such as the page shown in Figure 12.4. In this example, a booking chart is shown for a 100-bedroom hotel for five nights, Saturday 15 September to Wednesday 19 September. The hotel offers three price levels for identical rooms – £100, which gives the customer freedom to cancel and amend their booking and obtain a refund, even if a reservation is cancelled at the last minute; £70, which is available to customers who book at least one week in advance and has penalty charges for cancellation or amendment; and a third category of £40 rooms, which are sold to tour-group operators and made available through last-minute clearance websites. In this example, the hotel is not expecting much demand on Sunday night – traditionally a quiet night for hotels, so a large number of rooms are offered at the lower rate. On Wednesday night, a conference or sporting event in town may have led the hotel to reduce the availability of the cheaper-rate rooms. These allocations can be adjusted day by day to take account of differences between expected bookings on a particular night, and actual bookings achieved so far.

Figure 12.4 A hotel pricing chart

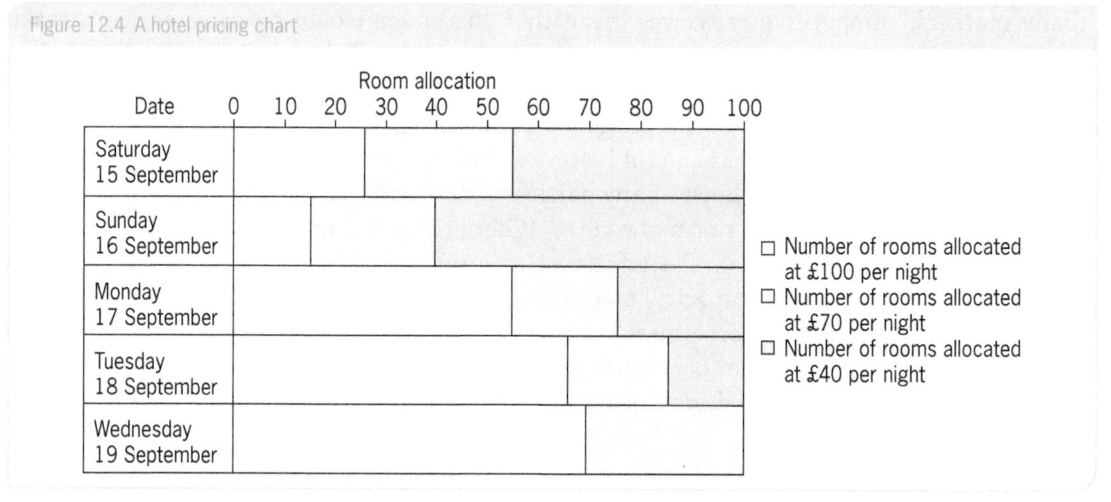


Overbooking occurs not just with respect to individual customer bookings, but also with respect to the utilization of components of the total service offer. Assumptions must be made in a service blueprint about how long each stage of a sequential process should take. For many service processes there will be variability in actual process times, for example the number of repair calls undertaken by an electrician or the number of journeys completed by a taxi. Services organizations are often tempted to overbook these resources, with insufficient recovery time allowed between services. So, if the engineer is delayed on one job, there may be insufficient time allowed prior to the next booked job. The result is that the quality of service perceived by customers will fall. Service providers must try to balance the need for high levels of reliable service delivery (which may imply having spare capacity in reserve) and the need for keeping costs to a minimum (which may mean reducing any spare capacity). In many markets, these considerations form part of companies' marketing mix, with the result that different service levels are targeted at different market segments. Within the UK aircraft charter market, for example, Civil Aviation Authority statistics have shown marked variation between airlines' levels of reliability, with many low-price, no-frills airlines providing poorer reliability performance than comparable full-service rivals.

### 12.5.1 Limitations of yield management practices

Against the theoretical benefits of yield management are numerous operational challenges. It has been noted that the practice of 'holding out' for the best available price involves good forecasting techniques, based on both explicit and tacit knowledge. The simple extrapolation of previous years' trends and the development of rules-based approaches to predicting demand cannot in themselves provide a complete picture of the future. Inputs to the forecasting process rely on judgements of sometimes quite unpredictable factors. For example, an airline must consider the likelihood of a football team gaining a place in a championship final, or the change in image of a destination as a result of media coverage. Incorporating tacit knowledge into operationally driven rules-based systems can be a major challenge.

Revenue management often requires that the yields of a business unit as a whole are maximized, rather than the yields of its component parts. A hotel room booking made at a low price may nevertheless achieve a high yield in the hotel's restaurant, possibly higher than a business guest paying the full price and eating out. Again, human inputs can be crucial to achieving organization-wide maximum yields, by avoiding a 'silo' mentality in which individual departmental managers' pursuit of maximum departmental yields results in a sub-optimal yield for the business unit as a whole.

Another human-behaviour issue is based on consumers' potential mistrust of an organization that uses variable prices. Service companies that use a relatively simple range of fixed prices achieve operational efficiency, and can achieve a consistent price positioning in consumers' minds. In service industries where prior evaluation of quality is difficult, price may be the most important indicator of expected service quality. Indeed, yield-management practices often have the apparently perverse effect of reversing the link between service quality and price. At times of peak demand, congestion (such as longer queues to check in at a hotel, standing-room only on a busy commuter train) result in lower perceived quality, yet customers are charged more than in off-peak periods when quality of service is higher. It follows, therefore, that if price is variable, consumers may have greater difficulty in assessing the likely quality of a service.

There is some evidence that buyers may mistrust a company that uses flexible pricing, especially if this is not transparent and the 'rules' are not clearly explained (Streitfeld, 2000; Wolverton, 2000). This would appear to be troubling, because many of the same firms that have developed yield-management practices have also been strong in their development of relationship marketing (RM) strategies. The published literature on relationship marketing has pointed to the central importance of trust as a means of sustaining a relationship between a buyer and seller (e.g. Morgan and Hunt, 1994). Yield management may therefore undermine the development of such relationships. This undermining of trust may be particularly pronounced where consumers pay higher prices during peak times, but at the same time perceive a deterioration in quality as the service provider seeks to process as many people as possible (Armistead, 1994).

Against this, Choi and Mattila (2006) have contended that the provision of an appropriate level of information on the hotels' pricing policy has a positive impact on customers' perceived fairness of RM. This is consistent with Rohlfs and Kimes (2005) who concluded that consumers (of hotels) will accept the idea of variable prices as long as they understand that they are receiving the 'best-available rate'. It can be argued that consumers are becoming increasingly savvy about pricing methods, and as long as the rules for variable pricing are made clear and well understood, they will accept variability and occasional high prices as the flip side of being able to obtain bargain deals.

### 12.5.2 Yield management or uniform pricing?

Many services organizations have resorted to offering standardized prices, or 'everyday low prices', instead of finely segmented prices. This would appear to be contrary to the principles of marketing and of yield management, but does appear to have a number of advantages. First, the process of setting prices is simplified, resulting in less administrative effort being required by staff and less potential for confusion among customers. Second, there may be communication advantages of offering a single price. A price position can be readily established in the minds of potential consumers. Simple price structures may help develop trust among buyers, who may otherwise feel deceived by not being able to obtain promotional prices or by comparing the price they paid with a lower price paid by another customer for a basically similar product.

There are many recent examples of services organizations that appear to have gone against the philosophy of marketing by offering near-uniform prices for all customers. The hotel sector, for example, has been a leading adopter of yield-management techniques, yet the Premier Inn chain grew rapidly by offering basically standard prices for each similar unit of output sold. Is this position sustainable? There is some evidence that organizations that have initially adopted uniform prices subsequently revert to more sophisticated pricing systems based on the price sensitivity of individual segments for a basically similar product. Even Premier Inn, which initially promoted one single price, has since made promotional voucher offers to fill spare capacity during off-peak times and often charges different rates for weekends compared with weekdays and at different locations.

## Case study

### Cultural change needed to manage hotel yields more effectively

Una McMahon-Beattie, University of Ulster

Yield management (or revenue management) can be seen in a wide variety of industries, such as airlines, hotels, car rentals, cruising, casinos, television advertising, apartment rentals, retailing distribution, logistics, sports and performing arts. In the international hotel industry, revenue management practices and procedures are now so well accepted that they are seen as the competitive advantage of the future. Indeed one commentator has stated that 'The mantra "location, location, location" is fast becoming replaced with "revenue management, revenue management, revenue management"' (Hales, cited in Chase, 2007). However, it has long been recognized that its introduction is far from plain sailing and that the successful implementation of revenue management requires far more than having the right dedicated technology. There are a variety of managerial and organizational factors that have an enormous impact on the levels of benefits obtained from such a system. One critical success factor is effective management of people behind the system. An analysis by Huyton and Peters (2000) of a large 180-bedroomed hotel in Warwick illustrated some of the problems that can occur during implementation.

Prior to introducing a yield-management system, the hotel had used the Champs management information system, which provided a good method for providing occupancy reports and statistics, but had only a limited use for forecasting, which is a fundamental part of yield management. It was essentially retrospective and was not able to provide meaningful forecasts about the future. Forecasting of demand is crucial to give rooms managers the confidence to 'hang out' for the highest possible rate. This idea of 'hanging out' for a higher rate, rather than taking the first available customer that comes along, is an essential part of yield management. One implication is that the volume of business for a hotel may remain constant but, through effective yield management, the amount of profit yielded by each customer may increase. Knowing when to 'hang out' for a higher rate is a management skill, helped by reliable data and forecasting methods. In addition to the forecasting system, an effective yield-management

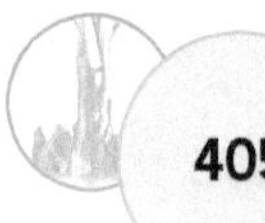



system calls for a computerized decision support system, such as Fidelio, which was used in the case study hotel, and effective communications within the hotel.

Perhaps the biggest challenge facing management was to change the attitudes of front-desk staff, who had previously been happy to register anybody who came along. Now they had to learn to 'hang out' by saying no. As one of them commented following introduction of the new yield management system: 'The reservation staff sit there and say to prospective cutomers "we're terribly sorry, we are fully booked", but in actual fact we have got 15 to 20 rooms to sell (but because of the rate offered by the client we won't take it).' Sales staff had been used to a culture in which rewards are given according to the volume of sales, rather than the profit they yield. An early part of the training programme for reservation staff was to teach them to say no. In practice, this proved to be quite difficult, so the rooms manager resorted to going into the system and blocking off rooms so that reservations staff could see that there was no availability. Reservations staff had to learn not to be afraid of quoting the full rack rate to an enquirer. It is much easier to subsequently offer a discounted price than to try to recover margin from a customer who has been sold a room at a low price. Management has the confidence to hold out for a higher rate because they know, on the basis of probability, that they will get someone else who will pay the full or second-highest 'rack rate'. Staff incentives, which were previously based on the volume of sales made, were changed to reflect the number of sales made at higher rates.

Just as a conductor unifies the diverse talents and capabilities of the musicians in an orchestra, yield management plays a key role in co-ordinating the selling activities of a number of areas in the hotel. As such, the hotel formed a forecasting team that involved a number of departmental managers:

- general manager;
- rooms manager;
- food and beverage manager;
- financial controller.

The authors were surprised to note that the sales manager was not included in this forecasting team, although the results of each meeting were communicated to him in the form of sales targets.

The forecasting team met once a month to discuss forecasts for the coming months. The yield-management ethos helped to identify trends in demand, and in particular shifts in the balance between the main market segments of corporate, leisure and conferences.

Regular meetings, armed with appropriate information, allowed the hotel to see ahead. For example, during the previous year the hotel had found itself with a very quiet Friday and Saturday in June. There had just been two bank holidays and everybody who wanted to come to Warwick for the weekend had been and gone, so there was not much more that the rooms manager could do at the time to stimulate demand. But, with a yield-management system, the forecasting team could have been more proactive earlier in the year when it should have been able to spot, on the basis of previous experience, the potential quiet spot in June. Back in January or February, the hotel would have had enough time to book in a relatively low-yielding coach group for that weekend – some revenue would have been better than no revenue.

Another issue that arose was the need to manage the yield of the hotel as a whole, rather than of individual elements within it. As an example, food and beverage sales may suffer as a result of the hotel holding out for a higher proportion of corporate customers paying a high rate, because business people are more likely to eat out in the evening, thereby depriving the restaurant of revenue. On the other hand, a conference may yield less per room, but this could be made up by high spending on catering and beverages.

The hotel persevered with implementation of its yield-management system. Was it all worth the effort? Within the first year of implementing the system, the hotel noticed an average improvement in yield per room of £5 per night, ahead of the general change in prices within the sector, and very credible given the competitive nature of the industry. Indeed, experts state that implementing yield- or revenue-management systems can generally increase revenue 3–7 per cent or more and all this comes from using existing assets more effectively.

This case clearly shows that a revenue- or yield-management system is not just a piece of dedicated software that, once installed, should be left alone so that it can provide the benefits it is capable of delivering. Such a system only operates with maximum efficiency when the people in the organization understand and capitalize on its strengths and weaknesses, and accept it as a normal part of their daily activities. This need for cultural change is also a key finding of Okumus's (2004) recent study of the yield-management implementation process in an international hotel chain. He argues that implementing yield or revenue management is not a rational, linear process, but rather it is a dynamic and continuous process where the organizational culture, structure and dynamics of the company play important roles.

*Source*: adapted from Huyton and Peters (2000).

### Case study review questions

1 Summarize the issues that are likely to detract from an organization-wide pursuit of maximum yields.
2 What techniques can be used to improve a hotel's accuracy in forecasting demand?
3 To what extent do you think that fluctuating prices, which are associated with yield-management systems, may undermine customers' trust in a hotel brand?

## Summary and links to other chapters

Marketing in the services sector is made more complex by the perishability and inseparability of the service offer, with the consequence that supply and demand must be closely matched by time and place. This demands close integration of marketing and operations-management functions. Fluctuating patterns of demand are often seen as a problem within the services sector, but can also be seen as an opportunity that yield management practices address.

Capacity management is closely related to study of the service encounter (Chapter 2). This chapter has taken a broader management overview to supplement the previous discussion of service design. A critical aspect of making a service organization more flexible lies in the flexibility of its employees, discussed in Chapter 10. Capacity management, and the way in which customers are processed, can be facilitated by ongoing relationships (Chapter 5). The handling of customers during queuing processes can be a major contributor to customers' perceptions of service quality, discussed in Chapter 9.

### Chapter review questions

1 Identify the likely effects on a cinema chain of uneven patterns of customer demand. Critically assess the methods that the cinema could use to overcome problems encountered.
2 Discuss the view that it is not so much variable pricing in itself that may undermine consumers' trust in a brand, but the transparency of the 'rules' by which variable pricing is applied.
3 Given that yield-management methods require an accurate forecast of demand, critically assess methods by which an airline can forecast demand for flights across its route network for the following six-month period.

## Activities

1 Take a look at a selection of websites for airlines that fly between popular destinations, e.g. London–Paris or Frankfurt–Milan. Check the price of flights next week, at different times of the day and on different days of the week. Now repeat the process for dates one month ahead. What principles do you observe being applied by the airlines? If you observe differences between two airlines for flights at roughly similar departure times, how do you explain these differences?

2 Conduct a small survey among your colleagues about the price they paid for recent train journeys. Identify whether they were charged relatively high 'peak' fares or lower 'off-peak' fares. Now try to correlate the price paid to the perceived level of service quality. Are the two issues related?

3 Universities typically face uneven demand patterns throughout the year, and throughout the week. Identify problems arising from uneven demand for an educational establishment with which you are familiar. Now identify and critically appraise possible solutions to overcome the problems that you have identified.

## Key terms

Bottleneck A stage in a process that causes the entire process to slow down or stop.

Consumer surplus Difference between the price consumers are willing to pay and the actual price paid.

Core workers Employees who are generally functionally flexible and perform activities central to an organization.

Multi-tasking Ability to execute two or more tasks simultaneously.

Peaks in demand The greatest demand placed on a product or service.

Queuing system A system for handling temporal excess of demand relative to capacity.

Reservation systems Matching customers' specific requests for service with actual availability of capacity.

Yield management Methods used to maximize revenue from each unit of finite and perishable capacity. Also often referred to as revenue management.

## Selected further reading

*Some of the basic principles of matching service capacity to demand through the techniques of yield management are discussed in the following:*

**Yeoman, I. and McMahon-Beattie, U.** (2010) *Revenue Management: A Practical Pricing Perspective*, Palgrave Macmillan, Basingstoke.

**Wand, X.L. and Bowie, D.** (2009) 'Revenue management: the impact on business-to business relationships', *Journal of Services Marketing*, 23 (1), 31–41.

*Methods of handling queuing situations are discussed in the following:*

**McGuire, K.A., Kimes, S.E., Lynn, M., Pullman, M.E. and Lloyd, R.C.** (2010) 'A framework for evaluating the customer wait experience', *Journal of Service Management*, 21 (3), 269–90.

**Sheu, C., McHaney, R. and Babbar, S.** (2003) 'Service process design flexibility and customer waiting time', *International Journal of Operations & Production Management*, 23 (8), 901–17.

## References


**Armistead, C.** (1994) *The Future of Services Management*, Kogan, London.

**Atkinson, J.** (1984) 'Manpower strategies for flexible organizations', *Personnel Management*, August, 15–26.

**Bitner, M.J., Booms, B.H. and Tetreault, M.S.** (1990) 'The service encounter: diagnosing favorable and unfavorable incidents', *Journal of Marketing*, 54 (1), 71–84.

**Chase, N.** (2007) 'Revenue management redefined', *Hotels*, February, 59–62.

**Choi, S. and Mattila, A.S.** (2006) 'The role of disclosure in variable hotel pricing', *Cornell Hotel and Restaurant Administration Quarterly*, 47 (1), 27–35.

**Cowley, E., Farrell, C. and Edwardson, M.** (2005) 'The role of affective expectations in memory for a service encounter', *Journal of Business Research*, 58 (10), 1419–25.

**Deery, M. and Jago, L.K.** (2002) 'The core and the periphery: an examination of the flexible workforce model in the hotel industry', *International Journal of Hospitality Management*, 21 (4), 339–51.

**Hornik, J.** (1984) 'Subjective vs objective time measures: a note on the perception of time in consumer behavior', *Journal of Consumer Research*, 11 (1), 615–18.

**Huyton, J.H. and Peters, S.D.** (2000) 'Application of yield management to the hotel industry', in A. Ingold, U. McMahon-Beattie and I. Yeoman (eds), *Strategies for the Service Industries*, 2nd edn, Cassell, London.

**Katz, K.L., Larson, B.M. and Larson, R.C.** (1991) 'Prescription for the waiting-in-blues: entertain, enlighten, and engage', *Sloan Management Review*, 32 (Winter), 44–53.

**Kimes, S.** (1997) 'Yield management: an overview', in A. Ingold, U. McMahon-Beattie and I. Yeoman (eds), *Strategies for the Service Industries*, 2nd edn, Cassell, London.

**McMahon-Beattie, U. and Yeoman, I.** (2004) *Revenue Management and Pricing*, Thomson Learning, London.

**Morgan, R.M. and Hunt, S.D.** (1994) 'The commitment–trust theory of relationship marketing', *Journal of Marketing*, 58 (3), 20–38.

**Okumus, F.** (2004) 'Implementation of yield management practices in service organizations: empirical findings for a major hotel group', *The Service Industries Journal*, 24 (6), 65–89.

**Rohlfs, K.V. and Kimes, S.E.** (2005) *Best-rate Pricing at Hotels: A study of Customer Perceptions and Reactions*, Cornell University School of Hotel Administration Center for Hospitality Research, Ithaca, NY.

**Streitfeld, D.** (2000) 'On the web, price tags blur', *Washington Post*, 27 September, A01.

**Taylor, S.** (1994) 'Waiting for service: the relationship between delays and evaluation of service', *Journal of Marketing*, 58 (2), 56–69.

**Wolverton, T.** (2000) 'Some Amazon.com customers are fuming over random discounts on some of the e-tailer's most popular DVDs', *News.Com*, available at http://news.cnet.com/2100-1017-245326.html (accessed 8 July 2013).

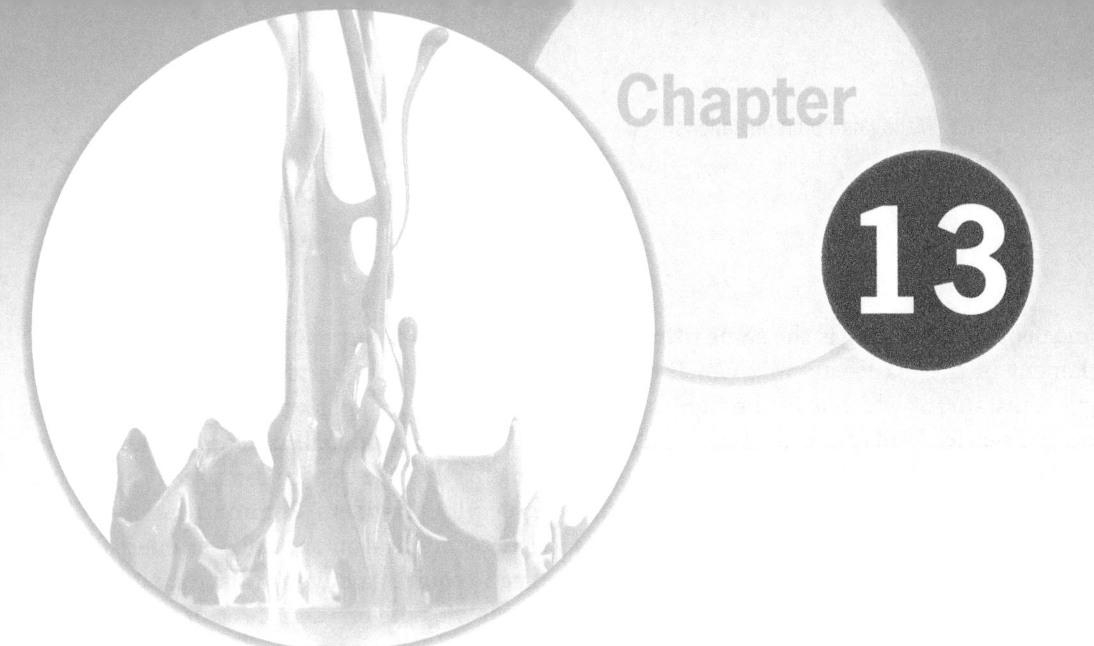


# Managing communications

*For British Airways, the opening of its new Heathrow Terminal 5 involved carefully planned communications in the build-up to the launch. The public had been kept informed of development of this exciting new £4.3 billion state of the art terminal through carefully planned press releases, behind the scenes television documentaries and the promise that the misery of travelling through the aged and cramped Heathrow would be transformed with the new terminal. Then when the terminal finally opened in March 2008 calamity struck and the years of carefully planned communications seemed to be undone in just a couple of days. The baggage system failed in a big way, resulting in piles of baggage going missing. Flights had to be cancelled and British Airways, which the British still had an affection for, was humiliated and became the laughing stock of the world. News reports carried endless stories about missing bags and ruined holidays. Bloggers were active warning travellers to avoid Terminal 5 and YouTube carried videos of mountains of misplaced baggage and angry customers. British Airways had seemingly lost control of its carefully thought-out communication plan. The Terminal 5 fiasco reminds us that communication planning can be much more difficult for service rather than goods-based companies. The variability of services, caused in part by the live, inseparable nature of production, creates problems which are explored in this chapter.*

## Learning objectives

After reading this chapter, you should understand:

- The basic processes involved in communicating a brand or service offer
- The need for services companies to build and maintain their reputation through communication
- The effects of service intangibility on buyers' perception of risk and the role of communication in addressing this perceived risk
- The extended promotional mix for service
- The importance of word-of-mouth recommendation for services

## 13.1 Introduction

To some people, marketing is the same thing as advertising. This is quite wrong. Advertising is just one element of the marketing mix which helps to sell a service. If a service is well designed, for example a restaurant which is in the right part of town and has earned a good reputation through its food and service, it may not need to do any advertising. This is unusual, and most organizations will need to put some effort into communicating the benefits of their service compared to the competition. The focus of this chapter is communication by service providers. Communication is about more than advertising the benefits of a particular service to potential and actual customers. We will see in this chapter how the intangibility of services often requires a buyer to have a high level of trust in a service provider, and to be reasonably sure that it will deliver a service as promised. Given the fact that services cannot be examined before purchase, a large part of service organizations' communication effort is therefore directed at building a strong organizational image, and to provide reassurance that it can be trusted to deliver what it promises, no matter how broad its portfolio of services. We saw in Chapter 8 that brands become increasingly important as services businesses grow, and customers cannot rely on the personal reputation of the business owner him or herself. A brand must communicate the values of the organization so that customers can be reassured of consistent service processes and outcomes, wherever and whenever they deal with the organization.

Service providers' communication is also likely to be targeted at a wide range of other stakeholders, including government agencies, employees, suppliers and intermediaries. In highly regulated service sectors, such as telephone and electricity supply, communicating the benefits of a large quasi-monopolistic company to competition authorities may be key to long-term success. In labour-intensive service industries, communicating the values of the organization to employees may be crucial for ensuring that front-line staff share the same expectations as customers.

There is an argument that communication goes beyond the boundaries of marketing management's responsibility, and many organizations have central communications functions that cover a wide range of communication issues relating to marketing, operations, finance and human resource management. Announcements of a company's financial results may not be seen as specifically a marketing communications issue, but, nevertheless, particularly good (or bad) financial results may have an indirect impact on a company's marketing efforts. If a company's results are particularly good, will customers see the company as successful, or simply greedy? (In 2011, the retailer Tesco made record profits, but was keen to play these down to avoid accusations from customers and regulatory authorities that it was abusing its dominant market position.) Particularly bad results may lead customers to question whether the company will be able to afford to deliver the services that it promised or, indeed, whether the company will be around at all in the future. Where a company provides its services through a network of intermediaries and co-producers, these may become concerned about the long-term viability of the company as a network partner.

Effective communication can be particularly important when a company faces a crisis. We have seen that services are generally much more variable than manufactured goods, and occasionally services organizations face major crises, such as an aeroplane crash or an outbreak of food poisoning at a restaurant. Communication is crucial to reassure customers that the company can still be trusted and, indeed, if handled well, a crisis can even add to a company's credibility.

Communication essentially involves a company sending a message through a channel of communication to reach an intended target. Whether the communication is successful depends on a number of factors:

- *The nature of the message itself.* Does it address the concerns/needs of those at whom it is aimed? Does it use language that is understood?
- *Correct identification of the target audience.* A communication aimed at the wrong people may be as bad as having no communication at all. In the case of communication aimed at potential customers, target audiences for the communication should derive from segmentation studies and the selection of target markets. We saw in Chapter 6 that buyer behaviour can be complex, involving large numbers of people, with a decision-making process spread over a long period of time. Communication of service benefits should therefore target the right members of the decision-making unit, at the right time in the buying process.
- In order to address a target audience, the most appropriate channels of communication need to be selected. Which websites do members of the target audience visit? When do they visit them? What are their preferred television channels? Which newspapers do they read? The selection of channels involves assessment of cost-effectiveness – how many members of your target audience do you get access to for each pound of expenditure?
- The message that a company sends out is not necessarily the one that the audience picks up. A whole range of 'noise' factors can result in a different interpretation by the audience, compared to that intended by the sender of the message. An advert that worked well last month may not work as well this month, because of the effects of competitor activity, news media stories, the weather, etc. For many messages, there are likely to be big individual differences between individuals in how they interpret a particular message – an individual who has had bad experiences with a bank may see its advertising for loans with scepticism, whereas somebody desperate to borrow money for the first time may see the message more positively as a means of satisfying their needs. The channel of communication may itself influence the way in which a message is perceived. For example, a package holiday may be perceived as exclusive if it is advertised in an up-market magazine such as *Country Life*, but cheap and ordinary if the same holiday is advertised in a tabloid newspaper such as the *Sun*.

A model of the essential elements of the communication process is shown in Figure 13.1. This portrays a process by which sometimes complex messages are abbreviated into coded form for

Figure 13.1 The communication process

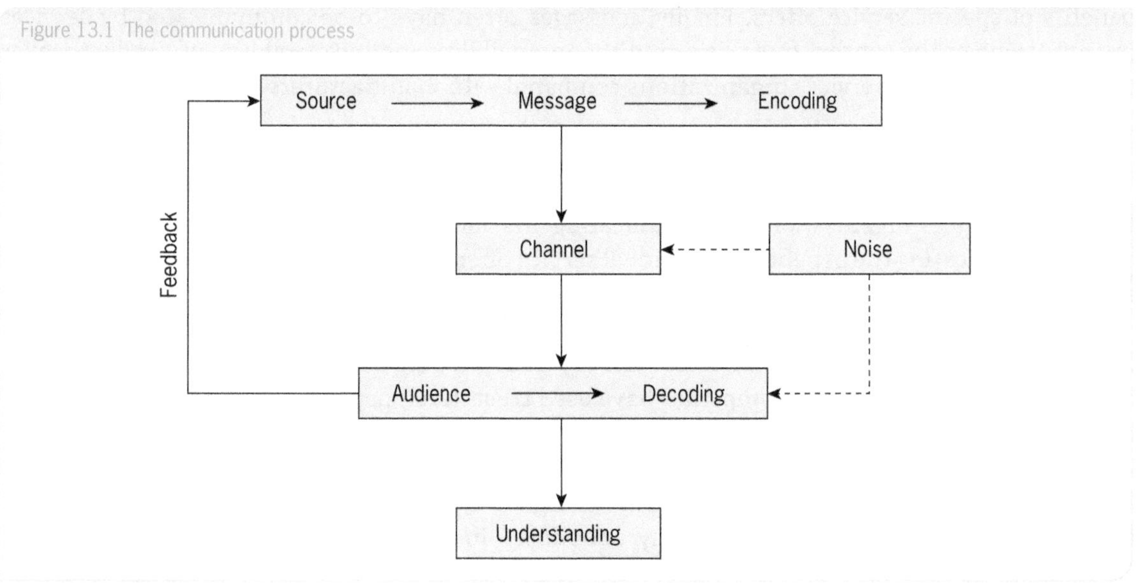

communication through various channels of communication, and are then decoded by the receiver. Some messages will be understood and then acted upon, but most will fail to have an effect on the target audience. They may fail because the audience for the message was wrongly specified; the message may have been coded in a form that was inappropriate for the target audience; the channels chosen may have been inappropriate to the target market; or the message may have been drowned by the 'noise' created by other competing messages.

This chapter will begin by exploring the nature of the messages that service organizations seek to communicate to their various audiences. It will then consider the decisions that services organizations make about how to allocate their communication expenditure between different channels of communication. We will see how services organizations face an extended promotion mix, compared with the promotion mix of manufacturing companies. In addition to the conventional promotional channels, the inseparable nature of services gives rise to new opportunities (and challenges) for communication. Front-line service personnel, the visibility of service production processes and the physical environment in which a service is produced all have potential to communicate messages in a way that is not usually possible for a car-manufacturing company.

Finally, it should not be forgotten that the promotion industry is a major service sector in its own right. Public relations agencies, direct-mail operators and advertising agencies not only provide vital inputs to other firms' marketing efforts, but they themselves have to develop promotional plans for their own businesses.

## 13.2 The message

Central to an organization's communication effort is the message that it wants to communicate. This must be derived from a sound analysis of an organization's service offer and the positioning of its brand. To be effective, a message must identify the target audience and communicate in a manner that addresses its needs and expectations. In this section, we will look at a number of contexts for services organizations' communications efforts. We first consider the importance of communicating core brand values that encourage customers and other stakeholders to trust the organization and its brands. We then consider approaches to communicating the features and benefits of specific service offers. Finally, messages often have to be communicated by services organizations in the context of a crisis, and the intangibility and inseparability of services makes this a bigger issue for services organizations compared with manufacturers.

### 13.2.1 Communicating the corporate brand

For many services organizations, communicating the values of their brands is more important than communicating the benefits of individual service offers. We have seen how the intangibility of services implies that buyers are generally unable to assess a service before they consume it, so how can they trust that a company which promises a service will actually deliver what it promised? Service-based organizations have invested heavily in developing and communicating their corporate reputation, and successful companies have used trust developed in one service area to develop new service offers in completely unrelated areas. In the UK, the retailer Boots has used consumers' high level of trust in its pharmacy chain to develop optician and dentistry services. Similarly, the Virgin Group has used a reputation as a trusted organization to diversify from music to aviation, banking, phones and trains. The company announced in 2006 a proposal to develop its 'Virgin Gallactica' project to take tourists into outer space, something that demands a high level of trust

## In practice: A smarter way to communicate

Matching the target market with media audiences is key to successful communication. A message sent to the wrong audience is a message wasted. For this purpose, target markets have traditionally been defined in terms of economic, social and demographic factors, and the stage that a consumer has reached in the buying process. Timing has always been crucial, and a message that is too late or too early for the target audience may be wasted. Increasingly, the place that a message is received is becoming a basis for defining a target audience. Newspapers, television and radio stations have for a long time segmented their audience by time and place (e.g. leisure attractions advertising in the local press just before the weekend). With the advent of smartphones, the ability to target messages to geographically very specific audiences is greatly increased. This is particularly important for inseparable and perishable services, so for example a restaurant with spare capacity can send special offer messages to people on its database who are in the area at the time. Smartphones also offer the chance of two-way feedback communication; for example, the recipient of a message may use their smartphone to book a table at the restaurant immediately. There is some evidence that a message received at exactly the right location may increase a consumer's expenditure (Hui et al., 2013).

Figure 13.2 A new generation smartphone. (Reproduced courtesy of Apple)

from consumers. Would you want to be taken literally out of this world by a company that you perceive cannot even be trusted to tell the truth in its financial accounts, or is perceived as having a poor record of safety maintenance in other areas of its activities?

Communicating the corporate brand therefore becomes crucial for services organizations. Ind (1997) defines corporate branding as the 'sum of values that represent the organization'. This concept implies the need to communicate the values of the organization to a network of stakeholders, both internal and external to the organization, through corporate as well as marketing communication vehicles (Balmer and Greyser, 2006). We will see later in this chapter that communications with employees, government agencies and local communities can be crucial for marketing success, and sometimes communicating the values of an organization to customer groups may have secondary importance. Successful services organizations are able to manage effectively the several dimensions of corporate brand communication, such as strategic corporate vision, organizational culture and addressing the needs of different customer and stakeholder groups (Balmer and Greyser, 2006).

Many services organizations have to protect their corporate brand against attack by pressure groups. Repeated campaigning by pressure groups against the practices of an organization may deter some customers, but, more seriously, may eventually lead to government regulation that has the effect of increasing the sector's costs and/or reducing its appeal to customers. Sometimes, pressure may derive from a company's general association with an issue, rather than a specific grievance with its operations. Starbucks Coffee, for example, was subject to widespread public criticism in the UK in 2012 when it was revealed that despite making high profits, it had managed to pay almost no tax on its profits to the UK government. What it had done was not illegal but the ethics were challenged by many, including the campaign group Uncut which organized demonstrations outside the company's stores in December 2012. The company subsequently agreed to pay £10 million in tax to the UK government, but many saw this as too little and too late, and furthermore, some critics were further angered at the idea that Starbucks should treat tax on its profits as if it were a voluntary contribution which the company itself could decide.

Services organizations are not only on the receiving end of pressure groups' activities – they also frequently join together to influence government policy formation. As an example, many pub operators in the UK are members of the Portman Group and have used this organization to put pressure on government to resist further taxation on alcohol which would be against the interests of members (Figure 13.3). The group has also communicated a message of responsible drinking to a wider group of stakeholders, including customers, local and national government agencies and health-promotion organizations. Although communication through pressure groups may be attractive to services organizations, there can be problems. If the industry is divided on an issue, it may be unable to communicate its case effectively. For example, the British Retail Federation had difficulty in communicating its views to government on proposed food labelling regulations, because its members were divided over what would be the best policy to pursue. If a sector co-operates too closely to communicate its views, it may be accused of illegally operating a cartel, which has the effect of restricting consumers' choice.

## In practice: Last orders?

Like many bars, the one in Figure 13.3 promotes a 'happy hour' period during which alcohol is sold at a reduced price. For pub operators, such communication may be vital to boost margins, especially if all bars in the area are offering equally low prices. Unfortunately, one consequence of cheap alcohol and 'buy one, get one free' offers is to increase 'binge drinking', with many British town centres becoming noisy and violent areas at night-time, fuelled by excessive drinking. For any individual pub, how does it balance the need for aggressive price promotion to customers with the need to appear socially responsible, for fear of further government regulation of the sector? Adverts for alcohol now routinely include warnings about the consequences for the customer of excessive drinking, but often in much smaller print than the main price information. Should a pub simply stop two-for-one offers and earn a higher margin on a smaller volume of sales? Although this may seem to be a responsible and profitable approach, it is unlikely to work if other pubs continue with their two-for-one offers – determined drinkers will simply make their way to the cheapest pub that has communicated the best offers. To illustrate the complexity of the task facing the sector, bar owners in some towns have voluntarily got together to try to agree collectively to stop price promotions that many believe lead to binge drinking. Agreement of all bar owners would be crucial, because otherwise drinkers would simply find out the cheapest outlet and other bars would be forced to cut their prices defensively to retain business. But did government see this as a benign example of socially motivated co-operation? Not the Office of Fair Trading, which gave a veiled threat to a group of Essex bar owners that they could be prosecuted for operating a cartel and illegally fixing prices.

Figure 13.3 Happy hour

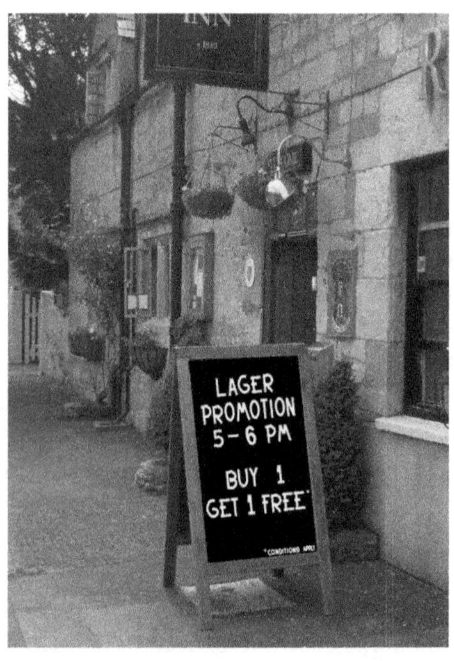

## Thinking around the subject: A war of words over green airline claims

Global warming has emerged as a major concern to consumers throughout the world. Initially, awareness of the causes and consequences of global warming was confined to a small part of the population, but linkages with the destructive tsunami of December 2004 and Hurricane Katrina of 2005 brought home to many people the possible long-term harmful consequences of excessive emissions of $CO_2$ into the atmosphere. Global warming was no longer a humorous subject, where people in the developed countries of northern Europe and the United States focused on the benign consequences of mild winters and exotic new plants that they would be able to grow. Destructive winds, rising sea levels and devastation of low-lying areas were increasingly coming to be seen as a consequence of our prodigious use of fossil fuels.

Reduction of $CO_2$ emissions had already been taken on board by many manufacturing companies, the largest of which had seen reductions through a system of carbon trading initiated by the Kyoto Treaty. Nevertheless, one service sector – civil aviation – had been quite notable in many people's eyes for its failure to embrace the principles of reducing carbon emissions. Critics of the sector pointed out that, as a result of worldwide agreements, aviation fuel was not taxed, in contrast to the steep taxation on most other forms of fuel. Although aircraft had become more efficient in their use of fuel during the 1990s, this was more than offset by booming demand for flights with no-frills airlines such as easyJet and Ryanair. It seemed that the budget airline companies were very effective in communicating their low-price message to customers, who filled their planes, often with more thought about a cheap weekend break by the Mediterranean, rather than the unknown and remote possibilities of global warming.

However, the no-frills airlines increasingly needed to address their communication efforts to politicians, some of whom were becoming frustrated by the airlines' seeming lack of willingness to address issues of climate change. Already, the Bishop of London had described air travel as 'immoral', for the way that wealthy Western travellers could inflict harm on people in the developed world through climate change. Could a large group of airline passengers really begin to feel guilty about flying away for a cheap weekend break, and cut back their purchases?

In January 2007, the communications battle was stepped up when a UK government minister described Ryanair as 'the irresponsible face of capitalism'. He had argued that, while other industries and consumers were cutting down their emissions, Ryanair had expanded at a phenomenal rate, churning out more $CO_2$ into the atmosphere at a time when other industry sectors were reducing their emissions. Friends of the Earth (2000), in a report *Aviation and Global Climate Change*, noted that commercial jets were adding 600 million tonnes of $CO_2$ a year to global warming, almost as much as the whole of Africa. With such negative communication, would Ryanair suffer as people felt guilty about flying, and governments increasingly moved to regulate civil aviation and make it more expensive, especially for the price-sensitive segments that the no-frills airlines had been targeting?

Rarely known to be quiet, the chief executive of Ryanair, Michael O'Leary, went on a communications offensive. Dismissing the minister as 'knowing nothing', he presented Ryanair as a friend rather than an enemy of global warming. He argued that travellers should feel reassured that Ryanair used one of the world's most modern and fuel-efficient fleets of aircraft. Moreover, Ryanair's business model of filling seats at the lowest price really meant that the carbon emissions per passenger were much lower than traditional full-service airlines, which often flew half-empty planes. And the fact that budget airlines operated an extensive point-to-point network avoided the costly and environmentally harmful effects of taking two indirect flights via a central-hub airport.

The war of words that has ensued over airlines' contribution to global warming demonstrates the difficulty that many ordinary consumers have in evaluating rival claims. Many may have taken to heart governments' and church leaders' claims that made them feel guilty about flying. Governments may have had in mind to raise the cost of aviation fuel, so that marginal customers may be priced out of flying. This was all potentially bad news for the airlines, who realized that they needed to go on a communications offensive, not just to promote their low fares, but also the very idea of cheap, guilt-free travel.

### 13.2.2 Communicating service features and benefits

For many services organizations, a large proportion of communication messages will be aimed at encouraging purchase of specific service offers, rather than the brand of the service provider in general.

A message must be able to move an individual along a path from awareness through to eventual purchase. In order for a message to be received and understood, it must gain attention, use a common language, arouse needs and suggest how these needs may be met. All of this should take place within the acceptable standards of the target audience. However, the service itself, the channel and the source of the communication also convey a message and therefore it is important that these do not conflict.

Three aspects of a communication message can be identified – content, structure and format. It is the content that is likely to arouse attention, and change attitude and intention. The appeal or theme of the message is therefore important. The formulation of the message must include some kind of benefit, motivator, identification or reason why the audience should think or do something. Appeals can be rational, emotional or moral.

Messages relating to specific service offers can be classified into a number of types, according to the dominant theme of the message. The following are common focal points for messages:

- *The nature and characteristics of the organization and the service on offer*. For example, television advertisements for the airline Cathay Pacific emphasize the high quality of its in-flight service.
- *Advantages over the competition*. Promotion by the airline Ryanair has emphasized the low cost of its fares compared to its competitors'.
- *Adaptability to meet buyers' needs*. Many insurance companies stress the extent to which their policies have been designed with the needs of particular age segments of the population in mind.
- *Experience of others*. In this way, testimonials of previous satisfied customers are used to demonstrate the benefits resulting from use.

Recipients of a message must see it as applying specifically to themselves and they must see some reason for being interested in it. The message must be structured according to the job it has to do. The points to be included in the message must be ordered (strongest arguments first or last) and consideration given to whether one-sided or two-sided messages should be used. The actual format of the message will be very much determined by the medium used, for example the type of print if published material, the type of voice if broadcast media is used, etc.

A second important characteristic of the audience justifying research is its degree of perceived risk when considering the purchase of a particular category of service. For purchases that are perceived as being highly risky, customers are likely to use more credible sources of information (e.g. word-of-mouth recommendation) and engage in a prolonged search through information sources. People differ markedly in their readiness to try new products and a number of attempts have been made to classify the population in terms of their level of risk taking. Rogers (1962) defined a person's 'innovativeness' as the 'degree to which an individual is relatively earlier in adopting new ideas than the other members of his social system'. In each product area, there are likely to be 'consumption pioneers' and early adopters, while other individuals only adopt new products much later. A message has to reflect the position of a service in its life cycle and differences between buyers in their motivations to try new services. Rogers described a diffusion model (see Figure 13.4) in which a small group of 'innovators' are first to respond to a new service offer, and a message to them may emphasize the novelty of the purchase and the social benefits that may derive from being a consumption pioneer of an exclusive product. Over time, ownership will become diffused

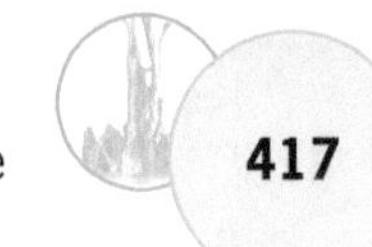

Figure 13.4 A diffusion model of adoption

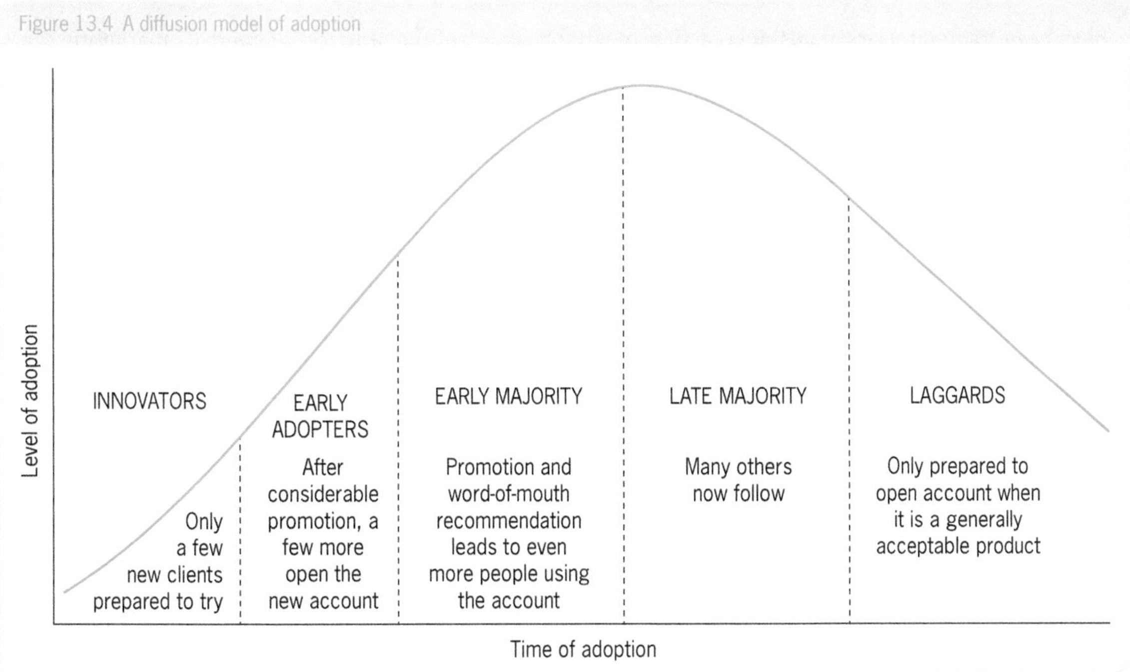


to progressively wider audiences, helped by falling costs and increasing competitive pressure. Instead of stressing exclusivity, the advertising message is likely increasingly to emphasize easy availability and an affordable price. A final group of 'laggards' may only become receptive to a message if it implies that what was once an exclusive product has now become a necessary item that even they can afford. As new services go through their life cycle, the dominant message could be expected to change, initially emphasizing the innovative new features and being the first to own the product, and gradually increasing the emphasis on affordable price and easy accessibility.

Mobile phone services as a category have gone through this diffusion process, with previous 'snob appeal' messages about mobile phone messages giving way to more general price-based promotion. Nevertheless, mobile phone operators are continually developing new services, such as location-based services, which have the effect of starting the process again with a new group of innovators, before this new service itself becomes adopted by a mainstream audience.

## Thinking around the subject: Guerrilla tactics

In the world of military warfare, the most dangerous enemy is the surprise attacker whose behaviour is unpredictable and who can have an impact disproportionate to their efforts. So too with promotion by commercial organizations. When advertising begins to blend in with the wallpaper, it can take guerrilla tactics to grab buyers' attention.

The term **guerrilla marketing** is not new and can be traced back to the mid-1980s. Jay Conrad Levinson describes the concept as being all about achieving conventional goals, such as increased awareness, with unconventional methods, such as investing energy instead of money (Levinson, 2007). Just as guerrilla warfare tactics can serve the interests of small dissident terrorist groups, guerrilla marketing is particularly suitable for smaller services businesses. Nightclubs, bars and online information services have been frequent users of guerrilla tactics. Inevitably, many of the practices of guerrilla marketing can be questioned on ethical grounds.

One of the principles of guerrilla marketing is to get a message through to the target audience when the audience would least be expecting a selling message. Instead of perceptually filtering out what might be seen as a sales message, the target may be more amenable to persuasion.

When guerrilla tactics get linked to the Internet, the results can be even more ethically questionable. FriendGreetings.com built up a mailing list of email addresses and thousands of people followed its link to a greeting card that the company claimed was waiting for the recipient. Users were then invited to install an ActiveX control in order to view their e-card. Two lengthy end-user licence agreements were displayed stating that by running the application the user is giving permission for a similar email to be sent to all addresses found in the user's Outlook address book. Of course, most users did not bother to read the licence agreement and therefore allowed numerous unwanted emails to be sent from their email address. Such a 'worm', which creates a flood of unwanted emails, can be just as much a nuisance as a virus. Guerrilla tactics had achieved their aim of attracting attention. As the message took the form of an e-card sent by somebody that the user knew, they did not suspect that clicking onto the link would result in anything untoward occurring.

Are the practices of companies such as FriendGreetings.com ethical? Would such practices be self-defeating because the company would simply acquire a bad reputation for itself? Is it right that 999 people may be inconvenienced so that the company can get profitable business from just one person out of each 1000 that it targets? Is it possible to stop practices of this type? After all, users had technically given permission for a worm to get into their computer, even if the request was deviously hidden in a lengthy licence agreement.

### 13.2.3 Message purpose and response

Companies send out messages for a variety of reasons, and achieving a short-term sale is often not the main purpose of a message. We have already seen that developing a strong brand reputation is often an important reason for a message, and achieving an immediate sale is often a subsidiary purpose of a message.

A communicator may be seeking any one or more of three audience responses:

- *Cognitive responses.* The message should be considered and understood.
- *Affective responses.* The message should be liked and lead to some change in attitude.
- *Behavioural responses.* Finally, the message should achieve some change in behaviour (e.g. a purchase decision).

In most cases, customers go through a series of stages before finally deciding to purchase a service, especially for high-involvement services. It is therefore critical to know these buyer-readiness stages and to assess where the target is at any given time.

Many models have been developed to show how marketing communication has the effect of 'pushing' recipients of messages through a number of sequential stages, finally resulting in a purchase decision. One of the oldest, AIDA (Awareness, Interest, Desire, Action), can trace its origins back almost a century (Strong, 1925), and like many simple models has stood the test of time. This and two other sequential models, the hierarchy of effects and innovation–adoption models, are shown in Figure 13.5.

Communication models portray a simple and steady movement through the various stages, although communication should not be seen as ending when a sale is completed. It was noted in Chapter 5 that services organizations increasingly seek to build relationships with their customers, so the behavioural change (the sale) should be seen as the starting point for making customers aware of other offers available from the organization and for securing repeat business. Smooth

Figure 13.5 Models of buyer states. The communication process often has to take prospects from the stages of being unaware of the existence of a service, to awareness, liking and eventual purchase. In addition, prospects who have actually become customers must have their positive attitude towards the service reinforced, so that they repurchase and recommend the service to friends.

| Domain | AIDA model | Hierarchy of effects model (*Lavidge and Steiner, 1961*) | Innovation–adoption model (*Rogers, 1962*) |
|---|---|---|---|
| Cognitive | Awareness | Awareness | Awareness |
| | | Knowledge | |
| Affective | Interest | Liking | Interest |
| | Desire | Preference | Evaluation |
| | | Conviction | |
| Behavioural | Action | Purchase | Trial |
| | | | Adoption |

progress through these stages is impeded by the presence of a number of 'noise' factors, which are discussed below. The probabilities of success in each stage cumulatively decline as a result of noise and therefore the probability of the final stage achieving an actual purchase can be very low.

A number of 'noise' factors can get in the way between the message sent out and the eventual response. The nature of 'noise' factors can be examined in terms of a simple 'black box' model of buyer response. A communication of some sort (originating either from within a company or extraneously) is seen as a stimulus to some form of customer response. Response can be expressed in terms such as quantity purchased, frequency of purchase or even non-purchase. The final response, however, is not a straightforward response to the initial stimulus.

The initial stimulus can be distorted, resulting in different individuals responding in different ways to a similar stimulus. Noise factors can be divided into two major types:

- *Those that relate to the individual, i.e. psychological factors.* Both positive and negative previous experiences predispose an individual to decode messages in a particular way. Also, the personality of specific members of an audience can significantly influence interpretation of a message – for example, an extrovert may interpret a message differently from an introvert. Similarly, an individual's motives can influence how a message is decoded. An individual who has just come home from work hungry, and is about to eat dinner, is unlikely to be amenable to information communicated by a life assurance salesperson, which may satisfy some higher-order need for family security.
- *Those that relate to other groups of people, i.e. sociological factors.* Important sociological influences on behaviour include culture and social class. Individual members of different cultures and classes are likely to interpret messages in different ways. In this way, communications offering credit facilities may be interpreted with suspicion within certain social groups who have been conditioned to live within their means, whereas members of other social groups may welcome the opportunities represented by the message.

## 13.2.4 Message source

The source of a message – as distinct from the message itself – can influence the effectiveness of any communication. A number of factors will influence the effectiveness of a communication:

- If a source is perceived as having power, then the audience response is likely to be compliance.
- If a source is liked, then identification by the audience is a likely response. Important factors here include past experience and reputation of the service organization, in addition to the personality of the actual source of the communication. A salesperson, any contact personnel, a television/radio personality etc. can all be important in creating liking.
- If a source is perceived as credible, then the message is more likely to be internalized by the audience. Credibility can be developed by establishing a source as important, high in status, power and prestige or by emphasizing reliability and openness.
- For many low-risk, low-involvement services, endorsement by an individual's peer group can be important. 'If people like me are happy using this service, then I will be happy as well' is a typical rationalization. A company may build on this by using an ordinary person as the message source.
- Celebrities are often used to endorse a service or an organization. We have a tendency to impute to the endorsed product the qualities that we have come to like about our favourite celebrity characters. There have been numerous studies of the effects of celebrity endorsement (e.g. Chung-kue and McDonald, 2002). To be effective, the celebrity must be carefully chosen to match the aspirations of a product's target market (for example, the television chef Jamie Oliver has developed a loyal following among ethically minded, aspirational cooks that has been exploited by the grocery retailer Sainsbury's, who employed him to front its advertising campaign demonstrating meals made with Sainsbury's groceries).

Closely related to the notion of credibility is the 'halo effect'. Coulson-Thomas (1985) defined this as the 'tendency to impute to individuals and things, the qualities of other individuals and things with which they are associated'. The closer the perceived link between 'personality' and a service, the stronger the halo effect. However, there is also a phenomenon known as the 'sleeper effect', in which the credibility of a source – and hence message retention – is built up over a period of time. The implication of this is that company and service reputation need regular reinforcement, both from formal advertising and from satisfying contacts between customers and front-line employees.

## Thinking around the subject: University of fun?

How do you strike a balance between an advertising campaign being eye-catching and accessible on the one hand, while preserving the core values of the product on the other? Retailers, banks and insurance companies have all encountered problems when their traditional mature audiences have been alienated by advertising that was aimed at increasing the number of younger customers. Wacky advertising may attract attention, but what does it say about the nature of the product on offer? Liverpool-based John Moores University is among the many UK universities that has tried to redesign its communications using an approach that may appear cool in the eyes of target students. In 1999, its prospectus paid relatively little attention to the details of the courses on offer, but gave great emphasis to the pubs and clubs in town. It may well be that this was based on a sound analysis of the factors that influence students' choice of university. Most prospective students have only a limited ability to distinguish between the academic credentials of competing courses, whereas nightlife is an easier point of reference. But the media picked up the story, claiming that this was further evidence of 'dumbing down' in education generally, and at this university in particular. Even existing students claimed that the value of their degrees would be demeaned by advertising that made their institution appear to the outside world like a 'good-time university'. But if the university went back to stuffy advertising and prospectuses, would it lose a point of difference with its competitors? Would the target audience even bother stopping to read its messages?

### 13.2.5 Communication in a crisis

Because services can be highly variable, there is always the possibility that the media will pick up on one bad incident and leave its audience thinking that this is the norm for that organization. This is particularly a problem for highly visible public or quasi-public services for which audiences enjoy reading bad-news stories to confirm their own prejudices. Furthermore, service organizations, by the very nature of their operating environment, face unpredictable major crises, such as a train crash or a fire at a nightclub. External events may also lead to bad publicity, or the negative actions of similar service organizations may lead to a generally poor reputation of the sector as a whole. In all of these situations, an organization needs to establish communication contingency plans to minimize any surprise and confusion resulting from the publicity. Bad publicity is more likely to be effectively managed if an organization has previously invested time and effort in developing mutually supportive good relations with the media.

How can communication help a service-based organization out of a crisis? There is a lot of evidence that being proactive rather than reactive is crucial to both short-term and long-term recovery (Elliott et al., 2005; Smith, 2005). Services organizations have facilitated recovery from a crisis by developing contingency plans. The nature of these plans depends on the type of service provided, so, for example, an Internet-based service company may focus on the consequences of its main server being unavailable, perhaps because of fire or terrorist attack. One contingency plan may be to have geographically dispersed back-up servers and call centres that can be brought into operation at very short notice. Even with equipment-based services such as those of an Internet service provider, recovery plans may fail if every small detail is not fully thought through. For example, is the power supply at a back-up centre sufficient to cope with suddenly increased usage? How quickly can staff be transferred to the back-up centre, and how will they get there? Who will communicate to staff about where to go? Is there an up-to-date list of staff contact numbers so that the company can keep in touch with its employees, even though its operating centre is no longer accessible to them?

For labour-intensive services involving a high degree of customer co-creation, predicting the precise nature of a crisis can sometimes be difficult, even if the general nature of potential crises can be identified. For a restaurant operator, possible crises may derive from issues of health and safety (a food poisoning outbreak), from death or injury to customers (e.g. a fire or bomb attack at branch of the restaurant) or from issues of corporate governance (e.g. allegations of institutionalized racial discrimination). Even though the details of a particular crisis may be unpredictable, an organization should be able to develop contingency plans for a general type of crisis. These may include, for example, being able to commission a call centre to handle customer enquiries at short notice and ensuring that adequate lines are open with suitably trained staff. Within the organization, there should be well-practised communication channels that can be used when normal internal channels are not available.

Sometimes, a crisis may be exacerbated by a part of the media that has revelled in reporting stories of previous service failures by the company. For example, a train crash that occurred in the UK in 2000 at Hatfield, involving a London–Edinburgh train, came following a series of widely reported failures, and appeared symptomatic of everything that was wrong with Britain's railways. Partly because of the public's general distrust of Britain's railway operators, the industry, through its regulatory agencies, was forced to respond with drastic and costly measures, including system-wide speed restrictions. The industry was under intense scrutiny by the media, which sensed that more bad practice would be found if it looked hard enough. It took several years for the sector to recover its trust in the eyes of its users. By contrast, the coach operator National Express had a long history of safe operation, with very few causes for complaints by its customers. It had been a long while since the public had read stories of overcrowded coaches travelling at excessive speed, driven by poorly trained, overworked and tired drivers. When one of the company's coaches crashed in January 2007, killing two passengers and injuring several others, the media was generally sympathetic to the company. Senior executives were made available to answer media questions and the company provided an efficient and effective helpline for customers and the relatives of those affected. Above all else, the company had invested in a good reputation and even the most adversarial investigative reporters could not find a history of bad management to prolong the crisis and open a 'can of worms' that would come back to haunt the company.

## In practice: Crisis? What crisis?

A catastrophic failure is always a possibility for services operating in a risky environment where a technical failure or sabotage can have an immediate impact on customers. Despite improvements in safety standards, air operators live with the possibility of customers being injured or killed by a service failure. Unfortunately, an air crash makes a newsworthy story, and is likely to be extensively covered by the media. The perception may be created that air travel is unsafe, whereas in reality air travel is considerably safer than most other forms of transport. Air operators probably cannot do much to reduce newspaper and television editors' desire to reproduce pictures of carnage, but they can work hard to ensure that a bad-news story does not get out of control. Honesty in dealing with the media is crucial, and any sign of inconsistency or falsehoods will be seized upon by the media, who may open a 'can of worms' of previous bad practice by the company. Media relations must be proactive rather than reactive, and companies who have a good record of integrity and openness with the media can actually turn a catastrophe into an event that enhances their reputation for caring for customers.

Figure 13.6 Disasters always attract media coverage.

AIR CRASH HORROR

By our staff reporter

A catastrophic failure is always a possibility for services operating in a risky environment where a technical failure or sabotage can have an immediate impact on customers. Despite improvements in safety standards, air operators live with the possibility of customers being injured or killed by a service failure. Unfortunately, an air crash makes a newsworthy story, and is likely to be extensively covered by the media. The perception may be created that air travel is unsafe, whereas in reality air travel is considerably safer than most other forms of transport. Air operators probably cannot do much to reduce newspaper and television editors' desire to reproduce pictures of carnage, but they can work hard to ensure that a bad news story does not get out of control. Honesty in dealing with the media is crucial, and any sign of inconsistency or falsehoods will be seized upon by the media, who may open a 'can of worms' of previous bad practice by the company. Media relations must be proactive rather than reactive, and companies who have a good record of integrity and openness with the media can actually turn a catastrophe into an event that enhances their reputation for caring for customers.

## 13.3 Channels of communication

After consideration of 'who says what to whom and with what effect', the next area of concern is 'how?'. This entails selecting and blending different channels of communication in order to achieve the promotional objectives of the marketing mix. Specifying the objectives of a communication is important if appropriate messages are to be accurately targeted through the most appropriate channels in the most cost-effective manner possible. Typical promotional objectives might be:

- to develop an awareness of, and an interest in, the service organization and its service product(s);
- to communicate the benefits of purchasing a service;
- to influence eventual purchase of the service;
- to build a positive image of the service firm;
- to differentiate the service from its competitors;
- to remind people of the existence of a service and/or the service firm.

Ideally, these objectives should be quantified as far as possible and thus promotional objectives for a new type of motor insurance policy may begin with an objective to achieve awareness of the brand name by 30 per cent of the 25–55-year-old UK insurance-buying public within one year of launch.

The promotion mix refers to the combination of channels that an organization uses to communicate with its target markets. Communication is received by audiences from two principal sources – sources within an organization and external sources. The latter includes word-of-mouth recommendation from friends, editorial in the press, etc., which it has already been noted may have high credibility in the service evaluation process. Sources originating within an organization can be divided into those originating from the traditional marketing function (which can be divided into personal two-way channels such as personal selling and impersonal one-way channels such as advertising) and those originating from front-line production resources. Because services normally involve consumers in the production process, the promotion mix has to be considered more broadly than is the case with manufactured goods. Front-line operations staff and service outlets become a valuable channel of communication. The elements of the extended services promotion mix are illustrated in Figure 13.7.

Figure 13.7 The extended promotion mix for services, showing communication channels deriving from marketing and non-marketing sources.

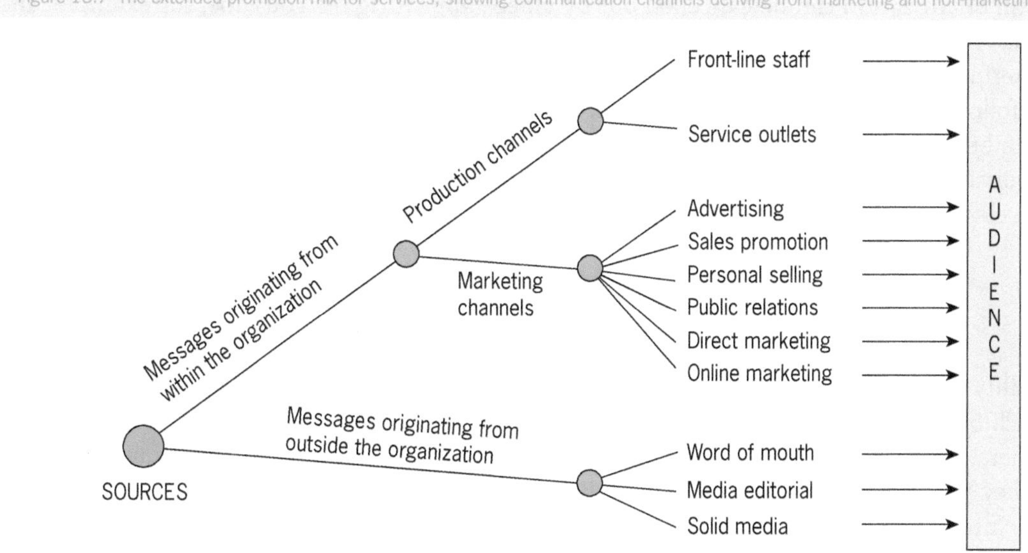

The choice of a particular combination of communication channels will depend primarily on the characteristics of the target audience, especially its habits in terms of exposure to messages. Other important considerations include the present and potential market size for the service (advertising on television may not be appropriate for a service that has a local niche market, for example), the nature of the service itself (the more personal the service, the more effective the two-way communication channel) and, of course, the costs of the various channels.

A very important consideration is the stage that a service has reached in its life cycle (see Chapter 7). Advertising and public relations are more likely to form important channels of communication during the introductory stage of the life cycle, where the major objective is often to increase overall audience awareness. Sales promotion can be used to stimulate trial and, in some instances, personal selling can be used to acquire distribution coverage. During a service's growth stage, the use of all communication channels can generally be reduced as demand during this phase tends to produce its own momentum through word-of-mouth communications. However, as the service develops into its maturity stage, there may be a call for an increase in advertising and sales promotion activity. Finally, when the service is seen as going into decline, advertising and public relations are often reduced, although sales promotion can still be quite usefully applied. Sometimes, services in decline are allowed to die quietly with very little promotion. In the case of many long-life financial services, which a company would like to delete but cannot for contractual reasons, the service may be kept going with no promotional support at all.

The nature of promotion channel decisions has been changing rapidly in recent years. Although the following sections distinguish between apparently separate components such as advertising and sales promotion, these are becoming increasingly integrated and one media channel is likely to be used alongside other channels as reinforcements. But perhaps the most fundamental change that has occurred has resulted from Web 2.0 technologies which make it much easier for communication messages from ordinary customers to be heard by very large audiences. 'Word of mouth' has always been important to service companies, keen to grow their business through personal recommendation, but now social network media allow individuals to spread their messages much more widely and quickly. Many services organizations are still grappling with the issue of how to exploit the opportunities of social network media, and to restrict the possible damage that they can cause to brand reputation. As the chapter opening demonstrated, a lot of planned communication effort by an organization can be cancelled out by videos appearing on YouTube, for example, and links to the video being spread virally through social network sites. We will return to the subject of viral marketing later in this chapter.

In the following sections, each of the elements of the promotion mix through which communications can be directed is discussed. Before the traditional elements of advertising, sales promotion, personal selling and public relations are considered, attention is given to the role of the additional elements of the promotion mix that are specific to services.

## 13.4 The extended services promotion mix

Inseparability results in consumers being involved in a series of encounters with service producers. During each of these encounters, a service organization has an opportunity to communicate with its customers. Without any effort on the part of an organization, customers will pick up messages, whether they are good or bad. With more planning, an organization can ensure that every encounter is turned into an opportunity to convey positive messages that encourage repeat business from customers and encourage them to pass on the message to others. Two important sources of non-marketer-derived messages can be identified within the extended promotion mix of services – front-line employees and the physical environment of the service encounter. These represent communication opportunities (and possible problems) for services organizations that are not usually available to manufacturing firms – very few people buying a car, for example, would come into contact with the workers where their car was built or see the production processes and factory.

### 13.4.1 The promotional role of employees

The important role played by front-line operational personnel as 'part-time marketers' has been stressed on many previous occasions in this book. It has also been noted that the activities of such staff can be important in creating an image of an organization that can live on to influence target customers' perceptions of an organization. Simply by being in the front line, employees are communicating messages; for example, the standard of dress may give messages about a service process to follow – scruffy dress, careless service; smart dress, careful service?

Staff who have front-line encounters with customers should be trained to treat these encounters as promotional opportunities. Without appropriate training and explanation of expectations, a call for such employees to promote their service more effectively can be little more than rhetoric. Training might seek to develop a number of skills in front-line staff:

- An ability to spot cross-selling possibilities can call for empathy on the part of front-line staff. A bank clerk who sees a customer repeatedly using a service that is not adequately fulfilling his or her needs could be trained to try to sell another service that better meets the customer's needs. In practice, firms often struggle to create conditions that are conducive to employees' concurrent engagement in both selling and delivering service (Jasmand et al., 2012).
- Many operational staff have quite clearly defined sales responsibilities; for example restaurant waiters may be expected to encourage customers to spend more on their visit to the restaurant.
- The general manner of staff interaction with customers is important in encouraging customers to return and to tell their friends about their good experience. Again, training should emphasize those behaviours that have a positive effect on customers' evaluation of their encounter.
- Staff can directly influence future purchases by encouraging customers to book a repeat service or by giving them literature to pass on to friends.

It can be difficult to draw a distinction between production staff and marketing staff in terms of their contribution towards the promotion of an organization. Organizational boundaries should not prevent operational staff being considered an important element of promotion-mix planning.

### 13.4.2 The promotional role of service outlets

From the outside, service outlets can be seen as billboards capable of conveying messages about the services that take place within them. They are therefore powerful tools in appealing to both customers and non-customers. The general appearance of an outlet can promote the image of a service organization. A brightly coloured and clean exterior can transmit a message that the organization is fast, efficient and well run. Outlets can be used to display advertising posters, which in heavily trafficked locations can result in valuable exposure.

Service outlets can also provide valuable opportunities to show service production processes to potential customers, something that is much more difficult to achieve through conventional media. A fast-printing shop displaying sophisticated printing equipment and a tyre retailer's large stocks and tidy appearance both help to promote an organization's processes as much as its outcomes.

## 13.5 Advertising and the media

Advertising is mass, paid communication that is used to transmit information, develop attitudes and induce some form of response on the part of the audience. It seeks to bring about a response by providing information to potential customers, by trying to modify their desires and by supplying reasons why they should prefer that particular company's services.

### Thinking around the subject: Imposing building, trustworthy business?

Figure 13.8 Is it a church or a bank?

The idea that buildings should form an important part of a service organization's promotion mix is not new. Today, a grand reception area and an imposing atrium in an accountant's headquarters may send out a message that the firm of accountants is a substantial one and has the resources to be a reliable long-term service provider. A century ago, before the age of modern regulation, banks needed to earn the trust of their customers. With lots of small, regional banks competing for business, and frequent bankruptcies robbing investors of their savings, how could anyone be sure that the bank where they invested their savings was not going to disappear with their savings? One solution adopted by many banks was to construct substantial buildings, often designed to look like cathedrals (see Figure 13.8). This bank may now stand out as a listed building, but its design could send out a message to customers that the bank would be around for as long as the cathedrals that the building emulated. Following the banking crisis of 2008, did the presence of solid-looking banks such as this one, owned by Lloyds TSB, provide customers with reassurance which was not present with newer online banks such as Iceland's Landsbanki bank which went bankrupt in 2008?

Having provided a seemingly clear definition of what advertising is about, recent developments have blurred this definition, with online blogs being used to support television or newspaper advertising, for example. Although advertising has been central to many companies' promotional efforts, there is evidence that the importance of advertising within the promotion-mix is declining. Many have argued that stand-alone media advertising is becoming less relevant in today's increasingly online world. One survey found that the majority of respondents felt less positively about advertising messages than they did a year previously (Wegert, 2004).

Advertising objectives should be clearly specified in terms of target audiences and desired effects. However, in monitoring the performance of advertising, it can be extremely difficult to prove that this alone is responsible for a sales increase. Sales, after all, can be the result of many intervening variables, some of which are internal to the organization (e.g. public relations activity, pricing policy), while others are external (e.g. the state of the national economy). It is therefore too simplistic to set advertising objectives simply in terms of increasing sales by a specified amount. Given the existence of diverse adopter categories and the many stages in the communication process, as described earlier, more appropriate objectives can often be specified in terms of levels of awareness or comprehension.

### 13.5.1 Media characteristics

The choice of media is influenced by the characteristics of each medium and their ability to achieve the specified promotional objectives. The following are some of the most common types of media and their characteristics.

#### Newspapers

Daily newspapers tend to have a high degree of reader loyalty, reflecting the fact that each national title is targeted to specific segments of the population. This loyalty can lead to messages being perceived by readers as having high credibility. Newspapers can be used for creating general awareness of a product or a brand, as well as providing detailed product information. In this way, banks use newspapers both for adverts designed to create brand awareness and a liking for the organization, as well as adverts for giving specific details of savings accounts. The latter may include an invitation to action in the form of a freepost account-opening coupon. The popularity of newspapers for promotion has been falling sharply in recent years, especially for specialized, local, searchable services. Many newspapers have transformed themselves from printed to online media.

#### Magazines/journals

Within the UK, there is a wide range of magazine and journal titles available to advertisers. While some high-circulation magazines appeal to broad groups of people (e.g. *Radio Times*), most titles are specialized in terms of their content and targeting. In this way, *Which Mortgage* can be a highly specific medium for banks to promote mortgages. Specialist trade titles allow messages to be aimed at service intermediaries – for example, a tour operator seeking to promote a holiday offer may first gain the confidence and support of travel agents through such magazines as *Travel Trade Gazette*. Although advertising in magazines may at first seem relatively expensive compared to newspapers, they can be good value to advertisers in terms of their high number of readers per copy and highly segmented audiences. As with newspapers, many magazines have sought to integrate their printed editions with online versions.

#### Outdoor advertising

The effect of a television advertisement can be prolonged if recipients are exposed to a reminder poster on their way to work the following day. If strategically placed, the posters can appeal to segmented audiences – for example London Underground sites in the City of London are seen by large numbers of affluent business people. The sides of buses are often used to support new service facilities (e.g. new store openings) and have the ability to spread their message as the bus travels along local routes. Posters can generally only be used to convey a simple communication rather than complex details.

#### Television

This is an expensive, but very powerful, medium. Although it tends to be used mainly for the long-term task of creating brand awareness, it can also be used to create a rapid sales response. The very fact that a message has been seen on television can give credibility to the message source and many smaller service companies add the phrase 'as seen on TV' to give additional credibility to their other media communications. The power of the television medium is enhanced by its ability to appeal to the senses of both sight and sound, and to use movement and colour to develop a sales message. Television advertising has become an increasingly flexible medium, with cable and satellite channels offering geographical and lifestyle targeting of audiences. Digital television is also able to offer an immediate response function, so a pizza delivery company can use television not only for creating brand awareness, but also for immediate need fulfilment.

A major limitation of television advertising is its cost – for most local service providers, television advertising rates start at too high a level to be considered. Also, is the target viewer actually in the room when an advertisement is being broadcast? If the viewer is present, is he or she receptive to the message? The distinction between television and Internet has become blurred, with a tendency for young people in particular to increase their use of the Internet, at the expense of television viewing. One survey found that 28 per cent of respondents claimed they were more likely to pay attention to an online video advertisement than television advertisements (Knight, 2009).

### The Internet

Most services organizations have their own websites, which are used to disseminate messages to customers and potential customers. Getting viewers to a company's website is a continuing challenge, especially for people who are not looking for a company specifically, but seeking a category of service through a search-engine enquiry. Search-engine optimization (SEO) has become a specialist skill to ensure that a company's website comes top of the list when the user of a search-engine enters specified keywords. Many models exist by which companies can pay to improve their search engine ranking, for example by paying per 'click through'. Many other approaches are used to get visitors to the company's website, such as sponsored links from affiliates. The essential point is that in a competitive environment, it is not sufficient to just have a website, it is important to have a strategy for getting visitors to the website.

The greatest power of the Internet is that it can become a medium for personalized messages, thereby not strictly falling within the definition of advertising given earlier. For this reason, further consideration of the Internet as part of an organization's promotion mix will be given in the later section on online marketing.

### Cinema

Because of the captive nature of cinema audiences, this medium can potentially have a major impact. It is frequently used to promote local services such as taxi operators and food outlets, whose target market broadly corresponds to the audience of most cinemas. However, without repetition, cinema advertisements have little lasting effect, but do tend to be useful for supporting press and television advertising.

### Commercial radio

Radio advertising has often been seen as the poor relation of television advertising, appealing only to the sense of sound. The threshold cost of radio advertising is much lower than for television, reflecting much more local segmentation of radio audiences and the lower production costs of radio adverts. A major advantage over other media is that the audience can be involved in other activities – particularly driving – while being exposed to an advertisement. Although there are often doubts about the extent to which an audience actually receives and understands a message, it forms a useful reminder medium when used in conjunction with other media.

## 13.5.2 Media selection criteria

In addition to the characteristics of the media themselves, a number of other important factors must be taken into account in selecting the media mix for a particular advertising campaign:

- the characteristics of the target audience;
- the level of exposure of the target audience to the communication;
- the impact that advertising will have on the target audience;
- the extent to which the effects of a particular advertising message 'wear out' over time;
- the cost of advertising through the medium.

### Target audience

The media habits of the target audience must be fully understood. If a firm's target market is not in the habit of being exposed to a particular medium, much of the value of advertising through that medium will be wasted. As an example, attempts to promote premium credit cards to high-income segments by means of television commercials may lose much of their value because research suggests that the higher socio-economic groups tend to spend a greater proportion of their viewing time watching BBC rather than commercial channels. On the other hand, they may be heavy readers of Sunday newspaper magazine supplements.

Information about target audiences' media habits is obtained from a number of sources. Newspaper readership information in the UK is collated by the National Readership Survey. For each newspaper, this shows reading frequency and average issue readership (as distinct from circulation), broken down into age, class, sex, ownership of consumer durables, etc. Television viewing information is collected by the Broadcasters' Audience Research Board (BARB). This indicates the number of people watching particular channels at particular times by reference to two types of television ratings (TVRs) – one for the number of households watching a programme/advertising slot and one for the number of people watching.

### Advertising exposure

The number of advertising exposures of a particular communication is determined by two factors, cover/reach and frequency. 'Cover' or 'reach' is the percentage of a particular target audience reached by a medium or a whole campaign, while 'frequency' is the number of times a particular target audience has an 'opportunity to see/hear' (OTS/OTH) an advertising message. The combination of these two factors results in an index of advertising exposure, which is usually stated in terms of 'Gross Rating Points' (GRPs). For example, if an objective is to reach 50 per cent of the target audience three times a year, this would be stated as a GRP of 150 (i.e. $50 \times 3$). Within a given budget, there has to be a trade-off between coverage/reach and frequency.

### Advertising impact

Impact is usually more closely related to the message than the media. If, however, the medium is the message, then advertising impact should be an important criterion for media selection. Different media vehicles can produce different levels of awareness and comprehension of an identical message. In this way, the image of Ronald McDonald presented via television is very much more powerful than that presented via radio.

### Wearout

The concept of advertising exposure assumes that all advertising insertions have equal value. However, the effect of additional insertions may in fact decline, resulting in diminishing returns for each unit of expenditure. There is usually a threshold level of advertising beneath which little audience response occurs. Once over this threshold, audience response tends to increase quite rapidly through a 'generation' phase until eventually a saturation point is reached. Any further advertising may lead to a negative or declining response, that is, 'wearout'.

### Cost

The cost of using different media varies markedly and, while a medium that at first sight appears to be expensive may in fact be good value in terms of achieving promotional objectives, a sound basis for measuring cost is needed. There are generally two related cost criteria:

- *Cost per gross rating point.* This is usually used for broadcast media and is the cost of a set of commercials divided by the gross rating points.
- *Cost per thousand.* This is used for print media to calculate the cost of getting the message seen by one thousand members of the target market.

These measures can be used to make cost comparisons between different media vehicles. However, a true comparison needs to take into consideration the different degrees of effectiveness of each medium. In other words, the strength of the media vehicle needs to be considered, as does the location, duration, timing and – where relevant – size of the advertisement, plus a variety of more complex factors. These are all combined to form 'media weights', which are used in comparing the effectiveness of different media. Cost-effectiveness, therefore, is calculated using the following formula:

$$\text{Cost-effectiveness} = \frac{\text{Readers/viewers in target} \times \text{Media weight}}{\text{Cost}}$$

## Thinking around the subject: Selling an organization to its employees

Although the primary target audience of an advertisement may be customers, its effects on employees should not be forgotten. This is especially true of labour-intensive services industries where an advert can provide encouragement for front-line employees to perform their jobs with pride, as well as encouraging customers to buy. If cabin crew of British Airways see the airline's advertisements casting them in the role of helpful and friendly problem solvers, they should be able to identify with this role and carry it out effectively and with pride. Employees can become highly involved in the advertisements where they are used in place of professional actors. The do-it-yourself (DIY) retailer B&Q has for a long time used its own employees from different branches to promote its store offers, providing a sense of realistic credibility to customers and involvement from employees.

Employees who have heard rumours about poor financial prospects for a company amid talk of falling sales may have some of their confidence restored by the sight of advertisements to drum up new business.

At times, however, advertisements can only serve to demotivate staff. Advertising claims may be made that front-line staff are simply incapable of delivering, perhaps due to inadequate training or insufficient resources to keep promises made in an advert. If employees do not believe the claims of an advert, why should customers? On occasions, adverts can actually annoy staff by casting them in a demeaning role, something that the retailer Sainsbury's learnt to its cost following a series of adverts in its 'Value to shout about' adverts. These used the actor John Cleese to promote the grocery retailer's low prices, but in doing so the scenes belittled staff and their knowledge of the new low prices. After representations from staff – and some suggestion that the campaign was not working with customers – the adverts were pulled.

## 13.6 Sales promotion

Sales promotion involves those activities, other than advertising, personal selling and public relations, that stimulate customer purchase and the effectiveness of intermediaries. Although it can be used to create awareness, sales promotion is usually used for the later stages of the buying process, that is, to create interest, desire and, in particular, to bring about action. Sales promotion can quite successfully complement other tools within the promotion mix, for example by reinforcing a particular image or identity developed through advertising.

Over the past few years there has been a rapid increase in the use of sales promotion, for a number of reasons:

- As a result of the proliferation of brands and increasing competitive pressure, buyers are more 'deal orientated' and this has led to pressure from intermediaries for better incentives from manufacturers and service principals.
- Companies are increasingly likely to want a 'quick result' which sales promotion can often deliver.
- It has been argued by many that advertising efficiency is declining as a result of increasing costs and media clutter.
- New technology in targeting has resulted in an increase in the efficiency and effectiveness of sales promotion.
- The public and professional services sectors have increasingly accepted the role of sales promotion. For example, sales promotion activity by opticians in the UK would have been almost unthinkable before the 1980s, but now opticians such as Specsavers routinely target individuals with limited-time promotional offers.

### 13.6.1 Sales promotion planning

Sales promotion contributes in a number of ways to achieving overall promotional objectives. While it can be used merely to gain attention for a service, it is more likely to be used as an incentive incorporating an offer that represents value to the target audience. It can also act as an invitation to engage in a transaction now rather than later. Sales promotion usually attracts brand switchers, but is unlikely to turn them into loyal brand users without the use of other elements of the promotion mix. In fact, it is usually considered that sales promotion is used to break down brand loyalty, whereas advertising is used to build it up. Sales promotion can gain new users or encourage more frequent purchase but it cannot compensate for inadequate advertising, poor delivery or poor quality.

It has been suggested that the role of sales promotion for services is much more limited than is the case with goods. The fact that services cannot be stored may appear to limit the ability of a service firm to offload unused services at a cheap price, something that is commonly undertaken by goods manufacturers using sales promotion. On the other hand, off-peak sales promotional activity can help to alleviate such a problem in the future. There is also a view that some promotional tools – such as the use of free samples – cannot be used for services as the sample would have to involve the whole service. However, a free first consultation by a solicitor, for example, could be thought of as an equivalent form of sales promotion.

As in the case of advertising, effective sales promotion involves an ongoing process with a number of distinct stages:

- *Establishment of objectives.* These could include the encouragement of increased usage or the building of trial among non-users or other brand users.

Figure 13.9 In many markets where services are perceived by buyers as being basically similar, it may be necessary to offer an incentive in order to initiate a dialogue. Eager to enter buyers' choice set, many insurance companies, such as this one, offer incentives, which are given following a completed purchase. Sales promotion activities of this type may be particularly important where consumers' ability to differentiate between competing products is low and an incentive offers a tangible basis for differentiation. (Reproduced courtesy of Axa Wealth Ltd)

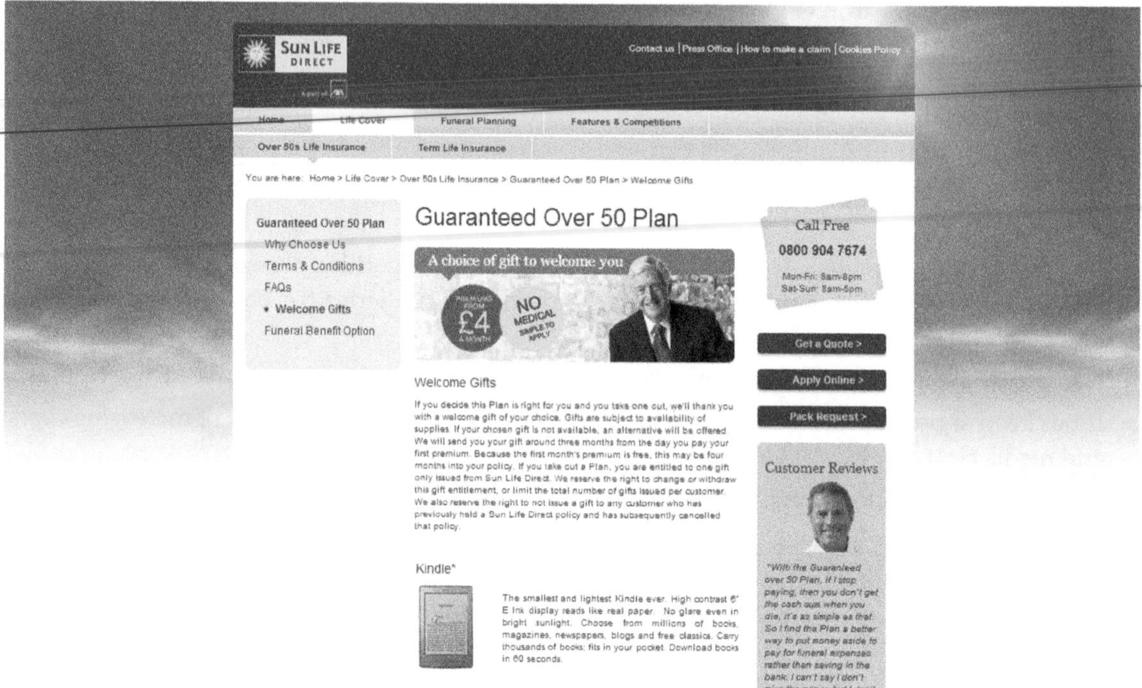


- *Selection of promotional tools.* These can include free samples/visits/consultations (which can be an important means of demonstrating an intangible service process), money-off price incentives (although these tend to be expensive to the service provider, as the incentive is given to customers regardless of its motivational effect on an individual customer), coupons/vouchers (which can offer targeted invitations to try a new service or to reward customer loyalty), gift offers (which can help to give tangible cues of the service company's offering as well as offering an incentive for immediate purchase) and competitions (which can add to the perceived value of a service).
- *Planning the sales promotion programme.* The timing and size of incentive to be offered are especially important.
- *Pre-testing.* In order to ensure that potentially expensive problems are discovered before the full launch of a promotion (e.g. false assumptions of redemption rates for an incentive may lead to the budget being exceeded, or unacceptably long queues developing if there is insufficient capacity to cater for free-trial services).
- *Implementation.* This must specify the 'lead time' (the time necessary to bring the programme up to the point where the incentive is to be made available to the public) and the 'sell in time' (the period of time from the date of release to when approximately 90–95 per cent of incentive material has been received by potential customers).
- *Evaluation.* With the use of customer databases, methods of evaluation are improving. However, it can be extremely difficult to separate out the effects of sales promotion activity from other promotional activity – or indeed from other marketing-mix and extraneous factors.

## In practice: Amazon targets book lovers

Coupons have been used by marketers for a long time to promote sales. They allow groups of prospective or actual customers to be targeted with an incentive to encourage them to become a new customer, or to become a bigger-spending customer. By restricting the distribution of coupons to those in whom it is most interested, a company avoids giving a price reduction to everybody, including those who are loyal and probably find its prices good value. The Internet has allowed electronic coupons to be distributed more efficiently and effectively. By studying site visitors' previous behaviour, unique coupons can be generated. These can either be used online or be printed for use elsewhere. The online retailer Amazon.com has made extensive use of coupons to promote sales, such as this one, which is configured according to the information that the company has available about specific targets. Combined with a carefully planned Internet-based promotion programme and an active affiliates programme, Amazon has become the leading online book retailer in the UK.

Figure 13.10 An online coupon from Amazon. (© 2010 Amazon.com Inc. and its affiliates. All rights reserved. Reproduced with permission of Amazon.co.uk)

Sales promotion activity can be aimed at intermediaries as well as at the final consumers of a service. Sales promotion activity aimed at intermediaries includes: short-term increases in sales commission; competitions and gifts (useful motivators where individual sales personnel benefit directly from the incentive); point-of-sale material (e.g. tour operators who arrange a film evening for their travel agencies' clients); and co-operative advertising, where a service principal agrees to subscribe to local advertising by an intermediary, often in conjunction with a significant event (e.g. the opening of a new outlet by the intermediary). Sometimes, a service principal targets sales promotions at individual employees of its intermediaries (e.g. tour operators have given free holiday vouchers to travel-agency clerks who sell a certain quota of the tour operator's holidays). This can raise ethical issues about whether employees should accept incentives when their first duty is to their employer, who in turn seeks to develop the best long-term relationship with its customers.

## 13.7 Personal selling

Personal selling is a powerful two-way form of communication. It allows an interactive relationship to be developed between buyer and seller in which the latter can modify the information presented in response to the needs of the audience. Personal selling allows for the cultivation of a friendship between buyer and seller, which can be an important element of a relationship marketing strategy. It can also be powerful in creating a feeling of obligation by the customer to the salesperson, thereby helping to bring about a desired response.

Although the principles of personal selling are basically the same for goods and services industries, services sales personnel are more likely to combine their sales duties with other operational duties, for example in the way that a travel agent – as well as being an expert on travel reservation systems – is expected to perform a selling role.

### 13.7.1 The salesperson's activities

The actual selling act is only a small part of the overall salesperson's role. In addition to their specific selling role, two further principal roles can be identified – servicing and intelligence.

The servicing element can be an important contributor to the development of long-term customer relationships where the service in question is perceived as being highly risky. Such relationships need to be regularly attended to, even if there is no short-term prospect of a sale. In a study of the life assurance sector, George and Myers (1981) found that customers viewed their purchases as being highly risky and therefore unpleasant. As a consequence, they attached particular importance to the level of support they received from a salesperson in particular, and their organization in general. There have now been many studies to identify the factors that contribute towards relationship satisfaction between buyer and seller (e.g. Crosby et al., 1990; Cho, 2006).

As well as being the mouthpiece of an organization, sales personnel can also be its ears. They can be extremely useful in marketing research, for example by reporting on customers' comments, or providing information about competitors' activity. Organizations should develop systems for capturing information collected by sales personnel.

In respect of their selling role, a number of types of selling situations can be identified:

- *Trade selling.* Here, the salesperson's role is to facilitate sales through intermediaries.
- *Technical selling.* This involves giving advice and technical assistance to customers in the process of making a sale.
- *Missionary selling.* Here, the salesperson is not expected to take orders but to 'prepare the ground' by building goodwill.
- *New business selling.* This involves the acquisition of new accounts and may sometimes involve 'cold calling'.

The task of selling can be broken down into a number of sequential stages:

- *Prospecting, i.e. finding new customers.* Sales leads can be developed in a number of ways, for example, records of past customers, past enquiries and referrals from existing customers and suppliers.
- *Preparation and planning.* A salesperson should attempt to gain as much information as possible about a prospect before actual contact takes place, for example in regard to their previous buying behaviour or aspirations.
- *The sales presentation.* The salesperson should be recognized as a surrogate for the service and the sales presentation should help 'tangibilize' an intangible service. Samples of supporting goods and brochures can often give a more credible description of a service process than a salesperson alone. The sales presentation should not offer what cannot be delivered – this applies to both goods and services but is particularly important where abstract expectations of service quality are not matched by actual performance. Customers should be given early opportunities to assess service quality, either by producing evidence of previous outcomes (e.g. previous performance of an investment fund) or by sampling the service process. Appearance and demeanour of the salesperson are very important in creating the right impression of the service offer.

- *Handling objections.* Objections to the sales presentation can be rational (e.g. objections to the price or to the service itself) or irrational (e.g. objections based on resistance to change, apathy, prejudice, etc.) and need to be acknowledged, isolated and discussed.
- *Closing the sale.* This is a difficult stage as knowing how and when to close is a skill in itself.
- *Follow-up.* This stage is often neglected but is essential to ensure customer satisfaction and repeat business. A letter of thanks or a phone call can help to reduce post-purchase dissonance, which is especially valuable for services where benefits are to be delivered in the distant future.

### Thinking around the subject: Overenthusiastic selling of insurance?

Can a salesperson be too successful? Many sales people have responded to bonus or other incentives offered by their employers to vigorously achieve sales that looked good at the time, but later came back to haunt the company. One of the key characteristics of a good salesperson is their ability to listen and to gain a good understanding of a buyer's needs. But what happens when the customer does not really have a very good understanding of their own needs? Furthermore, what happens when this is coupled with a salesperson who would prefer to earn his sales commission as easily as possible rather than probing the true needs of the customer? The result has been a series of mis-selling scandals that have tarnished the reputation of a number of business sectors, especially financial services.

The term *caveat emptor* ('let the buyer be aware') has been used to excuse the situation where a salesperson sold an individual an item that was not at all suited to their needs. It was assumed to be the buyer's fault for buying wrongly, rather than the seller's fault for selling wrongly. The balance is now tilting in the consumer's favour as society's expectations of sellers rise. This has been demonstrated through the mis-selling of a range of financial services. From 2007, many UK financial services companies had become involved in selling 'Payment Protection Insurance' (PPI), which in principle should have provided great benefit and reassurance to buyers, by guaranteeing to pay off their debts if they lost their job or became unable to work. However, the conditions of the insurance often contained exclusion clauses which would make the policy useless for the buyer, So a salesperson, keen to earn their bonus, may have sold a policy to a 62-year-old, even though they knew the customer's age and that the policy would not pay out to anyone over 60 years old.

Did the salesperson mis-sell or did the buyer mis-buy? The buyer may have thought that they were buying into a good deal, but many buyers were not able to understand the complexities of the 'small print' of the policy. Given the intangibility of the service, they probably felt inclined to rely on the advice of the salesperson, especially if they were employed by an organization that they knew and thought they could trust.

The overenthusiastic selling of PPI policies resulted in the big financial services companies being fined by their industry watchdog and forced to pay billions of pounds in compensation to customers. Lloyds TSB alone had by 2013 set aside £6.7 billion for compensating its customers (Guardian, 2013). Banks were forced to rethink the way they managed and rewarded their sales personnel, but much of the change simply involved going back to traditional best practice for the sales force: listening to the customer and understanding what they really need; training the sales force with greater product knowledge; and structuring their rewards to recognize a balance between the need for short-term incentives and long-term relationships.

## 13.8 Direct marketing

Direct marketing has been defined by the UK Direct Marketing Association (2006) as 'an interactive system of marketing which uses one or more media in acquiring a measurable response at a given location'. Its aim is to create and exploit a direct relationship between service producers and their customers. In recent years, there has been a dramatic increase in the use of direct marketing for promoting services, largely due to the development of new technology, which enables organizations to target their messages accurately. Travel companies, retailers and hotels have been more recent adopters of direct marketing methods on a large scale. While direct marketing may include personal selling, it is the other elements of direct marketing that are of interest here, including telemarketing, direct mail and directories.

The key elements of a direct marketing system are the following:

- an accurate record of the names of existing customers, ex-customers and prospective customers classified into different groups;
- a system for recording the results of communications with targets; from this, the effectiveness of particular messages and the responsiveness of different target groups can be assessed;
- a means of measuring and recording actual purchase behaviour;
- a system to follow up with continuing communication where appropriate.

Direct marketing is closely linked to a firm's efforts to build long-term relationships with its customers (Chapter 5). Direct marketing helps a company to assess each of its customers' and potential customers' likely level of profitability and to deliver services and messages that are very closely related to their unique needs.

The three most common media used by services organizations are telemarketing, direct mail and electronic media. (Electronic media is considered in Section 13.11.)

### 13.8.1 Telemarketing

**Telemarketing** involves two-way communication by telephone – 'outbound' telemarketing occurs where suppliers take the initiative and 'inbound' where customers act in response to another stimulus, such as a newspaper advertisement. There has been a rapid increase in the use of inbound telemarketing using toll-free 0800 numbers, particularly by the financial services sector. Companies need to be able to handle surges in incoming calls, otherwise the cost of generating leads is wasted and prospective customers who cannot get through may get such a bad impression of the company that they may not bother calling back. Research by Mintel into 2000 users of call centres found that by far the biggest complaint when telephoning a call centre was the time spent waiting on hold, with some 60 per cent complaining about this. Those aged between 25 and 34 were the least tolerant towards call centres, with around 35 per cent abandoning calls. Just 5 per cent of consumers had never experienced a problem with a call centre (Mintel, 2002).

Outbound telemarketing has sometimes been used as an alternative to personal selling, especially where some customers are seen as potentially less profitable than others and telemarketing is used for these instead of more expensive face-to-face personal selling.

The effectiveness of telemarketing can be assessed in a number of ways. One possibility is to measure the cost per telephone call and, from this, the cost per successful call. Alternatively, effectiveness can be measured in terms of the cost per telephone hour, which includes the costs incurred in managing the system. A more useful approach is to assess effectiveness in terms of benefits as well as costs. The simplest measure of benefit is the number and quality of enquiries received. It can often be possible to measure the cost-effectiveness of telemarketing in terms of the value of sales generated, especially where there is little extraneous media advertising that could itself have explained sales success.

### 13.8.2 Direct mail

Direct mail describes the way in which an organization targets printed material aimed at specific individuals or companies with a view to carrying on direct interchange between the two parties. A number of important advantages that it has over the other promotional tools can be identified:

- It can be used very selectively to target quite specific groups.
- The sales message can be personalized to the needs of individual recipients.
- Direct mail offers a very versatile and creative medium and is flexible in the range of materials that can be used.
- It can be timed effectively to fit in with the overall marketing strategy and is quick to implement and to produce results.
- Direct mail can include tangible evidence of a highly intangible service offer (e.g. pictures of hotels).

Direct mail can be employed to achieve a number of promotional objectives, including the generation of enquiries, keeping prospects interested, keeping customers informed of new developments and improving the effectiveness of the salesperson (i.e. it can be used as a 'door opener').

#### Thinking around the subject: Telecoms companies are particularly bad at communicating, says report

The phenomenal development of telecommunications (telecoms) over the past couple of decades should have opened up tremendous new opportunities for two-way communication between a company and its customers – actual and potential. However, there is still evidence that service companies can be slow to embrace the interactive communication abilities of the telephone and Internet. Research undertaken in 2006 by the e-services provider Transversal showed that the UK telecoms sector – which should have been at the forefront of the telecommunications revolution – was actually performing badly at communication. The report found phone companies to be among the slowest at answering their phones, with some, such as Carphone Warehouse, apparently being overwhelmed at their call centres. Answering a phone is generally more expensive than having customers communicating through a website, entering all data themselves and using the customer's time rather than a call-centre operator's time to search for results. But the phone companies did not seem to do well here either. The report found that only a third provided an online customer search function, down from 70 per cent a year earlier. Furthermore, the telephone companies' websites could answer an average of just two out of 10 most basic customer questions such as 'How do I upgrade my phone?'. Online users who sent an email to the company to resolve a problem would typically wait 48 hours for a reply, and many email requests for information simply did not get answered.

It is easy to say that telecommunications improve the ability of companies to communicate with their customers, but technology alone will not improve communication. Telecommunications companies should be at the leading edge when it comes to the enabling technology, but did they have the management abilities to put the technology to good use? Or were they simply victims of their own success and, as they grew, their capacity to handle calls continually lagged behind customer demand? Had the communications revolution led to higher expectations by customers, who may have been happy to wait several days for an answer, but now want an instant response, 24/7? And, with communication costing money, could facilitating easier communication simply result in more calls from customers, adding to a company's costs and putting it at a disadvantage in a price-sensitive market?

Compared to advertising, the direct mail message can be more detailed. Much more space is available on a direct mailshot and this allows long and complex messages to be presented – a point that partly explains the popularity of direct mail with financial services companies, whose sales messages are typically very complex. Leaflets, inserts, pop-ups, etc. can also be included in the mailshot. The response medium serves a variety of purposes. It can be used to obtain expressions of interest, to obtain sales orders and to measure the effect of the promotion.

With the use of reply-paid envelopes and freephone numbers, response from recipients of direct mail is facilitated. The results of individual targeted mailshots can be assessed quite easily and through further refinement of customer profiling and targeting, the cost of contact per person can be reduced to a low level. It is also important to consider non-respondents and why they did not respond.

## 13.9 Public relations

**Public relations** is an indirect promotional tool, which aims to establish and enhance a positive image of an organization and its services among its various publics. It is defined by the Institute of Public Relations as 'the deliberate, planned and sustained effort to establish and maintain mutual understanding between an organization and its publics'. It seeks to persuade people that a company is an attractive organization with which to relate or do business, which is important for the services sector because it has already been noted that services are evaluated very subjectively and often rely on word-of-mouth recommendation. Public relations facilitates this process of subjective evaluation and recommendation.

Because public relations is involved with more than just customer relationships, it is often handled at a corporate level rather than at the functional level of marketing management. As an element within the promotion mix, public relations presents a number of valuable opportunities as well as problems. Some of its more important characteristics are described below:

- *Low cost.* The major advantage of public relations is that it tends to be much cheaper in terms of cost per person reached than any other type of promotion. Apart from nominal production costs, much public-relations activity can be carried out at almost no cost, in marked contrast to the high cost of buying space or time in the main media.
- *Audience specificity.* Public relations can be targeted to a small specialized audience if the right media vehicle is used.
- *Believability.* Much public-relations communication is seen as credible because it comes from an apparently impartial and non-commercial source. Where information is presented as news, readers or viewers may be less critical of a message than if it is presented as a biased advertisement.
- *Difficult to control.* A company can exercise little direct control over how its public-relations activity is subsequently handled and interpreted. If successful, a press release may be printed in full, although there can be no control over where or when it is printed. At worst, a press release can be misinterpreted and the result can be very unfavourable news coverage.
- *Competition for attention.* The fact that many organizations compete for a finite amount of attention puts pressure on the public-relations effort to be better than that of competitors.

### 13.9.1 The publics of public relations

Public relations can be distinguished from customer relations because its concerns go beyond the creation of mutually beneficial relationships with actual or potential customers. The following additional audiences for public relations can be identified:

- *Intermediaries.* These may share many of the same concerns as customers and need reassurance about the company's capabilities as a service principal. Service organizations can usually develop this reassurance through the use of company newsletters, trade journal articles, etc.
- *Suppliers.* These may need assurances that the company is a credible one to deal with and that contractual obligations will be met. Highlighting favourable annual reports and drawing attention to major new developments can help to raise the profile and credibility of a company in the eyes of its suppliers.
- *Employees.* Here, public relations overlaps with the efforts of internal marketing (see Chapter 10) and assumes great importance within the services sector, where personnel become part of the service offer and it is important to develop participation and motivation among employees. In addressing its internal audiences, public relations uses such tools as in-house publications, newsletters and employee-recognition activities.
- *Financial community.* This includes financial institutions that have supported, are currently supporting or who may support the organization in the future. Shareholders – both private and institutional – form an important element of this community and must be reassured that the organization is going to achieve its stated objectives.
- *Government.* In many cases, actions of government can significantly affect the fortunes of an organization and therefore relationships with government departments – at local, national and supra-national level – need to be carefully developed. This can include lobbying of Members of Parliament, communicating the organization's views to government enquiries and civil servants and creating a favourable image for itself by sponsoring public events.
- *Local communities.* It is sometimes important for an organization to be seen as a 'good neighbour' in the local community. Therefore, the organization can enhance its image through the use of charitable contributions, sponsorship of local events, being seen to support the local environment, etc.

### 13.9.2 The tools of public relations

A wide range of public-relations tools are available and the suitability of each is dependent upon the promotional objectives at which they are directed. In general, the tools of public relations are best suited to creating awareness of an organization or a liking for its services and tend to be less effective in directly bringing about action in the form of purchase decisions. While there can be argument as to just what constitutes public-relations activity, some of the important elements that are used within the promotion mix are described below:

- *Press releases.* These are activities undertaken by firms to obtain editorial space in the media, which is likely to be seen or heard by the company's target customers. The aim of the press release is more likely to be promoting the image of an organization than achieving an immediate sale. Because of its important contribution towards the promotion mix, press relations is considered in more detail below.
- *Lobbying.* Professional lobbyists are often employed in an effort to inform, and hence influence, key decision-makers who may be critical in allowing for elements of a marketing plan to be implemented. Lobbying can take place at a local level (e.g. a bus company seeking to convince a local authority of the harm that would result to the public in general if streets in a town centre were closed to buses), at a national level (e.g. lobbying by British Telecom to reduce the regulatory constraints on its pricing) and at a supra-national level (e.g. lobbying by airlines to the

European Commission to tone down the effects of proposed measures to reduce $CO_2$ emissions by aircraft).

- *Education and training*. In an effort to develop a better understanding – and hence liking – of an organization and its services, many services organizations aim education and training programmes at important target groups. In this way, banks frequently supply schools and colleges with educational material that will predispose recipients of the material to their brand when they come to open a bank account. Open days are another common method of educating the public by showing them the complex 'behind the scenes' production processes involved, a tactic commonly employed by theatres.
- *Exhibitions*. Most companies attend exhibitions not with the intention of making an immediate sale, but to create an awareness of their organization, which will result in a sale over the longer term. Exhibitions offer the chance for potential customers to talk face to face with representatives of the organization and the physical layout of the exhibition stand can give valuable tangible evidence about the nature of the service on offer. Exhibitions are used for both consumer services and business-to-business services. As an example of the latter, the annual World Travel Market in London offers the chance for a wide range of tourism-related service industries to meet quite narrowly targeted customers and to display tangible cues of their service offering (e.g. brochures and staff).
- *In-house journals*. Many services organizations have developed their own magazines, which are given to customers or potential customers. By adopting a news-based magazine format, the message becomes more credible than if it was presented as a pure advertisement. Usually, outside advertisers contribute revenue, which can make such journals self-financing – this commonly happens with in-house magazines published by banks. Travel operators often publish magazines that are read by a captive travelling public.
- *Special events*. In order to attract media attention, organizations sometimes arrange an event that is in itself newsworthy and will create awareness of the organization. One example was the world's first non-stop passenger plane flight between Britain and Australia, made by a Qantas aircraft. Although Qantas had adapted the aircraft and the journey could not be made under normal operating conditions, the fact that it was a 'first' made it newsworthy and created significant awareness of Qantas. Of course, if badly managed, a special event can turn into a public-relations disaster.
- *Sponsorship*. There is argument about whether this strictly forms part of the public-relations portfolio of tools. It is, however, being increasingly used by services companies and is described in more detail below.
- *Online interaction*. The public-relations function increasingly interacts with online blogs and forums by 'seeding' ideas within these groups and responding to issues raised. There has been much discussion of the ethics of PR professionals lurking in forums and providing comments without revealing their true identity, but in most cases their credibility may be enhanced by being identified as the 'official' voice of the company.

### 13.9.3 Media relations

Service organizations realize that an important way of promoting a favourable corporate image is through effective relationships with the main media. They aim to create over the longer term a feeling of mutual understanding between the organization and the media, which is achieved by means of the following:

- *Press releases*. These are the most frequent form of press-relations activity and are commonly used to announce new service launches, new appointments or significant achievements. Press releases are increasingly issued electronically and have the advantage of being a relatively inexpensive promotional tool that can reach large audiences with a high degree of credibility. Against this, a major disadvantage is the lack of control that the generator of a press release has over how it is subsequently handled, in terms of appearance, timing and content (it is likely to be edited). Because of the competition from other organizations for press coverage, there can be no guarantee that any particular item will actually be used.
- *Press conferences*. These are used when a major event is to be announced and an opportunity for a two-way dialogue between the organization and the media is considered desirable.
- *Availability of specialist commentators*. Faced with a news story that the media wishes to report on, a newspaper or radio station may seek specialists within an industrial sector who are knowledgeable on the issues involved. For example, a local tour operator may be asked by a local newspaper to comment upon the consequences of a hurricane in an overseas resort. This helps both the reporter and the service organization in question, whose representative is fielded as an expert.

## Thinking around the subject: Spotting dissent through the Internet

The Internet is not just a tool that organizations can use to send messages to customers, suppliers and intermediaries – it is increasingly being used by organizations to monitor their business environment. Monitoring chat groups and critical websites has become an important activity for organizations and their public-relations (PR) agencies, anxious to spot any general shifts in attitudes and specific comments that may harm the organization. News now crosses geographical frontiers quicker than a blink of the eye and corporate reputations can be savaged as disgruntled customers and shareholders swap comments via the Internet. Thorns in the side of PR people include the McSpotlight site (www.mcspotlight.org), which carries information critical of McDonald's Restaurants, and untied (www.untied.com), which is a forum for disgruntled United Airlines passengers. Such sites can be created without the companies' knowledge, if they are not monitoring and contributing to the forums and chat rooms. The sites can end up being a damaging mix of rumour and untruths.

Public-relations agencies that have the technical expertise have set up monitoring services. One PR consultancy, Edelman, monitors the Internet, checking on 33,000 user groups and bulletin boards and regularly prepares web pages for its clients in anticipation of crises. These are then 'hidden' on the website, ready to be activated if needed.

Businesses have had to face up to the new realities of the Internet. Response times need to be immediate, with no specific deadlines that are typical of conventional published media. At the same time, activists are changing the nature of the game that companies have to deal with. In 2013, protesters campaigned against 'fracking' (oil recovery from underground rocks) in southern England, causing large-scale disruption. It has been suggested that much of the planning for the protest took place through bulletin boards and blogs.

Quite aside from the battle of information technology is the fundamental question: Why did a company allow itself to get into the position of exposing itself to criticism? Could this not have been foreseen? If there is little for people to campaign about, the dissident websites would probably lose much of their support.

## 13.10 Sponsorship

One way that services organizations can try to 'tangibilize' their service is to attempt to get customers to link the image of its organization or of specific services with a more tangible event or activity. While publicity can successfully perform this function, sponsorship can also have long-term value.

**Sponsorship** involves investment in events or causes in order that an organization can achieve objectives such as increased awareness levels, enhanced reputation, etc. Sponsorship activities include such examples as a bank sponsoring cricket matches (e.g. the NatWest Trophy) and the sponsorship of specific television programmes (such as an insurance company sponsoring a television channel's weather forecasts).

Sponsorship is attractive to service companies as it allows the relatively known characteristics of an event or activity being sponsored to help enhance the image of an organization's own inherently intangible services. As an example, an insurance company wishing to associate itself with high quality may seek to sponsor the activities of a leading arts organization noted for the quality of its productions. A further advantage of sponsorship is that it allows a company to avoid the general media clutter usually associated with advertising. Furthermore, audiences can be segmented and a sponsorship vehicle chosen whose audience matches that of the sponsoring company, in terms of socio-economic, demographic and geographic characteristics. In this way, a regional insurance broker might sponsor a local theatrical group operating solely in its own business area.

Sponsorship of sporting events allows a company's brand name to be seen by viewers of the event and to associate the brand with the values of the sport concerned. Cheltenham & Gloucester (C&G) is the third-largest provider of household mortgages in the UK and has to compete with dozens of other banks and building societies for buyers' attention. By sponsoring a public activity (via the Cheltenham Cricket Festival – see Figure 13.11) the brand name is exposed to potential buyers, especially, in this case, cricket fans, for whom C&G may be high on the list of brands that are spontaneously recalled. The company's financial services products are also likely to be attributed with some of the characteristics of cricket – traditional, very English, reliable, etc.

It is difficult to evaluate sponsorship activities because of the problem of isolating the effects of sponsorship from other elements of the promotion mix. Direct measurement is only likely to be possible if sponsorship is the predominant tool. Sponsorship should therefore be seen as a tool that complements other elements of the promotion mix.

Figure 13.11 Through sponsorship, C&G has been associating itself with the values of cricket. (Reproduced with permission of Gloucestershire County Cricket Club)

Entertain in style at the world famous

**C&G Cheltenham Cricket Festival**

C&G Cheltenham & Gloucester

## 13.11 Online communication

The Internet is a versatile element of the promotion mix, which often combines a promotional function with a distribution function. In the early days of online marketing, there were many claims that the Internet would come to dominate companies' promotion mix. Of course, many people's early expectations for the Internet have since been moderated and it may be more realistic to regard online communication not as a stand-alone activity, but as just one component of a company's **integrated marketing communications**.

We have already mentioned some of the advantages of online marketing in our previous discussion of the elements of the promotion mix and noted the overlap between promotion-mix elements:

- Our definition of advertising includes web pages that broadcast to large numbers of people but are not interactive.
- Personal selling is increasingly relying on online communication to support the efforts of sales personnel.
- Public-relations professionals have understood the impact of chat rooms and dissident websites on a company's reputation and have developed web-based tools of their own.
- Online media have become an integral element of direct marketing by opening up an additional channel through which a company can enter an interactive dialogue with its customers.

### 13.11.1 Objectives and development of online media

Communication using online media involves a number of stages of development. At the most basic level, a company's website can simply give additional information about its services; for example, many hotels have websites that give information about their location and the facilities available. At this stage of development, the Internet is being used simply as an online form of the traditional printed brochure. Although a static, one-to-all website may now seem quite unadventurous, we should nevertheless recognize the advantages that web pages have over traditional printed brochures:

- They are much less expensive to produce.
- They can be updated very rapidly (e.g. in response to a price change) without the need to destroy existing stocks of brochures.
- Information can be provided immediately to prospective customers anywhere in the world, without the need to wait for a postal delivery.
- Comprehensive information can be provided within the site – more than could realistically be provided within the confines of a printed brochure.
- Links can be provided to other related information (for example, a hotel can include a link to local tourist attractions).

The second stage of online development allows some degree of interactive dialogue between a company and visitors to its website. At its simplest, this can take the form of a facility for visitors to enter a dialogue with the company by email, perhaps to find out further information. Interactivity could be added by creating a help facility that allows the visitor to ask simple questions and for the site to generate answers that are of direct relevance to the customer. This could take the form of a simple ready-reckoner type of calculator to allow the user to calculate the monthly repayments on a mortgage, in which they are invited to enter various loan amounts and repayment periods. More complex interactivity can be developed by linking the customer's request to a database of information. This is used by railway operators (e.g. www.nationalrail.co.uk) to provide precise information on possible rail journeys in response to a customer's request for information on train times between two specified points at a specified time. Many online service providers use targeted email services to encourage customers to visit their sites. The travel and leisure company Lastminute.com, for example, claims to send more than two million emails to customers every week. The content of the email is tailored to fit the recipient's age, lifestyle and other factors.

The third stage of online development is to allow immediate fulfilment of a request, such as confirmation of a hotel booking or reservation of a plane ticket. By linking a customer's online request to a real-time database of availability, the company is able to immediately communicate a specific price/product offer. Many airline and hotel companies have used the principles of yield management to continually change their price and product offer to reflect the changing balance between supply and demand, so the message that it sends to a site visitor may be quite different from one that it sent even just half an hour ago.

The fourth stage of online development embraces user-generated content. It was noted earlier that where a purchase decision is perceived as highly risky, buyers are likely to seek the opinions of their friends and fellow consumers. Many websites therefore incorporate customer review and discussion facilities in an attempt to facilitate the evaluation process.

The Internet is extensively used for comparison shopping and a lot of research has gone into understanding which sites produce the best results in terms of moving an individual through the stages of purchase. A regularly updated site that contains information of direct relevance to a user and that is fast to download has become a minimum requirement for most users of the medium.

In most Western countries, the majority of the population now has access to the Internet, at home, at work or at their place of study, and increasingly, through a mobile handheld device. The Internet is now firmly established as a communication medium in most organizations, and, in a growing proportion of households, use of broadband Internet is becoming as commonplace as switching on the television. An important consideration to marketers is that those households who have innovated with fixed and mobile Internet access tend to be the high-income households and opinion leaders, whom many companies are particularly keen to target. Online communication is particularly attractive for services, such as travel and financial services where the cost of delivering tangible elements is not a major constraint. The availability of high-speed mobile Internet will increase the possibilities for communication to customers while they are on the move and dependent upon their current location.

## In practice: Battle of the search engines

For many generic types of services which can be searched using easy to specify criteria, search engines have become an important battleground for capturing the attention of buyers. If you are a hotel offering budget accommodation in London, you would want to be top of the list of results for people who enter the term 'London budget hotel' into a search engine such as Google, rather than being lost somewhere on page 24, which very few users would click through to. If you are a big hotel with lots of other websites providing links to your site, you may just come close to the top of the list without much effort. But in reality, you may need to bid for key words so that you come top of the page as a sponsored link. Generic and popular search terms can be expensive to purchase. Further complication arises because your agents may be bidding against you for the same keywords. Even if you include your hotel name as a paid-for search term, competitors might have outbid you, in the hope that anybody looking for your site will instead find the competitor's site at the top of their search results. In the early days of the Internet, many

Figure 13.12 A typical search website. (Reproduced courtesy of Google)

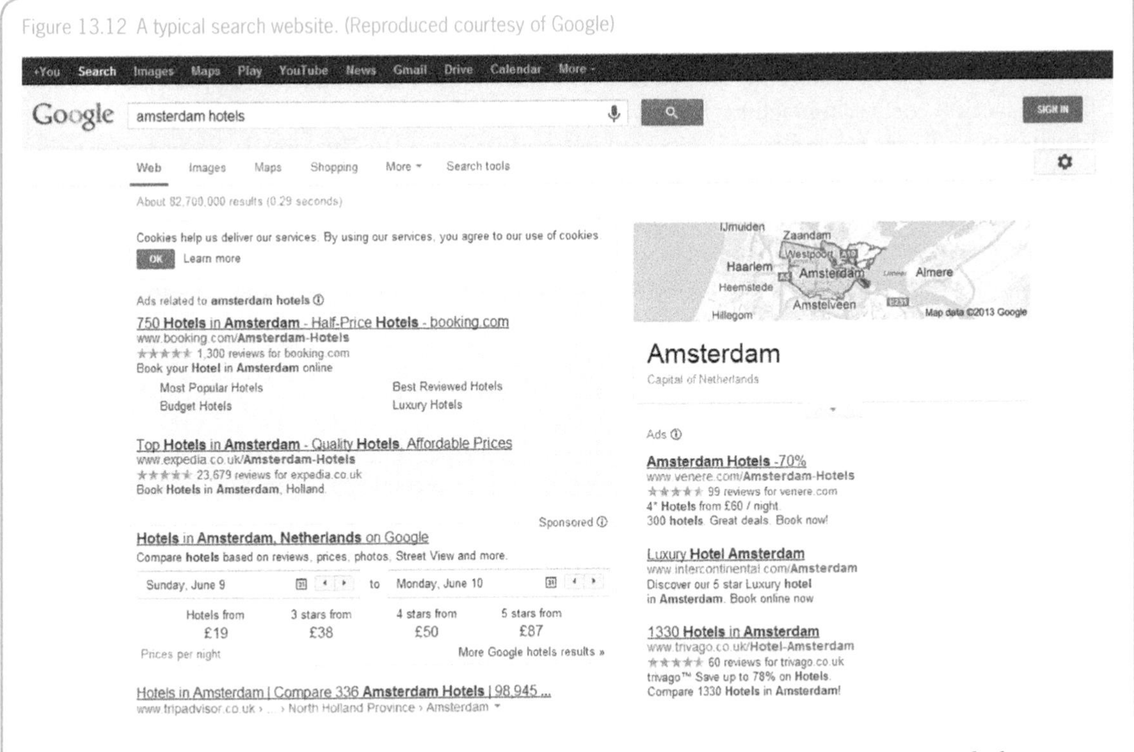


people expected the Internet to make inexpensive advertising available to all. However, with the growing sophistication of online promotion, many companies have had to sharply increase their budgets for search engine optimization and employed specialists to undertake the task.

## 13.11.2 Limitations of online media

Online media have developed rapidly over the past decade and provided benefits to buyers and sellers that would previously have been almost unimaginable. Rapid growth inevitably brings developmental problems and some of the limitations of online media are summarized below:

- Systems often require high capital outlay, and there may be a slow return on investment. Compatibility within the technological architecture of an organization can be a limitation, with new technologies continually requiring additional investment from companies.
- As use of the Internet as a communication medium has increased, it has become increasingly cluttered. This effect has been seen during the development of all media, and companies using the Internet have faced increasing challenges in drawing people to their websites. Getting a high ranking in search engines has become a critical skill and specialist companies are often employed to raise a client's rankings. Although the Internet is a very cheap source of messages, companies have to spend increasing amounts of money promoting their web presence, both online and offline. A new generation of 'informediaries' has appeared to simplify communication between online buyers and sellers. Buying access to target customers on the Internet has become an important activity, with portals such as Yahoo! charging premium prices for the use of **banner advertisements** on their popular websites. A number of companies, such as Google Analytics (www.google.com/analytics), exist to collect information about individuals' usage patterns with a view to improving the targeting of advertisements through paid-for websites.

- Many companies have been keen to move communication with customers to the Internet and away from other, more expensive media. Research undertaken by Oxford Associates in a number of US-based industries has suggested that most companies achieved a 20–40 per cent reduction in transaction costs when selling through distributors and partners, 40–45 per cent when selling through call centres and over 50 per cent when selling over the Internet. However, they warned against following a cost-reduction strategy that does not take account of buyer behaviour. A company could too easily lose key customers as it cuts back its sales force and call centres, hoping that buyers will migrate to the Internet. There have been many cases of online systems that have faced lengthy teething problems, costing a lot in lost customer goodwill.

## Thinking around the subject: Switch in Amazon promotion strategy

One of the early paradoxes of the 'new media' of the late 1990s was their reliance on 'old' media. To those who had advocated a revolution in media channels, it would seem odd that some of the biggest newspaper and television advertisers in recent years have been Internet-related services companies, with companies such as Expedia and Yahoo! spending huge amounts to promote their Internet-based services.

Among the big spenders was Amazon.com, which had soaked up billions of dollars of its investors' capital in developing a high-profile brand, backed up by high levels of service. Up until 2002, Amazon had used its television advertising for both brand building and driving immediate sales. The company's television advertising campaign – which in 2001 cost an estimated $50 million – focused on the advantages of shopping online versus going to a shopping mall. The company had not generally promoted specific products via television advertisements. Instead, the company had an impressive web presence that promoted the company and its products.

In 2002 Amazon decided to stop all television advertising. Was this just another wild idea by a company, whose chairman Jeff Bezos had ruffled the feathers of many investors through his seemingly wacky ideas? Or was the decision simply a reflection of the fact that the promotional objectives of Amazon had changed, and therefore called for new communication tools?

The company had carried out extensive research into what was now a substantial customer base. Simply encouraging existing customers to buy more (for example, through new product ranges) was one way of securing additional sales. But its research also showed that shipping costs were a major point of contention with existing and would-be customers. With local high-street bookstores offering attractive prices and long opening hours, plus free ordering and collection services, people often felt miffed about having to pay a £5 shipping charge for an item that only cost £10. Although the company felt that the creative message of its television advertisementss was working, it thought that free shipping and lower prices would bring an even greater return on its investment.

The company switched its advertising budget, initially just in the USA, to fund a sales promotion of free shipping costs for purchases over $25. During 2001, Amazon reported in its financial results a $41 million loss on its shipping costs. After an initial trial, the free shipping promotion was extended in 2003 to the British market for purchases over £39 and was gradually reduced to a qualifying threshold of £15 by 2007.

Amazon had another promotional tool up its sleeve in which it planned to use fully its network of associates who place a banner ad on their website and take a small percentage of sales revenue when a visitor to their website clicks through to Amazon and makes a purchase. The company had also been a big spender on banner adverts on other companies' sites, and strengthened this form of promotion, helped by a slump in charges for banner ads during 2002–03 as other dot.com advertisers were removed from the market through bankruptcy.

Stopping all television advertising is an unusual move for a major brand such as Amazon. Its brand had been successfully built, to the extent that it scored highly in unprompted recall of booksellers' names. But could it have built the brand entirely online without television and newspaper support? Would the brand need refreshing with further TV advertising to protect it against new 'clicks and mortar' bookstores?

*Source*: based on Kawamoto (2003).

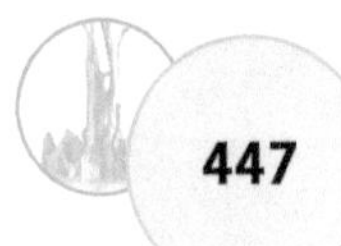

## 13.12 Word of mouth and social network media

An organization's image and reputation can be derived through channels other than the formal communication process. There is a lot of evidence, for example, that when differentiating between professional and personal services providers, customers prefer to be guided by information from friends and other personal contacts rather than the usual promotion mix (e.g. Susskind, 2002; Walker, 2001). Of course, positive word-of-mouth recommendation is generally dependent on customers having good experiences with an organization and studies have shown how unexpectedly high standards of service from a company can promote recommendation (Derbaix and Vanhamme, 2003). On the other hand, a bad experience can rapidly be spread as negative word-of-mouth discouragement. An important communication objective is therefore often to leverage this 'free' form of positive promotion and to limit the damage caused by negative word of mouth by encouraging dissatisfied customers to resolve their problems before they tell others. In addition to providing a good service that people would want to recommend to their friends, firms facilitate word-of-mouth recommendation through such means as customer referral cards (Figure 13.13).

### In practice: The voice of the people

It should never be forgotten that the most powerful form of promotion is word-of-mouth recommendation. For many people, booking a hotel may involve a high level of perceived risk. Rather than relying on the hotel's own description, buyers are increasingly turning to customer review sites to find out whether other customers would recommend a hotel. Maybe the official hotel website did not say anything about the factory opposite, whose workers noisily and abruptly woke people up at 6 a.m. Hiding this on the official hotel website wouldn't be a lie, but increasingly people are prepared to volunteer the whole story to other potential customers. However, even customer review sites can be ambiguous, with competitors trying to sabotage other hotels while covertly praising their own. Many companies have realized that they cannot ignore customer review sites, or hope to control them, so they need to find a way of engaging with them.

Figure 13.13 Customer reviews on TripAdvisor. (Reproduced courtesy of TripAdvisor.co.uk)

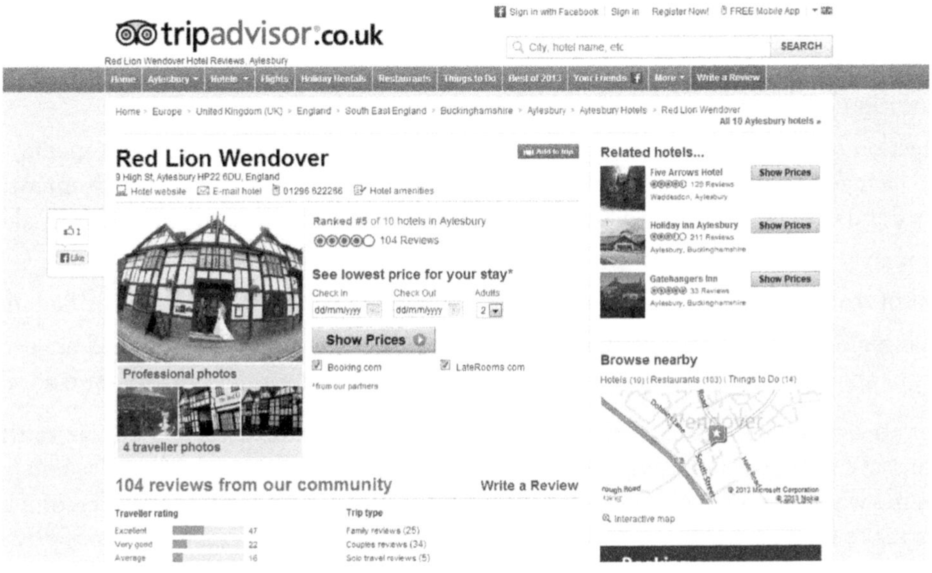

Word-of-mouth referral has been greatly facilitated by the Internet. As well as telling their friends, messages left with bulletin boards and chat rooms can spread a message very rapidly. Many companies have embraced the Internet to develop 'viral' marketing, in which a message can be rapidly spread from one person who informs a handful of friends, who each in turn inform a handful of their friends (Cruz and Fill, 2008). 'Word of mouth' has become 'word of mouse' and has the capability to spread a message very quickly.

There are many examples of viral marketing campaigns that have been very successful, and allowed a message to be spread with very little paid-for advertising support. In its early days, the Internet-based phone company Skype used viral marketing to expand very quickly. Even apparently uninteresting subjects for messages can be spread very quickly using viral techniques. An example from the public sector was Transport for London's 2008 campaign to improve the safety of cyclists. In an effort to demonstrate the need to pay attention to cyclists, visitors to its website were shown a game of basketball and asked to count the number of basketball passes. Somebody in a bear suit danced through the team, but this was initially unseen by the majority of people until they were told about it afterwards. The film acquired a cult status and was reportedly viewed by over 8 million people in the month after its launch, almost entirely through word-of-mouse referral (Readon, 2009). Of course, although millions of people might have visited the site, it cannot be assumed that the attitude of visitors had been changed in the way that Transport for London had intended.

## 13.13 Developing a promotional campaign

A campaign brings together a wide range of media-related activities so that, instead of being independent activities, they can act in a planned and co-ordinated way to achieve promotional objectives. The term 'integrated marketing communication' is often used to describe the bringing together of media so that they reinforce a message in a cost-effective way.

The first stage of campaign planning is to have a clear understanding of promotional objectives (see above). Once these have been clarified, a message can be developed that is most likely to achieve these objectives. The next step is the production of a media plan. Once the target audience has been defined in terms of its size, location and media exposure, media must be selected that achieve desired levels of exposure/repetition with the target audience. A media plan must be formulated that specifies:

- the allocation of expenditure between the different media;
- the selection of specific media components – for example, in the case of print media, decisions need to be made regarding the type (tabloid versus broadsheet), size of advertisement, whether use of a Sunday supplement is to be made and whether there is to be national or local coverage;
- the frequency with which the message will be repeated;
- the cost of reaching a particular target group for each of the media vehicles specified in the plan;
- the linkages between different media, for example the way in which billboard adverts remind readers of an advertisement on television the previous night, or direct readers to a website.

While the principles of planning a campaign for a services organization are similar to those for a manufacturing company, the intangible, inseparable and variable nature of services do need to be borne in mind when a campaign is planned. Advertising alone is unlikely to be successful in helping customers make services purchase decisions, but their effectiveness can be increased by following a few guidelines. To summarize from the points raised earlier in this chapter, a service provider should:

- Use clear and unambiguous messages.
- Build on word-of-mouth communication.
- Provide tangible cues of the service offer.
- Promise what can be delivered.
- Include employees in the promotion campaign.
- Remove post-purchase anxiety.

### 13.13.1 Determining the promotion budget

Promotional expenditure can become a drain on an organization's resources if no conscious attempt is made to determine an appropriate budget and to ensure that expenditure is kept within the budget. A number of methods are commonly used to determine an advertising budget:

- *What can be afforded.* This is largely a subjective assessment and pays little attention to the long-term promotional needs of a service. It regards promotion as a luxury that can be afforded in good times, to be cut back during lean times. In reality, this approach is used by many smaller service companies to which promotional spending is seen as the first and easy short-term target for reducing expenditure in bad times.
- *Percentage of sales.* By this method, expenditure rises or falls to reflect changes in sales. In fact, sales are likely to be influenced by promotional spending rather than vice versa and this method is likely to accentuate any given situation. If sales are declining during a recession, more promotion may be required to induce sales, but this method of determining the budget implies a cut in expenditure.
- *Comparative parity.* Promotional expenditure is determined by the amount spent by competitors. Many market sectors see periodic outbursts of promotional expenditure, often accompanying a change in some other element of firms' marketing mix. However, merely increasing advertising expenditure may hide the fact that it is the other elements of the marketing mix that need adjusting in order to gain a competitive market position in relation to competitors.
- *Residual.* This is the least satisfactory approach and merely assigns to the promotional budget what is left after all other costs have been covered. It may bear no relationship whatever to promotional objectives.
- *Objective and task.* This approach starts by clearly defining promotional objectives. Tasks are then set that relate to specific targets. In this way, advertising is seen as a necessary – even though possibly risky – investment in a brand, ranking in importance with other more obvious costs such as production and salary costs. This is the most rational approach to setting a promotional budget.

## Case study

### Promoting an 'ethical bank'

Banks had never been popular among the general British public, but from 2008 their reputation fell to a new all-time low. Many media commentators, politicians and the public saw bankers in general as a greedy, short-sighted group of people whose selfish pursuit of big bonuses had brought about the near collapse of the national economy. Many people were outraged when the UK government spent billions of pounds rescuing Royal Bank of Scotland and Lloyds Banking Group from collapse, only to see these banks continuing to pay bonuses to their senior staff, while restricting the loans they advanced to ordinary small businesses and private households. To many people, one bank is quite indistinguishable from another, and loyalty to a bank often derives from historical inertia – the pain of switching banks may be perceived as greater than the pain of simply putting up with their current bank. Very few banks have successfully communicated a message that allows them to stand out as something quite different from their competitors. A few, such as First Direct, have acquired loyalty through high levels of customer satisfaction. But one UK bank – the Co-operative Bank – has gone one step further by clearly communicating its ethical credentials and acquiring a high level of loyalty from its customers. Its long-term communication strategy seemed to be paying dividends in the depths of the banking crisis when other banks were being ridiculed.

The Co-operative Bank can trace its origins back to 1872 when it was established by the Co-operative Wholesale and Retail Societies. By the mid-1980s it had enjoyed a period of steady growth and its branch size passed 100, helped by several innovative new products such as free in-credit banking, extended opening hours and interest-bearing cheque accounts. However, the bank found its market position being steadily eroded by increased competition from the major clearing banks and particularly building societies that were able to enter the personal banking sector, following deregulation of the banking sector. As a result of increased competition following deregulation, the bank saw its market share fall from 2.7 per cent in 1986 to 2 per cent by 1991. Alongside this trend the bank faced a changing customer profile. Traditionally, the bank had attracted a high proportion of its customers from the more affluent ABC1 social groups. By 1992 an increasing number of new accounts were being attracted from the C2DE social groups, while at the same time the bank was losing its core ABC1 accounts.

The bank's research showed that, outside of its customer base, it lacked a clear image, being seen mainly as rather staid, old-fashioned and with left-wing political affinities. Furthermore, spontaneous recall of its name had steadily fallen despite extensive advertising of a series of innovative new products.

The bank realized that immediate action was necessary to rebuild its image and stem the loss of its ABC1 accounts. The size of the bank and its profitability meant that the advertising budget had to be modest and therefore a focused campaign with maximum effectiveness was crucial.

BDDH was appointed as advertising agency to devise a promotional campaign. The agency 'interrogated' the Co-operative Bank to identify any distinctive competencies that it could build a campaign upon. It discovered that the bank's heritage offered a unique positioning opportunity against other mainstream banks. This derived in particular from its sourcing and distribution of funds, which had been governed by an unwritten ethical code, with the effect that the bank never lent money to environmentally or politically unsound organizations. BDDH set out to transform the results of its interrogation into a relevant and motivating proposition that would appeal beyond the bank's current customer base. A key strategic decision was made to target promotional activity at the growing number of 'ethical consumers' who, importantly, were found to have a more upmarket ABC1 profile.

The 1990s had seen a great growth within the financial services sector of investment funds that claimed to invest only in businesses that are run ethically. Initially, some City people described them as 'Brazil Funds' – they were simply 'nuts'. Ethical investment funds started out as funds that merely excluded investment in specific activities or industries such as tobacco, gambling, alcohol and armaments. Other funds have taken a more proactive stance, actively looking to invest in companies involved in environmentally sound, socially progressive businesses. A more recent approach goes further and is based on the belief that financial institutions should proactively create a dialogue with companies in their portfolio on a specific number of social and environmental issues. The aim is to encourage them to adopt the best business practices.

Ethical investment funds may have appealed to middle-class investors who could afford to put concern for ethics before concern for achieving the maximum return (although many would argue that ethics and maximum returns are not incompatible). But how could this approach be used by a bank that was facing fierce competition for basic banking services?

The 'ethical bank' formed the foundation upon which BDDH built its campaign. Initially this was tested on its existing customer base, where it gained a high level of approval. The bank recognized that advertising claims must be met by actual practice and incorporated its ethical stance into its customer charter. The bank was well aware that the media enjoy making trouble for companies that claim to be ethical but in fact are caught out by undertaking unethical practices. Advertising was initially used to raise awareness of the bank's positioning. The creative work was deliberately provocative and motivating, while at the same time maintaining the bank's credentials as a high-street lender. The creative images used were often simple and stark.

The key objectives of the campaign were:

- Build customer loyalty and so stem the outflow of ABC1s.
- Expand the customer base, targeting ABC1s.
- Expand the corporate customer base.

National press and regional television in the bank's 'northern heartland' were the primary media used in the initial stages of the campaign. Cinema advertising was used as the campaign progressed.

The marketing objectives were exceeded as a result of the promotional campaign. The bank established a strong and differentiated brand platform, which it subsequently used to launch new services, including its 'Smile' Internet banking service (www.smile.co.uk). The campaign was carefully targeted with the aim of achieving maximum impact, which enabled the message to be delivered cost-effectively. The case clearly demonstrates how effective promotional activity, linked closely to business and marketing objectives and strategy, can provide a long-term sustainable competitive position in the marketplace.

In 2009, the bank reported its tenth year of increased operating income, of £755.4 million, and profits of £113.2 million. The bank's mortgage loan-to-value ratio of 42 per cent – considered good for the banking sector – provided further evidence that the bank was not reliant on poorer socio-economic groups who tend to borrow a higher proportion of a property's value. In 2009 the Co-operative Bank effectively came to the rescue of the Britannia Building Society, which like many building societies had suffered as a result of the 'credit crunch'.

Communicating an ethical position had served the Co-operative Bank well, and this position continued to evolve in response to changes in its customers' concerns. The Co-operative Group has led the way in responsible business practices and in 2008, was voted the UK's most ethical brand in the GfK NOP Ethical Brands Survey. At a time when many people were questioning the ethics of business in general, and banks in particular, this was a very welcome position.

However, with other financial services organizations increasingly going out of their way to state their ethical credentials, the Co-operative Bank has had to communicate the nature of the difference between itself and its competitors. The company also had to be on guard for a growing number of commentators who were critical of the whole idea of ethical investment. A report by the Social Affairs Unit was scornful of ethical investment, because ethics is about judgements on what people do with products. It cited the example of funds' refusal to invest in the nuclear industry, which implied that the industry was totally bad, despite the valuable role that nuclear radiation plays in medicine, and potentially to reducing global warming.

Some began to question the sustainability of the Co-op bank's activities, especially in 2013 when instead of profits, the bank reported a loss of £674 m for the previous financial year and was forced to sell its insurance business to raise capital. Worse still, Moodys, a leading credit rating agency, downgraded its risk assessment of the bank. It seemed that in rescuing the Britannia Building Society, the Co-operative Bank had done what many of its bigger bankrupt banks had done previously – spent a lot of money in pursuit of growth by buying an institution without rigorously investigating the quality of its debts. Lloyds TSB may have been brought down by its acquisition of HBoS – could the Co-operative Bank be brought down by an ideologically based acquisition of a fellow mutual bank?

## Case study review questions

1. Critically evaluate methods that could be used by the Co-operative Bank to assess whether its promotion as an ethical bank has been effective.
2. Discuss the dangers that the Co-operative Bank could face in promoting an ethical position.
3. Critically assess the promotional positioning of other banks with which you are familiar.

## Summary and links to other chapters

This chapter has explored the role of communication in the marketing of services. While many of the principles of communication for services are similar to those for goods, the promotion of services poses additional problems and opportunities. Perceived risk, caused by intangibility, must be addressed by communication, and techniques for seeking to achieve this have been discussed. The presence of consumers in the production process for services opens possibilities for promotion that are not generally available to the goods manufacturer.

There is a strong link between this chapter and Chapter 8, which introduced branding – as services organizations grow, development and communicating a trusted brand reputation becomes very important. Communication has a vital role in guiding buyers through the purchase decision process (Chapter 6). With the development of relationship-marketing strategies (Chapter 5), the promotional emphasis in many companies has moved from recruitment of new customers to retention of existing ones. With the development of direct marketing, promotion and accessibility strategies are becoming increasingly closely connected (Chapter 4). Promotion strategy can be particularly important where a company is launching new services (Chapter 7). New communication challenges arise when a service organization expands to a foreign market (Chapter 14).

### Chapter review questions

1. Critically evaluate the differences between goods and services in the development of a communication strategy.
2. 'A good service should not need any promotion – reputation built on service quality should be sufficient to sell the service.' Critically discuss this statement in the context of a service sector of your choice.
3. What additional factors need to be considered by a public-sector service organization developing a communication strategy for its service, compared with the factors facing a private-sector organization?

### Activities

1. Undertake a critical assessment of the last time you purchased a reasonably high-involvement service such as a holiday or university course. Identify the main sources of communication that influenced your eventual choice, noting the effects of messages derived from within and beyond the service provider. Now repeat the exercise on friends to see if a consistent pattern emerges.
2. Go through a newspaper or magazine and select adverts for services organizations. Critically assess the messages contained in the adverts and, in the context of a buyer-response model, try to understand what the intended response of the message might be.
3. Gather together a selection of university/college brochures, or look through their websites. Critically evaluate how these universities balance their message between the need to appear scholarly and the need to be accessible to all. Do you notice any difference in the message content of 'top' universities compared with lower-rated universities?

## Key terms

**Adoption** Rate at which individuals start buying a product.

**Advertising** The process by which an advertiser communicates with target audiences through paid-for messages.

**AIDA (Attention, Interest, Desire, Action)** A mnemonic used to describe the process of communicating a series of messages.

**Banner advertisements** Paid-for advertisements on other companies' websites.

**Channel of communication** Medium used to convey information from a sender (or transmitter) to a receiver.

**Cross-selling** Strategy of selling other products to a customer who has already purchased (or intends to purchase) a product from the vendor.

**Diffusion model** Process by which a new idea or new product is accepted by the market.

**Direct marketing** Direct communication between a seller and individual customers using a method of promotion other than face-to-face selling.

**Extended promotion mix** The traditional goods promotion mix, with the addition of elements related to visible service processes.

**Guerrilla marketing** The use of unconventional promotional tactics that are unexpected by the target audience.

**Integrated marketing communications** Promotional planning designed to ensure that all brand communications received by a customer or prospect for a service or organization are relevant to that person and consistent over time.

**'Noise' factors** Causes of distortion between the message that a communicator sends out and the message that a receiver perceives.

**Post-purchase dissonance** A buyer's feelings after making a purchase are not in accordance with reality.

**Promotion mix** Combination of advertising, personal selling, sales promotion and public relations.

**Public relations** The deliberate, planned and sustained effort to establish and maintain mutual understanding between an organization and its publics.

**Sales promotion** Techniques and incentives used to increase short-term sales.

**Search engine optimization (SEO)** Strategies and tactics to put a company's web page at the top of the list of results seen by people using a search engine.

**Sponsorship** Payment by a company to be associated with a particular event or activity.

**Stakeholder** Person or organization that has an interest in a project or entity.

**Telemarketing** Sales activity that focuses on the use of the telephone to enter into a two-way dialogue with present and potential customers.

**Viral marketing** Using friends and friends of friends to spread a message rapidly.

**Web 2.0** A general term used to describe a range of web-based communication technologies that allow simultaneous communication between multiple users.

**Word of mouth** Passing of information by verbal means, especially recommendations, but also general information, in an informal, person-to-person manner.

## Selected further reading

*For a fuller discussion of the general principles of promotion, the following texts cover the main elements of the promotion mix:*

**De Pelsmacker, P., Feuns, M. and Van den Bergh, J.** (2010) *Marketing Communications: A European Perspective*, FT Prentice Hall, London.

**Fill, C. and Zook, Z.** (2011) *Marketing Communications: Integrating Offline and Online with Social Media*, Kogan Page, London.

*During the early days of the services marketing literature, a number of articles sought to define the ways in which the promotion of services differed from that of goods. Early articles, and more recent discussion, can be found in the following:*

**Firestone, S.H.** (1983) 'Why advertising a service is different', in L.L. Berry, G.L. Shostack and G.D. Upah (eds), *Emerging Perspectives in Services Marketing*, American Marketing Association, Chicago, IL.

**George, W.R., Kelly, J.P. and Marshall, C.E.** (1983) 'Personal selling of services', in L.L. Berry, G.L. Shostack and G.D. Upah (eds), *Emerging Perspectives in Services Marketing*, American Marketing Association, Chicago, IL.

**Mortimer, K.** (2000) 'Are services advertised differently? An analysis of the relationship between product and service types and their information content', *Journal of Marketing Communications*, 6 (2), 121–34.

*For an overview of direct marketing and online media, the following provide useful background:*

**Chaffey, D. and Ellis-Chadwick, F.** (2012) *Internet Marketing: Strategy, Implementation and Practice*, 5th edn, Pearson, London.

**Fox, V.** (2010) *Marketing in the Age of Google*, John Wiley, New York.

**Weber, L.** (2009) *Marketing to the Social Web: How Digital Customer Communities Build Your Business*, 2nd edn, John Wiley, Chichester, UK.

**Tapp, A.** (2008) *Principles of Direct and Database Marketing*, 4th edn, FT Prentice Hall, London.

## References

**Balmer, J.M.T. and Greyser, S.A.** (2006) 'Corporate marketing: Integrating corporate identity, corporate branding, corporate communications, corporate image and corporate reputation', *European Journal of Marketing*, 40 (7/8), 730–41.

**Cho, J.** (2006) 'The mechanism of trust and distrust formation and their relational outcomes', *Journal of Retailing*, 82, 25–35.

**Chung-Kue, H. and McDonald, D.** (2002) 'An examination on multiple celebrity endorsers in advertising', *Journal of Product & Brand Management*, 11 (1), 19–29.

**Coulson-Thomas, C.T.** (1985) *Marketing Communications*, Heinemann, London.

**Crosby, L.A., Evans, K.R. and Cowles, D.** (1990) 'Relationship quality in services selling: an interpersonal influence perspective', *Journal of Marketing*, 54 (3), 68–81.

**Cruz, D. and Fill, C.** (2008) 'Evaluating viral marketing: isolating the key criteria', *Marketing Intelligence & Planning*, 26 (7), 743–58.

**Derbaix, C. and Vanhamme, J.** (2003) 'Inducing word-of-mouth by eliciting surprise: a pilot investigation', *Journal of Economic Psychology*, 24 (1), 99–116.

**Direct Marketing Association** (2006) *The Direct Marketing Industry in 2005*, Direct Marketing Association, London.

**Elliott, D., Harris, K. and Baron, S.** (2005) 'Crisis management and services marketing', *Journal of Services Marketing*, 19 (5), 336–45.

**Friends of the Earth** (2000) *Aviation and Global Climate Change*, Friends of the Earth, London.

**George, W.R. and Myers, T.A.** (1981) 'Life underwriters' perceptions of differences in selling goods and services', *CLU Journal*, April, 44–9.

**Guardian** (2013) 'PPI – facts and figures from the "biggest mis-selling scandal of all time"', *The Guardian*, London, 4 March.

**Hui, S.K., Inman, J., Huang, Y. and Suher, J.** (2013) 'The effect of in-store travel distance on unplanned spending: applications to mobile promotion strategies', *Journal of Marketing*, 77 (2), 1–16.

**Ind, N.** (1997) *The Corporate Brand*, Macmillan, Oxford.

**Jasmand, C., Blazevic, V. and de Ruyter, K.** (2012) 'Generating sales while providing service: a study of customer service representatives' ambidextrous behavior', *Journal of Marketing*, 76 (1), 20–37.

**Kawamoto, D.** (2003) 'Amazon switches off TV ads', *CNET News.com*, 10 February, available at http://news.cnet.com/2100-1017-984007.html (accessed 8 July 2013).

**Knight, K.** (2009) 'Study: television still tops with consumers', *BizReport*, 21 April, available at http://www.bizreport.com/2009/04/study_television_still_tops_with_consumers.html (accessed 8 July 2013).

**Lavidge, R.J. and Steiner, G.A.** (1961) 'A model for predictive measurement of advertising effectiveness', *Journal of Marketing*, 25 (October), 61–5.

**Levinson, J.C.** (2007) *Guerrilla Marketing: Cutting edge strategies for the 21st century*, Houghton Mifflin, Boston, MA.

**Mintel** (2002) *Optimising the Power of Call Centres*, Mintel, London.

**Readon, J.** (2009) 'Viral marketing: Alternative reality' [Electronic version], *Brand Strategy*, 44, 23 February, www.accessmylibrary.com/coms2/summary_0286-36821291_ITM (accessed 11 August 2010).

**Rogers, E.M.** (1962) *Diffusion of Innovation*, Free Press, New York.

**Smith, D.** (2005) 'Business (not) as usual: crisis management, service recovery and the vulnerability of organisations', *Journal of Services Marketing*, 19 (5), 309–20.

**Strong, E.K.** (1925) 'Theories of selling', *Journal of Applied Psychology*, 9 (1), 75–86.

**Susskind, A.M.** (2002) 'I told you so! Restaurant customers' word-of-mouth communication patterns', *Cornell Hotel & Restaurant Administration Quarterly*, 43 (2), 75–85.

**Walker, L.J.-H.** (2001) 'The measurement of word-of-mouth communication and an investigation of service quality and customer commitment as potential antecedents', *Journal of Service Research*, 4 (1), 60–75.

**Wegert, T.** (2004) 'When consumers love advertising', *ClickZ Networks*, 22 April, available at www.clickz.com/clickz/column/1696299/when-consumers-love-advertising (accessed 8 July 2013).

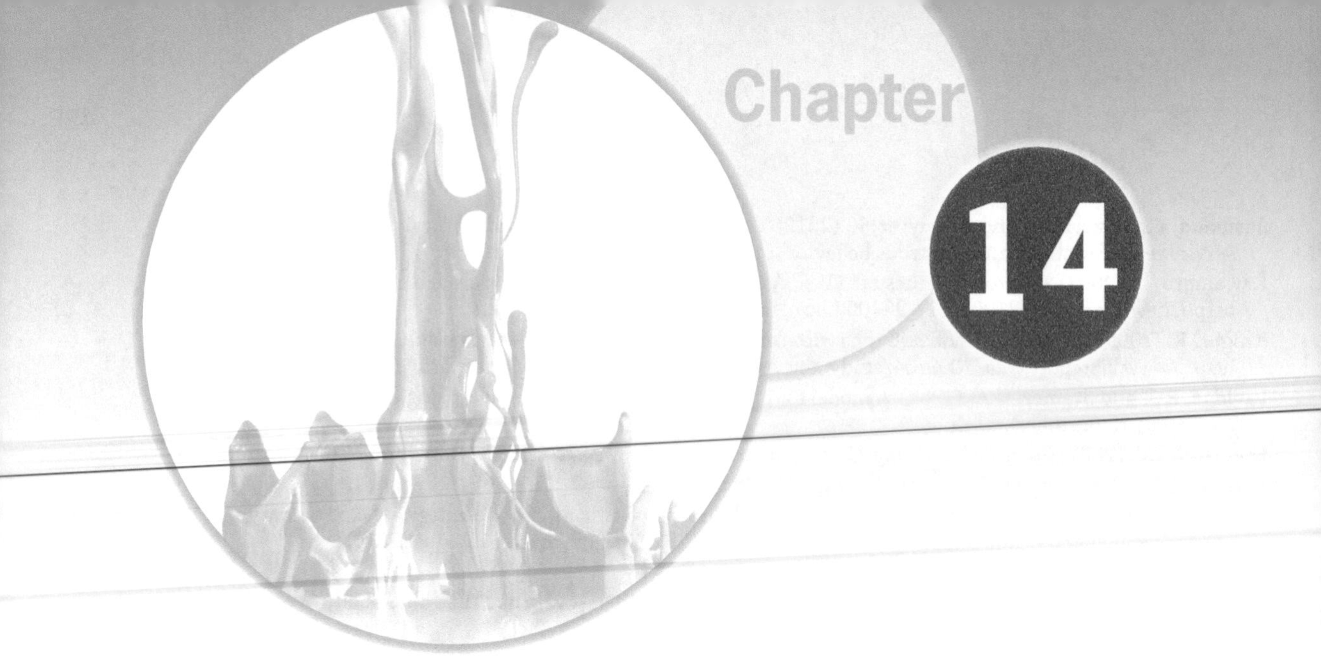


# Globalized services marketing

*Jessica lives in a small town in the English Midlands. She has just received her quarterly bill from her electricity supplier EDF Energy, part of the state-owned Électricité de France. There seems to be a problem with the payment from her bank account with Santander, based in Spain. She speaks to someone in a call centre somewhere in India, using her mobile phone connected to the $O_2$ network, now owned by the Spanish company Telefonica. She leaves the house and catches a bus operated by the French firm Veolia, then goes to London on a train whose operator is owned by German DB Railways. In the part of London that she is visiting she sees a street cleaner wearing the uniform of the French company GDF Suez. She is visiting a hospital for a routine scan, and finds that this has been outsourced by the NHS to the South African-based company Netcare. After all that, she stops for a spot of lunch at a fancy Italian restaurant, Zizzi. Actually, that is owned and operated by a British company – Gondola Holdings – but the waiters and waitresses are mainly from Eastern Europe. She then heads to Oxford Street to do some shopping where she finds an array of foreign-owned retailers, and relaxes in an American-owned Starbucks coffee shop. Just in the space of a few hours, Jessica is made aware that globalization is not just about big business, affecting 'somebody else' – we encounter the globalized service economy in almost everything we do.*

## Learning objectives

After reading this chapter, you should understand:

- The nature of international trade in services and reasons for its development
- Methods used by services firms to assess the attractiveness of overseas opportunities
- The development of marketing plans that are sympathetic to local market needs
- Market entry strategies, including the need to balance risk and control

## 14.1 Introduction

Globalization has become a dominant theme for many services organizations. The number of companies who can regard their markets purely in terms of their home country is rapidly diminishing. Airlines, commercial banks and consulting engineers have for a long time seen their markets in world terms. Companies operating in sectors such as electricity supply, office cleaning and bus services would only a few years ago have most likely considered globalization to be something which only concerned other sectors, and not theirs. However, all of these sectors have seen companies expanding outside of their domestic market.

It may be fair to say that 'going global' is no longer an additional activity which companies may decide to become involved in. The reality for more and more companies is that they are already part of the globalized service environment. Even if they are not taking their service to overseas customers, they are quite likely to be facing competition from companies who are based abroad.

The purpose of this chapter is to review some of the additional challenges that the service-based business faces in a globalized rather than a purely localized business environment.

Many of the fundamental principles of marketing management that have been applied to a firm's domestic market will be of relevance in an international setting. The processes of identifying market opportunities, selecting strategies, implementing those strategies and monitoring performance involve fundamentally similar principles to those that apply within the domestic market. One study found that foreign operations in service firms are driven by a similar set of variables to those of manufacturing companies, but that the intensity and direction of some key relationships require modification and adaptation (Cicic et al., 1999). The major challenge to services companies seeking to expand overseas lies in sensitively adapting marketing strategies that have worked at home to the needs of foreign markets, the environments of which may be totally different from anything previously experienced.

New challenges face the international marketer. According to Naomi Klein, global services brands such as Shell, Wal-Mart and McDonald's have become metaphors for a global economic system gone awry, evidenced by growing concern about the pay and conditions of Third World workers. She believes that brands and their multinational owners, rather than governments, will increasingly become the target for activists (Klein, 2010).

The purpose of this chapter is to identify the main differences facing the task of marketing management when services are provided in an international rather than a purely domestic environment. Some of the key differences between trade in goods and trade in services are emphasized, in particular the diverse nature of buyer–seller interaction, which causes international trade in services to take a number of forms. The chapter, as well as extending knowledge of services marketing to the international context, provides a useful integrative revision chapter.

## 14.2 The importance of international trade in services

At some point, many services organizations recognize that their growth can only continue if they exploit foreign markets. However, entering foreign markets can be an extremely risky business for services companies, as evidenced by examples of recent failures where companies failed to foresee all of the problems involved:

- The mobile phone company $O_2$ invested over £1.5 billion in the Dutch mobile phone operator Telfort but failed to achieve higher than fifth ranking in the Dutch market. In April 2003 the company admitted defeat and sold the entire Dutch operation for just £16 million.

- The grocery retailer Sainsbury's pulled out of Egypt in 2001, only two years after investing in a chain of 100 supermarkets. Egypt had no tradition of supermarket shopping, and the company was not helped by persistent rumours of links with Jewish owners. Sainsbury's two years of involvement in the Egyptian market had incurred a loss of over £100 million.
- Even the fast-food restaurant chain McDonald's initially failed to make profits when it entered the UK market in the 1970s and had to rapidly adjust its service offer in order to achieve viability.

Nevertheless, a company that has successfully developed its marketing strategy should be well placed to extend this development into foreign markets. There are many examples of companies that have successfully developed foreign markets, including the following:

- The retailer Tesco has successfully reduced its dependence on the saturated UK grocery market by developing outlets in Ireland, the Far East and Eastern Europe.
- The mobile phone company Vodafone has expanded from its UK base and now provides service in 30 countries, reducing the company's unit costs through economies of scale and offering seamless, added-value services to international travellers.
- The Irish airline Ryanair started life with a route network that focused on Dublin. With successful expansion of its route network, most of its services now do not call at its Irish base.
- Carphone Warehouse was the brainchild of entrepreneur Charles Dunstone and, after a small-scale start in London, it has successfully expanded to operate more than 1100 stores throughout Europe, operating under the Carphone Warehouse banner in the UK and The Phone House in France, Spain, Germany, Sweden and the Netherlands.

Many national economies have come to rely heavily on foreign-currency earnings generated by their services industries. Notable examples include the Bahamas and Malta, whose financial services and tourism sector earnings offset the countries' need to import many manufactured goods and agricultural products. The UK is typical of many Western developed economies in relying on a trade surplus in services to offset a deficit in manufactured goods trade.

## 14.3 Defining international trade in services

Analysis of international trade in services is complicated by the diverse nature of producer–supplier interaction, stemming from the inseparability of service production/consumption processes.

The form that international trade takes is dependent on the mobility of both producer and consumer and the separability of the production/consumption process (see Figure 14.1). From the diversity of producer–consumer interaction, three important patterns of trade can be identified:

- *Production of a service in one country for consumption in another country*. While manufactured goods are commonly traded on this basis, this can only occur for services where production and consumption can be separated. The Internet and falling costs of telecommunications have created new opportunities; for example, call centres provide a service to a customer who may be located thousands of miles from the call centre.
- *Production of a service by a domestic company in a foreign market for foreign consumption*. Where the problem of inseparability cannot be overcome, a domestic service producer may only be able to access a foreign market by setting up production facilities in that market. Examples include catering and cleaning services, which must deliver a tangible outcome at a point of the customer's choice. While this type of international trade can be very important to services

organizations, it only appears in a country's balance of payments in the form of capital movements, remitted profits and trade in the tangible components of a service offer.

- *Production of a service at home for sale to foreign customers for consumption in the domestic market.* It is often expensive or impossible to take a service production process to foreign customers, therefore customers must travel to consume the service. This can occur for a number of reasons:
  - Demand for a highly specialized service may be very thinly dispersed, making it uneconomic to take highly specialized staff and equipment to the market. As an example, it is common for patients to travel long distances to visit specialist doctors in London's Harley Street.
  - The laws of a foreign country may make the provision of a service in that market illegal, forcing those seeking the service to travel overseas. Countries that forbid abortion operations often do so to the benefit of abortion clinics in countries such as Britain where the law allows more freedom.
  - Production costs may be lower in an organization's own country, making it attractive for foreign customers to travel in order to obtain a service. As an example, the lower price of labour in many less-developed countries makes it attractive for shipowners to send their ships away for major overhaul work to be undertaken.
  - A country may possess unique geographical features that form an important element of a service offer and, in order to receive the benefits of related services, customers must travel to that country. This is very important for tourism-related industries, where the benefits of services associated with heritage sites or climatic differences cannot be taken to consumers. If American citizens wish to visit the Tower of London, they must travel to London.

Figure 14.1 Patterns of producer–consumer interaction in foreign trade for services

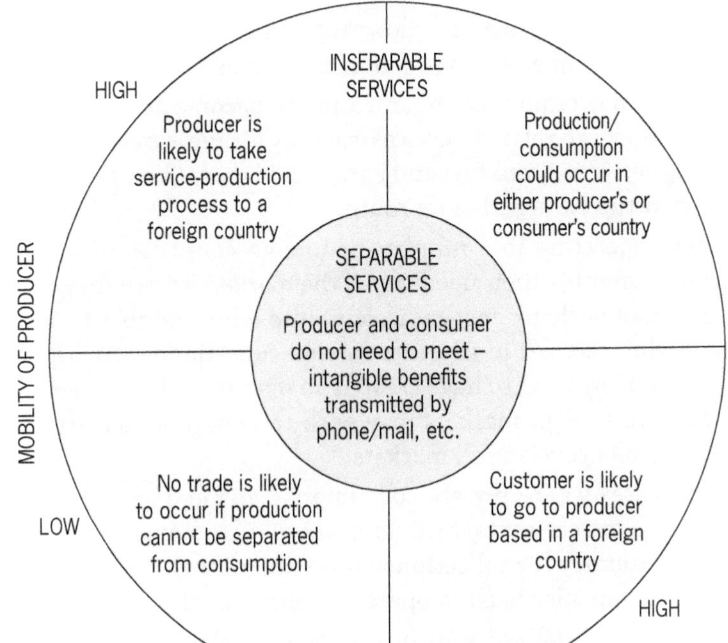

## 14.4 Reasons for service firms going global

For an individual company, development of foreign markets can be attractive for a number of reasons. These can be analysed in terms of 'pull' factors, which derive from the attractiveness of a potential foreign market, and 'push' factors, which make an organization's domestic market appear less attractive:

- For firms seeking growth, foreign markets represent new market segments, which they may be able to serve with their existing range of products. In this way, a company can stick to producing services that it is good at. Finding new foreign markets for existing or slightly modified services does not expose a company to the risks of expanding both its product range and its market coverage simultaneously.
- Saturation of its domestic market can force a service organization to seek foreign markets. Saturation can come about where a service reaches the maturity stage of its life cycle in the domestic market, while being at a much earlier stage of the cycle in less developed foreign markets. While the market for fast-food restaurants may be approaching saturation in a number of Western markets – especially the USA – they represent a relatively new service opportunity in the early stages of development in some Eastern European countries.
- Regulations may make it difficult for a company to exploit its service concept fully in its domestic market, forcing it to look overseas for opportunities. As an example, restrictions on new out-of-town retail developments in the UK during the 1990s led many retailers to seek expansion of their format in foreign markets such as Ireland and Eastern Europe.
- As part of its portfolio management, an organization may wish to reduce its dependence upon one geographical market. The attractiveness of individual national markets can change in a manner that is unrelated to other national markets. For example, during 2012 many service providers in Western Europe suffered a downturn in consumer expenditure, but consumer spending continued to grow in emerging economies such as Turkey, India and Brazil.
- The nature of a service may require an organization to become active in a foreign market. This particularly affects transport-related services such as airline services and courier services. A German airline flying between Frankfurt and Paris would most likely become involved in exploiting a foreign market at the Paris end of its route.
- Industrial companies operating in a number of foreign countries may require their services suppliers to be able to cater for their needs in all the markets where they operate. For example, a car manufacturer may wish to engage accountants who are able to provide auditing and management accounting services in all of its foreign subsidiaries. To achieve this, the firm of accountants would probably need to have created an operational base overseas. Similarly, firms selling their products in foreign markets may wish to engage an advertising agency that can organize a global campaign covering all markets.
- There are also many cases where private consumers demand a service that is internationally available. An example is the car-rental business, where customers frequently need to be able to book a hire car in one country for collection and use in another. To succeed in attracting these customers, car-rental companies need to operate internationally.
- Some services are highly specialized and the domestic market is too small to allow economies of scale to be exploited. Foreign markets must be exploited in order to achieve a critical mass which allows a competitive price to be reached. Specialized aircraft engineering services and oil exploration services fall into this category.

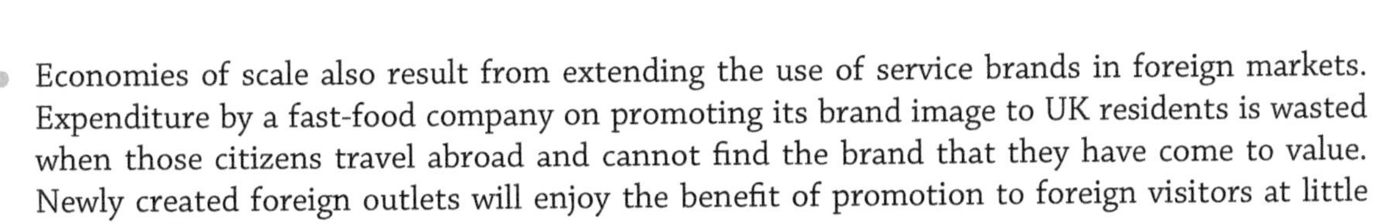

- Economies of scale also result from extending the use of service brands in foreign markets. Expenditure by a fast-food company on promoting its brand image to UK residents is wasted when those citizens travel abroad and cannot find the brand that they have come to value. Newly created foreign outlets will enjoy the benefit of promotion to foreign visitors at little additional cost.

## 14.5 Analysing opportunities for overseas development of services

Foreign markets can represent very different opportunities and threats compared with those that an organization has been used to in its domestic market. Before a detailed market analysis is undertaken, an organization should consider in general terms whether the environment of a market is likely to be attractive. By considering in general terms such matters as political stability or cultural attitudes, an organization may screen out potential markets for which it considers further analysis cannot be justified by the likelihood of success. Where an exploratory analysis of a foreign marketing environment appears to indicate some opportunities, a more thorough analysis might suggest important modifications to a service format, which would need to be made before the service could be successfully offered to the market.

This section first identifies some general questions that need to be asked in assessing the marketing environment of foreign countries and then considers specific aspects of researching such markets.

### In practice: Is the glass half full or half empty?

In a twist to an old tale, the story is told of a business development team from a tour operator that was sent abroad to investigate the possibilities for offering package holidays in the format that had worked well at home. The main finding was that very few people in that market bought package holidays. But what did this mean? One member of the team concluded that the current level of sales indicated a lack of interest in the product and the market should therefore be best avoided in favour of other possible markets. But, to another member of the team, this was the sign of huge potential – 'Just wait until these people discover the advantages of buying package holidays!'. This simple example emphasizes that any analysis of overseas market potential can only be based on a combination of factual analysis and judgement.

## 14.6 The foreign marketing environment

The combination of environmental factors that contributed to success within an organization's domestic market may be absent in a foreign market, resulting in the failure of attempts to export a service format. In this section, questions to be asked in analysing a foreign marketing environment are examined under the overlapping headings of the political, economic, social, demographic and technological environments.

### 14.6.1 The political environment

Government and quasi-government organizations influence the legislative and economic frameworks within which organizations operate. Although the most important political influences originate from national governments, inter-government agreements can also be important in shaping a national market.

At a national level, individual governments can influence the attractiveness of a market in a number of ways:

- The stability of the political system can affect the attractiveness of a national market. While radical change rarely results from political upheaval in most Western countries, the instability of some African governments has led to uncertainty about the economic and legislative framework in which services will be provided.
- Licensing systems may be applied by governments to protect domestic producers. Licences can be used to restrict individuals practising a particular profession (e.g. licensing requirements for accountants or solicitors may not recognize experience and licences obtained overseas) or licences can be used to restrict foreign owners setting up a service operation (e.g. the US government does not allow non-US investors to own more than 25 per cent of the shares in its domestic scheduled airlines).
- Regulations governing service standards may require expensive reconfiguration of the service offer to meet local regulations, or may prohibit its provision completely – gambling-related and medical services often fall into this category.
- Import controls can be used to restrict the supply of goods that form an integral part of a service. A restaurant seeking foreign outlets may be forced to source its materials locally, leading to possible problems in maintaining consistent quality standards and also possibly losing economies of scale.
- Service production possibilities can be influenced by government policies. Minimum wage levels and conditions of service can be important in determining the viability of a service. For example, many countries restrict the manner in which casual or seasonal staff can be employed.
- Restrictions on currency movements may make it difficult to repatriate profits earned from a foreign service operation.
- Governments are major procurers of services and may formally or informally give preference in awarding contracts to locally owned services organizations.
- Legislation protecting trademarks varies between countries – in some countries, the owner may find it relatively hard to legally protect itself from imitators.

The political environment can include actions of local, regional and national governments, and supra-national governmental organizations, such as the European Union and World Trade Organization.

### 14.6.2 The economic environment

A generally accepted measure of the economic attractiveness of a foreign market is the level of GDP per capita. As we saw in Chapter 1, the demand for most services increases as this figure increases. However, organizations seeking to sell services overseas should also consider the distribution of income within a country, which may identify valuable niche markets. As an example, the relatively low GDP per head of Nigeria still allows a small and relatively affluent group to create a market for high-value foreign holidays (see Figure 14.2).

An organization assessing a foreign market should place great emphasis on future economic performance and the stage that a country has reached in its economic development. While many Western developed economies face saturated markets for a number of services, less developed economies may be just moving on to that part of their growth curve where services begin to appeal to large groups of people.

Figure 14.2 This graph shows, for selected countries, the tendency for GDP per capita to be closely correlated with per capita expenditure on tourism services. (Based on World Travel & Tourism Council (2007) and World Bank (2008) data)

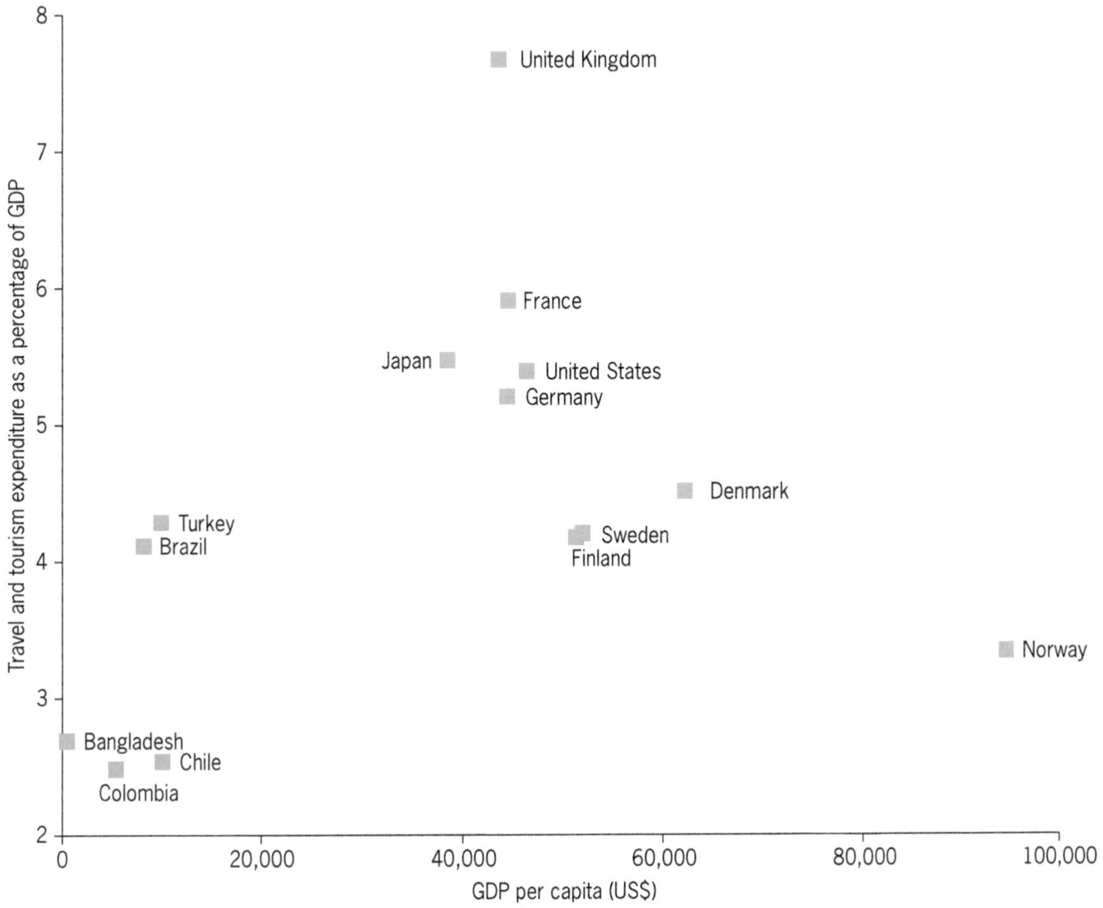

*Note*: Tourism expenditure is based on WTTC estimates of personal expenditure by residents of each country. Figures refer to 2008 or the most recent estimates available.

A crucial part of the analysis of a foreign market focuses on the level of competition within that market. This can be related to the level of economic development achieved within a country – in general, as an economy develops, its markets become more saturated. This is true of the market for household insurance, which is mature and highly competitive in North America and most Western European countries, but relatively new and less competitive in many developing economies, where better margins may be achieved.

## Thinking around the subject: Where in the world?

If you were planning to expand your restaurant chain to an overseas market, which of the countries listed would appeal to you most? A casual glance at the data in Figure 14.3 will reveal that many of the poorest countries of the world are associated with lower levels of political freedom and a high level of corruption. However, should you instinctively go for a country such as Switzerland, which has a high level of GDP and a relatively open, incorruptible system of government? At first sight, Switzerland may appear much more attractive than Tanzania or Zambia, where it may be necessary to bribe your way into

Figure 14.3 This table reports data for a selection of countries linking annual GDP per capita with an index of political freedom within the country (for example, the extent of universal voting rights). It also gives a ranking of economic freedom (for example, the ease with which new entrants can enter a market) and ranking of corruption.

| | GDP per capita 2011 | Index of political freedom 2013 | Ranking of economic freedom 2013 | Ranking of corruption 2013 |
|---|---|---|---|---|
| | | | | |
| BURUNDI | 604 | 5.0 | 148 | 165 |
| LIBERIA | 585 | 3.5 | 147 | 75 |
| TANZANIA | 1512 | 3.0 | 98 | 102 |
| HAITI | 1171 | 4.5 | 152 | 165 |
| PAKISTAN | 2745 | 4.5 | 121 | 139 |
| INDIA | 3650 | 2.5 | 119 | 94 |
| ZAMBIA | 1621 | 3.5 | 93 | 88 |
| NIGERIA | 2533 | 4.5 | 120 | 139 |
| PHILIPPINES | 4119 | 3.5 | 97 | 105 |
| CHINA | 8400 | 6.5 | 136 | 80 |
| UNITED ARAB EMIRATES | 47,893 | 6.0 | 71 | 27 |
| CANADA | 40,420 | 1 | 6 | 9 |
| UK | 35,598 | 1 | 14 | 17 |
| IRELAND | 40,868 | 1 | 11 | 25 |
| SWITZERLAND | 51,227 | 1 | 5 | 6 |
| NORWAY | 60,392 | 1 | 31 | 7 |

the country, only to find a very poor population. The problem with this simplistic analysis is that a country that is attractive to you will also be attractive to your competitors. So, the competitive pressure for a restaurant is likely to be much greater in Switzerland than Zambia. If you invest time and effort into Zambia, you may have the market to yourself, reasonably secure in the knowledge that a new overseas competitor would first have to go through the pain barrier that allowed you to enter the market. Also, the figures for GDP per person can be quite misleading, because what really matters is the number of people in the population who have disposable income above the level at which they start eating out in restaurants. In many emerging economies, a low GDP may mask big differences in income distribution. A small but expanding middle class may be a very attractive proposition for a new entrant to the market.

The measure of political freedom comprises a composite of two separate indicators, political rights and civil liberties. The combined score is between 1 and 7, 1 being the most free and 7 being the least free. The organization Freedom House considers countries with scores of between 1.0 to 2.5 'free'; those scoring between 3.0 and 5.0 as 'partly free'; and those scoring between 5.5 and 7.0 as 'not free'. The ranking of economic freedom consists of one index, in which the most free economy (Hong Kong) is ranked 1 and the least free economy (North Korea) ranks 179. Ranking of corruption is based on data provided by Transparency International (2013), with the least corrupt country being ranked 1.

*Source*: based on United Nations (1998); World Bank (2013); Freedom House (2013); Transparency International (2013); *World Factbook* (2013); Heritage Foundation (2013)

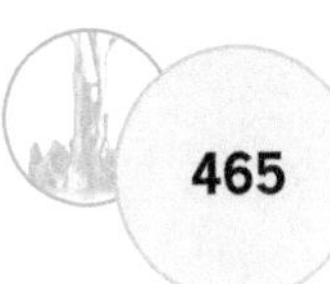



### 14.6.3 The social and cultural environment

An understanding of culture and, in particular, an appreciation of cultural differences are clearly important for marketers. Individuals from different cultures not only buy different services, but may also respond in different ways to the same service. Examples of differing cultural attitudes and their effects on international trade in services include the following:

- Buying processes vary between different cultures – for example, the role of women in selecting a service may differ in a foreign market compared with the domestic market, thereby possibly requiring a different approach to service design and promotion.
- Some categories of services may be rendered obsolete by certain types of social structure. As an example, extended family structures common in some countries have the ability to produce a wide range of services within the family unit, including caring for children and elderly members. Extended families also often reduce the need for bought-in financial services by recirculating funds within a very close system. A European budget hotel chain that has attracted people who are visiting friends and relatives, but do not actually want to stay with them, may find its proposition less acceptable in a country such as India where it may be perceived as discourteous not to stay with friends or relatives when visiting their town.
- A service that is taken for granted in the domestic market may be seen as socially unacceptable in a foreign market – interest charged on bank loans may be regarded as a form of usury in some Muslim cultures, for example.
- Attitudes towards promotional programmes differ between cultures – the choice of colours in advertising or sales outlets needs to be made with care because of symbolic associations (for example, the colour associated with mourning/bereavement varies across cultures).
- What is deemed to be acceptable activity in procuring sales varies between cultures. In some Middle Eastern markets, for example, a bribe to a public official may be considered essential, whereas it is unacceptable in most Western countries.

It should, however, be remembered that no society is totally homogeneous. Every culture contains smaller subcultures, or groups of people with shared value systems that are based on common experiences and situations. These identifiable subgroups may be distinguished by race, nationality, religion, age, geographical location or some other factor, and share attitudes and behaviour which reflect subcultural influences.

It has been common to talk about cultural convergence, implying that individuals are becoming more alike in the way that they think and behave. Advocates of the concept of cultural convergence remind us that needs are universal and therefore there should be no reason why satisfaction of those needs should not also be universal. If a Big Mac satisfies a New Yorker's need for hygienic, fast and convenient food, why should it not satisfy those similar needs for someone in Cairo? Against this, many observers have noted individuals' growing need for *identity* in a world that is becoming increasingly homogenized. Support for regional breakaway governments (e.g. by the Kurdish and Basque peoples) may provide some evidence of this. A number of writers have noted the rise of identity with Islam, with a suggestion that following the Iraq war in 2003, many consumers in Arab countries used purchases of Muslim products to identify themselves with an anti-American cause. Many Western service brands have become despised by some groups as symbols of an alien identity. Banks in many Muslim countries have reported increased interest in sharia-based banking services.

### Thinking around the subject: Saturated burgers for less saturated markets?

A saturated domestic market is often the spur for companies to seek new foreign markets. But is there a moral case against companies seeking to promote a Western style of service consumption in countries with well-established and sustainable lifestyles? Fast-food companies have stepped up their efforts to develop new foreign markets as Western markets for fast food become saturated. Is it responsible to promote burgers, which are high in saturated fats, to people whose diets are inherently healthier? Is it right that fast-food companies should develop low-fat burgers for the American market, partly out of fear of litigation, while selling higher-fat burgers to less-developed countries where legislation and consumers' awareness of health issues may be more lax? Defenders of fast-food companies point to the fact that they are providing hygienic food prepared in conditions that may be far superior to the norm in many developing countries. They have offered jobs to individuals, which may be the envy of peer groups. Should the solution be greater education of consumers in healthy eating, rather than more regulation? Is greater education a realistic prospect in a culture where Western-style fast food may have become a cultural icon?

## 14.6.4 The demographic environment

It is also important to consider the demographic structure of a foreign market. Within the EU countries, the total population in recent times has increased at a natural rate of about 1.0 per 1000 population (that is, for every 1000 deaths, there are 1001 births). However, this hides a range of rates of increase, with, at each extreme, Ireland having a particularly high birth rate and Germany a particularly low one. This has major implications for future age structures and consumption patterns. By 2030, people over 65 in Germany will account for almost half the adult population, compared with one-fifth in 2000. And, unless the country's birth rate recovers from its present low of 1.42 per woman, over the same period its population of under-35s will shrink about twice as fast as the older population will grow. The net result will be that the total population, now 82 million, will decline to 70–73 million, and the number of people of working age will fall by a quarter, from 40 million today to 30 million. In Japan, the population was expected to peak in 2010, at around 126.8 million and, by 2030, the share of the over-65s in the adult population will have grown to about half (*World Factbook*, 2013). Much faster population growth is expected to occur in Africa and Latin America.

In addition, the geographical distribution of the population and structure of household units may be significantly different from that which had brought about success in the domestic market. For example, recent EU statistics show a number of interesting contrasts in geodemographic characteristics between member states, which could have implications for the marketing of a service:

- Very significant differences occur in home ownership patterns, with implications for demand for a wide range of home-related services. The proportion of households living in rented accommodation ranges from 21 per cent in Spain to 53 per cent in West Germany, while the proportion with a mortgage ranges from 8 per cent in Spain to 44 per cent in the UK.
- The proportion of the population living within metropolitan areas varies from 13 per cent in Italy to 44 per cent in France. The resulting differences in lifestyles can have implications for services as diverse as car-repair services, entertainment and retailing.
- The proportion of self-employed people ranges from 45 per cent in the Netherlands to 17 per cent in Italy, with implications for the sale of personal pension schemes, etc.
- Average household size ranges from a low of 2.26 in Denmark to a high of 4.16 people in Ireland, having implications for the types and quantities of services bought by household units.

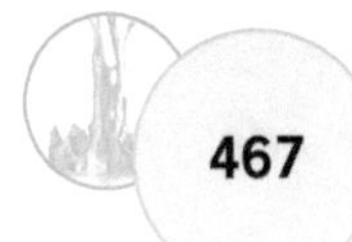



### 14.6.5 The technological environment

An analysis of the technological environment is important for services organizations that require the use of a well-developed technical infrastructure and a workforce that is able to use technology. Communications are an important element of the technological infrastructure – poorly developed telephone and postal communications may inhibit attempts to make credit cards more widely available, for instance.

### Thinking around the subject: A hotel for lunatics?

Hilton International, owner of many of the world's most prestigious hotels, has joined the race to build the first hotel on the moon. It has developed a project called the Lunar Hilton, which would comprise a complex with 5000 rooms. Powered by two huge solar panels, the resort would have its own beach and sea as well as a working farm. Experts disagree on the practicalities of life on the moon, but barriers seem to be diminishing as new discoveries are made.

'Space tourism' received a boost in April 2001 when the determined multimillionaire Dennis Tito paid $20 million for a round-trip ticket to the International Space Station. Such is the interest in exploiting the moon for tourism that there is now a Space Tourism Association and a lot of national pride is at stake. The Russians placed the first man in space and now the first tourist in space. In Japan, the Kinki Nippon Tourist (KNT) Company, the country's second largest wholesale tour operator, set up a space travel club in 2002. Back in 1998, KNT helped a Japanese Pepsi franchisee launch a sweepstake for a sub-orbital flight. The company received 650,000 applications for five tickets, each valued at $98,000. The company is convinced that excursion-class spaceships will become a driving force for the travel industry in the twenty-first century.

Three Japanese companies have between them already spent £25 million on development work for their own moon projects. Compared with this, Hilton's expenditure to date of £100,000 looks quite modest. Is the company mad in believing that people will want to visit the moon? Or is this just the kind of long-term strategic thinking that so many businesses lack? With the world becoming smaller and increasingly saturated with goods and services, does the moon offer a unique opportunity for expansion?

## 14.7 Sources of information on foreign markets

The methods used to research a potential foreign market are in principle similar to those that would be used to research a domestic market. Companies would normally begin by using secondary data about a potential foreign market that is available to them at home. Sources that are readily available through specialized libraries, online services, government organizations and specialist research organizations include the UK Department for Business, Innovation and Skills information for exporters, reports of international agencies such as the Organisation for Economic Co-operation and Development (OECD), chambers of commerce and private sources of information such as that provided by banks. Details of some specific sources are shown in Figure 14.4.

Initial desk research at home will identify those markets that show greatest potential for development. A company will then often follow this up with further desk research of materials available locally within the short-listed markets, often carried out by appointing a local research agency. This may include a review of reports published by the target market's own government and specialist locally based market research agencies.

Figure 14.4 Some examples of sources of secondary information on foreign markets

**Government Agencies**
Home Government statistics – e.g. UK Department for Business, Innovation and Skills market reports
Foreign governments – e.g. USA Department of Commerce
Foreign national and local development agencies

**International Agencies**
European Union (Eurostat etc.)
Organisation for Economic Co-operation and Development (OECD)
World Trade Organization
United Nations
International Monetary Fund
Universal Postal Union
World Health Organization

**Research Organizations**
Economist Intelligence Unit
Dun and Bradstreet International
Mintel
Eurostat
Market research firms

**Publications**
*Financial Times country surveys (available at www.ft.com)*
*Business International*
*International Trade Reporter*
Banks' export reviews

**Trade Associations Chambers of commerce**
Industry-specific associations – e.g. International Air Transport Association (IATA)

Just as in home markets, secondary data has limitations in assessing market attractiveness. Problems in foreign markets are compounded by the greater difficulty in gaining access to data, although the development of online information services has helped in this respect. There may also be language differences and problems of definition, which may differ from those with which an organization is familiar. In the case of services that are a new concept in a foreign market, information on current usage and attitudes to the service may be completely lacking. For this reason, it may be difficult to use secondary data to try to assess the likely response from consumers to large out-of-town superstores in some emerging economies. The Internet now allows companies to undertake a lot of preliminary assessment of a foreign market from their office-based computer.

Primary research is used to overcome shortcomings in secondary data. Its most important use is to identify cultural factors that may require a service format to be modified or abandoned altogether. A company seeking to undertake primary research in a proposed foreign market would almost certainly use a local specialist research agency. Apart from overcoming possible language barriers, a local agency would better understand attitudes towards privacy and the level of literacy that might affect response rates for different forms of research. However, the problem of comparability between markets remains. For example, when a Japanese respondent claims to 'like' a product, the result may be comparable to a German consumer who claims to 'quite like' the product. It would be wrong to assume on the basis of this research that the product is better liked by Japanese consumers than German consumers.

Primary research is generally undertaken overseas when a company has become happy about the general potential of a market, but is unsure of a number of factors that would be critical for success, for example whether intermediaries would be willing and able to handle their new service or whether traditional cultural attitudes will present an insurmountable obstacle for a service not previously available in that market. Prior to commissioning its own specific research, a company may go for the lower-cost, but less specific, route of undertaking research through an omnibus survey. These are surveys regularly undertaken among a panel of consumers in foreign markets which carry questions on behalf of a number of organizations.

## 14.8 Refining the marketing programme for foreign markets

A crucial task of foreign marketing management is the design of a marketing programme that is sensitive to local needs. The following sections examine the extent to which adaptation of the marketing mix to local needs is either desirable or possible. In particular, should a company seek to develop one globally uniform service offer, or make it different in each of the foreign markets that it serves?

Whether services firms choose to standardize their products globally or to adapt them to the needs of local markets is dependent on the nature of the services that they offer. Some fast-food restaurants have, for example, adapted their menus, architectural designs and staff-training methods to suit local needs, while retaining a common process formula worldwide. Services can often enjoy the best of both worlds, retaining their competitive advantage by remaining true to their basic managerial approach, while changing their product to meet local needs, in a process sometimes referred to as '**glocalization**'.

### 14.8.1 Product and promotion decisions

At the heart of international marketing-mix strategy are product and promotion decisions. Five generic strategies can be identified, based on the extent to which the configuration of the service offer and the promotional effort differ from a global norm.

#### Maintain a uniform product and promotion worldwide

This approach effectively develops a global marketing strategy as though the world were a single entity. The benefits of this approach are numerous. Customers travelling from one market to another can immediately recognize a service provider and the values that its global brand stands for. If, on the other hand, the service formulation was different in a foreign market, a traveller visiting a foreign outlet might come away confused about the qualities of the brand. As an example, a car rental company with an established position in its home market as the operator of a very modern fleet of cars could harm its domestic image if it pursued a strategy of operating older cars in a foreign market. Standardization of the service offer can also yield benefits of economies of scale, which include economies in market research and the design of buildings and uniforms, etc., although the greater adaptability of services often renders these benefits less than in the case of manufactured goods. The use of a common brand name in foreign markets for either the service provider or for specific services also benefits from economies of scale. Travellers to foreign markets will already be familiar with the brand's values as a result of promotion in the domestic market. However, care must be taken in selecting a brand name that will have no unfortunate connotations in foreign markets – the 'Big Mac', for example, translated in French as 'Gros Mec', was understood as the 'big pimp'. There can also be problems where legislation prevents an international slogan being used. In Quebec, for example, companies have been fined for using standard Anglicized advertising material without changing it to French as required by the province's legislation.

In the case of transport services that operate between different markets, it may not be feasible to adapt the service offering to each of the local markets served, and either a compromise must be reached or the needs of the most important market given precedence. Airlines flying between two countries may find the pricing of in-flight services, the décor of the aircraft and catering having to satisfy very different market needs at either end of the route.

### Retain a uniform service formulation, but adapt promotion

This strategy produces an essentially uniform global service, but adapts promotional effort to meet the sensitivities of local markets. The manner in which brand values are communicated in advertisements is a reflection of the cultural values of a society. For this reason, an airline may use a straightforward, brash hard-sell approach in its American market, a humorous approach in its British market and a seductive approach in its French market, even though the service offer is identical in each market. Similarly, certain objects and symbols used to promote a service may have the opposite effect to that which might be expected at home. Animals are often used in Britain to promote a range of home-based goods and services because they present a caring and comfortable image; however, in some markets, such as Japan, animals are seen as unclean, disgusting objects.

### In practice: Spinning an Irish yarn?

How do you promote the image of a tourist destination in foreign markets? The destination itself cannot be adapted to suit the needs of individual markets. The Tower of London will always be the same for tourists whether they are from Manchester, Madras or Melbourne. But the promotional message can be fine-tuned to stress the aspects on which different markets place high value. Take the case of the Brand Ireland campaign, a joint effort by the Northern Ireland Tourist Board and Bord Failte to increase the number of visitors to Ireland, north and south. Several hours of footage were filmed featuring tourist attractions around Ireland. This was reduced to a series of 15- and 30-second television commercials, but a different cut was made for each of the major markets targeted by the campaign. The German cut stressed the wild, rugged nature of the country, the Italian cut stressed the romance of the island, the American cut stressed Ireland's history and the English cut stressed that Ireland is so close, but so different. The strap line 'Live a different life' worked well in most markets, but had to be changed in the USA after focus groups identified unfortunate associations with cross-dressing.

### Adapt the service offering only

This may be done in order to meet specific local needs or legislation, while retaining the benefits of a global image. For this reason, a car rental company may offer a range of predominantly compact cars in areas where average journeys are short (e.g. the Channel Islands), while offering jeeps and vans in areas such as the USA, where motoring costs are lower and distances generally much greater.

### Adapt both product and promotion

In practice, a combination of slight service and promotion modification is needed in order to meet both differing local needs and differences in local sensitivity to advertising.

## In practice: Miniaturized hotels for miniaturized people?

How does a large American hotel chain adapt its service offer to the Japanese market? Hotels operated by Hilton International in the USA have bedrooms that, to many visitors from overseas, are surprisingly large. But what would an American think of a typical Japanese hotel? Land prices in America are generally fairly low outside of the main metropolitan areas; hence the relatively spacious facilities offered. But in Japan, space is at a premium and has given rise to all sorts of miniaturized hotel formats, aimed at keeping prices at an affordable level. How could Hilton International remain affordable yet retain its generic brand values? Following extensive research, the company developed a hotel format that was appropriate to the Japanese market. To avoid the problem of visitors from America being shocked by the relatively cramped hotels, Hilton International developed a separate brand format, *Wa No Kutsurogi*, providing comfort and service the Japanese way.

#### Develop new services

Markets may emerge overseas for which a domestic company has no service offering that can be easily adapted. In the field of financial services, the absence in some foreign countries of state provision for certain key welfare services may create a market for insurance-related products (e.g. dental health insurance cover) that are largely absent in the domestic UK market, where the welfare state is relatively comprehensive. Similarly, the social and economic structure of a country can result in quite different products being required. For example, the pattern of property ownership in Malaysia has given rise to a novel two-generation property mortgage not generally found in Western European markets.

### 14.8.2 Pricing decisions

The issue of whether to globalize or localize the service offer arises again in respect of pricing decisions. On the one hand, it might be attractive for an organization to be able to offer a standard charge for a service regardless of where in the world the service is consumed – consumers will immediately have an idea of how much a service will cost and this helps to develop a long-term relationship between client and company. However, a variety of factors generally cause global service operators to charge different prices in the different markets in which they operate. There is usually no reason to assume that the pricing policies adopted in the domestic market will prove to be equally effective in a foreign market. Furthermore, for those overseas-produced services that are consumed mainly by the local population, it may be of no great importance that comparability between different markets is maintained.

There are a number of factors that affect price decisions overseas:

- Competitive pressure varies between markets, reflecting the stage of market development that a service has reached and the impact of regulations against anti-competitive practices.
- The cost of producing a service may be significantly different in foreign markets. For services that use people-intensive production methods, variations in wage levels between countries will have a significant effect on total costs. Personnel costs may also be affected by differences in welfare provisions that employers are required to pay for. Other significant cost elements that often vary between markets include the level of property prices or rental costs.
- Taxes vary between different markets; for example, the rate of value added tax (or its equivalent sales tax) can be as high as 38 per cent in Italy compared to 15 per cent in Luxembourg. There

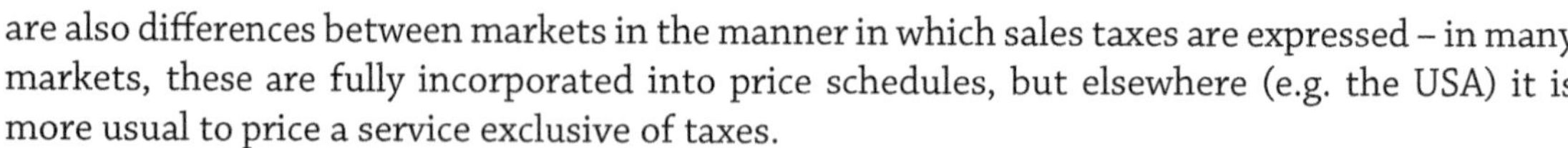

are also differences between markets in the manner in which sales taxes are expressed – in many markets, these are fully incorporated into price schedules, but elsewhere (e.g. the USA) it is more usual to price a service exclusive of taxes.

- Local customs influence buyers' expectations of the way in which they are charged for a service. While customers in the domestic market may expect to pay for bundles of services, in a foreign market consumers may expect to pay a separate price for each component of the bundle, or vice versa. Also, in some countries, it is customary to expect customers to pay a tip to the front-line person providing a service, whereas other cultures expect to pay an all-inclusive price without the need to subsequently add a tip. Formal price lists for a service may be expected in some markets, while, in others, the prevalence of bartering may put an operator who sticks to a fixed price list at a competitive disadvantage.
- Government regulations can limit price freedom in foreign markets. In addition to controls over prices charged by public utilities, some governments require 'fair' prices to be charged over a wide range of services – e.g. tourism-related services – and for the prices charged to be clearly publicized.
- The price charged for a service can reflect the stage of development in a market. For a category of service that is already established in a foreign market, a newcomer may only be able to gain market share by offering significant price incentives. In the early stages, discounting may have to be used to establish a trial of the service until the brand is sufficiently strongly established that the company can charge a premium price. As an example of this, international airlines often charge premium prices at the domestic end of a route (where their brand is well known), compared with the overseas end (where the brand is relatively unknown).

Services organizations are generally much better able to sustain discriminatory pricing policies between countries compared to exporters of manufactured goods. If wide differences in the pre-tax price of goods emerge between countries, it is open to entrepreneurs to buy goods in the lower-priced market and sell them in the higher-priced market (evidenced by the large volumes of cigarettes and alcohol that are imported from the relatively low-price French market to the high-price UK market). The inseparability of production and consumption generally prevents this happening with services – a low-priced hotel room cannot be taken from the relatively cheap Spanish market and offered for sale in the London market.

### 14.8.3 Accessibility decisions

Where a service organization is launching a service into a new foreign market, intermediaries can have a vital role in making the service available to consumers. The selection of intermediaries to facilitate the introduction of a service to a new foreign market is considered in more detail below. Consideration is given briefly here to the place and manner in which a service will be made available.

The analysis of location decisions presented in Chapter 4 can be applied equally to foreign markets. However, a service provider must avoid assuming that a locational strategy that has worked in one market will work just as effectively in a foreign market. A revised strategy may be required on account of differences in the geography of the foreign market, differences in consumer expectations, differences in current methods of making that type of service available and differences in legislative constraints:

- Geographical differences can be important where land-use patterns differ greatly in the target foreign market. As an example, the extensive nature of many urban areas within the USA results in there being a series of suburban commercial areas rather than a clearly defined central business district. A European retail bank with a city-centre service format that had worked well in its domestic market may only be able to succeed by developing out-of-town formats of its branches for a proposed expansion in the USA.

- Consumer behaviour may differ significantly in foreign markets. What is a widely accepted outlet in one country may be regarded with suspicion in another. The idea of a coffee shop located within a bookstore may appear quite ordinary within the USA, but may seem unusual in other countries. Customers' expectations about ease of access may differ, for example in relation to the availability of car-parking facilities or the distance that they are prepared to travel.
- Differences in the social, economic and technical environments of a market can be manifested in the existence of different patterns of intermediaries. As an example, the interrelatedness of wholesalers and retailers in Japan can make it much more difficult for a foreign retailer to get into that market compared with other foreign opportunities. In some markets, there may be no direct equivalent of a type of intermediary found in the domestic market – estate agents on the UK model are often not found in many markets where the work of transferring property is handled entirely by a solicitor. The technological environment can also affect accessibility decisions – the relatively limited and unreliable postal and telecommunications services of many less-developed countries make direct availability of services to consumers relatively difficult.
- What is a legal method of distributing a service in the domestic market may be against the law of a foreign country. Countries may restrict the sale of financial services, holidays and gambling services – among others – to a much narrower set of possible intermediaries than is the case in the domestic market.

### 14.8.4 People decisions

Where overseas service delivery involves direct producer–consumer interaction, a decision must be made on whether to employ local or expatriate staff. The latter may be preferable where a service is highly specialized and may be useful in adding to the global uniformity of the service offering. In some circumstances, the presence of front-line expatriate serving staff can add to the appeal of a service; for example, a chain of traditional Irish pubs established in mainland Europe may add to their appeal by employing authentic Irish staff.

For relatively straightforward services, a large proportion of staff would be recruited locally, leaving just senior management posts to be filled by expatriates. Sometimes, an extensive staff development programme may be required to ensure that locally recruited staff perform in a manner that is consistent with the company's global image. This can sometimes be quite a difficult task – a fast-food operator may have difficulty developing values of speed and efficiency among its staff in countries where the pace of life is relatively slow.

Where staff are recruited locally, employment legislation can affect the short- and long-term flexibility of service provision. This can affect the ease with which staff can be laid off or dismissed should demand fall – for example, in Germany, the Dismissals Protection Law (*Kundigungsschutzgesetz*) gives considerable protection to salaried staff who have been in their job for more than six months, allowing dismissal only for a 'socially justified' reason.

## 14.9 Market-entry strategies

A new foreign market represents both a potential opportunity and a risk to an organization. A company's market-entry strategy should aim to balance these two elements. The least risky method of developing a foreign service market is to supply that market from a domestic base, something that can be possible for separable services. A wide variety of financial and information services can be provided to foreign markets by Internet or telephone, avoiding the cost and risk of setting up local service outlets.

Where the producer must go to the consumer to provide its service process, local outlets must be established. Risk can be minimized by gradually committing more resources to a market, based on experience to date. Temporary facilities could be established that have low start-up and close-down costs and where the principal physical and human assets can be transferred to another location. A good example of risk reduction through the use of temporary facilities is found in the pattern of retail development in Eastern Germany following reunification. West German retailers who initially entered East Germany were reluctant to commit themselves to building stores in specific locations in a part of the country that was still economically unstable and where patterns of land use were rapidly changing. The solution adopted by many retailers was to offer branches of their chain in temporary marquees or from mobile vehicles. These could move in response to the changing pattern of demand. While the location of retail outlets remained risky, this did not prevent retailers from establishing their networks of distribution warehouses, which were considered to be more flexible in the manner in which they could respond to changing consumer spending patterns.

In emerging services markets, timing can be a crucial aspect of market entry strategy (see Figure 14.5). In the past two decades, major opportunities for hotel operators have emerged as the economies of China, India, Eastern Europe and Latin America have grown rapidly. When these economies emerged as centres for economic growth, one of their first requirements has been for hotels to accommodate the army of architects, engineers and business people who headed out to these countries to create new infrastructure and trading links. The result was that, in the early stages of rapid

Figure 14.5 A supply and demand model for the hotel industry over time

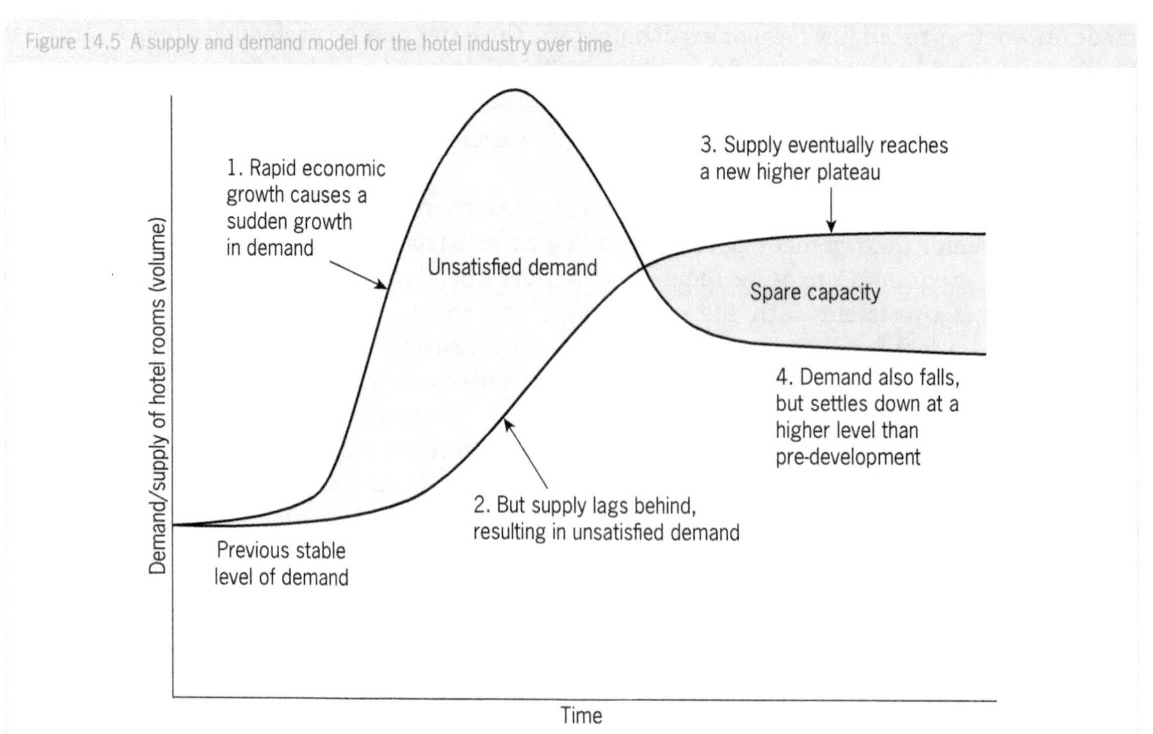

growth, hotels were very scarce and operators could charge premium prices. As an example, China and Eastern Europe are associated with low costs of labour and many manufacturers and service businesses have moved operations there to exploit these low costs. However, their capital cities often had some of the highest hotel costs in the world, reflecting their scarcity at a time of rapid economic growth. This has been a signal for more hotel chains to move into the market, but eventually the steam goes out of the economic boom, probably just at the time when the additional hotel capacity is becoming available. The result is greater pressure on prices, and a less attractive overseas investment opportunity for newly arrived companies compared with that achieved by earlier arrivals. Of course, it is easy with hindsight to spot the right time to invest, but much more difficult to predict which economies are going to grow, when and by how much.

While there may be long-term benefits arising from being the first company to develop a new category of service in a foreign market, there are also risks. If development is hurried and launched before service quality can be guaranteed to live up to an organization's international standards, the company's long-term image can be damaged, both in the new foreign market and in its wider world market. In the turbulent marketing environment of Eastern Europe in the late 1980s, two of the world's principal fast-food retailers – McDonald's and Burger King – pursued quite different strategies. The former waited until political, economic, social and technological conditions were capable of allowing it to launch a restaurant that met its global standards. In the case of Burger King, its desire to be first in the market led it to offer a sub-standard service, giving it an image from which it subsequently struggled to recover.

Where the inseparability of a service offer generally makes it impossible for an organization to supply the service to a foreign market from its home base, an assessment of risk is required in deciding whether an organization should enter a foreign market on its own or in association with another organization. The former maximizes the strategic and operational control that the organization has over its foreign operations, but it exposes it to the greatest risk where the foreign market is relatively poorly understood. The most common overseas market entry strategies are noted below.

### 14.9.1 Direct investment in foreign subsidiary

A company can acquire an existing foreign company or invest in a new start-up. This option gives a service organization maximum control over its foreign operations, but can expose it to a high level of risk on account of the poor understanding that it may have of the foreign market. Direct investment in a foreign subsidiary may be made difficult by legislation restricting ownership of certain services by foreigners – civil aviation is an example where many countries prevent foreign companies owning a controlling interest in a domestic airline.

### 14.9.2 Franchising

As with the development of a domestic franchise service network, franchising can allow an organization to expand rapidly overseas with relatively low capital requirements. Franchising in a foreign market can take a number of forms. At one extreme, the organization seeking to develop overseas could enter into a direct franchising relationship with each individual franchisee. The problem of this approach is the difficulty in monitoring and controlling a possibly large number of franchisees in a country far from home. To alleviate some of these problems, the franchisor would normally establish its own subsidiary in the foreign territory, which would negotiate and monitor franchisees locally or, alternatively, grant a master franchise for an area to a franchisee where the latter effectively becomes the franchisor in the foreign country.

### 14.9.3 Management contracting

Rather than setting up its own service organization overseas, a company with a proven track record in a service area may pursue the option of running other companies' businesses for them. For a fee, a foreign organization that seeks to develop a new service would contract a team to set up and run the facility. In some cases, the intention may be that the management team should get the project started and gradually hand over the running of the facility to a local management.

### 14.9.4 Joint ventures

An international joint venture is a partnership between a domestic company and a foreign company or government. Joint ventures can balance a company's desire for control with risk minimization and can be attractive in many situations: a joint venture can spread financial and market risks, and may be essential where foreign governments insist on a local partner being involved in a project; it can allow the operation to be fronted by a domestic producer with whom customers can be familiar, while allowing the foreign partner to provide capital and management expertise.

### 14.9.5 Strategic alliances

These are agreements between two or more organizations where each partner seeks to add to its competencies by combining its resources with those of a partner. A strategic alliance generally involves co-operation between partners rather than joint ownership of a subsidiary set up for a specific purpose, although it may include agreement for collaborators to purchase shares in the businesses of other members of the alliance. They are frequently used to allow individual companies to build upon the relationship that they have developed with their clients by allowing them to sell on services that they do not produce themselves, but are produced by another member of the alliance. This arrangement is reciprocated between members of the alliance. Strategic alliances are important within the airline industry, where operators share their route networks through 'code-sharing', thereby increasing the range of origin–destination opportunities that can be provided with a through ticket.

#### In practice: Costly alliances?

With the globalization of markets, strategic alliances are becoming increasingly important as a means of gaining competitive advantage. In the airline sector, an alliance such as the Oneworld Alliance allows one airline's services to be marketed by all other alliance members. For customers, Air Berlin is able to offer 'seamless' travel around the globe on services of fellow alliance members. However, although global airline alliances are highly visible, it should not be forgotten that the fastest-growing sector of civil aviation in recent years has been based on a low-cost, no-frills model, in which membership of a strategic alliance is seen as a costly burden, rather than a benefit that adds to competitive advantage.

Figure 14.6 Air Berlin's use of strategic alliances. (Reproduced courtesy of oneworld)

### 14.9.6 Global e-commerce

Many service providers now reach global audiences through the Internet. A consumer in the UK, for example, could find a hotel in Australia and book a room online. This strategy can be attractive for pure services organizations which do not require any tangible product to be delivered to the customer. However, using the Internet to enter foreign markets can pose many problems, including possible lack of awareness and trust in foreign markets, and issues of contract jurisdiction. Therefore, many companies who use e-commerce to enter global markets often do so in partnership with a locally based, or globally recognized, intermediary.

## Case study

### Indian call centres create new international trade

Dial an 0800 customer helpline in the UK and your call may be answered not in Bradford or Birmingham, but quite likely in Bangalore or Bombay. Operating call centres on behalf of Western clients has become an important new source of international trade for some less developed countries that have previously been associated with manufacturing cheap clothes and electrical items. In October 2012, over 250 call-centre providers from around the world exhibited at the UK Call Centre Expo to try to sell their services. In India alone, the value of handling overseas clients' telephone calls was estimated by Nasscom, an Indian trade body, to be $7bn in 2011. Having grown from almost nothing, the Indian call-centre sector would have been almost unthinkable only 20 years ago.

Handling customer service requirements emerged as a new international trade sector in the 1990s. Organizations of all kinds found increasing need to enter information into databases – records of customer sales, services performed, details of rolling stock movements, to name but a few. In the early days, most firms regarded this as a back-room function that they could perform most cost-effectively by using their own staff at their own premises. With time, an increasing volume of data to be analysed, the growing popularity of customer telephone support services, the growing sophistication of data analysis systems and the falling costs of data communication, many service companies emerged to take the burden of data processing off client companies.

At first, most data-processing and call-handling companies operated close to their clients. However, by the late 1980s, this activity began entering international trade, to be processed by companies in foreign countries where costs were lower, working regulations more relaxed and trades unions often non-existent. An important factor accounting for this development in international trade was the rapid pace of technological developments. Processed data and voice calls could now be transmitted very quickly and cheaply using satellites and fibre optic links.

Data processing and customer telephone support have established a firm foothold as an exportable service in areas such as India, the Caribbean and the Philippines. Each of these countries is characterized by relatively low wage rates and skills that are at least as good as those of workers in many more-developed countries.

In India, the outsourced call-centre industry has been growing at double-digit rates from the late 1990s. According to Datamonitor's estimates, the industry showed a compound annual growth rate of 56.4 per cent over the 2000–05 period, higher than any other industry sector in India.

The development of Genpact illustrates the way in which international trade can be developed. Genpact started as a customer-support centre for US-based General Electric in 1997. General Electric was looking for ways of cutting the cost of its customer-support and back-room operations. In 2004, the company employed about 18,000 people worldwide, including more than 12,500 in India, and also had customer-contact centres in China, Hungary, Mexico and Romania. Although General Electric accounted for 93 per cent of Genpact sales in 2004, Genpact has had an expansion strategy to increase the proportion of third-party client work that it undertakes.

Wages at Indian call centres such as those operated by Genpact are much lower than they would be in Britain. It is reported that many staff in 2004 would have earned as little as £2.90 a day and the total pay for an eight-hour shift could be below the minimum wage for one hour's work in Britain. Handling calls often involves antisocial hours, with night-time shifts a common feature of employment. National holidays such as Republic Day and religious festivals like Diwali and Holi are usually ignored by call-centre companies working for UK- and US-based clients. As for trades unions, these are rarely found.

Although wages may be considered very low by Western standards, a job in a call centre has been seen by many as highly prized. It has been reported that call-centre wages are typically double what a fully qualified local teacher can earn, allowing individuals to buy previously unattainable luxuries.

Despite the rapid growth of Indian call centres, many challenges are emerging. Most importantly, costs are rising and appear to be following the pattern of developing countries, gradually losing their competitive edge to countries with even lower costs. Staff turnover has become a major issue, with reports of annual staff turnover reaching 60 per cent. The UK's Financial Services Authority (FSA) in a study in 2005 found that the staff turnover at Indian call centres was approaching that in the UK and that managers were demanding comparable wages to their UK counterparts. Retaining women after they marry is a problem not generally encountered in the UK. Some staff have been deterred by the abuse they can face from callers, who may hold them personally responsible for the delay in getting their computer repaired or their insurance claim settled.

The FSA also warned that overseas call centres posed 'a material risk' to its aim of cutting financial crime, protecting consumers and retaining confidence in Britain's financial markets. The industry was not helped by the arrest in 2006 of an Indian call-centre employee of HSBC who was accused of stealing customers' details and selling them on to third parties. Overcoming these fears will inevitably involve more regulation, further forcing up Indian call-centre operators' costs, and cutting their international competitive advantage.

Some UK companies, such as the insurer Aviva, have enthusiastically extended their support operations in India. But it seems that polarization has been occurring, with Datamonitor suggesting in 2008 that over half of those companies who already used overseas call centres planned to increase their use, while the majority of companies would not consider sending any of its operations overseas. Some, such as NatWest Bank, have proudly proclaimed in their advertising that all of their telephone calls are actually answered in the UK.

The Indian call centre industry has been going through growing pains and many companies were badly affected by the recession in Western Europe and the USA from 2008, as recession-hit clients in the West cut their expenditure. Although call centres had developed new domestic sources of demand (US$600m in 2005 according to Nasscom, 2005), call centres still remained dependent on the health of their Western clients.

Some observers felt that the sector was struggling to shed its image for low-value work in which it had developed a cost advantage, but not a quality advantage over its competitors. Newer competitors in the call-centre market, such as the Philippines, had emerged and by 2012, over 400,000 Filipinos worked in call centres on behalf of Western companies. It seemed that not only were they cheaper, but quality could be better, with a suggestion that blue-chip US companies preferred Filipinos' American-friendly accents and deeper cultural affinity with the USA.

Further evidence of India's maturity as a call-centre provider occurred when Indian companies began taking their services overseas. Some moved to be closer to their Western clients, so in a 'coals to Newcastle' type of story, a leading Indian call-centre operator, ICICI OneSource, announced in 2007 that it was setting up two new call centres in Northern Ireland. Having gained expertise in handling calls for European customers, it was following these customers back to where many now preferred to have their calls answered and responding to changes in the comparative cost advantages of Europe and India. Other call centres played the game of outsourcing themselves by transferring some of their operations to low-cost countries. As an example, Mumbai-based Aegis, one of India's largest call-centre operators, had been steadily moving more operations to the Philippines and by 2013 had become one of the biggest call-centre providers in that country, with 13,500 employees.

*Sources*: based on http://www.biztechreport.com/ Ernst and Young (2009); Datamonitor (2008; 2009).

## Case study review questions

1 Why has data processing and call-centre handling emerged as a major new activity in world trade?
2 What are the advantages and disadvantages to a Western European-based insurance company of outsourcing its call-centre operation to a supplier in India?
3 What are the challenges and opportunities for the Indian economy of developing its call-centre industry?

## Summary and links to other chapters

This chapter has highlighted the increasingly competitive and global nature of services markets. The inseparable nature of services is reflected in quite different challenges for the development of foreign markets, compared with goods. Very often, a service organization can only develop an overseas market by locating there. Understanding a foreign market is crucial and firms have available to them a variety of techniques for assessing the cultural, economic and political acceptability of a service in a foreign market. Sensitive adaptation of a service formula is crucial to success and many services that have been successful at home have failed because of false assumptions about the needs of a proposed foreign market. The involvement of a joint venture partner can lessen the risk of entering an unknown market, but this has to be balanced against a loss of control.

All of the principles of services marketing that have been discussed in previous chapters in the context of the domestic market apply also to foreign markets. However, their application may differ. So the nature of the service offer and the processes involved in service encounters may need to be adapted (Chapters 1 and 2). Buyers may evaluate a service offer quite differently and be more or less amenable to the concept of relationship marketing (Chapters 5 and 6). Managing people in a foreign operation can be quite different, and inhibit the development of universal brands and standards of service (Chapters 8, 9 and 10). Issues of accessibility, pricing and promotion need to be sensitively managed (Chapters 4, 11 and 13).

### Chapter review questions

1 Discuss the macro- and micro-level reasons why a UK-based general insurance company might seek to expand into continental Europe.

2 Critically evaluate the methods that a bank might use to go about researching market potential for business development loans in a foreign country.

3 Evaluate the methods by which a firm of consulting engineers can minimize the risk of proposed foreign expansion.

### Activities

1 Choose two or three international service providers from the following sectors: hotels, airlines, fast food, car rental, accountancy services. Go to their websites and click through to a selection of their national sites in countries with a different socio-economic profile to your own. Analyse what is common between the service offer and the promotional messages between the different countries in which the company operates. Then try to identify ways in which the service offer has been adapted to meet local conditions.

2 Go to the website of an international hotel chain such as Hilton or Holiday Inn. Check out the price of a standard room on a particular date, for a selection of the company's hotels in different capital cities. What dispersion of prices for a basically similar room do you observe between cities? What factors may explain the differences in prices that you observed? Do you think such price differences are likely to persist?

3 Revisit Figure 14.3, which gives information about GDP per person and the level of corruption and economic freedom in a selection of countries. If you were a European hotel operator seeking international expansion for its budget hotel format, how would this information influence your choice of target country to expand into? What specific additional information would you need to further guide your choice between those countries listed?

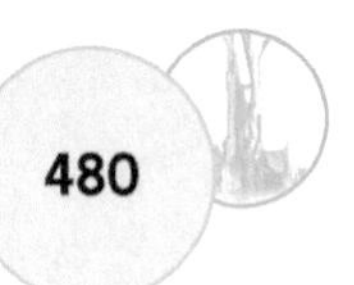


## Key terms

**Cultural convergence** A tendency for attitudes and values of previously distinct groups of people to gradually become more similar.

**Glocalization** Combining global standardization with adaptability to local markets.

**Joint venture** A partnership formed between two or more parties to share risk or expertise, with each sharing in revenues, expenses and control of the enterprise.

**Strategic alliance** A formal relationship formed between two or more parties to pursue a set of agreed goals or to meet a business need while remaining independent organizations.

## Selected further reading

*The following references offer a general review of the factors that influence firms' foreign expansion decisions:*

**Keegan, W.J. and Green, M.C.** (2012) *Global Marketing*, 7th edn, Pearson, Harlow.

**Lee, K. and Carter, S.** (2012) *Global Marketing Management: Changes, Challenges and New Strategies*, 3rd edn, Oxford University Press, Oxford.

**Doole, I. and Lowe, R.** (2008) *International Marketing Strategy*, 5th edn, Thomson.

*There is a growing body of literature that specifically relates to services organizations' foreign market-entry decisions:*

**Javalgi, R.G. and White, S.D.** (2002) 'Strategic challenges for the marketing of services internationally', *International Marketing Review*, 19 (6), 563–81.

**Javalgi, R.G., Joseph, W. and LaRosa, B.R.J.** (2009) 'Cross-cultural marketing strategies for delivering knowledge-based services in a borderless world: the case of management education', *Journal of Services Marketing*, 23 (6), 371–84.

**Kanso, A. and Kitchen, P.J.** (2004) 'Marketing consumer services internationally: localisation and standardisation revisited', *Marketing Intelligence & Planning*, 22 (2), 201–15.

## References

**Cicic, M., Patterson, P.G. and Shoham, A.** (1999) 'A conceptual model of the internationalization of services firms', *Journal of Global Marketing*, 12 (3), 81–106.

**Datamonitor** (2008) *Trends in Global Contact Center Outsourcing Pricing and Attrition Report (Strategic Focus)*, Datamonitor, London.

**Datamonitor** (2009) *Trends to Watch: Contact Center Outsourcing and Services*, Datamonitor, London.

**Ernst and Young** (2009) *Domestic BPO in India: Trends and Challenges*, Ernst and Young, London.

**Freedom House** (2013) 'Freedom in the world', available at www.freedomhouse.org/report-types/freedom-coored (accessed 18 July 2013).

**Heritage Foundation** (2013) 2013 Index of Economic Freedom, available at http://www.heritage.org/index/rankinzg (accessed 11 May 2013).

**Klein, N.** (2010) *No Logo*, 3rd edn, Picador, New York.

**NASSCOM** (2005) *IT in the Economy of India*, NASSCOM, New Delhi.

**Transparency International** (2013) '2013 Corruption Perceptions Index', Transparency International, Berlin, available at www.transparency.org/ (accessed 17 May 2013).

**United Nations** (1998) *Human Development Report*, available at http://hdr.undp.org/edreports/global/hdr1998/ (accessed 8 July 2013).

**World Bank** (2008), *World Development Report, 2007/2008*, available at www.worldbank. org/wdr/wdr98/contents.htm (accessed 17 June 2010).

**World Bank** (2013) World Development Indications database, World Bank, Washington, DC, available at http://data.worldbank.org/indicator/NY.GNP.PCAP.CD (accessed 18 July 2013).

***World Factbook*** (2013) available at https://www.cia.gov/library/publications/the-world-factbook/ (accessed 16 May 2013).

**World Travel & Tourism Council** (2007) *Travel & Tourism Navigating the Path Ahead: The 2007 Travel & Tourism Economic Research*, 8 March, London.

# Index

## C

## D

## Q

## T